HELP® 3–6 (2nd Edition)
Assessment Manual

Edited by
Patricia Teaford, M.S.

Contributors
Jan Wheat, M.S. ECE
Tim Baker, Ph.D.

VORT Corporation
PO Box 60132
Palo Alto, CA 94306
http://www.vort.com

Copyright © 2010

COPYRIGHT

This document is copyrighted by VORT under the U.S. Copyright Act. No part of this book may be reproduced in any form or by any means, electronic or mechanical, without prior written permission from VORT Corporation. (1st Edition was entitled *HELP for Preschoolers* © 1995 VORT Corporation.)

Copyright © 1995, 2010 VORT Corporation.
Printed in the United States of America. All rights reserved.
ISBN: 978-0-89718-206-5
Product Number: 659
HELP®, Hawaii Early Learning Profile®, and VORT® are registered trademarks of VORT Corporation.

Publisher's Note

We are pleased to have the opportunity to publish this important family support and information resource. It is concise and comprehensive, however, we cannot anticipate the circumstances under which a reader may apply its contents. We expressly decline liability for the techniques, activities, or results of conclusions you may reach about a child after reading and applying the contents of this book.

Disclaimers

The developmental information contained in this book is intended for supplemental support and not a replacement for developmental or medical evaluation, advice, diagnosis, or treatment provided by healthcare or other developmental professionals. This book is intended to provide accurate information, however, in a time of rapid change it is difficult to ensure that all information is entirely accurate and up-to-date. It is the professional's responsibility to review each behavior and skill and procedures for appropriateness for each child. The authors and publisher accept no responsibility for any inaccuracies or omissions and specifically disclaim any liability, loss, or risk, personal or otherwise, which is incurred as a consequence, directly or indirectly, of the use and or application of any of the contents of this book.

For Use by Professionals

These materials are intended for use by qualified child development professionals working with the child and the family. The child's doctor must be consulted under all circumstances if the child has special needs/health issues, or if there are any health or safety questions whatsoever. It is also important to remember that each child is unique and develops behaviors and skills at different rates and ages. No child is expected to demonstrate all behaviors and skills identified in *HELP 3–6 (2nd Edition)*. Age ranges listed are only a guide of the age range when a behavior/skill may typically emerge, not when a behavior/skill begins and ends.

Safety Guidelines

Although precaution and safety notes are included for behaviors and skills, there may be some which are not appropriate for some children, and some which have the potential for misinterpretation. It is your professional responsibility to carefully review the appropriateness of the information and activities for each particular child, and to alter the activity and/or add additional safety precautions as needed. It is extremely important to use caution with the child and to supervise the child carefully around sharp objects and utensils, appliances, small objects, scissors, hot water, etc. Be sure to check with the child's family/doctor regarding any food allergies or diet issues before providing or using snacks or food. Remind parents of these safety issues, and advise parents to always supervise their child. For example, the U.S. Consumer Product Safety Commission (CPSC) urges caregivers to be sure that toys and items used with or given to young children are safe and appropriate. Numerous toy safety guidelines and brochures are available through their website: www.cpsc.gov.

To be used as a reference

This book contains hundreds of activities and suggestions. For ease-of-use, use this book as a reference. Use the child's age as an approximate starting point, and use the assessment forms – *HELP 3–6 (2nd Edition) Strands* or *Checklist* or *Charts* – to identify the child's target behavior(s) and skill(s) to work on, and then look up the behaviors/skills in this book using the item ID number.

Contents

Introduction v
Purpose of HELP 3-6 years vii
Design of HELP 3-6 years ix
Structure and Link to HELP 0-3 x
Preparing for the Assessment – Quick Start xi
Conducting the Assessment xv
Other Assessment Considerations xv
What's New in the 2nd Edition xviii

Assessment:

1.0 Cognitive 1
2.0 Language 107
3.0 Gross Motor 177
4.0 Fine Motor 203
5.0 Social 233
6.0 Self Help 339

Introduction

The term "HELP" is derived from the product "Hawaii Early Learning Profile," which was first published by VORT in 1979. The original HELP materials consisted of a profile Chart and an Activity Guide for serving children, ages birth through three years (0-3).

In 1987, VORT published *Help for Special Preschoolers* (for serving children 3-6 years) which was adapted from the BCP (Behavioral Characteristics Progression) developed by VORT and the Santa Cruz County Office of Education.

To better link the 3-6 materials to the improved 0-3 materials, in 1995 VORT restructured the 3-6 year materials into *HELP for Preschoolers* to conform to the developmental Strand structure of HELP 0-3, thus offering a "seamless" birth-6 years HELP behaviors/skills continuum.

In 2010, a team of editors and reviewers completed a two-year revision of *HELP for Preschoolers* resulting in the new *HELP 3–6 (2nd Edition)* which includes an updating of the behaviors/skills (both text and ages and the removing of some skills; see page xvii), and updating the assessment materials, procedures, and adaptations. To improve use of the materials, the assessment portion of *HELP 3–6 (2nd Edition)* was separated from the curriculum activities resulting in two new books, the *Assessment Manual* and the *Curriculum Guide*. These books parallel the two books for HELP 0-3: *Inside HELP* and the *HELP Activity Guide*. **See page xviii for complete listing of What's New in this 2nd Edition.**

The *HELP® 3–6 (2nd Edition)* family of products includes:
    #659 – *HELP® 3–6 (2nd Edition) Assessment Manual*
    #652 – *HELP® 3–6 (2nd Edition) Curriculum Guide*
    #658 – *HELP® 3–6 (2nd Edition) Assessment Strands*
    #650 – *HELP® 3–6 (2nd Edition) Charts*
    #651 – *HELP® 3–6 (2nd Edition) Checklist*
    #656 – *HELP® 3–6 (2nd Edition) Activities at Home*

The combined HELP 0-6 materials cover over 1,250 unique behaviors and skills in six primary domains of: Cognitive, Language, Gross Motor, Fine Motor, Social, and Self-Help. The behaviors and skills (items) are linked by unique ID numbers to over 1,800 pages of assessment, curriculum, and family support materials. The six domains have been divided into 75 developmentally-sequenced strands. Each strand includes items which focus upon a specific underlying key concept and are hierarchical in nature; i.e., one item typically leads to or builds the foundation for the next item.

The HELP materials are not standardized. No child is expected to display all the behaviors or skills nor display all behaviors and skills for an age range. Be sure to consider individual, environmental, or cultural differences for each child. The age ranges reported in HELP are the ages at which a skill or behavior (for children who do not have disabilities) typically *begin to emerge* according to the literature. These age ranges are **not** when an item begins and ends. Some behaviors/skills are time-limited and emerge into more complex behaviors/skills, while others are lifetime skills.

Sometimes a behavior or skill stretches out over several months. This is not meant to imply that the item begins and ends within the age-range time frame. The age range reflects when the item typically emerges. Since there is not always agreement in growth and development literature, approximate age ranges are offered as a guide of when you can expect an item (behavior or skill) to typically be present. A child may develop the behavior or skill at any time within the age range to be "developmentally age appropriate." Descriptions of the child's behaviors and skills are more important than age levels for understanding a child's development and determining next steps in intervention or the child's educational plan.

Age ranges for HELP 3-6 are displayed in Months as well as Year.Month, e.g., 3.10-4.4 is 3 years 10 months to 4 years 4 months.

Note: The term "items" is used interchangeably to mean HELP 3-6 behaviors/skills.

Items listed on traditional developmental checklists and standardized tests, although generally listed in a developmental order according to age, are not generally hierarchical. Consequently, if a child "passes" one item it does not necessarily mean that he is ready to learn the next behavior or skill. Conversely, if a child "failed" an item, this does not mean that he cannot accomplish or is not ready to learn an item placed higher on the continuum. Without careful item analysis, it can be difficult to identify strengths and needs within a domain of development and difficult to identify "next steps" for planning. The *HELP 3–6 (2nd Edition) Assessment Strands* address these needs and provides an option for developmental assessment and monitoring.

Functional Outcomes

The HELP 3-6 curriculum-based assessment materials can be used to identify child needs and select a variety of activities designed to support the "Three Child Outcomes" presented by the U.S. Office of Special Education (OSEP).

The three OSEP Child Outcomes are:

1. Children have positive social-emotional skills (including social relationships)

2. Children acquire and use knowledge and skills (including early language/communication [and early literacy])

3. Children use appropriate behaviors to meet their needs

The outcomes are meant to be functional and "refer to things that are meaningful to the child in the context of everyday living" and "refer to an integrated series of behaviors or skills that allow the child to achieve the important everyday goals".

Functional means to refer to or include behaviors that integrate skills across domains instead of looking at a single behavior or skill and choosing just one item from the HELP 3-6 materials to achieve a single goal. In using the HELP 3-6 materials to develop functional child outcomes, you will want to consider the multiple domains associated with achieving the outcome.

For example, consider a child who does not play well with other children. All areas of development for this child should be investigated to help this child progress socially. A functional outcome for this child might be:

The child is to relate to adults and other children and follow rules related to groups or interacting with others.

For this sample outcome, you could use HELP 3-6 to help the child achieve success in play by:

1. Assessing the child on the items below using the *HELP 3-6 Assessment Strands* in conjunction with the *HELP 3-6 Assessment Manual*;

2. Using the *HELP 3-6 Curriculum Guide* for instructional activities linked by ID number;

3. Involving the child's family/parent by handing out and annotating the respective pages from the *HELP 3-6 Activities at Home* binder:

Cognitive:
    1.188…Works in small groups for 5-10 minutes
    1.239…Works in group for 10-25 minutes
    1.305…Role plays or organizes other children using props

Language:
    2.119…Carries on a conversation

Social:
    5.96…Plays with one or two others
    5.97…Exchanges items with another child
    5.98…Child engages in cooperative play with other children
    5.110…Looks at person when speaking
    5.112…Shares toys/equipment with another
    5.114…Stays with group during an activity

5.118...Takes turns
5.145...Obeys rules
5.163...Bargains with other children

All HELP 3-6 behaviors/skills are cross-referenced to the HELP curriculum materials and all HELP activities focus on the underlying concepts and skills that lead to functional child outcomes.

/*\ Safety First!

Although precaution and safety notes are often included for the activities, there may be some items or activities which are not appropriate for all children, and some which have the potential for misinterpretation. It is your professional responsibility to carefully review the appropriateness of the activities for each particular child, and to alter the activity and/or add additional safety precautions as needed. It is extremely important to use caution with the child and to supervise him carefully around sharp objects and utensils, appliances, small objects, scissors, hot water, etc. Be sure to check with the child's family/doctor regarding any food allergies or diet issues <u>before</u> providing or using snacks or food.

Involve families/parents

HELP 3–6 (2nd Edition) Activities at Home offers warm, at home suggestions for each item. These are written from the child's point of view and include an Introduction to the item, Materials in the home for teaching the skills, and Activities for the parent to follow to help the child develop the respective item. VORT products and publications are intended for use by and under the guidance of child development professionals. For example, families/parents interested in using the HELP materials must receive the materials through (ordered by) a qualified professional, and must work with and consult the professional on all procedures, including Gross and Fine Motor activities, Safety Issues, and any questions whatsoever. Be sensitive to, and adapt, the assessment items and procedures, and the instructional activities, as appropriate to the culture, customs, dress, appearance, and speech patterns of the child and his/her family.

Visit the VORT web site

The VORT web site (www.VORT.com) offers a wealth of current product information, training tips, instructions for use, and FAQs (answers to Frequently Asked Questions). Be sure to check out the web site, especially the FAQs, to supplement what is provided in the Introduction and Instructions in this book.

Purpose of HELP 3–6

HELP 3–6 (2nd Edition) is a curriculum-based assessment for use with both children who are exhibiting "typical" development and with those children who may have developmental delays. It is designed to be used by those working in early childhood settings and by those involved in a multi-disciplinary or transdisciplinary team approach. *HELP 3–6 (2nd Edition)* addresses the requirements for early childhood programs, including:

1. **Assessment and early identification**: Through family/parent interviews, observations, and exposure to different activities in all areas of development, individuals working with a child can get an overall picture of a child's skill levels. You can use the *HELP 3–6 (2nd Edition)* materials to document the child's growth and progress, both at home and in the educational setting. This can help you determine how a child is developing within and between developmental areas (strands). When there appear to be delays, mild or severe, it should be decided, with the family/parents involvement, whether the child needs to be referred for a more in-depth evaluation to determine eligibility for special services.

HELP 3–6 (2nd Edition) is a curriculum-based assessment, **not** a standardized test. The age ranges are provided to indicate when a skill "typically" emerges. You can use *HELP 3–6 (2nd Edition)* to record the child's development in a longitudinal manner from the age of three to six years. *HELP 3–6 (2nd Edition)* will **not** yield a definitive single age level or score. The primary purpose of *HELP 3–6 (2nd Edition)* as a curriculum-based assessment is <u>to identify curriculum outcomes, strategies and activities, and to plan next steps</u>. *HELP 3–6 (2nd Edition)* thus should not be used if your program requires standardized instruments to determine developmental delay. In addition, since *HELP 3–6 (2nd Edition)* cannot provide a single "score" or definitive developmental age, it should **not** be used to determine eligibility for children who may be experiencing mild developmental delays. In such cases, however, *HELP 3–6 (2nd Edition)* can be used to compliment standardized instruments to support "informed clinical opinion" requirements, and it can be used as an initial and ongoing assessment to help identify the child's unique strengths and needs, and the services appropriate to meet those needs. If your program does not require standardized instruments, *HELP 3–6 (2nd Edition)* can be used as an initial and ongoing assessment to help identify the child's unique strengths and needs.

2. **Program intervention and instructional teaching resource**: By recording a child's developmental progress using *HELP 3–6 (2nd Edition)*, strategies can be included in the curriculum to build and expand a child's skills. The child should be taught according to his rate and style of learning within the range of normal development. *HELP 3–6 (2nd Edition)* provides detailed instructional activities for each skill along with suggestions for adapting activities relative to the child's experience and abilities.

3. **Family/Parent involvement**: The parent/caregiver needs to be involved in the assessment and introduced to the teaching concepts that can be carried over into the home setting. As the parent becomes more involved, he or she will begin to feel more competent and effective in reinforcing skills at home that have been introduced in the educational setting. The *HELP 3–6 (2nd Edition) Activities at Home* binder provides practical, home-based activities that can easily be administered by the parents or the child's home-care provider. An introduction, a short list of easy-to-use materials and clear list of activities is included for most skills.

4. **Team approach and training guide**: Family members, the early childhood educator, and other school personnel, along with professionals such as audiologists, social workers and therapists, constitute the team that provides comprehensive services to meet the child's unique needs. *HELP 3–6 (2nd Edition)* can be used by the team to record growth and as a training guide for persons who are new to the field of early childhood education, particularly in working with young children who have a developmental delay or who may be considered to be at risk. *HELP 3–6 (2nd Edition)* can support early childhood teachers or administrator working with paraprofessionals, volunteers, or teachers' aides, and can be used to train staff in assessing the child's skill levels, as well as providing activities for teaching various skills. *HELP 3–6 (2nd Edition)* can be used as a resource for teachers whose classes include children with special needs.

Design of HELP 3–6

1. The *HELP 3–6 (2nd Edition)* (3-6) behaviors and skills are an extension of HELP 0-3. Thus, the item ID numbers for HELP 3-6 are based on domain (e.g., Cognitive = 1.0, Language = 2.0), and the 3-6 ID numbers start where the 0-3 ID numbers end. For example, Cognitive, 0-3 ends with item #1.159, and the first *HELP 3–6 (2nd Edition)* (3-6) Cognitive item is #1.160.

2. The age ranges provided with *HELP 3–6 (2nd Edition)* are based upon current literature. The age ranges are approximations as to when the behavior/skill "typically" emerges. The *HELP 3–6 (2nd Edition)* materials are **not** standardized, therefore, *HELP 3–6 (2nd Edition)* is not a formal "test" and you do not "score" a child. You use *HELP 3–6 (2nd Edition)* to credit a child's mastery of a behavior or skill and to plan next steps.

3. The activities in the *HELP 3–6 (2nd Edition) Activities at Home* binder are written from the child's point-of-view, which families/parents enjoy and which prevents any problems with gender. Some of the Instructions below are written using the male gender to avoid redundancy and confusion. No gender bias is intended.

4. *HELP 3–6 (2nd Edition)* covers 585 skills, ages 3 to 6 years. Activities and other content are written using both "he" and "she" to avoid gender bias. The references throughout this book to parents (in the plural) is meant to apply to all parents and caregivers, single, married, etc.

For each skill, this Assessment Manual provides:

Unique ID number and text identical across all the HELP 3-6 family of products.

   1.160 Counts orally to 3

Strand reference and Age range shown in both month-month(m), and year.month-year.month(y) formats.

   Strand: 1-10 Age: 28-36m 2.4-3y

Definition
   This clarifies the item; can be adapted to serve as a basis for criteria to determine mastery.

Assessment Materials
   For use in conducting the assessment. Play-based observations are often recommended.

Assessment Procedures
   Suggested Grouping, and step-by-step methods for conducting the assessment.

Credit
   The criterion for mastery of the behavior/skill.

Adaptations
   Techniques for adjusting the assessment and instruction to accommodate differences in children's abilities and experiences.

5. The behaviors and skills in *HELP 3–6 (2nd Edition)* follow a "normal" developmental sequence and are applicable to all children. However, four of the Strands of skills are provided for use with children with special needs: 2-8 Sign Language; 2-9 Speech Reading; 3-8 Swimming; 3-9 Wheelchair skills. These strands require special instruction; thus, *HELP 3–6 (2nd Edition)* does not provide parent/at home activities for these four strands.

Important Note: Assessment and instruction on some Self-Help items is not appropriate away from home. Follow proper local and agency policies and guidelines regarding these items.

Note: Throughout this *HELP 3–6 (2nd Edition) Assessment Manual*, sample words or sounds are identified in the activities, such as a, b, c, A, B, C. Normally these would be placed in quotes, but for consistency and ease of reading, the quotation marks have been omitted. Upon occasion this may make the grammar structure of the sentence appear awkward. Be sure to read the content carefully so these words/sounds are recognized as samples.

Structure and Link to HELP 0-3

The HELP 3-6 materials link directly to the HELP 0-3 materials according to the developmental strand structure of the 0-3 materials, thus offering a "seamless" Birth-6 continuum. The over 1,250 HELP 0-6 skills are grouped into 75 "concept-based Strands." There are some HELP 0-3 strands for which there are no 3-6 skills (e.g., 1-1 Symbolic Play), and likewise, there are some 3-6 strands that have no 0-3 counterpart (e.g., 1-8 Attention).

Following is the entire HELP 0-6 Strands structure: 0-3 Strands are shown as plain text, HELP 3-6 Strands are in **bold**, Strands that span *both* HELP 0-3 and HELP 3-6 in *italics*.

0.0 Self Regulation (Regulatory/Sensory Integration 0-3)	**4.0 Fine Motor:**
	4-1 Visual Responses and Tracking
1.0 Cognitive:	4-2 Grasp and Prehension
1-1 Development of Symbolic Play	4-3 Reach and Approach
1-2 Gestural Imitation	4-4 Development of Voluntary Release
1-3 Sound Awareness	4-5 Bilateral and Midline
1-4A Problem Solving/Object Permanence	*4-6A Pre-Writing*
1-4B Problem Solving/Means-End	*4-6B Blocks/Puzzles*
1-4C Problem Solving/Cause and Effect	4-6C Formboard
1-4D Problem Solving/Reasoning	**4-6D Paper Activities**
1-5 Spatial Relationships	*4-7A Manipulating Pages*
1-6 Concepts: A. Pictures B. Numbers	**4-7B Pegboard**
1-7A Discrimination/Classification:Matching/Sorting	*4-7C Stringing Beads*
1-7B Discrimination/Classification: Size	*4-7D Scissors*
1-7C Discrimination/Classification: Associative	**4-8 Perceptual Motor: Tactile**
1-8 Attention	
1-9 Reading Readiness	**5.0 Social:**
1-10 Math Readiness	*5-1 Attachment/Adaptive skills*
1-11 Writing Skills	*5-2 Development of Self Identification*
1-12 Dramatic Play	5-3 Emotions/Feelings
1-13 Time	*5-4 Expectations/Responsibility/Rules*
	5-5 Social Interactions and Play
2.0 Language:	**5-6 Social Manners**
2-1 Receptive: Understanding Words	**5-7 Social Language**
2-2 Following Directions	**5-8 Personal Welfare/Safety**
2-3 Expressive Vocabulary	
2-4A Communicating with Others: Gesturally	**6.0 **Self Help:**
2-4B Communicating with Others: Verbally	6-1 Oral-Motor
2-5 Grammar	*6-2A Dressing*
2-6 Development of Sounds	**6-2B Undressing**
2-7 Communication through Rhythm	*6-3A Feeding/Eating*
2-8 Sign Language Skills	**6-3B Drinking**
2-9 Speech Reading Skills	6-4 Sleep patterns and behaviors
	6-5 Grooming
3.0 Gross Motor:	*6-6 Toileting*
3-1 Prone	6-7 Household Responsibility
3-2 Supine	**6-8 Oral Hygiene**
3-3 Sitting	**6-9 Nasal Hygiene**
3-4 Weight-bearing	
3-5 Mobility/Trans. Movements	
3-6 A. Reflexes B. Reactions	
3-7A Balance/Standing	
3-7B Walking/Running	
3-7C Jumping	
3-7D Climbing	
3-7E Stairs (see 3-7B)	
3-7F Catching/Throwing	
3-7G Bilateral Play	
3-7H Balance Beam	
3-8 Swimming	
3-9 Wheelchair Skills	

Assessment/Instruction on some Self-Help skills may **not be appropriate outside the home.

Preparing for the Assessment — Quick Start

Collect and review preliminary information: e.g., review current and past medical reports for conditions the child might have that would influence the assessment; talk with the family regarding the child's strengths and needs, as well as any specialized equipment the child may need to use or have access to during the assessment, such as: glasses, hearing devices, orthopedic devices/equipment; communication systems; review reports from Early Start Programs to see where the child was functioning and what their specific outcomes were; review reports and/or get consent from the family to talk with specialists who previously worked with the child, such as: an occupational therapist, physical therapist, speech and language pathologist, etc.

Review the items (behaviors and skills) which you anticipate you will be observing or eliciting on the *HELP 3–6 (2nd Edition)* Strands, Checklist or Charts. This can be accomplished by identifying general developmental milestones via review of records and parent interview. Highlight several behaviors/skills above and below the child's approximate developmental level.

Some items may occur spontaneously within the classroom or home environment. By providing the child with certain materials, he/she may be observed naturally performing a specific behavior/skill that may be on the list of skills or behaviors to assess. It is important to make note of items that are observed during everyday activities. These can be used to build on the next developmental step/item (behavior/skill) and to indicate a starting place for instruction and further assessment opportunities. A more structured assessment period will be necessary to fully assess a child's levels in all the necessary areas.

A sample overall format for structuring an assessment may include:

- Free-play warm-up period ranging from about 10-15 minutes. Have developmentally appropriate play materials available that are likely to elicit some of the behaviors and skills that you have targeted to assess. During the initial part of this period, family members can be asked to play with their child any way they choose. During this time you can become familiar with the style and level of interaction that the child and family members are most comfortable with and begin to identify additional, more structured activities you may want to incorporate. During this free-play period you can observe family-child interactions, some of the child's toy preferences, how he solves problems, and the manner in which the child moves from one toy to another.

- Structured facilitation period ranging from about 15-30 minutes. Introduce selected eliciting toys, materials and activities directly with or through the parent. This may include table top activities, drawing, looking at books, playing in a dramatic play corner, etc., depending on the behaviors and skills which you are interested in assessing. Again, although you may be targeting specific items for assessment, be sure to capitalize on all areas of development and behaviors/skills that you may observe naturally during the child's play.

- Movement/motor activities and play period ranging from about 10-15 minutes. Provide mats, balls, and other large play equipment dependent upon the child's age and motor abilities, such as a tunnel, things to climb on, small slide, tricycle, or balance beam. Initially, it may be helpful to observe how the child approaches and plays on the equipment before structuring eliciting situations directly with or through the parents. For children with special motor needs, adaptive devices might be necessary for some equipment.

- Feeding or snack time period (about 10-20 minutes). This is an excellent opportunity to observe the child's oral motor skills, independent feeding abilities, food and texture preferences and any tactile reactions, posture during feeding, communication, and behavior. Include washing up before and after snack to observe the child's participation in washing, as well as his reactions to having his face washed. If the child is older, invite him to help clean up afterward by wiping the table and throwing away some of the trash.

When considering a behavior/skill, review each item of information:

1. Item ID Number and Text - Each behavior/skill is assigned a unique ID number that corresponds to the developmental domain for that skill. For example, 1.160 is a 1.0 Cognitive item and 2.133 is a 2.0 Language item. This ID number is used across all the HELP 3–6 (2nd Edition) materials to facilitate cross-referencing assessment procedures, activities, and related information. The items (behaviors/skills) are presented in a developmental sequence within each strand. After the child has been assessed, the text of the targeted skill may then be used as an objective in his educational plan. Items can be easily adapted to behavioral terms, which enables the teacher to select objectives to include in the child's plan or structured program.

2. Age Reference - The age references for each skill are in fact just that—age references and approximations of when the skill typically emerges. Because the data and research do not always agree, the placement of an item with an age level reflects current best thinking and judgment. Every child develops at a different rate and has strengths and areas of need based on abilities, environment, and culture.

The use of age references enables the teacher/staff:

a. To approximate an individual child's progress

b. To assist in the determination of a child's strengths and areas of need.

c. To pinpoint a beginning place for teaching and learning.

The developmental age levels are not to be used for placement, for comparison with peers, for in-class grouping, or for setting unrealistic objectives.

3. Definition - The stated definition clarifies the behavior/skill. The definition includes what the child is expected to do, what the adult involved is expected to do, and any additional contextual description of the item. The definition further clarifies the item text, and can be used to create the necessary criteria for determining credit for the item.

4. Assessment Materials - Items that can be used for assessing and crediting the child. For use in conducting the assessment. Play-based observations are often recommended.

5. Assessment Procedure - The assessments for each item are designed to be administered by a person involved with an early childhood setting.

Each assessment (Level One) includes the following elements:

a. Any special conditions required for the child to perform the assessment procedures.

b. Specific instruction to the person providing the assessment. It is recommended that these instructions be followed as closely as possible.

c. Any appropriate prompt(s).

Some assessment procedures include Level Two strategies that are designed so a child may also be observed informally when he is performing the same behavior/skill during interaction with others. The following are recommended for recording responses.

Group testing can sometimes make it difficult to ascertain a child's true performance since he may "echo" others, or he may refrain from responding because of peer involvement that prevents measuring his highest abilities. You may adapt any of the following as the basis for your credit criteria; however, be sure to record the criteria level for each item as part of his record (using the Strands, Charts, or Checklist), and be consistent in using this criteria so that subsequent staff or a different program can understand his abilities and needs.

<u>Suggested credit/mastery codes:</u>

- **+** if the behavior/skill is present
- **-** if the behavior/skill is not present
- **+/-** if the behavior/skill appears to be emerging
- **A** if the behavior/skill is atypical or dysfunctional
- **N/A** if the behavior/skill is not applicable or not appropriate to assess due to disability or parent preference.

If you create/adapt your own criteria, be sure to use criteria consistently across all items for all children. Record assists under Comments, e.g., "corrects with verbal prompt."

The selection of an assessment criterion depends on many variables. These include experiences, type of children, number of children, educational settings, procedures, and time. The important issue to consider when you select an assessment recording device is that it will provide the needed information and is easy to use and manage. The length of time a child is assessed at a given setting should be decided individually. Try to limit an assessment session to a 15 to 30 minute period. The individual behaviors/skills have been designed to be administered in a five- to eight-minute time period.

6. Assessment sessions should encompass the following:

a. The assessment should be curriculum-based, observational, direct intervention, or program-based to allow for linkage to the program objectives.

b. The assessment should be relevant to the child.

c. The assessment should be sensitive to the child's progress and correlated to the curriculum. It should be broad enough to permit continuous progress.

d. The assessment should be adaptive; if it is too structured, the evaluator may tend to underestimate the child's functioning level. Obvious stimulus and response limitations must be recognized and accommodated. The assessment should stress <u>how</u> the child completed a task as well as whether he completed it.

e. The assessment results should be shared with the entire team. Reporting forms should be organized around the curriculum objectives; therefore, the forms should be based on the curriculum instead of on the test result. The forms should reflect a total picture of a child's performance to determine whether he should be referred for further diagnostic evaluation.

To help a child to reach his optimal performance, encourage and affirm him each time he is involved with an assessment. It is up to the discretion of the person who administers the assessment to decide whether any modifications of the verbal prompts or the language are necessary. It is important to use language the child can easily understand and to accept verbal responses from him in his own words as long as his answers are in response to the assessment.

7. Assessment Adaptations - If a child does not have the prerequisite skill for an assessment procedure, he may have a problem responding to what he is asked to do. Assessment adaptations address the sub-skills the child needs to have mastered before he can attempt the targeted skill or objective. The adaptations may include references to other behaviors/skills that are learned prior to the skill being assessed. The adaptations may provide an explanation or offer some remedial procedures to help instruct the child.

For some specific conditions that have already been identified (including the Federal Special Education eligibility criteria), use the following suggestions to administer the assessment section:

- <u>Cognitive Delays</u> (including the Federal Special Education eligibility for mentally retarded, autistic-like behaviors, autism, learning disabled, or traumatic brain injury) - Use the assessment procedures as written, but modify as follows:

Allow additional time for responses;

Assist with any delayed speech;

Conduct the assessment in the environment where the activity will take place;

Repeat the instructions simply, slowly, and more than once (note how many times the instructions were repeated as this may be valuable information to reference when developing intervention strategies);

Take the child through a procedure by talking him through the assessment, modeling the assessment, asking him to respond independently with support prompts, and finally, asking him to respond without any assistance.

Provide positive feedback on the child's performance, e.g., "Teresa, I really like the way you're listening," or "You are really working hard Scott, keep it up!"

- Speech Disorders (including the Federal Special Education eligibility for Speech or Language Impaired) - Before giving the assessment, consult the child's speech therapist for specific suggestions and assistance. Find out if the child has a specific speech diagnosis that might impact his ability to respond clearly (such as: articulation, voice disorders, fluency issues). If the child is nonverbal, or has significant difficulty expressing himself verbally, a communication system may need to be established prior to the assessment. This could include using an object, picture, or icon system, electronic boards, or other technology or computer programs.

- Behavioral/Social Concerns (including the Federal Special Education eligibility for autistic-like behaviors, traumatic brain injury, or seriously emotionally disturbed) - The assessment procedures often include common behavioral reactions. You can assess the child as the procedure directs, but modify as follows:

  a. If the child's on-task behavior is a diagnosed concern, break the assessment into smaller parts, so he interacts for only a few minutes at a time.

  b. Use simple statements and model the directions as you verbally give them so as to be sure the child understands exactly what he is expected to do during the assessment.

  c. Reward the child for any part of the assessment he accomplishes. Provide positive reinforcement for attempting the task, like trying hard, listening carefully, and achieving goals. Make your compliments specific. If using tangible rewards (i.e., stickers, food items, etc.) change the rewards frequently.

  d. If the assessment is obviously not going to reflect the true performance of the child, stop the procedure and perform the assessment at another time.

- Blind/Visually Impaired (including the Federal Special Education eligibility for visually impaired and blind) - Depending on the degree of the child's visual impairment, you may need to request assistance from a teacher of the visually impaired or consult with the child's ophthalmologist or optometrist.

- Motor Involvement (including the Federal Special Education eligibility for severely orthopedically impaired) – The child has difficulty with motor output in performing purposeful movements. You may give most assessments as written, but modify as follows:

  a. Use patterns, templates, stencils, and/or guided drawings in place of any visual-motor tasks you expect the child to complete if hand coordination is an issue.

  b. Give verbal directions for any perceptual motor components of the assessment.

  c. Use motor devices such as structural aids, e.g., pencil grips, four-ring scissors or grip scissors, paper secured to work place, etc. (Note the effectiveness of the accommodations for the child for further program planning.)

  d. When seated at a table, make sure the child's feet can be placed flat on the floor. The height of the table should be at an appropriate level. (This accommodation should be done for all children regardless of any motor issue.)

- Hearing Impaired (including the Federal Special Education eligibility for hearing impaired or deafness)- The child should have the support of an audiologist, a speech therapist, and a teacher of the deaf and hard of hearing.

  a. Determine which assessment skills apply to the specific hard-of-hearing child.

  b. Verify what the child's communication process involves, whether it's total communication, oral, or signing; then administer the proper assessment in that receptive/expressive mode.

Conducting the Assessment

1. To determine where to begin the assessment process for a child, research his records and ask for observations from parents, teachers, and other persons who are directly involved with the child.

2. Using this collected input, formulate a starting point in a developmental domain. (It is recommended that motor precede communication, social, and cognitive.)

• Within each developmental domain, select a strand/goal area.

• Within the strand/goal area, consider the child's developmental age level, and begin the assessment and instruction at approximately six months below this level. Note: If the child is successful at six months below the developmental age level, move to six months ahead of his developmental age level and work backwards until he attains a success level. Or if the child is unsuccessful at six months below level, move six more months back and then move forward until he attains a success level. (The success level should be based on predetermined criteria.)

3. Remember that you can informally observe many behaviors and skills as the child interacts naturally during activities, with peers, and during group play.

4. Select a starting behavior/skill to begin the assessment. Remember that not all items are applicable to every child. Review the assessment procedure and activities, collect the recommended materials, secure an assessment form, and prepare the setting for the assessment. It is important that you define a criterion level for the item according to the policy established within your program.

5. Adapt the procedure to meet the child's unique needs as necessary.

6. Record the child's responses as indicated in the procedure.

7. Note the items that are not yet mastered, and use the matching Instructional Activities with any necessary adaptations.

8. Use *HELP 3–6 (2nd Edition) Activities at Home* to find appropriate activities to share with the parent(s), and encourage the parent to use the handout as a reinforcement of the instructional activities.

Other Assessment Considerations

• If you use a sequence of skills in a particular domain or developmental strand, and the child makes three incorrect responses in a row based on the predetermined criteria, stop the assessment and begin the instruction with the first item before the child's incorrect response.

• After assessing the child at least six behaviors/skills at six months or more below his developmental level, in which he has been unsuccessful, determine whether he must be referred for diagnostic testing. You may also make the decision before the six missed assessments by observing him in the setting.

• Reassess as necessary to decide whether the child has learned/mastered the behavior/skill and is maintaining mastery.

• Continue to use the recording form as an observational vehicle.

• Date each assessment session.

• It is not necessary to complete all items targeted for an assessment in a particular developmental domain before you move on to another domain.

Although the learning activities and assessments are appropriate for all preschool children, expect them to take a little longer and require modification for children with special needs.

Identifying Child Target skills and activities for instruction

1. Planning - Determine the items (behaviors/skills) the child has not mastered, and select one or more as an objective. Use the ID Number(s) to locate the appropriate instructional activity information in the *HELP 3-6 (2nd Edition) Curriculum Guide*. Review the activities for the target objective to determine any modifications you should make based on the child's unique needs, the availability of materials, teacher skills, physical surroundings, parental involvement, and schedules. **Note**: Some activities include suggested changes based on reducing the task levels, adjusting to the entry behavior of the children, timing, and physical adjustments. Collect or assemble the materials for the activity. Prepare the setting for the instructional procedure.

2. Preparation - Most of the curriculum activities involve directing the child or a group of children through a series of steps that with sufficient repetition and reinforcement will lead to the attainment of the item. It is important to encourage the child or group during the entire activity, and as much as possible, to allow each child to explore and experiment on his own.

3. Instruction - Conduct the suggested activities. You may adjust these to meet the needs of the child, but do not alter the intent of the learning experience. Note: Record any adjustments or modifications, as these notes may be helpful when the specific activity is repeated or is conducted by someone else.

4. Evaluation - At the conclusion of the activity, evaluate the procedure as to its effectiveness, ease of administration, and whether it met the interest level of the child, was motivational for him or the group, provided a vehicle for reviewing the child independently, or had skill-transferable features. Many activities have been designed for use as an evaluation continuum to determine whether the skill has been mastered.

Additional Tips: (adapted in part from *Inside HELP (0-3)*, by Stephanie Parks)

<u>Where do I begin?</u>

One of the most frequently asked questions related to the HELP is "Where do I begin? There are so many items on the assessment forms!"

- *HELP (0-3 and 3-6)* are ongoing curriculum-based assessments which are not intended to be completed in one assessment session. There are a large number of items but these are behaviors and skills which may be included in curriculum planning during an ongoing intervention program that may last for up to three years. As pertinent behaviors and skills are mastered, this can be recorded in the *HELP 3-6 (2nd Edition)* Charts, Checklist or Strands.

- All the behaviors and skills may not apply to all children. Many will not be pertinent due to the child's age and developmental level (e.g., items in the birth to 40-month range and items in the 44-46 month range would not be applicable to a child who is developmentally functioning in most areas at about the 32-35 month range); some behaviors/skills may not be functional due to a child's disability; other skills may not be necessary to assess because they are not judged to be important for a particular child, e.g., ability to walk on a balance beam if the child displays no difficulty in motor planning or balance skills.

- It is important, however, to have a general idea of where to begin an initial assessment, as this will have planning implications regarding the types of materials, settings, and times for observations. Parents can provide an enormous amount of information about their child to give you a general idea of level of functioning in most areas of development.

<u>Make assessments culturally relevant:</u>

It is important to assess and adapt items to reflect the child's relevant cultural and environmental experiences. Some behavior/skills listed in the HELP may not be culturally relevant or appropriate to assess.

Be sure to identify medical limitations and precautions:

It is important to review the child's medical history and current medical status carefully, including vision and hearing if available, before intervention and assessment. Many conditions may require a medical clearance from the child's physician for assessment and intervention.

Involve families in every step of the process:

Families should be invited to participate and make decisions during all phases of the assessment process. Curriculum assessment content, process and expectations should be adapted to respect and fit individual family priorities, beliefs and values. Parents are experts in their child's development and can provide valuable and valid assessment information related to their child's behaviors and skills. It is important to explain what you are assessing and why.

Adapt for disabilities:

Assessment adaptations should be made to help ensure that a disability or delay in one area of development does not interfere with a true assessment of the child's capacities in other areas of development.

What's New in this 2nd Edition of HELP 3–6

Over the past two years, all materials related to *HELP for Preschoolers* were extensively reviewed and evaluated to determine if the behaviors/skills continued to be relevant, age ranges coincided with current literature review, present safety trends and procedures were being followed, and what additional behaviors/skills needed to be addressed. Behaviors/skills that were considered dated, or no longer appropriate, were either modified or removed. Behaviors and skills that were viewed to emerge prior to the age of three, or beyond the age of six, were removed. Some age ranges were modified when necessary. Items related to safety were updated, however, professionals are cautioned to determine the appropriateness of any given skill for each child being assessed. Where gaps in behaviors/skills were noted, new skills were written and incorporated. In addition, three new Strands have been developed.

Suggestions related to what type of grouping might be used to assess the different behaviors/skills have been added. Be mindful that informal observation is a very effective way of assessing a child's abilities because the behavior/skills are occurring in a natural context and in the environment where the task is typically performed. Informal observation should always be considered when the behavior/skill allows. The child is more at ease and their behavior is more natural during an observation. Additionally, an assessor can observe skills they won't necessarily see when conducting a standardized assessment that may require a certain protocol and procedure due to standardization factors. When informal observation isn't appropriate, or the child's skills make it more of a challenge to assess a behavior/skill, one-on-one assessment or small group assessments can often be used.

Another new feature is a section for each behavior/skill that addresses how to "credit" the item. Suggestions are offered regarding when a child should be given credit for demonstrating competency or mastery of each skill. This facilitates consistency across assessments and between children.

The *HELP for Preschoolers Assessment and Curriculum Guide* has been divided into two separate books for ease of use. *HELP 3-6 (2nd Edition)* materials maintain the integrity of the original materials. The breadth of information covered through the behaviors/skills continues to make *HELP 3-6 2nd Edition* a valuable assessment tool for assessing and planning programs for young children. It continues in the tradition of *HELP 0-3* by providing the assessor a broad view of the child's capabilities as well as a giving them a clearer picture of a child's unique areas of strengths and needs. *HELP 3-6 (2nd Edition)* continues to be a helpful resource for professionals to use in conjunction with *HELP 0-3* because of the seamless transition of covering behavior/skills from birth to age six.

Note: To incorporate changes in a manner that makes *HELP 3–6 (2nd Edition)* compatible with the prior version (*HELP for Preschoolers*), the item ID numbering has remained unchanged. For easier cross-reference to "look up an item," the items (behaviors/skills) are listed in this book in <u>ID number sequence</u>. In some cases this means that items do not appear in age sequence. The ID number is strictly for easy cross-reference between assessment and curriculum materials and should not be considered to represent developmental sequence.

After thorough review and analysis of current literature and information, the editorial team made the following changes to HELP 3–6:

A. Three **new Strands** have been added:

<u>0-0 Self-Regulation:</u> Self-regulation is the act of regulating oneself. This requires the child to demonstrate the ability to self-monitor, self-evaluate, and adjust behavior. As a child matures, he becomes more capable of regulating himself. With adult guidance a child can learn to tolerate some anxiety and not go from an impulse to an action by reacting too quickly. Developing a Strand for self-regulation helps the assessor identify a child's skills in this area, which can lead to planning and developing strategies to help the child stop and think before he acts.

1-12 Dramatic Play: Dramatic play was added because so much can be learned about a child's skills by observing them while they are engaged in pretend play. Play is spontaneous, enjoyable, involves interaction with other children, and gives the assessors an opportunity to see how children can assume the roles of others. How elaborate, or simple, a child's play themes or play sequences are can tell a great deal about their developmental level of functioning. In formal, standardized assessments we don't often get the opportunity to observe the child engaged in pretend play. Current literature suggests that when children are playing they are performing close to their optimal developmental level.

1-13 Time: Skills related to time were incorporated in the Strand – Math Readiness. While some of the skills associated with "time" focus on reading numbers on a clock, the abstract understanding of the concept of time (e.g., "today," "tomorrow," and "yesterday") and the days of the week seem to suggest skills outside the realm of math readiness. Therefore, a separate category for Time has been added.

B. Twelve **new** items (behaviors/skills) have been **added**.

ID	Strand	Age (Y.M)	Behavior/Skill Text
1.303	1-12	3.0-3.6	Uses imaginary objects during play
1.304	1-12	3.0-3.6	Uses dolls or action figures to act out sequences
1.305	1-12	5.0-6.0	Role-plays or organizes other children using props
1.306	1-11	5.8-6.8	Prints the numbers 1 - 10 correctly, in sequential and random order, when requested without the use of a model
2.224	2-4B	3.6-3.11	Answers questions logically
2.225	2-4B	4.0-4.6	Responds appropriately to "where" questions
2.226	2-4B	4.6-5.0	Answers "why" questions by giving a reason
4.128	4-6A	3.0-4.0	Holds paper with one hand while drawing with the other hand
4.129	4-7D	3.6-4.0	Cuts out a circle with scissors
4.130	4-6D	4.0-5.0	Places a paper clip on paper
4.132	4-6A	4.6-6.0	Holds pencil/crayon using a dynamic tripod grasp to draw
5.233	5-5	4.0-5.0	Engages in rough-and-tumble play

C. The **text** of the following items was changed, primarily to make the item more consistent with the literature or with HELP 0-3, or to replace/merge it with another item (behavior/skill). A few other items received minor wording changes to improve readability.

ID	Strand	Age (Y.M)	New Text
1.180	1-7C	2.7-3.6	Identifies objects based on appearance (color, shape, or physical characteristic)
1.207	1-11	4.0-5.0	Draws a square, copying model
1.210	1-11	4.9-5.9	Draws a triangle, copying model
1.211	1-10	4.0-5.0	Counts orally to 10, with one-on-one correspondence
1.212	1-10	4.0-5.0	Names penny, nickel, dime and quarter
1.224	1-11	5.9-6.9	Draws diamond, copying model
1.273	1-10	5.4-5.10	Finds group having more, less, or the same number of objects as a given group up to 10
1.292	1-10	5.0-5.6	Reads numerals to 19
1.293	2-7	5.6-6.6	Sings verse of a new song by rote
1.294	1-11	5.8-6.6	Prints all letters of the alphabet correctly, without models
1.298	1-9	5.0-6.0	Answers questions about a story related to the interpretation of the content (was 2.172)
1.308	1-11	4.4-5.0	Draws diagonal lines, copying model (was 4.114)
2.103	2-1A	2.8-3.2	Responds correctly with a non-verbal response or with a single word answer to a stated question
2.104	2-1A	2.8-3.6	Points to or places an object on top/bottom

2.114	2-1A	2.6-3.6	Provides objects as they are requested by name or referenced by function
2.139	2-3	4.0-5.0	Uses negatives in sentences
2.147	2-4B	5.0-6.0	Uses timed events appropriately when explaining a happening (today, yesterday, tomorrow)
2.157	2-2	3.6-5.0	Acts out at least two, but no more than five, commands in the same order they were presented
2.161	2-4B	4.0-6.0+	Uses four- to eight-word sentences
2.176	2-1A	5.4-5.8	Identifies order of sounds in a word and blends the sounds together to make meaningful words
2.182	2-1A	5.8-6.6	Repeats a poem when prompted by the title, a subject clue, or the first line
3.148	3-7A	3.0-3.8	Balances on each foot for 5 seconds, without support
3.163	3-7A	3.0-3.6	Kicks a large ball when the ball has been rolled directly to him
3.164	3-7B	3.8-4.7	Runs and changes direction without stopping, avoiding obstacles
3.170	3-7A	4.0-5.6	Stands up without losing balance after lying on back
3.175	3-7B	5.0-5.5	Walks up and down stairs carrying an object, without support
4.94	4-6B	2.6-3.4	Puts together simple inset puzzles
4.96	4-7D	3.0-4.0	Cuts across paper following a straight line 6 inches long and then a curved line 6 inches long
4.110	4-6D	2.6-3.4	Spreads paste/glue on one side of paper and turns over to stick it to another paper
4.111	4-6A	4.0-5.0	Draws a picture of a person
4.115	4-8	4.5-5.0	Matches or chooses through tactile cues like objects that are circular, triangular, rectangular, and square
4.120	4-7D	5.6-6.0	Cuts cloth with scissors
5.96	5-5	2.6-3.2	Plays with one or two other children
5.97	5-5	2.8-3.2	Exchanges items with another child during play
5.98	5-5	2.8-3.6	Engages in cooperative play with other children
5.99	5-8	2.10-3.5	Avoids hazards and common dangers
5.110	5-5	3.0-3.8	Looks at person when speaking/spoken to
5.116	5-1	3.0-4.0	Transitions from one activity to another at the request of an adult
5.129	5-7	3.6-4.6	Shows an emerging sense of humor by laughing at the appropriate time
5.133	5-6	3.8-4.4	Cleans up spills independently
5.135	5-5	3.6-4.6	Plays with group of 3 or more children
5.137	5-7	3.4-4.5	Uses appropriate manners to request an object
5.184	5-5	5.0-5.6	Waits appropriately for attention in group situation
6.94	6-2B	2.6-3.6	Pulls shoes off completely, including undoing laces, straps (*Velcro*), and buckles
6.100	6-2A	3.6-4.6	Puts on appropriate clothing depending on the weather
6.101	6-8	3.0-4.0	Puts toothpaste on brush and wets
6.115	6-2A	2.6-3.6	Puts shoes on the correct feet
6.121	6-2B	3.2-3.6	Removes pull-over clothing off both arms and starts over head
6.122	6-3B	3.2-3.10	Refills a glass using a container with a handle and a spout
6.153	6-3B	3.2-4.0	Holds container with one hand while sucking liquid through a straw
6.167	6-6	4.4-5.0	Uses toilet properly by self with no accidents
6.175	6-9	4.6-5.6	Covers mouth with tissue, hand or the bend of the elbow when sneezing or coughing
6.181	6-2A	5.0-5.8	Ties shoes, following step-by-step demonstration/support
6.190	6-8	5.5-6.6	Uses proper brushing strokes to clean teeth
6.193	6-2A	5.6-6.6	Ties shoelaces independently

D. Forty-eight items were **removed** for reasons including overlap with HELP 0-3, similarity to other items, or the updated age places the items below three years or above six years.

1.232	2.121	2.210	4.127	5.196	6.124
1.247	2.122	3.150	5.100	5.198	6.125
1.266	2.132	3.151	5.102	5.202	6.126
1.271	2.134	3.154	5.106	5.214	6.128
1.297	2.200	3.156	5.146	5.226	6.165
2.110	2.201	4.95	5.148	6.102	6.173
2.115	2.203	4.107	5.166	6.103	6.179
2.116	2.209	4.109	5.194	6.120	6.187

E. **Ages** were removed for the behaviors and skills in the Strands of 2-8 Sign Language, 2-9 Speech Reading, 3-8 Swimming, and 3-9 Wheelchair because the emergence and development of these behaviors and skills is more dependent upon when the child is exposed to or given an opportunity to learn in the respective environment, such as swimming.

F. **Updated ages** are shown for the following items:

ID	Age (Y.M)	ID	Age (Y.M)	ID	Age (Y.M)
1.180	2.7-3.6	5.107	3.0-4.0	6.101	3.0-4.0
1.192	3.6-4.6	5.108	2.8-3.6	6.104	3.0-4.0
1.194	3.8-4.8	5.113	3.6-4.6	6.107	3.6-4.6
1.203	3.8-4.8	5.116	3.0-4.0	6.113	2.6-3.6
1.210	4.9-5.9	5.124	3.6-4.6	6.115	2.6-3.6
1.224	5.9-6.9	5.125	3.0-4.0	6.118	2.4-3.2
1.241	3.0-4.0	5.128	3.0-4.0	6.119	2.6-3.4
1.292	5.0-5.6	5.135	3.6-4.6	6.127	3.0-4.0
2.111	2.0-3.4	5.137	3.4-4.5	6.131	2.6-3.8
2.112	2.6-3.4	5.138	4.0-5.0	6.133	3.4-4.4
2.114	2.6-3.6	5.142	4.0-5.0	6.135	3.0-4.0
2.120	2.6-3.2	5.143	4.0-5.0	6.139	2.6-3.6
2.130	2.6-3.8	5.145	4.0-5.0	6.144	4.6-5.6
2.139	4.0-5.0	5.164	4.0-4.10	6.145	3.0-4.0
2.147	5.0-6.0	5.165	4.0-5.6	6.147	3.6-4.8
2.155	3.0-4.6	5.167	4.0-5.0	6.151	3.0-4.6
2.156	3.0-4.6	5.171	4.0-6.0	6.153	3.2-4.0
2.157	3.6-5.0	5.172	4.0-5.0	6.154	3.0-4.0
2.161	4.0-6.0	5.178	3.0-5.0	6.156	4.8-6.0
2.173	4.0-5.6	5.179	4.0-5.6	6.157	3.0-4.0
2.177	3.6-4.6	5.181	4.6-5.6	6.161	4.0-5.6
3.153	3.6-4.6	5.182	4.6-5.6	6.166	5.0-6.0
3.157	3.0-3.8	5.183	5.0-6.0	6.169	3.4-4.6
3.160	3.6-4.4	5.186	4.6-6.0	6.174	4.0-5.0
3.161	3.6-4.4	5.189	3.6-4.6	6.176	4.6-6.0
3.163	3.0-3.6	5.197	4.0-5.0	6.177	4.0-5.4
4.94	2.6-3.4	5.199	5.0-6.6	6.178	4.0-5.6
4.110	2.6-3.4	5.211	3.4-6.0	6.184	3.4-4.4
4.120	5.6-6.0	5.225	5.0-6.6	6.185	5.6-6.6
5.98	3.0-4.0	6.97	2.6-3.2	6.188	5.5-6.6
5.101	3.0-3.4	6.100	3.6-4.6		

G. **Definitions** were rewritten and improved for many of the behaviors/skills.

H. These items were **moved between Domains**:

Old ID	New ID	Old ID	New ID
1.167	4.131	4.114	1.308
2.148	1.307	5.193	1.309
2.172	1.298	5.227	1.310

I. These items were **moved** to **different Strands** (with new item ID in bold)

ID	To Strand	ID	To Strand
1.167	**4.131** in 4-6A	1.243	1-7A
1.175	1-7B	1.244	1-7A
1.192	1-7B	1.256	1-7B
1.222	1-7B	2.148	**1.307** in 1-4D
1.233	1-7A	2.172	**1.298** in 1-9
1.234	1-7A	4.114	**1.308** in 1-11
1.237	1-7B	5.193	**1.309** in 1-4D
1.238	1-7A	5.227	**1.310** in 1-4D

1.160 Counts orally to 3
Strand: 1-10 **Age:** 28-36m 2.4-3.0y

Definition
Many children sing number songs long before the counting process takes meaning. Even though the songs do not develop concepts of quantity, they establish the auditory sequence of numbers which is the prerequisite to counting. The child will count up to 3 items upon request.

Assessment Materials
Pegs and a pegboard, or beads and a string for stringing the beads.

Assessment Procedures
Grouping: This skill can be introduced and practiced in a group setting. However, when you are ready to assess the child's ability to orally count to 3, it is recommended that you do so one-on-one with the child.
1. Select one of the manipulative devices (pegs and pegboards, or beads and string for stringing).
2. Provide the child with at least 10 pegs or beads.
3. Ask the child to count each peg or bead she places.
4. Encourage the child to count as far as she can as she places the pegs or beads.
5. Record the child's responses verbatim, being sure to include the sequence she used and how far she was able to count accurately.
6. Place three beads/pegs in front of the child and tell her that you are going to point to each of the items one at a time, and that she is to count as you point.
7. Record the child's responses verbatim. Note if she is able to proceed beyond three.

Credit: + Child consistently counts to 3 in sequence.

Adaptations
If the child is having a problem counting to three, determine if she can look at a series of objects and count them aloud. It is important that counting be connected to an understanding of one-to-one correspondence, not just a rote activity. Some suggestions for assistance in this area are: (1) Cut a hole in the lid of a box, replace the lid and provide the child with blocks to drop into the box via the hole. Ask the child to count only when she drops a block into the box. After all the blocks have been dropped in, remove the lid to the box and ask the child to point to and count the blocks in the bottom of the box; (2) During a small group activity with at least three other children, ask the child to give each child one crayon (or other small item) while counting aloud; (3) If the child has motor issues and is unable to place pegs in a pegboard or string beads, ask the child how many crackers she would like to eat for snack. Have her count the crackers as you place them on the table in front of her. Provide assistance if needed.

1.161 Draws circle, imitating adult
Strand: 1-11 **Age:** 28-38m 2.4-3.2y

Definition
Using a crayon or pencil at least ½" in diameter, the child will copy a circle. The circle needs to be at least two inches in diameter. The child may construct the circle by one continuous movement or by forming two half-circles and then joining them.

Assessment Materials
Paper and pencils (large), crayons, or markers.

Assessment Procedures
Note: A child needs to be stable when sitting at a table, with their feet resting flat on the floor or placed on a footrest.
Grouping: This skill can be introduced and practiced in a group setting, such as drawing on a chalkboard or on the sidewalk. However, when you are ready to assess the child's ability to draw a circle in imitation of an adult, it is recommended that you do so one-on-one with the child.
1. Position yourself next to the child at a table. Place two sheets of paper on the table, one in front of the child and one in front of yourself.
2. Ask the child to watch you as you draw a circle on the sheet of paper.
3. Give the child a crayon or large pencil and ask him to look at your circle and draw one just like it on his sheet of paper.
4. Provide a five-minute break.
5. Show the child the paper that has the model circle on it.
6. Provide him with the necessary writing materials again and ask him to draw another circle.
7. Observe and record his circle-making skills (note which hand he uses to hold the crayon and his grasp on the crayon).

Credit: + The child draws a circle at least two inches in diameter that clearly resembles a circular shape. It does not need to be a perfect circle.

Adaptations

Pre-writing skills require small muscle coordination and eye-hand coordination. If a child has fine motor issues, provide them with adapted writing utensils such as chubby crayons that are approximately 2 ½ to 3 inches tall and ½ inch wide. Let the child practice drawing on a piece of paper taped to a chalkboard or slant board where they can make large strokes that do not require as much fine motor control. Play games with the child by having them imitate your strokes as you make a sound. For example, make a vertical line while saying "Zip!" a horizontal line while you say, "Zap!" or a circle while saying "Zoom!"

1.162 Completes task with some attention and reinforcing

Strand: 1-8 **Age:** 30-36m 2.6-3.0y

Definition

The child will complete a task, such as listening to a tape/CD, sorting blocks, or looking at a picture book for a specified period of time. It may be necessary to provide the child with a sequence of reinforcement activities to renew attention.

Assessment Materials

A set of at least five building blocks and a tennis ball.

Assessment Procedures

Grouping: This skill should be assessed one-on-one with the child.

1. Scatter the blocks on the table. Secure the child's attention by saying her name, tapping on the table, or saying, "Look at me and listen."
2. Tell the child that you want her to build a single tower with three of the blocks (if necessary demonstrate building a tower and then re-scatter the blocks). Explain to her that when she has the tower constructed, you will give her the ball so she can try to knock the tower down.
3. Say, "Ready, set, go! Build your tower!"
4. As the child is building the tower, reinforce her actions by saying such things as, "You are a good tower builder", "Good work!", etc. It is important to use verbal praise prior to using any subtle reinforcement. If the child becomes distracted, bring her attention back by tapping one of the blocks (physical prompt) or re-stating the directions (verbal prompt). Use each attention-getting technique only once.
5. Record the time it takes the child to build the tower. Also make a note of the number of reinforcement strategies used.
6. After the tower is built, give the child the tennis ball and tell her she is to use the ball to knock over the tower. Do not demonstrate, but allow the child to use a trial and error approach in deciding how to use the ball to hit the target.
7. Encourage the child by saying such things as, "You nearly got it!" or "You are really good at this," etc.
8. If the child becomes distracted, bring her attention back by asking her to let you have a turn with the ball. In this case, demonstrate how to roll the ball on the table, but do not knock the tower over.
9. Record the number of attempts it takes the child to knock down the tower and note the number of reinforcement strategies used.

Credit: + Child completes the task with some attention and reinforcement, using only one verbal and one physical prompt.

Adaptations

For some children, learning to focus attention, to stay on task, and to complete an activity is hard because they are easily distracted. Often these children need to pay attention to many of the auditory and visual stimuli that are occurring around them. To begin attention-span training, a quiet environment with fewer distractions (both auditory and visual) may be needed.

1.163 Repeats sequence by physical movements

Strand: 1-4D **Age:** 30-40m 2.6-3.4y

Definition

When shown a series of at least two and not more than six different, concept-related movements, the child will repeat the series. The child needs to be asked to repeat the sequence immediately after the demonstration and encouraged to add to the sequence if appropriate. The physical movements can involve fine or gross motor responses.

Assessment Materials

2 or 3 two-hand/body movements, 2 or 3 three-hand/body movements, and 2 or 3 four-hand/body movements predefined for easier administration and recording.

Assessment Procedures

Note: It is helpful to note in writing the various movement patterns you will be demonstrating for the child to reproduce. By having the movements recorded on paper, it will make it easier to record the child's movements and the order in which they were given.

Grouping: This skill can be introduced and practiced in a group setting. However, when you are ready to assess the child's ability to repeat a sequence by physical movements, it is recommended that you do so one-on-one with the child.

1. Discuss with the child the different ways he can move his hands and body (making a fist, clapping, waving, moving fingers, nodding his head up and down, nodding his head side to side, patting his knees, tapping his feet, etc.)
2. Tell the child to watch while you move your hands and body in two positions. Example: clapping, patting knees. Then ask the child to repeat the movements you just made.
3. If the child does not do the movements correctly, verbally prompt the child by saying, "Watch me!" and repeat your demonstration and remind the child to "Do what I did."
4. Show the child a series of three body movements, such as wiggling the fingers, nodding the head up and down, and tapping the feet. Then show a series of four body movements, such as waving, patting the knees, tapping the feet, and clapping the hands.

Credit: + Child repeats a series of at least two sequences immediately after demonstration. If the child repeated more sequences, note the number. If the child added to the sequence appropriately, note what he did.

Adaptations

If the child displays any motor issues, it may be best to begin the sequence tasks using gross motor skills (head, arms, legs). Perform the sequence slowly using two sequences to begin with. Once the child seems to understand the task, begin adding on to the number of movements being requested. If the child has difficulty with gross motor skills, simple hand and finger movements should be used. Breaking the task into smaller elements and then practicing each element until the child reaches a level of success is necessary prior to putting all the motor sequences together.

1.164 Names an item when shown parts
Strand: 1-4D **Age:** 32-42m 2.8-3.6y

Definition
The child is able to identify an object when only part of it is shown. This identification requires the child to utilize simultaneous thinking skills, by relating a part to a whole.

Assessment Materials
Six single item pictures that the children know (e.g., a picture of a boat, a dog, a house, etc.) The pictures should be at least 5 x 7 inches and mounted on tag board. Cut the pictures into at least two parts. One of the parts should show a recognizable section of the item.

Assessment Procedures
Grouping: This skill can be introduced and assessed in a small group setting, no more than three children. (You may need to have additional single pictures cut into at least two parts). Remind the children that they will be taking turns while playing the game and that they need to listen and wait for their turn. If you have a child who is easily distracted by other children, assess the skill one-on-one with them.

1. Place the six recognizable pictured parts on a table in view of the child. Place the other parts in a low flat box, with the picture side up.
2. Ask the child to select one of the picture pieces on the table. Ask the child, "What do you see?"
3. Present the child with the box of puzzle pieces and ask the child to locate the missing piece and put the puzzle together.
4. When the child has completed the picture puzzle, ask him what the picture shows. Review the first response that he made when he was exposed to the first piece of the puzzle/picture.
5. Continue the same procedure as outlined above for the remaining five picture puzzles.
6. If the child misses any of the pictures, record the error and the child's response.

Credit: + Child identifies at least two items when shown one recognizable section of the item.

Adaptations
If the child finds this task difficult, allow him to see the completed puzzles before he begins. Talk about the pictures noting the item, color and shape. Mix the puzzle pieces again. Have the child pick an item from the table. Allow ample time for processing what is seen, if

necessary use auditory cues. Then provide the child with the box of puzzle pieces to find the matching piece. Phase out the auditory cues when the child begins to feel comfortable with identification based on the picture displayed.

1.165 Locates pictured analogy
Strand: 1-4D **Age:** 32-44m 2.8-3.8y

Definition
The child will view and locate pictures that have like characteristics. The first level of difficulty will include sets of pictures with one odd color, shape or size. A more advanced level of analogy will include a picture that is different because of use or type.

Assessment Materials
Prepare five 8 x 10-inch picture cards. Divide the picture cards into four sections. On card number one, in three squares draw or place a cut-out of three red squares that are the same size; in the fourth square place a different colored square that is larger. On card number two, in three squares place three different color and size circles; in the fourth square place a circle that has a design. On card number three, in three squares draw or place a cut-out of items that are used for the same thing, i.e., place to live in, house, tent, bird-house; in the fourth square place a picture of a toy. On card number four, in three squares draw or place a cut-out of an orange, a ball and a balloon; in the fourth square place a rectangle box wrapped as a present. On card number five, in three squares draw or place cut-out pictures of a toothbrush, comb and soap; in the fourth square place a picture of a broom.

Assessment Procedures
Grouping: This skill should be assessed one-on-one with the child.
1. Explain to the child that she is going to look at some different picture cards. Each picture card has four pictures on it. She is to look at the pictures and point to the picture that does not belong with the rest.
2. Show her card number one. After she has pointed to a picture, ask her to justify her response. Record her response, and if she made an error, note the picture that she selected.
3. Continue with the same procedure using cards numbered two - five.

Credit: + Child locates the pictured analogy in three out of the five picture cards.

Adaptations
The child may need to work with concrete objects before being asked to identify pictures of objects. She may also need practice in perceiving relationships between facts, ideas and articles.

1.166 Sings parts and phrases of familiar songs
Strand: 2-7 **Age:** 32-44m 2.8-3.8y

Definition
The child will sing a part, a phrase, or the chorus of a familiar song. His singing does not need to be intelligible speech if the melody can be determined. He may also sing only parts of the lyrics if the melody can be determined.

Assessment Materials
A recording of a simple song that is repetitious and familiar to the child. A tune such as "Mary Had a Little Lamb" is appropriate. Equipment to play the song.

Assessment Procedures
Grouping: This skill can be introduced, practiced and assessed during a group activity. You may also hear the child singing while he is spontaneously playing and can assess his skills based on what you heard.
1. Invite the child to listen to the selected song. Play it several times and begin to sing along.
2. Encourage the child to sing along with the familiar tune.
3. Observe the parts that he sings, and note how he continues to sing more and more of the song.
4. If he has problems singing along, select a song that includes some physical movements, such as "The Wheels On the Bus" or "The Itsy Bitsy Spider." Invite him to listen and watch the actions to the song.
5. Play the song several times, doing the motions, and singing along.
6. Encourage him to join in doing the movements and singing along.
7. Emphasize singing the action parts of the song; for example, in "The Wheels On the Bus," emphasize as follows: "The wheels on the bus go round and round," and so on.
8. Sing the song several times, observing whether he participates in the movements and the singing.
9. It is important to reward his singing efforts and to give him plenty of opportunities to

enjoy singing along. Most children enjoy singing, and their enjoyment does not diminish unless someone discourages their efforts.

Credit: + Child sings part of the lyric, even if the child's speech is unintelligible, but you can recognize the melody.

Adaptations

Children are more apt to sing along with songs they have heard many times. Having visuals, like a book, or movements draws them in even more. Having a choice board with a picture to represent each song can give a child an opportunity to choose a song they would like to sing. Have the child stand next to you and lead a small group in singing the song. Providing props, such as a school bus for "The Wheels On the Bus" can encourage more interaction from the child. Also, you can sing a song one-on-one with a child and as you sing, pause to see if he will fill in the words that come next. Finally, using musical instruments as you sing can entice the child to join in with the singing of a song.

1.167 (Moved to Fine Motor, skill 4.132)

1.168 Names action when looking at a picture book

Strand: 1-9 **Age:** 36-42m 3.0-3.6y

Definition

The child will use verbs to explain what is happening in a picture. The action verbs the child might use are "running, jumping, the boys are climbing, riding a horse, the girls are playing with their dolls," etc.

Assessment Materials

Two pictures that show action. Picture one needs to show one person doing a single action. Picture two should show more than one person involved in more than one action.

Assessment Procedures

Grouping: This skill should be assessed one-on-one with the child.

1. Explain to the child that you are going to show him a picture and that he is to look at the picture carefully, because you are going to ask him some questions.
2. Ask such questions as, "What is the girl doing?" "Is she _____ fast/slow?" "Can you _____?" etc.
3. Make note of when the child answers with the correct description of the action.
4. Show the child the second picture and ask him to look at it carefully, because you are going to ask him some questions about what is happening.
5. Ask such questions as, "What is happening in the picture?" "Are all the people doing the same thing?" "Name the things that the people are doing." "Which one of the things that are happening in the picture would you like to do?"
6. Make note of when the child answers with the correct description of the action.

Credit: + Child consistently uses verbs to explain what is happening in the pictures.

Adaptations

It is important to select pictures that clearly show the action as the central theme. Some children find a need to focus on one segment and then quickly move to another part of the picture; thus when asked to locate the main action of a picture it is difficult unless a verbal discussion or story accompanies the picture/illustration.

1.169 Tells story when looking at a picture book that has been read many times

Strand: 1-9 **Age:** 36-42m 3.0-3.6y

Definition

The picture book should have much word repetition and the illustrations should have a direct relationship to the story content. It should be a story that the child has not only heard several times, but one that the child would request to hear again. Using memory and picture clues, ask the child to tell the story.

Assessment Materials

A short picture book that has rhyme and repetition in the dialogue.

Assessment Procedures

Grouping: This skill should be assessed one-on-one with the child.

1. Ask the child to sit next to you, so that you can read the story to her and so she can see the pictures that match the content.
2. Read the story to the child.
3. Read the story again, and point to the pictures that correlate with the script. Discuss the main character of the story, the sequence of events, and the ending.

© 2010 VORT Corporation. All rights reserved. Do Not copy.

4. Read the story again and begin to leave out words that rhyme or words that are repeated.
5. Read the story again and allow the child to begin sharing the story telling. If the child becomes unsure of the plot, provide assistance by giving leading clues as to what is going to happen next.
6. Read the story again and allow the child an opportunity to become the storyteller.
7. Ask the child if she would like to tell the story while you turn the pages.
8. Record whether or not the child told the story without any assistance; if prompts were needed, record the number of times you assisted.

Credit: + Child retells the main points of the story using memory and picture clues only.

Adaptations

A child may not remember a story plot or sequential happenings if it was not clearly perceived. That is the reason for making association with the pictures as you are reading a story, and for having words that rhyme and phrases that repeat. This allows for visual and auditory clarification. After the information has been "stored," it must be retrieved/recalled for retelling. Some children have difficulty recalling the correct information. Hence the child needs an opportunity to retell the story (with the support of the adult story book reader) before being expected to become the storyteller. An activity you can use to engage a child in telling a story would be to have a small group of children act out a well known story, such as "The Three Little Pigs" as you read the book. Some of the children can be actors by playing the various roles and the other children can help the adult with the telling of the story. The adult should frequently pause and allow enough time for the children to fill in the lines. The adult could also say the wrong thing, such as "Little goats, little goats! Let me go out!" Wait, and allow the children to correct you before moving on.

1.170 Moves body to music

Strand: 2-7 **Age:** 36-42m 3.0-3.6y

Definition

When presented with live or recorded music, the child will move his body to the music. The child may sway, rock, tap, clap or do any physical movement that indicates a "feel" for the music. The child need not move in correct rhythm to the music. The musical rhythm may be fast or slow.

Assessment Materials

Songs or musical selections that have a distinct rhythmic beat. The songs may lend themselves to fast movement or encourage slow reaction such as a waltz.

Assessment Procedures

Note: It is important to allow the child to have many opportunities to experiment with the sounds of music and to be able to swing and sway.

Grouping: This skill can be assessed in a group setting.

1. Explain to the child that you are going to play some music and that he is to listen. As the child listens to the selection, observe if his body begins to identify with the rhythm.
2. Observe such movements as a swing or sway, a gallop, a clap, tapping, etc.
3. If the child does not respond to the music, remember that the introduction to creating rhythmic movement is gradual and often begins with watching others and moving or dancing with others.
4. Encourage him to hold your hands and to move with you. You can show him how to move his body from side to side and then ask him to show you another way you might be able to move. Imitate his movements.
5. Change the tempo of the music, either faster or slower, whatever seems to match his temperament.
6. Often children will feel more comfortable moving to music when they see the adults around them dancing to music and having a good time.

Credit: + Child moves his body to the music. He does not need to move in the correct rhythm to the music in order to receive credit.

Adaptations

Some children are not comfortable moving to music because they are shy or they might have motor issues. Offering to dance with these children can them make feel more comfortable and may provide the physical support they need to move more freely. For children who are slow to warm up to the idea of moving to music, the introduction of musical instruments might encourage them to move their arms. Suggesting that the group march around the room while listening to music may encourage them to move their legs. Next combine the instruments with the marching to get the child to move more of their body. Also, children can take turns showing the group a specific way they can move their body to the music and then everyone imitates and takes turns showing their new moves.

1.171 Claps to music

Strand: 2-7   **Age:** 36-42m   3.0-3.6y

Definition
When the child is presented with live or recorded music, she will clap in imitation, but not necessarily in time to the music.

Assessment Materials
Simple, short, rhythmic, musical patterns.

Assessment Procedures
Grouping: This skill can be assessed in a group setting.
1. Invite the child to join you at the music center.
2. Explain that you are going to play some music and that you want her to listen.
3. Start clapping to the beat of the music.
4. Do not ask the child to clap with you; allow her to join in the clapping process spontaneously.
5. Observe if the child distinguishes the beat and expresses it through clapping.
6. If the child does not participate, clap a simple, short, rhythmic pattern. Ask the child to clap the pattern with you. Provide physical assistance if necessary, phasing out the hand-over-hand support as the child begins to "feel" the pattern.
7. Clap the pattern again.
8. Ask the child to repeat the clapped sequence.
9. As the child gains skills, play the music again (no prompting) and observe her participation.

Credit: + Child claps in imitation, but not necessarily in time to live or recorded music.

Adaptations
Some children may not be aware of what is expected with this activity. Return to a favorite song of theirs, preferably one that has hand movements that include clapping. Encourage the child to clap at the appropriate times in the song. If clapping is difficult for them because of motor challenges, have the child pat a drum. If necessary, provide hand-over-hand support to help the child clap. Pause during the song to see if the child will spontaneously move their hands together.

1.172 Taps to the beat of music

Strand: 2-7   **Age:** 36-42m   3.0-3.6y

Definition
When presented with live or recorded music that has a precise, slow, simple beat, the child will mark time to the selection using his fingers, feet or an object (stick). The tapping activity may or may not generate a sound.

Assessment Materials
A musical selection that has a precise, slow, and simple beat. Sticks, such as dowels.

Assessment Procedures
Grouping: This skill can be assessed in a group setting. You may also observe the child tapping spontaneously to music while playing and can assess his skills based on what you saw.
1. Explain to the child that you are going to play a song and that you want him to listen.
2. As the selection is being played, observe if the child begins to tap his fingers or toes, or if he picks up the dowel and starts to tap the beat on the table.
3. Continue your observation by determining if he changes the rhythm within the same musical selection by changing the movements in a noticeable manner.
4. If the child does not participate in tapping the beat, begin discreetly tapping your fingers or foot to the beat of the music.
5. Observe if the child follows the model.
6. Use the dowel stick to keep the beat. Give the child the other dowel stick and take turns tapping to the music.

Credit: + Child marks time to music with his fingers, feet or an object (stick). The tapping need not generate a sound in order to be given credit.

Adaptations
Most children are comfortable with musical rhythms. Children have been responding to sounds since infancy; they bang their silverware, they listen to and enjoy the rhymes of Mother Goose, they beat boxes, pots, pans, and toys and will clap to favorite tunes. It is important to allow the child to participate in these musical experiences, not only for the enjoyment but to assist in the understanding of the rhythmic aspect of language and the development of motor skills. Hand-over-hand support can be given to the child to help them tap to music.

© 2010 VORT Corporation. All rights reserved. Do Not copy.

1.173 Marches to music
Strand: 2-7 **Age:** 36-42m 3.0-3.6y

Definition
When the child is presented with a repetitive marching musical selection, she will march to the music, but not necessarily with the beat.

Assessment Materials
Marching props such as a scarf, flag or pompom. Marching music.

Assessment Procedures
Grouping: This skill can may be introduced, practiced and assessed during a group activity.
1. Play the marching music.
2. If the child begins to march, hand her a prop, and encourage her to participate by clapping or marching along.
3. If she does not march to the music, select a marching prop for yourself and give her the scarf or other marching prop.
4. Play the selection and begin marching, using your prop. Invite her to join you in the musical march.
5. If she joins in, phase out your participation; stop marching and begin to clap in place. Be prepared to begin marching again if she stops. Only enter into the marching activity two times.
6. If she does not join you in the march, encourage her to clap or tap to the beat.
7. Do not require her to perform the assessment at this time; however, allow her many more opportunities to march to music.

Credit: + Child marches to the music, but not necessarily the beat. You may prompt the child by marching with them no more than two times during the activity.

Adaptations
Some children have a difficult time performing activities in a patterned sequence. To perform certain tasks, certain body movements must follow others. In marching, the legs must move alternately in time to the musical beat, or the legs and arms must move in a precise manner to the marching beat. Children experience the timing of the movement and the temporal sequence of steps. All these are dimensions of auditory-motor responses. If a child is experiencing an auditory-motor response delay, deal with it through such activities as line walks, obstacle paths, animal walks, and hoop steps. Marching to music should be addressed as part of an enjoyable musical occurrence, not as a remedial technique for a motor skill.

1.174 Identifies and counts quantities of one, two, three or four
Strand: 1-10 **Age:** 36-42m 3.0-3.6y

Definition
The child has been manipulating objects and gaining insight into the pre-symbolic concepts of size, form and quantity. The child must first assimilate and integrate his nonverbal experiences, and then he will associate the numerical symbol with that experience. Finally, the child will use the language of mathematics to express the value of the quantity. When shown one to four objects, the child will associate and verbalize the correct word for the quantitative value.

Assessment Materials
A cup of edible items (small crackers, squares of cheese, cereal, etc.) Two sets of index cards, four to a set. Each set will be identical. Put one dot or sticker on card one, put two dots or stickers on card two, put three dots or stickers on card three, and put four dots or stickers on card four. Two blank sheets of construction paper.
Note: If food items are not appropriate, substitute other items such as: checkers, cars, counting bears.

Assessment Procedures
Grouping: This skill should be assessed one-on-one with the child.
A. Using cards:
1. Using the index cards, place one set of cards with dots or stickers on them in random order on the table in front of the child.
2. Hand the child one card from the second set of cards and ask him to match it to the same card on the table. As they match the cards, ask them how many dots or stickers are on the card.
3. Continue this same process by handing the child the remaining cards in random order and asking him to match them to the cards in front of him.
4. Note the child's two responses: (1) Correctly matches the amounts; (2) Saying the correct number.
B. Using paper:
1. Next, place one of the sheets of construction paper in front of the child and place the other sheet of construction paper in front of you.

Place a group of at least eight edible items on the table.
2. Explain to the child that you are going to place one type of food item on your piece of construction paper and that he is to put the same amount of food on his sheet of paper. Continue by telling him that you will ask him how many _____ he has on his paper.
3. Use the first activity as a teaching example.
4. Place two of the food items on your sheet. Say, "Look at the number of _____ on my sheet. Can you put the same amount on your piece of paper?" After the child has placed the items ask, "How many pieces of _____ are on your paper?"
5. Repeat if the child does not understand the assessment procedure.
6. Continue step five using the quantitative value of one, three, two, four.
7. Record his responses: (1) The correct food-number match; (2) Stating the quantitative amount by number name.
8. Eating the food items is an effective reward for tasks attempted or well done.

Credit: + Child associates and verbalizes the correct word for the quantitative value of one, two, three and four objects.

Adaptations

Some children do not have the concept of one-to-one relationships, therefore they will have a difficult time grasping the concept of numbers or counting. These children may count erratically; for example, when counting blocks they may say, "one, two" when touching the first block, "three, four" when touching the second block, and then could skip the next block altogether. Other children who find it hard to understand one-to-one relationships may have a problem grasping the concept that there are only four chairs around the table and when six people come to sit down there is not enough for every person. To assist the child in understanding the corresponding value of one-to-one the following are suggestions: (1) Have the child match rows of blocks. Arrange a row of blocks and give the child another set to arrange in exactly the same way. Do not permit him to skip any blocks or put more in than match the model row; (2) Use the child's auditory and visual modality to assist him in relating to numbers. Beat a drum or clap your hands, ask him to place a block on the table each time he hears the beat or clap of your hands.

1.175 Locates big and little objects in groups of 2
Strand: 1-7B **Age:** 36-42m 3.0-3.6y

Definition
The child needs to have an understanding and perception of different sizes in order to deal with such mathematical concepts as perimeters and areas. Without the basic notion of big and little, the child may find confusion in everyday activities, e.g., will this box fit into this drawer, will these keys fit into my pocket? By using models of two sizes, the smallest being at least 3 inches on a side or in diameter and the largest being 7 inches on a side or in diameter, the child will identify items according to size. The child will respond to the terminology large - big and small - little.

Assessment Materials
Collect a set of eight pictures that show four single items in two different size dimensions. The pictures can be drawn or cut and glued on poster board. Example: a picture of a big ball on one card, and a picture of a small ball on another card; a picture of a large tree on one card, and a picture of a small tree on another card; a picture of a big elephant on one card, and a picture of a small elephant on another card; a picture of a large bed on one card, and a picture of a little bed on another card, etc. Write down four questions about the relative sizes of the objects pictured in the Card Set. Example: Can you put a ball in a shoe box? Can you fit an elephant in a bath tub? Can you move the tree into your closet? Will a bed fit in the room that you sleep in? The more ridiculous the questions are, the more enjoyable they become.
Note: If food items are not appropriate, substitute other items such as: checkers, cars, counting bears.

Assessment Procedures
Grouping: This skill should be assessed one-on-one with the child.
1. Show the child the pictures of the balls.
2. Discuss the pictures with the child, asking questions about the color of the balls, what they are used for, which she would rather play with, etc. Do not ask any questions dealing with size.
3. Ask the Fun Question about the size of the ball. Example: "Can you put a ball in a bath tub?"
4. Following the question, ask the child to point to the ball that is small and then point to the ball that is big.

5. Ask the child to point to the ball that would fit in a bath tub (could be both sizes).
6. Record the child's response; both the verbal answer and pointing to the correct size.
7. Continue the above procedure, but only use the pictures and questions about the tree, elephant and bed. Record the child's response to each item.

Credit: + Child consistently locates big (large) and little (small) objects when presented in groups of two.

Adaptations

Using food items of different sizes can be motivating in learning the difference between large – big and small – little. Figure out what food item is their favorite. Have a large – big portion and a small – little portion in front of you. Ask the child which one they want. Typically, they will point to the larger serving. Explain which serving is large – big and which is small – little. You could negotiate with the child for the larger serving for yourself, while offering them the smaller serving. You could then ask which one they want. Allow time for them to respond and see if they use their words to describe which serving they would prefer.

1.176 Points to the same item in two different settings

Strand: 1-4D **Age:** 36-44m 3.0-3.8y

Definition

The child is expected to identify the same object even if the item has a modified spatial position, becomes distorted due to visual form change, or a different visual background.

Assessment Materials

Select a picture book that has at least one main character in the story plot. It is important that a main character be pictured on nearly every page, in different positions, with different backgrounds and doing different tasks.

Assessment Procedures

Grouping: This skill should be assessed one-on-one with the child.
1. Show the selected book to the child and locate the main character.
2. Turn the pages of the book with the child. Use the name of the character and ask the child to locate the character on the pages of the book.
3. The character should be illustrated in such positions as bending over, stretching, and climbing. Be sure that the character is shown in such settings as outside, inside, standing beside a tree, walking with a group of people, standing in a crowd, in a store, dressed differently, etc. It is important that this character also be behind an item, under something, beside a chair, on top of a ladder, etc.
4. As the child is responding, determine if he is having any problems, and if so, if they are related to the identification of the character when in a changed body position, when the character is viewed in a multi-object background or when the character is pictured differently in dress and activity. Note any area of concern.

Credit: + Child identifies the same object even if the item has been changed or modified in some way in two different settings.

Adaptations

Some children may have problems remembering an object in different settings because the content varies according to meaning and the content may be meaningless to the child. If this appears to be a problem, discuss the item with the child and what the item is doing in the setting, why the item is there and how the item looks alike and different in the various content situations. As an example, if the child is shown a picture of a car parked in a driveway, and on the next page the same car is going down a busy freeway, the child may have difficulty identifying the car on the freeway because the child only associates the car in the known context of the driveway.

1.177 Plays on rhythm instruments

Strand: 2-7 **Age:** 37-42m 3.1-3.6y

Definition

When presented with a basic rhythm instrument (triangle, maraca, tambourine, cymbals, sticks, clappers, sand blocks, bells, drum) and background music, the child will play the instrument. She should be exposed to the following instruments first: sticks, clappers, sand blocks, bells, and drum. It is not necessary for her playing to be rhythmic or exact.
Note: *Any item that is not too difficult to manipulate and that produces a distinctive sound may be used as a rhythm instrument.*

Assessment Materials

Wooden sticks (made of hard-enough wood to provide a resonant sound), clappers (blocks made of hard wood with a handle on one side), sand blocks (heavy duty sandpaper wrapped around a wooden block), bells (any variety of bells rung by hand or the wrist fitting variety), and a drum (made with padded heads or made of rubber, such as a hand drum, bongo drum, tom-tom). A rhythm instrument recording of a lively rhythm, a nursery rhyme, or a song such as "Row, Row, Row Your Boat" or "Old MacDonald Had a Farm."

Assessment Procedures

Grouping: This skill can be introduced, practiced and assessed either in a group setting or one-on-one with the child. If the child is easily distracted when other children are present, assess the skill one-on-one or in a small group. If the child is timid in a one-on-one setting assess the skill in a group.

1. Display the instruments on a table.
2. Invite the child to experiment with the musical instruments. Share with her in this exploration.
3. Provide any instruction needed for her to be able to play the instrument. She will no doubt wish to try out all five instruments.
4. After this investigation period, ask her to choose one of the instruments.
5. Put the remaining instruments away.
6. Play the music, and ask her to use the instrument she chose to play along with the selection.
7. If she plays it, select an instrument for yourself, and join her in a musical duet.
8. Allow her to change instruments at the end of the selection.
9. If she is not interested in participating, demonstrate the use of each instrument, and play the accompanying selection, but do not insist that she play.

Credit: + Child plays the instrument to background music. It is not necessary for her playing to be rhythmic or exact.

Adaptations

A formal, organized method to play a rhythm instrument may diminish creative expression and should be used sparingly. A stereotyped activity in which the child is supposed to follow the basic beat carefully will not nurture creativity. Free use of rhythm instruments allows her to become involved in music without having to be a musician. This builds success for children with special needs and provides them with an avenue of rewarded participation.

1.178 Marches in time to the music
Strand: 2-7 **Age:** 40-44m 3.4-3.8y

Definition
When she is presented with a marching song, the child will march in time to a repetitious beat.

Assessment Materials
Two recorded marches. A drum.

Assessment Procedures

Grouping: This skill can be assessed in a group setting. You may also observe the child marching in time to music spontaneously while she is playing and can assess her skills based on what you observed.

1. Do this activity in an area large enough so the child will have ample room to march.
2. Play the march.
3. Point out the marching area, and encourage her to move to the music.
4. Observe whether she marches in time to the music.
5. If she marches to the music, begin to clap or do other hand movements.
6. If she does not march to the music, ask her to watch while you demonstrate marching to the music.
7. Encourage her to join you in the marching exercise.
8. As she begins to model your marching, phase your marching out, but continue to emphasize the beat by clapping or beating a drum.
9. When she demonstrates that she feels the marching beat, phase out the support.
10. Play another march and ask her to march in time to the music.

Credit: + Child marches in time to a repetitious beat.

Adaptations

The inherent pleasure in the rhythmic movement of marching is a beginning vehicle for the interpretation of music. Children need to be allowed to interpret different marching motions and should not be required to perform in a stereotypical way. They need to realize that marching is not just a gross motor skill, but that it can include hand and head movements. Children who have difficulty learning to march, should be exposed to marching through fun and playful games. As you walk to another room, encourage the child to imitate what you do. March lifting your legs high in the air. Then ask the child to walk sideways or backwards. Return to marching and continue the game by marching loudly or marching quietly. Ask the child to take the lead and choose how the group should march.

1.179 Claps to beat of familiar songs or to speech patterns

Strand: 2-7 **Age:** 40-46m 3.4-3.10y

Definition
When he is presented with a familiar song or with speech cadence or patterns, the child will clap in time to the selection. He should clap the beat during the main musical theme or in cadence with the repeating phrases.

Assessment Materials
Choose a song with a distinct beat that is familiar to the child. Select a poem or chant that has ample repetition and can be read in a metered manner.
Example:
Where's Melissa?
Where's Melissa?
She is here.
When do we go?
I know.
Where's Judy?
She is here.
When do we go?
I know.
Where's Max?
He is here.
When do we go?
I know.
Everyone's here.
When do we go?
I know,
I know.

Assessment Procedures
Grouping: This skill can be assessed in a small group setting, no more than four children. Remind the children that they will need to listen and take turns during the activity.
1. Play the music or say the poem.
2. Ask the child to clap to the beat of the selection.
3. Start clapping to the beat if he pauses or hesitates.
4. Phase out the clapping as he picks up the beat. If he loses the rhythm at any time, resume clapping to re-establish the pattern.
5. If he has a difficult time keeping the beat, begin a tap--clap pattern.
6. Example: 1) Tap the table. Clap the hands; 2) Tap, Tap, Clap, Clap; 3) Tap, Clap, Tap, Tap; 4) Tap, Tap, Tap, Clap, Clap, Clap.
7. Repeat the above steps.
8. Observe whether he is able to clap to the beat.

Credit: + Child claps in time to a familiar song or the speech cadence and pattern in a poem or chant.

Adaptations
Children like to keep the beat of a musical selection, but they may think they are keeping the rhythm and never realize that their efforts are not quite right. However, the more a child becomes aware of rhythmic sounds, the more he will enjoy music. It is important to allow all children to experience the sound of cadence or beats; however, performing expectations and making them conform to set standards can easily take away their enjoyment. For a child who has receptive difficulties, clapping to rhythms enhances his listening skills and may be a motivational way to improve auditory responses.

1.180 Identifies objects based on appearance (color, shape, or physical characteristic)

Strand: 1-7C **Age:** 31-42m 2.7-3.6y

Definition
The child will identify objects that are based on: (1) Color; (2) Shape; and (3) Physical characteristics. The child will identify these objects by verbal response or by manipulation. The first objects presented to the child should be concrete (an apple, a ball, a cap, etc.) The child should then be asked to identify by visual representation (single item pictures). If the child experiences success in identifying these items, ask her to identify an object based on a verbal description of its appearance.

Assessment Materials
Concrete items, such as an apple, a ball, a paint brush, or a small toy car. Strips of colored paper (two 2 x 4-inch strips, two per color with at least four different colors). Five sets of single item pictures (two pictures of a banana, two pictures of a flag, two pictures of a car, two pictures of a chair, etc.)

Assessment Procedures
Grouping: This skill should be assessed one-on-one with the child.
A. Using the concrete items:

1. Place the concrete items in a random position on the table. Ask the child to point to the red apple.
2. Observe the child as she locates the item.
3. Continue with the other items on the table.
4. Place the color strips randomly on the table.
5. Ask the child to name the colors.
6. Explain to the child that you want her to locate the two strips that are alike and put them together.
7. Take note of the hesitancy of the child and the time involved in the assessment task.
8. After she matches the colors, place the similar single item pictures in view of the child and ask her to name the items.
9. After she has named the items, ask her to place the two that are exactly alike together.
10. Note the correctness of the task and the time required to complete the task.

B. Using single item pictures:
1. If the child is successful in the above assessment procedures, collect the single item pictures, explain to the child that you are going to look at one of the pictures, and describe it. After the description, ask the child to name what has been described. Reinforce the response by showing the child the picture.

Credit: + Child identifies objects based on appearance, which includes: color, shape, or physical characteristics.

Adaptations

There are many games you can play with children to help them learn to identify objects based on appearance. You can introduce a lotto game. There will be many sets of two identical picture cards. Hand the child one card from the set while you keep the second card in a stack in front of you. Randomly choose a card from the stack in front of you. Turn the card around to see if they can visually match the cards. This game can also be played in a small group.

1.181 Identifies objects based on category

Strand: 1-7C **Age:** 40-48m 3.4-4.0y

Definition

The child will identify objects based on category. The child will identify these objects by manipulation or verbally. The first objects presented to the child should be concrete. The child should then be asked to identify by visual representation (single item picture). If the child experiences success in identifying these items, ask him to identify an object based on a verbal description of its appearance.

Assessment Materials

Two red circles, two red squares, and two red triangles. Two blue circles, two blue squares, and two blue triangles. Two yellow circles, two yellow squares, and two yellow triangles. Three boxes large enough to hold the shapes.

Assessment Procedures

Grouping: This skill should be assessed one-on-one with the child.
1. Place the boxes and shapes in front of the child, point to the boxes, and request that the child put the circles in one box, the squares in another box, and the triangles in another box.
2. Record the number of items placed correctly and the time taken to respond.
3. Repeat the above asking the child to place the red shapes in one box, the green shapes in another box, and the blue shapes in another box.
4. Record the number place correctly and the time needed to respond. Repeat the directions if necessary but do not cue.

Credit: + Child identifies objects based on category. This can be done verbally or by putting like items together.

Adaptations

Some children have a difficult time when asked to deal with categories, because most items can fit into more than one class (for example, a glass is not just something that you can drink from; it is also clear and easily broken). These children will find success if the named category is something they are familiar with and if they have actually used the object in the mentioned class. To assist the child, it is best to present categorical requests that are concrete things that the child has experienced, and items that have a classification cue within their appearance. It is also important to make sure that descriptive words are used to expand the child's opportunity to understand the class and the objects.

1.182 Identifies objects based on function

Strand: 1-7C **Age:** 40-48m 3.4-4.0y

Definition

The child will recognize those objects that are used for the same purpose or have the same general performance qualities. The child will match items that carry things, things that clean, things that keep us warm, things that we play with, etc. It is important that the child understands that she is classifying items by what they do. When asked, the child should begin to state the function of the item with some prompting.

Assessment Materials

Four sets of two pictures per set. Set One - a picture of a piece of furniture (chair) and a picture of something that moves (car). Set Two - a picture of a toy (ball) and a picture of something we read (book). Set Three - a picture of a pan (frying) and a picture of a bar of soap or tube of toothpaste. Set Four - a picture of a tool (hammer) and a picture of a musical instrument (horn).

Assessment Procedures

Grouping: This skill should be assessed one-on-one with the child.
1. Show Set One to the child and ask her to point to the picture that shows something that moves.
2. Show Set Two to the child and ask her to point to the picture that shows something you could play with.
3. Show Set Three to the child and ask her to point to the picture that shows something that keeps us clean.
4. Show Set Four to the child and ask her to point to the picture that shows something that makes music.
5. Tabulate the responses. Continue the assessment using the following directions.
6. Show Set One to the child and to point to the picture of the car while saying, "A car is something that you would _____." Wait for the child to respond. Prompt if necessary.
7. Show Set Two to the child and point to the picture of the ball while saying, "A ball is something you use during _____." Wait for the child to respond. Prompt if necessary.
8. Show Set Three to the child and point to the picture of soap while saying, "Soap is something that takes away _____." Wait for the child to respond. Prompt if necessary.
9. Show Set Four to the child and point to the picture the horn while saying, "A horn is something that would make you want to dance and sing when _____." Wait for the child to respond. Prompt if necessary.
10. Tabulate the responses.

Credit: + Child identifies objects that are used for the same purpose or have the same general function. The child should begin to state the function of an item (with some prompting if necessary).

Adaptations

Some children find it difficult to understand the difference between function and appearance. A number of objects may have similar appearances but do not have the same function (toy cars look like big cars, but they do not transport people). It is important to discuss and compare items that look similar but are not functionally the same. To help clarify the differences, ask questions to encourage the child to make understandable comparisons. If the child has a long response time, after the directions have been given, make sure the child is familiar with the visuals; name the item in the picture but not the function, or ask the child what the item could be used for. It is important to involve the child in a general discussion of the items.

1.183 Tells a word that associates with another word

Strand: 1-4D **Age:** 40-50m 3.4-4.2y

Definition

For children to be able to associate words, they must have the ability to process the interpretation and the relationship of word meanings. The hierarchy of word association is important. For example, automatic word association (dog-cat, hot-cold, fire-warm, bath-water) is a primary task to stating functional similarities (places to live - houses, tents, nests, trailers, apartments) which is a lower level association activity than abstract concepts (does the child know that a table is a table, but it is also furniture; a pea is in a pod, but it is also food; a ball bounces but is also a toy).

Assessment Materials

Paper and a pencil for marking the number of correct responses given by the child.

Assessment Procedures

Note: Select a series of four functional categories that can be stated. Example: name objects that you can eat, name objects that you wear, name objects that you can ride in, and name objects that you can play with.

Grouping: This skill should be assessed one-on-one with the child.
1. Explain to the child that you are going to ask him to name some things, but he needs to

listen carefully, because you are going to give a direction first.
2. Get the child's attention prior to giving your instructions, such as saying, "Ready . . . listen!"
3. Say, "Name things that you can eat. Ready . . . go!"
4. Make a mark for each correct response. When the child appears to be out of responses, praise their work by saying something like "Good listening. Let me give you another question."
5. Say, "Name things that you can wear. Ready . . . go!"
6. Make a mark for each correct response. When the child begins to hesitate say, "You know a lot of things to wear."
7. Continue with the two other functional categories.

Credit: + Child uses functional similarities to associate words that go to a particular category.

Adaptations

If the child is having problems in the area of word association, it could be due to lack of concentration or an inability to integrate the received information. To assist the child with concentration, be sure to have a focus time cue, such as saying a word, tapping on the table, making eye contact, etc. If the concern is reception of the spoken word, make sure that the word given to the child represents something he has had a practical experience with. It might be helpful to have the child repeat the word said, prior to making any associations. A picture of the object shown to the child at the same time the word is said is another way to assist in receptive association; however, fading of the visual cue is needed.

1.184 Identifies missing parts of a picture storybook that has been read several times

Strand: 1-9 **Age:** 42-48m 3.6-4.0y

Definition

The child is read a story that he is very familiar with, and part of the story is left out on purpose. The child is able to identify the part that has been omitted and is able to retell the part correctly. This can also include the modification of the story content. The child is able to tell what has been changed, and what the original story-line was.

Assessment Materials
Select a short story with a clear story line and an easily identified sequence of events.

Assessment Procedures
Grouping: This skill can be introduced and practiced during a group activity. However, when you are ready to assess the child's ability to identify missing parts of a picture storybook that has been read several times, it is recommended that you do so one-on-one with the child.

1. Seat the child beside you so he can see the pictures in the book.
2. Read the story several times to the child. Point to the pictures that correspond with the events or actions in the story.
3. Discuss the plot of the story with the child and include the sequence of each episode, the characters, the ending, etc.
4. Read the story again, and if the child wants to assist in the storytelling, allow him to do so.
5. Read the story again, but this time leave out a segment, making sure that the part left out is pictured.
6. Make a note if the child recognized the error and if the child filled in the correct section.
7. If the child did not recognize the error, read the story again and eliminate another part. Make a note if the child recognized the error and if he filled in the correct section.

Credit: + Child identifies the part of a familiar story that has been omitted and is able to retell the missing story part correctly.

Adaptations

The child must be able to accurately recall what he has heard. Recall involves understanding what is said and making critical judgments. Many children can provide answers to questions, follow directions, and even draw conclusions, but when critical listening is involved, a child may have a tendency to not trust his recall. The "inner voice" says, "What you just heard is probably right, you just forgot that part." If you are working with a child that does not trust his "recall," ask him such questions as, "Do you think I read that right?" "Does that sound right to you?" "I think I just made a mistake in the story." You may need to prompt the child in advance that you are going to change the story and that their job is to listen carefully and let you know when a change has occurred. You can start by calling the main character by another name, then leaving out a major plot point, and eventually changing the ending.

1.185 Starts a task only when reminded, some prompting
Strand: 1-8 **Age:** 42-48m 3.6-4.0y

Definition
One of the most important elements of not beginning an activity until prompted is determining the cause. Some causes are: lack of motivation, sense of inability to achieve, preoccupation, low self-image, inappropriate role model, etc..

Assessment Materials
Select a topic that the child is interested in. Examples: cars, dogs, turtles, dolls, etc. Prepare or secure a variety of different activities (not more than four) within the scope of the child's interest levels and based on the selected topic. These activities could include picture books, puzzles, models, tracing activities, simple drawing tasks, etc.

Assessment Procedures
Grouping: This skill can be assessed in a small group (two or three children) or one-on-one with the child.
1. Engage the child in a discussion about the topic, including questions about factual information. Then move to questions that require interpretation and allow the child the chance to respond to judgmental questions. Conclude the discussion in a positive manner, recognizing the child's interest and knowledge of the topic.
2. Show the child the various activities that he can choose to do. Explain each activity/task and what the child needs to do to complete the task.
3. Allow the child time to explore the various options.
4. Tell the child he may begin a task when he has decided which one to do.
5. If the child does not begin a task remind him to begin.
6. Identify the number of times he was reminded before he began a task.

Credit: + Child starts a task when directed or when given only one or two prompts to begin. Attempt to determine the reason the child did not begin the activity and note your findings.

Adaptations
To assist children who are reluctant to begin a task, it is helpful to vary the mode of the presentations to include illustrations, discussions, demonstrations, motor involvement and any other multi-sensory approaches. The child needs to know that he is going to be an active learner and that recognition will occur.

1.186 Makes hand/foot rhythmic movements
Strand: 2-7 **Age:** 42-48m 3.6-4.0y

Definition
When the child is presented with a rhythmic selection, she will move to the selection using at least two different parts of her body, e.g., hands, fingers, arms, legs, feet, head, etc. The child needs to move her body parts in rhythm to the music.

Assessment Materials
A recorded rhythm selection. (Suggested artists: Ella Jenkins, Hap Palmer, Tom Glazer, Gary Rosen, Bill Shontz, Steve Millang, Greg Scelsa, "Miss Jackie.") Adequate space for moving to the music. Assorted props such as scarves, flags, and pompoms to aid children in being less inhibited. (Note: The overuse of props can become distracting and prevent concentration on the purpose of the task.)

Assessment Procedures
Grouping: This skill can be assessed in a group setting.
1. Explain to the child that she will be hearing some lively music and suggest that she may tap her feet and clap her hands, clap her knees and nod her head, tap her feet and clap her hands, or use any other part of her body to keep time to the music. Demonstrate these motions, and make sure she is aware of her choices and that she understands there is no right or wrong way.
2. Play the music. Observe whether she kept time to the music with her foot, hands, or fingers, and if she picked up the rhythmic beat.
3. Model for her if she has a problem getting started.
4. Ask her to stand up and march around the room. Encourage her to use her feet and another part of her body, such as swinging her arms, as she marches.

Credit: + Child moves at least two different parts of her body in rhythm to the music.

Adaptations

Most children develop the fundamentals of movement with normal maturation; however, some need specific involvement in the categories of locomotion, such as walking, hopping, jumping, and running. If the child's movements are uncoordinated at first, the best adaptive technique is to provide plenty of opportunity for her to move with guidance and encouragement. If the child has difficulty moving her lower body and legs, encourage her to move her upper body and arms. Allow the music to promote her natural body tempo.

1.187 Attends to task without supervision

Strand: 1-8 **Age:** 43-48m 3.7-4.0y

Definition

The child will stay on task without any prompting or any reinforcement. The number of seconds/minutes that the child is expected to stay on task is left up to the discretion of the adult. There are numerous variables that need to be considered when placing a specific time for on-task behavior. Those variables include: child's interest, child's attitude at that particular time, level of difficulty of the task, level of motivation, distractions, child's physical condition.

Assessment Materials

/*\ **Safety Note:** Provide scissors appropriate for the child. Remind the child of safety regarding scissors.

Select an activity that the child is capable of doing independently and one that the child is motivated to do. The activity could be completing a picture puzzle, drawing, coloring a picture, stringing beads, looking at a picture book, building with construction material, listening to a tape/CD, dressing a doll, making roads in a sandbox, playing a ball game, working with clay, etc. Any necessary supplies that the child will need to complete the activity (crayons, scissors, drawing paper, etc.)

Assessment Procedures

Grouping: This skill can be assessed in a small group (two or three children) or one-on-one with the child.

1. Present the activity to the child. Explain that he is to work at the task until you tell him to stop.
2. Based on the activity, the child, and any environmental conditions, determine the amount of time you will allow before saying stop.
3. Have the child begin the task/activity.
4. Say, "Stop" and praise the child for being on task, doing a good job, being such a super worker, etc. Record the number of seconds/minutes it took him to finish.
5. Tell the child he can continue his work, until he hears the word "Stop" again.
6. Re-determine the amount of time you will allow.
7. Say, "Stop" and record the number of seconds/minutes it took him to finish.

Credit: + Child stays on task without any prompting or reinforcement. The amount of time expected to stay on task is left up to the discretion of the adult. They should take into consideration the child's interest, child's attitude at the time of assessment, level of difficulty of the task, level of motivation, distractions, and the child's physical condition.

Adaptations

When the child becomes restless and efficiency is reduced, the task should be stopped and a switch made in an effort to allow the child to engage in a more motivating activity. Switches can include: resting, exercising, changing the material and the mode for learning, listening to music, and presenting a different but related topic.

1.188 Works in small group for 5-10 minutes

Strand: 1-8 **Age:** 43-48m 3.7-4.0y

Definition

A small group refers to four or five children; the project that these children work on should be designed to be completed within the 5-10 minute period. The group does not work independently, and should receive supervision. The amount of supervision will vary, depending on the group structure and the activity.

Assessment Materials

A picture puzzle with eight pieces (the puzzle needs to have a frame - a commercial puzzle or a picture cut into eight pieces that has been reinforced with heavy paper and mounted in a low rim box). The subject of the puzzle should be something the children are familiar with.

Assessment Procedures

Grouping: This skill should be assessed in a small group setting with four to five children.

1. Remove the eight pieces of the puzzle and randomly put two pieces of the puzzle together to make four sets of two pieces of the puzzle.
2. Ask four children to join you, give each child two pieces of the puzzle.
3. Explain that you are going to work together to complete the puzzle. Also explain that "we are going to take turns to see if the pieces you have can be placed in the puzzle."
4. Say, "When I call your name it will be your turn to try to fit your piece in the puzzle." Record the time when the group begins working.
5. Begin the activity by calling one of the children's name. If the child is confused as to what is expected of him, restate what the task is.
6. Continue by calling each child's name, allowing them time to decide if their puzzle piece can be put into place.
7. Record the time in which the group completed the puzzle. Add any comments about the children's behavior, such as taking turns, becoming distracted, reacting selfishly, assisting another child, being over competitive, etc.
8. After the puzzle has been completed, conduct a discussion about the picture, and observe any negative or positive group interaction concerns.

Credit: + Child works in a small group (four or five children) to complete a project within 5-10 minutes with adult supervision.

Adaptations

When children are introduced to a group situation, there are a few that may need special help with considering the feelings of others. Learning to share, take turns, and work in a group can be challenging for children with language or motor delays. Providing children with language issues verbal prompts may be helpful, as well as explaining the goal of the group before starting their work together. Children with motor delays may require the help and support of another group member or adult when it comes to manipulating objects or performing gross motor activities. Modeling appropriate behavior and praising children who are able to stay on task can help the whole group work together more effectively.

1.189 Remains on task when distractions are present

Strand: 1-8 **Age:** 43-48m 3.7-4.0y

Definition

The child is to remain involved with an activity when there is varied visual and auditory stimulation in the child's immediate environment. The activity the child is doing is an independent task, with no direct supervision. The recommended time for this on-task behavior is 5 minutes, however this is only a recommendation; the interest level of the child and the degree of the stimuli affect any timing.

Assessment Materials

A regular classroom environment with other children present or a pre-recorded audio tape/CD of typical things a person might hear in a classroom (children at play, a teacher reading a story, children asking questions) and people staged to come in an out of the classroom where the child is being assessed. An activity that is on the child's instructional level, but not an activity that the child can automatically perform. Example: bead pattern cards, parquetry pattern cards, maze, matching game.

Assessment Procedures

Grouping: This skill should be assessed one-on-one with the child, but the child is being assessed in a group setting with other children present.

1. Give the child the selected activity and explain the directions.
2. Tell the child that there may be some things going on around him while he is doing his task, but the important thing is for him to keep working.
3. If you do not have access to a regular classroom environment, activate the tape recorder (or CD player/MP3) and have someone go in and out of the room a few times while the child is working.
4. Note the time that the child begins work on the activity and also when the distractions began.
5. Observe the child, and record any actions that he does to "block out" the stimuli, such as covering his eyes, putting his hands over ears, or moving his seat. Also record if the child stops work to transfer attention to the tape or someone in the classroom and if he returns to the task.
6. Allow the child to complete the activity.

Credit: + Child remains focused on the task given to him when visual and auditory distractions are present in the immediate environment.

The recommended time for this on-task behavior is 5 minutes, with no direct supervision. The interest level of the child and the degree of stimuli present may affect the timing.

Adaptations

Some children involuntarily or voluntarily respond to visual and auditory signals in their immediate environment. When they are reminded to get back to work, it is often necessary for the child to review what he was doing, recall the directions for accomplishing the task and determine where he left off when he was distracted. If the child has to go through this process each time he reacts to a noise or a different visual scene, he soon becomes frustrated and the activity is not completed.

1.190 Places illustration in correct sequence
Strand: 1-4D **Age:** 44-52m 3.8-4.4y

Definition
Placing pictures in the sequence in which they occur is a cognitive process. This process helps children discover relationships which increase the learning of new information. Sequencing is also a conceptualizing skill used in many school-related tasks.

Assessment Materials
Prepare two sets of three cards each. Index cards work well, however, there are numerous sets of sequence cards available at teacher supply/learning stores. Set One should display three different steps related to a child's daily living skills (eating, going to bed, putting on a coat). Set Two should illustrate three different stages of an item (plant growth, ice cube melting, pop-corn popping).

Assessment Procedures
Grouping: This skill should be assessed one-on-one with the child.
1. Place the cards from Set One face down on the table in front of the child, being sure that the cards are not in the correct sequence.
2. Tell the child that you are going to turn the cards over and that the cards tell a story of something she does everyday.
3. After the cards have been turned face-up, ask the child to place them in the order in which the activity would occur.
4. If necessary provide an oral cue, once only.
5. Provide the child with an chance to tell the story following the sequence presented.
6. After the child has completed this task, remove Set One and repeat the above with the cards from Set Two.
7. When recording the outcome include achievement, trials taken, behaviors and any discrepancies in the story telling.

Credit: + Child places at least one set of three cards in correct sequence.

Adaptations
The ability to use sequential thinking skills is often dependent on the child's ability to conceptualize parts of a whole. If a child is having problems with this, she may need specific training in forward and backward chaining. An example of forward chaining is to take the child through the steps in getting a drink of water and using all modalities of learning to assist her in recognizing the parts related to getting that drink. An example of backward chaining is to show the child a drink of water and then review what had to happen in order for that drink to be available.

1.191 Puts manipulative shapes together to form same design as illustrated model
Strand: 1-4D **Age:** 44-54m 3.8-4.6y

Definition
The child will be presented with a picture that has been made of different basic shapes. The child will then use tangrams, construction paper shapes, wooden beads or templates to reproduce the basic shape picture on the model.

Assessment Materials
Popsicle sticks, five 8-inch cardboard squares.

Assessment Procedures
Grouping: This skill can be introduced and practiced in a small group setting. However, when you are ready to assess the child's ability to put manipulative shapes together to form the same design as an illustrated model, it is recommended that you do so one-on-one with the child.
1. Prepare the five cards by tracing around the popsicle sticks, forming different shapes and designs. Cards One and Two should be a square and a triangle respectively; cards Three, Four and Five should be simple designs. Give the child a group of popsicle sticks.

2. Show the child card number One and ask her to use the popsicle sticks to reproduce the shape that is on the card.
3. Continue showing the child the rest of the cards and asking her to use the popsicle sticks to reproduce the shape/design on each respective card.
4. Record the number the child got correct and how many tries she attempted per card.

Credit: + Child reproduces basic shape pictures from at least three of the models.

Adaptations

When beginning to use manipulatives to respond to various tasks, some children find the act of picking up beads, templates, pegs, etc. a fine motor challenge. They spend so much effort and time using their fine motor skills, that reproduction of the shape is secondary. For these children, and as a start in using manipulatives for all children, it is helpful to use an item that can be pushed into placement, rather than being picked up.

1.192 Sorts according to shape, size, and length

Strand: 1-7B **Age:** 42-54m 3.6-4.6y

Definition

The reasoning process for early quantitative conceptualization is largely based on visual interpretation; hence, the child must be able to observe general configurations of shapes, sizes, and lengths in order to determine how things are similar and to follow nonverbal operations. Use circles, squares, and triangles (at least two of each shape) which are at least three inches on a side or in diameter. Mix the shapes and the child will sort them when requested. Continue the procedure using shapes of different sizes and strips of different lengths.

Assessment Materials

Geometric shapes at least 4 inches in diameter (tag board or wallpaper sample books work well). The geometric shapes should be three squares, three circles, three rectangles, and three triangles. Using one color of paper, cut out two circles of each of the following sizes; the biggest circles should be 6 inches in diameter, the medium circles 4 inches in diameter and the smallest circles 2 inches in diameter. Finally, cut out paper strips of different lengths; one strip 14 inches long, one strip 12 inches long, one strip 10 inches long, and another strip 8 inches long.

Assessment Procedures

Grouping: This skill should be assessed one-on-one with the child.
1. Place the large geometric shapes (three squares, three circles, three triangles, and three rectangles) randomly on a table. Tell the child to put all of the squares in one pile, the circles in another, etc. Record if the child was able to accurately sort these shapes.
2. Place the circles of different sizes in the middle of the table. Ask the child to place all the big circles in one pile, all the small circles in one pile, and all the medium sized circles in one pile. Record if the child was able to match the shapes according to size.
3. Place the strips of paper on the table. Inform the child to find the longest strip and place it in front of him. Ask the child to find the shortest strip and place it in front of him. Remove these two strips.
4. While looking at the last two strips on the table in front of the child, say, "Point to the longest strip." Then say, "Point to the shortest strip."
5. Place all four-paper strips on the table. Tell the child to place them in order from the longest to the shortest.
6. Record the child's responses in identifying the correct length of the paper strips.

Credit: + Child sorts by shape (at least two of the following shapes: circle, square, or triangle), size (at least two of the following sizes: big, medium, or small), and length (at least two objects of the following lengths: longest and shortest).

Adaptations

Some children are not aware of shape, size and length without an adult bringing it to their attention. It is important to take advantage of everyday opportunities to discuss shape, size and length with these children in order to help them focus on the different characteristics of objects. Throughout the day talk about the things children commonly see. The cereal they eat in the morning may be small circles, while in comparison the bagel they eat for lunch is a bigger circle. The crayons they use to color may be short, while the pen or pencil their parents' use is longer. The washcloth they use to wash their face is a small square and the towel they use to dry with after a bath is a large rectangle. We see different shapes, sizes and lengths everyday so take time to point them out and talk about them. Encourage children to describe the objects they use with words that represent the size, shape, and length. Children learn through repetition, and this is a task mastered through use.

1.193 Draws square, imitating adult
Strand: 1-11   **Age:** 42-50m 3.6-4.2y

Definition
The child will use a crayon, marker or a pencil and draw a square equal or nearly equal on each side with all corners meeting at right angles. The child will draw a square after watching an adult draw a square. The child will reproduce the shape upon verbal request.

Assessment Materials
Three sheets of paper. Paper and crayons/pencils for the child. Square template; these can be made from cardboard, wood, plastic, etc.

Assessment Procedures
Grouping: This skill should be assessed one-on-one with the child.
1. Ask the child to join you at a table. Sit beside the child so he can see your paper and watch what you are doing. Tell him you are going to draw a square then proceed with making the shape.
2. Let the child look at your square.
3. Say, "I would like you to draw a square like this."
4. Allow the child time to draw the shape.
5. If he was successful write his name and the date on his paper and maintain it for reference and program planning.
6. If he is having difficulty, provide him with the square template and prompt him to trace around it, first with his finger and then with a crayon or pencil.
7. Show the child the model of the square, again. Then say, "Try to draw a square like this."
8. Write the child's name and the date on his paper and keep it for reference and program planning.

Credit: + Child draws a square equal or nearly equal on each side with all corners meeting at right angles.

Adaptations
   Some children find it difficult to visualize the design they are being asked to reproduce. A child may have difficulty sequencing the movements necessary to draw the figure; he may have problems with top to bottom and left to right, or he may demonstrate inconsistency. A child may also reproduce the figure too small or too large, the figure may be done quickly and inaccurately or may be done slowly and laboriously. Some children experience problems with copying figures without first tracing a model. Insert templates can be an effective media to assist these children. The child should begin by tracing around the inside of the template with his finger. Then have him trace two or three times with a pencil or crayon. Gradually reduce the above task sequence and use the process only as support. Another activity would be to provide the child with four straws of equal lengths. Talk about how you can take the four straws and make a square. Demonstrate and then have the child complete the task on his own. Talk about the four straight lines and how they come together at the corners to make a square.

1.194 Participates in singing songs with group
Strand: 2-7   **Age:** 44-56m 3.8-4.8y

Definition
The child will join in singing with a group. His singing does not need to be rhythmic or completely in tune and he does not need to sing the exact lyrics.

Assessment Materials
Two songs the child enjoys singing, one song he does not know. The new song should have a few phrases. It is best if the new song has repeated lyrics. Two or more other children. Pictures that represent the lyrics to the new song.

Assessment Procedures
Note: Both the old and new songs should be sung during the day at spontaneous times.
Grouping: This skill may be introduced, practiced and assessed during a group activity with two or more other children.
1. Sing the song the child knows and likes. If possible, sing this song from memory without accompaniment; sing directly to him with physical contact and enthusiasm.
2. Sing the song several times. Observe whether he joins in the singing.
3. Sing the new song several times during the day. Select a time to introduce the new song when the child is in transition from one activity to another, when he is in a more leisure mode or when he is engaged in a listening task.

4. Briefly introduce the new song by discussing its title or content and showing a picture that relates to the lyrics.
5. Sing the new song, emphasize the repeated parts or the chorus.
6. Sing the new song again. Be sure to involve the child with eye contact, facial expressions and physical gestures.
7. Sing the song again. Observe whether he joins in singing the new song.
8. If he does not respond after he hears the first few lines, continue, as he may need more time to recall the words and sometimes even longer to match the words with the melody.
9. It is important to allow him to join in when he is ready.

Credit: + Child joins in singing a song with a group. His singing does not need to be rhythmic and he does not need to sing the exact lyrics.

Adaptations

Some children choose not to join in group-singing. Often they are totally involved in watching and listening to others. Also, a reluctant child may be aware he is having difficulty matching tones, reproducing the pitch or the tune, or experiencing problems in voice control. When working with a reluctant singer, be sure to encourage and reassure him, not pressure him or require participation. Interaction will occur when he is motivated and comfortable.

1.195 Determines which of 2 groups has more and less, many and few

Strand: 1-10 **Age:** 46-56m 3.10-4.8y

Definition

The ability to view two sets (one with more objects than the other) and be able to determine which set has more or less (without counting each item) means reaching a stage of knowing that change in groups does not occur simply because the objects in a group are rearranged. Select objects that are close to the same shape, size and color. Place the objects in two groups and ask the child to point to the group that has more, less, many and few.

Assessment Materials

Collect small objects that can be held in a hand. Examples: buttons, small crackers, wooden beads, checkers, etc. Two pieces of yarn at least 18 inches long.

Assessment Procedures

Grouping: This skill should be assessed one-on-one with the child.
1. Ask the child to come to the table.
2. Place one of the small objects in one hand and four objects in the other hand. Show the objects to the child and say, "Which hand has more in it?"
3. Place three objects in one hand and five objects in the other hand. Show the objects to the child and say, "Which hand has more in it?"
4. Repeat the above using less or more objects.
5. Continue using the terminology "many" and "few."
6. Record the child's responses.
7. If the child is having any problems identifying the amount, allow the child to place the objects in her hand and to feel whether there is more or less.
8. Place the two pieces of yarn in a circle on the table. Put four buttons in one circle and two buttons in another circle.
9. Ask the child to point to the circle that has more buttons.
10. Ask the child to point to the circle that has less buttons.
11. Record the child's responses.
12. Place four buttons in a row in one of the circles. Randomly place the five buttons in the other circle. Ask the child to point to the circle that has more buttons.
13. Then ask the child to point to the circle that has less buttons.
14. Record the child's responses.

Credit: + Child points to which of two groups has "more" or "less," "many" or "few," without counting the items.

Adaptations

If the objects in a set are close in number, some children have a problem quickly viewing the areas to determine which set has more and which set has less. These children often need to match the objects in each set by correspondence to determine those that are left over. They also may become perplexed when the arrangement of the objects does not follow a consistent pattern. To assist the child in determining the concepts of more and less, the following activities are suggested: (1) Relating "more and less" in a story that includes illustrations, for example: there are four birds and each bird wants a birdhouse. There are only three birdhouses. Are there more birds than birdhouses? (2) Provide daily opportunities so that the language and concept of more/less begins to become commonplace (more crayons, less clouds in the sky, many children with sweaters, few children with coats).

1.196 Matches like items based on appearance

Strand: 1-7A **Age:** 48-53m 4.0-4.5y

Definition
Using more than one identical object or picture, the child will match the ones that look alike. Using more than one object or picture the child will match the ones that almost look alike.

Assessment Materials
Four sets of two pictures that are the same. Two of these sets should be of single item pictures and two sets should be of multi-object pictures.

Assessment Procedures
Grouping: This skill should be assessed one-on-one with the child.
1. Show the child the different pictures; no identification is required.
2. Place three of the single item pictures in front of the child, two of them being the same.
3. Ask the child to look carefully at the three pictures and then point to the two pictures that are the same.
4. Repeat with the other single item set and then the multi-object picture sets.
5. Identify the number of matches the child made as well as the amount of hesitation the child exhibited.

Credit: + Child matches more than one identical object or picture that look alike. Also credit if the child matches more than one object or picture that almost looks alike.

Adaptations
Some children may have a problem focusing on a single picture when other visual stimuli are present. These children have a need to look at everything within their visual range. When asked to match different objects/pictures, these children are "busy" responding to the other visuals. To assist these children, make sure that all other visuals are out of sight. When one set has been completed, remove it before placing the next group of pictures on the table.

1.197 Matches like items based on function

Strand: 1-7A **Age:** 48-53m 4.0-4.5y

Definition
The child will match objects based on functional use. The child will identify these objects verbally or by manipulation. The initial functional categories should be within the child's interest and experiences, such as: things that keep us clean, things that keep us warm, things that move, etc.

Assessment Materials
Three large (8 ½ x 11 inches) single item pictures of a functional class (e.g., things that keep us clean, things that we ride in, things that we write with, things that keep us warm, etc.) Nine smaller cards of which three have pictures matching each class shown on the larger cards. (e.g., three cards showing a picture of something that keeps us clean, three cards that show a picture of something we ride in, three cards that illustrate things that keep us warm).

Assessment Procedures
Grouping: This skill should be assessed one-on-one with the child.
1. Place the three large pictures in full view of the child.
2. Discuss with the child what the pictures are and what function the items shown in the pictures perform.
3. Give the child the nine smaller cards and instruct the child to look at each card carefully and decide what function the pictured item represents.
4. Tell the child to place the smaller card on the correct larger illustration.
5. Count the number of pictures the child correctly matched and record any indecisive behavior the child displayed when responding.

Credit: + Child matches more than one object based on functional use that is of interest and within the range of their experiences.

Adaptations
Some children find it difficult to understand the difference between function and appearance. A number of objects may have similar appearances but do not have the same function (toy cars look like big cars, but they do not transport people). It is important to discuss and compare items that look similar but are not functionally the same. To help clarify the differences encourage the child to make comparisons. If the child takes a long time to

respond after directions have been given, make sure that the child is familiar with the items shown, name the item in the picture (but not the function), or ask the child what the item could be used for. It is important to involve the child in a general discussion of the items.

1.198 Points to a word in a story being read
Strand: 1-9 **Age:** 48-53m 4.0-4.5y

Definition
When asked, the child will point to a word that is being read, or anticipates the word and points voluntarily.

Assessment Materials
Write a story on a chart/chalkboard.
Example:
<u>Whirling Leaves</u>
The little leaves are whirling,
Round, round, round.
The little leaves are whirling round,
Falling to the ground,
Round, round, round, round.
Falling to the ground.
Illustrate the story by drawing two leaves around the word "leaves", drawing a circle around the word "round," and a spiral-type figure around the word "whirling."

Assessment Procedures
Grouping: This skill can be introduced and assessed in a small group setting, no more than three children. Remind the children that they will need to listen and take turns during the activity.
1. Seat the child in front of the chart story and explain that it is a story about whirling leaves. Discuss and demonstrate a whirling motion. Read the story to the child, pointing to the word "round" as you are reading.
2. Repeat the story and point to the word "round." Ask the child to point to the word "round" whenever it appears in the story.
3. Read the story and observe if the child points to the word "round" each time it is read.
4. If the child is having problems, show him the circle around each occurrence of the word "round."
5. Repeat the story and observe if the child points to the word round. Record the children responses.
6. Continue with the word whirling, pausing on line three between whirling and round.
Record the child's responses.

Credit: + Child points to more than one word in a story being read. Visual cues can be used to draw attention to particular words in the story. The child can be asked to point to a word if he does not do so voluntarily.

Adaptations
As a prerequisite to identifying a word being read in a story, the child must be able to follow words across a line, starting at the left side, moving to the right, then bringing his eyes in one sweep back to the left and lowering them to the new line. With many children this becomes automatic, as they watch the eyes of readers. But with some children the left-to-right eye movement needs to be correlated to the words being spoken. A helpful instructional strategy is to assist the child in tracking under each word grouping, either with a pointer or his hand, as the words are being read. Make sure that at the right end of the printed line the pointer or finger track moves unbroken to the left and the next line down.

1.199 Repeats words that rhyme
Strand: 1-9 **Age:** 48-53m 4.0-4.5y

Definition
The child is expected to repeat the phoneme sound order of words. These words or syllables have the same patterns (usually CVC-consonant/vowel /consonant) and are presented to the child orally. The child is expected to say other words that have the same linguistic arrangement. Generally the words are said in rhymes or jingles (e.g., Little Miss Muffet - Sat on her tuffet) prior to isolation (e.g., Muffet - tuffet). However, an extended skill could include beginning consonant substitution (rat, cat, fat, mat, bat, spat.)

Assessment Materials
Select three well-known nursery rhymes (*Jack and Jill, Peas Porridge Hot, Little Bo Peep*). Additionally, write three verses that rhyme. Examples: (1) The boy got up to bat. He had on a funny hat; (2) A little mouse lived in a straw house; (3) When this cup of juice is done, I will give you another one.
Choose three simple rhymes, leaving the last word blank. Example: (1) We have fun when we_____; (2) See the silly cat sit on the _____; (3) I hear a bell but don't you _____.

Assessment Procedures
Grouping: This skill should be assessed one-on-one with the child.
1. Discuss the concept of rhyming words. Provide the child with examples of rhymes (tin - pin, run - fun).
2. Inform the child that you are going to say some rhymes and that when she hears the words that sound alike (rhyme), she is to say the words.
3. Use the first nursery rhyme as a teaching example.
4. Continue with the nursery rhymes. Tabulate if the child said the correct words and write down the words she said if she erred.
5. Continue with the three verses that rhyme. Tabulate the child's responses and record the errors.
6. Continue with the open-ended rhymes. Record the words stated by the child.

Credit: + Child says more than one set of rhyming words from a familiar nursery rhyme or they can fill in a word that rhymes with the word used in a simple verse.

Adaptations
Auditory discrimination can be a difficult task for those children who have a visual-modality preference. However, the ability to determine the likenesses and differences between sounds is basic to sound/symbol association. If rhyming is a challenge for the child, consider providing instruction in the following: (1) Sound location, (2) Identification of common sounds, (3) Distinguishing between different sounds. Providing the child with a picture and directing her to match pictures that rhyme can be a helpful assistance to auditory separation. The pictures should be phased out as soon as possible.

1.200 Colors within the lines of a circle
Strand: 1-11 **Age:** 48-53m 4.0-4.5y

Definition
The child will fill in at least half of a circle with a single color, showing no more than two lines outside the circle. The child should use a crayon that is comfortable for his grip.

Assessment Materials
Make three circles on white sheets of paper, one circle per sheet. Circle one should be 6 inches in diameter and outlined in black. Circle two should be 4 inches in diameter and outlined in black. Circle three should be 6 inches in diameter, but should have a raised outline. This raised outline could be made with glue (allow to dry thoroughly), clay (type that hardens), yarn that has been dipped in starch, etc. Crayons for the child to use. Extra sheets of white paper for additional circles if needed.

Assessment Procedures
Grouping: This skill can be assessed during a small group activity.
1. Provide the child with circle one. Tell the child that he may choose a crayon. Point to the area inside the circle and say, "Color the inside of the circle."
2. Remind the child that he is supposed to stay within the lines.
3. If the child was successful in coloring the 6-inch circle give him circle two and repeat the above instructions.
4. If the child was unsuccessful in coloring the 6-inch circle give him circle three.
5. Explain to him that the circle has a "fence" around it, and that the "fence" will stop the crayon. Tell the child to color inside circle three.
6. After the child has completed circle three, give him circle one and explain that the "fence" has been torn down. Point to the area inside the circle and say, "Color the inside of the circle."
7. Remind the child that he is supposed to stay within the lines.
8. Date the child's paper (note that he used the controlled model prior to completing the circle) and maintain it in his file.

Credit: + Child colors in at least half of the circle with a single color, with no more than two lines outside the circle. If circle three was used by the child before he was able to color within the lines of a circle independently, mark as an emerging skill and reassess the skill again at a later date.

Adaptations
Some children have a difficult time moving from the stage of scribbling with no perimeters to the stage of writing with visual restrictions. Coordination and fine motor strength are required to stay inside lines. The child needs to be aware when he is getting close to the line so that he can slow his movements down, begin a reverse or parallel direction and make decisions on how to complete the task. If the child has difficulty with these actions, he may need some prerequisite activities in visual/motor and in

strength development. The following exercises will address visual/motor integration: establishing a boundary using a raised outline like a template and adding verbal description (e.g., "move your crayon up when I say up and move your crayon down when I say down.") Strength development can be addressed by having the child squeeze clay and make shapes out of the clay. Both of these exercises are excellent ways for the child to increase his hand strength.

1.201 Sings and does actions with songs
Strand: 2-7 **Age:** 48-53m 4.0-4.5y

Definition
The child will sing a song and do actions that accompany the words. These actions may be creative or instructional and require either fine motor skills or gross motor skills. The child may sing along with live or recorded music.

Assessment Materials
An action singing song, such as *Teddy Bear, Teddy Bear* or *Two Little Apples*. Recorded songs and finger plays that encourage body movements are available from various commercial publishers. Some early childhood musical artists include Tom Glazer, Raffi, Ken Whitely, Ella Jenkins, and Hap Palmer. Some early childhood musicians who captivate creative melodies and rhythms are Hap Palmer, Raffi, Steve Millang and Greg Scelsa. Their musical selections encourage creative movement and creating different lyrics. However, some pieces by famous composers such as Debussy, Porter, Grieg, Rossini and Pachelbel are excellent for enhancing creative movement. Equipment to play the music.

Assessment Procedures
Grouping: This skill may be introduced, practiced and assessed during a group music time. You may also observe and hear the child singing and doing actions to familiar songs while she is spontaneously playing.
1. Tell the child that you will play a live or recorded song and ask her to listen carefully.
2. Play the song several times.
3. Sing along with the song and do the suggested actions. Encourage the child to sing along and do the actions too.
4. Observe her as she engages in the action and singing activity, noting the following: (1) If she enjoys the musical experience; (2) If she is able to participate in the singing and motions; (3) If she attempts any innovative variations; (4) If she is able to sing along in tune.
5. If she experiences difficulty in singing and doing the actions, support her by filling in the words or the actions. However, let her participate at her own rate and motivation.
6. Tell her you will play another recorded song and ask her to listen carefully. Play the musical piece to motivate her to explore movement and to create lyrics.
7. Encourage her to make up a song to go with the music.
8. Encourage her to make up movements to go with the lyrics and the music.
9. Praise and support all her efforts.
10. Observe her as she reacts to the music and generates expressions.

Credit: + Child sings a song and does the actions that accompany the words. The actions and words may be those that go to a familiar song, recorded music or made up by the child.

Adaptations
Some children have difficulty when they are asked to do two things at once, such as singing while doing hand movements or clapping and tapping. These multi-action activities require her to conceptualize two areas and require her to perform two motor responses. To help her, have her start this activity at a slower introductory pace to assure her success at one skill; for instance, have her sing along before doing the accompanying hand/body movements. Repeat the singing/action musical approach often and in different ways. Include visuals, devices for manipulation, and cue support when you present a dual involvement. Children with special needs often thrive within musical experiences.

1.202 Locates which out of 5 objects or pictures does not belong in same class/category
Strand: 1-7A **Age:** 48-54m 4.0-4.6y

Definition
The child is presented with five objects; four of the objects will belong to the same category and one will not. The child will identify the different object (object that does not belong) verbally or by manipulation.

Assessment Materials
Two sets of five objects; four objects out of each set should be representative of a single class,

while the fifth item should be from a different category, e.g., four pens and one pencil, or four small cars and an airplane.

Assessment Procedures

Grouping: This skill should be assessed one-on-one with the child.

1. Place all the five objects from one set in a box or sack.
2. Take the items out of the container one at a time and ask the child to name them as they are placed on the table.
3. After all the items are placed, explain to the child that there is one object that is different from the rest.
4. Request that the child locate the one object that is different. Allow the child time to respond.
5. Continue with the second set of five objects.
6. Record the two responses and enter any comments the child made to justify why he selected the object.

Credit: + Child identifies one object or picture out of a series of five objects/pictures that does not belong to the same category as the others. This can be done verbally or by pointing. The child does not need to justify his selection.

Adaptations

When some children are asked to locate the "wrong" answer (that is, what is different), they become confused and frustrated. They have an orientation of responding with right answers (that is, things that are the same). This "mind-set" needs to be reversed, as well as the child understanding that in some situations the "wrong answer is the right answer." To assist a child in this area, locate the "wrong" answer after identifying what the normally correct answer would be. Gradually phase out this reverse process, making sure that a reinforcement is included when locating the answer that is "different."

1.203 Places 3 pictures in sequence

Strand: 1-7A   **Age:** 44-56m 3.8-4.8y

Definition

The child is shown three pictures (in random order) depicting a sequence of events. The pictures/sequence should be of something that is familiar to the child. The child will put the pictures in the correct order and be given an opportunity to tell about each picture.

Assessment Materials

Three sets of three pictures that clearly show a sequence of events that is familiar to the child (a candle in a holder, a hand lighting the candle, and the candle burning; putting on pajamas, getting into bed, and falling asleep in bed; holding a milk carton, pouring milk, and drinking milk). Three 12 inch rulers and three cards with the numbers one, two, and three written on them. Commercial sequence cards are available to purchase through school supply stores.

Assessment Procedures

Grouping: This skill should be assessed one-on-one with the child.

1. Place the three rulers horizontally on a table in front of the child. Place the numbered cards above the three rulers to show the sequence.
2. Sit next to the child facing the rulers and numbers.
3. Place one set of three pictures in random order on the table and tell the child that you are going to place the pictures in an order which tells a story. Have the child watch as you place the pictures under the rulers in the correct sequence (1, 2, 3), and then tell the child a story about the pictures.
4. Give the child a set of three pictures and tell him to place them by the correct rulers just as you did. Explain that the pictures need to be in the right order to tell a story. After the pictures have been placed, ask the child to tell the story. If by watching the pictures he realizes the pictures are in a different sequence than the story, let him rearrange the pictures and begin the story again.
5. Repeat with the other set of pictures.
6. Note the number of attempts the child made to place the pictures in sequence. When telling the story, accept verbal responses of single words, phrases, and incomplete sentences.

Credit: + Child places at least two sets of picture cards in correct order and attempts to tell a story about what is happening in the pictures.

Adaptations

Some children become confused when they have to deal with more than one visual. It is important to make sure that the three pictures represent a sequence the child is familiar with. It is also helpful to discuss each picture, naming the objects in the picture, asking questions which will define what is occurring, accepting the child's responses, and then modifying as necessary and reviewing the sequential events several times.

1.204 Matches like items based on category

Strand: 1-7A **Age:** 48-56m 4.0-4.8y

Definition
The child will match at least six objects or pictures according to a class/category. The initial classification categories should be within the child's interest and experiences, such as: things she plays with, things to eat, things to wear, etc.

Assessment Materials
Six pictures or objects, three representing one category and three representing another category. The categories need to be something relative to the child's environment and experiences. Examples might be food, clothing, things that move, toys, animals, etc.

Assessment Procedures
Grouping: This skill can be introduced and practiced in a group setting. However, when you are ready to assess the child's ability to match like items based on their category, it is recommended that you do so one-on-one with the child.

1. Discuss with the child how things belong to different groups. This discussion could be an outcome of looking at a book or pictures and talking about characteristics that place things in categories, or it could be related to concrete items, such as what the child is wearing, what she ate for lunch, or what toys she plays with.
2. Following the discussion, show the child the six pictures.
3. Ask the child to name each picture. Point to the picture to be named.
4. Explain to the child that the picture cards show two different groups (or categories.)
5. Tell the child to place the two different types of pictures into two different stacks.
6. After the child has placed the pictures, ask her to tell you what the two categories are and to name the pictures in each group.
7. If the child hesitates, do not provide any clues or verbal assistance.
8. Note the correct placement of the pictures in the two categories and record the naming of categories and reasons for placement that the child stated.

Credit: + Child matches at least four objects or pictures according to class/category (present only two categories at a time).

Adaptations
When asked to group objects or pictures, some children may have difficulty because they try to classify by irrelevant characteristics. When looking at an object/picture, classifying the shape, color, features, or position of an object can become distracting and prevent the child from generalizing. It is important that the objects/pictures selected are those that represent things that the child has had a concrete experience with and that are easily put into obvious classes.

1.205 Repeats sequence of words with meaning association

Strand: 1-4D **Age:** 48-58m 4.0-4.10y

Definition
The child associates words in a meaningful way and interprets how the spoken word reflects relationships. The child needs to be able to use a series of words to express a sequence of activities, categorical events, expression of feelings, recreational purposes and creativity.

Assessment Materials
A small rubber ball.

Assessment Procedures
Grouping: This skill should be assessed one-on-one with the child.

1. Show the child the rubber ball and explain that you are going to do some different things with the ball. Tell him to watch and listen carefully.
2. Bounce the ball on the table and say "Bounce." Throw the ball against a hard object and say "Throw." Throw the ball in a manner in which you can catch the ball and say "Catch." Place the ball in your hand and squeeze and say "Squeeze."
3. Explain to the child that you are going to repeat the actions with the ball and he is to say the words that go with the sequence of actions.
4. Bounce the ball and pause for the child to say "Bounce." Throw the ball and pause for the child to say "Throw." Continue with the action/words "Catch" and "Squeeze."
5. Note the child's correct responses.

6. Without using the ball, ask the child to repeat the words in the order in which the action happened.
7. Demonstrate with the ball only if a cue is needed.

Credit: + Child uses a series of words to express a sequence of activities, categorical events, expression of feelings, recreational purposes and creativity. The sequence should consist of three to five words used in a meaningful way to demonstrate the relationship between the word and the action.

Adaptations

The abstraction of words and their meaning can be a concern for some children. It is important for the child to be exposed to a concrete experience (use of an actual object) or semi-concrete (use of a visual of the actual object) that is associated with the words, prior to the use of the words in isolation.

1.206 Points to pictures that represent sequence of events in a story

Strand: 1-9 **Age:** 48-60m 4.0-5.0y

Definition

When presented with not more than five pictures, the child is able to place them in a sequence that reflects the order of events in a story. When asked the child will point to the first thing that happened and when asked will point to the last thing that occurred.

Assessment Materials

Prepare four large size index cards with a single picture on them. The pictures needs to tell a story about doing an activity. Example: Making a clay pinch pot (picture one - rolling a ball of clay, picture two - pushing down the center of the clay ball, picture three - enlarging and smoothing the inside of the pot, picture four - smoothing the outside of the pot and making a flat bottom); peeling a banana (picture one - a banana with skin on, picture two - a hand starting to peel the banana, picture three - the banana with the peel almost off, picture four - a bite taken out of the banana); or putting a puzzle together (picture one - puzzle pieces laying on a table, picture two - a few pieces of the puzzle put together, picture three - the last piece being held by a hand and about to be placed in the puzzle, picture four - the completed puzzle). Gather the necessary material to demonstrate one of the above, e.g., clay, banana, puzzle.

Assessment Procedures

Grouping: This skill should be assessed one-on-one with the child.

1. Seat the child at a table across from you. Explain to the child that you are going to show her how to get a banana ready to eat. As you are demonstrating this task, make up a story about a zoo keeper that had to teach a monkey how to peel a banana. Include in your story a name for the zoo keeper, a name for the monkey, the setting in which the training occurred, how the other monkey friends watched and how pleased the monkey was to learn how to prepare a banana for eating, etc. Make sure that your story and demonstrations include the events that are pictured on the four cards.
2. At the conclusion of the demonstration/story, shuffle the deck of the four banana cards.
3. Place the mixed up cards on the table in front of the child.
4. Ask her to put them in the right order, based on what happened in the demonstration/story.
5. Direct the child as to where to place the first card.
6. Tabulate the child's response and the number of attempts made before placing the pictures in the correct sequence. Based on the picture order, identify if the child re-told the story correctly.

Credit: + Child places no more than five pictures in sequence to reflect the order of events in a story. When asked the child correctly points to the first thing that happened in the story, as well as the last thing that occurred.

Adaptations

Sequencing is a skill of organization. Often young children are not able to understand the steps of a process or the order of events. For these children, events tend to run together and there is little understanding of the total sequence. They put their shoes on before putting on their jeans or they comb their hair and then put on a shirt. When they have completed building a block structure, they knock it down or take it apart and put the blocks back in the bag. Then they immediately take the blocks out of the bag to build another item. Understanding sequential order is important to problem solving, language, and reading. To provide children assistance with sequencing, organize the objects that the child will interact with in the proper sequence of events. Discuss with the child what event would come first and what would come next. It is important to provide only two options at the beginning.

1.207 Draws a square, copying model
Strand: 1-11   **Age:** 48-60m   4.0-5.0y

Definition
The child will be presented with a drawing of a square (3 inches) and upon request he will copy the picture of the square, showing four clearly defined sides that are nearly equal in length with the lines meeting or close to meeting at the corners to form the beginning resemblance of a right angle.

Assessment Materials
A sheet of paper with a drawing of a square (3 inches). Paper and crayons/pencils for the child. Square template made from cardboard, wood, plastic, etc.

Assessment Procedures
Grouping: This skill should be assessed one-on-one with the child.
1. Ask the child to join you at a table. It is important that you sit beside the child, not across from him.
2. Provide the child with paper and markers.
3. Show the child the model of the square.
4. Say, "Draw a square like this."
5. Allow the child time to construct the shape.
6. If he is having difficulty, allow him to trace the model with his finger. Note that this cue was used.
7. Show the child the model of the square again.
8. Then say, "Draw a square like this."
9. If the child has difficulty, provide him with the square template and ask him to trace around it. Note that this support cue was used.
10. Again, show the child the model of the square.
11. Then say, "Draw a square."
12. Write the child's name and the date on his paper and maintain it for reference and program planning.

Credit: + Child draws a square copying a pattern without support cues. The square shows four clearly defined sides, nearly equal in length, and meeting at the corners to form the beginning resemblance of a right angle.

Adaptations
Children vary in their development of eye-hand coordination. If a child has not had the necessary visual-motor experiences or is showing delays, help him by working on the following activities: (1) Small muscle coordination—Ask him to string a series of beads of various sizes; (2) Eye-hand coordination—Ask him to draw a line by connecting a series of dots; (3) Copying ability—Give him a paper that has been folded in half; on one half draw a simple form (right angles, square). Ask him to draw the same thing on the other half; (4) Square recognition—Ask him to find items around the room that are in the shape of a square; (5) Tracing—Draw a large square on a sheet of paper. Have the child trace the square with his finger, keeping his finger in contact with the paper the entire time. Now, have him trace the square again this time using a crayon. Remind him to keep his crayon on the paper the entire time as he traces the square. Additionally, provide the child with four straws of the same length. Demonstrate how the straws can be put together to make different shapes like a square, triangle and a diamond. Talk about the straight lines and angles. Give the child his own straws and allow him to construct the designs himself. Encourage him to use his finger to trace around the shapes he makes.

1.208 Identifies own name when printed
Strand: 1-9   **Age:** 48-60m   4.0-5.0y

Definition
The child will point to her first name when it is printed on a sheet of paper with no other printing. The child will point to her first name when it is printed next to another name. The child will point to her first name when it is printed in a row of four other names which do not start with the same first letter as the child's name. The child will point to her first name when it is in a list of four other names, of which at least one starts with the same letter as the child's. If the child is successful in the identification of her first name, the above should be repeated with her last name.

Assessment Materials
Prepare five 3 x 10-inch flashcards; one of the cards should have the child's first name printed on it. The other flashcards should have other names printed on them; at least one of those names should start with the same letter as the child's name and be of the same basic length/look. Have one 3 x 10-inch blank flashcard.

Assessment Procedures

Grouping: This skill can be introduced and practiced in a group setting. However, when you are ready to assess the child's ability to identify her own name, it is recommended that you do so one-on-one with the child.

1. Seat the child at a table. Inform the child that you are going to lay some cards on the table. Place the card that is blank and the card with the child's name on it on the table.
2. Point to the card that has the name on it and say, "Do you know what this says?" If the child says her name, verbally praise her.
3. If the child does not know what it says, tell her that it is her name. Ask her to repeat her name as you point to it. Review each letter in her name.
4. Place her name card and the blank card on the table. Ask the child to point to her name, and if she does so verbally praise her.
5. Place her name card and another name card on the table (select one that starts with a different letter than the child's name).
6. Request that the child point to her name.
7. Note if she was correct and if there was hesitation.
8. Place her name card on the table along with the name card that starts with the same letter and has the same configuration. Ask the child to point to her name.
9. Note if she was correct and if there is any hesitation.
10. Randomly place all the name cards on the table.
11. Tell the child to point to her name.
12. Record if she was correct and if she hesitated.

Credit: + Child correctly identifies her first name when it is present with four other names, of which at least one starts with the same letter and has the same configuration as the child's.

Adaptations

After instruction and practice, the child should instantly identify her printed name. The ability to recognize her name on sight is based upon visual memory of the word image. If the child has difficulty with automatic name recognition, an instructional procedure for increasing visual image should be considered. Many young children respond to outlining the word image and focusing on the "pictured" word. If her name is such that a mnemonic visual could be added, this may be helpful in triggering her visual memory. Example: if the child's name is Teddy, draw a bear face around the T or dd's. Using kinesthetic printed letters (sandpaper) is another strategy that assists in imagery.

1.209 Identifies number symbols of 1 - 5

Strand: 1-10 **Age:** 48-60m 4.0-5.0y

Definition
Shown numerical symbols 1 - 5, the child will verbally give the name of the number.

Assessment Materials
Make a set of number cards 1 - 5. Each individual number should be a cut-out made from a tactile medium, such as sandpaper, poster board covered with textured material, or rippled plastic foam. Make a set of number cards (index cards), with the numbers 1 - 5 written (black marker works well) on the cards. Number card one should have the number 1, number card two should have the number 2, etc.

Assessment Procedures
Grouping: This skill should be assessed one-on-one with the child.

1. Explain to the child that you are going to show him a number and that you want him to tell you the name of that number.
2. Show him the tactile number one and ask, "What is the name of this number?"
3. Show the child the tactile number two and ask, "What is the name of this number?"
4. Continue the above steps with the numbers 3, 4 and 5.
5. Note the child's response.
6. Show the child the tactile number three and ask, "What is the name of this number?"
7. Show the child the tactile number five and ask, "What is the name of this number?"
8. Show the child the tactile number two and ask, "What is the name of this number?"
9. Show the child the tactile number four and ask, "What is the name of this number?"
10. Show the child the tactile number one and ask, "What is the name of this number?"
11. Note the child's response.
12. Shuffle the number cards and randomly place them on the table in view of the child.
13. Explain to the child that you are going to point to a number card and that he is to tell the number on the card.
14. Randomly point to the number cards and note the child's response.

Credit: + Child identifies verbally the number symbols 1 – 5 when presented in random order.

Adaptations

Many children are able to visually recognize number symbols when they are presented in sequence (1 - 2 - 3 - 4 - 5). However, when the number symbol is out of sequence, the "rhythm" of the order is missing and the reliance on the number before and after is unavailable. It is important that the numbers 1 - 5 be introduced first. After the child has recognized the numbers in sequence, begin by presenting the child with number 2, then 4, then 3, then 5, and finally 1. If the child is confusing one number with another, color cues may be used: make the top of the five blue and the bottom red. To assist in making the numbers less confusing, use visuals to represent the quantitative amount. For example, put two animal stickers on the number 2. The use of tactile numbers gives the child an opportunity to feel the corners, edges, and curves of the graphic number. However, visual assistance for number recognition should be phased out as soon as possible.

1.210 Draws a triangle, copying model
Strand: 1-11 **Age:** 57-69m 4.9-5.9y

Definition
The child will be presented with a drawing of a triangle (3 inch base) and upon request he will copy the triangle with three clearly defined sides with the lines nearly equal in length, meeting at the corners at approximate angles (45 degrees - 90 degrees).

Assessment Material
A sheet of paper with a drawing of a triangle (3 inch base). The shape should be drawn with a black wide-point marker. Paper and crayons/pencils for the child. Make a triangle template; these can be made from cardboard, wood, plastic, etc.

Assessment Procedures
Grouping: This skill should be assessed one-on-one with the child.
1. Ask the child to join you at a table. Sit beside the child.
2. Provide the child with paper and markers.
3. Show the child the model of the triangle.
4. Say, "Draw a triangle like this."
5. Allow the child time to construct the shape.
6. If she is having difficulty, allow her to trace the model with her finger.
7. Note that this cue was used.
8. Show the child the model of the triangle again.
9. Then say, "Draw a triangle like this."
10. If the child demonstrates difficulty, provide her with the triangle template and ask her to trace around it.
11. Note that this support cue was used.
12. Show the child the model of the triangle.
13. Then say, "Draw a triangle."
14. Write the child's name and the date on her paper and maintain it for reference and program planning.

Credit: + Child draws a triangle from a pattern without support cues. The triangle should have three clearly defined sides with the sides being nearly equal in length and meeting at the corners at approximate angles (45 degrees - 90 degrees).

Adaptations
Some children experience problems in the ability to copy a series of lines, a shape, a number, or a word without first tracing a model. They find it difficult to visualize the design that they are being asked to reproduce. To help the child have a visual image of the design, the use of the sense of touch is important. For example, have the child make triangles out of clay, ask her to trace the shape of a triangle in material (such as salt or sand), cut triangles out of textures (such as carpet, sandpaper, corrugated paper), glue chenille pompoms on a sheet of paper in the shape of a triangle, etc. Ask the child to use her finger and trace the tactile shape; gradually transfer the feeling experience to asking the child to draw a triangle.

1.211 Counts orally to 10, with one-on-one correspondence
Strand: 1-10 **Age:** 48-60m 4.0-5.0y

Definition
Many children learn to count verbally, but without attaining the concept that each number corresponds to one object. In order to establish the counting principle, the child should first be involved in a motor and tactile response (placing pegs in a pegboard, clipping clothespins on a line, or stringing beads). The child should count aloud to ten, while pointing at one object at a time (point to a block and say "One").

Assessment Materials
A pegboard and ten pegs, or a clothesline and ten clothespins. Ten blocks or ten chips.

Assessment Procedures

Grouping: This skill should be assessed one-on-one with the child.

1. Place the pegboard in front of the child. Give him the ten pegs. Tell the child that he needs to count the pegs aloud as he places them in the board.
2. To assist the child in getting started, place a peg on the board and say, "One." Say, "You put the next peg in and say the next number." (two)
3. Make any notation of errors, numbers repeated, pauses, skipping of pegs or holes, etc.
4. Place the ten blocks randomly before the child.
5. Tell the child that he is to point to each block and count it aloud.
6. To assist the child in getting started point to a block and say, "One." Say, "You point to the next block and say the next number." (two)
7. Observe if the child arranges the blocks in a systematic order for counting.
8. If the child becomes mixed up because the blocks are not in an order, stop the child and place the blocks in a row.
9. Explain to the child that he may now start pointing to and counting the blocks.
10. Make any notation of errors, numbers repeated, pauses, skipping of blocks, etc.

Credit: + Child verbally counts objects up to ten with one-on-one correspondences (points to one object at a time, stating the number, and continuing to count in consecutive order until he reaches the number 10, without missing or repeating any number). He shows an understanding of the concept that each number corresponds to one object.

Adaptations

When a child begins to count, he uses a thought process to find how many objects there are in all. Some children cannot look at a series of objects and count aloud; they cannot hold the auditory sequence (1,2,3) while simultaneously following (pointing) the visual pattern. With these children it may be necessary to first minimize the task. The following procedures are suggested: (1) Ask the child to close his eyes and concentrate on listening and counting beats of a drum. As a next step, ask him to open his eyes, listen for the drum beats and make a mark on a paper for each sound he hears. After he has learned to listen, count, and mark correctly, have him recount his marks without the aid of the drum beat; (2) Ask the child to count objects in a manner that require a strong auditory motor response. Such an activity as dropping marbles in a can encourages the child to say the number while he is handling the marbles and hearing them drop.

1.212 Names penny, nickel, dime and quarter

Strand: 1-10 **Age:** 48-60m 4.0-5.0y

Definition

When presented with one coin at a time, the child will name the coin. The first presentation to the child should be based on value amount and in the following sequence: a penny, a nickel, a dime and a quarter. The second presentation should be based on appearance (size, color, engraving) and in the sequence of dime, penny, nickel and a quarter. The third presentation should be random. **Note:** *It is important to use the same side (head or tail) of the coin when doing the presentations. It is also important to use real coins when introducing money concepts.*

Assessment Materials

A penny, nickel, dime and a quarter. Locate a coin bank, or make a bank by putting a slit in a small box.

Assessment Procedures

Grouping: This skill can be introduced and practice in a group setting. However, when you are ready to assess the child's ability to name coins, it is recommended that you do so one-on-one with the child.

1. Place the coins in your hand and show the child the coins.
2. Instruct the child that you are going to show her one coin at a time.
3. Explain that when she sees the coin she is to name it, and if she gives the coin it's correct name, she can place the coin in the bank.
4. Show the child a penny and say, "What is the name of this coin?"
5. If the child says penny, give her the bank to put the coin in.
6. Show the child a nickel and say, "What is the name of this coin?"
7. If the child says nickel, give her the bank to put the coin in.
8. Continue in the same manner with the dime and the quarter.
9. Record how many coins are in the bank.
10. Empty the bank and show the child the coins once again.

© 2010 VORT Corporation. All rights reserved. Do Not copy.

11. Show the child the dime and ask, "What is the name of this coin?"
12. If the child says dime, give her the bank to put the coin in.
13. Continue with the penny next, then the nickel and finally the quarter.
14. Record how many coins are in the bank and which coins were correctly identified.
15. Empty the bank and place all the coins on the table.
16. Tell the child to pick up any coin, say it's name, and then place it in the bank.
17. If the child is unable to say a coin's name, remove the coin from the group.
18. Record how many coins are in the bank and which coins were named correctly.

Credit: + Child names a penny, nickel, dime and quarter correctly in all three trials.

Adaptations

If the child was unable to recognize coins when randomly presented, it maybe an indication that the child has not gone beyond rote memory, i.e., the child has learned to repeat the name of the coins as long as they were in the same order: penny, nickel, dime, quarter. The organization of the way new material is presented has a great deal to do with random recall. The more a child can attach what they are learning to what they already know, the better they will remember by association. An activity that is often helpful is to place the coins in the rote memory order that the child knows (penny, nickel, dime quarter), point to each coin, and ask the child to name them. Then rotate the coins (nickel, dime, quarter, penny) and ask the child to name them in the new order presented. Continue the rotation and naming. Collect the coins and put down only three coins (dime, quarter, penny). Ask the child to name the coins when pointed to. Change the order and the coins, then ask the child to name the coins. Collect the coins and put down only two coins (penny, quarter). Change the order and the coins, then ask the child to name the coins. Collect the coins and put down only one coin. Change the coins and ask the child to name the coins. This activity takes into consideration the following skills: sequential memory, associations, memory skills, recall, and auditory visual matching.

1.213 Traces own name
Strand: 1-11 **Age:** 48-60m 4.0-5.0y

Definition
The child will trace her first name with her finger when it is printed in manuscript form on a lined sheet of paper. She will use a highlight marker/primary pencil and trace her first name. The child will trace (write-over) her first name which has been written on lined paper.

Assessment Materials
A sheet of lined paper that has the child's first name printed in manuscript form. Secure a highlight marker. Prepare a sheet of paper that has the child's first name printed in a raised texture. A raised texture can be made by using white glue; trace the letters of the name and allow the glue to dry.

Assessment Procedures
Grouping: This skill should be assessed one-on-one with the child.
1. Present the child with the sheet of paper that has her name on it and the highlight marker.
2. If the child has not had any experience with a highlighter, allow her time to experiment with it. Discuss with the child the attributes of the marker.
3. Draw the child's attention to the paper.
4. Instruct the child to use the marker and trace her name.
5. Upon completion of the task, date the paper and place it in the child's records.
6. If the child had a problem in the tracing activity, show her the paper with the raised texture.
7. Request that she use her finger and trace her name.
8. Allow her to finger trace her name several times.
9. Give the child the sheet of paper with her name on it and the highlight marker.
10. Repeat the above steps using the marker and the paper.
11. Upon completion of the task, date the paper and make a notation that a tactile experience was involved prior to the tracing. Place the child's work in her file.

Credit: + Child traces over her first name, which has been written on lined paper, with a highlight marker. She should begin with the first letter and end with the last letter, making the strokes or marks necessary to complete each letter. If a tactile experience was needed, mark the skill as emerging and reassess at a later time.

Adaptations

It is important, when a child begins writing words, that she understands that words have meaning. As the child begins to trace her first name she should concentrate on learning the correct order of the tracing strokes and the spacing involved. However, with some children it is beneficial to discuss what the child is writing (her name), why it is important to know how to write her name, where her name may be written, etc. Words that have meaning for the child should be considered when beginning the writing process.

1.214 Constructs set of objects

Strand: 1-10 **Age:** 48-60m 4.0-5.0y

Definition

Using objects at least 3 inches on a side or in diameter, the child will make a set by separating a requested number of items from a group. Example: the child is presented with ten blocks and is asked to separate three blocks from the group of ten. Construction of sets should begin at the concrete level, by establishing set boundaries (string circles, sheets of paper, lids of boxes) and determining if the members of the set belong together (blocks, buttons, chips, shape templates). The child will need to use her knowledge of classification by attributes and one-to-one correspondence in order to develop sets. The child's first experience at constructing a set should deal with objects that are alike and should allow the child to discover the meaning of equal items per set.

Assessment Materials

Collect or construct sets of objects that are alike. There needs to be at least 6 items per set. The objects need to be the same size, shape and color. Examples: 6 blocks, 6 chips, 6 drinking straws, 6 plastic forks, etc. Collect 6 wooden beads that are different colors and shapes. Two pieces of yarn or string.

Assessment Procedures

Grouping: This skill should be assessed one-on-one with the child.
1. Have the child sit at a table or on the floor.
2. Show the child one set of similar objects (four blocks). Say, "What are these?" Pause for the child to respond.
3. Put a yarn circle around the blocks.
4. Say, "These blocks belong to a group. This is a set of blocks." Say, "What are these blocks called?" Pause for the child to say "a set of blocks." Prompt if necessary by saying, "This is a set of blocks."
5. Ask the child to use the blocks to make a set that has just two blocks.
6. Note the child's response.
7. After the child has separated two blocks from the group of four, give her a piece of yarn with which to make a circle around her set of two.
8. Ask the child to look at the two sets of blocks.
9. Ask the child to discuss the two sets of blocks.
10. If the child does not volunteer that the two sets are alike, cue her with questions that will generate the conclusion of like sets.
11. Remove the blocks and place four different colored/shaped wooden beads on the table.
12. Place the yarn circle around the set of four beads. Say, "These beads belong to a group. This is a set of beads." Say, "What are these beads called?" Pause for the child to say a "set of beads." If necessary repeat, "This is a set of beads."
13. Hand the beads to the child and ask her to use the beads to make a set of two. Note the child's response.
14. After the child has separated two beads from the group give her a piece of yarn to place around her set of two.
15. Observe the child's selection of beads to make a set, and if she chose the same color, the same shape, or just any two beads.
16. Ask the child to look at the two sets of beads.
17. Ask the child to discuss the sets, particularly that they are like sets, that they are beads, but that they are unlike sets due to their different colors/shapes.
18. Hand the child six chips (the same size, shape, and color) and ask her to separate four chips from the group of six.
19. After the child has separated four chips to make a set, give her a piece of yarn to place around her set of four, and another piece of yarn to place around her set of two.
20. Ask the child to discuss the sets, how they are alike (they are all chips and they are all the same color) and how they are different (the number of chips in each set is different). Record her responses.

Credit: + Child makes a set by separating a requested number of items from a group. The child should be able to construct a set of objects when the items are identical (have a same attributes).

Adaptations

If the child has not developed the language related to "sets of objects" through the process of classifying, this needs to be addressed. The language of sets includes "alike," "equal," "the same," "a pair," "unlike," "identical," etc. The language of sets can be developed when likenesses and differences are known. For the child to understand the verbal explanations and directions of sets, she needs to comprehend the terms, "some of one set are alike" and "some of the set are different." To assist the child in these concepts it is helpful to use the child's natural experiences. For example, a pair of shoes, a set of dishes, a collection of rocks, a box of ribbons, and a set of books. Talk about how these items are alike and discuss how they are different. It is also helpful if these everyday items are placed in sets.

1.215 Locates first, middle, and last in group of objects
Strand: 1-10 **Age:** 48-60m 4.0-5.0y

Definition
The child will point to or place an object in the first position when asked. The child will point to or place an object in the middle position when asked. The child will point to or place an object in the last position when asked. The first group of objects should be completely different (e.g., a toy car, a ball, a block), the second group of objects should be different by only one attribute (e.g., color--a blue block, a red block, a yellow block) and in the third group each object should be alike.

Assessment Materials
Obtain nine rubber or plastic farm animals. Three animals need to be different (cow, horse, pig). Three animals need to be the same but different colors (spotted cow, black cow, brown cow). Three animals need to be the same and look exactly alike. A miniature pail and a sign in front of the pail that says breakfast.

Assessment Procedures
Grouping: This skill should be assessed one-on-one with the child.
1. Line up the three rubber or plastic farm animals that are different. Place the bucket and the breakfast sign at the front of the line. Invite the child to the farm scene.
2. Ask the child to identify who is first, middle, and last in line.
3. Tell the child to place a given animal in the specified last, middle, or first position.
4. Reinforce the child for correct response by letting him feed breakfast to the first animal in line.
5. Model the correct response if the child is incorrect in his positioning of an animal and let him try again.
6. Repeat several times so the child has several turns.
7. Modify the above activity by replacing the three different animals with the three different colored cows and finally replacing the cows with the three animals that are exactly alike.

Credit: + Child identifies correctly the first, middle, and last in a group of three objects. He completes this skill when the objects used are all different, when the items share only one attribute, and when each object is alike.

Adaptations
Some children have problems with visual analysis and synthesis. When given three parts they are unable to put them together in a requested order. Hence, when a child is shown a three-part visual, he is able to identify the first, middle, and last, but when asked to put together three parts in an order, he may find the task difficult, indicating that he cannot relate the parts (first, middle and last) to the whole. Try the following example to provide assistance to the child: always begin a position task from the whole and then break the whole into parts, e.g., place the three animal pieces together and then start by designating the first piece (head) and saying, "The head is the first part of this animal." Continue with the other pieces. This activity takes into consideration the following skills: sequencing, left to right directionality, parts versus whole relationships, spatial relations, serial order, and spatial orientation.

1.216 Matches coins
Strand: 1-10 **Age:** 49-58m 4.1-4.10y

Definition
Initial instruction using money needs to be a very concrete experience and it is best to allow the child to manipulate real coins. A fundamental aspect of understanding money is to become familiar with the appearance (engraving), the size, the shape and the metal color of the coins. The child will match like coins, stack like coins, arrange coins by size, identify coins by sides (heads or tails) and begin to

understand the value of a penny, nickel, dime and quarter.

Assessment Materials
Four pennies, four nickels, four dimes and four quarters. A small box.

Assessment Procedures
Grouping: This skill should be assessed one-on-one with the child.
1. Place one penny, one nickel, one dime, and one quarter in a row on a table in front of the child.
2. In another row place one dime, one quarter, one penny, and one nickel.
3. Ask the child to match the coins by putting the ones that are alike next to each other.
4. Observe if the child is able to put the penny by the penny, the nickel by the nickel, the dime by the dime, and the quarter by the quarter.
5. Randomly place three pennies, three nickels, three dimes, and three quarters in a pile.
6. Place a penny in a small box.
7. Say, "Find all the pennies and put them in this box."
8. After the child has placed the pennies in the box, put them back on the pile.
9. Place a nickel in the small box.
10. Say, "Find all the nickels and put them in this box."
11. After the child has placed the nickels in the box, put them back on the pile.
12. Place a dime in the small box.
13. Say, "Find all the dimes and put them in this box."
14. After the child has placed the dimes in the box, put them back on the pile.
15. Place a quarter in the small box.
16. Say, "Find all the quarters and put them in this box."
17. After the child has placed the quarters in the box, put them back on the pile.
18. Observe if the child was able to match the coins. Repeat the activities if the child had a problem with any of the coin matching tasks.

Credit: + Child matches coins in a variety of ways. He matches coins in at least two of the following ways: matches like coins, stacks like coins, arranges coins by size, and identifies coins by their side (heads or tails).

Adaptations
Some children may match the coins based on detail. These children often feel a need to pick up each coin and scrutinize it carefully. These children would benefit from some training in looking at the whole of an object rather than a part. To assist the child in recognizing a more general appearance of an item, stamp a picture (both sides) of a penny on a piece of paper. Do the same with a nickel, dime and quarter. Ask the child to match a real coin, to the card with the stamped picture.

1.217 Starts task with no reminding or prompting
Strand: 1-8 **Age:** 49-60m 4.1-5.0y

Definition
The child will be assigned a task to start at a specific time, and when the appointed time arrives, the child will begin without any prompting. The assignment will be given verbally.

Assessment Materials
A story to read to the child. The story should not be longer than five minutes, and should have one main character who is easy to illustrate. Drawing paper and a pencil, plus crayons, or paints, or colored markers.

Assessment Procedures
Grouping: This skill should be assessed one-on-one with the child.
1. Have the child sit next to you. Tell the child that you are going to read her a story (show her the book, talk about the cover and the title). Tell the child that when you finish reading the story, she is to draw the main character in the story (it may be necessary to explain the term main character).
2. Show her where the drawing paper, pencils, crayons, paints, or colored marking pens are located.
3. Read the story to the child.
4. At the end of the story, ask the child if she enjoyed the story, and what she liked best about it.
5. Pause to determine if she is going to get her materials to begin drawing the picture.
6. If not, take a sheet of the drawing paper and hand it to her.
7. Pause to determine if the child is going to take the paper and begin drawing the picture.
8. If not, say "Do you remember what you are to do now?"
9. Pause to determine if the child is going to take the paper and begin drawing the picture.
10. If not, repeat the assignment.
11. Write down if the child started the task without any reminding, and if not, record

how many cues were needed and if the child needed to hear the assignment once again.

Credit: + Child starts a verbally assigned task at the appointed time without prompting of any kind.

Adaptations

It is important when making a delayed assignment that only one assignment is given, with only one direction. As an example, "I am going to read you a story and at the end of the story I want you to draw a picture of the person/thing that the story was about." Do not say, "I am going to read you a story and at the end of the story, I want you to draw, color, cut-out and glue a picture of the person/thing that the story was about." Some children will have difficulty recalling the four activities (draw, color, cut-out, glue) in the order to be done. Also, do not say, "I am going to read you a story and at the end of the story I want you to draw a picture of the person/thing that the story was about, including in your picture something in the story that made the person/thing happy, and where the person/thing lived." This requires the child to recall three things that she is to illustrate. The child will become so pre-occupied with trying to recall the assignments that listening to the story will be secondary.

1.218 Attends to task without supervision for 10 minutes

Strand: 1-8 **Age:** 49-60m 4.1-5.0y

Definition

The child will stay on task without any prompting or any reinforcement for ten minutes. The task should be something he is motivated to do and there should be a limited amount of distractions.

Assessment Materials

/*\Safety Note: Provide scissors appropriate for the child. Remind the child of safety regarding scissors.

Select an activity that the child is motivated to do and is capable of doing independently. The activity could be completing a puzzle, drawing, coloring a picture, looking at a picture book, building with construction material, listening to a tape, working at the computer, playing a ball game, modeling with clay, etc. Any necessary supplies that the child will need to complete the activity (crayons, scissors, drawing paper, etc.)

Assessment Procedures

Grouping: The skill should be assessed one-on-one with the child

1. Present the activity to the child. Explain that he is to work at the task until the timer goes off.
2. Show the child the timer and explain that you will be unable to help him, or check on his task until the timer has buzzed.
3. When the timer goes off, go to the child and praise him for working until the timer rang, for doing a good job, for just being a super worker, etc.
4. Record if the child stayed on task for the ten minute period and note any distracted behaviors that the child displayed.
5. If the child has not completed his work and expresses a desire to continue, allow him the necessary time.
6. Set the timer for an additional ten minutes; however, if the child completes the task before the buzzer, record that time.

Credit: + Child stays on task for 10 minutes without supervision or prompting.

Adaptations

If a child is unable to stay on task for the ten minute period and becomes restless, angry or frustrated, the task should be stopped. Some children reach a high frustration level if they are being timed; all they concentrate on is "beating" the clock, not on accuracy or enjoyment. Another consideration is that the child might misplace his frustration and blame the learning activity, not the timing. Often a child needs to make some switches before going back to the task. Switches can include: resting, exercising, listening to music, or being presented a different but related topic.

1.219 Remains on task for 5 to 10 minutes when distractions are present

Strand: 1-8 **Age:** 49-60m 4.1-5.0y

Definition

The child is to remain on task with an assignment, while there are distractions in the child's immediate setting. The activity the child is doing is an independent task, one that is within the child's ability range and that she is motivated to accomplish. The assignment is done with no individual supervision. As children get older their attention span increases.

Assessment Materials

A typical classroom environment with auditory and visual distractions present. An activity that is on the child's instructional level, but not an activity that the child can automatically perform. Example: playing a game, completing a puzzle, looking at a book, doing a matching worksheet, drawing a picture, modeling clay, etc. A timer.

Assessment Procedures

Grouping: This skill should be assessed in a group environment, such as a typical classroom. You should be assessing only one child at a time so you can observe what she is doing and whether she can stay on task.
1. Give the child the selected activity and make sure she understands how to accomplish the assignment.
2. Tell the child that there may be some things going on around her, but it is important that she remembers to keep on working.
3. Explain that you are going to be a Starter and a Stopper. When you tell her to "Start", she should begin and when you tell her to "Stop", she should stop.
4. If using a timer, set it now and say "Start."
5. Observe the child for the following: (1) Stops working and pays attention to the action around her; (2) Stops working and becomes disinterested in the task and the surrounding distractions; (3) Demonstrates any behaviors that are an attempt to block out the distractions; (4) Seeks assistance.
6. At the end of the ten minutes, tell the child to stop and record if the child was task-oriented.
7. Recognize the child for her accomplishments and if she wants to complete the activity, allow her to do so.

Credit: + Child remains on task and completes the assigned activity even though visual and auditory distractions were present.

Adaptations

Some children involuntarily or voluntarily need to respond to the visual and auditory signals that are happening in their immediate environment. When they are reminded to get back to work, it is often necessary for the child to review what she was doing, recall the directions for accomplishing the task and determine where she left off when she was distracted. If the child has to go through this process each time she reacts to a noise or a different visual scene, she soon becomes frustrated and the activity is not completed. If she is not reminded to get back to work, the learning experience will not happen. Initially, she might be placed in a learning carrel or a study room to minimize the distractions.

1.220 Draws line between 2 parallel lines

Strand: 1-11 **Age:** 49-60m 4.1-5.0y

Definition

The child will be presented with a sheet of paper that has parallel lines draw on it. The lines need to be at least four inches in length and about 1-2 inches apart. The child will draw a line between the two parallel lines when asked.

Assessment Materials

Prepare a sheet of paper that has two parallel lines drawn on it; the lines should be straight, at least four inches long, and about 1-2 inches apart. Highlight the lines with a marker. Secure a blank sheet of paper, a ruler, a marker, and a pencil.

Assessment Procedures

Grouping: This skill should be assessed one-on-one with the child.
1. Seat the child at a table. Present him with the sheet of paper that has the two parallel lines.
2. Ask him to look at the two lines and allow him to trace the two lines, moving from top to bottom.
3. Give the child a marker or a pencil and say, "Draw a line between the two lines on the paper."
4. If the child hesitates, indicate the starting point and say, "Draw a line between these two lines and start here."
5. Allow the child time to respond.
6. If the child was successful, date the sheet of paper and place it in the child's file.
7. If the child was unsuccessful, make sure that he understands the concept of "between" by asking him to watch while you draw two parallel lines on a sheet of paper.
8. Point to the area between the two lines and explain the concept of between.
9. Using another sheet of paper, draw two parallel lines and ask the child to point to the part that is "between" the lines.
10. After the child has pointed to the area, say, "Draw a line between the two lines."
11. Date the paper and place it in the child's file.

Credit: + Child draws a line between two parallel lines (at least four inches in length and about

1-2 inches apart) without going outside the lines.

Adaptations

Some children may need assistance in understanding terms that relate to spatial relations. When the child is asked to react to between, under, on top of, etc., he may only understand these terms when dealing with three-dimensional objects, not when viewed on a flat plane. Hence, he may not be successful because of a comprehension problem, not a writing problem.

The following activity will assist a child in transferring spatial relations from one dimension to another. First, place blocks in various positions and ask the child to point to the block that is between the red one and the blue one, to the block that is behind the green one, etc. After he has located the block position using the real objects, show the child a picture of the blocks placed in the same or similar positions and ask the child to point to the block that is between the red one and the blue one, to the block that is behind the green one, etc. If necessary, the same block positions that are shown in the picture can be reconstructed using the real blocks. Make sure that the terms related to spatial positions are used in the discussion.

1.221 Shifts body rhythm when music tempo changes

Strand: 2-7 **Age:** 49-60m 4.1-5.0y

Definition

When presented with a musical selection that includes various tempos, the child will move her body in rhythm to the music. The tempo change should represent either slow or fast beats. The musical selection may be live or recorded.

Assessment Materials

A few musical pieces that have different and distinct tempos. Examples: *"Stars and Stripes Forever"* (march), *"The Nutcracker Suite"* (twirl, circle and leap), *"Blue Danube"* (sway and glide). A musical piece that is based on a theme and has exacting tempos. Examples: Themes such as Circus, Space, Animal, Storm, or Jungle. Equipment to play the music.

Assessment Procedures

Grouping: This skill may be introduced, practiced and assessed during a group music activity.
1. Invite the child to listen to the march.
2. Say, "You may move to the music." or say, "Show me the music by moving." or say, "Show me how this music makes you feel."
3. Observe and reinforce her for her creative efforts.
4. If she does not participate, make a note of her reluctance and substitute a music selection with a tempo that suggests designated movements.
5. Invite the child to listen to the twirling, circling, leaping tempo.
6. Repeat the above requests for participation.
7. Invite her to listen to the swaying, gliding tempo.
8. Repeat the above requests for participation.
9. Select the "theme" recording. Be sure it is within the child's experiences and a recording that has at least two separate tempos.
10. Talk with her about the theme, asking questions such as: What would you see if you were there? How would things look? Where would you go first? How would you feel?
11. Play the recording.
12. Say, "Show me how you would move if you were in the [jungle]."
13. Observe her and praise her for her creative movements.
14. If she does not participate, make a note of her reluctance, and play only one tempo of the theme recording at a time.
15. As you make the assessment, remember that as she begins to feel free to move to the music, she will become more imaginative with interpreting the tempos.

Credit: + Child's body movements shift as the tempo of the music changes (such as fast or slow movements).

Adaptations

Some children need specific directions and guidelines. When a child is asked to do an activity that requires spontaneity, she may become frustrated and choose not to take a risk. To encourage such a child to participate, listen to a tempo, discuss and demonstrate movements, help her execute a simple motion and reward her for her effort. If she becomes frustrated or feels uncomfortable, provide her with a simple instructional pattern for moving to the tempo. Praise her when she adds to or improvises from the pattern.

1.222 Selects long, longer, longest from group of objects

Strand: 1-7B **Age:** 50-56m 4.2-4.8y

Definition
A child will develop the concepts of length and the idea of constant units of measurement by interacting with concrete objects. Understanding that the length of an object does not change if the item has been moved is established after active experiences with lengths and the rearrangement of items. The child will point to the longest of two or more objects, when requested. The child will point to the longest of the same two or more objects, after the objects have been moved.

Assessment Materials
Cut strips of poster board, 1 x 3-inch, 1 x 5-inch, 1 x 7-inch, and two strips 1 x 9-inch. The strips should be the same color.

Assessment Procedures
Grouping: This skill should be assessed one-on-one with the child.
1. Place one 1 x 3-inch and one 1 x 5-inch strip on the table. Seat the child at the table and call attention to the two strips of paper.
2. Say, "Point to the longest of these two strips of paper." Pause and allow the child to respond. Note his response.
3. Remove the 1 x 3-inch strip of paper. Place the 1 x 5-inch and the 1 x 7-inch strips of paper on the table.
4. Say, "Point to the longest of these two strips of paper." Pause and allow the child to respond. Note his response.
5. Remove the 1 x 5-inch strip of paper. Place the 1 x 7-inch strip and the 1 x 9-inch strip on the table.
6. Say, "Point to the longest of these two strips of paper." Pause and allow the child to respond. Note his response.
7. Place all three strips on the table.
8. Point to the strip that is 1 x 7-inch and say, "Point to the strip that is longer than this one." Pause and allow the child to respond. Note his response.
9. Point to the strip that is 1 x 5-inch and say, "Point to a strip that is longer than this one." Pause and allow the child to respond. Note his response.
10. Place one 1 x 9-inch and one 1 x 7-inch strip of paper parallel to each other.
11. Ask the child if the strips are the same length. After the child decides that they are different lengths with one being longer, move one strip about 2 inches to the right of the other.
12. Say, "Are the two strips the same length or is one strip longer than the other?"
13. Pause and allow the child to respond. Note his response. If he does not reason that the strip of paper is still different in length, move the paper back until both strips are in a parallel position.
14. Discuss what happens when the strips are moved.
15. Demonstrate by moving the other strip 2 inches to the right and then moving the second strip to the right and parallel to the first moved strip.

Credit: + Child consistently points to the longest of two or more shapes of different length. Additionally, the child consistently points to the longest of two or more objects, even after the objects have been moved.

Adaptations
It is important to allow the child ample time to decide which strips are longer or shorter. Some children need a base in which to place the "bottom" of the strip; if this is not available then the strips do not begin with a leveled line. Example: the strip that is 1 x 2-inch is placed 4 inches from the base line, the strip that is 1 x 5-inch is placed on the base line, hence the 1 x 2-inch strip appears to be 1 inch longer than the 1 x 5-inch strip. The more the child is exposed to the manipulation of the strips, dowels, sticks, etc. the more he will seek out and select the longest strip (or maybe the shortest), then the next longest and so on.

1.223 Plays simple rhythmic patterns

Strand: 2-7 **Age:** 52-60m 4.4-5.0y

Definition
The child will play a simple rhythmic pattern--one steady beat with the music. A percussion instrument such as rhythm sticks, wood blocks, drums, rattles, or bells can provide the most effective way to create a steady beat.

Assessment Materials
A percussion rhythm instrument, which you can purchase or make one of the following instruments:
Drum--(a) Save a large #10 food can or coffee can. Remove both ends of the can. Cover the top and the bottom of the can with inner tube rubber. Cut the tubing at least 2 inches wider

than the can and punch holes around the edge of the tubing. With lacing leather shoestrings, twine, or strips of tubing string, lace through the holes in the inner tube rubber, and pull it taut and tie; (b) Stretch a damp chamois over the opening of a circular wooden box. Secure it tightly and allow the cloth to dry; (c) Turn a stainless steel bowl upside down. For a drumstick, use the eraser end of an unsharpened pencil with a big eraser, a slender dowel with a tightly wrapped piece of cloth over the end, or a wooden spoon.

Rhythm Sticks--Cut round sticks of various thicknesses, such as dowels or broomsticks, into 8 to 12-inch lengths. Sand the wood if necessary. Finish by staining or painting.

Wood Blocks--Sand 4- to 6-inch-square scraps of wood not more than an inch thick. Finish by staining or painting. Put a handle in the center of the wood square. Use spools, smaller wooden blocks, cupboard pulls or drawer pulls to make the handles.

Rattles--Put some dried beans, gravel or rice in a container with a tight-fitting lid, such as a tin box, tin salt shaker, or frozen orange juice container. Attach a small dowel stick for a handle. Paint and decorate the container.

Bells--(a) Fill drinking glasses with varying amounts of water to be tapped gently with a spoon; (b) Hang spoons from a string on a dowel stick or a clothes hanger; (c) Sew jingle bells on elastic for wearing around a wrist or an ankle, or attach them to a stick for shaking. Some recorded march music (examples: John Philip Sousa, Ella Jenkins and Her Rhythm Workshop, Georgiana Stewart and Her Playtime Band). Words to *Twinkle, Twinkle, Little Star* or *Hickory, Dickory, Dock*. Equipment to play the music.

Assessment Procedures

Grouping: This skill can be assessed in a group setting.

1. Place one of the percussion instruments on a table, and prepare to play the recorded march.
2. Let the child handle and play the rhythm instrument. When he appears to be comfortable with it, tell him you are going to play a march.
3. Tell him that he may use the rhythm instrument to play along with the music.
4. Observe if he keeps the beat of the music and if he responds to the accented and the unaccented beat. It is important that you do not expect him to follow established rhythmic signatures.
5. Playing on rhythm instruments should help him become involved in music without metered or timed expectations.
6. If he appears to be confused and is uneasy with the manipulation of the instrument, demonstrate how to use the instrument, using the rhyme *Twinkle, Twinkle, Little Star*, as follows:
Twinkle - two beats
twinkle - two beats
little - two beats
star - one beat hold
How I - two beats
wonder - two beats
what you - two beats
are - one beat hold.
7. Give the instrument to the child and tell him to use it to beat out the rhythm to the poem.
8. If he continues to have problems in the handling of the instrument, tell him that you will say the rhyme again, and point when he is to hit the drum or the sticks.
9. Repeat *Twinkle, Twinkle, Little Star* and point to indicate the beats.
10. Phase out the point cues.
11. After he becomes comfortable in keeping the beat to the rhyme, play the march again.
12. Observe whether he keeps the beat with his instrument.

Credit: + Child plays a simple rhythmic pattern with a steady beat.

Adaptations

Some children exhibit inappropriate behavior with a rhythm instrument. They may pound the drum vigorously or hit the sticks rapidly, exhibiting extreme reactions when they are dealing with some musical patterns. Try to determine if a child demonstrates such behaviors because he is uncomfortable with how to use the instruments, is seeking attention, or the music, with a single, exact beat is acting as the catalyst that triggers a strong reaction. Giving him clear instructional procedures in the use of the instrument should assist in these extreme reactions. However, if demanding musical beats create frustrating responses, use a waltz or a lullaby (such as, "*Are you Sleeping?*" or "*All Through the Night*"). It is important to remember that simple rhythmic patterns may not be "heard" by the child, either due to maturity or aptitude in musical reception. Hence, forcing the child to participate before he is "musically ready" could affect his appreciation for music.

1.224 Draws diamond, copying model
Strand: 1-11 **Age:** 69-81m 5.9-6.9y

Definition
The child will be presented with a drawing of a diamond at least 2 inches in diameter and upon request he will copy the shape to display fairly close right angles and four straight lines of nearly equal length.

Assessment Materials
Secure sheets of white paper, a black marker, pencil or crayon, and a diamond template.

Assessment Procedures
Note: The diamond does not have to be in a vertical position.
Grouping: This skill should be assessed one-on-one with the child.
1. Ask the child to join you at the table. Provide the child with a sheet of paper and a writing tool.
2. Show the child the model of the diamond. Say, "Draw a diamond like this."
3. Allow the child time to construct the shape.
4. If her diamond reproduction has all four corners meeting and resembles the figure, date the paper and add it to her file.
5. If the child is having a problem in her attempt, show her the diamond model again, and ask her to trace the lines with her finger.
6. After she has traced the diamond, repeat the above.
7. If she can draw the shape, date her paper and make a notation that she needed to have the tracing experience.
8. If the child is still unable to reconstruction the diamond, provide her with the template and ask her to draw around it.
9. Allow her to trace around the template several times.
10. Repeat the above assessment and if she is successful, date the child's paper making a note that she traced around a diamond template prior to making the diamond.

Credit: + Child draws a diamond copying a model without support cues. The diamond should have four straight lines of nearly equal length and fairly close right angles at the four points.

Adaptations
Drawing a diamond can be a frustrating experience for those children that have difficulty with eye-hand control. Often the side lines of the diamond become scribble-like, due to the attempt by the child to match the four points. In creating this figure the child may exert excess pressure on the pencil and lose control, hence the line will go off track. To assist the child with eye-hand control, begin with kinesthetic activities. Another helpful method is to provide the child with half of the shape and ask her to complete the rest, as it involves a semi-model and a mirrored response.

1.225 Tells or draws a picture to provide a solution for a given problem
Strand: 1-4D **Age:** 52-66m 4.4-5.6y

Definition
When presented with a problem, the child will be able give a solution based on anticipated needs to a situation (You are invited to a birthday party, what will you need to do to get ready?), the anticipated next happening in a situation (You have accidentally spilled some milk on the carpet, what will you do now?), the anticipated outcome to a problem based on known information (The picnic basket is ready, the car will be here in a minute, when should I get ready?), and the anticipated cause and effect of a situation (What would you do if you lost your favorite toy?)

Assessment Materials
A series of questions that present a problem :
(1) You are invited to a birthday party, what will you need to do to get ready? (2) You have accidentally spilled some mild on the carpet, what will you do now? (3) The picnic basket is ready, the car will be here in a minute, when should I get ready? (4) What would you do if you lost your favorite toy? Crayons or pencil for the child to use and paper.

Assessment Procedures
Grouping: This skill should be assessed one-on-one with the child.
1. Tell the child you are going to ask him some questions. Each question will have a problem for him to solve.
2. Give him the option of answering you verbally or drawing a picture to show his solution to the problem.
3. Ask the first question, "You are invited to a birthday party, what will you need to do to get ready?"
4. Allow the child time to process the question.
5. If he answers the question verbally, record his response.
6. If he decides he would like to draw a picture that solves the problem, give him paper and

crayons or a pencil. When he finishes his drawing ask him to tell you about what he has drawn.
7. If he is having difficulty solving the problem, provide him with several possible solutions and have him draw a picture about the one he thinks will work best.
8. When he finishes his drawing, encourage him to tell you about his drawing.
9. Continue with the remaining questions.
10. Record his verbal responses or have him describe what he draws.

Credit: + Child tells you how he would go about solving a problem, anticipating what will happen next, the outcome and the anticipated cause and effect. The child's responses can be given verbally or drawn in a picture.

Adaptations

When some children are asked to transfer a solution to a problem to either an auditory explanation or a visual response, they need to transfer the understanding of relationships, symbolism, abstraction and concept formation. When asked to conceptualize a problem, a child must understand that there may be various solutions and he needs to select the solution that appears to be the best from his perspective. This requires the process of classifying, categorizing, selecting a common denominator and dealing with abstraction. Often a good strategy is to provide the child with several solutions and ask him to select one and tell/draw about his choice. This provides an immediate scenario for telling or drawing his response; it also allows the child to build a "bank" of solutions to modify, alter, add to, etc. as he is asked to conceptually determine outcomes. The process of thinking problems through will come only after the child learns for himself how to solve problems by using past experiences, trial and error, observation, natural consequences, etc. Allowing the child to explore problem-solving strategies is an important phase of cognitive development.

1.226 Names item(s) that would assist with a problem-solving situation
Strand: 1-4D **Age:** 52-66m 4.4-5.6y

Definition
After viewing a concrete problem, the child will locate the object that is needed to solve the problem. Example: the child needs one more circle to finish the picture, one more block to finish the house, or a chair to get to the cookie jar. From the concrete problem the child will look at a picture of a problem and select another picture or name an object(s) that would solve the problem. Finally, after hearing about a problem, the child is able to name an item(s) that would assist in the solution.

Assessment Materials
Use a set of attribute blocks, or from construction paper cut the following: a set of four medium size circles, squares and triangles and a set of small size circles, squares and triangles. Each size shape should be of four different colors (use red for one medium size circle, square and triangle, use red for one small circle, square and triangle, repeat with three other colors).

Assessment Procedures
Grouping: This skill should be assessed one-on-one with the child.
1. Tell the child that you are going to ask her to solve a puzzle.
2. Place the following in front of the child: a medium and small square in one color and a medium and small circle in a different color and finally a medium and small triangle in still a different color.
3. Take the medium-size square and place it in front of the child, then place the small square below the medium-sized square.
4. Take the medium-size circle and place it next to the medium-size square.
5. Point to the empty spot below the circle and ask the child to look at the other shapes. Request that the child find the correct shape for this spot.
6. Make up other problem-solving patterns with the shapes.
7. It is important to increase the difficulty of the patterns, by first adding more shapes, then more complex patterning and mixing of colors.
8. Encourage the child to say the name of the shape that completes the pattern and solves the problem.
9. Note the patterns that the child got correct. After the first miss, stop the assessment and record the shape combination that was missed.

Credit: + Child names what would assist in a problem-solving situation. Assess using the method described above. Start with the shapes all being the same color and move on to more difficult patterns by adding more shapes, then more complex patterning and by mixing the colors. Credit if the child correctly completes two out of three tasks by verbally identifying what color and shape is needed to solve the problem.

Adaptations

If the child finds this use of intuitive thought a difficult concept to understand and is unable to complete the patterns independently, consider lowering the level of self-exploration and solution by doing the following: place a medium-size square in front of the child and next to it place a small square. The two squares should be of the same color. Place the medium-size circle next to the medium-size square, making sure it is also the same color.

Name the shapes and the colors while pointing to them. Ask the child to repeat. "Big red square.", "Little red square.", "Big red circle." Take the small circle of the same color and place it under the medium-size circle and name the shape "Little red circle." Place the circle in position and repeat naming all the shapes. It is helpful if this can be done in a rhythm type manner. Ask the child to join in the verbalization. Verify that the small size circle should remain in the position, by asking the child whether that shape solves the problem.

1.227 Selects an item based on appearance

Strand: 1-7C **Age:** 53-60m 4.5-5.0y

Definition

When the child is shown a group of items or a picture with multi-items in it, he will identify at least one item in the picture based on appearance. The child will identify the items after an oral description. The child will identify these objects by manipulation or a verbal response.

Assessment Materials

A picture book that interests the child and is consistent with her experiential background.

Assessment Procedures

Grouping: This skill can be assessed in a small group setting, no more that four children. Remind the children that they will need to listen and take turns during the activity.
1. Tell the child that she is going to look at some pictures and that she needs to listen carefully.
2. Show the child a picture from the book. Select a single part of the picture, such as a person, animal, flower, house, etc. and describe it using qualities of color, shape, size, expressions, etc. For example, say, "Can you point to the little girl that has on a red dress and a silly hat?"
3. Ask the child to point to the item that has been described.
4. Continue sharing pictures from the book with the child and requesting that the child locate items described.
5. Vary the descriptions to include as many descriptors having to do with appearance as possible.
6. Record the number and type of descriptors given to the child and if she was able to find the correct item.

Credit: + Child selects an item from a group of items, based on the verbal description of its appearance.

Adaptations

Some children may find it hard to respond to oral presentations. These children's primary characteristic is their concern in comprehending the spoken words. Often they have a problem with abstract language and some parts of speech. Nouns are usually easier to comprehend than words that represent actions, qualities, feelings, or ideas (verbs). When descriptive words (adjectives) are used, these children need to understand that objects can be described as well as named. To assist these children, it is important for them to comprehend that the steady flow of words is made up of separate, meaningful units; these units need to be differentiated. Single-item visuals can help with this interpretation. Example: show the child a picture and (1) ask the child to name the object (noun), (2) Ask the child to tell what the item is doing (verb), (3) Ask the child to tell what color the item is, (4) Ask the child to tell one thing about the item, (5) Continue with other questions which require words that describe as answers.

1.228 Selects an item based on category

Strand: 1-7C **Age:** 53-60m 4.5-5.0y

Definition

When the child is given a category (food), he is able to select, from objects or pictures, the item that meets the criteria of that category. Beginning categorical requests should be those that the child is familiar with within his environmental experiences. As the child becomes familiar with classifications and categories, the selection requests can become more abstract.

© 2010 VORT Corporation. All rights reserved. Do Not copy.

Assessment Materials
A red apple, a cup, a red ball, and a radish.

Assessment Procedures
Grouping: This skill can be assessed in a small group setting, no more that four children. Remind the children that they will need to listen and take turns during the activity.
1. Place the apple and the cup on the table. Ask the child to point to the item that is a food and is good to eat. Record the child's answer.
2. Place the apple, the cup, and the red ball on the table.
3. Ask the child to point to the one that is round, red, and that we eat. Record the child's response.
4. Place the apple, the cup, the red ball, and the radish on the table.
5. Request that the child point to the one that is round red, edible, and that grows on a tree. Record the child's response.
6. Compare the three responses.

Credit: + Child selects an item based on category. Begin with categories that are within the child's experience.

Adaptations
Some children have a difficult time when asked to deal with categories, because most items can fit into more than one category (a glass is something that you drink from, holds liquids, is considered a dish, goes into a cupboard, you put on a table, you can see through, that may break easily, etc.) A child will find success if the named category is something he is familiar with and if he has actually used the object. Sorting an object based on category often requires comprehension beyond physical appearances and function. If a child has been involved with the item in the item's major category (a glass is something we drink out of), the understanding is facilitated. To assist him, it is best to present categorical requests that are concrete, things that he has experienced, and items which have a classification cue within their appearance. It is also important to make sure that descriptive words are used to expand the child's opportunity to understand the class and the objects.

1.229 Selects an item based on function
Strand: 1-7C **Age:** 53-60m 4.5-5.0y

Definition
The child will select those objects that are used for the same function or have the same general performance qualities. The child will match items such as: things that carry items, items that clean, things that keep us warm, objects that we play with, etc. It is important that the child understands that she is selecting items by what they do (their function). When asked, the child will be able to state the item's function.

Assessment Materials
Four sets of picture cards. Each set shows items for each of the following four functions: items that holds food (bowl, carton, pot, basket, etc.), items that clean (soap, toothpaste, wash cloth, sponge, etc.), something to rest on (bed, chair, hammock, sleeping bag, etc.), and something that lights up a room or area (light bulb, flashlight, candle, headlight on a car, etc.)

Assessment Procedures
Grouping: This skill can be assessed in a small group setting, no more that four children. Remind the children that they will need to listen and take turns during the activity.
1. Place one card from each set on the table.
2. Ask the child to name the cards that are in view. Tell the child that you are going to say some words that describe what one of the items is used for. Say, "Point to the picture of the item that is used to hold food." Continue until all the pictures have been identified.
3. Place another card from each set on the table.
4. Repeat the above directions with the different cards.
5. Write down the number of cards the child identified correctly.

Credit: + Child selects an item based on its function and can state the item's function.

Adaptations
The ability to classify and associate permits children to react to stimuli in a concise manner. Some children find classifying objects difficult since they may not have clearly received the various perceptions common to an object. Prior to asking a child to select an item based on function, the child should be required to group things which are alike. The first criterion for determining "likeness" should be very general. Encourage the child to verbalize about the items. Ask her questions about the object and prompt her to see the relationships which exist among

them. After the child is comfortable in identifying likenesses and differences, function should be introduced, using the like/different characteristics as part of the cue to function. It is important to discuss and compare items and to ask questions to encourage the child to make comparisons.

1.230 Selects items that are different from a set/group

Strand: 1-7C **Age:** 53-60m 4.5-5.0y

Definition
When presented with an established set of four items, the child will identify at least one object that is different from the rest of the set. The set should include at least two items identical in shape, color, size, appearance, function, object class, etc.

Assessment Materials
Four blue squares, one yellow triangle, three red circles of different sizes, three yellow octagons of the same size, and one bigger yellow octagon. Three pieces of chalk and a pencil. One rubber band.

Assessment Procedures
Grouping: This skill should be assessed one-on-one with the child.
1. Explain to the child that you are going to show him some objects, some of which will be alike and some of which will be different.
2. Tell him that you will be giving him directions on what to do with the items.
3. Lay out two blue squares, the yellow triangle, and another blue square.
4. Say, "Find the one that is different."
5. Record the child's response and make any notation of hesitancy or his comments.
6. In random order, lay out the three red circles of different sizes and a blue square. Repeat the request and record responses.
7. Randomly lay out the octagons and repeat.
8. Present the three pieces of chalk and a pencil to the child and ask him to find the one that does not belong to the group.
9. Record his response and any comments.
10. Add a rubber band to the chalk/pencil grouping and request that the child find the one that does not belong.
11. Record his response and any comments.
12. Discuss with the child what happened when the rubber band was added to the set.

Credit: + Child correctly identifies at least one object from an established set that is different from the rest of the set. The child should be able to perform this task correctly at least three times (each time the identical objects should vary, that is one set should have objects of the same shape, the next set should have objects of the same color, then the objects should be the same size, then the objects should have the same appearance, then the objects should have the same function, etc.)

Adaptations
When presented with a collection of visual items or pictures, some children become overwhelmed and frustrated with the excess stimuli/choices, and when they are asked to do a specific task with the items, their focus needs to be modified. Often this change requires time, additional explanations, removal of some items, adjustment of the task level, repetition of the directions, and practice. To assist these children, the following is recommended: (1) When placing the first set of shapes in front of the child, be sure that the predominate group is together; (2) Arrange the items in such a way that the like set is clustered and the odd object is semi-isolated; (3) Place one item at a time on the table, rather than placing all of them on the table at once; (4) Provide verbal support by pointing to each item and naming it and then asking the child to name the object that is being pointed to.

1.231 Tells suitable ending to a simple story

Strand: 1-9 **Age:** 53-60m 4.5-5.0y

Definition
After the child hears an unfamiliar story with a single plot and not more than four sequences, the child will provide an appropriate ending. The ending should include making inferences and drawing a conclusion.

Assessment Materials
Select or write a simple story.
Example: Big Red
Big Red was a friendly dog.
Big Red liked to walk with his buddy Bill.
One day Bill and Big Red were walking in the woods.
All of a sudden Big Red saw a bush move.
Big Red ran to the bush.
A rabbit jumped out of the bush.
Big Red ran after the rabbit.
The rabbit ran fast.
Big Red wanted to go back to Bill.

But he was lost.

Assessment Procedures
Grouping: This skill should be assessed one-on-one with the child.
1. Tell the child you are going to read a story. Explain that she is to listen carefully.
2. After sentence number 1, ask, "What is Big Red?" After sentence number 2, ask, "What did Big Red like to do?" After sentence number 3, ask, "Where were Bill and Big Red walking?" After sentence number 6, ask, "What jumped out of the bush?" After sentence number 7, ask, "What happened before Big Red ran after the rabbit?" After sentence number 9, ask, "Is the main idea of this story about a nice day for a walk, or is the main idea about a dog who wanted to go back to his friend?"
3. After sentence number 10, ask, "Will you finish the story...?"
4. The ending should be related to the details, including the sequence of events and encompassing the main theme. Make note if the child developed an ending that required making judgments and reaching a conclusion.

Credit: + Child provides an appropriate ending to an unfamiliar story that has been told, making inferences and drawing a conclusion. The story should contain no more that four sequences.

Adaptations
In developing conclusions, some children need to be given direct instruction on the prerequisite skills. These skills include listening for: (1) Detail; (2) Sequence of events; (3) Main idea; and (4) Inferences. To assist in the skill of listening for detail, it is necessary to read a story and stop often to ask who?, what?, and where? - type of questions. To assist in determining sequence of events, after reading a story, give the child a series of pictures that show the various events and ask her to put them in the correct order. To help a child with the main idea, read a story and conduct a discussion of what it is "really" about (often the title is a clue). For the child who is having problems with inferences, read a part of the story, stop at an exciting part, and ask the child to guess what happens next.

1.232 (Removed, see page xviii)

1.233 Sorts 5 multiple-classed objects or pictured objects according to class/category
Strand: 1-7A **Age:** 54-60m 4.6-5.0y

Definition
Given five objects or pictures that represent different classification groups, such as doctor, barber, truck, car, and firefighter, the child will sort into two groups the pictures that represent people that help us and the pictures that represent a form of transportation. The child will sort these objects verbally or by manipulation. The first objects presented to the child should be concrete, then by visual representation. If the child experiences success in sorting these items, ask her to classify based on a verbal description only.

Assessment Materials
Twelve pictures that are single illustrations of two different class/categories, e.g., dog, horse, cat and tree, flower, bushes or house, tent, trailer home and chair, stool, bench etc.

Assessment Procedures
Grouping: This skill should be assessed one-on-one with the child.
1. Take six of the cards and place them face up in front of the child.
2. Name the picture on each of the cards.
3. Explain that the pictured cards can be divided into two groups. Name each of the groups by class. Arrange the pictures so there are three cards from one group together and three cards from the other group together.
4. Give the child six of the pictured cards.
5. Tell her to look at the cards and to sort them into the two sets that go together.
6. Record if the child sorted correctly and how long it took her.

Credit: + Child sorts five multiple-classed objects or pictures by classification groups, either verbally or by manipulation.

Adaptations
When some children are asked to interact with sets and groupings, they will chose quickly, usually on the basis of appearance (color, shape) and often become ambiguous over the selections. These children perform grouping tasks using automatic-perceptual processes and when they complete the members of a set, the grouping predominates over other possible arrangements. To assist these children in creating sets, identify the common elements of the set items, and locate the "odd" objects,

beginning with identifying shapes and colors. Once the children have created a set of like color/shapes, assist them in creating sub-sets. Gradually move the set identification tasks from shapes and colors to those classes which are familiar to the children.

1.234 Names classes/categories of sorted objects
Strand: 1-7A **Age:** 54-60m 4.6-5.0y

Definition
When the child is presented with pre-sorted objects in at least two different categories, the child will name each of the categories. The child may determine his own criteria for classifying objects and naming the set. (e.g., This category is called "Toss Toys", because they are things to play with and throw.)

Assessment Materials
Pictures of objects that can be sorted into one classification (e.g., colors, cars, places to live, birds, or dogs). There should be at least three pictures per grouping and four different categories.

Assessment Procedures
Grouping: This skill should be assessed one-on-one with the child.
1. Display one set of pictures to the child. Point to and name each object.
2. Ask the child if he can name the category that the pictures belong to (for example, red, blue and green are all colors; the category is colors).
3. Continue the above procedure with the rest of the sets of cards.
4. Record the child's correct answers and write down any comments made as to what the pictures have in common.

Credit: + Child names the category of at least two sets of sorted objects.

Adaptations
Children will identify a categorical grouping based on their knowledge of the items involved. If the children have had a direct experience with the objects they may classify them differently than those children who are less familiar with the items. To assist children it is important to: (1) Begin by selecting items that the child is familiar with; (2) Name a category and discuss the items in it. Include in the discussion the appearance and the function of each; (3) Accept the child's response; if the name needs to be modified, expand the child's information about the items rather than rejecting the stated label.

1.235 Identifies and counts quantities of at least 6
Strand: 1-10 **Age:** 54-60m 4.6-5.0y

Definition
As the child becomes proficient in counting out loud, she discovers numbers, both printed and stated. The child also realizes that these numbers represent a specific quantity and that a specific quantity can be expressed by the spoken symbol ("three"), by the number (3), and by the written word (three). The child will say the numerical word that represents a set of objects and she will match the written number that corresponds to a set of objects.

Assessment Materials
Twelve (5 x 3-inch) index cards and dot stickers (21 stickers). You will be making two sets of number cards. The first set of cards should have the numbers 1 through 6 written on them. Write one number on each of the six cards. The second set of six cards should have the quantities 1 through 6 depicted on them using the dot stickers.

Assessment Procedures
Grouping: This skill should be assessed one-on-one with the child.
1. Seat the child across from you and place the number cards in order, 1 through 6.
2. Shuffle the six quantity cards.
3. Tell the child that you are going to show her some cards with stickers on them. Her job is going to be to count the number of stickers on each card.
4. Randomly choose a quantity card. Hold up the card so the child can see it. Ask her, "How many stickers does this card have?" Record her response.
5. Have the child look at the number cards on the table. Ask her to find the card that shows the same number as the number of stickers shown on the card you are holding. Record her response.
6. Place the number card back on the table and place the quantity card in a separate pile.
7. Shuffle the quantity cards and repeat the process.
8. Continue with the remaining cards.
9. Record the child's answers.

Credit: + Child verbally identifies the number of objects and she also matches the written number that correspondence to that set of objects. She identifies and counts quantities at least up to six.

Adaptations

Some children may find it difficult to maintain an auditory sequence with a visual sequence. These children recognize the quantity of four blocks but may not be able to associate the correct spoken number and instead say, "There are three blocks." Or they may say, "There are four blocks" but are unable to visually calculate four.

A strategy to deal with this is to present visual symbols in dot configurations such as those found on dominoes. Extra-large dominoes should be used with indented dots so that the child can feel, as well as see, the grouping. When the child makes the association between the quantities and the numbers, the dots should be arranged in other ways so that she will not think that the number refers only to a specific dot configuration.

1.236 Places 4 pictures in sequence
Strand: 1-7A **Age:** 54-62m 4.6-5.2y

Definition
When the child is shown four pictures depicting a sequence of events, the child will put the pictures in the correct order and tell the picture story.

Assessment Materials
Two sets of three separate picture cards that tell a story. For example, picture one shows a deflated balloon, picture two shows a person blowing up the balloon, and picture three shows a happy child holding an inflated balloon. Two set of four separate picture cards that tell a story. Sequence cards can also be purchased commercially.

Assessment Procedures
Grouping: This skill should be assessed one-on-one with the child.
1. Place the set of three pictures in front of the child, making sure that they are not in the correct story order.
2. Tell the child that when these pictures are placed in the right order they tell a story. Discuss each picture with the child and decide which one should go first, second, and third. Ask the child to look at the pictures and tell a story.
3. Place the second set of three pictures in view of the child and tell him to place those pictures in the correct order to tell a story. After the child has placed the pictures, encourage him to tell the story.
4. Present the child with the set of four pictures and repeat the directions.
5. Place the second set of four pictures in view of the child and tell him to place those pictures in the correct order to tell a story. After the child has placed the pictures, ask him to tell you the story.
6. Record the responses of the second set of three pictures and the two sets of four pictures.

Credit: + Child places at least one set of four pictures in sequence to tell a story and tells a story that describes what is occurring in the pictures.

Adaptations
Some children become confused when having to deal with more than one visual. It is important to make sure the pictures represent an action that the child has experienced before. It is also helpful to discuss each picture, naming the objects in the illustrations, asking literal questions which will generate what is occurring, accepting the child's responses and then modifying as necessary, and reviewing the sequential events several times.

1.237 Locates big, bigger, biggest and small, smaller, smallest in group of objects
Strand: 1-7B **Age:** 54-64m 4.6-5.4y

Definition
The child will compare and contrast objects of different sizes, formulating the concept of big, bigger, biggest and small, smaller, smallest. When the child is looking for the smallest item in a group, she will understand that this item is smaller than all the ones that she will select later. When the child is looking for the biggest item in a group, she will understand that this item is bigger than all the items she will select.

Assessment Materials
Cut five circles: circle one should be 5 inches in diameter, circle two 4-inch in diameter, circle three 3-inch in diameter, circle four 2-inch in diameter, and circle five 1-inch in diameter. Make a model of the five circles by drawing the circles on a sheet of paper from the smallest to the largest. Cut five rectangular strips: strip one should be 1 x 6-inch, strip two should be 1 x 5-inch, strip three should be 1 x 4-inch, strip four should be 1 x 3-inch, and strip five should be 1 x

2-inch. Make a model of the five rectangles by drawing the rectangles on a sheet of paper from the smallest to the largest. A strip of tape to act as the base.

Assessment Procedures

Grouping: This skill should be assessed one-on-one with the child.

1. Place the strip of tape on the table and then put the five circles in mixed order on the table. Seat the child at the table and ask her to arrange the circles in a row beginning with the smallest and working toward the biggest.
2. If the child is hesitant, select the smallest circle, place the edge of the circle on the base tape, and ask the child to continue.
3. After the child has placed the circles in size sequence, say, "Give me the biggest circle."
4. Say, "Give me a bigger circle than this one," while pointing to one of the circles on the table.
5. Say, "Give me a big circle."
6. Record the child's responses.
7. If the child has any problems with these activities, show her the model and ask her to place/match the cut out circles with those drawn on the paper model. After the child has had an opportunity to superimpose the circles, repeat the above steps.
8. Record the child's responses.
9. Place the five rectangle strips on the table. The strips should be in random order.
10. Ask the child to arrange the strips in a row beginning with the biggest and work toward the smallest.
11. If the child is hesitant, select the biggest strip, place the bottom of the strip on the base tape, and ask the child to continue.
12. After the child has placed the strips from the biggest to the smallest, say, "Give me the smallest strip."
13. Say, "Give me the strip that is smaller than this one," pointing to a strip that is in the sequence.
14. Say, "Give me a small strip."
15. Record the child's responses.
16. If the child has any problems with the strip activities, show her the model and ask her to place the cut out strips on the paper model. After the child has had an opportunity to superimpose the strips, repeat the above steps.
17. Record the child's responses.

Credit: + Child locates big, bigger, biggest and small, smaller, and smallest in a group of objects. Child completes the task without the need of a model.

Adaptations

The placement of objects in sequence based on size is a visual task. To assist children, who are having difficulty with a sequencing task present licorice ropes cut to different lengths (6 inches, 4 inches, and 2 inches). Food can often be highly motivating for a child. Arrange the licorice according to size. Mix up the pieces and then have the child arrange the licorice by big, bigger, biggest. Mix up the three pieces again and have the child identify the biggest piece. Ask the child which piece of licorice she would like to eat. Most children will probably ask for the biggest piece. Ask the child which piece of licorice you can eat. Next have her identify who has the big piece, followed by the bigger piece, and then the biggest piece. Take a break and eat the licorice. Discuss how the biggest piece took longer to be eaten than the big piece.

1.238 Sorts items by category
Strand: 1-7A **Age:** 54-65m 4.6-5.5y

Definition
When the child is given a category (e.g., food), he is able to sort objects or pictures which meet the criteria of that category. Categorical sorting should begin with items the child is familiar with and which are within his experiences. After sorting objects into a single category, the child will be presented with additional categories and items, as well as an emphasis on subtle differences of the categories.

Assessment Materials
Two sets of five picture cards. Each set should illustrate a separate category (e.g., things that fly, things that we wear, things that we eat, etc.) Two boxes that are larger than the cards.

Assessment Procedures
Grouping: This skill should be assessed one-on-one with the child.

1. Take one card from each set and show it to the child. Tell the child that it is a picture of something that flies, that you wear, that you eat, etc. Place the card in one of the boxes and tell the child the name of the box. For example, "Things that _____ box." Continue by showing the child a picture from the other category and placing it in the correct box.
2. Shuffle and place the rest of the cards from each set face down in front of the child. Tell the child that he is to draw one card at a time,

look at it, and decide if it should go in the "Things that____ box" or in the "Things that we____ box." After he decides, he should place the picture card in the correct box.
3. Note the number placed correctly.
4. After the child has completed this sorting task, remove all the cards from the boxes, replace them face down in front of the child, and add another qualifier to the categorical sorting (e.g., things that fly but that we don't ride in, items we wear to go to a party, things we eat without cooking, etc.)
5. Repeat the verbal directions to the child and ask him to place the cards in the correct boxes.
6. Note the number of cards placed correctly and the amount of time needed.

Credit: + Child sorts items by category, emphasizing subtle differences of the categories.

Adaptations

Some children have a difficult time when asked to deal with categories, because most items can fit into more than one category. For example, a glass is something that you drink from, that holds liquids, that is considered a dish, that goes into a cupboard, that is put on a table when setting it, etc. These children will be successful if the named category is something they are familiar with and if they have actually used the object as part of the mentioned category. Sorting an object based on a category often requires comprehension beyond physical appearances and function. If a child has been involved with the item in the item's major category (a glass is something we drink out of), the understanding is facilitated. To assist a child, present categorical requests that are concrete, things that the child has experienced and items which have a classification cue within their appearance. It is also important to make sure that descriptive words are used to expand the child's opportunity to understand the class and the objects.

1.239 Works in small group for 10-25 minutes

Strand: 1-8 **Age:** 54-72m 4.6-6.0y

Definition

A small group refers to four or five children. The project that these children do should be designed to be completed within the 10-25 minute period. The group does not work independently, but receives supervision. The amount of supervision will vary, depending on the group structure and the activity.

Assessment Materials

A picture puzzle or floor puzzle with at least twenty interlocking pieces. The puzzle should not be one that the children have completed before, and should be on a subject the children are familiar with.

Assessment Procedures

Grouping: This skill should be assessed in a small group setting, no more than four to five children. Remind the children that they will need to listen and take turns during the activity.

1. Remove the pieces of the puzzle and randomly put five pieces of the puzzle together to make four sets of at least five pieces.
2. Ask four children to join you, and give each child at least five pieces of the puzzle.
3. Explain that they should work together to complete the puzzle. Also explain that they are going to take turns to see if the pieces they have can be placed in the puzzle.
4. Say, "When I call your name it will be your turn to try to fit your piece in the puzzle." Record the time when the group started working.
5. Begin the activity by calling one of the children's names. If the child is confused as to what is expected of him, restate the directions.
6. Continue by calling each child's name, allowing them time to decide if their puzzle pieces can be put into place.
7. Record the time when the group completed the puzzle.
8. Add any comments about the children's behavior, such as taking turns, becoming distracted, reacting selfishly, assisting another child, being over competitive, etc.
9. After the puzzle has been completed, conduct a discussion about the puzzle, and observe any negative or positive group interaction concerns.

Credit: + Child works in a small group of four to five children and is able to stay on task for 10-25 minutes. Supervision is provided as the children work together on an activity.

Adaptations

When children are introduced to a group situation, there may be some children who need extra help with recognizing the attitudes and feelings of others. These children need assistance in understanding the manifestations of aggressive and passive behavior. If a child demonstrates a behavior that becomes the catalyst in which group attention is diminished, that child needs to be made aware of the inappropriate behavior and be reminded of the proper way to act.

1.240 Tells as many solutions as possible for a given problem situation
Strand: 1-4D **Age:** 54-72m 4.6-6.0y

Definition
The problems presented to the child should be those that begin with such statements as "What are some of the things that could happen if_____?" or "If _____ happened, what are some of the things you could do?" Make sure that the problems presented are those that are within the realm of the child's experiences. Example: "What are some of the things that could happen if you lost one of your shoes?" or "If your ball got caught in the tree what are some of the things you could do to get it down?"

Assessment Materials
Prepare at least two problem-solving situations that have several possible solutions. Example: "Pretend that you are going to your friend's birthday party and you have lost the present you were going to give her. What would you do?" or "You and your mother are shopping. What would happen if she went down one aisle and you went down another, and all of a sudden you were lost?"

Assessment Procedures
Grouping: This skill should be assessed one-on-one with the child.
1. Explain to the child that you are going to tell her a short story, but that stories need endings. Encourage the child to listen carefully and be ready to tell as many different endings to the story as she can think of.
2. Give the child a point for each appropriate ending that she says. Judge the quality of the responses by how appropriate they are, how creative they are, and if they solve the presented problem. Response time may also be noted.

Credit: + Child gives at least two or three solutions for a given problem presented to them.

Adaptations
Reasoning skills are developed in children by giving them different chances to think. To develop these skills, it is important to begin with simple questions that can be answered by simple responses. (What can fly?) The next consideration should be those questions that need to be answered by using some form of analytical thinking. (Which circle is the biggest?) Then the ability to do reasoning that requires the child to answer with a new or unknown solution to a problem. (What would you do if your friend got hurt when she fell down the stairs?) If a child has difficulty developing the unknown solution, it may be necessary to first ask her questions relative to simple and then analytical reasoning.

1.241 Draws recognizable face with eyes, nose, mouth
Strand: 1-11 **Age:** 36-48m 3.0-4.0y

Definition
The child will draw a face with eyes, a nose and a mouth when asked. The face needs to be recognizable and the features in approximate facial positions.

Assessment Materials
Prepare or secure a picture of a face. The face (front view) should be an oval with two eyes, a nose, and a mouth. White drawing paper and crayons or markers. Prepare a "Paddle Face" (an oval made from heavy paper the actual size of a head; with the eyes, nose and mouth cut out. The circle should be mounted on a ruler).

Assessment Procedures
Grouping: This skill can be introduced and practiced in a group setting. However, when you are ready to assess the child's ability to draw a recognizable face, it is recommended that you do so one-on-one with the child.
1. Invite the child to the working area.
2. Ask the child to point to his face.
3. Ask him to point to his eyes.
4. Ask him to point to his nose.
5. Ask him to point to his mouth.
6. When the child has successfully noted his facial features, give him a sheet of white drawing paper and markers/crayons.
7. Say, "Use the markers and draw a face on this paper."

8. Allow the child ample time to complete the drawing. Allow the child one opportunity to start over.
9. Date the child's completed picture and place it in his file.
10. If the child is having difficulty with the task, present him with the picture of the face. Point (circular movement around the outside of the face) and ask, "What is this?"
11. Point to the eyes and say, "What are these?"
12. Point to the nose and say, "What is this?"
13. Point to the mouth and say, "What is this?"
14. After the child has answered all the questions, give him a sheet of paper and say, "Draw a picture of a face and give it eyes, a nose, and a mouth."
15. Allow the child ample time to complete the drawing.
16. Allow the child one opportunity to start over.
17. Date the child's completed picture, note that verbal and visual cueing was necessary, and place it in his file.
18. If the child has difficulty with this task, place the Paddle Face over your face and circle the face area saying, "This is my face." Point to the eyes (cut out) and say, "These are my eyes." Point to the nose (cut out) and say, "This is my nose." Point to the mouth (cut out) and say, "This is my mouth."
19. Allow the child to put the Paddle Face over his face and repeat the steps.
20. Place the Paddle Face on a sheet of paper and trace around it, tracing the holes for the eyes, the nose, and mouth.
21. Point to each facial feature and ask the child to name it.
22. Remove the Paddle Face and the traced drawing.
23. Give the child a sheet of paper and ask him to draw a face.
24. Allow him ample time to complete the assignment.
25. Date his paper and make a note physical, verbal, and visual cueing used prior to the drawing.

Credit: + Child draws a recognizable face with eyes, nose, and mouth without any prompting.

Adaptations

Some children will have a difficult time trying to illustrate the dimensions of real items such as facial features. Face outlines are viewed as round, and eyes are conceptualized as round and dot-like, but the nose can cause concern for these children, as it is viewed as a dimension; hence the child becomes confused as to what angle to represent the nose. If looked at straight-on, the nose is two curved lines, if looking upward, the nose is two holes and if looking side ways it is an elongated right angle. Often the drawing of real items is not a graphic concern but a problem of wanting proper representation. To assist those children in focusing on drawing the figure as they perceive it (and not be concerned about realism), provide them numerous chances to trace, connect lines, reproduce from flat visuals, compare figures from different dimensions and use a medium that can be altered quickly.

1.242 Names capital and lower case letters when shown printed letters

Strand: 1-9 **Age:** 58-72m 4.10-6.0y

Definition

When shown a letter of the alphabet the child will be able to name the letter. The child will be shown one letter at a time, capital and lower case together. The letters should be printed on cards not less than 2 x 2-inch. Next present only the capital letters of the alphabet. Follow by presenting just the lower case letters of the alphabet. The letters in each group should be randomly presented.

Assessment Materials

Make three sets of cards at least 2 x 2-inch (index cards work well). Print the letters of the alphabet, upper and lower case, on cards (Set One). Print the capital letters of the alphabet on cards (Set Two). Print the lower case letters of the alphabet on cards (Set Three). The letters should be printed in one color and the capital should be first (Bb). For scoring purposes, a sheet needs to be prepared that has all the letters on it with three columns: column one for both the capital and lower case together, column two for the capitals only, and column three for lower case only.

Assessment Procedures

Grouping: This skill can be introduced and practiced in a group setting. However, when you are ready to assess the child's ability to name capital and lower case letters, it is recommended that you do so one-on-one with the child.

1. As a warm-up, ask the child to join you in saying the alphabet. Singing the *Alphabet Song* would also be an excellent warm-up.

2. Inform the child that you are going to show her some cards with letters on them and when you point to the letters, you want her to tell you the letter's name.
3. Show the child the letter Aa. Point to the letter and say, "Tell me this letter's name." On the scoring sheet put a check after the letter if the child said the correct name.
4. Continue showing the child other letters in random order.
5. If the child correctly named each letter, use Set Two and repeat the steps.
6. If the child correctly named each letter, use Set Three and repeat the steps.

Credit: + Child correctly names all the capital and lower case letters in print. The letters need to be presented in random order to verify that the child actually knows the individual letters and has not just memorized the *Alphabet Song*.

Adaptations

Because most children learn to say the alphabet in rote-clusters or by learning the *Alphabet Song*, it is often hard to give a letter name out of sequence. Children often have to look at the letter presented and then think to themselves, "ABCD EFG HIJK LMNOP" etc., until they come to the letter being shown to them. Children also have a tendency to say the letter's sound rather than the letter's name, because the letters are often referenced to as "A is for Apple," "B is for Baby," etc. To assist the child in these often confused responses: (1) Present the letters to be named in their familiar rote clusters. Prepare cards that have the following: Card One - ABCD, Card Two - EFG, Card Three - HIJK, Card Four - LMNOP, Card Five - QRS, Card Six - TUV, and Card Seven – WX, Card Eight - YZ. Show the child Card One and ask her to say the letters as you point to them. Start by pointing to the letter A, then B, C, and D. Continue with the other cards. When the child is comfortable naming the letters by card cluster, show her Card One and point to only one letter, e.g., C, and ask the child to tell the letter name. This way, if the child needs to use verbal recall, she only has to deal with the letters on the individual cluster cards. As the child becomes more comfortable with individual letter naming, phase out the multi-lettered cards; (2) To deal with the confusion of letter name and sound, when the child is shown a letter, e.g., B, and she responds "Ba-a-a," tell her, "Ba is the sound of the letter that is named B." Tell the child that letters have both a name and a sound. It is often helpful to use analogies during the discussion, such as a baby chick makes a sound of "peep", but is named chicken, hence the letter B can sound like "Ba" in the word Baby but has the name B.

1.243 Sorts items by appearance
Strand: 1-7A **Age:** 60-65m 5.0-5.5y

Definition
Using more than one identical object or picture, the child will sort the ones that look alike. Using more than one object or picture, the child will sort the ones that look nearly alike.

Assessment Materials
Red, yellow, and blue paper. From the yellow paper cut a large circle, a medium size square, and a small triangle. From the blue paper cut a large square, a medium triangle, and a small circle. From the red paper cut a large triangle, a medium circle, and a small square.

Assessment Procedures
Grouping: This skill should be assessed one-on-one with the child.
1. Mix up the shapes and place them on a table. Tell the child to sort them by color. Record responses.
2. Mix up the shapes and place them on a table. Tell the child to sort them by size. Record responses.
3. Mix up the shapes and place them on a table. Tell the child to sort them by shape. Record responses.

Credit: + Child sorts at least two groups of items by appearance.

Adaptations

Some children may have a problem focusing on a single picture when other visual stimuli is present. These children sense a need to look at everything within their visual range. When asked to sort different objects/pictures, the directions may be ignored/deferred because the child is too "busy" responding to the other visuals. To assist these children, make sure that all other visuals are out of view. When the child has completed sorting one set, remove it before placing the next group of pictures in front of the child.

1.244 Sorts items by function
Strand: 1-7A **Age:** 60-66m 5.0-5.6y

Definition
Children begin by sorting objects that are of opposite function (e.g., things we wear and things that we cannot wear); gradually approaching sorting items by finer definition (e.g., things we wear to keep us warm and things we wear to keep us cool); and finally expanding the concept to the affective (e.g., things that I wear that make me laugh and things that I wear that make me feel special).

Assessment Materials
Make three lotto-type game boards divided into three sections horizontally and vertically. On game board one the following pictures should be in the divided sections: shoes, an apple, a blouse, a bowl, a cap, a cup, a dog, a jacket, and a wrist watch. On game board two the following pictures should be in the divided sections: boots, shorts, a warm hat, a swim suit, a heavy coat, thongs, a parka, mittens, and a straw hat. On game board three the following pictures should be in the divided sections: a queen or king's crown, a clown costume, a party dress, a funny hat, a painted fun face, a fancy bow, a Halloween costume, a Your Special Button, and shoes on the wrong feet. Markers, such as checkers or chips, should also be available.

Assessment Procedures
Grouping: This skill should be assessed one-on-one with the child.
1. Show the child game board one and name the pictures illustrated on the board. Give the child the markers.
2. Tell the child to place a marker on all the pictures that show things that are made to be worn.
3. Identify the number the child got.
4. Show the child game board two and name the pictures illustrated on the board. Give the child the markers.
5. Tell the child to place a marker on all the pictures that show things that we wear to keep us warm.
6. Identify the number the child got right.
7. Show the child game board three and name the pictures illustrated on the board. Give the child the markers.
8. Tell the child to place a marker on all the pictures that show things that make him laugh.
9. Identify the number the child got right.

Credit: + Child sorts at least two groups of items according to function.

Adaptations
Some children find it difficult to understand the difference between function and appearance. A number of objects may have similar appearances, however, they do not have the same function (toy cars look like big cars, but they do not transport people). It is important to discuss and compare items that look similar but are not functionally the same. To help clarify the differences, ask inquiry-type questions and encourage the child to make comparisons. If the child takes a long time to respond after the directions have been given, make sure the child is familiar with the items, name the item in the picture but not the function, or ask the child what the item could be used for. It is important to involve the child in a general discussion of the items.

1.245 Uses tactile terms to describe properties of items
Strand: 1-7C **Age:** 60-66m 5.0-5.6y

Definition
The child will describe an object by using such words as hard or soft, rough or smooth, round or flat, big or little, dark or light, large or small, and conclude by naming the object.

Assessment Materials
A group of at least six small objects of different textures and properties, such as a spool of thread, a cotton ball, a rock, sandpaper, wool fabric, tissue paper, wood sample, etc.

Assessment Procedures
Grouping: This can be introduced and practiced in a group setting. However, when you are ready to assess the child's ability to use tactile terms to describe the properties of an item, it is recommended that you do so one-on-one with the child.
1. Take one of the items (rock) and give it to the child. Tell the child to look carefully at the rock. Then ask the child how the rock feels; prompt if necessary by asking if the rock is hard or soft. Ask the child how her fingers feel as she touches the rock. Prompt if necessary by asking if it feels smooth or rough. Continue with other identifying properties of the rock (e.g., heavy, light, bumpy, sticky, etc.)

2. After the child has become familiar with the procedure, explain that she will be given an object and that she is to answer questions about it.
3. Give the child an object and ask, "How does the _____ feel? Tell me all the things you can about the_____." No prompting.
4. If the child responds with a comparison statement such as ,"It feels like the rug in my mother's room." Say "Can you think of a word(s) that tell about the rug and the_____?"
5. Record all the tactile words the child uses to describe the item.
6. Repeat the above with at least five different objects.

Credit: + Child uses tactile terms to describe the properties of at least three different items and then identifies the item by name.

Adaptations

Some children demonstrate a dislike for touching certain things. This dislike may be related to sensory issues and avoiding certain textures, or a touch association has been made with an unpleasant experience. To assist these children, discuss the way the object feels, gradually rub the item on the child's inside arm and "play-down" the reaction. Some children may not be able to use tactile terms to describe items, because these words are not within their expressive vocabulary. To assist these children, use words that describe how something feels, asking the child to repeat the words in association with the object. Encourage the child to select one item and "tell about it," making sure that the child discusses how it feels.

1.246 Sings or dances to different songs

Strand: 2-7 **Age:** 60-66m 5.0-5.6y

Definition

The child will sing at least two different familiar songs (he will sing them mostly in tune and remember most of the lyrics). He will dance to at least two different musical selections. His dance may be either created or in a learned pattern.

Assessment Materials

An accompanying instrument such as a drum, rhythm sticks, or wood blocks. A musical selection with a tempo and a "feeling" for creative dancing (suggested musicians: Offenbach, Mendelssohn, Tchaikovsky, Cohan, Raffi, Mr. Al, Hap Palmer).

Assessment Procedures

Grouping: This skill can be introduced and practiced in a group setting. However, when you are ready to assess the child's ability to sing or dance to different songs, you may need to do so in a smaller group or one-on-one.

Singing Assessment:
1. Whenever the child begins to sing a song spontaneously during the day, observe whether he is singing the tune and remembering most of the words.
2. If he has problems with the tune, sing the song with him. If he is having problems with remembering the words, cue him by singing the unknown words distinctly and phasing out on the familiar words. His singing will improve with practice.
3. If a more structured assessment is desired, the following is recommended.
4. Invite him to join you in playing an instrument.
5. Say, "I would like us to play your favorite song," or " Can you tell me what you would like to sing?"
6. If he does not respond, begin singing and keeping rhythm to a song that he enjoys and you think he knows.
7. Encourage him to join in. If he choose not to sing, either change songs and repeat it, or move to another activity.

Dance Assessment:
8. Invite the child to join you in a large area (large enough for dancing and creative movement).
9. Explain that you are going to play the drum to accompany him as he does a special drum dance.
10. Demonstrate the following dance steps, using the drum to maintain a steady beat:
Two claps
Two taps with the right toe
Two claps and two taps with the left toe
(Repeat this series several times.)
Four claps
Four taps with the right toe
Four claps and four taps with the left toe
(Repeat this series several times.)
11. Having the child move in the same way each time or follow a specific step pattern can stifle rather than support his creative expression. Let him interpret the rhythmic movements in his own way.
12. Allow him to do dance independently.

13. Others dances that he will enjoy doing are include *Hokey Pokey, Skip to My Lou, Here We Go Round the Mulberry Bush,* or *Put Your Little Foot In*.
14. Tell him that you are going to play some special music. Discuss with him how music often makes us want to dance and move. Tell him to listen to the music and to dance to it in any way it makes him feel.
15. Observe and encourage him to enjoy the freedom of creative dance.

Credit: + Child sings at least two different familiar songs or he dances at least two different musical selections (his dance can be creative or a learned pattern).

Adaptations

Some children have difficulty remembering the tune and the words of a song. This is particularly true if the words do not have meaning to him. For most children, the ability to sing a favorite song develops with natural maturation and practice. However, singing, like other learning skills, proceeds through levels of task accomplishments. Some children need instruction and practice at each level. A recommended sequence of development for the child is: (1) Accompanies his own playing with humming or singing to himself; (2) Begins to listen to others singing; (3) Begins to recognize songs he has heard others sing; (4) Responds to a song with actions to the words or to the tune; (5) Joins in singing a few words with others; (6) Sings with others but does not match the tune or rhythm; (7) Sings with others and is able to match pitch and rhythm; (8) Sings a song by himself, knowing all the lyrics and maintaining the melody and rhythm.

Children often have favorite songs. Allowing them the opportunity to choose a song from the various songs you sing may increase his interest in joining in with the singing. Also, using props to go along with the words to a song can encourage a child to join in. The same is true for dancing. Children might be more apt to dance to a preferred song, as well as to dance with a prop that goes to a song so they are not dancing alone.

1.247 (Removed, see page xviii)

1.248 Locates object of given number in group of 10
Strand: 1-10 **Age:** 60-66m 5.0-5.6y

Definition
The child, upon request, will select from a row of objects the item that is first, second, third, fourth and fifth. As an extension of this skill: the child, upon request, will select from a row of objects the item that is sixth, seventh, eighth, ninth and tenth. It is necessary that the child be able to count in cardinal order to five prior to using ordinal position to five. It is necessary that the child be able to count in cardinal order to ten prior to using ordinal position to ten. Special emphasis should be placed on first and second, because they are different contextual words than the number words one and two. Focus should also be on the words third and fifth as they are also contextually different from their counterparts three and five.

Assessment Materials
Ten bean bags and a basket or a box big enough to hold the bean bags when thrown. Ten paper plates.

Assessment Procedures
Grouping: This skill can be introduced and practiced in a group setting. However, when you are ready to assess the child's ability to locate objects of a given number in a group of ten, it is recommended that you do so one-on-one with the child.

1. Place ten paper plates in a row on the table and place one bean bag on each plate. The paper plates will serve as place markers for the bean bags. Place the basket within throwing distance of the child.
2. Ask the child to stand/sit in front of the row of bean bags.
3. Tell the child to count the bean bags on the table. Explain to him how the paper plates will save the bean bags place once he has thrown the bean bag into the basket.
4. Explain to the child that you are going to ask him to throw a bean bag into the basket. For each bean bag that lands into the basket he gets a point.
5. Say, "Throw the first bean bag into the basket."
6. Say, "Throw the second bean bag into the basket."
7. Say, "Throw the third bean bag into the basket."
8. Say, "Throw the fourth bean bag into the basket."

9. Say, "Throw the fifth bean bag into the basket."
10. Continue the directions up the tenth bean bag.
11. Tell the child how many points he has and record if he selected the bean bags in the order they were stated.
12. Have the child count the paper plates before returning the bean bags.
13. Explain that you want him to play the game again.
14. Place the bean bags in a row on a table on the paper plates.
15. Say, "Throw the third bean bag into the basket."
16. Say, "Throw the first bean bag into the basket."
17. Say, "Throw the fifth bean bag into the basket."
18. Say, "Throw the second bean bag into the basket."
19. Say, "Throw the fourth bean bag into the basket."
20. If the child is able to recognize placement, continue with the same directions for beans in the sixth through tenth position in random order.
21. If the child is not able to recognize placement, hand him the bean bags, one at a time, until all have been thrown into the box.
22. Tell the child how many points he has and record if he selected the bean bags in the order they were stated.
23. Make any notations as to how the child approached the task. Example: he counted 1 - 2 - 3 - 4 - 5 – 6 – 7 – 8 – 9 – 10 before responding to third, first, second, fifth, fourth, etc.

Credit: + Child correctly locates objects in the first, second, third, fourth, and fifth positions, randomly, in a group of 10.

Adaptations

When a child first learns to count, he learns the cardinal system which tells how many (2, 4, 7). The ordinal system indicates the place of the number in a sequence (e.g., first, second). Some children have a difficult time understanding that first, second, third, fourth, etc. refer to positions or locations within a sequence. It is important that the child who is having a problem with ordinals begins by discovering that objects are used as reference points, and that the position in a row is not specific enough. An example is: Place three or four toy farm animals in a line near a barn. Say, "Which animal is closest to the barn? Which animal is the farthest away? Which animal is at the end of the line? Which animal is at the beginning of the line?" When the child responds to the questions, be sure to extend his answer by saying "The animal at the beginning of the line is first. The next animal is second. The last animal is fourth." The child will be able to see the animal's position in reference to the barn and then in reference to the position in the row.

1.249 Matches groups having equal numbers of objects up to 10

Strand: 1-10   **Age:** 60-66m 5.0-5.6y

Definition

The child will match two equal groups of the same objects. When the child views objects in two sets of one, two sets of two and two sets of three, she will be able to point to the sets having the same number of objects upon verbal request. The presentation of sets should be done in clusters of one, two and three objects. Then in a cluster of four, five and six objects and in the final cluster of seven, eight, nine and ten objects.

Assessment Materials

Twenty blank 5 x 8-inch index cards. At least 110 stickers (no more than ½" in diameter).
Attach the stickers to the index cards in the following patterns:
Set One:
Card One: one sticker in the middle of the card.
Card Two: identical to Card One.
Card Three: two stickers side by side.
Card Four: identical to Card Three.
Card Five: three stickers side by side.
Card Six: identical to Card Five.
Set Two:
Card One: four stickers in two rows of two stickers.
Card Two: identical to Card One.
Card Three: five stickers in a position of one row of two, one row of one and one row of two.
Card Four: identical to Card Three.
Card Five: six stickers in two rows of three.
Card Six: identical to Card Five.
Set Three:
Card One: seven stickers in a position of one row of three, one row of one and one row of three
Card Two: identical to Card One.
Card Three: eight stickers in two rows of four.
Card Four: identical to Card Three.
Card Five: nine stickers in a three rows of three stickers.

© 2010 VORT Corporation. All rights reserved. Do Not copy.

Card Six: identical to Card Five.
Card Seven: ten stickers in a position of one row of four, one row of two and one row of four.
Card Eight: identical to Card Seven.

Assessment Procedures
Grouping: This skill should be assessed one-on-one with the child.
1. Ask the child to come to the table. Place all the cards in Set One face down on the table.
2. Tell the child to turn over two cards.
3. Say, "Are your cards the same?" If the child has a matched pair, she may keep the cards and turn over two more cards. If the child selected two cards that show unequal sets tell the child to place the two cards face down on the table and turn over two more cards.
4. Record the child's correct and incorrect answers.
5. Repeat the procedures using Card Set Two.
6. Repeat the procedures using Card Set Three.

Credit: + Child matches groups having equal numbers of objects up to 10 objects. First, start with one, two and three objects. Next, assess four, five and six objects. Finally, cluster seven, eight, nine and ten objects.

Adaptations
Some children will have difficulty visually identifying sets that have the same members. Often these children will count each item in the two sets, they will try to superimpose the items of each set, or they will lay another object on top of each item in each set. These types of problem-solving behaviors may indicate that the child needs to begin set matching by using three-dimensional objects which allow the child to move the items he is about to match. After the child has matched the number of objects by moving from one set to another, the child should place a piece of yarn or draw a line from one three-dimensional object in one set to a three-dimensional object in the other set. Another technique to consider for those children who are having difficulty visually matching groups is to establish sets that are logically realistic, such as two apple trees in one group to be matched with two apples in another group, or three birds in one group to be matched with three nests.

1.250 Completes task with little prompting
Strand: 1-8 **Age:** 60-66m 5.0-5.6y

Definition
The child will complete an activity, with not more than two reminders. The reminders need to be of a positive nature. Such statements as "You have completed the hardest part of the _____(picture)! It is going to really look nice when you are done." or "I am really proud of the way you have been working, keep it up." The reinforcement prompt should be based on progress, not on accuracy. Continue the reinforcement strategies as described, then fading should begin.

Assessment Materials
Prepare an activity that is within the child's achievement level. This task could be completing a puzzle, playing game, drawing, stringing beads, looking at a book, doing a worksheet, etc. Secure any supplies that may be needed to complete the activity (crayons, markers, drawing paper, glue). Select a reward, something that the child will work for and enjoy.

Assessment Procedures
Note: In recording the number of prompts needed, also record the type of reinforcement that was used (verbal, non-verbal, tangible).
Grouping: This skill should be assessed one-on-one with the child.
1. Explain to the child that he is to do the activity. Provide the child with directions if necessary.
2. Pause to see if the child will begin the activity without any prompting.
3. If prompting is necessary, make a note.
4. Observe the child as he does the activity, and use the reinforcement prompts if the child discontinues the task.
5. When the child has completed the activity, give him the earned reward.

Credit: + Child completes a task with little prompting and no more than two reminders. The reminders need to be positive statements related to the progress the child is making on the task, not the accuracy.

Adaptations
Some children have the feeling that the important issue in doing an activity is being the best. The issue here is task completion, and so the prompting/reinforcement needs to emphasize working hard, staying on task, and

completing the task. As some children become older, their concern with failing and not being the best may lead to such behavior as being reluctant to begin a task, particularly if the activity requires coloring a picture, building a design, etc. These children may "play around" rather than start a task. They may draw something and then tear the paper up, hide the work, etc. To help these risk-reluctant children, it is important that the skill be within an instructional level, and that the first attempts be positively received. Beginning limitations should be given to the child and resources made available to enable the child to find out that what he has done is correct.

1.251 Reads and writes numerals to 5
Strand: 1-10 **Age:** 60-68m 5.0-5.8y

Definition
When the child is presented with the written numerals 1, 2, and 3 he will read them. The numbers should be presented in the following manner: first present number 1, with a set of one object; after the child has responded, remove the number and object. Then present number 2, with a set of two objects; after the child has responded, remove the number and the set of two objects and present numbers 3, 4, 5 in the same way. The child should then say each number (1 - 5) when the number and set are presented randomly. Using pencil, crayon, marker and paper, the child will write the numerals 1, 2, 3, 4, and 5 when verbally presented in random order.

Assessment Materials
Cut out twelve 3-inch circles from poster board. On each of two circles draw a caterpillar's head. Set One should have five circles in it. Circle one should have the number 1 written on one side and one dot on the other side; circle two should have the number 2 on one side and two dots on the reverse side; circle three should have the number 3 on one side and three dots on the reverse side. Continue with numbers 4 and 5. Set Two should be made up of 5 blank circles with a pencil line drawn at the bottom of each circle. A pencil or marker.

Assessment Procedures
Grouping: This skill should be assessed one-on-one with the child.
1. Invite the child to join you at the table. Place one of the head circles on the table.
2. Explain to the child that the caterpillar only has a head, and that together you are going to make the body of the caterpillar.
3. Select from Set One the circle with the number one on it.
4. Show the child the circle with the number one and say, "What is this number?"
5. After the child responds, place the 1 circle next to the caterpillar's head.
6. If the child has any problems with the numeral name, turn the circle over and have him count the dots.
7. Show the child the circle with the number two and say, "What is this number?"
8. After the child responds, place the number two circle next to the number one circle.
9. Continue the above steps using circles 3 - 5.
10. Record the child's responses.
11. Collect the Set One circles, leaving the caterpillar's head. Shuffle the circles and present them randomly to the child.
12. Show the child the first circle and ask the child to tell what number is on it.
13. Place it next to the caterpillar's head if the child gives the correct answer. If the child gives an incorrect answer show him the reverse side and ask him to count the dots.
14. Replace the missed circle with the remaining group.
15. Record the child responses and make a note if the cueing of the quantity (sets of dots) assisted the child in a responding correctly the next time the number appeared.
16. Remove Set One circles, leaving the caterpillar's head.
17. Tell the child that you are going to give him a blank circle and a marker.
18. Explain to the child that the line on the circle is like a line on a sheet of paper, to help him write some numbers.
19. Give the child the first circle and ask him to write the number one.
20. Allow time for the child to complete the task.
21. After the child has written the number one, ask him to place it next to the caterpillar's head.
22. Give the child the second circle and ask him to write the number two.
23. Allow time for the child to complete the task.
24. After the child has written the number two, ask him to place it next to the caterpillar's head.
25. Continue with the other circles and the numbers to five.
26. Record the child's responses.
27. Place the two caterpillar heads on the table.

© 2010 VORT Corporation. All rights reserved. Do Not copy.

28. Using Set One, place the dot side of the circles randomly beside the caterpillar head. Example: Caterpillar head, circle with three dots, circle with two dots, circle with four dots, circle with one dot, and circle with five dots.
29. Give the child Set Two and request that the child locate the circle number that matches the first circle of the completed caterpillar. When the child has located the number, instruct him to place it next to the second caterpillar head (Caterpillar head one, circle with three dots - Caterpillar head two, circle with number three).
30. After the child has placed all the circle numbers, ask him to read the numbers.
31. Continue matching the circles.
32. Record the child's responses.

Credit: + Child reads and writes the numerals (1 – 5) when randomly presented.

Adaptations

The writing of numerals should emerge from the concepts of grouping and creating sets. Some children will experience problems moving from the concrete group of three blocks to the abstraction of the graphic symbol for the number 3. An additional step may be necessary to help these children understand that three blocks has equal meaning to the symbol 3. A suggested step is: On an 8 ½ x 11-inch sheet of poster board, write a large number 1 and beside the number draw one object (apple). On another sheet write a large number 2 and beside the number draw a set of two things (ducks). Continue making the chart set.

After the child has become familiar with the semi-abstract charts, provide him with five blank sheets of paper and ask him to write the number 1 on a sheet and draw a set of one (item). Continue until he has made his own set of 1 - 5 number charts.

1.252 Counts orally to 20

Strand: 1-10   **Age:** 60-68m 5.0-5.8y

Definition

The child will verbally count from 1 - 20. She will be asked to count by rote, count items, count in groupings (count 1 - 5, 5 - 10, 10 - 15, 15 - 20) and count to 20 from a given number (start with 7 and count to 20).

Assessment Materials

Pegboard and 20 pegs.

Assessment Procedures

Grouping: This skill should be assessed one-on-one with the child.
1. Ask the child to rote count from one to twenty. If the child is unable to count to twenty, stop her at the point where she was counting successfully. Record the last number that she orally counted correctly.
2. Place 20 pegs in the pegboard. Ask the child to point to and count each peg. Record the last number that she orally counted correctly.
3. Arrange the pegs in the pegboard in groupings of five. Ask the child to point to and count each group of pegs. (Note if the child continued counting from one group to the other, or started each group with the number one). Record responses.
4. Place the pegs in the pegboard. Point to the 7th peg and say, "This peg is number seven; I want you to start with this peg (point to number 8) and count the pegs to twenty." Record the child's responses.
5. Compare the recorded responses to assist in determining the child's instructional level.

Credit: + Child independently counts from 1 – 20, by rote, one-to-one correspondence (counting items), counting items in groupings of five, and counting to 20 from a given number.

Adaptations

Some children can "chant"-count from 1 - 20, without having any knowledge of ordinal or cardinal numbers, or that the process of calling number names involves adding one more number each time. As a strategy for making sure that the operation of counting is understood, have the child point to and count objects. It is also important that she is able to start with any number and continue counting in correct sequence. It is also important to start with smaller counting clusters (first step, 1 - 5; second step, 1 - 8; third step, 1 - 10).

1.253 Names days of week in succession

Strand: 1-13   **Age:** 60-68m 5.0-5.8y

Definition

The child will name the days of the week in order, but it is not necessary to start with Sunday. When learning the days of the week the child should begin to respond with an activity that he does on a given day (Monday go to school, Saturday play at home, Sunday visit friends, etc.)

Assessment Procedures

Grouping: This skill can be introduced and practiced in a group setting. However, when you are ready to assess the child's ability to name the days of the week in succession, it is recommended that you do so one-on-one with the child.

1. Discuss with the child things that happen on certain days of the week. Ask such questions like: "What day is it today?" "What day of the week is your favorite?" "What day of the week do you get to watch TV? "
2. After the child is familiar with the content of the questions, say, "Name the days of the week in order, starting with Sunday."
3. If the child hesitates in his response say, "Please start with Sunday." Prompt as necessary.
4. Record if the child was able to name the days of the week in succession with no prompting.
5. Record any prompting needed.

Credit: + Child names the days of the week in succession without prompting.

Adaptations

Some children have difficulty affixing a verbal name with a period of time, such as, "Monday is the first day of the week when I go to school, and Friday is the last day of the week." The concepts of naming the days of the week should be presented in relationship to events that take place during that particular time period. An activity that is often helpful in making the days of the week meaningful is to ask the child to draw a picture of something that he does on Monday, Tuesday, Wednesday, etc. After the seven pictures have been completed, point to the first day (Sunday or Monday) and ask the child to name the day. The illustration acts as a cue to the name of each day. Continue until all the days of the week have been named.

The book "Today Is Monday" by Eric Carle is a book that demonstrates how something different occurs each day of the week.

1.254 Relates "today," "tomorrow," "yesterday" to days of the week

Strand: 1-13 **Age:** 60-68m 5.0-5.8y

Definition

The child will respond when asked "What day is today? What day was yesterday? What day will tomorrow be?" by stating the day of the week or by indicating a visual representation of the day.

Assessment Materials

Secure a calendar for the current month, seven 5 x 8-inch cards, and seven blank word strips. On the cards place a picture of a typical activity the child would participate in for each day of the week. Example: Monday - give lunch money to teacher. Tuesday - go to the gym for exercises. Saturday - go to the grocery store with family, etc. On a word strip place the words for the days of the week. Example: word strip one has Sunday, word strip two has Monday, etc.

Assessment Procedures

Grouping: This skill should be assessed one-on-one with the child.

1. Invite the child to a work area. Place the monthly calendar in front of the child.
2. Explain that this is a calendar for this month. Continue by pointing to the current week. Point to the day of the week and say, "If today is_____ (pause for child response; if the child does not respond say the day), what day of the week was yesterday?" Record the child's responses.
3. Point to the day of the week and say "If today is_____(pause for child response; if the child does not respond say the day), what day will tomorrow be?" Record the child's responses.
4. Remove calendar and place one of the word strips in front of the child.
5. Point to the strip and say, "If today is Tuesday, what day of the week was yesterday?" Record the child's responses.
6. Point to the strip and say, "If today is Tuesday, what day of the week will tomorrow be?" Record the child's responses.
7. Continue with the rest of the word strips making sure they are randomly placed.
8. If the child had difficulty with identifying the passage of time by responding to the word strips, continue by using the pictures.
9. Place three picture cards in the following sequence: yesterday's picture card, today's card, and then tomorrow's card.
10. Point to the middle card (today), discuss what is occurring, and say, "If today is _____, what day of the week was yesterday (point to the first card)?" Record the child's responses.
11. Point to the middle card (today) and say, "If today is_____, what day of the week will tomorrow be (point to the last card)?" Record the child's responses.

Credit: + Child correctly relates "today," "tomorrow," and "yesterday" to the days of the week.

Adaptations
Some children need to associate a visual image with sequences. The child may be able to say the days of the week in "rote" but when asked what day it is, what day of the week yesterday was, or what day of the week tomorrow will be, the child's thought process needs to associate the first day of the week with a visual image. For example, she thinks of the word Sunday and a visual representation of what happens on that day, or she thinks of the word Monday and a visual representation of what occurs on that day, etc. When asked about today, yesterday, or tomorrow the child needs to review the sequence of symbols and images from the first day in the rote order.

It is important to include a verbal description of the activities for each day. Example: Today is Monday and on Monday you give me your lunch money for the week. Yesterday was Sunday and on Sunday you spend time with your family. Tomorrow is Tuesday and on Tuesday we go to the gym to do our exercises. It is also important to point to the days on the calendar as you are discussing them.

Phase out the activity descriptions as soon as the child is showing an understanding of the relation of days to the week.

1.255 Prints own first or last name, copying model
Strand: 1-11 **Age:** 60-70m 5.0-5.10y

Definition
The child will print his first or last name when shown a model. The model needs to be in manuscript form and the letters should be on a base line. The child's letters should be recognizable, however the strokes need not be made in the correct sequence, the lines need not be constructed perfectly, the spacing does not need to be equal between the letters, and the density of the lines may be different.

Assessment Materials
Two 5 x 8-inch cards with the child's first name written on one and his last name written on the other. The names need to be on a base line and written with a black marker. A tactile model of the child's first and last names (a tactile model may be made by cutting the letters of the child's first and last names out of sandpaper letters and then gluing the letters on a 5 x 8-inch card). Paper and an appropriate writing tool for the child.

Assessment Procedures
Grouping: This skill should be assessed one-on-one with the child.
1. Explain to the child that his first name is _____ and that his last name is _____.
2. Write his first name on a sheet of paper.
3. Ask the child to write his first name.
4. Discuss with the child why he has a last name, how it is used, who else has a last name like his, etc.
5. Ask the child to watch while you write his last name on a sheet of paper. Say each letter as you write his last name.
6. Show the child the card with the written model of his last name. Point to and say each letter.
7. Ask the child to look at the cards that have his first and last names on them. Give the child a sheet of paper and a pencil. Request that the child write his first and/or last name on the sheet of paper. Allow him to look at the model.
8. If the child successfully writes his first and/or last name, date the paper and place it in his file.
9. If the child had a problem writing his first or last name, or if you observed that it was a difficult task for him, then do the following: (1) Provide the child with the tactile name cards; (2) Demonstrate tracing each letter, saying the name of each letter; (3) Ask the child to trace each letter; (4) After the child has numerous chances to trace the tactile names, repeat the above sequence using the print card.
10. Date the child's paper and make a notation that a tactile experience was a prerequisite.

Credit: + Child prints his first or last name when shown a model. The letters should be recognizable, but the lines and spacing do not need to be perfect.

Adaptations
Those children who have a difficult time in the formation of letters may have a problem in written expression, not due necessarily to lack of expressive ideas, but to the difficulty in reproducing letter forms. Often children who have a difficult time forming letters benefit from individual instruction. Some techniques to consider in providing individual instruction are: (1) Copying letters. Copying provides the child

with practice in visual memory that leads to writing from memory, without any added support; (2) Tracing of letters, using a gradual removal of the end of a stroke first, followed by the preceding stroke, and continuing until the entire process of tracing has been faded out; (3) Practice writing letters on a large area, such as a chalkboard, unlined paper, newsprint, in a sandbox, etc. Writing on a large area assists the child with a kinesthetic feel of the letter form and a large visual image. For these children it is important to follow a sequence of instruction in letter formation. The following are recommended steps: (1) Ask the child to print a letter, his name, or a simple word. If the child prints the configuration, move on to another letter or word; (2) If the child is unable to print the letter or word, print it for the child, saying the letters aloud as you are printing them and asking the child to repeat the letters after you; (3) Ask the child to print the letter or word; if he is successful move on to the next letter or word, if the child is unsuccessful, place your hand over the child's and guide his hand to print the word. Say each letter aloud while printing them, asking the child to repeat the letters after you. Gradually fade out the naming of the letters but continue the physical direction; (4) Repeat holding his hand but do not say the letters, encouraging the child to say each letter while your hands are making them.

1.256 Arranges objects in order of size from smallest to largest

Strand: 1-7B **Age:** 60-72m 5.0-6.0y

Definition

In order to grasp the idea of numbers, the notion of relations is as important as classification and matching one-to-one. By providing the child with different sized objects and asking her to put them in order from the smallest (a 3-inch object) to the largest (an 8-inch object), she will understand the concept of order and position.

Assessment Materials

Cut one circle with a 3-inch diameter, cut one circle with a 6-inch diameter, and cut one circle with an 8 inches diameter. Cut one 3-inch square, one 6-inch square, and one 8 inches square. Cut one triangle with a 3-inch base, cut one triangle with a 6-inch base, and cut one triangle with an 8-inch base. The shapes should be all the same color.

Assessment Procedures

Grouping: This skill should be assessed one-on-one with the child.
1. Call the child to the table. Place the circles in the following pattern: 6 inches, 3 inches, and 8 inches.
2. Ask the child to point to the smallest circle.
3. Ask the child to point to the largest circle.
4. Ask the child to put the circles in order from the smallest to the largest. It is important to prompt the child to place the small circle on her left to start the order. Note the child's response.
5. Place the squares in the following pattern: 3 inches, 8 inches, and 6 inches.
6. Ask the child to point to the smallest square.
7. Ask the child to point to the largest square.
8. Ask the child to put the squares in order from the smallest to the largest. Refrain from prompting. Note the child's response.
9. Place the triangles in the following pattern: 8 inches, 6 inches, and 3 inches.
10. Pause to determine if the child will automatically place the triangles in the correct sequence. Note the child's response.
11. Randomly place a 3-inch circle, a 6-inch triangle and an 8 inches square in front of the child.
12. Ask the child to place the shapes in the order from the smallest to the largest. Note the child's response.

Credit: + Child demonstrates the concept of order and position by putting different sized objects in order from the smallest to the largest.

Adaptations

At an early age children gain insight into the pre-symbolic concepts of order by stringing beads, putting different size pegs in a board, and playing with stacking forms. They are learning aspects of the language of math (small, large, big, little) by exploration and simulation. They also follow a sequence of assimilating the information; first they learn to integrate nonverbal experiences, then they associates a numerical symbol with the experience, and finally they express ideas of size and order by using the language of mathematics. For children who are having difficulty manipulating different sized objects according to size, go back to some of those activities they did when they were younger like putting cups of graduated size together. Reintroduce this activity, but incorporate the mathematical language we are teaching. Talk about the smallest cup, a bigger cup, an even bigger cup, continuing to the largest cup. In addition to nesting the cups, have the child reverse the task and stack the cups upside down, going from the largest to the smallest to build a tall tower. Begin with three to five cups and expand up to eight to 10 cups. Again incorporate the language of largest to smallest. Next, have the child line the cups up from smallest to largest. Sometimes returning to a familiar and previously mastered task can help us expand and build on the learning of a new skill. If necessary, model the activities but begin fading out the model as soon as possible.

1.257 Says the sound a letter makes when shown the letter

Strand: 1-9 **Age:** 60-72m 5.0-6.0y

Definition

The first letters shown to the child should be consonants in both capital and lower case. Vowels (short sound only) should also be shown to the child in both capital and lower case. The letters should be printed on cards (which are no less than 2 x 2-inch) and displayed to the child one letter at a time. The consonants can be presented in alphabetical order, with emphasis placed on the fine auditory discrimination between m and n, s and t, and v and w. At the beginning levels, with those phoneme/grapheme consonants (c, g, s, and x) that have two sounds, the initial and most frequently used sound should be presented to the child (c - cat, g - go, s - sack, and x - xylophone). When presenting the vowels (a,e,i,o,u), caution and emphasis needs to be placed on the e and i due to the fine auditory discrimination.

Assessment Materials

Secure or develop a set of sound, letter, and picture cards. These alphabet sound cards are available from commercial sources or can easily be made by gluing a picture of an object whose name has the same beginning sound as the letter printed on the card and the word that names the object. Example: a - apple, b - boat, c - cat, d - duck, e - egg, f - fork, g - goat, h - house, i - ice cream, j - jump, k - kite, l - lamp, m - man, n - nest, o - orange, p - pan, q - queen, r - ring, s - sack, t - tack, u - umbrella, v – violin, w - wagon, x - xylophone, y - yellow, z - zebra. A set of letter cards with only the capital and lower case letters (Tt) printed on the card. A scoring sheet that has all the letters listed with two places to check right or wrong and two places to write the sound given. The two places are for: (1) When the child responds to Set One, which is the picture/letter/word card; (2) When the child responds to Set Two, which is the card with just letters.

Assessment Procedures

Grouping: This skill should be assessed one-on-one with the child.
1. Place the child next to you at a table. Inform the child that you are going to show him some picture cards that are also sound cards. Tell the child he is to finish the sentence that you are going to say.
2. Present the cards in alphabetical order.
3. Use the first card as a teaching card. Say "A is for _____. The sound of A is_____."
4. Cue the child if his response is uncertain.
5. If necessary, use the second card as a teaching card. Say "B is for_____. The sound of B is_____."
6. Continue showing the child the picture/letter/word cards and asking for picture name and letter sound.
7. Record the responses on the Scoring Sheet. The recording should include a mark for correct or incorrect, and if incorrect what sound was sound stated.
8. After the child has completed Set One, inform him that you are going to show him some cards that only have letters on them. Tell the child that he is to finish the sentence that you are going to say.
9. Present the cards in alphabetical order.
10. Use the first card as a teaching card. Say "The sound of A is_____ as in _____."
11. Continue showing the alphabet cards. Record the responses on the Scoring Sheet. The recording should include a mark for correct or incorrect, and if incorrect what sound was stated.
12. Compare the scores on the recording sheet. By comparing the two scores, you can tell if the child is depending on the picture for the sound association or if he is being successful with the phoneme-to-grapheme connection.

Credit: + Child says the sound a letter makes when shown the letter only. Start with consonants in both capital and lower case and then vowels also in capital and lower case.

Adaptations

When a child has gained the skill of visually perceiving elements within words, it does him little good to simply see that a "b" is different from a "d," or that an "m" is different from an "n." He needs to know the sounds of the different letters. Single letter sounding is a fundamental of synthetic phonics, which involves building words from letter-to-letter sounding. This part of synthetic sounding has disadvantages for many early learners. Learning sounds in isolation can be boring and uninteresting, especially for those children who have some picture/word recognition. It must be recognized that some letter sounds are meaningless to the child and unrelated to his listening and speaking vocabulary. The child needs to be able to see the letter, see the letter in a word, and hear its sound. Instruction in hearing the letter sound can be given only when the sound is in its natural setting - that of a whole word.

1.258 Matches (visually) identical letters in group of different letters

Strand: 1-9 **Age:** 60-72m 5.0-6.0y

Definition

The child will recognize all the letters in a row that are the same. The sequence of letters to match will be: (1) Upper case open letters, (2) Upper case round letters (3) lower case open letters and (4) lower case round letters. It is not necessary that the child provide the letter name or the letter sound.

Assessment Materials

Prepare six paper strips (3 x 10-inch). Divide the paper strips into sections measuring 3 x 2 inches. The first section should have a double line to designate its importance from the other spaces. In strip one, first section, place the letter M, and in the other sections place the letters O, M, V, and P. In strip two, first section, place the letter L, and in the other sections place the letters T, A, L, and B. In strip three, first section, place the letter D, and in the other sections place the letters C, N, R, and D. In strip four, first section, place the letter t, and in the other sections place the letters a, t, b, and h. In strip five, first section, place the letter g, and in the other sections place the letters j, e, r, and g. In strip six, first section, place the letters Ss, and in the other sections place the letters Kk, Ss, Ww, Yy. The letters can be printed, cutout and glued on the cards, or stamped.

Assessment Procedures

Grouping: This skill should be assessed one-on-one with the child.

1. Place the first strip on a table in front of the child. The first strip is an instructional strip. Point to the first letter and ask the child to look at the other letters in the squares. Then ask the child to point to another letter that looks just like the first one.
2. Continue with the other five strips
3. Record the number that the child got correct and record any form of the letters that she had problems with (upper case-open, upper case-closed, lower case-open, lower case-closed).

Credit: + Child visually matches identical letters in a group of different letters in five out of the six different strips presented.

Adaptations

Some children may have difficulty because they cannot discriminate between different letters. To these children the letters may appear in various positions, such as reversed, rotated, elongated, incomplete and suspended. Remediation strategies should include some activities prior to letter matching. Matching should begin with shapes: (1) Matching shapes that are solid; (2) Shapes that are outlines; (3) Open shapes (a gradual introduction of letters can be made).

1.259 Matches (visually) identical words in group of words

Strand: 1-9 **Age:** 60-72m 5.0-6.0y

Definition

The child will match words that are visually alike. The first matching the child is asked to do will be words that are grossly different in configuration. The second area of matching will be words that are similar in configuration. The child does not have to read the words.

Assessment Materials

Prepare six paper strips (3 x 10-inches). Divide the paper strips into sections measuring 3 x 2-inch. The first section should have a double line to designate its importance from the other spaces. In strip one, first section, print the word "ball"; in the other sections print the words "pat," "him," "ball," and "sun." In strip two, first section, print the word "make;" in the other sections print the words "tape," "make," "seat," and "play." In strip three, first section, print the word "little;" in the other sections print the words "matter," "apple," "dollar," and "little." In strip four, first section, print the word "cat;" in the other sections print the words "cat," "rat," "car," and "cot." In strip five, first section, print the word "ride;" in the other sections print the words "hide," "rode," "ride," and "side." In strip six, first section, print the word "funny;" in the other sections print the words "sunny," "funny," "fuzzy," and "runner." The words should be printed in the same color.

Assessment Procedures
Grouping: This skill should be assessed one-on-one with the child.
1. Place the first strip on the table in front of the child. The first strip is an instructional strip.
2. Point to the first word and ask the child to look at the other words in the squares. Then ask the child to point to another word that looks just like the first one.
3. Continue with the other five strips
4. Record the number the child got correct. Record if he had difficulty with strips 1 - 3 (grossly different) or 4 - 6 (close visual representation). Record if he had difficulty with strip 3 or 6 (two syllable words).

Credit: + Child visually matches identical words in groups of words. Remember the does not have to read the words. Start with matching grossly different words and then matching words that look similar. Child correctly identifies matching words on four out of the five examples given. Do not count example one, which is the instructional strip.

Adaptations
Some children may have difficulty because they cannot interpret what is seen; they do not have the ability to comprehend the visual presentation of written words. These children need additional time to process what is being viewed and to be taught to look for the details in a graphic representation. When remediation is needed, the following are examples of techniques that are helpful: (1) The child traces the word; (2) The child says each letter out loud; (3) The adult points to the target word and then shows the choices one by one covering the other words; (4) The target word is written on a separate card that the child can use to compare to the choices (moving the card closer to each word they can choose from). Children benefit from being reminded to look carefully at each word, being given enough wait time before responding, and having practice in activities with letters and words.

1.260 Prints letters and numbers, copying model
Strand: 1-11 **Age:** 60-72m 5.0-6.0y

Definition
When a letter or a number is demonstrated to the child, she will reproduce the letter's configuration. The letter/number should be recognizable. It should have a base and the lines, circles, etc. that form the figures should be made from left to right, and the child does not have to know the letter or the numbers. The letters need to be written in manuscript form and can be upper or lower case. Present only one letter (e.g., A) and one number (e.g., 7) at a time. The child will use a marker large enough to facilitate writing control.

Assessment Materials
Writing paper and pencils.

Assessment Procedures
Grouping: This skill should be assessed one-on-one with the child.
1. Explain to the child that you are going to write some letters and that after she has seen each letter, she is to write one like it (present the first letter as a teaching example).
2. Write no more than five upper case manuscript letters, one at a time. The beginning letters should represent broadly different configurations. Such as: a simple continuous line, L; one movement, O; two lines, T; one line and a curve, D; three lines with focal points, N.
3. Ask the child to watch carefully. Write the letter L.
4. Provide the child with a sheet of paper and a pencil. Tell her to look carefully at the letter you just wrote, and ask her to write the letter L.
5. Continue with the other four letters.
6. If the child is successful, date the paper and place it in the child's records.
7. If she is unable to write the letter L, ask her to watch as you write the letter again.
8. Ask her to write the letter L.
9. If she is successful, date the paper and make a notation that she had to see the writing of L again.
10. Continue with the other upper case letters.
11. At the completion of the upper case letters, select five lower case letters with different visual configurations. Such as: single stroke, l (lowercase L); curved single stroke, c; two single lines with one focal point, v; a single

line with retrace and curve, n; and a curve, retrace and line, a.
12. Ask the child to watch carefully. Write the letter l.
13. Say, "Write the letter l."
14. Continue as above with the other four lower case letters.
15. Repeat the above using the numbers 1, 3, 7, 6, and 4.

Credit: + Child prints letters (both upper and lower case) and numbers that are recognizable when copying a model. Letters and numbers should be presented one at a time. The child copies at least 10 out of the 15 letters and numbers presented.

Adaptations

Some children find it difficult to recall the strokes necessary to make a letter. Often they are able to construct the first part of the symbol but are unable to complete the figure. It is important to begin with letters that have easier strokes and to use lined paper for aligning and spacing. Some strategies that can be useful in dealing with stroke recall are: "talk out" strokes (n - short line down, back up, around and down), dot-to-dot formation of letters, numbering the strokes or color coding the strokes (green for the first line, red for the second, etc.) Remember that these children cannot recall what they did to reproduce a letter or number, so they need to have ample practice and varied activities.

1.261 Imitates actions in the order told

Strand: 1-9   **Age:** 60-72m 5.0-6.0y

Definition

When given not less than three verbal directions, the child is able to do the following: listen to the directions, recall the commands when requested, and perform the actions in the correct sequence. At the beginning, the child will be expected to perform the actions immediately after being instructed (short term sequential memory). Gradually the child will be asked to perform the tasks after a delay (long term sequential memory). The first sequential actions presented to the child should be related (stand up, turn around, sit down). As the child becomes more astute in responding, the actions need to become less related (The girl puts on her coat. The girl went to the door. The girl picked up a book.)

Assessment Materials

Secure or write two levels of at least three sequential directions.

Level One should involve the child's motor skills. Example: Clap your hands, stand up, and turn around.

Level Two should involve unrelated commands. Provide the child with the following items, a shoe, a hat, a crayon, a car and a doll. Ask the child to listen carefully and then give them the following verbal directions. Put the crayon in the shoe. Take the car to the kitchen. Move the doll to floor. Throw the hat in the air.

Assessment Procedures

Grouping: This skill should be assessed one-on-one with the child.
1. Call the child to the chair next to you. Make sure there is ample room for movement around the area.
2. Tell the child to listen carefully, because you are going to give her some directions.
3. Explain that she is not to begin doing anything until you say "Go".
4. Make sure the child is paying attention and give the sequential directions in Level One.
5. Pause 5 - 10 seconds, say "Go", and ask the child to follow the directions in the order in which they were given.
6. Note if the child did the actions in the order that they were stated.
7. Tell the child to listen carefully again, because you are going to give her some more direction. This time it will be more difficult.
8. Make sure the child is listening and give the unrelated directions in Level Two.
9. Note if the child dramatized the sequence in the proper order without any review of the directions or prompting.

Credit: + Child imitates at least three verbal directions in the order they were given without prompting.

Adaptations

The skill of remembering the order of events is the ability to recall the words or sentences heard in the correct sequence. Often children cannot recall because they were not paying attention, they did not focus on the concepts of the sequencing, or they can not retrieve information to which they have been exposed. Those children who are not paying attention often receive only part of a message which may be far removed from the order of events. They also do not realize that the sequence of events is usually related to action, and they listen for other elements (names), happenings to a specific thing (ball), or feelings (tired). When given a series of directions, often these children can only concentrate on one or two at a time. If such a child is told to go in her room, put on her shirt, comb her hair, brush her teeth, and put on her shoes, the child may only be able to recall one or two of the directions. To assist those children who are having problems with sequential memory, the following are helpful training techniques: (1) Limit the number of ordered actions and after achievement add others, (2) Include visual cues, (3) Have the child echo each directions after stated, (4) Organize the sequential information in such a manner that it will aid the child in recall.

1.262 Scans letters of word left to right
Strand: 1-9 **Age:** 60-72m 5.0-6.0y

Definition
Beginning reading not only involves the differentiation of letters but the patterning of letters within a word. This patterning of letters requires left-to-right movement. The letters of cat are written in this left-to-right pattern, and cannot be written in any other order. The first step to establishing the concept of left-to-right sequencing is to make sure that the child comprehends that letters in a word need to be in a particular order.

Assessment Materials
Prepare four shape strips; the strips should be 3 x 12-inches. On Shape Strip One, place the following shapes (at least ½" tall): circle, square, square (draw a perpendicular line), square, square, circle (space), circle, square, square (space), circle, circle, square. On Shape Strip Two, place the following shapes (at least ½" tall): circle, circle, square (draw a perpendicular line), square, square, circle (space), square, circle, circle (space), circle, circle, square. On Shape Strip Three, place the following shapes (at least ½" tall): square, triangle, square (draw a perpendicular line), triangle, square, square (space), triangle, square, triangle (space), square, triangle, square. On Shape Strip Four, place the following shapes (at least ½" tall): triangle, circle, triangle (draw a perpendicular line), triangle, circle, triangle (space), circle, triangle, circle (space), circle, circle, triangle. Prepare four word strips; the strips should be 3 x 12-inches. On Word Strip One, place the following words (at least ½" tall): "hot" (draw a perpendicular line), "can," "bat," "hot." On Word Strip Two, place the following words (at least ½" tall): "man" (draw a perpendicular line), "pet," "cut," "man." On Word Strip Three, place the following words (at least ½" tall): "sat" (draw a perpendicular line), "sat," "cat," "saw." On Word Strip Four, place the following words (at least ½" tall) "pit" (draw a perpendicular line), "pat," "pit," "put."

Assessment Procedures
Note: The speed of recognition is important. If the child is slow in matching, he could have difficulty learning letters or words by instant recognition.
Grouping: This skill should be assessed one-on-one with the child.
1. Call the child to the table, and ask him to sit across from you.
2. Use Shape Strip One as an instructional strip. Point to the first shapes (circle, square, square), making sure that you point to the shapes in a left-to-right sequence. Ask the child to find another group of shapes that are in the same order.
3. Continue the activity using the other Shape Strips.
4. Record the child's responses and the time required. Also observe the child's eyes to determine if he is scanning from left to right.
5. Repeat the above procedure using the Word Strips, One to Four.
6. Record the child's responses and the time required. Also observe the child's eyes to determine if he is scanning from left to right.
7. Compare the Shape Strip responses with the Word Strip responses.

Credit: + Child scans letters of word from left to right. This is a prerequisite skill to reading.

Adaptations
Problems of scanning left-to-right sequences are common, and some children do not realize that there is a particular letter order which should be visualized. Often these children will look at one letter at a time, even pointing to single letters, not necessarily in a left-to-right pattern. If the left-to-right deficit is not addressed and the child continues in his reading program, he may look at any letter in a word and start auditory recognition with that letter sound (keep becomes peek) or he may look at a sight word and reverse the letter rotation (saw becomes was). To assist the child in conceptualizing the fact that there is a particular order, the use of non-symbolic activities is recommended. Such activities as: (1) Arranging blocks according to a left-right model (red, green, yellow, blue) etc.; (2) Stringing colored beads in the same left-right pattern as an

example (blue, green, green, red, blue, blue); (3) Saying the order of objects (create a row of pictures: dog, cat, dog, cow, cat. Ask the children to name the pictures as you point to them in a left-to-right order. Continue in a verbal chanting mode); (4) Making paper chains of colored strips of paper, and requesting that they develop a pattern; (5) Developing tracking worksheets such as: Draw a balloon floating away on the right side of a worksheet. Draw a child running after it from the left side of the worksheet. Connect the child and the balloon with a dotted line. Draw a picture of a ball rolling from the left side of the worksheet to the right side, include a dog running after the ball (provide the child with a copy of the worksheet and ask him to trace the path the objects are following).

1.263 Identifies missing or incongruous element of picture

Strand: 1-4D **Age:** 60-72m 5.0-6.0y

Definition
Being able to locate those things that are not correct, proper, or logical, or things that are missing, is related to developing the ability to understand that everything that is seen is not always the way it is.

Assessment Materials
Prepare two sets of cards with six cards to a set (index cards work well). Set One should show unrealistic situations, items with missing or misplaced parts (a cat without ears or boy with hats on his feet instead of shoes), animals doing things that are strange (a dog eating at a table), or people who look or dress differently (a child all dressed up for a wintry cold day and sitting by a swimming pool with other children enjoying the summer day and pool).
Set Two should show the part of the Set One cards that will correct the situation. Example: (1) A cat with ears; (2) A boy with shoes on his feet and a hat on his head; (3) A dog eating from dog dishes on the floor; (4) All children at the pool dressed for the summer.

Assessment Procedures
Grouping: This skill should be assessed one-on-one with the child.
1. Place Set One face down in front of the child. Place Set Two face down near the child, but so that it is not accessible to him.
2. Tell the child to turn over the top card of Set One and to tell you what is different, wrong, or missing from the picture.
3. After the child has identified what is wrong, request that she lay the card face up.
4. Continue the above sequence, turning the cards over in Set One.
5. Present Set Two to the child, asking her to turn over the top card and to look at it carefully. Explain that there is a card on the table that has a different, wrong, or missing part, and that the card the child holds shows the correction.
6. Ask the child to place the pictured cards together.
7. Write down the number of cards where the child identified what was wrong and also note the number of correct pairs the child made.

Credit: + Child correctly identifies missing or incongruent elements of a picture in at least eight of the pictures shown.

Adaptations
Difficulty with identifying what is missing or wrong with a picture can be related to focus and attention. Sometimes, removing extraneous stimuli can be helpful, such as moving to a quiet area where there is limited auditory and visual distractions. Some children need to be reminded to look closely at the pictures and to scrutinize the detail. They see the bigger picture, but miss the details. Some children become frustrated when things do not appear as they really are. These children prefer to deal with things that are actually tangible or an event that is really going to occur. If a child is having a problem with identification of inconsistencies in real things, it may be necessary to deal with this conceptual skill through a non-real personage or make-believe.

1.264 Makes judgments in time and speed

Strand: 1-7B **Age:** 60-72m 5.0-6.0y

Definition
The child will make a determination as to which of three time periods is the longest/shortest and will determine which of three objects move the fastest/slowest. The child will indicate the different times and speed by physical involvement, visual conclusions and conceptual decisions.

Assessment Materials
One page from a calendar and three pictures that represent objects that move at different speeds (e.g., jet, bicycle, car, or turtle, horse, cat).

Assessment Procedures
Grouping: This skill should be assessed one-on-one with the child.
1. Show the calendar page to the child. Tell the child that it is the month of _____ and that each section represent weeks or days.
2. Tell the child you are going to ask her some questions about the calendar page.
3. Say, "Which is the longest amount of time, a day (point to one square), a week (point to a row that represents a week), or a month (indicate the whole page)?"
4. Repeat using the word "shortest" instead of "longest."
5. Place the pictures of the vehicles or the pictures of the animals in front of the child.
6. Tell the child to look at the pictures and name each vehicle or animal.
7. Say, "One of the pictures you are looking at goes faster than the others. Point to the picture that shows the item that goes the fastest."
8. Say, "One of the pictures you are looking at goes slower than the others. Point to the picture that shows the item that goes the slowest."
9. Note the responses made by the child.

Credit: + Child correctly makes judgment in time and speed by correctly identifying the longest and shortest amount of time on a calendar and the fastest and slowest moving items from a group of pictures of vehicles and animals.

Adaptations
Some children have a difficult time judging the abstraction of time and speed, and some children lack the vocabulary to express the concepts of time and speed. To assist children with the abstraction, substitution of a more concrete experience is recommended. An example would be: ask the child which would take the longest amount of time, to walk from her seat to the door or to walk from her seat to the play area. If the child is hesitant, take her on the two "trips" and assist her in determining which was the longest. Repeat using a different situation and the concept of shortest. To address the concept of speed, show the child a picture of a water faucet with just a drip coming out and another picture of a faucet with a steady stream.

Ask the child to point to the picture that would fill a glass first. Making sure that the child hear words that accompany the concepts, since hearing the words provides her with the necessary expressive terminology.

1.265 Finds the incongruous/out-of-place/misdirected object
Strand: 1-7C **Age:** 60-72m 5.0-6.0y

Definition
The child will first locate a part of a picture that is missing, such as a man's ear; then the child will find a part of an illustration that shows a misplacement; an example would be rabbit ears on a cat; finally the child will locate the part of a scene that is not relative, like a child dressed in swimming trunks with a winter cap and scarf on, about to jump into a swimming pool.

Assessment Materials
A set of five pictures that show something out-of-place. Magazines and catalogs are good sources, though you can make your own. Some suggestions for incongruous pictures are: a horse smaller than a dog, flowers growing in a bathtub, a cat with shoes on, a boy with eyes in the back of his head, and a rabbit wearing a scarf. Another set of five pictures that shows the correct version of the first five. This would include a horse of the right size, flowers growing in a garden, a cat without shoes, the boy with eyes in the correct position, and a rabbit without a scarf.

Assessment Procedures
Grouping: This skill should be assessed one-on-one with the child.
1. Tell the child that sometimes he sees things that really are not right or the way they should be.
2. Place the correct set of five cards face up on the table in view of the child. Ask the child to name the items.
3. Explain to the child that you have another deck of cards in your hand and that the pictures on these cards show some things that are out-of-place or wrong. Tell the child that you are going to show him one card at a time and he is to find a picture on the table that shows the right way the picture should look. Encourage the child to tell what is wrong with the picture and why the one on the table is correct.

Credit: + Child finds the incongruous/out-of-place or misdirected object in a picture and can point it out.

Adaptations

Some children become frustrated when dealing with unrealistic items or absurdities. These children have little objectivity, or relativism; they refrain from looking at things from another's point of view, from another angle in space or time, or imaging how it would be if they were somewhere else. When these children are asked to deal with unrealistic situations or items and they are not in the "fantasy" thinking mode, realism is predominate. Other children can play/pretend to be someone else, in fact they are so good at this role-playing that they often lose themselves in the role. To assist these children, it is important to "set-the-stage" and assure them that what they are seeing is make-believe, out-of-place, or incongruent.

1.266 (Removed, see page xviii)

1.267 Improvises body movements to follow tempo/rhythm

Strand: 2-7   **Age:** 60-72m 5.0-6.0y

Definition
The child will do creative movements to music. He does some rhythmical movements without direction. The musical selection prompts creative dance and creative expression--its tempo may be fast or slow. The child may also move to a percussion instrument such as a drum, a tambourine, shakers, sticks, or blocks.

Assessment Materials
A drum, a tambourine or a shaker. A prerecorded musical selection representative of a movement theme, such as circus music, animals, or weather, and a prerecorded selection to enhance a child's feel of music. Large space to move to music. Equipment to play recording.

Assessment Procedures
Grouping: This skill can be introduced, practiced and assessed either in a group setting or one-on-one with the child. If the child is easily distracted when other children are present, assess the skill one-on-one or in a small group (two children). If the child is timid in a one-on-one setting, assess the skill in a group.

1. The following are three examples of observing a child as he moves to music. The movement suggestions are in a hierarchy ranging from the simple creative movements to the more involved. It is not recommended that all three examples be done during one period. (1) Tell the child that you will beat a rhythm on the drum or that you will create a musical pattern with the tambourine or shaker. Ask him to move to the music any way he chooses. In observing his movement, adjust the rhythm or the pattern to enhance his creative dancing experience. If he does not wish to participate, demonstrate simple movements of beat (clapping, head movements, swaying, twisting) and pattern (clap, bob, clap bob, twist, clap, bob). Encourage him to participate; however, creative movement should be spontaneous, not instructional; (2) If he enjoyed moving to the rhythm instrument, talk about the theme of the prerecorded selection. Involve him as you demonstrate how a circus clown flops and tumbles, how a kangaroo hops, or how the wind blows branches of a tree; (3) Play the theme selection, and invite him to listen to the music and to move as if he were a circus performer, an animal in a field, or a balloon on a windy day. Reinforce his efforts regarding the dynamics of his movements and his interpretation of the theme.

2. You can learn a great deal about the child by observing his movements. How a child moves is often a mirror of his attitude, self-esteem, and intentions. In the observation process, movement can reflect immaturity, precocity, steadiness, lethargy, or resilience. Because movement is basically a reflection of the development of body control, look for pride as he walks, hesitation in the way he moves his head and torso, caution in his stance, or an assured manner in his change of movements.

Credit: + Child moves rhythmically to music without directions being given.

Adaptations
Some children are not ready to demonstrate and perform without inhibitions. Like other children, they possess the normal urges to use their gross motor skills for whirling, rolling, twirling, and jumping, but often they have been repressed because restrictions have been placed on them to be quiet, to sit still, or to stop jumping. Such a child will take a longer time to liven up and feel comfortable with freedom and imagination. To help him, provide him with

some ideas to get him started. Encourage him to wiggle up and down, roll in the grass, jump up and down and around, stretch his arms in front, up and down, tap fast and slowly, or sway and swing. Remember that movement is natural to children, but it can take them time to overcome their hesitations. A child's natural rhythm will help him establish an awareness of the relationship between music and movement, thus developing his sense of creativity.

1.268 Prints simple words, copying models

Strand: 1-11 **Age:** 62-70m 5.2-5.10y

Definition
The child will copy at least three simple words (cat, bee, hot, if) when presented with a model. The child will write the words with a writing tool that is comfortable and easy to control. The words should be readable, but each letter need not be the correct angle, spaced consistently, constructed in sequence, or totally aligned on a line.

Assessment Materials
Paper and pencils. Four word cards; each word on a card should be printed in manuscript form and the letters should be based along a line. The words need to be printed in black ink/marker. Word card one should have the word "cat," word card two should have the word "bee," word card three should have the word "hot," and word card four should have the word "if." On four sheets of paper write the words "cat," "bee," "hot," and "if" (one word per sheet), only make the letters with dots instead of with a solid line.

Assessment Procedures
Grouping: This skill should be assessed one-on-one with the child.
1. Explain to the child that you are going to show her a card with a word on it and that you want her to look at it carefully.
2. Show her word card one, tell her that the word says "cat," point to each letter, and say the letters (c - a - t).
3. Continue by telling her that you will place the card on the table and that she is to write the word using the paper and pencil.
4. Say, "Write the word cat, c - a - t."
5. If the child successfully copies the word cat, continue with the other three words.
6. If there is a problem, show the child the sheet with the dotted word "cat." Ask her to connect the dots to make the word "cat."
7. After she has connected the dots and written the word "cat," show the child word card one and say, "Write the word 'cat'."
8. If she completes the word "cat," date the paper, adding an explanation that a tracing task had been involved prior to copying the word.
9. Continue with the other words in the same manner.

Credit: + Child copies at least three simple words from a model. The words should be readable, but they do not need to be perfect in there presentation.

Adaptations
Some children have a problem with copying letters and words from another location because they have difficulty with sequencing. These children often place the letters in the wrong position in the word. The child may have to look at the model for each letter and may make errors due to incorrect memory sequencing. Hence "cat" becomes "atc," "run" becomes "nur," etc. It is important that the child be given an opportunity to trace each letter prior to reproduction. Drawing a line around the configuration of a word helps the child realize the whole (word) rather than each part (letter). Another useful technique is to draw a different colored line under each letter; this acts as a point of focus for the child.

1.269 Colors within heavy outlines/within faint outlines

Strand: 1-11 **Age:** 62-70m 5.2-5.10y

Definition
The child will color the inside of a circle that is outlined with a thick dark black line. The circle should be 4 inches in diameter. The child will color inside the line. The child will color the inside of a circle that is outlined with a thin faint black line. The circle should be 4 inches in diameter. The child will color inside the line.

Assessment Materials
Two sheets of paper. Sheet one has a circle 4 inches in diameter that is drawn with a thick dark black line. Sheet two has a circle 4 inches in diameter that is drawn with a thin faint black line. Prepare three copies of sheet one and three copies of sheet two.

A template that is a circle inset or use corrugated cardboard or foam and cut out a 4-inch circle. The template needs to have a ridge that will act as a block to stop a crayon from going out of the line.
Blank sheets of paper, a set of crayons, and a black marker.

Assessment Procedures

Grouping: This skill should be assessed one-on-one with the child.

1. Give the child the sheet of paper that has the circle with the dark black line. Invite the child to select one crayon from the set.
2. Tell him to color the inside of the circle with the crayon, and explain that he is not to go outside the black line.
3. Allow him time to complete this task.
4. Observe the child as he is coloring, make note of such behaviors as gripping the crayon tightly, moving too closely to his work, coloring in the same direction, slowing down as he gets to the dark line, becoming discouraged, losing interest, etc. If the child colors inside the circle, praise him and date his paper and file it.
5. If the child colors outside of the line, give him another copy and ask him to try again.
6. If he colors outside of the line or if it appears that he is unable to do the task, remove the paper and give him a blank sheet.
7. On the blank paper, place the insert circle template and ask the child to watch as you draw a heavy black line around the inside of the template.
8. Do not remove the template, and ask the child to color the inside of the circle.
9. It may be necessary to hold the template in place as the child colors.
10. After the child has finished coloring inside the circle, remove the template to show the completed work.
11. Give the child another sheet of paper with the pre-drawn heavy black line circle.
12. Ask him to color the inside of the circle and to pretend that there is a "wall," like the template, around the circle.
13. Allow him time to complete the task.
14. If he successfully stays within the line, date the paper making a notation that the task was assisted.
15. Repeat the above steps, using sheet two. If the child needs to use the inset template, draw the black outline faintly.

Credit: + Child colors inside the lines of a circle with a thick dark black line, as well as a circle with a thin faint black line.

Adaptations

Some children have a difficult time when they are required to write or color. These children may lack the eye-hand coordination and the conceptual processing to internalize the need to slow the hand movement down as the stop point/boundary becomes closer. They often become discouraged and will scribble over the outline. A technique that is helpful in teaching children to stay within lines is the addition of a second outline. Example: draw a circle with a four inch diameter using a heavy black line. Then, one inch inside the circle, draw another circle using a heavy black line. Or from a coloring book select a simple illustration and draw a line around the printed outline. The line should be no less than ½ inch from the original. Explain to the child that there are two lines and that the inside line is a warning line; it says, "Slow down, you are getting close." Demonstrate for the child a back and forth coloring movement, slowing down near the inside line and cautiously coloring to the outside edge.

1.270 Prints own first name without a model

Strand: 1-11 **Age:** 62-72m 5.2-6.0y

Definition

The child will print his first name without looking at a model or without being told the letters to write, and without any verbal assistance, physical help, or tactile experiences.

Assessment Materials

Paper (ruled) and pencil.

Assessment Procedures

Grouping: This skill should be assessed one-on-one with the child.

1. Ask the child to write his first name on the paper. Observe the child as he does the task.
2. During the observation, determine if the child's shoulder is stable so that his arms can perform separate actions without losing precision. Also be aware if the child has control of his forearm; particularly from a palm-down position to a thumb-up position. It is very important that his wrist be stable to provide the support needed for finger control.

Finally, observe how the child grasps the writing utensil.
3. Note how the child forms the letter; does he hesitate in an attempt to recall the next letter, does he use the lines on the paper as guides and are the letters of the same proportions.

Credit: + Child prints his first name independently, without looking at a model or being told the letters to write.

Adaptations

Some children learn to make visual motor associations very early. They soon become aware that they can produce a particular visual pattern by moving their arm/hand/fingers in a certain way; they discover that they can make pictures, shapes, and letters by changing the direction of these movements. Often a child will enjoy a picture created or a written name, etc., but when he tries to remember what to do in order to reproduce the item, he gets frustrated. The child has a difficult time making associations and has problems when expected to transfer information into a coordinated motor response. To assist the child: (1) Ask the child to imitate pretend movements, such as washing hands, holding a paint brush, etc. It is best not give any verbal commands; reduce the auditory stimulation and simply perform an action and then ask the child to imitate the motion; (2) Ask the child to close his eyes and then guide his hand in a particular graphic pattern until he can do it by himself; (3) Include verbal directions as the child is involved with a writing activity. By saying such things as: "Draw a straight line from here (point) to here (point). Go down-turn right; go across-go up." Regardless if the child learns best by a visual-to-auditory to visual-motor approach or a kinesthetic to visual-motor or a kinesthetic-to-auditory to visual-motor approach, the important issue is to find the best way to involve the child in a successful writing experience.

1.271 (Removed, see page xviii)

1.272 Identifies an object that does not belong to a group based on one or more characteristics

Strand: 1-7C **Age:** 62-72m 5.2-6.0y

Definition

The child will select an item that is different from a group, first based on one criteria and then on two. The characteristics may include size, shape, color, function, etc. or any combination of these.

Assessment Materials

Prepare four 8 x 10-inch cards with a picture on the top half and four smaller pictures on the bottom. The four smaller pictures should include three that go with the top picture and one that does not. On two of the large cards, the four smaller pictures should have one picture that is different, based on only one characteristic. On the other two large cards, one of the smaller pictures should be different, based on two characteristics. An example would be the top picture shows a playground with children playing. The four smaller pictures include a swing, a ball, a jump rope, and a chicken.

Assessment Procedures

Grouping: This skill should be assessed one-on-one with the child.
1. Place a sheet of paper over the small pictures at the bottom of the page.
2. Tell the child that he is to look at the top picture. Discuss what the picture is about, what is happening, where it is located, etc.
3. Explain to the child that you are going to remove the sheet of paper at the bottom of the picture. Explain that there are four small pictures, and that one of the pictures does not belong with the large illustration. The child is to point to the one that does not belong.
4. After the child has identified the picture, ask him why the one selected does not belong.
5. Repeat the above with the other three cards.
6. Note the responses and annotate the child's justification statements.

Credit: + Child identifies an object that does not belong to a group based on one or more characteristics. He correctly responds to three out of the four picture cards shown.

Adaptations

For those children who have limited core language, it is important to be consistent in the use of the descriptive words. Use same and different, or alike and unlike, or not alike and similar, or identical and different. Do not interchange the words when providing instruction or directions.

1.273 Finds group having more, less, or the same number of objects as a given group up to 10

Strand: 1-10 **Age:** 64-70m 5.4-5.10y

Definition

Use objects such as blocks or shapes. Make 4 groups; two groups of two objects, one group of one object, and one group of 5 objects. The example group is one of the two object groups and the other 3 groups are control groups. When asked, the child points to the group having more objects in it than the example group. Repeat using less objects and using same amount of objects. Repeat the requests of more, same and less using different numbers in the groups. The control group can change with each example group.

Assessment Materials

Cut four pieces of string or yarn at least 12 inches long. One of the string/yarn pieces needs to be one color (red) and the other three string/yarn pieces need to be the same color (blue). Secure 25 objects, such as play chips, blocks, or shapes. (The objects selected need to be small enough to fit inside the string circle.)

Assessment Procedures

Grouping: This skill should be assessed one-on-one with the child.
1. Place the four yarn circles flat on a table. In the red circle place 3 objects, in one of the blue circles place 3 objects, in another blue circle place 2 objects, and in another blue circle place 5 objects.
2. Ask the child to join you at the table.
3. Point to the four circles and explain that there are objects in each circle. Ask the child to count the objects in the red circle (3).
4. Then say, "Point to the circle that has more objects (blocks) in it than the red circle." Note the child's response.
5. Then say, "Point to the circle that has the same amount of objects (blocks) in it as the red circle." Note the child's response.
6. Then say, "Point to the circle that has less objects in it than the red circle." Note the child's response.
7. Collect all the objects in the circles.
8. Replace the objects, using different amounts than above. Example: Red circle - 5 objects; one blue circle - 5 objects; one blue circle - 3 objects; one blue circle - 7 objects.
9. Repeat the procedure described above.

Credit: + Child finds the groups having more, less, and the same number of objects as a given group without counting. Quantities vary up to 10 items in a group.

Adaptations

Some children have difficulty with the meaning of the words "more," "less," and "the same" when used in a comparison situation. The comprehension of these concepts requires the ability to reverse a thought process. Some children will need to count the items in each circle. If a child has to count the items prior to responding to the question of which has more, less, etc., she often forgets the requested question/answer. The child needs assistance in viewing a group of objects and determining which has the asked quantity. To assist the child in this area, ask her to do some manipulative exploring prior to being asked to respond to the verbal commands. For example, say, "Give me more marbles than are in the dish. Which has more marbles?" Continue, using the concept of "less" and then "same."

1.274 Reads hour and half-hour time

Strand: 1-13 **Age:** 64-72m 5.4-6.0y

Definition

The child will identify the hour and half-hours on a conventional clock (hour and minute hands). The child will specify the hour and half-hours by reading the clock, relating the hour or half-hour by activities or by setting a conventional clock to the hour or half-hour requested.

Assessment Materials

Make a clock face with movable hands, or illustrate a set of four cards that show 1:00, 5:00, 8:00 and 11:00 and a set of four cards that show 2:30, 4:30, 9:30 and 10:30.

Assessment Procedures

Grouping: This skill should be assessed one-on-one with the child.
1. Invite the child to sit across from you. Explain that she is going to see some clocks and that she is to look carefully at the time on the clocks. Continue by telling her that you will ask her what time is shown on each clock.
2. Show the child either the clock face set at 1:00 or the clock card with 11:00.
3. Say, "What time does this clock show?" Note the child's response.
4. Show the child the clock displaying 5:00.

5. Say, "What time does this clock show?" Note the child's response.
6. Continue with the other two hour times and the four half-hour times.
7. The child's responses should indicate if she is comfortable with reading time when on the clock-wise position before the number 6 (1:00, 5:00, 2:30, 4:30) and the clock-wise position after the number 6 (8:00, 11:00, 9:30, 10:30). This is often a challenge when learning to tell time, as 2:30 and 4:30 are read going down and 9:30 and 10:30 are read going up.

Credit: + Child reads the hour and half-hour time on a clock correctly.

Adaptations

A prerequisite to the telling of time is the understanding of time itself. An understanding is needed that certain things happen at certain times, like getting up, having breakfast, eating lunch, playing, and going to bed. Telling time is abstract in nature. It requires the child, when reading hours, to read the number the short hand is pointing at and then saying "o'clock" for the number the long hand is pointing at, as well as conceptualizing that the time read is an indication of an activity to happen or one that will occur. To assist those children who find learning to tell time a difficult task, integrate a schedule of events and the time these events are to happen (a picture of going to lunch and the time, 11:30, written beside the illustration) prior to presenting the clock face. When the child is comfortable in understanding that 11:30 is the time to go to lunch, then add a clock that shows 11:30. Gradually phase out the written 11:30 and the set clock. Use the room clock to tell the child that it is time to go to lunch.

1.275 Matches time with daily activities
Strand: 1-13 **Age:** 64-72m 5.4-6.0y

Definition
When an activity is stated to the child, he will say, point to, or set a clock to the time that the activity takes place. Example: "What time do you go to bed?" The child will say 9:00, point to a written 9:00 or set a clock to show 9:00.

Assessment Materials
Prepare a list of questions regarding five daily activities that the child is involved in, such as: (a) What time do you get up in the morning? Show me the time you get up in the morning; (b) What time do you go to school? Show me the time you go to school; (c) What time do you have lunch? Show me the time you have lunch; (d) What time is playtime? Show me the time you have playtime; (e) What time do you go to bed? Show me the time you go to bed.
Make a cardboard clock with moveable hands. Prepare a sheet of paper that has the hours and half-hours written on it. The times should be written clearly, in numbers at least ½ inch tall with ample space between each numbers.

Assessment Procedures
Grouping: This skill should be assessed one-on-one with the child.
1. Ask the child to join you at a work area. Explain to the child that you are going to ask him some questions about the time he does certain things each day. Also explain that there are no right or wrong answers.
2. Say, "What time do you get up in the morning?"
3. Pause for the child's response, making sure his answer is a time.
4. Say, "What time do you leave for school?"
5. Pause for the child's response.
6. Continue asking the child the remaining three time activity questions. Note the child's responses.
7. Give the child the cardboard clock. Tell him that you are going to ask him the same questions, only this time he is show you the time by moving the hands on the clock.
8. Say, "What time do you get up in the morning?"
9. Pause, while the child moves the clock hands.
10. Continue asking the child the remaining four time activity questions. Note the child's response.
11. Replace the cardboard clock with the sheet of paper with times written on it.
12. Explain to the child that the sheet of paper has various times written on it and you are going to ask him the same questions, only this time he is to point to the correct time.
13. Say, "What time do you get up in the morning?" (It is important to recall the response the child made to this question in the prior assessment sections.)
14. Pause, while the child points to one of the written times. Record the child's response.

Credit: + Child matches time by saying, pointing or setting a clock to the time a scheduled activity takes place.

Adaptations

Children must have an understanding of time, concepts of today, tomorrow, yesterday, next week, tonight, this morning, etc., because these are basic to the comprehension of "clock time." An understanding that certain things happen at certain times, like getting up, going to school, lunch, playtime, storytime, dismissal, dinner, bed, etc. is needed. To assist those children who find learning to associate time with activities difficult, post a schedule of daily activities and the time that these activities will occur. The time should first be shown on a teacher-made clock and then the numerical time may be written. It is also helpful if the child has his own schedule of daily events shown by a clock face and the noted time.

1.276 Adds 1's and 2's in a story format
Strand: 1-10 **Age:** 64-72m 5.4-6.0y

Definition
The child will solve word problems involving adding 1's and 2's when no unnecessary information is given. The child will state or demonstrate the story problem answers.

Assessment Materials
Prepare no more than four 5 x 8-inch cards with visual addition story problems involving 1's. Example: Card One - 1 (picture of a ball) and 2 (picture of two balls) are _____ (picture of three balls). Card Two - 3 (picture of three bananas) and 1 (picture of one banana) are _____ (picture of four bananas). Card Three - 1 (picture of one flower) and 4 (picture of four flowers) are_____ (picture of five flowers) in all. Card Four - 5 (picture of five cups) and 1 (picture of a cup) are _____ (picture of six cups) in all. Prepare no more than four 5 x 8-inch cards with visual addition story problems involving 2's. Example: Card One - 2 (picture of two cherries) and 2 (picture of two cherries) are _____ (picture of four cherries). Card Two - 3 (picture of three suckers) and 2 (picture of two suckers) are _____ (picture of five suckers). Card Three - 2 (picture of two clown faces) and 1 (picture of one clown face) are _____ (picture of three clown faces) in all. Card Four - 2 (picture of two boxes) and 4 (picture of four boxes) are _____ (picture of six boxes) in all.

Assessment Procedures
Grouping: This skill should be assessed one-on-one with the child.

1. Take Card Set One, the 1's story problems, and instruct the child to join you.
2. Show the child Card One and say, "One ball and 2 balls are how many balls in all?"
3. Wait for the child's answer and note if she pointed to the illustrated balls and counted them one at a time.
4. Show the child Card Two and say, "Three bananas and one banana are how many bananas in all?"
5. Wait for the child to answer and note if she pointed to the illustrated bananas and counted them one at a time.
6. Show the child Card Three and say, "How many flowers in all?"
7. Note the child's response and any devices used to determine the answer.
8. Continue with Card Four in the same way as Card Three.
9. Record the child's response.
10. Show the child Card One, the 2's story problems, and say, "Two cherries and two cherries are how many cherries?"
11. Pause for the response.
12. Show the child Card Two and say, "Three suckers and two suckers are how many suckers?"
13. Pause for the response.
14. Show the child Card Three and say, "How many clowns are there in all?"
15. Note the child's response and any devices used to determine the answer.
16. Continue with Card Four in the same way as Card Three.

Credit: + Child solves word problems involving the adding of 1's and 2's. They provide the correct answer to at least three of the four story problems presented.

Adaptations
When children have learned about one-to-one correspondence and can recognize numbers from one to nine, adding simple number combinations with visuals is the next step for basic computation. For those children who find pictorial representation of addition problems a concern, their first story combinations should be introduced and practiced using concrete objects. These children also need to follow the appropriate sequence of instruction when dealing with addition story problems. This sequence of instruction is: (1) Understanding one-to-one correspondence; (2) Recognizing numbers one to nine; (3) Using concrete items to solve story equations; (4) Gradually making a transition to numerical pictorial representations;

(5) Replacing the pictorial illustrations with the number symbol and signs.

1.277 Subtracts 1's in a story format
Strand: 1-10 **Age:** 64-72m 5.4-6.0y

Definition
The child will solve word problems involving subtracting 1's when no unnecessary information is given. The child will state or demonstrate the story problem answers.

Assessment Materials
Prepare no more than four 5 x 8-inch cards with visual subtraction story problems involving 1's. Example: Card One - A picture of 3 inflated balloons, then a picture of 1 popped balloon and a line that says, "How many balloons are left?" Card Two - A picture of a basket with 5 apples in it, then a picture of 1 apple core and a line that says, "How many apples are left?" Card Three - A picture of 4 flowers growing in a garden, then a picture of 1 flower picked and a line that says, "How many flowers are left?" Card Four - A picture of six pencils in a box, then a picture of 1 pencil laying on a table and a line that says, "How many pencils are left?" Prepare no more than four 5 x 8-inch cards with visual subtraction story problems involving 1's. Example: Card One - 2 (picture of two cherries with stems) - 1 (picture of one stem only) = _____ (picture of a cherry). Card Two - 3 (picture of three suckers) - 1 (picture of one sucker stick only) = _____ (picture of a sucker). Card Three - 5 (picture of five clowns with hats on) - 1 (picture of one clown without a hat) = _____ (picture of four clowns). Card Four - 6 (picture of six glasses full of water) - 5 (picture of five empty glasses) = _____ (picture of a full glass).

Assessment Procedures
Grouping: This skill should be assessed one-on-one with the child.

1. Take the card's from Set One (1's story problems) and instruct the child to join you.
2. Show the child Card One and say, "There are three balloons. One of the balloons has popped. How many balloons are left?"
3. Wait for the child's answer.
4. Show the child Card Two and say, "There are five apples in the basket. One apple has been eaten. How many apples are left?"
5. Wait for the child's answer.
6. Show the child Card Three and say, "There are four flowers growing in the garden. One flower has been picked. How many flowers are left?"
7. Wait for the child's response.
8. Show the child Card Four and say, "There are six pencils in the box. One pencil has been taken and is laying on the desk. How many pencils are left in the box?"
9. Wait for the child's answer and note if he pointed to or made any "primitive" marks to determine the answers.
10. Show the child Card One, the 1's story problem, and say, "Two cherries. One of them has been eaten. How many are left?"
11. Pause for the response.
12. Show the child Card Two and say, "Three suckers. One of them has been eaten. How many are left?"
13. Pause for the response.
14. Continue the same procedure with Cards Three and Four.
15. Note the child's response and his techniques used to determine the answer.

Credit: + Child solves word problems involving subtracting 1's. The child gives the correct response in at least three of the word problems presented.

Adaptations
Subtraction is the opposite process of addition. Many of the skills learned during addition will be used by the child to solve subtraction problems. Instruction should proceed from total use of concrete objects to abstract forms, as in addition. Some children are confused by the subtraction terms of minus and equals; when the child is engaged in the initial activities in subtraction, using the terms "take away" and "leave" is helpful. It is also effective if the first subtraction story problems have an element of "vanish" (example: the apple was eaten, the flower was picked, the water was emptied, the pencil broke, etc.)

1.278 Reads numerals on clock face and associates time with routine activity
Strand: 1-13 **Age:** 64-72m 5.4-6.0y

Definition
The child will read the numerals on a clock face at least 5 inches in diameter. Numerals should be in Arabic. A working clock or poster board clock face may be used. The child should be able to tell what time it is (i.e., time for lunch, time for play, time for

bed, etc.) The child should read the clock at least three different times (hours and half-hours only).

Assessment Materials
Prepare a cardboard clock with movable hands, and a series of five cards that each show a picture of a daily activity. The cards could illustrate activities such as eating lunch, going to school, playing, doing a daily home task, going to bed, etc.

Assessment Procedures
Grouping: This skill should be assessed one-on-one with the child.
1. Explain to the child that you are going to show her a clock.
2. Tell her that she is to tell the time that is on the clock and then she is to describe an activity that would occur at that time.
3. Set the clock on an hour (e.g., 9:00) and say, "What time is it?"
4. If the child does not respond or responds with a wrong answer, review clock hand placement with her. Example: "The long hand points to the number 12 and the short hand points to the time, 9. It is 9:00."
5. Set the clock on an hour (e.g., 10:00) and say, "What time is it?"
6. Pause, and when the child responds with 10:00, say, "What happens at 10:00?" Pause for the child to respond. Example: "We go outside and play."
7. If the child is unsure what occurs at the specific time, use the Activity Cards as prompts, being sure to show the child the correct card and at least one other.
8. Continue with at least one more hour time.
9. Record the responses.
10. Set the clock on a half-an-hour (e.g., 2:30) and say, "What time is it?"
11. If the child does not respond or responds with the wrong answer, review clock hand placement for half-an-hour.
12. Set the clock on a half-an-hour setting (e.g., 11:30) and say, "What time is it?"
13. Pause, and when the child responds with 11:30, say, "What happens at 11:30?" If the child is unsure what occurs at the specific time, use the Activity Cards as described above.
14. Continue with at least one more half-an-hour time.
15. Record the responses.

Credit: + Child reads numerals on a clock face and associates the time with a routine activity. The child should be able to read at least three different times (hours and half-hours only).

Adaptations
Children usually do not have trouble with telling hourly times. However, half-hours are often more difficult due to reading the half-way-between numbers in different positions from 12:00 to 6:00 and 6:00 to 12:00. For those children who find this a concern, it is important to tell them to always read the number behind the short hand or the number that the short hand has just past.

Some children find associative thinking a difficult task. When the child is confronted with the questions, "What happens at 11:30?" or "What happens when the clock says this time?" she is required to "sort-out" different thought images and determine which is the most appropriate answer. As an example, when a child is asked, "What happens at 11:30?" her conceptual patterns may include getting out of her chair, walking down a hall, carrying a heavy lunch tray, washing her hands, eating, etc. The child then needs to take the pieces and formulate a general concept (lunch), when often the like or dislike of a food is foremost in her thoughts.

1.279 Makes judgments in weight without being confused by the object's size
Strand: 1-7B **Age:** 64-78m 5.4-6.6y

Definition
The child will determine which of four objects, varying in size, is heaviest by lifting each one to feel its weight versus focusing on its size.

Assessment Materials
Four empty opaque plastic bottles (e.g., small water bottle 8 oz, medium water bottle 16 oz., tall water bottle 1 liter, and ketchup bottle 24 oz.). Cover the bottles with paper. Some gravel, sand, or beans.

Assessment Procedures
Grouping: This skill can be introduced and practiced in a group setting. However, when you are ready to assess the child's ability to make judgments in size, length, and weight, it is recommended that you do so one-on-one with the child.
1. Completely fill the 16 oz bottle with sand. Beans or gravel (make sure that the child can't see what you've put inside). Fill the 8 oz.

bottle half full, the 24 oz bottle one fourth full, and leave the 1 liter bottle empty.
2. Explain to the child that all the bottles are different in size and weight.
3. Have the child guess which bottle he thinks will be heaviest without lifting the bottles.
4. Next have him pick up the bottles one at a time.
5. Ask him is the bottle is heavy or light.
6. Once he has had an opportunity to pick up each of the bottles, ask him which one he now thinks is heaviest. Place that bottle to the side.
7. Out of the remaining bottles ask which one is the lightest. Place that bottle to the side.
8. Ask the child which of the remaining two bottles is heaviest.
9. Talk about his original guess and why he thought that bottle would be heaviest.
10. Mix up the bottles.
11. Have the child lift all the bottles again, one at a time and place them in order, the heaviest one first.
12. Record the order.

Credit: + Child makes judgment in weight that is not based on appearance.

Adaptations

Some children have a difficult time judging the abstraction of size and weight, while others lack the vocabulary to express the concepts of size and weight. To address the concept of weight, show the child two objects of different weights. Ask the child to select the heaviest one and then the lightest one. Show the child two objects which are the same size but one is heavier tan the other. Ask the child to select the one he thinks is the heaviest. Discuss how they both look alike but do not weigh them. Make sure the child hears words that accompany the concepts. Hearing the words provides him with the necessary expressive terminology.

1.280 Attends to task without supervision for 15 minutes

Strand: 1-8 **Age:** 64-78m 5.4-6.6y

Definition

The child will stay on task without any verbal or nonverbal prompting or any reinforcement for 15 minutes. The activity that the child is asked to do within the 15 minute span should be on her leisure level and something that she is motivated to do, with a limited amount of distractions.

Assessment Materials

Select an activity that the child is capable of doing independently. The activity could be reading or looking at the pictures in a book, drawing, coloring a picture, building with construction materials, listening to a tape/CD, working at the computer, playing a ball game, modeling with clay, etc. Any supplies that the child will need to complete the activity (crayons, scissors, drawing paper, etc.)

Assessment Procedures

Grouping: This skill should be assessed one-on-one with the child.
1. Present the activity to the child. Explain that she is to work at the task until the timer goes off.
2. Show the child the timer and explain that you will not be able to help her or check on her work until the timer has buzzed.
3. Set the timer for fifteen minutes.
4. When the timer goes off, go to the child and praise her for working until the timer rang, for doing a good job, for being a super worker, etc.
5. Record whether or not the child stayed on task for the 15 minute period and note any distracted behavior that the child displayed.
6. If the child has not completed her work and expresses a desire to continue, allow her the necessary time.
7. Set the timer for an additional 15 minutes. However if the child completes the task before the buzzer, record how long it took her to finish.

Credit: + Child stays on task without verbal or nonverbal reinforcement for 15 minutes while engaged in a preferred leisure activity.

Adaptations

If a child is unable to stay on task for the 15 minute period and becomes restless, angry, or frustrated, the task should be stopped. Some children are easily frustrated if they are being timed - all they concentrate on is "beating" the clock, not on being accurate or enjoying the task. Also consider that the child might misplace her frustration and blame the learning activity, not the timing. If this frustration isn't diminished, the child may develop a dislike for reading, drawing, or whatever the activity is. Allow the child to take breaks before going back to the task. Breaks can include: resting, exercising, listening to music, or being presented with a different but related topic.

1.281 Compares items by appearance
Strand: 1-7C **Age:** 65-72m 5.5-6.0y

Definition
The child will perceive significant differences and likenesses in the appearance of objects. It is important to avoid those visual discrimination tasks that require the child to seek minute details. The comparisons should be based on such visual appearances as size, color, designs, parts, etc.

Assessment Materials
Collect pictures of animals and objects. Make a set of seven cards, each showing three items that go together and one that doesn't. The relationship of the items on the cards should be based only on appearance.

Assessment Procedures
Grouping: This skill should be assessed one-on-one with the child.
1. Present the first card of the set as the teaching card for the assessment procedure.
2. Show the child the card and ask him to look at the items on the card.
3. Discuss with the child how the pictures are alike and how they are different.
4. Have the child point to the one picture on the card that is different.
5. Give the child the opportunity to tell why he selected the picture that he did.
6. Continue showing the child the rest of the cards, one at a time. Each time a card is shown ask the child to find the picture that is different and encourage the child to justify his choice.
7. It is important that the choices be made on appearance only.

Credit: + Child perceives significant differences and likenesses in the appearance of objects. The comparisons should be based on visual attributes like size, color, design, etc. The child correctly responds to five out of the seven cards presented.

Adaptations
When asked to compare or sort objects, some children have difficulty grasping the concept of consistent criteria. When these children are asked to compare/sort objects, they may group a yellow square with a red square because the items are the same shape and then add a red circle because it is red. When comparing items, it is important for the child to recall why he made his first choice and then make similar choices based on that same reason.

Consider the following when helping a child to remain consistent: (1) Absolute Comparison - the child identifies large and small members of different pairs of objects--the biggest rock, the smallest cookie; (2) Relative Comparison - the child perceives the same object as now large, now small, relative to the size of another object; (3) Additive Activity - add to a series of objects already identified by common appearance.

1.282 Compares items by category and function
Strand: 1-7C **Age:** 65-72m 5.5-6.0y

Definition
The child will compare at least two objects from different classes. The selection of the classes should be determined by the entry level of the children and the experiential background. The following are suggested categorical classifications: things that move versus objects that are stationary, clothing that keeps us warm versus clothes we wear for cooler weather, animals that live on a farm versus those that live in zoos, items that are used in the kitchen versus tools that are used to build things.

Assessment Materials
Collect three sets of five pictures or cut-outs each. Set One should be of things we wear, Set Two should picture things we eat with and Set Three items that we use to keep clean.

Assessment Procedures
Grouping: This skill should be assessed one-on-one with the child.
1. As a teaching item, select one picture from each of the sets.
2. Place the three pictures in front of the child and ask her to name the items.
3. Request that the child tell what each pictured item is used for. If necessary, present questions to the child that will relate to comparing the pictured categories.
4. After the child has successfully completed and understands the teaching item, place the three pictures in a row in front of the child.
5. Hand the child one picture or cut-out at a time and tell her to look at it carefully and then place it under the picture that it goes with.
6. Continue until all twelve pictures have been placed.
7. Encourage the child to explain the different categories and why certain pictures were placed together.

8. Record the number the child placed correctly, the amount of time required, and any pertinent responses.

Credit: + Child compares at least three objects from different classes by category and function.

Adaptations
Prior to comparing by classification, it may be necessary to direct the comparison, by requesting that the child match by size, shape, color, texture, etc. An example might be dividing toys into two groups: small toys and large toys, or hard toys and soft toys. Continue by requesting that the toys be divided into groups that you throw and those that roll.

1.283 Groups objects by two analogies
Strand: 1-7C **Age:** 65-78m 5.5-6.6y

Definition
The child will be able to identify likeness in things even though the objects are totally different. The child will determine the like relationships by using different criteria. An example: A mug and a glass are alike because a person can drink from them. A sweater and a stocking cap are alike because they keep us warm. An apple and a radish are alike because they are both red, plus you can eat them.

Assessment Materials
A collection of picture books, magazines, catalogs, picture worksheets and picture cards. (Single item pictures are better to use than multi-object visuals.)

Assessment Procedures
Grouping: This skill should be assessed one-on-one with the child.
1. Select one of the picture collections.
2. Explain to the child that he is to look through the pictures that you have given him and find at least two pictures that go together for one reason.
3. If the child displays any difficulties, prompt him by showing a picture and asking him to name the object in the picture. After the child has completed this task, ask him to find another picture that goes with the one just named.
4. It is important to provide time for the child to explain how the two items relate.
5. Continue until the child has compared four pictures by a single analogy.
6. Write down the name of the pictures matched and the reason stated.
7. Provide the child with another picture collection and ask him to find an item.
8. When he has selected a picture, request that he find another picture that goes with it, based on two analogies. It is important to provide time for the child to justify his rational for selection.
9. Continue until the child has compared four pictures by two analogies.
10. Record the name of pictures matched and the reasons stated.

Credit: + Child groups at least four pictures by two analogies.

Adaptations
Some children have difficulty categorizing two or more elements. These children need to abstract or to categorize at least three objects in terms of at least two characteristics. Often these children think literally and have a difficult time understanding analogies. To assist these children, limit the amount of items they have to choose from, discuss the different aspects/characteristics of each item, and begin verbal comparisons. As an example: Give the child an apple, a potato and an orange. Discuss the appearance of each, talk about how they grow and what they are used for. After the discussion, ask the child to point to two items that grow on trees and are both fruits.

1.284 Determines realistically when task is done
Strand: 1-8 **Age:** 65-78m 5.5-6.6y

Definition
When given just one task to do, the child will decide when the task is completed. Examples: all the questions answered, colored all of the picture, reached the end of the book, put the last piece of a puzzle in, matched the pegboard design, etc. When given one task to do, the child will decide if the completed task is done correctly and is her best quality work.

Assessment Materials
Divide a large sheet of paper (10 ½ x 17 inches) into two sections.
On the left side, draw or cut and glue a group of eight recognizable objects in detail. Example: animals, houses, plants, cars, toys, etc.
On the right side, draw the same objects in a different position; fill them to look like a shadow or a silhouette.
Duplicate the right side drawings on another sheet of paper and cut the objects out.

Assessment Procedures

Grouping: This skill should be assessed one-on-one with the child.

1. Give the child the sheet of figures and instruct her to draw a line from the object on the left side to its match (shadow) on the right side.
2. If the child is having any problem with the directions, do the first item using a broken line. Request that she fill in this line before doing the rest.
3. Tell the child that she is to match all the figures on the paper.
4. Show her the cut-out objects of the shadowed items, and explain that when she has finished drawing the line to match the items, she is to use the cut-outs to see if she has made the correct matches. Limit the information that she is given about how to use the silhouettes to check accuracy.
5. Request that the child raise her hand when she has completed the task.
6. Before she raises her hand, observe the child to determine if she completes the matching and uses the self-checking objects to assure a quality activity.
7. Note if she accomplished matching and if she used self-checking.

Credit: + Child determines realistically when a completed task is done correctly and to the best of her ability.

Adaptations

Structured limitation of a task is sometimes necessary when the child is overwhelmed with what she is asked to do. For example: there are too many things on a page, the book is too thick, the picture to color has too much detail, the stack of pattern cards is too high, the tape is too long, etc. The child may develop an attitude of "I'll never get done." To assist the child in dealing with this concern, divide the activity in manageable parts (do the first row, read to the marker in the book, color everything that is blue, look at only a few cards at a time, stop the tape after five minutes).

Some children will hurry to complete a task without any concern for quality. A task is complete only when everything has been done to the best of the child's ability. In this regard, begin by giving the child tasks that will be simple for her to do, so that she will achieve her goal of finishing all parts of the task. Deal with the quality level by making sure the child has instruction on the difficult aspects or has a resource to refer to for assistance. Make sure that the child is also aware of the two expectation levels; provide a separate reinforcement for each.

1.285 Groups objects by at least two analogies

Strand: 1-4D **Age:** 65-78m 5.5-6.6y

Definition

The child is expected to place objects in groups based on the objects being alike in two or more ways. The objects could be very dissimilar, but could be alike in function or position. Example: oranges and radishes are both round and are both edible.

Assessment Materials

A set of attribute blocks that contain triangles, squares, circles and diamonds in two sizes and four colors. If attribute blocks are not available, the shapes can be cut from construction paper.

Assessment Procedures

Grouping: This skill should be assessed one-on-one with the child.

1. Place the blocks on a table in front of the child.
2. Ask the child to sort the blocks by size and shape.
3. If the child has difficulty, end the assessment at this point; if not, continue.
4. Ask the child to sort the blocks by color and shape.
5. If the child has difficulty, end the assessment at this point; if not, continue.
6. Ask the child to sort the blocks by color, size and shape.
7. Record the groupings that are correct.

Credit: + Child correctly groups objects by at least two analogies.

Adaptations

Some children need to sort by a single attribute/characteristic prior to selecting by/using mixed analogies/attributes. It may be necessary to start by asking the child to sort first by color, then by size and then by shape. After the child has mastered this sorting activity, request that he place all the same colors together. When this task has been completed, demonstrate how to place red, blue, yellow, and green circles of the same size on top of each other. Continue with the other blocks of different sizes and shapes. Be sure to discuss what you are doing during this demonstration. At the conclusion, mix up the blocks and ask the child to put all the colors together, then ask him to stack the blocks. Continue the above process, this time stacking the blocks by size. Finally, stack the blocks according to their shape.

1.286 Reads simple 3-letter words paired with pictures

Strand: 1-9 **Age:** 66-72m 5.6-6.0y

Definition
The ability to match and read simple words is one of the first skills in learning to read. This beginning level of word recognition closely follows the child's developmental stage of recognizing a particular word form as being the same each time she sees it, and being able to name two words that sound alike after hearing a series of words. It is desirable that the child's first reading experience with words be associated with pictures. The initial pictures recommended are those that the child is familiar with, and the initial words should be of a consonant-vowel-consonant (CVC) pattern (cat, dog, man, cup, etc.) In presenting the word/picture models to the child, it is important to have only one picture and one word on the material.

Assessment Materials
Develop three sets of Lotto materials.
Set One should have a child Lotto card; each card should be divided into six squares, three across and two down. In each square there should be a single item picture (these can be either drawn or cut out and glued in the squares) of something that the child is familiar with. Under each picture should be written the name of the object. Examples: first row across - Dog, Cup, Hat; second row across – Jet, Pig, Mug. Set One also needs a deck of single cards that have the same pictures and words on them. Note: When making the child Lotto cards, make another set just like it and cut on the lines to make a deck of single object cards.
Set two should have the same child Lotto card as in Set One. Set Two does not require the single picture/word cards; instead make a set of word cards only (Dog, Cup Hat, Jet, Pig, Mug); no pictures.
Set Three should have a child Lotto card, and each card should be divided into six squares, three across and two down. In each square there should be only the words (Dog, Cup, Hat, Jet, Pig, Mug); no pictures. Set Three also needs single picture cards of each of the words on the child Lotto card (Dog, Cup, Hat, Jet, Pig, Mug); no words. Markers/chips.

Assessment Procedures
Grouping: This skill should be assessed one-on-one with the child.
1. Ask the child if she would like to play a game of Lotto.
2. Give the child a card from Set One. Explain to the child that each square has a picture and a word that tells what the picture is. Point to and name each of the six pictures, inviting the child to say the words with you.
3. Shuffle the single deck of picture/word cards. Present one card to the child (picture and word of a Cup) and ask the child to read the word and place the card on top of the picture/word Cup on her Lotto card. Markers/chips may be used in place of the picture/ word cards.
4. Continue until all the squares on the Lotto card have been covered.
5. Remove the picture/word cards from the child's card.
6. From Set Two get the word cards only.
7. Tell the child, "This time your card is not going to have a picture on it."
8. Show the child the first word card (Dog), and ask the her to read the word and place it on the correct space on her Lotto card.
9. Continue until all the word cards have been read and all the squares on the Lotto card have been covered.
10. From Set Three, give the child the Lotto card that has only the words in the squares. Secure from Set Three the picture cards.
11. Tell the child that her new card only has words on it. Explain that she is going to have to place the correct picture in the square and then read the word.
12. Show the child the first picture card (Hat), and ask her to place the picture in the right square and read the word.
13. Continue until all the picture cards have been placed and the words read.
14. Make a listing of the words that the child read correctly when using the Lotto card from Set Three.

Credit: + Child reads simple 3-letter words that have been paired with pictures.

Adaptations
The number of times a child needs to look at a picture and a word before the word becomes part of a sight vocabulary will vary tremendously. Most children find it easier to learn words if the words are meaningful and familiar through everyday expression. Example:

It would be easier to learn the word "mug," if the child was told daily, "I will pour your milk in the mug," or "Bring me your mug and I will get you a drink." Some children learn the words more easily if they have distinctive shapes or features. Example: Many words provide visual clues to aid in recall (look - two oo's look like eyes, Hat - first letter looks like a tall hat). Other words are easily recognized because of their unusual configuration (baby, pretty). Some children learn the words more easily if they are emotionally pleasing. Example: A child may learn to recognize the word "cookie" after one exposure, because the word cookie refers to something she likes. Some children have difficulty learning the word in isolation, even when accompanied with a picture. For those children the word needs to be expressed in a sentence. Example: Write, "The jet was high in the sky." Show the sentence to the child with a picture of a jet over the word "jet." Read the sentence. Read the sentence again with the picture removed showing the word "jet." Allow the child to say the word jet with you as you read the sentence. It is important to expose the child to as many different learning strategies as possible and to repeat the picture/word experience.

1.287 Blends letter sounds to say the word as a unit

Strand: 1-9 **Age:** 66-72m 5.6-6.0y

Definition

As soon as the child has learned some of the consonant sounds and the short sounds of two vowels (preferably short a and short i), he needs to receive instruction on how to blend these sounds into meaningful words. The blending must be done smoothly to prevent mispronunciation of words and distortions. It is often helpful to begin with words composed of nasal consonants with a short "a" so there are no sound pauses between the letters (man, nap, map, mat, etc.) Once the child is able to sound blend a few words (man), consideration should be given to initial consonant substitution and the forming of other words by sound blending (pan, fan, ran).

Assessment Materials

Make up twenty wooden blocks (at least 1 ½" square). A black marking pen.
On five blocks, write one letter per side. Randomly place the following consonants: b, c, d, f, g, and h. Both capital and lower case letters can be used.
On five blocks, write one letter per side. Randomly place the following consonants: j, k, l, m, n, and p. Both capital and lower case letters can be used.
On five blocks, write one letter per side. Randomly place the following consonants: r, s, t, v, w, and z. Both capital and lower case letter can be used. At this time, the consonants q, x, y are not included.
On five blocks, write one letter per side. Randomly place the vowels a, e, i, o, and u. Use only lower case.

Assessment Procedures

Grouping: This skill should be assessed one-on-one with the child.
1. Select blocks that have the letters on them to make the following words: map, man, mud, mit, nan, nat, nap, lot, got, rug, hug, jug, jet, vet, wet. (Other consonant-vowel-consonant words may be used.)
2. Present words with the short sound of "a" at the beginning of the assessment. Separate the presentation of the short sound of "e" and "i," because the sounds are so similar.
3. Prepare a scoring sheet listing the words to be used.
4. Ask the child to join you at the table.
5. Align three blocks to form the word "tan."
6. Instruct the child to say the word.
7. If the child has difficulty in sound-blending the word "tan", move the "t" block away from the "an" and ask the child to sound the "t" as you quickly move the block to meet the "an" blocks. As the "t" block connects with the stationary "an" blocks, request that the child sound the complete word. The child needs to sound-blend at the following duration: "t" (half-second interval) "an."
8. Continue the above procedure with the other letter blocks.
9. On the scoring sheet, indicate the words the child could sound-blend without any prompting, those that he needed assistance with, those that he took longer than a half-second interval with, and those with which he sounded each letter (M---a---n).

Credit: + Child blends letter sounds to say a word as a unit. The child can blend at least five to ten words.

Adaptations

One of the big concerns of sound blending is the rate at which sounds are expressed. The closer they are presented in time, the more readily the child will be able to blend a word as a unit. Many children, when presented with a decoding process, need about two seconds to identify the letter and recall the sound associated with it. The child then must hold that sound, while moving on to the next letter(s) and recalling that sound (s). The child needs to reach the level of proficiency in which he is only concentrating on recalling the sound/symbols, not having to recall each letter sound and having to focus on blending successive sounds. The first task in dealing with auditory sound blending is time, the rate at which sounds are introduced. The closer they are presented the more accurately they will be blended. Ask the child to repeat a word after you, then to repeat it when you say it slowly. Example: Say, "What is this word: tr (pause1/2 second) ee?" If the child cannot respond with the word "tree," ask him to say "tree." Then say "What is this? Tr-tr-tr-tr-ee-ee," holding each sound but blending them together. Ask the child to say the word. Continue this practice, until the child can process sounds into words with at least two second intervals.

1.288 Fills in a word when read a passage with words missing

Strand: 1-9 **Age:** 66-72m 5.6-6.0y

Definition

The child is expected to use the meaning of words, phrases or sentences that she hears to fill in any missing word(s). Learning to use context clues to determine the unknown word should begin with an oral presentation with a visual cue to accompany it. This should be followed by showing the child a printed phrase or sentence; read the selection and provide a picture stimulus. Gradually, the picture needs to be phased out and the child's response based on the word that would fit in because of the meaning of the other words.

Assessment Materials

Prepare a set of five picture cards (large size index cards work well). For Set One some picture examples are: a bed, a ball, an apple, a coat, and a car. Prepare picture card Set Two, which is a duplicate of Set One, except that the word of each object is written at the bottom of each card. Prepare another set of cards, Set Three, which is a set of the words without the pictures.

Develop five incomplete sentences that require one of the cards from Set One. Example: I sleep in a _____. John threw the _____. Lisa ate a big red_____. Jack put on a warm_____ to go outside. We went to the store in the_____. Develop five incomplete sentences that require one of the cards from Set Two. Example: The man had to put a new tire on his_____. John was sound asleep in his _____. The boy picked a big _____. I went to the store to buy a new hat and_____. It was my turn to catch the_____ .

A Scoresheet that is divided into three columns: column one heading Set One, column two heading Set Two, and column three heading Set Three. Each column needs to have an area for recording whether or not the answers were correct or incorrect, and the child's response if incorrect.

Assessment Procedures

Grouping: This skill should be assessed one-on-one with the child.

1. Explain to the child that you are going to read some sentences, but that there is a word missing and that she is to tell you that word. Provide the child with an example: Your name is_____. Place Set One in view of the child. Explain that the pictures may help her decide the missing word and she is to point to the picture card that represents the word.
2. Say, "I sleep in a_____." Pause and wait for the child to select the picture that shows a bed and to say bed. Record the child's response on the scoring sheet.
3. Continue with the other four sentences and pictures.
4. Collect Set One pictures.
5. Place Set Two picture/word cards in view of the child.
6. Discuss with the child Set Two picture/word cards, mentioning that these cards have the word of the object printed at the bottom.
7. Explain that you are going to read some sentences, but that there is a word missing and that they are to tell you the missing word. Place Set Two in view of the child. Explain that the picture/word cards may help her decide the missing word and that she is to point to the card that represents the word.
8. Say, "The man had to put a new tire on his_____." Pause and wait for the child to select the picture that shows the car and to say car. Record the child's response.

© 2010 VORT Corporation. All rights reserved. Do Not copy.

9. Continue with the other four sentences and pictures associated with Set Two. Record the child's responses on the Scoresheet.
10. Collect Set Two picture cards.
11. Place the Set Three word cards in view of the child.
12. Discuss with the child the Set Three word cards, mentioning that these cards only have words on them.
13. Select a sentence from Set One or Set Two and write it on a sheet of paper. Example: Lisa ate a big red_____.
14. Tell the child that you are going to show her a sentence and that you will read it to her. Point to the words and read the sentence, leaving out the last word.
15. Ask her to say the word and find the word card that fits in the sentence. Request that she place the word card in the blank.
16. If the child is having any problems, refer to Set Two.
17. Read the sentence together.
18. Record the child's responses on the Scoresheet.
19. Continue with the other four sentences and word cards.

Credit: + Child fills in a word when read a passage with a word missing. Child correctly identifies the missing word in three of the four examples in Set One and Set Two.

Adaptations
Some children may have a difficult time with generalization skills. When asked to complete a sentence with a missing word, the child needs to conceptualize the individual word meanings and infer the missing meaning. In the sentence, "Jack put on his warm_____," the child needs to process an analysis of the parts of the sentence, such as, "'put on' means an action of dressing" and "'his warm' means something Jack has that will keep him from feeling cold." She must first put those elements together and then make a generalization of what Jack might have that he would use to dress himself to keep away the cold. Some of the options might be a sweater, coat, shawl, newspaper, blanket, plastic bag, etc. After considering the options, the child needs to respond with the most appropriate selection. Often the selection is based on the child's experience in a similar situation; however, it is important to realize that there may not be one right answer. The child that has a problem with using specific information to make a generalization needs some additional instruction, such as: (1) Asking the child to supply as many words as she can that would make sense in the sentence and then discussing the words that would be best; (2) Sounding the beginning consonant of the missing word as a clue ("Jack put on his warm (c)_____") limits the possible responses.

Some children will be able to generalize the response, but because of a language concern, they may have a problem recalling words. They understand words, but they cannot retrieve them for usage. It is important for these children to have ample time to recall and to be given a visual to assist.

1.289 Reads simple phrases/sentences
Strand: 1-9 **Age:** 66-72m 5.6-6.0y

Definition
The child will read a fictional story that he has not been exposed to before. The story should have less than 60 words. The child is allowed to read the story orally or silently. After not more than two readings, the child will retell the story.

Assessment Materials
Select a fictional story within the child's word recognition level and experiences. The selection should also include pictures that relate to the story content.

Assessment Procedures
Grouping: This skill should be assessed one-on-one with the child.
1. Show the child the storybook that you would like him to read.
2. Discuss with him the title of the story and any pictures on the front of the cover. Also ask him some motivational questions (Do think this is going to be a scary story? I wonder what is going to happen to the Teddy Bear? etc.) Build enthusiasm and excitement prior to the reading.
3. Explain to the child that you are going to give him time to read this fun story. Tell him that you will help him with any words that he is having a problem with.
4. Tell him that he can read the story to himself or out loud.
5. Give the child the story to read. If the child decides to read the story silently, begin to read your own book. If the child chooses to read aloud, listen attentively.

© 2010 VORT Corporation. All rights reserved. Do Not copy.

6. Observe the child as he reads the story; do not make any written notes during the reading time.
7. If the child asks for help with a word, tell him the word, but do not assist him in any decoding skills.
8. If the child read the story silently, ask him some general questions such as, "What was the story about? Was it a funny story?," etc. Ask him to tell you the story.
9. If the child read the story aloud, tell him that you enjoyed the story so much that you would like him to tell it again.
10. After the session, record any observations made during the reading experience, any words that he asked, and how accurately he retold the story.

Credit: + Child reads an unfamiliar fictional story of less than 60 words, silently or aloud, and after the first or second reading, he retells the story.

Adaptations

A child might have trouble reading a total story for many reasons: he could have problems with maintaining his attention, the words of the story could be too difficult, he might not be motivated with the content, the reading could be a time-consuming task for him, or reading might not be a rewarding experience. If the child is experiencing an attention problem, place a limit on how much he is expected to read the first session. Give him a break after the limit has been reached and retry another "small bite" before trying an another alternative strategy. If the problem is that the material is too difficult, reduce the readability level. If the child is to read the selection, he must recognize that completing the task will prove to be satisfying, and the story is more inviting and more easily read if he can relate to the story situation. Reinforcement is an important issue for early readers. In the beginning, the child wishes to read since it is a "grown-up" act. He is satisfied because he is reading. However, some children find the task so difficult that additional motivation needs to be explored.

1.290 Identifies what number comes before and after a given number, or between 2 numbers

Strand: 1-10 **Age:** 66-78m 5.6-6.6y

Definition

The child will be presented with three numbers in sequence. The middle number will be the example number and the child will pick the number that comes before. The middle number will be the example number and the child will pick the number that comes after. When shown two example numbers, the child will pick the number that goes between.

Assessment Materials

Poster board numerals (0 - 10). The numerals should be at least 2 inches high. The numbers can be either cut out or written on cards.

Assessment Procedures

Grouping: This skill should be assessed one-on-one with the child.

1. Sit across from the child and say, "Tell me the number that comes before 6." Note the child's answer.
2. Say, "Tell me the number that comes after 6." Note the response.
3. Say, "Tell me the number that comes between 3 and 5." Note the response.
4. Continue the above three steps using other numbers between 0 and 10.
5. If the child makes errors or is hesitant in her response, continue with the following assessment activities.
6. Place three of the number cards in front of the child. The numbers should be in order. Example: 5, 6, 7 or 2, 3, 4 or 8, 9, 10.
7. Point to the middle number (6) of the group of three and say, "What number is this?" After the child has answered, say, "What number comes before 6? What number comes after 6?" Record the child's response.
8. Continue using the number cards and do another cluster set (2, 3, 4, or 8, 9, 10, or 4, 5, 6, etc.) Record the child's response.

Credit: + Child identifies what number comes before and after a given number, or between two stated numbers. She gives the correct answer in three out of four examples given.

Adaptations

Prerequisite to identifying the numbers before and after are: (1) Being able to count by rote from 1 - 10. (2) Being able to put an object in front of and in back of another object and locating the object between. (3) Being able to state if an item is in back of, in front of, or between another item. (4) Being able to say individual numbers when they are presented out of sequence.

Some children may not have mastered these prerequisites. They are unable to implement the combination of before, after, between, or recall the name of the numbers. If the child has to begin counting from one to say the numbers, the spatial position of "before" and "after" is affected. Besides reteaching the prerequisites, these children may be assisted by highlighting the number requested. Example: The numbers from 1 - 10 are written on the chalkboard or a chart as follows: 0, 1, 2, 3, 4, 5, 6, 7, 8, 9,10. The numbers 2, 5, and 8 are circled, the numbers 1, 4, and 7 are written in red, and the numbers 3, 6, and 9 are written in blue. Ask the child to say the numbers in the clusters. Then ask the child to look at cluster one and the number that is circled. Using the color cues, discuss the number that comes before and after. When the child has difficulty, encourage her to say only the numbers in the clusters (e.g., 1, 2, 3, - "1 comes before 2, and 3 comes after 2, and 2 is in the middle").

Continue using the clusters 4, 5, 6 and 7, 8, 9. Fade the cues as the child becomes successful.

1.291 Makes judgments in distance

Strand: 1-7B **Age:** 66-78m 5.6-6.6y

Definition
The children will determine which of a given number of objects is closest to, or farthest from, them. As the child experiences judgments in distances relative to themselves, the skill should be transferred from one object to another.

Assessment Materials
Four different colored balloons attached to four different lengths of string. Four different colored small balls (ping-pong balls, marbles, or rubber balls) or large beads (stringing type), two pieces of different colored yarn.

Assessment Procedures
Grouping: This skill can be introduced and practiced in a group setting. However, when you are ready to assess the child's ability to make judgments in distance, it is recommended that you do so one-on-one with the child.

1. Select two of the balloons that are in the air at different heights. Give the child the strings of the two balloons. Ask the child to tell you what color the balloon is that is the closest to him.
2. Give the child the other two balloons. Ask the child to tell you what color the balloon is that is the farthest from him. Record the child's correct responses.
3. Place one of the colored balls/beads on the table close to the child; place the other ball farther away from the child. Ask the child to tell you the color of the ball/bead that is closest to him.
4. Switch the position of the ball/bead and ask the child which one is the farthest from him.
5. Record the child's responses.
6. Place both pieces of colored yarn on the table, about 18 inches apart. Place one of the colored balls closer to one of the yarn pieces than the other.
7. Ask the child which color of yarn the red ball is closest to.
8. Repeat, using which is the farthest.
9. Record the child's responses and compare to the above.

Credit: + Child makes judgments in distance, indicating which item is closest to or farther from the them.

Adaptations
Some children may have difficulty making judgments about distances because they easily misunderstand the language of distance, e.g., words such as: near, nearer, nearest, far, farther, farthest, close, closer, closest, etc. These words are abstract in nature and need to be demonstrated for comprehension and practical application. If the child is having problems with these words, allow him to have experiences in which he hears the words used (e.g., I am putting this box "close" to the ball.) Provide the child with the opportunity to manipulate items (e.g., ask the child to place the ball close to the book), and describe what has occurred (e.g., ask the child to tell you about the objects - prompt if necessary - "The ball is _____ to the box."). Provide the child many opportunities to interact with distances and judgment decisions.

1.292 Reads numerals to 19
Strand: 1-10 **Age:** 60-66m 5.0-5.6y

Definition
The child will say a number between 0 - 19 when shown a number randomly.

Assessment Materials
Prepare number cards or cut-out numbers from 0 - 19. The numbers should be at least 2 inches high. Paper and pencils or markers.

Assessment Procedures
Grouping: This skill should be assessed one-on-one with the child.
1. Ask the child to join you at a table. Tell the child that you are going to show her a number and that she is to tell you what the number is.
2. Using the number cards, show her 5, 17, 3, 8, 12, 19, 7, 10, 1, 4, 16. Record any numbers that the child did not get right.
3. Talk to the child about her performance so far, praising her for on task behavior.
4. Using the number cards, show her 13, 18, 2, 6, 11, 15, 9, 14. Record any numbers that the child did not get right.

Credit: + Child reads numbers 0 – 19 when presented randomly.

Adaptations
Some children have a hard time retaining visual symbols; they may reverse part of the number, or graphically misjudge shapes. To assist these children in mastering the correct visual image, begin instruction with direct visual matching, using templates, and patterning the formation of the numbers and kinesthetic techniques.

1.293 Sings verse of a new song by rote
Strand: 2-7 **Age:** 66-78m 5.6-6.6y

Definition
The child will learn at least one verse of a new song by rote. Teaching a song by rote can be defined in two ways: (1) Teaching a song by singing one line at a time and repeating the lines as they are introduced. Note: Teaching every new song using the "line-by-line" approach may create a negative reaction because a child does not hear or learn a song as a total entity; therefore, learning a new song is fragmented and may become a dreaded process. Using the line rote approach is effective in teaching him how to pronounce the words and for putting the melody with the words; (2) Teaching a song by the whole method. This approach allows him to sing along with words or phrases that are easy to remember. The phrases become cumulative, and he learns entire songs with enthusiasm.

Assessment Materials
A song the child does not know. In selecting a new song, consider: the subject matter, the words that are within his understanding and interests, the length of the song, and a song that has a repeated word pattern.

Assessment Procedures
Grouping: This skill should be assessed one-on-one with the child.
1. Tell the child that you are going to sing a new song. Tell him the title of the song. Briefly discuss what the song is about and any other characteristics pertaining to its content.
2. Read him the words, slowly and clearly. Emphasize the repeated phrases, key words and word patterns.
3. Ask him to listen carefully.
4. Sing the new song for him.
5. Repeat it several times.
6. Invite him to join in singing the song, even if he doesn't know all the words or the tune.
7. Sing the song again, and encourage him to sing along.
8. When he has learned the song fairly well, sing along quietly or silently so that he can hear himself; this enhances his ability to carry the tune alone. If he hesitates, provide support by singing strongly.
9. Observe him to determine if he feels successful in learning the new song.
10. Be positive about his achievement level, and stress the importance of having a pleasant singing experience.

Credit: + Child sings at least one verse of a new song by rote. The song can be taught one line at a time or by singing the whole song.

Adaptations
Some children have a problem remembering words, phrases, and sounds they hear. When these children are expected to recall words to a new song and its melody, they become frustrated and do not attend to the task. When they focus on the words of the song, the tune is blocked, and when they attend to the tune the words are blocked. To assist a child who has this problem: (1) Use visuals to provide cues to the words; (2) Teach him the words by speaking them, not singing them; (3) Use the line-by-line rote approach; (4) Teach to over-achievement;

(5) Teach the words first; (6) Provide many different opportunities for him to practice the new song in natural settings. Having a tape of the song is helpful because the child can then listen to it over and over; (7) Make the experience positive, not a laborious task. Teaching him a love of singing is the issue; the number of songs he knows should not be as important.

1.294 Prints all letters of the alphabet correctly, without models

Strand: 1-11   **Age:** 68-78m 5.8-6.6y

Definition
The child will print all letters of the alphabet using lined paper and a comfortable writing tool. The letters will be both upper and lower case. The letters should be legible, positioned on the paper correctly, with correct stroke sequence and a common stroke pressure.

Assessment Materials
A model of upper and lower case manuscript letters in alphabetical order. Lined paper for the child and a pencil.

Assessment Procedures
Grouping: This skill can be introduced and practiced in a group setting. However, when you are ready to assess the child's ability to print all the letters of the alphabet, it is recommended that you do so one-on-one with the child.
1. Tell the child that you want her to write the alphabet starting with Aa. Give the child a sheet of paper and a pencil.
2. On the top line of the paper, write the letter Aa, explaining to the child that you want her to write the letter Bb next to the Aa. Point to the space that the child is to write the Bb. After the child has written the Bb, point to where she should write the Cc. Continue until you get to the letter Ff.
3. Tell the child to complete all the rest of the letters.
4. If the child successfully writes the alphabet, date her paper and place it in her writing folder.
5. Observe the child as she is working. If she has a problem recalling the next letter, tell her the letter, and pause to see if she can write it. If she is unable to write it, tell her to go on to the next letter which is ____.
6. Allow enough time for the child to complete the assignment.
7. If the child completes some letters of the alphabet but needs reminders for others, indicate that verbal prompting occurred (note the letters that were prompted). Make a notation of the letters she could not form properly, date her paper, and place it in her folder.
8. At any point where the child is unable to continue, thank her for her efforts.
9. Show her the alphabet model, point to the letters that were a problem to her, and then ask her to write those letters.
10. Indicate on the paper that a model was shown to assist her in completing the assessment.

Credit: + Child prints all the letters, both upper and lower case, from memory on lined paper. The letters are legible, positioned correctly, and were made with the correct stroke sequences.

Adaptations
Children who have problems in writing letters from memory usually do not have a problem with the writing of the letters, but recalling the letters when they are presented in different configurations. They can copy the letters and can say letter names when they see them, especially when the letters are in an order. To assist the child in visual memory, all letters should be clear and have well-defined lines. The models should be written in black, with adequate space between each letter, and should be viewed by the child on the same plane and in close relationship to her paper. The child should have access to an alphabet model until proficiency has been achieved. It is often beneficial for her to work from recognition, to partial recall, to total recall. Example: she is asked to recall and write the letter H. The first requirement is to see and work with the entire letter, then with only a partial part of the letter, and finally to revisualize it without external assistance.

1.295 Prints simple words without a model

Strand: 1-11   **Age:** 68-78m 5.8-6.6y

Definition
The child will print in manuscript form at least three simple words. The words should not have more than three letters (cat, dog, run, it, to).

The words should be printed on lined paper with a pencil or similar writing tool. The words should be readable and based on a line. The strokes should be consistent and even, with appropriate spacing between letters, and the size/width of letters should be in proportion. The child will write the words on request.

Assessment Materials
Writing paper and pencils. A list of words that are meaningful to the child, such as the names of people, places, and things which he is familiar with, and a listing of linguistic word families (cat, pat, mat). A sheet of paper and a pencil.

Assessment Procedures
Grouping: This skill should be assessed one-on-one with the child.

1. Point to a line on the paper and ask the child to write his first name.
2. Tell the child that you are going to ask him to write another word. Explain that he should listen to the word very carefully.
3. Say one three-letter word that is familiar to the child. Example: a friend's name, a pet's name, a favorite toy, a town name, etc.
4. Ask the child to write the word.
5. Tell the child that you are going to ask him to write another word. Say one three-letter linguistic family word (cat). Ask the child to write the word.
6. Say another three-letter (same linguistic family) word that requires a different beginning letter (hat).
7. Repeat with another three-letter linguistic word.
8. Change the linguistic family and ask him to write three more words.
9. If the child successfully writes the words, reward him and place his first "Word Writing" paper in his folder.
10. If the child was unsuccessful in writing the words, print the word on a sheet of paper.
11. Tell the child the word, then point to and name each letter of the word.
12. Allow the child a chance to repeat the word and name each letter.
13. Remove the sheet of paper with the word on it and ask the child to write the word.
14. Repeat with the other words.
15. After the child has watched the word being written, read the word, named the letters, and written the word without a model, say the first word again and ask him to write it.
16. If the child was successful in writing the words, reward him and place his practice paper and his final paper in his folder.

Credit: + Child prints at least three simple words, which are no longer than three letters, on request from memory.

Adaptations
Writing words is a skill in which there is only one pattern or arrangement of letters that is acceptable. Some children have a difficult time writing words because they lack the visual memory to reproduce without seeing a model. Other children have a problem when asked to write a word, due to the fact that the task requires only encoding. The opportunity to draw upon other cues is greatly reduced. To assist the children who find writing a word in isolation a problem, the following are helpful strategies: (1) Make sure that the child is able to recognize and pronounce the words that he is trying to write; (2) Present the words that the child is asked to write in a systematic manner, such as linguistic families and CVC patterns; (3) Incorporate tracing, listening, drawing, copying, and finally writing from memory; (4) Give the child a stem (it) and have him form words by beginning consonant substitution; (5) Ask the child to fill in the missing letters of a word, then phase out the letter placement, requiring the child to write the complete word.

1.296 Plays rhythm instruments in various rhythm patterns
Strand: 2-7 **Age:** 68-78m 5.8-6.6y

Definition
The child will play an instrument that is familiar to her using a song that changes rhythmic patterns, and she will change rhythm patterns with the music.

Assessment Materials
Collection of rhythm instruments. Prerecorded or live music that changes in rhythmic patterns. Equipment to play music.

Assessment Procedures
Grouping: This skill can be introduced, practiced and assess either in a group setting or one-on-one with the child.

1. Ask the child to choose a rhythm instrument she has played before and that she likes to play.
2. Give her some time to practice and explore playing the instrument.

3. Ask her to listen to some music and then to play her instrument along with the music.
4. Play the music. Observe her as she plays along with the music.
5. Let her choose another rhythm instrument familiar to her and repeat.
6. If she displays uncertainty playing the instrument or keeping the rhythm, stop the assessment.
7. Give her time to explore using the instruments on her own.
8. Let her discover that playing certain instruments in certain ways creates different sounds. (A drum makes a different sound when it is hit by a hand instead of a stick. A rattle makes a different sound when it is shaken in the air instead of hit against a body.)
9. After allowing her adequate practice playing the instrument, say, "I am going to play some music; use the [tambourine] to keep time to the music."
10. Play the music.
11. Observe him, reinforce for effort, creativity, the ability to change rhythms, enjoyment, and exploration.

Credit: + Child plays a familiar instrument to a song that has various rhythm patterns, changing rhythm patterns with the music.

Adaptations

Children who have difficulty playing rhythm instruments may have problems in one or more of the following: (1) Maintaining attention; (2) Coordinating fine motor skill with auditory reception; (3) Doing two things at one time; (4) Dealing with frustration; (5) Being overly stimulated.

To help the child stay on the task, keep the listening time and the playing time short. To deal with the integration of multiple tasks, clap a simple beat for her to accompany instead of a musical selection. To deal with a child who becomes frustrated and begins to react with inappropriate behavior, stop the activity immediately. Try to involve her in a different music experience, such as listening to a lullaby or an instrumental ballad, humming a familiar song, or moving to a soft, gliding presentation. For these children, creativity, patience, understanding, and guidance, plus a wide variety of musical activities, will enhance and broaden their music participation and appreciation.

1.297 (Removed, see page xviii)

1.298 Answers questions about a story related to the interpretation of the content
Strand: 1-9   **Age:** 60-72m   5.0-6.0y

Definition
After hearing a story, the child will be able to answer questions that relate to the interpretation of the content. Typically the questions are based on making predictions, inferences, comparisons and generalizations. A prediction type of question is one that requires the child to assimilate some details, think ahead and guess the outcome. (What do you think will happen next?) An inference type of question requires the child to use deductive reasoning. (If Jane did____what do you think Bill will do?) A comparison question requires the child to examine the things that are similar and the things that are different and draw conclusions. (At the beginning of the story Jean was not happy, what happened to change Jean's feelings?) A generalization question is one that requires the child to take bits of information and put them together to reach a decision. (Why did the lady decide to go?)

Assessment Materials
Select or write a short story. The story should not be something that the child has heard before. It should also contain vocabulary that the child is familiar with and events that are within the child's experiences.
Example: Alice Plays With Her Doll
1. One day Alice was playing outside.
2. She was playing with her best doll.
3. Alice made a bed for her doll.
4. She made the bed in deep, deep grass.
5. She put the doll in the bed and covered her up.
6. Soon a dark cloud covered up the sun.
7. Alice felt a drop of water on her arm.
8. She jumped up and ran for the house.
9. All of a sudden Alice remembered her doll.
10. She got a umbrella and went after her doll.
11. Alice and her doll were both dry in the house.

Assessment Procedures
Grouping: This skill should be assessed one-on-one with the child.
1. Read the story to the child. Explain that you are going to ask the child some questions about the story.
2. Re-read sentences 1 and 2.

© 2010 VORT Corporation. All rights reserved. Do Not copy.

3. Say, "Alice was playing with her best doll. What do you think her best doll looked like?"
4. Re-read sentence 3. Say, "Can you think of anything else Alice could have done with her doll?"
5. Re-read sentences 4 and 5. Say, "How do you suppose this doll bed was different than the one the doll had in the house?"
6. Re-read sentences 7 and 8. Say, "Why do suppose Alice ran for the house?"
7. Re-read sentence 9. Say, " What might have happened if Alice had not remembered her doll?"
8. Re-read sentence 10. Say, "If Alice had not been able to find her umbrella, what could she have done?"
9. Re-read sentence 11. Say, "Why was the doll dry?"
10. Say, "What do think Alice and her doll are going to do now?"
11. Say, "Do you think this story took place in the winter? Why or Why not?"
12. Since many of these questions have no right or wrong answers, it is helpful to make any annotations relative to the child's responses.

Credit: + Child correctly answers questions related to a novel story that has just been read relating to the interpretation of the content (making predictions, inferences, comparisons, and generalizations).

Adaptations

In order to be able to interpret what an author is saying in a story, the child must be able to understand the meaning of the words, have a background of related experiences, and have a reasonable attention span. If a character in the story is running in a meadow, and the child doesn't know what the word meadow means, she will be unable to answer an interpretive question such as; "How would you feel if you were in a meadow?" If the story the child heard was about riding on a subway, and the child had never had that experience, it would be difficult for her to make any inferences or comparisons dealing with subway questions. And if the child has any problems staying on task, she may miss some of the elements of "listening between the lines." Making sure that the words and experiences in the selected stories are relevant to the child is extremely important when moving from literal to interpretative listening comprehension.

1.299 Names numbers that represent more than and less than

Strand: 1-10 **Age:** 70-78m 5.10-6.6y

Definition
When the child is presented with a number, he will say a number that is more than and less than that number. When presented with a group of objects the child will create more objects and create less objects. The child will identify the number of beginning objects, the number added that makes more and the number taken away that makes less.

Assessment Materials
Collect at least 10 small objects, such as beans, buttons, plastic chips, beads, etc. Locate three containers.

Assessment Procedures
Grouping: This skill should be assessed one-on-one with the child.
1. Explain to the child that you are going to say a number and then you are going to ask a question about the number. Inform the child that he is to listen carefully.
2. Say, "The number is six. Tell me a number that is more than six."
3. Pause for the child's response.
4. Say, "Tell me a number that is less than six."
5. Pause for the child's response.
6. Continue with at least four more numbers. The numbers should be between two and 18.
7. Record the child's answers.
8. Select one of the containers and place six objects in it. Ask the child to count the objects and to tell you how many there are in the box.
9. Give the child the second container with the rest of the objects in it. Say, "Yes, there are four buttons in this box."
10. Ask the child to take buttons from the second box and add them to the first box to make more buttons.
11. Say, "How many buttons did you add to your box?" Wait for his response.
12. Then ask, "How many buttons do you have now?" Wait for his response.
13. Record the child's answers.
14. Say, "Make less buttons in your box and tell me how many you have left."
15. Pause for the child's response.
16. Say, "How many buttons did you take away?"
17. Pause for the child's response.
18. Record the child's answer.

Credit: + 1. Child names number between two and 18, indicating which number is more than and less than a given number. 2. When given a group of objects, the child creates groupings that are more than and less than a given number. 3. The child identifies the number of objects he has, and then identifies the number of objects he needs to add or take away in order to produce a particular number that was asked for. The child needs to correctly demonstrate all three tasks in order to receive credit.

Adaptations

Often children understand the terms "more" and "less" when presented in one setting, such as having more popcorn or having less crackers than another. But when that child is confronted with the same terms ("more" and "less") in a different situation, he is unable to transfer the concepts. Remediation of this problem depends upon determining exactly what terms are not understood by the child. After the terms have been identified, a strategy of comparison is often helpful, like comparing more popcorn (seven popped kernels to six kernels), and comparing less popcorn (five popped kernels to six kernels).

1.300 Counts orally to 100

Strand: 1-10 **Age:** 70-78m 5.10-6.6y

Definition

The child will count orally from 1 - 100 when requested.

Assessment Materials

Secure a jar large enough to hold 100 items, such as beans, buttons, marbles, etc. Collect 100 items.

Assessment Procedures

Grouping: This skill should be assessed one-on-one with the child.

1. Invite the child to join you at the table. Place the empty jar and a container with the 100 items in it on the table
2. Explain to the child that you want her to take one object at a time and put it in the jar.
3. Explain that she is to count the objects as she drops them in the jar.
4. Continue by telling the child that you will tell her the number that she is to start with.
5. Begin by saying, "I want you to start counting with the number one and count as far as you can up to 100."
6. Observe the child as she counts. If she appears to need a break, you can stop her, let her rest and then reminder her where she left of counting and ask her to begin from there.
7. Continue to observe the child as she counts, noting numbers missed or repeated.
8. If the child is having difficulty, prompt as needed. If the child is unable to rote count to 50, request that she stop, and record the last number she counted successfully.
9. Observe the child as she counts to 100. Prompt as needed and stop the process if the child becomes frustrated or cannot reach 100.
10. Record the responses.

Credit: + Child counts orally to 100 without prompting.

Adaptations

Counting from 1 - 100 may require too much sustained attention. If a child displays a short attention span, she may appear to be off-task or give the impression that the activity is beyond her capabilities. If this disorganization occurs or if the child appears to be distracted, it is important to reduce the required counting to smaller units. Ask her to use counters and to count from, for example, 1 - 20, or cluster 10 sticks in a package and have her count one package starting from 1, request that she count another package starting with 11, etc. Be sure to allow the child "breaks" from the activity, making sure to record where she left off before the break and where she needs to start.

1.301 Reads and writes numerals to 49

Strand: 1-10 **Age:** 70-78m 5.10-6.6y

Definition

Using paper and a marker, the child will write the numbers from 1 - 49. The child will say a number when shown in random order (e.g., point to 14, 26, and 9) upon request.

Assessment Materials

Prepare two worksheets. Each paper has a series of numbers and blanks, such as: 0, 1, 2, ___, 4, ___ 6, 7, ___, ___, 10, ___, ___, 12, ___13, 14, 15, ___, 17, ___, 18, 19, ___, (continue to number up to 50). This will be the first worksheet. Make a second worksheet that is the opposite of the first paper, it will have a blank where there was a number and a number where there was a blank.

Prepare a set of number cards (index cards work well) with one number (1 - 50) per card.

Assessment Procedures

Grouping: This skill should be assessed one-on-one with the child.
1. Give the child the first worksheet with the series of numbers and ask him to fill in the blanks.
2. Allow the child ample time to complete the task; however, if he becomes frustrated, remove the paper and praise him for his efforts.
3. Retain the completed paper as a record of the assessment.
4. Give the child the second worksheet. Ask the child to fill in the blanks.
5. Allow the child ample time to complete the task; however, if he becomes frustrated, remove the paper and verbally reward him for his efforts.
6. Shuffle the number cards. Show the child a number card and ask him to tell you what number it is.
7. Continue with the other number cards.
8. Record the number correctly stated.

Credit: + Child reads and writes the numbers 1 – 49 correctly and without prompting.

Adaptations

Some children may not have reached the level of writing numbers, so they will be preoccupied in the construction of the graphic symbol rather than the sequence of the numbers. To assist those children, it is often helpful to provide a model of the formation of the numbers. These models may have numbered line strokes, color coded cues, stencils, raised figures, etc.

When children are presented with a written number out of sequence, the child may have to sub-vocalize the order in which the number occurs. Example: If the number presented is 22 and the child is unable to name it, he may have to verbally "think" (20, 21, 22, 23) and then will say 22. Or he may have to "think" a visual image of 20, 21, 22, 23, and then say 22.

To help this child, consider repeated exposure to a series of numbers which serve as a model. Demonstrate the second number sequence, 0, 1, 2, 3, 4, etc. and the change of the 10's number (10, 11, 12, 13, - 20, 21, 22, 23, - 30, 31, 32, 33 etc.) and ask the child to place the number cards in sequence and say each number's name.

1.302 Locates day of week on calendar
Strand: 1-13 **Age:** 70-78m 5.10-6.6y

Definition
The child will locate all the days of the week in correct sequence and will locate the days of the week when they are presented out of sequence.

Assessment Materials
A calendar that is large enough for the child to view and point to the days of the week.

Assessment Procedures

Grouping: This skill should be assessed one-on-one with the child.
1. Show the child the calendar and briefly discuss the areas of the calendar.
2. Identify where the days of the week are listed, where the weeks are shown, where the first day of the month is, and where the last day of the month is.
3. Explain to the child that you want her to listen carefully and do what you ask her to.
4. Say, "Point to each day of the week and say the name of the day of the week."
5. If necessary, model how to point to the days of the week while saying the first day (Sunday, Monday).
6. Record the child's response.
7. Say, "Tell me the day of the week that I point to."
8. Point to the days of the week in sequence and then point to the days randomly.
9. Note the child's responses.

Credit: + Child names all the days of the week in correct sequence and will name the days of the week when they are presented out of order, without prompting.

Adaptations

Some children may become confused by the way days of the week are written on different calendars (Mon., Monday, etc.) These children cannot always generalize that different visual configurations mean the same things. It is important that the same spelling be used when the child is first dealing with naming the days of the week. It is also important that the child be able to name the days of the week in order prior to being asked to name them when presented randomly. If the child is unable to name the days of the week in order, assist her by pointing to the days of the week while saying them in order. Ask the child to say each day immediately after you. Repeat until the child can pronounce each day right after you. Start at the beginning of the week and name each day as you point to it. Request that the child say the name right after you; however, stop at the last day and ask the child to name it. Continue requesting that the child name other days in the sequence.

1.303 Uses imaginary objects during play
Strand: 1-12   **Age:** 36-42m   3.0-3.6y

Definition
The child begins to use imaginary objects during play. At first he may use one object in place of the actual object, for example he will use a banana for a telephone. He may also pretend to do something even though he does not have the props, for example he will pretend to serve and eat imaginary food.

Assessment Materials
A selection of toys for playing dress-ups.

Assessment Procedures
Grouping: When you assess a child's ability to use imaginary objects during play, the most effective procedure is play-based observation. An observational assessment can either be spontaneous or occur in a semi-structured situation.
1. If the choice is semi-structured, provide the children with some props and observe what occurs naturally.
2. During the observation, determine if the child uses one object in place of another object or if he pretends to act out something using imaginary items.
3. If the use of imaginary objects does not come up naturally during the play, make a suggestion that they do something, such as feed the babies, even though they do not have bottles, spoons, bowls, etc.
4. Note his response and what imaginary object he incorporated into the play.

Credit: + Child uses imaginary objects during play, either using one object in place of the actual object or pretending to do something even though he does not have the props.

Adaptations
Children learn how to use their imagination by observing other people pretending. Begin to introduce a child to simple pretend play experiences. Pretend that you need to make a telephone call, but you have no telephone. Pick up a banana or a block and pretend to dial and speak on the telephone. If necessary, explain to the child that you are "just pretending" to make a phone call. Encourage the child to join in. When opportunities arise during play, or when the child wants to do something but does not have the appropriate props, suggest that he use something else in place of that object. Eventually, pretend to do something even though you have no props. Pretend to cook while playing in the sandbox and "just pretend" to eat what you have made. Involve the child in your pretend play.

1.304 Uses dolls or action figures to act out sequences
Strand: 1-12   **Age:** 36-42m   3.0-3.6y

Definition
The child uses dolls or action figures to create situations from real life that they act out. The situations should include multiple sequences or steps to the scenario being played out.

Assessment Materials
A variety of dolls, action figures, dollhouse, doll furniture, doll accessories, and miniature objects from everyday life.

Assessment Procedures
Grouping: When you assess a child's ability to use dolls and action figures to act out sequences, the most effective procedure is play-based observation. An observational assessment can either be spontaneous or occur in a semi-structured situation.
1. If the choice is semi-structured, provide the children with dolls, action figures, a dollhouse and other materials they may use when playing with dolls and observe what occurs naturally.
2. During the observation, determine if the child is able to act out sequences from real life experiences. This might be done on their own or with another child.
3. If the child does not spontaneously begin playing with the dolls/action figures, take a doll and begin acting out a scene for the child to watch.
4. When the child shows interest in what you are doing, incorporate them into the sequences by giving them a doll or an action figure and engage them in the process.
5. Act out simple sequences such as having the doll/action figures walk into the kitchen of the dollhouse and announce, "Boy, I am hungry! I wonder what I could eat?" Sit the doll/action figures at the table and invite the

child's doll or action figure to join your doll for a meal.
6. Include the child in a conversation about what their doll or action figure likes to eat, how they might prepare that food, and what they will do when they finish eating.
7. Once the child seems comfortable, begin backing out of the play and observe whether the child can sustain the play either by himself or with another child.
8. Note his response and what sequences are incorporated into the play.

Credit: + Child uses dolls or action figures to create situations from real life that they act out using multiple sequences to the action.

Adaptations

The issue of whether boys should play with dolls is a common question or concern raised by parents and school staff. Developmentally speaking, dolls and action figures serve the same purpose. Children learn how to respond to different situations through their play and by imitating the people they are around most frequently, like their parents and teachers. Doll/action figure play takes on an important role in a child trying on or experimenting with being different people (such as the mother, father, teacher, doctor, etc.) Using dolls/action figures during play gives children a fun opportunity to work on their imitation skills, expressive and receptive language skills, and social interactions. Practice with dolls/action figures will help improve their social interactions with others. If there is a concern about a boy using dolls that are not obvious action figures (such as superhero figures), incorporate vehicles and blocks in the play so the child can construct a building and have their doll or action figure be the boss of the construction site. Act out common scenes from school or home using the dolls/action figures so the child can experience taking on the role of someone else.

1.305 Role-plays or organizes other children using props

Strand: 1-12 **Age:** 60-72m 5.0-6.0y

Definition

While engaged in pretend play the child organizes other children to use props while they role-play some event they have previously observed or experienced. The child orchestrates the role-playing event.

Assessment Materials

Dramatic play area with dress-up clothing, a kitchen area, and props used in the kitchen.

Assessment Procedures

Grouping: When you assess a child's ability to role-play and organize other children using props, the most effective procedure is play-based observation. An observational assessment can either be spontaneous or occur in a semi-structured situation.

1. If the choice is semi-structured, invite the children to the dramatic play area and encourage them to play.
2. During the observation, determine if the child takes on the lead and organizes the other children in role-playing some situation they have experienced in real life.
3. If the child does not spontaneously begin role-playing and organizing the other children, provide some verbal prompts to help set up the play scene. For example, suggest that the child be the mother, another child be the father, a third child be the baby, and the fourth child be the mail carrier.
4. Suggest that mother needs to prepare a package for the mail carrier to pick up and she needs everyone's help.
5. See if she can direct the father to do something to help prepare the package.
6. If she cannot, verbally prompt her by telling her what props might be helpful in this situation.
7. Do the same thing with the baby and the mail carrier.
8. Provide encouragement, but step back to allow the child the opportunity to take over and direct the play and use of the props as soon as they are comfortable.
9. Continue to observe the child, note the themes and props they pick for their performance.

Credit: + Child engages in role-playing and organizes other children using props during their play.

Adaptations

Role-playing provides a child with the opportunity to link related schemes into a sequence to tell a story. A child can be encouraged to link schemes from everyday life. The schemes will start off simple (stirring a cup) and become more complex (acting out the nighttime routine at home). Learning to sequence events will help a child learn how to tell a story with a beginning, middle, and end. It will lead to the ability to conceptualize time.

Allow the child to assume the role of another person performing a task that has a specific sequence of events. For example, ask the child to be the teacher and to run the morning circle. See if he follows the sequence of events, such as saying "Good morning" to everyone; singing songs; counting how many children are present; and reviewing the calendar, including what month it is, the days of the week, and determining the date. As you go through sequences during the day, pause to see if the child knows what will come next. Encourage him to use props to act out frequently occurring events during the day.

1.306 Prints the numbers 1 - 10 correctly, in sequential and random order, when requested without the use of a model

Strand: 1-11 **Age:** 68-80m 5.8-6.8y

Definition
The child will print the numbers 1 – 10, in sequential and random order, when dictated by an adult without the use of models. The child will use lined paper and a comfortable writing tool. The numbers should be legible, positioned on the paper correctly, with correct stroke sequence and a common stroke pressure.

Assessment Materials
Lined paper for the child and a pencil. A model of the numbers 1 – 10 in numerical order.

Assessment Procedures
Note: A child needs to be stable when sitting at a table, with their feet resting flat on the floor or placed on a footrest.
Grouping: This skill should be assessed one-on-one with the child.
1. Give the child a sheet of paper and a pencil. Tell the child you want him to write some numbers.
2. Begin by requesting the numbers in numerical order.
3. If the child successfully writes the numbers, date his paper and place it in his writing folder.
4. Next, request the numbers in random order.
5. Allow enough time for the child to complete each number.
6. Observe the child as he is working. If he has a problem recalling the number you requested, show him the number model, pointing to the number.
7. If the child completes the numbers, but has difficulty writing certain numbers, make a notation of the numbers he had difficulty forming, and indicate if visual prompting occurred. Place this note in his file.
8. At any point when the child is unable to continue, thank him for his efforts and stop the assessment.
9. Show him the number model, point to the numbers that were a problem for him, and then ask him to write those numbers.

Credit: + Child prints the number 1 – 10, in sequential and random order, when requested without the use of a model.

Adaptations
Children who have difficulty writing their numbers from memory may need help with visual memory skills. To assist the child with their visual memory skills, you should write all numbers clearly, with well-defined lines. The models should be written in black ink and have adequate space between each number. Provide the child with a number line or number model until they demonstrate proficiency in writing their numbers.

1.307 Locates left and right
Strand: 1-4D **Age:** 48-60m 4.0-5.0y

Definition
The child will indicate his right hand/foot upon request. The child will indicate his left hand/foot upon request.

Assessment Materials
A chair.

Assessment Procedures
Grouping: This skill should be assessed one-on-one with the child.
1. Ask the child to sit on the chair.
2. Standing behind the child, ask him to raise his right hand.
3. If the child is unable to raise the correct hand or is overly hesitant, prompt him by touching his right shoulder.
4. Standing behind the child, ask him to raise his left hand.
5. If the child is unable to raise his left hand or is overly hesitant, prompt him by touching his left shoulder.
6. Note the child's response and if prompting was necessary.
7. Repeat the above with no prompting.
8. Facing the child, ask him to raise his left hand.
9. Facing the child, ask him to raise his right hand.

10. Note the child's response and indicate any hesitancy.
11. Continue by asking the child to point to his left leg/foot, and then his right leg/foot.

Credit: + Child correctly indicates his right hand/foot and left hand/foot upon request.

Adaptations

Some children often confuse spatial relations such as front/back and left/right. To assist children in spatial concepts it is important to demonstrate the direction and to verbalize what is occurring. Example: Put a block in front of a box and say, "I am putting a block in front of this box." Ask the child to stand in back of or in front of an object and ask "John, are you standing in front of or in back of the toy?" Continue by using the directionality of standing on the left side of the toy and standing on the right side of the toy. It is important when dealing with left and right that the instructor be on the same body plane as the children (standing beside, not in front, when modeling).

1.308 Draws diagonal lines, copying model

Strand: 1-11 **Age:** 52-60m 4.4-5.0y

Definition

The child will copy a right-to-left diagonal line from a model. Then she will copy a left-to-right diagonal line from a model.

Assessment Materials

Sheets of white paper, a black marker, pencil or crayon, a diagonal template, chalkboard, chalk, Q-tips or straws.

Assessment Procedures

Grouping: This skill should be assessed one-on-one with the child.

1. Ask the child to join you at the table. Explain that you are going to draw a line called a diagonal line.
2. After making the right to left diagonal line, discuss the configuration of the line. Explain to her that the line begins at the top and slants to the left. As you make the line, explain your movements.
3. Provide her with a sheet of paper and a writing tool. Say, "Draw a diagonal line like this," as you point to the model of the right to left diagonal.
4. Give her enough time to complete the line.
5. Observe her as she makes the line.
6. Explain that you are going to draw another line that is also called a diagonal line, but that it goes from left to right.
7. After making the left to right diagonal line, discuss the configuration of the line. Explain that the line begins at the bottom and slants to the right. As you make the line, explain your movements.
8. Provide her with a sheet of paper and a writing tool. Say, "Draw a diagonal line like this," as you point to the model of the left to right diagonal.
9. Give her enough time to complete the line.
10. Observe her as she makes the line.
11. If she has difficulty making the diagonal (left/right or right/left) lines, the following activities are suggested before you reassess her: (1) A tactile experience may be helpful. Show her how to make horizontal, vertical, and diagonal lines by lying on the floor, standing tall, and leaning on the wall. Draw models on a chalkboard to show lines that go across, lines that go up and down, and lines that are slanted; (2) Draw several lines (horizontal, vertical, diagonal), and point out the diagonal lines to the child. Remove the models and then draw more lines, asking her to clap each time that you draw a slanted or a diagonal line; (3) Give her a box of several small sticks, such as Q-tips or straws, and a sheet of paper with diagonal lines drawn on it. Ask her to place the sticks on the pre-drawn lines; (4) Ask her to trace over pre-drawn or dotted diagonal lines; (5) Provide her with a diagonal template to trace; (6) Provide physical assistance by placing your hand over her hand to guide her in making diagonal lines.

Credit: + Child draws diagonal lines from a model, without help.

Adaptations

Drawing diagonal lines may be a frustrating experience for some children, especially those who have difficulty with visual-motor control. Drawing a diagonal line requires more motor control and more detailed visual perceptual skills than drawing vertical or horizontal lines. In forming a diagonal line, a child may have a tendency to make the lines inconsistent or in a "reclining" position. Also, she may exert excess pressure on the pencil and lose control, causing the line to go off the track. To assist her with eye-hand control, begin your efforts with kinesthetic activities. Provide the child with a dotted shape and ask her to join the dots together. A ruler or a template gives the child a stabilizing method for making the diagonal lines.

1.309 Locates self in relation to other objects

Strand: 1-4D **Age:** 60-78m 5.0-6.6y

Definition
When the child is asked to take a position in relationship to another object or person, he will move to that position. Examples: If he is asked to stand on the left side of the chair, he will move to that position. If he is asked to turn right, he will make the correct turn.

Assessment Materials
An object, such as a chair, a table, or stacking blocks. Chalk.

Assessment Procedures
Note: If the child is unable to identify his left and/or right hand, postpone this assessment.
Grouping: This skill should be assessed one-on-one with the child.

1. Ask the child to hold up his left hand. Ask him to hold up his right hand.
2. Ask him to point to your right hand. Ask him to point to your left hand.
3. Place the chair in such a way that leaves space on the right side and the left side.
4. Ask the child to go to the chair, to stand in front of it, and then to stand on the left side of it.
5. Note his response.
6. Ask him to go to the chair, to stand in front of it and then to stand on the right side of it.
7. Note his response.
8. Ask him to take four steps, turn right and go four steps, and stop.
9. Note his response.
10. Ask him to take four steps, turn left and go four steps, and stop.
11. Note his response.
12. If he is able to identify his and your right and left hands but has difficulty either standing on the correct side of the chair or turning correctly, the following is recommended: (1) When you ask him to go to the chair and stand on the right side, walk with him to the chair, stop in front, and ask him to hold up his right hand. Ask him to use his right hand and point to the right side of the chair, and to move to the right side of the chair. Repeat the above, only ask him to move to the left side of the chair; (2) Use chalk to place an R on the right side of the chair and a L on the left side. Tell him that the R stands for right side and the L stands for left side. Ask him to go to the chair, hold up his right hand and move to the letter R. Then tell him that he is standing on the right side of the chair. Continue using the left side of the chair. If he has a problem moving to his left or his right, the following is recommended: (1) Using a water-base marker or chalk, place an X on the floor. On the left side of the X put an arrow going left with the letter L written beside it. On the right side of the X put an arrow going right with the letter R written beside it. Tell him to walk to the X and turn right; explain that he should follow the arrow that has the R beside it. Walk with him, if necessary. Repeat using the arrow moving left and the letter L; (2) Ask him to hold his left arm out in front of him, elbow bent. After he has his arm in position, ask him which arm he has in front of him. Tell him to walk forward until you tell him to turn left, and then he must turn the direction in which his arm is extended; demonstrate, if necessary. Repeat with the right arm, walking and turning right. After he has participated in these lower skill levels, repeat the assessment above and note his response.

Credit: + Child locate himself in relation to other objects.

Adaptations
Note: Directionality and orientation are important to his school experience (e.g., paper/pencil tasks, physical activities, classroom games) and his everyday experiences.

Understanding his position in space may be difficult for a child. This understanding includes a knowledge of the various parts of his body in relationship to other parts of the body, and it also includes the relation of these parts to the environment. He must have the ability to relate himself to a fixed point. This point is a part of his body (left hand/right hand), or it may be perceived by him as space outside his body (standing on the left side of the table). Sometimes this orientation develops slowly, is inconsistent, related to body imagery, affects judgment, and creates frustration and embarrassment. To assist him, make him aware of both sides of his body and how they relate to directions in space. It is often helpful to ask him to close his eyes and then touch him on his left hand. Then ask him to raise the hand that was touched and to open his eyes and point to the part that was touched. To help him understand his position in space, ask him to close his eyes, listen for a sound, and then turn his head toward the sound. Ask him to open his eyes and look toward the source of the sound. Cueing is also important: put a green dot on his left hand and a red dot on his right hand. Then give simple directions (e.g., Hold up your left hand, put your right hand on top of your head, etc.) As soon as he becomes comfortable with the manipulation of his right and left hands, expand the concept to include position-in-space directions (e.g., Step forward and turn left. Walk to the chair and turn right. etc.)

1.310 Uses left and right to direct others in concrete situation

Strand: 1-4D **Age:** 68-78m 5.8-6.6y

Definition
The child will give others directions using the terminology "left" and "right." Example: "Go past the door, turn right, and go straight ahead; when you come to the window, go left." She will give directions that relate to concrete experiences and situations. The left and right directions will have to do with a person's relationship to the spatial world and her orientation to other objects and persons and not to sides of a body.

Assessment Materials
A sheet of white paper, ruler, markers, a toy car, masking tape.
On the sheet of paper, draw a simple map that includes streets, corners, houses, stores, etc. (Map should be drawn so that a toy mini-car can go down a street, turn left, turn right, etc.)

Assessment Procedures
Grouping: This skill should be assessed one-on-one with the child.
1. Place the map and the toy car on a table. Ask the child to take the toy car and "drive" it up and down the streets, turning at corners, etc.
2. After she has ample time to play with the car and the map, tell her that you want to drive the car but ask her to tell you where to go.
3. As an instructional procedure, "drive" the car down a road and when you come to an intersection, ask her whether you should turn left or right.
4. Continue until she begins to give you directions before you ask.
5. Explain to her that you are going to drive down a street and that you want her to tell you the direction to turn the car.
6. Observe as she gives directions.
7. If she has difficulty giving directions, the following is recommended to lower the task level: (1) Reverse roles: ask the child to drive the car and you give the directions; (2) At the intersections on the map, mark an L for a left turn and an R for a right turn. Tell the child to drive the car and when you say, "turn left," she must turn her car toward the L. When you say, "turn right," she must turn her car toward the R; (3) Place masking tape on the floor that duplicates the streets on the map. Tell her to pretend that she is a car and drive down the street. Explain that you will tell her which direction to turn when she comes to an intersection. After she has a turn being the car, exchange places with her; you become the driver as she provides the directions.
8. After she has additional practice using the drawn map and the toy car, repeat the assessment above.
9. Observe her responses.

Credit: + Child gives others directions using the terms "right" and "left."

Adaptations
Some children have a difficult time giving left and right directions to others, unless they are actually experiencing the same moves. To visualize a visual-motor action is to understand the direction in which the person will be going and then the left or right turns necessary to achieve the point of destination. A child may be comfortable when she is actually involved in the directional experience, but when left to right orientation in space is dependent on visual recall and imagery, she feels confused and uncertain.

To assist her: (1) Invite her to walk through the concrete situation and verbally echo the movements and directions. For example, say, "I am walking down the hall. I am at the corner of the hall, and I am turning left. I will walk until I get to the clock. I am at the clock; now I will turn right. A few more steps, and I will be at the door. Now I will open the door and turn left to go to the playground." It may be necessary to go with the child and provide the verbalization of what is happening. After she has walked and talked the directional route, ask her to tell you the directions without being there. (2) Provide her with a simple map of a neighborhood, including houses, parks, and stores. Ask her to use her finger to walk through the neighborhood, taking left and right turns. After she takes her finger stroll, ask her to tell your fingers where to go for a walk in the neighborhood. Provide assistance; for instance, when your finger arrives at a cross street, ask her which way you should turn; (3) Ask her to direct someone else to a location that requires only one left or right turn. Gradually add another turn and then another. Giving left to right directions is a lifelong skill and should be considered important; however, a child needs to have reached a developmental level that allows her to recall visually, understand left and right, and be able to clearly express information.

2.101 Names sounds heard in the immediate environment

Strand: 2-1A **Age:** 30-42m 2.6-3.6y

Definition
When the child is presented with known voices or laughs (such as family members, a teacher, a friend, a care provider, cartoon characters, or favorite characters from TV, or a talking toy), the child will name the person. When she is presented with different sounds heard in her environment (the classroom, on a walk, at home, in the car, playing outside, on a picnic, in the park) and is asked to name what made the different sounds, she will be able to respond correctly. When the child is presented with an audio recording of different sounds (animals, transportation, weather, toys), she will name the object or thing that is making the sound.

Assessment Materials
Prepared audio tapes/CDs: Tape/CD One--at least four different animal sounds familiar to the child. Illustrated or cutout and mounted pictures of the animals that are on the tape. (Please note, other categories can also be used such as transportation, weather, or toys.) Tape/CD Two--different sounds in a specific environment, such as the classroom, playground, on a walk, or at home. This tape can easily be made by allowing a tape to run in the identified location. Tape/CD Three—Voices or laughs of people the child is familiar with. Tape or CD player.

Assessment Procedures
Grouping: This skill should be assessed one-on-one with the child.
1. Ask the child to sit at the table across from you. Have Tape One in the tape recorder on the table, and say, "I want you to listen to this tape."
2. Play one sound, and stop the tape. Say, "What animal made that sound?" Prompt the child, if necessary. Rewind the tape/CD and play the first sound again, and stop the tape. Say, "What animal made that sound?"
3. If she responds with the correct answer, continue with the other sounds on the tape. Note her responses.
4. If she was successful with Tape One, move to Tape Two and Tape Three, repeating the above procedure.
5. If she was unsuccessful with Tape One, place the pictures of the animals on the table face-up. Point to each animal and name the animal. Play one sound, and stop the tape. Say, "Point to the animal who made that sound."
6. If she points to the correct animal, continue with the tape, stopping after each sound and asking her to point to the animal picture.
7. If she is unable to point to the animal after she hears the sound, play one sound and stop the tape, hold up the picture of the animal that made the sound and say, "This is the animal that made the sound you heard. This is a [sheep]."
8. Continue with the rest of the animal sounds and pictures. Play one sound, and stop the tape. Say, "Point to the animal that made that sound." If the child points to the correct animal, continue with the tape, stopping after each sound and asking her to point to the animal picture.
9. Note her responses, including the need to drop the assessment task level.
10. Continue with Tape Two.

Credit: + Child correctly identifies different voices and environmental sounds from real life or a recording.

Adaptations
When some children listen to different sounds from an environmental setting (playground, classroom), this could easily create interference of receptive information. This interference comes when one input modality is unable to focus on a single receiving devise (a ball bouncing on the playground) because another bit of auditory information is in the background (a child yelling and someone else skating), or the interference intersects the primary sound the child is concentrating on. When assisting these children, present single sounds prior to any combinations of sounds. When you do offer multiple sounds at once, make sure the sound you want the child to identify is one they are familiar with.

2.102 Performs appropriate action when self pronouns (me, my, mine) are used

Strand: 2-1A **Age:** 32-36m 2.8-3.0y

Definition
Level 1 - When the child is shown an object that he owns, he will say, "Give me my ball." When he has an object that belongs to him and is asked, "Whose ball do you have?" he will respond by saying, "The ball is mine," or "It is mine."
Level 2 - When the child is shown at least two items, he will give one of them to someone else upon request

e.g., the recipient says, "Give me the blue ball." After the recipient receives the blue ball, the recipient will say, "This is my ball." The recipient will then place the balls together and ask the child, "Point to the ball that is mine."

Assessment Materials
At least one item that belongs to the child. Three items familiar to him with different characteristics such as three different colored balls, three different shaped cookies, or three different toys.

Assessment Procedures
Grouping: This skill should be assessed one-on-one with the child.

Formal assessment:
1. Sit beside the child and place the item that belongs to him on the table. Discuss the item and what ownership means.
2. Say, "Give me your [toy]." If the child is reluctant to give up his possession, say, "Give me your [toy] to hold for just a minute," or "Give me your [toy], and I will give it right back."
3. Give the item back and ask the child, "Who does the [toy] belong to?" Pause for him to respond.
4. Observe both his receptive response to you and his expressive response to you.
5. Place the three items on the table in front of the child. Ask him to point to each item as you name and describe it.
6. Repeat this several times, so that he is familiar with the items and how they are different.
7. Say, "Give me the [red ball]."
8. After he has responded, say "This is my [red ball]." Replace the item and ask him, "Point to the red ball that is mine." Pause to allow him to react.
9. Observe him to determine his receptive association with "me," "my" and "mine."
10. Record the individual pronoun use.
11. Repeat the procedure if needed.

Informal assessment:
1. When you are engaged with the child in a cooperative activity, such as painting a picture or building with blocks, ask him to give you an item of needed equipment. Say, for example; "Give me the red paint please," "The blue paint is mine--it is for the sky," or "My little block is next to you, please give it to me."
2. Observe his response to the requests, his use of "me" and the ownership usage of "mine" and "my."

Credit: + Child understands and uses the appropriate action when self pronouns (me, my and mine) are used.

Adaptations
Some children have a problem with the pronouns I, my, mine and me, because the meaning is dependent upon who is speaking the word and under what circumstances. These words may refer either to the child or to another person, depending on the speaker. This receptive switch often results in responses such as, "Me is a boy." The child often comprehends the meaning of these words when he is asked to perform an activity with another, such as, "Show me your ball"; however, when he is asked to respond without an activity, his confusion of reference occurs. To assist such a child: (1) Expose him to a request that requires a physical response ("Give me the round cookie."); (2) Look at a picture of an adult and a child, and say, "Point to the person in this picture who is like me"; (3) Take him on a "my walk," and ask him to point to everything that is his and to tell you that it belongs to him. Give him a receptive lead: point to his cap and say, "This is not my cap. Whose cap is it?" Wait for a response using the word "mine", cue as needed.

2.103 Responds correctly with a non-verbal response or with a single word answer to a stated question
Strand: 2-1A **Age:** 32-38m 2.8-3.2y

Definition
When the child is asked a question concerning a particular concept, she will answer correctly with a nonverbal response (nodding head yes or shaking head no). When asked a simple question (what color is this?) the child will respond correctly with a single word answer.

Assessment Materials
Prepare concrete questions to be answered by the child correctly. Examples: (1) Do you like peas? (2) Do you like ice cream? (3) Do you like to go on picnics? (Questions 1 to 3 can be answered by saying yes or no, or nodding or shaking the head) (4) What color do you like the best? (5) How old are you? (6) Who is your friend? (Questions 4 to 6 can be answered by at least one word.)

Assessment Procedures

Grouping: This skill can be assessed one-on-one with the child. However, you can also informally assess the child by asking her questions during a group activity time.

Level One:
1. Tell the child that you are going to ask her some questions and you want her to answer any way she chooses.
2. Begin by asking the yes/no type questions (1 to 3), and then move to the questions that require single word answers (4 to 6). Note her responses.
3. If she has difficulty with the responses, evaluate the questions to be sure she is capable of answering them.
4. If the questions are within the realm of her knowledge, provide cues to assist her response. Example: (5) How old are you? Ask her to hold up her hand to count out the fingers that show her age. Repeat the question. Count the fingers if necessary. Repeat the question.

Level Two:
5. When you are engaged in a cooperative activity or playing a game, ask the child questions that pertain to the concepts. For example, when putting a puzzle together, ask questions such as, "Where does this piece go?" "Have you put this puzzle together before?" "What do think it will be when we are finished?" Take a piece of the puzzle and put it in a box, and ask her, "Is there a puzzle piece in the box?" Put the puzzle piece under the box, and ask, "Is the puzzle piece in the box?"
6. During game time, give her an item to hide. After she has hidden the object, try to find it. Ask questions such as, "What did you hide?" "Did you hide it by the book?" or "Am I getting close?"
7. During this more informal assessment, note her responses to the questions that are integrated into the activity.

Credit: + Child responds correctly to a question with a nonverbal response, such as nodding her head yes, shaking her head no, or using a single word response.

Adaptations

Some children have misconceptions which are often related to their experience and cognitive development. Without general knowledge, a child may conclude varied answers to questions. Example: Question--"How old are you?" Answer--"I'm not old, I am little." Question--"Do you have a brother?" Answer--"No, I am my brother." These type of answers often indicate a need for varied experiences. And during the experiences, it is important to talk, describe, link, and provide her with a process of networking information to be able to order new events into a thought classification pattern.

2.104 Points to or places an object on top/bottom

Strand: 2-1A **Age:** 32-42m 2.8-3.6y

Definition

When the child is asked, she will point to an object that has been placed in a spatial position (e.g., "Point to the ball that is on top of the box.") When the child is asked, she will place an object in a spatial position (e.g., "Put your shoes at the bottom of the stairs.")

Assessment Materials

Box (such as a shoe box) and several blocks.

Assessment Procedures

Grouping: This skill should be assessed one-on-one with the child.
1. Place a box and a block on a table in front of the child. Demonstrate how you can move the block in different positions, relative to the box. Include in the demonstration the concepts listed.
2. Explain to the child that you are going to ask her to place the block in different places around the box. Provide the child with a sample activity. For example, say, "(Name of child), take the block and put it on top of the box."
3. Reward the child for a correct response and explain that you will be telling her other places to put the block.
4. Continue giving the child directions using the other spatial position words, such as, "Put the block at the bottom of the shelf."
5. Note the child's responses.

Credit: + Child correctly points to or places an object on top/bottom when asked.

Adaptations

Some children lack sufficient fine motor skills to manipulate the blocks. These children have not developed their pincer grasps or they need additional practice in this movement. These children may understand spatial positions, but are unable to demonstrate them.

For these children, increase the size of the blocks or move the block and then ask the child to explain the block's position.

2.105 Points to or places object up, down
Strand: 2-1A **Age:** 34-42m 2.10-3.6y

Definition
When the child is given a small object such as block or a ball, he will place it up on a box or down on the floor on command.

Assessment Materials
At least four different colored blocks or other similar small objects, a shoe box.

Assessment Procedures
Grouping: This skill can be assessed one-on-one with the child. However, you can also informally assess the skill as the child is engaged in a spontaneous activity.
Level One:
1. Invite the child to join you at a table. Show him a block and the shoebox. Give him the block. Say, "Put the block up on the box." Observe him as he positions the block.
2. Say, "Put the block down on the table." Observe the child as he positions the block.
3. Remove the block.
4. Explain that you are going to put some blocks on and near the box. Put a block on top of the box and another block down on the table.
5. Say, "Point to the block that is up on the box." Observe him as he responds.
6. Say, "Point to the block that is down on the table." Observe him as he responds.
7. If he has any problems responding to the assessment, have him become involved physically in these spatial concepts; for example, ask him to step up on the stool and sit down on the floor.
8. It may be necessary to ask him to respond physically several times doing different tasks.
Level Two:
9. During a singing game, play with blocks, or pretend play, observe the child as he reacts to up and down directions. For example, when he is singing an action song, does he "make the balloon go up and then come down?" When doing a finger-play, does "the spider climb up and climb down the spout?" When building with blocks, does he put one block up on top of another, and does he knock them down when asked? When doing dramatic play, does he "hang up the hat and sit down on the chair?"

Credit: + Child correctly places an object up or down on command.

Adaptations
Some children become confused with the meaning of up and down. When a child hears the word "up" and the expected response is placement, he may perceive the word to mean to increase the volume (turn the TV up), to stop talking ("shut up") or a geographic location (going up town). When he hears the word "down" and the expected response is placement, he may perceive the word to mean to decrease the volume, to "quiet down," or to go downtown. Due to the multiple meanings of words, he may receive the information, but not be able to determine how to apply the request. To be certain he is conceptualizing the correct meaning of the word, demonstration is an important prerequisite to an expected receptive response.

2.106 Carries out 2 simple unrelated successive commands in order
Strand: 2-2 **Age:** 34-46m 2.10-3.10y

Definition
The child will respond correctly to a two-step command in which the steps are not logically related.

Assessment Materials
At least five two-step commands. Examples: Clap your hands and sit down. Put on your coat and pick up the glass. Get your sweater and close the door. /*\Safety-Supervise! Jump over the rock and climb the tree. Lay down on the floor and sing a song. Pick up the crayon and go into the kitchen. Be sure the child is capable of doing the motor skills involved. Be sure that the commands are within his experience. Include some silly commands; the child will enjoy them.

Assessment Procedures
Grouping: This skill can be assessed in a small group setting, no more than four children. Remind the children that they will need to listen and take turns during the activity.
1. Explain to the child that you are going to tell him some things to do so he should listen carefully.
2. Say, "Begin when I say Go."
3. State one of the commands and say "Go." Observe the child.

4. If he completes the first part of the command and then pauses, repeat the second part of the command only.
5. If he chooses not to respond at all, repeat the entire two-step command.
6. If he still does not respond, say and model the command, saying, for example, "Clap your hands" (clap your hands), and then say, "Sit down" (sit down).
7. Assist him in performing the two behaviors in the command.
8. Once he has demonstrated that he can clap his hands and sit down, repeat the two-step command. Record his responses.
9. Continue with the other commands. Be sure to enjoy the silly ones with the child.

Credit: + Child carries out a two-step command in which the steps are not logically related.

Adaptations

Children who have difficulty following oral directions are probably experiencing either a problem comprehending what has been spoken or in retaining the directions. If a child is able to carry out the first part of the two-step related command and then cannot complete the second step, this may indicate a short-term memory problem. If the directions given are within his motor skill ability, but he is not successful, he may lack word comprehension. It is important for him to understand exactly what to do. If he does not respond promptly and correctly to the directions given, repeat the directions. It is also necessary to take a look at each sub-skill of the task to make sure he understands each part. For example, in the command, "Clap your hands and sit down," does the child know what the words "clap," "hands" and "sit" mean? And does he comprehend the words "down" and "hands" in the context of the sentence? Before you assume that the child cannot perform the command, repeat the directions, clarify word meanings, and if possible, simplify the directions to make sure they are understandable.

2.107 Uses noun plurals. Uses verb plurals

Strand: 2-3 **Age:** 36-38m 3.0-3.2y

Definition

When a child is involved with a verbal situation or with a visual picture, she will respond by using noun plurals (e.g., shoes, girls). When she is presented with a situation or picture, she will respond by using verb plurals (e.g., girls run).

Assessment Materials

Two or more objects familiar to the child that she names in her normal conversation (Example: shoes, cookies, books). Pictures of persons or objects doing some form of action. (Example: two girls running and another girl walking.)

Assessment Procedures

Grouping: This skill could be assessed one-on-one with the child. However, the most important assessment procedure is made by observing the child in a natural conversational setting to determine her usage of plural nouns and plural verbs.

Level One:
1. Hold up one of the objects and say, "This is a shoe." Then select another shoe and ask the child to tell you what she sees while looking at both shoes. Pause for her response.
2. Continue with the other objects, observing her usage of noun plurals (books, cookies, children).
3. Show her an action picture (e.g., two girls running and one girl walking). Point first to the girls running and then to the girl walking and say, "These girls ____ but this girl ____?" Pause for her response (run, walks).
4. Continue with the other objects, observing her usage of verb plurals.

Level Two:
5. Observe the child in a free discussion or conversation period for appropriate verbalization of noun plurals and verb plurals.

Credit: + Child uses noun and verb plurals during a natural conversation or when presented with action pictures.

Adaptations

The primary approach to teaching simple, concrete nouns is to establish the process of naming. A child learns that the word "apple" represents the name of an object. The following are recommendations for teaching nouns:

(1) Nouns should be taught using real objects, progressing to models of the real object, and then to pictures of the object. Make sure the child understands that real items may be represented in pictorial form.

(2) As the child progresses, it is important to teach nouns that are more abstract or that have added inflected endings. Using categorical nouns is an effective method to deal with expanded meaning and usage. For example, have her sort the pictures into two categories, clothes and food. After she has sorted the

pictures, provide her with the appropriate words, phrases, and sentences: "We wear these; these are clothes," and "We eat these; these are foods."

The first objective in assisting a child to learn verbs is for her to understand that a word represents an action, not the name of an object. If a word, such as drink is used in association with milk, the child must understand that it means an action, not another item. When a word such as running is used, the child needs to know that it is not the name of a person, a place, or a thing, but that it means something that a person, place, or thing is doing. The following are recommendations for teaching verbs:

(1) Involve the child in simple activities such as walking, running, or jumping. Say the appropriate word during the activity. Repeat it until she comprehends the word and uses a noun with the action verb. For example, tell the child to run, or run with her, and say, "Sarah is running," and expand to, "Sarah is running down the walk."

(2) Although personal experience is most valuable, you may also use visuals. For example, show the child a picture of two animals and a girl running. Help her understand that the word run refers to an action, and that the girl and the two animals are not named "Run." Point to one of the running animals and say, "Tell me what this animal is doing." If she has difficulty say, "The dog is running." Point to the dog and say, "Tell me what this animal is doing."

(3) Some verbs are not easily dramatized or visually represented. For example, mix dough for making cookies. As you place the cookies in the oven for baking, look at them often and say, "The cookies are baking in the oven." Discuss that the longer they bake, the darker they get.

2.108 Identifies sounds, words just spoken

Strand: 2-1A **Age:** 36-39m 3.0-3.3y

Definition

(1) The child will look at an object that has just been named; he will look at a person who has just been named. (2) When a sound is produced, he will answer the question, "What was that?" or when someone speaks, he will answer the question, "Who was that?"

Assessment Materials

Level One: Five familiar objects (such as: ball, telephone, book, doll and apple). Five photographs of familiar people (such as: mother, father, teacher, classmate, sibling).

Level Two: Involve the child in a listening activity, such as "A Listening Walk," and observe him as he walks and listens closely to the sounds along the way. Discuss the sounds you hear and identify their source. Record the listening walk on a tape/CD recorder/cell phone. When you return, gather pictures of the things that you heard. For example, a car, bird, dog, familiar people you heard talking, motorcycle.

Assessment Procedures

Grouping: This skill can be introduced and practiced in a group setting. However, when you are ready to assess the child's ability to identify sounds and words just spoken, it is recommended that you do so one-on-one with the child.

Level One:
1. Set the five familiar objects on the table in front of the child. Tell him to listen carefully and to do as you say.
2. Say, "Point to the book." Record his response.
3. Say, "Point to the ball." Record his response.
4. Repeat the above with the remaining objects. Record his responses.
5. Remove the objects from the table and place the five photographs in front of the child.
6. Remind the child to listen carefully and then repeat the activity, this time naming the people and having the child point to the correct photograph. Record his responses.

Level Two:
7. Introduce the recording from the "Listening Walk" along with the pictures of the things you heard.
8. Explain to the child that you are going to play the tape/CD from the listening walk and he is to listening carefully. Tell him when he hears a sound, for example, of the motorcycle, he is to point to the picture that matches the sound he just heard.
9. Stop the tape/CD after each sound and allow the child to look at the pictures. If necessary, prompt the child to point to the sound he just heard.
10. Continue with all the sounds on the tape/CD. Record the child's responses.

Credit: + Child identifies an object or person when they have been named. Additionally, when the child hears a sound he can identify the source of the sound (the person, animal, or object that produced the sound).

Adaptations

Some children have difficulty identifying sounds they have just heard. It might be that they were distracted by something else in the environment, that they have problems discriminating certain sounds, or they may have a hearing problem. To help a child who is easily distracted, make sure that you prompt them and gain their attention before introducing the sounds. For a child who has difficulty discriminating sounds introduce some noise making toys like a drum, bells, an animal that makes noise, etc. Let the child experience the toys himself, producing the sounds and naming the different items. After the child has had an opportunity to fully explore the toys, ask him to sit down. Remove the toys and place them behind a screen (a divider, a curtain, etc.) Prompt the child to listen carefully while you go behind the screen and activate the toys one at a time waiting for the child to respond. If the child correctly identifies the sound, show him the toy and continue with another toy following the same procedure. If the child was incorrect, show him the toy and have him help you activate the toy. Go behind the screen and use a different toy. Make sure the child knows the label for each item. If the child has a hearing problem, they may benefit from being seated closer to the sound source. You may need to make sure that other sounds in the environment are reduced, such as turning off music that might be playing, having other children go outside to play, and turning off telephones. If the child wears hearing aids, make sure they are in good working order.

2.109 Identifies loud and soft sounds

Strand: 2-1A **Age:** 36-40m 3.0-3.4y

Definition

When the child is exposed to a loud and soft sound, she will identify each according to volume. She may identify a loud or a soft sound by a physical movement (raises arm high if the sound is loud, lowers arm if the sound is soft), by verbal expression (says "loud" to identify a loud sound or says "soft" to identify a soft sound), by visual representation (a tall line means a loud sound and a short line means a soft sound), or by looking at pictures of a loud and a soft sound maker (an airplane and a kitten) and pointing to the airplane when asked which one makes a loud sound and pointing to the kitten when asked which one makes a soft sound.

Assessment Materials

At least three objects that make loud and soft sounds. For example, a radio, a recorder/CD player, a drum, a piano, a beeper. At least six pictures of things that make loud and soft sounds, three representing loud sounds and three representing soft sounds. Example: Loud--airplane, siren, tuba. Soft--kitten, tiny bell, trickling stream.

Assessment Procedures

Note: If the child can determine the volume by seeing you create it, ask her to close her eyes or position her so she can not see you as you are making the sounds.

Grouping: This skill should be assessed one-on-one with the child.

1. Demonstrate to the child how the objects make loud and soft sounds.
2. Explain that you are going to select each object and play a sound. Ask the child to be ready to identify each sound as loud or soft.
3. Make one object sound loud. Ask the child to name the sound as loud or soft.
4. Continue with the other objects.
5. Observe and note her responses.
6. Place two of the pictures, one showing a loud-sounding object and the other a soft-sounding object on a table in front of the child. Ask her to look at the pictures and point to the one that makes a loud sound.
7. If she points to the correct picture, ask her to imitate the sound of the object.
8. Ask her if she could imitate the sound and make it loud and then soft.
9. Continue the above, using the other four pictures.
10. Observe her responses.

Credit: + Child correctly identifies when sounds are loud and soft. This includes actual noise they have heard as well as identifying pictures of things that are either loud or soft.

Adaptations

Some children have difficulty modulating themselves and therefore may have difficulty recognizing when something or someone is loud or soft. Using a visual to represent loud and soft can be a very useful tool. For example, if the child herself is being too loud, have a picture of a thermometer with the temperature level high (red in color), when they are soft a picture of a thermometer with the temperature level low (yellow in color) and when they are just right the temperature level will be green. Explain the thermometer to the child. When the temperature is too high the meter is red and goes all the way to the top. The red color is to remind them to stop. When the thermometer is low, the meter is yellow and only goes up a little, the child is being soft/quiet with their sounds. When the level is just right, the temperature will be up part of the way and the color will be green. The green color is to remind the child that the sound level is a "go" and the level of sound/noise is just right.

2.110 (Removed, see page xviii)

2.111 Uses noun with possessive
Strand: 2-3 **Age:** 24-40m 2.0-3.4y

Definition
When he is presented with a situation or a visual and a verbal prompt, the child will respond by using a noun with a possessive.

Assessment Materials
A collection of objects belonging to the child. A collection of objects that do not belong to him. A puppet or stuffed animal for demonstration purposes.

Assessment Procedures
Note: Prompt by imitating and expanding a response.
Grouping: This skill should be assessed one-on-one with the child. If possible, the best way to assess the child is by observing him in a natural conversational setting to determine his usage of possessives.

Level One:
1. Hold up one of the articles that belong to the child and say, for example, "Whose ball is this?"
2. Pause to allow him a response such as, "My ball."
3. Hold up one of the articles that does not belong to him and say, "Paul, is this your cap?"
4. Pause to allow his response such as, "Mom's cap" or "That cap belongs to Mom."
5. If he has a problem using possessives with a noun, prepare a presentation in which you play two characters, creating one character by using a puppet, using a different voice, or using a stuffed animal. Have the other character be yourself.
6. Have the puppet character, different voice character or the stuffed animal select an item that belongs to you and say, "Whose sweater is this?"
7. Respond to the question by saying, "It is my red sweater."
8. Repeat the above process with another item that belongs to you.
9. Gradually change from items that belong to you to items that belong to the child.

Level Two:
10. Observe the child in a free discussion or conversation period for appropriate verbalization of nouns with possessives.

Credit: + Child uses a noun with a possessive. Visual or verbal prompts may be used.

Adaptations
Nouns should be taught as concepts, not as just words or labels. A coat stands for a child's coat as well as an adult's coat or a dog's coat. Your instruction should include the general and specific meanings; many words represent many things, while others, such as names, denote a single meaning. As an example, point to the child's coat and say, "Your coat is red." Point to another coat and say, "Bob's coat is brown." Point to another coat and say, "This coat is very warm."

Nouns should be taught using real objects, progressing to models of the real objects and then to pictures of the objects. Make sure the child understands that real items may be represented in pictorial form.

2.112 Uses verb with noun (see dog, push wagon)
Strand: 2-3 **Age:** 30-40m 2.6-3.4y

Definition
The child uses a verb with a noun.

Assessment Materials
Objects that can be maneuvered. Examples: a marker, a hairbrush, a ball, a hand puppet.

Assessment Procedures
Grouping: This skill can be introduced and assessed in a small group setting. However, the most important assessment procedure is made by observing the child in a natural conversational setting and listening for her grammatical usage. Listen to what the child is saying and assess her skills at using a verb with a noun during her play.

Level One:
1. Ask the child to watch carefully.
2. Select one of the objects and create an action. For example, use the marker to draw a picture, use the brush to brush your hair, roll the ball, make the hand puppet clap.
3. After your performance, ask the child, "What was the ball doing?" Expect response from her such as, "Ball roll," "The ball is rolling," or "Roll the ball."
4. Observe and record her response.
5. Continue the above process with other manipulative items.
6. If she has difficulty, perform the action and state what is occurring at the same time. Repeat several times. Give her the item, and ask her to do the same thing and to say what is happening. Encourage her to do the action and make the statement several times.
7. Select another item, and perform an action and state what is occurring at the same time. Repeat several times. Give the item to the child and ask her to do the same thing and to tell what is happening. Encourage her to do the action and make the statement several times.
8. Select another object and create an action. After your demonstration, ask the child, "What was the hairbrush doing?"
9. Record her response.
10. Continue the above process with other manipulative items.

Level Two:
11. Observe the child when she is involved in a discussion or during a conversation for appropriate verbalization of noun/verb usage.

Credit: + Child uses a verb with a noun.

Adaptations

The following are examples of interventions that can be used to help a child in using a verb with a noun: (1) Ask her to verbalize her actions when she plays and as you conduct daily tasks; (2) Use pictures and ask her to name the objects. Encourage her to use the named objects in sentences and in a sequence of sentences; (3) Elicit a response from her by stating a sentence, leaving out a word, and asking her to supply it; (4) Give her two sentences in different order and ask for the correct sequence to promote ordering, or sequence of thought; (5) Use pictures and ask her to respond to questions that address actions, emotions, and cause-and-effect relationships. Show her three pictures, for example: (1) A boy riding a bicycle; (2) The boy hitting a rut and falling off his bicycle; (3) The boy lying on the ground next to her bicycle. Say, "Show me the picture that shows the boy fell." Ask her to point to the picture and tell what is happening. Provide words or model as needed. You may use this same approach (item 5) to elicit responses with other parts of speech and usage. The primary objective for a child with structural concerns should be to help her develop a correct, natural, spontaneous flow of language.

2.113 Uses pronouns appropriately (him, he, his, her, she)

Strand: 2-3 **Age:** 36-40m 3.0-3.4y

Definition
When the child is involved in a verbal situation or presented with a visual, he will respond by using the correct pronoun. Consideration should be given to the use of subjective pronouns (I, you, he, we, she) before objective pronouns (me, him, her, us, them) or possessive pronouns (your, his, our, their).

Assessment Materials
Pictures of different characters. Prepare by drawing a picture or securing a photograph of the following: (1) The child; (2) Yourself; (3) A boy; (4) A girl; (5) Several children; (6) An adult man; (7) An adult woman; and (8) A dog.

Assessment Procedures
Grouping: This skill can be introduced and assessed in a small group setting. However, the most important assessment procedure is made by observing the child in a natural conversational setting and listening for her grammatical usage. Listen to what the child is saying and assess his skills at using pronouns during his play.

Level One:
1. Place the pictures face-up on a table, and invite the child to come to the work area. Point to each picture and discuss it, being sure to use the associated pronoun.
2. Explain to him that you are going to tell a story using the pictures.
3. Collect the pictures, and place the picture of yourself on the table in front of the child and begin the story. For example, point to the appropriate pictures and say, "I decided to take a walk one day. The sun was shining brightly, and it was very warm. As I (point to the picture of yourself) walked along, I (point to the picture of yourself) saw my friend Tim.

He (point to the picture of the boy) was busy pulling weeds in his (point to the picture of the boy) flower garden. Soon I (point to the picture of yourself) met four children. They (point to the picture of the children) were getting ready to play ball in the park. I (point to the picture of yourself) decided that it was a perfect day to play ball, and I wished I could join them. All of the sudden I found myself humming a new tune. A lady passed me and she (point to the picture of the adult woman) asked me (point to the picture of yourself) what the name of my cheery tune was. I thought and thought, but I could not remember the name of the song. Still, we (point to the pictures of the adult woman and yourself) had a wonderful time humming the tune together. As I was about to reach my house, I (point to picture of yourself) saw my favorite dog sitting on the porch. He (point to the picture of a dog) was barking a big hello. What a grand day for a walk and a grand welcome home!"

4. Tell the child that you are going to tell the story again, and that you would like him to point to the pictures.
5. Tell the story once again. Omit the pronouns and encourage him to fill in the missing word. Example: "As I walked along, _____ saw my friend Tim. _____ was busy pulling weeds in his flower garden. . ."
6. Allow him an opportunity to use the pictures and tell a simple story.

Level Two:
7. Observe the child in a normal discussion or conversation period for appropriate verbalization of pronouns.

Credit: + Child uses pronouns (him, he, his, her, and she) appropriately.

Adaptations

The primary direction for teaching pronouns is the understanding that pronouns replace known nouns. The use of pronouns addresses the terms of number, gender, tense, subject, object, and indefinite. Singular (I) and plural (we) pronouns are often confused; pronouns (this, that, those) that refer to a noun that is understood or mentioned earlier are conceptually abstract; some pronouns referents depend on their emphasis in a spoken sentence. Examples: (1) John pushed Tom and Sue pushed HIM; (2) John pushed Tom AND Sue pushed him. In sentence 1 the meaning indicates that Sue pushed John, but in sentence 2. the meaning indicates that Sue pushed Tom. Consideration should be given to the following pronoun sequence: (1) Subjective pronouns (I, you, he, we, they); (2) Objective pronouns (me, you, him, us, them); (3) Possessive pronouns (my, your, his, her, their); (4) Possessive-replacive pronouns (mine, ours, theirs). The following are recommendations for teaching pronouns:

(1) State a sentence using a noun, and then repeat the sentence and substitute a pronoun for the noun.

(2) Act out and say a sentence to help establish pronoun usage. For example, say, "I give the cookie to Jim." then give a cookie to the child. Say, "Jim has a cookie," then hold up Jim's (child's) hand with the cookie. Say, "He will eat the cookie," then let Jim eat the cookie.

(3) Sentences unaccompanied by an activity may be used for practice in the use of pronouns. Omit the pronoun and require the child to complete the thought. Use an incorrect pronoun and ask him to correct the sentence.

(4) Say a riddle or play a guessing games that involves the use of pronouns. Say, for example, "Somebody is hiding behind the bookcase. Who is hiding behind the bookcase?" Or say, "A girl in this room is wearing a blue ribbon. Who is she?" Or say, "Bill has a blue shirt. Is he the only one wearing a blue shirt?"

(5) Demonstrative pronouns are best differentiated when you use them with a concrete activity. For example, touch and point to immediate pronouns (this, these) and distant pronouns (that, those) assists for determining differences in meaning.

2.114 Provides objects as they are requested by name or referenced by function

Strand: 2-1A **Age:** 30-42m 2.6-3.6y

Definition

When the child is presented with several different known objects and a verbal cue, for example, "Give me the spoon" or "Pick up the comb," she will select the correct item. When she is presented with known objects that also have a function such as a hairbrush, a glass, a spoon, or a hat, she will respond to the request, for example, "Give me the hairbrush." She may respond to a request to demonstrate the function of the item, for example, "Show me which one you would drink from."

Assessment Materials

Some objects familiar to the child that interest her. Example: miniature toy car, set of keys, small whistle. Duplicates of at least three items. Example: two cups, two toothbrushes, two flowers. Two trays.

Assessment Procedures

Grouping: This skill should be assessed one-on-one with the child.

Level One:
1. Set the collection of objects on a table in front of the child. Tell her you are going to ask her to do some things upon request.
2. Say, "Point to the cup." Then say, "Give me the keys."
3. Continue until all the items have been identified.
4. Note her responses.
5. If she has a problem locating the objects, repeat the request and then point to the item.
6. Then say, "Point to the cup." Observe her reaction.
7. If she is still unsuccessful, repeat the request and gently take her hand and locate the object.
8. Then say, "Point to the cup."
9. If she is still unsure of her response, lower the assessment level by doing the following: (1) Set two trays on the table, one for her and one for you; (2) Put one identical object on each tray; (3) Say to the child, "Point to the cup"; (4) While giving the child the direction, point to the object (cup) on your tray.
10. Observe whether she points to her object; if not, provide physical assistance.
11. Repeat at least two times.
12. Remove the items from both trays and place another item on her tray and your tray. Repeat the above procedures.
13. Continue with the third object.
14. Place another object with the one now on her tray. Say, "Point to the toothbrush."
15. Note her response.
16. Continue the above until all three objects are on each of the trays and she is able to point to the requested object independently.
17. Remove your tray and repeat.
18. If she is successful, remove the tray and place a collection of known objects on the table in front of her.
19. Ask her to point to or give you an object. (Follow the procedure above.)

Level Two:

20. During an activity time that requires children to share material, observe the child's response when another child asks her to give her a crayon, a book, or a block.

Credit: + Child provides a known object upon request and understands the function of familiar items.

Adaptations

A child with receptive language problems often has trouble sorting out "what means what." She cannot differentiate sounds or words and relate them to the proper experience. It is important to reduce the amount of language used and explain all new words that you introduce. For example, instead of saying, "Give me the cup," isolate the key word--"cup," and reduce the carrier phrase--"Give cup." Then graduate to "Give me a cup." As soon as she understands a word in isolation, reintroduce it into the context or short sentences.

2.115 (Removed, see page xviii)

2.116 (Removed, see page xviii)

2.117 Correctly answers questions concerning a message just spoken

Strand: 2-1A **Age:** 36-42m 3.0-3.6y

Definition

The child will answer a literal question related to a short story told, some factual information provided, an activity that is going to happen, etc.

Assessment Materials

Locate or write a short story that is of interest to the child and contains content that is within the child's experiences.

Locate or write at least two sentences which provide factual information about a single subject that the child is familiar with. Example: Cows eat grass. Cows give us milk.

Locate or write at least two sentences which provide information on an activity that is about to happen. Example: It will soon be time for lunch. We are having pizza today.

Assessment Procedures

Note: Begin the questions with such words as "Did you..., What..., Who..., Where..., When..., How.... If the child expands on the answers, consider asking questions that begin with

Who do you think..., What would happen if,... What would you do..., Do you think it was..."

Grouping: This skill can be introduced and assessed in a small group setting. For example, during a group activity that requires active participation, observe the child's responses to questions asked about what just happened during the activity (i.e., questions about a story you just read, questions related to an activity you just completed, questions related to directions you just shared, etc.)

<u>Level One:</u>
1. Explain to the child that you are going to read him a short story. Say, "Listen carefully while I read you the story."
2. After the story has been read, ask the child at least three questions about what happened. The required answers can be Yes/No, one word, a phrase, a sentence or several sentences.
3. Record the child's answers.
4. If the child had a difficult time answering the questions, say, "Now I want you to listen to something I am going to tell you." Say the two sentences that provide information about a single subject.
5. After the factual sentences have been read, ask the child at least two questions about the information. Begin the questions with such words as What.., Who..., or questions that require a yes or no answer.
6. Record the child's answers. If the child had a difficult time answering the questions. Say, "Now I want you to listen to something I am going to tell you."
7. Say the two sentences about an activity that is going to happen immediately. After the sentences have been read, ask the child at least two questions about the information. The questions should be of a literal nature or can be answered by yes or no.
8. Record the child's answers.

<u>Level Two:</u>
9. During the story time period, pause and ask the child questions about the story. Make a mental note about the child's responses.

Credit: + Child correctly answers literal questions related to a story, factual information provided, or an activity that is going to happen.

Adaptations

Some children will find responding to questions difficult. These children may have a problem in learning which word represents what experience. The same word can have different meanings depending on the context in which it is used. Example: A word such as "break" represents a period of time in one situation and an action in another. Not only does the same word represent dissimilar experiences but also a single object may have one or more names (e.g., pail/bucket). The complexity of the language is a real concern, especially when the symbolic process is disrupted. These children need to hear a steady flow of words, and the words need to be broken down into meaningful units.

2.118 Sequences a 3-picture story that has been read

Strand: 2-1A   **Age:** 36-44m   3.0-3.8y

Definition
After the child has heard a simple story with three events, she will be given a set of pictures showing the story sequence, and she will arrange the pictures in the correct order. The set of pictures will clearly depict the sequence of the story.

Assessment Materials
A simple story based on the child's activities. Example: Story One--"The child calls her dog. The dog comes. The child pets her dog. The dog and child are very happy." Pictures to correspond--(1) A child calling her dog, (2) a dog running to her, (3) the child petting the dog, both looking happy.

A simple story with a familiar content to the child, but not about her activities. Example: Story Two--"The girl was outside swinging. It started to rain very hard. The girl ran to get out of the rain." Pictures to correspond--(1) a girl swinging on a swing, (2) a dark cloud and rain coming down, (3) the girl running to get under a cover.

A simple story not within the child's realm of experiences. Example: Story Three--"Once upon a time a little bear put on a heavy coat. The little bear went outside, and her feet got very cold. She had forgotten to put on her heavy boots. The little bear ran inside and put on her boots." Pictures to correspond--(1) a little bear putting on a heavy coat, (2) the little bear stepping outside the door and into a snow drift with her bare paws, (3) the little bear inside her house putting on boots.

Three frames, larger than the story pictures for the child to place the pictures in sequence. (If frames are not available, removable tape works well.)

Assessment Procedures

Grouping: This skill should be assessed one-on-one with the child.

1. Place the frames on the table and ask the child to come to the table. Tell her that you are going to tell her a story, and ask her to listen carefully.
2. Tell her Story One.
3. Place the three pictures that go with Story One face-up on the table. Ask the child to find the picture that shows what happened first in the story and point to the frame to place it. Ask her to find the picture that shows what happened next and to point to where she should place it. Ask her to find the picture that shows what happened last and point to where she should place it.
4. Note whether she was successful in the sequencing task.
5. Allow her to retell the story and point to the pictures.
6. If she was unsuccessful, retell the story, as you hold up the picture that matches the sequential content.
7. Randomly place the three pictures on the table and ask the child to put them in the correct order.
8. If she is unsuccessful, retell the story, moving the pictures to the correct positions as you tell the story.
9. Shuffle the three pictures, place them on the table, and ask her to put them in the correct order.
10. Tell her that you are going to tell her another story and that she must listen carefully. Tell her Story Two.
11. Follow the procedure outlined for Story One.
12. Note whether she was successful in the sequencing task.
13. Tell her that you are going to tell her another story, and ask her to listen carefully. Tell her Story Three.
14. Follow the procedure outlined for Story One.
15. Note whether she was successful in the sequencing task.

Credit: + Child sequences three-pictures showing the events of a story in the correct order after hearing a simple story. The child completes the task without prompting.

Adaptations

Regarding sequential memory, some children are overly influenced by irrelevant verbal information and have a difficult time focusing on what is relevant. For her, a single event or a word may trigger a totally new thought chain. For example, the word "dog" in a spoken sentence or story leads to a linkage of dog, bark, bite, hurt, cry, bandage, bad dog, etc. In this process of mind wandering, her comprehension of spoken words is minimized. Using visuals with the expressed words and stories is an effective way to center the child's concentration.

2.119 Carries on a conversation
Strand: 2-3 **Age:** 36-44m 3.0-3.8y

Definition
The child will organize and verbally present his ideas to others, listen to ideas expressed by others, converse informally, engage in conversational give-and-take during interaction periods, make up and tell stories, talk about the interpretation of visuals, repeat sayings, and share experiences by oral expression.

Assessment Materials
An object placed in a box with a lid on the box. The object in the box should be familiar to the child. It should have unique characteristics that stimulate and motivate verbal expression. Same type of object placed in a closed paper bag.

Assessment Procedures
Grouping: This skill can be introduced and assessed in a group setting. However, the most important assessment procedure is made by observing the child in a natural conversational setting interacting with others. Listen to what the child is saying and assess his verbal skills in carrying on a conversation.

Level One:
1. Show the child the box. Ask him to take the lid off the box and to look inside.
2. Ask him to describe the object in the box.
3. Carry on a conversation with him about the object. Prompt the interaction with questions about the object. When you ask questions, it is important to begin with literal questions such as, "What color is it? What is its name?" and then to ask analytical questions such as, "What can the object be used for? Where do you think it came from?", and finally to engage him in interpretive questions such as, "What do you think it would eat? What game would you play with it?"
4. If the child has difficulty discussing the object, ask him to listen to you closely. Speak a sentence about the object and leave out one or more words, asking the child to fill in the left

out words. For example, say, "The object in the box is a _____." (Wait for the child to complete the sentence.) Next describe the object by color and shape. For example, say, "It is the same color as a banana. What color is that?" "It is also the same shape as a ball. So, what shape would that be?" (Again, allow time for the child to respond.) Now, say, "I want to put it on the _____. Do you think it will roll off?" (Leave pauses for him to answer.) Say, "Why not?" (Pause for his answer.)

5. Show the child the paper bag.
6. Ask him to open the bag and to look inside. Ask him to describe the object in the bag.
7. Carry on a conversation with him about the object. Prompt the interaction with questions about the object. When you ask questions again, begin with literal questions (e.g., What color is it? What is it?), then ask analytical questions (e.g., What can the object be used for? Where do you think the object came from?), and finally ask interpretive questions (e.g., What do you think the object would eat? What game would you play with it?).
8. Observe the child as he engages in verbal conversation pertaining to the objects.

Level Two:

9. Observe the child's conversations during various activities. Listen for verbal skills such as organization and presentation of ideas to another, listening attentively to others, use of words, sentence structure, clarifying of ideas, formulating thoughts and then putting the concepts into words, clarity of expression, and enthusiasm.

Credit: + Child carries on a conversation presenting his ideas in an organized fashion and listening to the ideas expressed by others. The conversation shows a give-and-take interaction with another person.

Adaptations

A child may have the ability to understand the spoken word, but he may be deficient in using it to express himself. Although he can understand and recognize words, he may not be able to retrieve them for spontaneous usage. Sometimes a child has a problem saying words; he comprehends, but he has problems executing the motor patterns necessary to formulate the construction. He may also be unable to plan and organize words for the expression of ideas in complete sentences. He may omit or distort the arrangement of words, use incorrect tenses, and make other grammatical, syntactical errors. If the child has difficulty with word retrieval, some strategies for you to consider are: (1) Emphasize recalling useful words; (2) Organize the materials you present to make the most efficient use of recall; (3) Provide him with a means of determining the recall of words.

Some children respond best to visual cues, some to the context of the other words used in a sentence, and some to the use of associated words.

If the child has a problem with motor planning when it comes to speaking, some strategies for you to consider are: (1) Listen carefully to note the sounds he emits and then attempt to make him aware of the sounds and the movements used to produce them; (2) Allow him to observe another's lip movements; have him watch in order to learn how to say words and phrases; (3) Instruct him how to make the necessary motor movements. For example, say, "Put your tongue behind your front teeth. Make your lips into a circle. "

If he has a problem formulating sentences, some strategies to consider are: (1) Plan a verbal presentation based on his experience that is coordinated with sentence patterns in keeping with his language level. As an example, tell a positive story about the child; (2) Arrange and discuss meaningful experiences, using play activities or pictures; (3) Provide a series of sentences auditorially that are structured with experiences so that he will retain and internalize different sentence patterns. A child should be given varied and frequent training to improve his language and conversational skills. This training should be related directly to his needs.

Note: It is important to refer a child experiencing language problems to a language specialist for an evaluation and to determine if the child would benefit from or be eligible to receive therapy.

2.120 Describes an action using a verb
Strand: 2-4B **Age:** 30-38m 2.6-3.2y

Definition
The child will answer questions about common occurrences related to a person involved in an action. He will state the action by using a verb.

Assessment Materials
At least five questions that require the child to respond with an action word. Example: (1) What do you do when you are cold? (2) What do you do when you are thirsty? (3) What do you do

when you get dirty? (4) What do you do when you are hungry? (5) What do you do when you get tired?

Assessment Procedures
Grouping: This skill should be assessed one-on-one with the child.
1. Tell the child that you are going to ask him some questions. Remind him to listen carefully.
2. Say, "What do you do when you are cold?"
3. Pause for a response. (Answers such as "Put on a sweater," "Turn up the heat," "Go inside," or "Stand by the fire" are appropriate.)
4. If the child responds with "I don't know" or gives an inaccurate answer, repeat the question one more time and then move on to the next question.
5. Record his response.
6. Say, "What do you do when you are thirsty?"
7. Pause for a response. (Such answers as. "Get a drink," "Go to the sink," or "Pour from the pitcher" are appropriate.)
8. Record his response.
9. Continue with questions 3 through 5.

Credit: + Child describes an action using a verb when shown a picture of a person or animal involved in an action.

Adaptations
Verbs are most easily learned when they can be experienced: The child can learn by doing the verbs: run, jump, skip, hop, throw, etc. For example, say, "Charlie, run to the door." As he runs to the door say, "Look! Charlie is running to the door." Ask him to repeat the action, but before he runs, have him say, "I will run to the door." While he runs to the door, ask him to say, "Look! I am running to the door."

Act out action stories and state the action words in sentence form.

2.121 (Removed, see page xviii)

2.122 (Removed, see page xviii)

2.123 Imitates common syllables (da, ka, wa)

Strand: 2-4B **Age:** 36-48m 3.0-4.0y

Definition
When the child is presented with a cue, she will say a correct imitation of the following syllables (either consonant + vowel (short) or vowel (short) + consonant): (1) (m + vowel) me as in meat, mi as in mitt, mo as in mop, ma as in mat; (2) (vowel + m) em as in hem, um as in hum, im as in him; (3) (t + vowel) te as in test, tu as in tub, ta as in tap; (4) (vowel + t) et as in get, ut as in cut, at as in at; (5) (p + vowel) pe as in pet, po as in pot, pa as in pat, pi as in pit; (6) (vowel + p) ep as in kept, up as in up, ap as in cap, ip as in tip; (7) (d + vowel) de as in depth, du as in dump, da as in dab, di as in did; (8) (vowel + d) ed as in wed, ud as in mud, ad as in add, id as in lid; (9) (n + vowel) nu as in nut, na as in nap, ni as in nip; (10) (vowel + n) un as in under, an as in fan, in as in pin; (11) (l + vowel) le as in sled, la as in lamb, li as in lit; (12) (vowel + l) el as in fell, al as in alley, il as in ill; (13) (s + vowel) su as in sum, sa as in sat, si as in sit; (14) (vowel + s) es as in dress, us as in bus; (15) (k + vowel) ki as in kick; (16) (vowel + k) uk as in luck, ak as in pack, ik as in pick; (17) (r + vowel) ri as in rip, re as in red, ro as in rod; (18) (b + vowel) bi as in bid, ba as in bad, be as in bed, bu as in bum: (19) (vowel + b) ib as in rib, ob as in rob, ab as in dab, ub as in tub; (20) (f + vowel) fe as in fed, fa as in fan, fu as in fun, fo as in fog; (21) (vowel + f) uf as in gruff, if as in if, af as in after; (22) (g + vowel) ge as in get, go as in got, gu as in gun; (23) (vowel + g) ig as in jig, ug as in mug, ag as in bag, eg as in peg, og as in jog; (24) (h + vowel) ho as in hot, ha as in ham, hu as in hum; (25) (w + vowel) wi as in wit, we as in wet.

The presentation of the verbal model will be done by an adult who will exaggerate the facial movements as she creates the sounds. The child will be instructed to watch the adult as the sound syllables are being presented. This is not a skill related to phonic or linguistic instruction in reading, but a skill to determine whether the child is developing her articulation (voice folds) in such a manner as to reproduce all vowels and those voiced consonants that are produced by vocal folds vibrations and those consonants unvoiced that are produced without vibration from the vocal folds.

Assessment Materials
At least ten consonant vowel syllables; five of the syllables should be consonant + vowel and five syllables should be vowel + consonant. Example: (1) (consonant + vowel) mi as in mit, pa as in pat, nu as in nut, fe as in fed and ro as in rob; (2) (vowel + consonant) ib as in rib, es as in dress, ud and in mud, ak as in pack, og as in jog.

Assessment Procedures
Grouping: This skill should be assessed one-on-one with the child.

1. Ask the child to sit directly across from you where she has a good view of your face. Ask her to listen closely and to watch your mouth very carefully.
2. Tell her that you are going to say a sound and she is to say the sound exactly the same.
3. Say in an exaggerated manner, "mi" (as in mitt). Pause to allow her to say the syllable sound "mi."
4. Note her response.
5. If she is unable to respond or if her response is incorrect, repeat the sounds. Pause to allow her to say the syllable.
6. If she is unable to respond or if her response is incorrect, ask her to say "mitt."
7. Note her response.
8. Say in an exaggerated manner, "pa" (as in pat). Pause to allow her to say the syllable sound "pa."
9. Note her response.
10. If she is unable to respond or if her response is incorrect, repeat the sounds. Pause to allow her to say the syllable.
11. If she is unable to respond or if her response is incorrect, ask her to say "pat."
12. Note her response.
13. Continue in the above manner with the other syllable sounds.

Credit: + Child correctly imitates common syllables consisting of either consonant + vowel (short) or vowel (short) + consonant.

Adaptations

While language seems to be acquired in a relatively natural and easy manner without the need for the direct teaching of talking, some children have difficulty with the phonology of language, the differentiating and producing of appropriate sounds. The frequency of confusion between the various consonants suggests that the voiced and unvoiced sounds are often interchanged. A child often confuses the sounds of voiced b as unvoiced p, voiced d as unvoiced t, voiced g as unvoiced k, voiced v as unvoiced f, voiced z as unvoiced s. Other confused patterns are g as d and z as either b or v. Confusion among vowels in language processing can also create significant problems, the most frequently involved vowels are i as in sit, e as in set and ae as in sat. To help a child in the production of sounds, the following are recommendations: (1) Use a mirror which you and she are both facing, and slowly say the sounds in isolation. Ask the child to imitate your movements. Begin with the following single sounds: m, p, b, k, g, n, t, d, l, r, and then the following syllable sounds: mi as in mit, pe as in pet, da as in dab, etc.; (2) Place her hand on your throat as you make the sound so she can feel the movements. Ask her to place her hands on her own throat to feel the vibrations; (3) Provide her with verbal directions as needed. For example, say, "Close your lips tightly and act as if you are humming to make the sound of m," or say, "Act as if you are blowing out a candle and make the sound of p"; (4) Hold a picture of tongue and mouth positions that are used for certain sounds up to a mirror. Ask the child to imitate the position she sees in the mirror; (5) Gradually blend sounds together after the child feels comfortable with the production of the sounds in isolation.

2.124 Says a favorite rhyme
Strand: 2-4B **Age:** 36-48m 3.0-4.0y

Definition
The child will recite the words of a familiar rhyme correctly. If he has not memorized the rhyme, he may be provided with prompts, visuals, or motor activities, but then these prompts must be phased out, and he will recite the rhyme without any cues.

Assessment Materials
A selected rhyme the child knows. (Nursery rhymes are often the first memorized rhymes.)

Assessment Procedures
Grouping: This skill can be introduced and practiced in a group setting. During a group activity observe to see if the child can recite a memorized song or rhyme by himself.

Level One:
1. Tell the child that you are going to ask him to say a rhyme. Say, "Jeff, please tell me the rhyme, *Twinkle, Twinkle, Little Star.*"
2. If he is hesitant to begin, prompt him by giving him the first few words of line one, "Twinkle, twinkle, little . . ."
3. If he is unable to recite the rhyme, prompt him by giving him the first few words of each line: "Twinkle, twinkle, little. . . ,
   How I wonder . . .
   Up above the world so. . .
   Like a diamond . . ."
4. As soon as he joins you in saying the rhyme, stop prompting.
5. Say, "Jeff, please say the rhyme, *Twinkle, Twinkle, Little Star.*"
6. Observe his response.
7. Repeat the above, using another rhyme.

Level Two:
8. During music or language time, observe the child to determine whether he is able to memorize a song or a rhyme. Also, observe whether he is able to recite the learned selection when asked.

Credit: + Child says a favorite or memorized rhyme by himself, without prompting.

Adaptations

Some children have a difficult time memorizing words, phrases, and sentences. This is particularly true when the selection does not have meaning to the child, when certain words are not within his understanding, and when the selection does not have a beat or meter. He feels much like an adult who is asked to memorize and state the moves of a chess game when he does not know how to play chess and does not want to learn. To assist the child to develop memorization skills, begin with selections that have a meter and consistent rhyming words. These include nursery rhymes, jump rope chants, finger plays, action songs and rhymes.

2.125 Names common objects and actions

Strand: 2-4B **Age:** 36-48m 3.0-4.0y

Definition

When the child is presented with a visual model (a picture) of common objects (nouns) and common actions (verbs), she will name the objects and the action. The pictures should be of single items.

Assessment Materials

At least 10 single-item pictures of common objects such as a door, a dog, a car, a foot, a cap, a fish, a clock, a spoon, a leaf, an ear. At least 10 single-item pictures of a common action taking place such as: eating, running, jumping, pushing, riding, sleeping, washing, throwing, falling, drinking.

Assessment Procedures

Note: If appropriate, establish an exposure time for the picture and a response time for the child. This timing should be based on the child's entry behaviors and her characteristics. When you establish timing, it is important to base the number of minutes or seconds on her instructional level, not her frustration or leisure levels.

Grouping: This skill can be introduced and practiced in a group setting. During a group story time, point to picture and ask the child to identify what the object is. Do the same things, only this time point to an action in the picture and ask the child to tell you what is happening.

Level One:
1. Tell the child that you are going to show her some pictures and ask her to name what she sees.
2. Show her the first common object picture (a door), and say, "This is a picture of a _____ ?"
3. Pause to allow her time to respond.
4. If she is unable to respond correctly, say, "This is a picture of a door," and place it at the bottom of the stack.
5. Show her the second common object picture (dog), and say, "This is a picture of a_____ ?" If she answers "puppy," probe by asking questions such as, "Yes, but what is the name of a grownup puppy?" If she says a dog's name (e.g., Spot), probe by asking her, "Yes, but what kind of an animal is Spot?" If she says the dog's breed (e.g., collie), probe by asking her questions such as, "Yes, this is a collie but what kind of animal is a collie?"
6. Pause to give her time to respond.
7. Record her response.
8. If she is unable to respond correctly say, "This is a picture of a dog," and place it at the bottom of the stack.
9. Continue with the other common object pictures, including any that she missed or did not respond to.
10. If she is unable to respond after being shown three different exposures, discontinue the assessment.
11. Tell her that you are going to show her some pictures and that she is to name what she sees.
12. Show her the first action picture (eating), and say, "What is this person doing?"
13. Pause to give her time to respond. Accept the words "eat" or "eating."
14. If she is unable to respond correctly, say, "This is a picture of a boy eating," and place it at the bottom of the stack.
15. Show her the second common action picture (run), and say, "What is this girl doing?"
16. Pause to give her time to respond. Accept the words "run" or "running."
17. Record her response.
18. If she is unable to respond correctly, say, "This is a picture of a girl running," and place it at the bottom of the stack.
19. If she is unable to respond after being shown three different exposures, discontinue the assessment.

© 2010 VORT Corporation. All rights reserved. Do Not copy.

20. Continue with the other action pictures, including any she missed or did not respond to.
21. Record her response.

Level Two:

22. During story time or any activity that involves a picture, point to an object in the picture and ask the child to tell you what it is. Point to an action in the picture and ask the child to tell you what is happening.

Credit: + Child correctly names common objects and actions.

Adaptations

Some children have problems determining what to call an object or an activity due to the fact that naming an object is more than a simple visual-auditory association. It is a conceptual process that requires categorical thinking, divergent thinking, and associative thinking. When the child sees a picture of a cup, she must know that the picture represents objects of varying sizes and colors, and that they are used to hold liquids. She must learn that another object from which she drinks is not a cup, but a glass. She must also realize that glass or glasses can be objects that are worn to see better, that glass is a material used to make jars, and that glass is also in windows. Words also change from an object to an action, as in the words "point" and "feast." The understanding of object name and action name comes with numerous and varied experience in which language is involved. Word meanings cannot be taught in drill sessions; experiences must be arranged to promote understanding and visual-auditory association. Provide the child an opportunity to respond differentially to a word with a dual meaning. For example, say, "Show me the point on your pencil. Now point with your finger."

2.126 Uses past tense by adding "ed" to verb

Strand: 2-3 **Age:** 36-48m 3.0-4.0y

Definition

When he is involved in a verbal situation or presented with a picture, the child will respond by using a past tense verb, adding "ed". Examples: pushed, jumped, skipped.

Assessment Materials

At least five pictures that show actions that have happened in the past. Example: (1) Candle or match that has burned; (2) A boy climbing down from an apple tree with a bucket of apples; (3) A dog running after a cat and the cat is climbing a tree; (4) A boy walking away from a pond with a fish on a line; (5) A person with a raincoat on closing an umbrella, with the sun coming out from behind a cloud.

Assessment Procedures

Grouping: This skill can be introduced and assessed in a small group setting. However, if possible listen to the child when he is involved in a discussion or conversation for appropriate verbalization of past tense verbs with "ed."

Level One:

1. Invite the child to join you at a table. Place picture 1 on the table. Ask him what has happened in the picture.
2. Expected responses: "The candle has burned down," or "The candle is all burned up."
3. Observe and record whether he mentions the past tense verb with an "ed."
4. Continue the same procedure with the additional pictures 2 through 5.
5. If he has difficulty using the past tense of the verb, assist him by: (1) Show him the picture, point to the burned candle, and say, "The candle has burned down"; (2) Ask him to repeat the sentence; (3) Repeat the pointing and statement, if necessary, and ask him to echo what he heard; (4) Show him picture 2, point to the boy climbing down the tree, and say, "The boy has picked all the apples"; (5) Ask him to repeat the sentence; (6) Repeat the pointing and statement, if necessary, and ask him to echo what he heard.
6. Show him picture 1 again. Ask him what has happened in the picture.
7. Observe whether he mentions the past tense verb with an "ed" (e.g., burned).
8. Continue with pictures 2 through 5.

Level Two:

9. Observe the child when he is involved in a discussion or a conversation for appropriate verbalization of past tense verbs with "ed."

Credit: + Child uses past tense by adding "ed" to verb.

Adaptations

The child needs to be aware that he uses one verb form when he talks about things in the past and another when he talks about things that are to happen in the future. A child is not conscious of structure and grammar, so he must associate certain experiences with a stated form. Listen to him carefully to determine whether he speaks only in the present tense, using statements as "Go to the store" and "Have breakfast in." Neither one indicates if it is from the past or if it relates to the future. The child needs to understand the experience and associate it with the correct grammatical structure. When this is internalized, he will use appropriate expressive construction. For example, place two or three visuals in front of him, say a sentence, and ask him to point to the one that represents what has been said. Then show him two more pictures, the first picture shows a dog eating, and the next one shows the dog standing by an empty bowl. Point to the picture of the dog eating and say, "What is the dog doing?" After he responds, point to the picture of the dog standing by an empty bowl and say, "What has happened in this picture?" If he has difficulty, prompt as needed.

2.127 Carries out 3 simple related successive commands in order

Strand: 2-1A **Age:** 36-48m 3.0-4.0y

Definition

When presented with a three-step command in which the steps are logically related, the child will respond by completing the necessary steps in order.

Assessment Materials

Note: The sequence of steps for each activity might vary according to the particular classroom routine, but you should be able to find a number of three-step commands that naturally occur within the regular daily schedule. Make sure that the motor skills and the vocabulary used are within the range of the child's ability.
At least four different activities each consisting of three steps which logically follow one another. These activities may commonly occur in the child's typical daily routine. Example: Activity One - (arriving at school) Hang up your backpack, go to the bathroom, and come to group time. Activity Two - (lunch time) Wash your hands, get your lunch box, and find a seat at the table. Activity Three - (outside play) Put your toys away, put on your jacket, and line up at the door. Activity Four - (end of the day) Put your lunch box in your backpack, put on your jacket, and put on your backpack.

Assessment Procedures

Note: It is important to consider the procedures for learning analysis when you ask a child to deal with multi-step tasks. The learning analysis is: (1) Tell the child what you want her to do and allow time for a response. If she does not respond: (2) Demonstrate what you want her to do and allow time for response. If she does not respond: (3) Tell and demonstrate what you want her to do and allow time for response. If she does not respond: (4) Tell her what to do and provide physical cueing as needed. If she does not respond (5) Tell her what to do and physically assist her through each step. Repeat any of the above as needed.

Grouping: This skill should be assessed one-on-one with the child.

1. Before giving the commands, explain that you are going to give the child some directions, and ask her to listen carefully.
2. Tell her not to start until you say, "Begin now."
3. Say, "Hang up your backpack, go to the bathroom, and come to group time."
4. Say, "Begin now."
5. Observe her response.
6. If she has a problem performing the task, repeat the directions very slowly.
7. If she continues to have a problem, break the sequences down by saying, "Hang up your backpack," pause for her to react, then say, "Go to the bathroom," pause, say, "Come to group time," and pause for the child's response.
8. The next day, repeat the three-step command without pausing.
9. If she is successful, continue with the other activities at the appropriate times.
10. Observe her responses.

Credit: + Child carries out a three-step command in which the steps are logically related.

Adaptations

Children who have difficulty following oral directions are probably experiencing either a problem comprehending what has been spoken or in retaining the directions. If a child is able to carry out the first part of the two-step related command and then cannot complete the second step, this may indicate a short-term memory problem. If the directions given are within her motor skill ability, but she is not successful, she may lack word comprehension. It is important for her to understand exactly what to do. If she does not respond promptly and correctly to the directions given, repeat the directions. It is also necessary to take a look at each sub-skill of the task to make sure she understands each part. For example, in the command, "Clap your hands and sit down," does the child know what the words "clap," "hands" and "sit" mean? And does she comprehend the words "down" and "hands" in the context of the sentence? Before you assume that the child cannot perform the command or prompt his response, repeat the directions, clarify word meanings, and if possible, simplify the directions to make sure they are understandable.

2.128 Uses four to six words in a sentence

Strand: 2-4B **Age:** 36-54m 3.0-4.6y

Definition
The child will spontaneously say a four- to six-word sentence.

Assessment Materials
A collection of summer and winter clothes for dress-up, such as hats, scarves, dresses, shirts, blouses, shorts, pants, jackets, sweaters, boots, shoes, slippers, capes, formal gowns, robes, sleep wear, raincoats, bathing suits, etc.

Assessment Procedures
Grouping: This skill can be introduced and assessed one-on-one with the child. However, it is more appropriate to listen the child when she is involved in a conversation, discussion, or play activity, to observe her use of sentences. Record what she says and note the number of words used in a sentence.

1. Place the dress-up clothes next to the child. Tell the child that she is going to get to dress up.
2. Ask her to think about who she will be, what she is going to do, and where she will be going after she gets dressed up.
3. Give her time to choose her clothes and get dressed.
4. After she has donned the clothes, ask her questions about who she is, where she is going, and what she is going to do. Word the questions in such a way that the child must answer in more than one word.
5. Encourage her to answer in complete sentences.
6. To modify this activity, dress up yourself, and join the child in a conversation about the make-believe setting you are both enjoying.

Credit: + Child uses four to six words spontaneously in a sentence.

Adaptations
A child may be able to use a pivot word (ball), and then develop short phrases from the pivot (big ball, play ball, my ball), but she is not able to generate longer syntactic units or sentences. Often she has not learned to internalize sentence patterns so she cannot create sentences. To create sentences from pivot words or pivot phrases, the child needs to understand language, to remember word sequences, and to formulate words based on grammar structures. When a child begins to develop sentence structure, it is usually due to two factors: (1) Imitation and reduction. Example: A person may say, "This is a big red ball," and the child will respond with "big ball"; (2) Imitation and expansion. Example: The child says "big ball," and a person who hears the phrase might say, "Can you throw the big ball to me?", which is an expansion of the phrase and something the child can respond to. The more the child is immersed in syntactical sentences, the more natural grammar and sentence structure will become to her.

2.129 Uses pivot verb "is" to form kernel sentences

Strand: 2-3 **Age:** 37-40m 3.1-3.4y

Definition
When the child is involved in a verbal situation or presented with a visual, he will respond by using the pivot verb "is" to form a kernel sentence. Examples: That is a cat. The cup is broken. (A kernel sentence is a simple declarative sentence in the active voice from which both simpler and more complicated English sentences may be derived).

Assessment Materials
At least six pictures that demonstrate an object (noun) in which the verb "is" becomes the core for a verbal response. Examples: a house, a boy sleeping, a broken toy, a dog, a baby crying, a bird flying.

Assessment Procedures
Grouping: This skill can be introduced and assessed one-on-one with the child. However, the most important assessment procedure is made by observing the child in a natural conversation and listening for his language usage.

Level One:
1. Show the child the picture of the house, point to it, and say, "This is a house."
2. Show him the picture of the boy sleeping and say, "The boy is sleeping."
3. Show him the picture of the broken toy and say, "What has happened to the toy?"
4. Pause for his response.
5. If he has difficulty, show him the picture of the boy sleeping again and say, "The boy is sleeping."
6. Then ask him to tell you what the boy is doing.
7. Pause for his response.
8. Show him the picture of the broken toy again and say, "What has happened to the toy?"
9. Pause for his response.
10. Continue with the other pictures: a dog, a baby crying, and a bird flying.

Level Two:
11. Observe the child when he is involved in a discussion or a conversation for appropriate use of a pivot word in sentence formation.

Credit: + Child uses the pivot verb "is" to form a kernel sentence.

Adaptations

The child must be aware that he uses one verb form when he talks about things in the past and another when he talks about things that are to happen in the future. A child is not conscious of structure and grammar, so he must associate certain experiences with a stated form. Listen to him carefully to determine whether he speaks only in the present tense, using statements such as "Go to the store" and "Have breakfast in." Neither one indicates if it is from the past or if it relates to the future. He must understand the experience and associate it with the correct grammatical structure; when this is internalized, he will use appropriate expressive construction. For example, place two or three visuals in front of him, say a sentence, and ask him to point to the picture that represents what you said. One picture shows a dog eating, and the next picture shows the dog standing by an empty bowl. Point to the picture of the dog eating and say, "What is the dog doing?" After he responds, point to the picture of the dog standing by an empty bowl and say, "What has happened in this picture?" If he has difficulty, prompt as needed.

2.130 Combines noun phrase and verb phrase to form kernel sentences

Strand: 2-3 **Age:** 30-44m 2.6-3.8y

Definition

When the child is involved in a verbal situation or presented with a visual, she will respond by using a noun phrase with a verb phrase. She may express the phrases with an article, a noun, the verb "is," and a verb (e.g., The dog is barking). (A kernel sentence is a simple declarative sentence in the active voice from which both simpler and more complicated English sentence may be derived).

Assessment Materials

A few objects that can be maneuvered. Examples: child-safe scissors, a spoon, a toy car, a hand puppet.

Assessment Procedures

Grouping: This skill can be introduced and assessed in a small group setting. However, the most important assessment procedure is made by observing her in a natural conversational situation.

Level One:
1. Select one of the objects and create an action with it. For example, use the scissors to cut out a picture, use the spoon to eat, move the toy car, or make the hand puppet clap.
2. After your performance, ask the child what the puppet did. Expected responses include: "puppet clap," "The puppet clapped her hands, " or "I saw the puppet clap her hands."
3. Observe and record her response.
4. Continue the above process with the other manipulative items.
5. If she has difficulty, perform the action, and state what is occurring at the same time. Repeat several times. Give her the item, and ask her to do the same thing and to say what is happening. Encourage her to do the action and make the statement several times.
6. Select another item, perform an action and state what is occurring at the same time. Repeat several times. Give her the item, and ask her to do the same thing and to say what is happening. Encourage her to do the action and make the statement several times.
7. Select another object and create an action. After demonstrating, ask her, "What was the [puppet] doing?"
8. Observe and record her response.
9. Continue the above process with other manipulative items.

Level Two:
10. Observe the child when she is involved in a discussion or a conversation for appropriate verbalization of noun/verb usage.

Credit: + Child combines a noun phrase and a verb phrase to form simple kernel sentences.

Adaptations

As the child progresses in her use of nouns, it is important for you to teach nouns that are more abstract or that have added inflected endings. Using categorical nouns is an effective method to deal with expanded meaning and usage. as an example, have her sort pictures into two categories--clothes and food. After she sorts the pictures, provide her with the appropriate words, phrases, and sentences: "We wear these; they are clothes," and "We eat these; they are foods."

When teaching verbs, remember the first objective is for her to understand that a word now represents an action, not the name of an object. Although personal experience is most valuable, you may also use visuals. Show the child a picture with two animals and a girl running. Help her understand that the word run refers to an action, and that the girl and the two animals are not named "Run." Point to one of the running animals and say, "Tell me what this animal is doing." If she has difficulty say, "The dog is running." Point to the dog and say, "Tell me what this animal is doing."

Some verbs are not easily dramatized or visually represented. The meaning of these verbs must be mastered over a period of time, but as often as possible, provide an actual experience. For example, mix dough for making cookies. When you place the cookies in the oven for baking, look at them often and say, "The cookies are baking in the oven." Talk about how the longer they bake, the darker they get, etc. The child needs to be aware that she uses one verb form when she talks about things in the past and another when she talks about things that are to happen in the future. The child is not conscious of structure and grammar, so she must associate certain experiences with a stated form. Listen to her carefully to determine whether she is speaking only in the present tense, using such statements as, "Go to the store," and "Have breakfast in." Neither one indicates if it is from the past or if it relates to the future. The child needs to understand the experience and associate it with the correct grammatical structure, when this is internalized, she will use appropriate expressive construction.

As an example, place two or three visuals in front of her, say a sentence, and ask her to point to the one that represents what has been said. The first picture shows a dog eating, and the next picture shows the dog standing by an empty bowl. Point to the picture of the dog eating and say, "What is the dog doing?" After she responds, point to the picture of the dog standing by an empty bowl and say, "What has happened in this picture?" If she has difficulty, prompt as needed.

2.131 Asks questions using "is" and "have" forms
Strand: 2-3 **Age:** 37-42m 3.1-3.6y

Definition
When the child is involved in a verbal situation or presented with a visual, he will respond by asking a question using either "is" (e.g., "Is that a dog?") or "have" ("Do you have the cracker?")

Assessment Materials
A few objects familiar to the child. Examples: a flower, a book, a rock, a cookie. A box, a sack, or a basket.

Assessment Procedures
Grouping: This skill can be introduced and assessed in a small group setting. However, the most important assessment procedure is made when you observe him in a natural conversation and listen for the words he uses when he asks a question.

Level One:
1. Place one of the items in one of the containers so it is out of the child's view.
2. Make up a riddle about the hidden item. Example: "It is pretty. It grows in a garden. You can pick it. You can put it in a vase. It smells good."
3. After telling the riddle, ask the child "What is it?"
4. Give him a few opportunities to guess, but encourage him to use the following format, "Do you have a [flower]?"
5. Exchange roles with him, so that he gives the riddle and you become the one who guesses.
6. Continue the above procedure with other objects.

Level Two:
7. Observe the child when he is involved in a discussion or a conversation for his appropriate use of "is" and "have" questions.

Credit: + Child asks questions using "is" or "have" appropriately.

Adaptations
See #2.129.

The first objective in assisting the child in learning verbs is for the child to understand that a word now represents an action, not the name of an object. If a word, such as drink, is used in association with milk, he must understand that it means an action, not another item. When a word like running is used, he needs to know that it is not a name of a person, a place, or a thing, but it means something that a person, place or thing is doing. The following is recommended for teaching verbs:

The child needs to be aware that he uses one verb form when he talks about things in the past and another when he talks about things that are to happen in the future. A child is not conscious of structure and grammar, so he must associate certain experiences with a stated form. Listen to him carefully to determine whether he speaks only in the present tense, using statements such as, "Go to the store" and "Have breakfast in." Neither indicates if it is from the past or if it relates to the future. The child must understand the experience and associate it with the correct grammatical structure; when this is internalized, he will use appropriate expressive construction. For example, place two or three visuals in front of him, say a sentence, and ask him to point to the one that represents what has been said. The first picture shows a dog eating, and the next picture shows the dog standing by an empty bowl. Point to the picture of the dog eating and say, "What is the dog doing?" After he responds, point to the picture of the dog standing by an empty bowl and say, "What has happened in this picture?" If he has difficulty, prompt as needed.

2.132 (Removed, see page xviii)

2.133 Uses predicate phrases with noun phrases

Strand: 2-3 **Age:** 37-43m 3.1-3.7y

Definition
When he is involved in a verbal situation or presented with a visual, the child will respond by using the correct predicate phrase with a noun phrase (The boy is my brother). Attention should be given to the basic sentence patterns used in our language. The basic sentence patterns fundamental for early language development are: noun phrases and verb phrases, noun phrases divided by a determiner and a noun; as well as subdividing a verb phrase. Beginning sentences are all simple, active, declarative and referred to as kernel sentences.

Assessment Materials
A series of five pictures depicting contents such as: (1) Boys run. (2) Boys play games. (3) The girl is my sister. (4) The girl is short. (5) The girl became sick.

Assessment Procedures
Grouping: This skill can be introduced and assessed in a small group setting. However, listening to the child when he is engaged in natural conversation is the most important assessment procedure.

Level One:
1. Display the pictures one at a time to the child. Ask him what is happening in the pictures.
2. Observe whether he uses appropriate phrase structure.
3. If he has a difficult time responding to the pictures or uses incorrect phrasing, show him picture 1 and say, "Boys run." Ask him to look at the picture and repeat, "Boys run." Continue with the rest of pictures in the same manner.
4. After he looks at the picture and repeats what he heard, display the pictures one at a time for him. Ask him what is happening in each picture.
5. Observe whether he uses appropriate phrase structure.

Level Two:
6. Observe the child in a free discussion or conversation period for appropriate verbalization of noun phrases.

Credit: + Child uses predicate phrases with noun phrases.

Adaptations
See #2.129.

General Strategies:

The following are recommendations for teaching nouns:

(1) Nouns should be taught as concepts, not just as words or labels. A coat stands for a child's coat as well as an adult's coat or a dog's coat. Your instruction should include the general and specific meanings; many words represent many things, others, such as names, denote a single meaning. For example, point to the child's coat and say, "Your coat is red." Point to another coat and say, "Bob's coat is

brown." Point to another coat and say, "This coat is very warm."

(2) Nouns should be taught using real objects, progressing to models of the real object and then to pictures of the objects. Make sure the child understands that real items may be represented in pictorial form.

The following are recommendations for teaching verbs:

(1) Although personal experience is most valuable, you can also use visuals. Show the child, for example, a picture of two animals and a girl running. Help him understand that the word "run" refers to an action, and that the girl and the two animals are not named "Run." Point to one of the running animals and say, "Tell me what this animal is doing." If he has difficulty, say, "The dog is running." Point to the dog and say, "Tell me what this animal is doing."

(2) Some verbs are not easily dramatized or visually represented. The meaning of these verbs needs to be mastered over a period of time, but as often as possible, provide an actual experience.

2.134 (Removed, see page xviii)

2.135 Categorizes sounds
Strand: 2-1A **Age:** 43-46m 3.7-3.10y

Definition
The child will be presented with a sound that can be associated with a category, for example, an animal sound, a transportation sound, a people sound, or a musical sound, and he will be asked to identify each of the sounds by category. He will be asked to say the category (animal) or to point to a picture that represents the category (a picture of several different animals). Note: When selecting the sounds for the tape category, use sounds that are within his realm of experience.

Assessment Materials
Tapes (or CDs) prepared as follows: Tape One--a dog barking, a cat meowing, a cow mooing, a sheep baaing, etc. Tape Two--sounds of a drum, a horn, a piano, a whistle, etc. Tape Three--baby crying, a person laughing, a child singing, a woman talking, etc. Tape Four--a dog barking, a cow mooing, a whistle, a drum beat, a cat meowing, a piano, a horn, etc. When preparing these tapes, allow a pause after each sound to allow the child a chance to respond. A group of animal pictures cut and glued on a sheet of white construction paper, a group of musical instruments cut and glued on a sheet of white construction paper, and a picture of a baby crying, a child singing, a person talking and a person laughing cut and glued on a sheet of white construction paper. A tape player to play the pre-recorded tapes.

Assessment Procedures
Grouping: This skill should be assessed one-on-one with the child.
1. Ask the child to join you at the worktable. Tell him you are going to play a tape that has different sounds and that he is to name the sounds as he hears them.
2. Play Tape One.
3. If he does not say "dog" after the barking sound, cue him, and continue with the other animal's sounds.
4. At the end of the tape say, " You named a dog, a cat, a cow, and a sheep. All those sounds were sounds that are made by ____."
5. Pause, allowing him to say "animals." If he does not say "animals," show him the picture of the animals.
6. Replay the tape and when he hears the dog bark, say, "That animal was a dog."
7. Continue with the other animal sounds on the tape. Be sure to say, "That animal was a [animal name]" after each sound.
8. Remove all the pictures.
9. Play Tape Two and repeat the above procedure.
10. Explain to the child that you are going to play another tape. Tell him that some of the sounds he will hear are the sounds of an animal and some are sounds of music. Tell him that instead of saying the name of the animal or the musical instrument, all he has to say is "animal" if it is an animal sound and "music" if it is a musical sound.
11. Play Tape Three. Repeat the above process.
12. Play Tape Four.
13. Use the first sound as a teaching item.
14. Allow the child to hear the sounds and to name the categories.
15. Note his responses.
16. If he has a problem naming the categories, replay the tape using the categorical pictures to assist in the discrimination.
17. Note his responses and indicate that visual assists were used.
18. Remove the pictures and replay the tape.

Credit: + Child categorizes sounds from at least two different groups correctly, with or without visual assists.

Adaptations

Often children who have a problem with identification of environmental sounds are thought to have an auditory acuity problem. These children should be referred to their pediatrician to see if audiological testing is indicated. Determination of an auditory acuity issue should be made as soon as possible because the education for a child who has an auditory receptive problem (with no hearing loss) is different than for a child who has a hearing loss. Professional audiometric testing and diagnostic instruction is necessary in determining intervention strategies for such a child.

2.136 Describes action in a picture using the present tense

Strand: 2-3 **Age:** 43-46m 3.7-3.10y

Definition
When she is presented with a visual, the child will respond by using descriptive words. She will describe the action occurring in the picture.

Assessment Materials
A picture showing people involved in some form of action. Examples: a birthday party, a picnic, giving a dog a bath, a baseball game.

Assessment Procedures
Grouping: This skill can be introduced and assessed in a small group setting. However, observe the child when she is looking at a book and listen to what she says, record any response that shows she can describe actions in a picture using present tense.

Level One:
1. Show the picture to the child. Ask her to describe what is happening in the picture.
2. If she begins to describe what has happened or what will happen, stop her and say, "No, tell me what is happening right now."
3. Listen to her verbal description to determine the correct use of present tenses. Record her response.
4. If she is hesitant to describe what is happening or has problems with present tense, point to one action in the picture and prompt her by asking questions. Examples: What is the boy doing? Where is he? Who is with him?
5. Encourage her to describe other areas of the picture.

Level Two:
6. Observe the child when she is involved with a visual, and listen for her description in the present tense.

Credit: + Child uses descriptive words to describe the action occurring in a picture (using present tense).

Adaptations
Some children understand what they hear, and they can use words and phrases, but they cannot formulate and organize words according to correct structure. They may tend to omit words, change the order of words, use incorrect tenses, and make other grammatical errors. The ability to form sentences requires the ability to understand, to recall word sequence, and to generalize principles for sentence construction. Even though a child may recognize correct sentence structure, she may be unable to reproduce words in a meaningful sequence. Recognizing correct order and reproducing sentences heard are important expressive elements; however, the role of memory must also be considered. A child must retain what she hears and apply the principles to other settings. In making the application, she may lack the ability to manipulate language structures. She hears certain models, perceives the order of words, but she lacks the ability to construct sentences on her own. She may understand certain grammar forms automatically, and she chooses words to fit into the grouping that are semantically and syntactically correct, but she is unable to transfer this automatic grammar placement. She does not realize that a correct structural pattern can be used in another structural setting. During everyday activities, talk about what the child is doing. Structure the sentences you use around her experiences. This will assist her in the retention and internalization of various sentence patterns.

2.137 Repeats simple words in the order presented

Strand: 2-1A **Age:** 43-48m 3.7-4.0y

Definition
When he hears no less than three or more than four familiar related words, he will be able to repeat them in the order presented. When he hears no less than three or more than four unrelated words, he will be able to repeat them in the order presented.

Assessment Materials

Four familiar objects: Set One--an apple, a rock, a crayon, a book. Four single-syllable related familiar words: Set Two--cup, bowl, glass, plate. Four single-syllable unrelated words: Set Three--sun, coat, grass, bat. Four phrases or sentences that contain a word that will be emphatically said.

Assessment Procedures

Grouping: This skill should be assessed one-on-one with the child.

1. Invite the child to sit across from you at the table. Explain that you are going to say some words and that when you say "begin now," he is to say the words that he just heard. Tell him it is important for him to say the words in the order he heard them.
2. Place the three familiar objects (Set One) on the table. Point to each object and say its name.
3. After the child has named each item, take away the items and say, "Apple, Rock, Book."
4. Say, "Begin now."
5. Listen to his response and record.
6. If he has any concerns, place the items back on the table and repeat the above.
7. Explain that you are going to say some words (Set Two), and that he is to listen carefully.
8. Say, "Cup, Bowl, Plate."
9. Say, "Begin now."
10. Listen to his response and record.
11. If he has any concerns, repeat the words, very slowly, and then say, "Begin now."
12. If he continues to have problems, tell him that you are going to say the words and for him to repeat each word after you say it.
13. Say, "Cup" (pause for the child to say "cup"). Say, "Bowl" (pause for him to say "bowl"). Say, "Plate" (pause for him to say "plate").
14. Explain that you are going to say the words and that he is to listen carefully.
15. Say, "Cup, bowl, plate."
16. Say, "Begin now."
17. Listen to his response and record.
18. Tell him that you are going to say some words (Set Three) and that he is to listen carefully. Say, "Sun, Coat, Grass."
19. Say, "Begin now."
20. Listen to his response and record.
21. Indicate the sets the child gave the correct response. The set assessment levels are: Set One--Naming words with objects for support; Set Two--Naming words that are related in content, with single word cueing; Set Three--Naming words that are not related.
22. Repeat the activities above but this time using four words.

Credit: + Child repeats simple words (at least three and no more than four) in the order presented.

Adaptations

Children with receptive language difficulties may have a problem comprehending the spoken word. Some can understand simple words such as nouns, but not words that represent actions, qualities or ideas. If a word has multiple meanings and the determination is based on its usage in the sentence, the child will find it easier to name the word when it is a noun than to name the same word when it is a verb. However, when he is asked to name words that he has just heard, he is involved in receptive memory skill without comprehension. He may make a visual/experience association with the words he has just heard. This association assists in sequential memory recall.

2.138 Uses noun with demonstrative (this dog, that car)

Strand: 2-3 **Age:** 43-48m 3.7-4.0y

Definition

When she is involved in a verbal situation or is presented with a visual, the child will respond by using a noun with a demonstrative pronoun. This demonstrative pronoun is used to indicate the one referred to and distinguishing it from other noun-related items during a conversation or in an illustration.

Assessment Materials

Three sets of single-item pictures that include three different positions or types of one subject. Examples: Set One--(1) A little, black dog; (2) A big, white dog; (3) A spotted dog. Set Two--(1) A pair of sports shoes; (2) A pair of high-heeled pumps; (3) A pair of boots. Set Three--(1) A picture book; (2) A coloring book; (3) A little board book.

Assessment Procedures

Grouping: This skill can be introduced and assessed in a small group setting. However, the most important assessment procedure is made by observing the child in a natural conversational setting and listening for appropriate verbalizations.

Level One:
1. Place Set One pictures, picture side-up, on a table in view of the child. Say, "Look at the pictures."
2. Point to picture 1 in Set One and say, "Tell me about this picture. When you tell me about the picture, start with these words: 'This dog is...'"
3. Pause to allow her time to discuss the picture.
4. Listen for her to use the phrase, "this dog," and then continue to describe it.
5. Continue with the other two dog pictures in Set One.
6. Observe her use of the noun with a demonstrator.
7. Repeat the above, using Sets Two and Three.
8. If she has difficulty, model the response. For example, look at picture one from Set One and say, "This dog is black." Then ask the child to look at the picture and to repeat what you stated, "This dog is black." Then look at picture two from Set One and say, "This dog is white." Ask the child to look at the picture and repeat what you stated, "This dog is white." Repeat with picture three from Set One. Then ask the child to look at picture one from Set One again and say, "Tell me about this picture. When you tell about the picture start with these words: 'This dog is...'"

Level Two:
9. Observe the child when she is involved in a discussion or a conversation for appropriate verbalization.

Credit: + Child uses a noun with a demonstrative pronoun correctly.

Adaptations

See #2.136.

Throughout the day model the appropriate use of pronouns by talking about things you see in the child's environment. For example, when the child is getting dressed, describe her clothing, such as, "This jacket is blue." "This dress is green." Describe the toys she is playing with, "That cow is white with black spots." Children continue to learn language through imitating what they hear.

2.139 Uses negatives in sentences

Strand: 2-3 **Age:** 48-60m 4.0-5.0y

Definition

When the child is involved in a verbal situation or presented with a visual, he will respond by using negatives in sentences ("The car is not broken."). He may also start to use contractions in sentences ("The car isn't broken.")

Assessment Materials

At least four different pictures that include a central character or theme. Examples: (1) A colored picture of a cat curled up on a pillow; (2) A clown with a sad face, plaid pants, and juggling balls; (3) A girl with a blue sweater on, carrying a basket and being followed by a dog; (4) A boy running in the rain pushing his bicycle with wet clothing and hair; (5) A boy crying; (6) A car that has a flat tire; (7) A girl trying to reach a top shelf; (8) A child sick in bed.

Assessment Procedures

Grouping: This skill can be introduced and assessed in a small group setting. However, the most important assessment procedure is made by observing him in a natural conversation to determine his use of syntax and sentence structure.

Level One:
1. Explain to the child that you are going to show him some pictures. Show him picture 1 and say, "The cat is not white. The cat is not sleeping. The cat is not jumping."
2. Show him picture 2 and say, "Tell me about this picture and you must use the words, "is not."
3. Prompt him, if necessary.
4. Continue the above procedure using pictures 3 and 4.
5. Observe and record his use of the negative "is not."
6. If he has difficulty with this verbal task, ask him to repeat the sentences after you. Show him picture 2, and say, "The clown is not happy." Ask him to repeat the sentence. After he repeats the sentence say, "The clown does not have on blue pants." Ask him to repeat the sentence. After he repeats the sentence say, "The clown is not throwing balls." Ask him to repeat the sentence.
7. Show him picture 3 and 4 and say, "Tell me about this picture; you must use the words, 'is not.'"
8. Explain to him that you are going to show him some more pictures. Show him picture 5 and say, "The boy isn't happy."
9. Show him picture 6 and say, "Tell me what this car can't do."
10. Prompt as needed, for example, "This car _____ move."
11. Continue the above procedure using pictures 7 and 8.

12. Observe and record his use of negatives and contractions.

Level Two:
13. Observe the child when he is involved in a discussion or a conversation for appropriate verbalization of contractions and salience of negative aspects.

Credit: + Child uses negatives in sentences during verbal situations or when shown a picture. Child may begin using contractions in sentences, too.

Adaptations

The comprehension of negatives can be difficult for some children. When a child encounters the word "not," it signifies that one of the expressed aspects must be deduced through a logical operation. For example, consider these sentences: "The toy truck is not red. It is blue." In a negative sentence, the quality of the color, its redness, must be subtracted from the attributes of the truck. The second thought re-establishes the color by saying that the truck is blue. This example is relatively simple because the negative is directly followed by a true statement. When a "truth" sentence does not directly follow a "not" concept, it is difficult for some children to reach an adequate understanding. The ambiguities that exist in most negative statements are often difficult to express with meaning. When you work with a child who has difficulty in expressing negatives, follow a sequence of imitation: (1) The negative is directly followed by clarity--The ribbon is not pink. It is blue; (2) A negative and a positive stated about the same item--The ribbon is blue, but it is not in a bow; (3) The proximity and sequence of the not statement--The ribbon is not on the tray; (4) The logical complexity--The ribbon is not the smallest. This ribbon is not smaller than that ribbon.

A child may be very comfortable in using "no more," "no drink," "coat bye-bye," or "all gone," but when he must express a negative using the word "not," his comprehension may be vague.

2.140 Uses conjunctions in sentences

Strand: 2-3 **Age:** 43-48m 3.7-4.0y

Definition

When the child is involved in a verbal situation or presented with a visual, she will use a conjunction (e.g., and, but, or) in a sentence.

Assessment Materials

Set of several clauses to which you can add a clause by using "and" or "or."
Examples:
(1) Mary went to the store and Bill _____ .
(2) The bird flew up in the tree and the cat _____ .
(3) John will eat the big apple or the _____ .
(4) The red flower is in the vase, and the _____ .
(5) Mother is going to fix soup or she is going to fix _____ .
(6) We can have cheese pizza or _____ .

Assessment Procedures

Grouping: This skill can be assessed one-on-one with the child. However, listen and observe the child when she is involved in a discussion or a conversation for appropriate verbalization of two clauses joined by a conjunction.

Level One:
1. Explain to the child that you are going to say some sentences and that she is to finish each of them.
2. Say, "Mary went to the store and Bill _____ ."
3. Give her time to complete the sentence.
4. Provide assistance as needed, such as, "Where do think Bill went?" Repeat the sentence, say a word after "Bill," such as "stayed," and allow the child to complete the rest.
5. Continue with clauses 2 through 6.
6. After she completes the sentences, repeat the procedure, only stop before you say the conjunction. For example, "Mary went to the store _____ Bill stayed home."
7. Ask the child to repeat the sentence.
8. If she is comfortable using the conjunctions "and" and "or," repeat the clauses using other joiners such as "but," "if," "when," "because," "before," "so," "after," "as soon as," "while," "unless," "as," and "although."
9. If the child exhibits any difficulty, provide her with a practical experience and verbalize her actions. For example, ask her to walk across the room and then to sit on a chair. As she walks across the room, say "Jannelle is walking across the room;" as she is about to sit on the chair, say, "and she is going to sit on a chair."
10. Give her an opportunity to give directions for you or another child to act out, using two clauses. Be sure she verbalizes the actions (clauses) and the conjunction while the directive is being carried out.

Level Two:
11. Observe the child when she is involved in a discussion or a conversation for appropriate verbalization of two clauses joined by a conjunction.

Credit: + Child correctly uses conjunctions in sentences.

Adaptations
See 2.136.

Continue to model sentences using a conjunction while interacting with the child. Encourage the child to describe what they are doing and to use conjunctions in her sentences.

2.141 Uses infinitive verb forms in sentences
Strand: 2-3 **Age:** 43-48m 3.7-4.0y

Definition
When the child is involved in a verbal situation or presented with a visual, he will respond by using an infinitive verb form in a sentence. ("I want to...")

Assessment Materials
Four pictures collected that show a person or groups of persons doing some action. Examples: (1) A boy sitting at a table and eating; (2) A girl packing a suitcase; (3) People getting on a bus; (4) People walking down a path and waving good-bye.

Assessment Procedures
Grouping: This skill can be assessed one-on-one with the child. However, the most important assessment process is made by observing him in a natural conversation and listening for his usage of semantics and syntactics.

Level One:
1. Tell the child that you are going to show him two pictures. Place pictures 1 and 2 on the table face-up.
2. Ask him to listen while you tell him something about the picture.
3. Say, "Finish your breakfast. I want you to eat all your cereal."
4. Ask him to point to the picture that relates to that sentence.
5. Observe and record his response.
6. Ask him to listen once again.
7. Say, "Tomorrow the girl will go to visit her grandmother."
8. Ask him to point to the picture that relates to that sentence.
9. Observe and record his response.
10. Continue the above steps, using pictures 3 and 4.
11. After he is comfortable pointing to the correct pictures, ask him to say a sentence so that you will point to the correct picture.
12. If he has a problem using the correct form of an infinitive verb phrase, ask him to imitate your sentences.
13. For example, remove all the pictures except the one of the boy sitting at a table and eating. Discuss the picture, what is happening, who might be in the room, what he is eating, and so on. Then ask the child to listen to a sentence. Point to the picture and say, "Finish your breakfast. I want you to eat all your cereal."
14. Continue with the other three pictures.
15. After you have shown him the three pictures, discussed them, stated the model sentence, and had the child repeat the sentences, and then show him picture 1 again.
16. Ask him to tell you something about the picture.
17. Observe and record his response.

Level Two:
18. Observe the child when he is involved in a discussion or a conversation for appropriate verbalization of verb phrases.

Credit: + Child uses infinitive verb forms in sentences when involved in a verbal situation or presented with a visual.

Adaptations
See #2.129.

Continue to model sentences using an infinitive verb. Ask the child what he would like to play with, but have him respond with, "I want to _____." Do the same during mealtime by having the child request what he would like to eat by saying "I want to eat _____."

2.142 Uses auxiliary verbs "am," "is," "are" with present participle
Strand: 2-3 **Age:** 43-48m 3.7-4.0y

Definition
When the child is involved in a verbal situation or presented with a visual, she will respond by using auxiliary verbs, "am," "is," "are," with present participle (e.g., is running).

Assessment Materials
Four pictures that show a person or groups of people doing some action. Examples: (1) A boy

is sitting at a table and is eating. (2) A girl is packing a suitcase. (3) Two children are swinging. (4) Six boys are playing football.

Assessment Procedures

Grouping: This skill can be assessed one-on-one with the child. However, the most important assessment process is made by observing her in a natural conversation and listening for her usage of semantics and syntactics.

Level One:
1. Tell the child that you are going to show her two pictures. Place pictures 1 and 2 on the table face-up.
2. Ask her to listen while you tell her something about the picture.
3. Say, "John is eating his breakfast." Ask the child to point to the picture that relates to that sentence.
4. Observe and record her response.
5. Ask her to listen once again.
6. Say, "The girl is packing a suitcase. I am sure she is going on a trip." Ask her to point to the picture that relates to that sentence.
7. Observe and record her response.
8. Place pictures 3 and 4 on the table face-up. Tell her to listen carefully.
9. Say, "Bill and Sara are having fun on the park swings." Ask her to point to the picture that relates to that sentence.
10. Observe and record her response.
11. Ask her to listen while you tell her something about picture 4.
12. Say, "The boys are playing football. I am sure they are getting dirty." Ask her to point to the picture that relates to that sentence.
13. Observe and record her response.
14. After she is comfortable pointing to the correct pictures, ask her to say a sentence about the pictures so you point to the correct picture.
15. Encourage her to use auxiliary verbs "are," "is" and "am."
16. If she has a problem using the correct form of an auxiliary verb, ask her to imitate your sentences.
17. For example, remove all the pictures except the boy eating. Discuss the picture, what is happening, who might be in the room, and what the boy is eating, and then ask the child to listen to a sentence. Point to the picture and say, "John is eating his breakfast."
18. Continue with the other three pictures.
19. After you have shown and discussed the three pictures, stated the model sentence, and had the child repeat the sentence, show her picture 1 again.
20. Ask her to tell you something about the picture while you listen. Then point to the picture that relates to her sentence.
21. Observe and record her responses.

Level Two:
22. Observe the child when she is involved in a discussion or a conversation for appropriate verbalization of verb phrases.

Credit: + Child uses auxiliary verbs ("am," "is," or "are") with present participle in a sentence correctly.

Adaptations

In dealing with auxiliary verbs and infinitives, young children should understand that these words do not change the basic meaning of the verb they accompany. The child needs to understand that words such as "the short girl" and "the girl is short" express identical meanings. When the child uses the word "laugh," she needs to understand that it has the same meaning no matter what the tense or sentence structure is. For example, "I have laughed" or "I plan to laugh" or "I am laughing" or "She is laughing" or "They are laughing" or "I laugh" do not change the meaning of laugh. Modeling correct usage of auxiliary verbs and infinitives is the most important process for child imitation. If the child is unsure of the constant verb meaning, discuss the sentence meaning with her.

2.143 Points to common objects according to function based on verbal cues

Strand: 2-1A **Age:** 45-48m 3.9-4.0y

Definition

The child will be able to identify objects or pictures by their use and function.

Assessment Materials

Four sets of pictures cut from magazines or drawn, and glued on large cards, of the following functions: Set 1--To hold food: a bowl, a carton, a pot, a basket. Set 2--To keep clean: soap, toothpaste, a washcloth, a sponge. Set 3--To rest on: bed, chair, hammock, sleeping bag. Set 4--To light up a room or an area: a light bulb, a flashlight, a candle, headlight on a car.

Assessment Procedures

Grouping: This skill can be assessed in a small group setting. Remind the children that they

will need to listen and take turns during the activity.
1. Place one card from each set on the table.
2. Ask the child to name the cards that are in view.
3. Tell him that you are going to say some words that tell what one of these pictures is used for.
4. Say, "Point to the picture that is used to hold food." Continue until he has identified all the pictures.
5. Place another card from each set on the table.
6. Repeat the above directions with the different cards.
7. Write down the number of pictures the child identified correctly and the time he took to respond to each card.

Credit: + Child points to objects and pictures by their use and function based on verbal cues.

Adaptations

It is important that the child be very familiar with the objects presented. Example: If the child has never seen a pair of ear-muffs, has never seen anyone wear them, etc., he needs an opportunity to explore the function of the item. When the child is presented with an object and a discussion occurs as to the function of the item, a complete description, a demonstration of the item's use and any comparisons should be introduced.

2.144 Identifies words that rhyme

Strand: 2-1A **Age:** 48-52m 4.0-4.4y

Definition

The child will repeat the phonemic sound order of words. These words or syllables have the same patterns (usually consonant-vowel-consonant-CVC) and are presented to the child orally. She is expected to say other words that have the same linguistic arrangement. Generally the words are said in rhymes or jingles (Little Miss Muffet--Sat on a tuffet) prior to isolation (Muffet - tuffet); however, an extended skill could include beginning consonant substitution (rat, cat, fat, mat, bat, spat.)

Assessment Materials

Three well-known nursery rhymes (*Jack and Jill, Peas Porridge Hot, Little Bo Peep*). Three made-up verses that rhyme. Examples: (1)The boy got up to bat. He had on a funny hat. (2) A little mouse lived in a straw house. (3) When this cup of juice is done, I will give you another one. Three simple rhymes, leaving the last word blank. Examples: (1) We have fun when we _____. (2) See the silly cat sit on the _____. (3) I hear a bell but don't you _____.

Assessment Procedures

Grouping: This skill can be assessed one-on-one with the child, or in a small group with no more than four children. Remind the children that they will need to listen and take turns during the activity.
1. Discuss the concept of rhyming words with the child. Provide her with examples of rhymes (tin--pin, run--fun).
2. Tell her that you are going to say some rhymes, and that when she hears the words that sound alike, or rhyme, she is to say the words.
3. Use the first nursery rhyme as a teaching example.
4. Continue with the nursery rhymes. Tabulate if she says the correct words and write down the words she said if she made an error.
5. Continue with the three verses that rhyme. Tabulate her responses and record the wrong words.
6. Continue with the open-ended rhymes. Record the words stated by the child.

Credit: + Child identifies or says words that rhyme. The words or syllables have the same pattern (typically CVC).

Adaptations

Auditory discrimination can be difficult for some children who learn best through visual modality. However, the ability to determine the likenesses and differences between sounds is basic to the sound/symbol association. If rhyming is a concern, consider providing instruction in the following: (1) Sound location, (2) Identification of common sounds, (3) Distinguishing between grossly different sounds, (4) Designating words that sound the same from a group of words--man, bat, man, put, (5) Providing her with a picture and directing her to match pictures that rhyme can be a helpful assistance to auditory separation. It is recommended that the pictures be phased out as soon as possible.

2.145 Carries out simple one-part commands that denote difference in sensory qualities

Strand: 2-2 **Age:** 48-53m 4.0-4.5y

Definition
The child will complete a command when presented with two items that are visually different, or two different volumes of sound, or two materials that have tactile differences, or two materials of different weight.

Assessment Materials
Items that show differences: Visual differences--four toys of different sizes (example: two toy animals and two balls); auditory differences--one noisemaker (a drum or a pan lid); tactile differences--two pieces of fabric (silky material, sandpaper, plastic, straw, emery board); Proprioceptive differences--two items of different weights (a heavy rock, a piece of foam, a paper weight, a ball of cotton).

Assessment Procedures
Note: There are a number of synonyms for small and big, whichever one you choose to use during the assessment, use it exclusively.

Grouping: This skill can be introduced and assessed in a small group setting, no more than four children. Remind the children that they will be taking turns while playing the game and that they will need to listen and wait for their turn.

1. Invite the child to join you at the work area. Place the two toys of different sizes on the table. Allow the child to play with the two toys.
2. Pick up the largest toy and say, "This is the big truck."
3. Put the toy down and ask the child to give you the big truck.
4. Repeat the above, using the small toy.
5. Replace the two toys with two different toys.
6. Place the two different toys on the table. Say, "Give me the big ball." Pause to allow him time to respond to the command.
7. Place the big toy on the table next to the small toy.
8. Say, "Give me the small ball." Pause to allow him time to respond to the command.
9. Observe his response to the command.
10. Place the two items of different weights on the table. Allow the child to handle the two items.
11. Ask him to point to the item that is the heaviest and then to the lightest.
12. If he is having a problem with this task, demonstrate the heavy item by the way you hold it. Demonstrate the light item by the way you hold it.
13. Say, "Give me the heaviest thing on the table." Pause to give him time to select and hand you the heaviest object.
14. Replace the item on the table.
15. Say, "Give me the lightest thing on the table." Pause to give him time to select and hand you the lightest object.
16. Observe his response to the command.
17. Place the drum on the table. Using drumsticks, hit the drum loudly. Pause and then hit the drum softly.
18. Say, "Play the drum loudly." Give him time to respond.
19. Say, "Play the drum softly." Give him time to respond.
20. Observe his response to the directive.
21. Place the two different pieces of material on the table. Invite him to touch the material.
22. Say, "Give me the thing on the table that feels rough." Pause for his response.
23. Replace the material on the table.
24. Say, "Give me the thing on the table that feels smooth." Pause for his response.
25. If the child is comfortable in responding to directions containing adjectives that involve sensory differences, mix up the visual, tactile, and weight objects and follow the above procedures. To expand this assessment, add the sensory elements of gustatory (sweet/sour), depth perception (thick/thin) or climatic (hot/cold).

Credit: + Child completes a command when presented with two items that are visually different, two different volumes of sound, or two materials that have tactile difference.

Adaptations
Some children have a problem comprehending the comparative characteristics of objects and situations. These children often have a predetermined base from which to view similarities. For example, the child has a toy car that is tiny; hence, he refers to all toy cars that are larger than his toy car as big. When a noise isn't as loud as a car horn, he calls it soft. It is difficult for this child to understand varying degrees: loud is the loudest sound he has ever heard and identified as a loud noise. To assist him in understanding degrees varying from the standard, establish a standard in this manner:

Draw a big face on a sheet of paper or on the chalk board, and label it as "the face," and then illustrate a bigger face and a smaller face. Discuss and compare the two extremes with "the face," which is the standard. It is also helpful to use the object or the situation that the child is viewing as his standard, such as bringing in his small car and establishing it as a standard.

2.146 Speaks with inflection when describing an event or action

Strand: 2-4B **Age:** 48-53m 4.0-4.5y

Definition

When he is telling about an exciting occurrence, the child will speak with voice inflections that indicate enthusiasm, surprise, and spirit. He may increase or decrease his volume and/or pitch to emphasize a part of the description, or he may imitate sounds or dialogue he heard for effect.

Assessment Materials

A short story selected or written that leads up to an exciting ending. It should be told to a climactic part, and then the child is asked to finish the story.
Examples:
Story One--Bill went to visit his grandmother in a strange city. When the plane landed and Bill got off, he looked for his grandmother. She was not there, so Bill was all alone. Bill said, "_____."
Story Two--Sue swam out onto the lake with her float raft. She was lying on it and floating far away from the shore. Suddenly Sue saw a big fish jump out of the water. It looked like a shark. Sue cried, "_____!"

Assessment Procedures

Note: It is important to become an enthusiastic listener as the child becomes excited telling his story.
Grouping: This skill can be introduced and assessed in a small group setting. However, the most important assessment procedure is made by observing the child in a conversation and listening for his intonation and inflection as he relates his own experiences to someone else.
Level One:
1. Explain to the child that you are going to tell a story without an ending. Tell him that he is to make up the ending.
2. Read or tell Story One, stopping after you say, "Bill said," and pause to let the child finish the story.
3. Note the intonation he uses to complete the story.
4. If he speaks in a monotone and without expression, repeat the ending he used to complete the story, saying it with noticeable changes in inflection.
5. Ask him to repeat the ending, saying it as you said it.
6. Continue with Story Two.
Level Two:
7. During conversation time, a group activity, or show and tell, observe the child's voice intonation and inflection as he relates an experience or an event.

Credit: + Child uses inflection when describing an exciting event or action.

Adaptations

Some children experience voice problems that prevent intonation and inflection. The three aspects of voice response are: (1) Pitch-- usually in a monotone; (2) Intensity--talking too loudly or too softly; (3) Quality--hyper-nasality (talking through the nose), hypo-nasality (sounds like the nose is plugged up, metallic voice (sounds like a cartoon character), or raspy (sounds as if gravel is in the throat). If the child's voice reflects a problem with pitch, intensity, or quality, recommend that he have a medical evaluation . Some voice problems are also related to hearing losses; the child cannot hear himself speak and is, therefore, not aware that he should be changing his pitch to make the normal intonation patterns. Other causes include abuse or misuse of the voice, or an emotional condition.

However, there are children who do not have voice problems and still lack inflection in their speech. A child who does not show voice enthusiasm when he talks about the witch visiting on Halloween may not understand that a witch is scary, especially on Halloween. A child who does not use a whisper when he puts his teddy bear to sleep may not understand that there is a need to be quiet when someone else is sleeping. If a medical evaluation confirms there are no physical problems, the child may need to be referred to voice therapy with special emphasis placed on understanding of words and settings that represent different moods.

2.147 Uses timed events appropriately when explaining a happening (today, yesterday, tomorrow)

Strand: 2-4B **Age:** 60-72m 5.0-6.0y

Definition

When the child is presented with a question such as, "Tell me, what you are going to do today?", "What are you going to do tomorrow?" or, "What did you do yesterday?" her response will reflect the timed happening correctly.

Assessment Materials

A series of prepared questions or statements requiring the child to respond. Examples: What are you going to do today? What did you do yesterday? What will you do tomorrow? Tell me what you did last night. Name one thing that you like to do during the day. Current calendar.

Assessment Procedures

Grouping: This skill can be introduced and assessed in a small group setting. However, the most important assessment procedure is made by observing whether the child is comfortable and knowledgeable using words that represent time during a conversation.

<u>Level One:</u>
1. Tell the child you are going to ask her some questions and you want her to answer them.
2. Say, "What you are going to do today?"
3. Pause for her response. Note her answer.
4. If she has a difficult time, discuss the meaning of timed words and events with her. Say, for example, "What does today mean? It means now or the present day. For example, today I will go to school and after school I will go to the park with my mother."
5. After reviewing the meanings and providing some examples of timed events, say, "Tell me what you are going to do today."
6. Pause for her response. Note her answer.
7. If she still has difficulty, use a calendar to point to today, yesterday, and tomorrow
8. After using the calendar, say, "Tell me what you are going to do today."
9. Pause for her response. Note her answers.

<u>Level Two:</u>
10. When the topic during a class discussion, story time, or listening time deals with timed events, observe the child when she is asked to explain or respond to a question. Example: When you read a story that included events that happened yesterday and today, and a future activity, ask her to relate what happened on those days. Or when you identify what day it is, include a discussion of the kind of weather it was yesterday and something fun that is going to happen tomorrow.

Credit: + Child explains timed events appropriately by responding to questions related to today, yesterday, and tomorrow.

Adaptations

Some children have difficulty with conceptualizing symbols. To use words as a tool for thinking, reasoning or problem solving means that a large number of past experiences impact present behavior by way of verbal communication. Even if the child can speak well, she may not be able to form judgments in relation to time of day, day of the week, season of the year, or estimated time until an event. Terms such as "today," "yesterday," and "tomorrow" are symbolic of the day, the day before today, and the day after today. She refers to times of the day as "after I get up," or "just before I take a nap," because this way of thinking allows her a point of reference; morning, afternoon, and evening are often incomprehensible. When you help her deal with time event words, it is important that they be attached to an activity. Say, for example, "In the morning after you get up, we will go to the store." For a symbolic word to take on meaning, it must represent a given unit of experience.

2.148 (Moved to Cognitive, skill 1.307)

2.149 Answers specific questions based on spoken material

Strand: 2-1A **Age:** 48-60m 4.0-5.0y

Definition

After hearing a story, the child will be able to answer questions that relate to understanding the primary, direct, or "literal" meaning of the content. The questions are based on "who was it," "what did they do," "when did they do it" and "where did it happen," etc.

Assessment Materials

A simple story you find or write that has the following elements: at least one character who does something at a given time and place.
Example:
<u>Time to Feed Sam</u>
1. Jenny heard Sam meow.

2. Jenny knew it was time to feed Sam.
3. Sam wanted his breakfast.
4. Jenny got Sam's bowl.
5. She opened the refrigerator door.
6. Jenny took out the milk.
7. She poured the milk into Sam's bowl.
8. She put the bowl close to Sam.
9. Sam started to drink the milk.
10. He made a licking noise.
11. Sam made a purring noise that said, "Thank You" in cat-talk.

Assessment Procedures

Grouping: This skill can be assessed in a small group setting, no more than four children. Remind the children that they will need to listen and take turns during the activity.
1. Explain to the child that you are going to read him a short story. Tell him that after the story you will ask him some questions about what he heard.
2. Read the story to the child.
3. Reread sentence number one of the story, "Jenny heard Sam meow."
4. Ask the child, "Who heard Sam meow?"
5. Reread sentences two and three.
6. Ask the child, "What did Sam want?"
7. Reread sentence number four.
8. Ask the child, "What did Jenny get?"
9. Reread sentence number five.
10. Ask the child, "Where did Jenny go?"
11. Reread sentences six and seven.
12. Ask the child, "What did Jenny put the milk in?"
13. Reread sentences eight.
14. Ask the child, "Where did Jenny put the bowl of milk?"
15. Reread sentences nine and ten.
16. Ask the child, "When did Jenny hear a noise?"
17. Reread sentence number eleven.
18. Ask the child, "What did Sam do to say thank you?"
19. Identify the number of correct answers the child responded to and if he had any errors, make a note of whether it was to a who, what, when, or where question.

Credit: + Child answers specific questions based on a story he has just heard. The questions should be based on "who," "what," "where," and "when."

Adaptations

Literal understanding is necessary in the beginning stages of listening comprehension. When you work with story materials, encourage a child to respond with interpretation rather than just to parrot the words exactly as he heard them. Literal questions give a child practice in recall and reproducing statements or facts.

A child who is very successful in answering literal questions often gives the impression of being well skilled in auditory comprehension; however, the significance of what is heard is associated with the thinking processes of interpretation and critical judgment. When you involve a child in a story's content, first ask questions of a literal nature, encouraging him to expand in answering, and then follow up those literal queries with questions that require interpretation.

2.150 Points to or places object before, after, above, below based on verbal cues

Strand: 2-1A **Age:** 48-60m 4.0-5.0y

Definition

When the child is given the prepositions before, after, above and below as a verbal direction, she will complete the activity/task correctly. Example: (1) Put your cap above the shelf; (2) Place the apple before the banana; (3) Take the ball and put it below the bat.

Assessment Materials

A set of at least eight directions using the prepositions "before," "after," "above" and "below." Examples: (1) Put the ball before the box; (2) Place the pencil on the table after the box; (3) Hold the paper above the box; (4) The book belongs below the window; (5) Put the toy car before the toy truck; (6) Move the apple after the orange; (7) This balloon goes above the table; (8) This balloon goes below the table.
The necessary articles that are mentioned in the directions, for example: a box, a ball, a pencil, paper, an apple, an orange, a book, two balloons, a small toy car, a small toy truck, a table.

Assessment Procedures

Grouping: This skill should be assessed one-on-one with the child.
1. Ask the child to come to the assessment table. Explain that you have several items on the table and that you will ask her to move the items around.
2. Explain that she is to listen very carefully and that she is not to move the items until you say "Go."
3. Put aside all the items except the ball and the box.

4. Say "Listen. Put the ball before the box. Go."
5. Pause, allowing her time to react to the directions.
6. Note her response.
7. If she exhibits any problems, provide the following assistance: (1) Point to the ball and say, "This is a ball." Point to the box and say, "This is a box"; (2) Pick up the ball and say, "I am going to put the ball before the box"; (3) Demonstrate the appropriate placement; (4) Hand the ball to the child; (5) Say, "Listen. Put the ball before the box. Go."
8. Observe her after the task modification.
9. Continue the above procedure using the other directives (2 through 8).

Credit: + Child points or places objects correctly based on verbal directions using the following prepositions: before, after, above, and below.

Adaptations

Some children have a difficult time with prepositional modifiers and the multiple meanings often connected with them. As an example, children have heard "before" to mean "in front of" (In a parade, the band comes before the horses), to mean "in the presence of" (I will go before the king to ask for permission), to mean "in preference to" (Judy would like her ice cream before her cake), to mean "earlier than" (Jan will leave before Bill). To be given a directive such as "Put the ball before the box" requires her to sort through the various meanings of "before" and to react. This sorting process can create confusion and frustration. When you deal with the clutter of word meanings, it is important that you demonstrate the concept before you ask the child to carry out a direction. Phase out the demonstration step when she has comprehended the meaning.

2.151 Uses past participle to form past tense

Strand: 2-3 **Age:** 49-54m 4.1-4.6y

Definition
When the child is involved in a verbal situation or presented with a visual, he will respond by using a past participle to form a past tense. (e.g., He had run to the car.)

Assessment Materials
Six groups of two sentences, one using an incorrect form of a past tense verb and the other a correct sentence using a past participle in past tense. Examples: (1) Bill rided his bicycle. Bill had ridden his bicycle; (2) She runned to the car. She had run to the car; (3) The bird eated the worm. The bird had eaten the worm; (4) I see-ed a pretty rainbow. I had seen a pretty rainbow; (5) Mother come-ed to school. Mother came to school; (6) John telled about his fun ride. John had told about his fun ride. Six pictures that depict the sentence groups.

Assessment Procedures
Grouping: This skill can be assessed one-on-one with the child. However, the most important assessment procedure is made by observing him in a natural conversation and listening for his sentence structure and syntax usage.

Level One:
1. Explain to the child that he is going to hear some sentences. Tell him that one sentence will sound silly and the other will sound right. Tell him to laugh if the sentence sounds silly and to clap if it sounds right.
2. Say, "Listen! Bill rided his bicycle."
3. Pause for him to laugh; if he is hesitant to respond, repeat the sentence, stressing the word "rided," and begin to laugh.
4. When he laughs, assure him that he is correct in doing so because "rided" is a funny word.
5. Say, "Bill rode his bicycle; he had ridden it."
6. Pause for him to clap; if he hesitates, repeat the sentence, stressing the words "rode," and "had ridden" and begin to clap.
7. When he starts to clap, assure him that he is correct in doing so because "rode" is the correct word.
8. Continue the above steps with sentences 2 through 3.
9. Explain to him that he is going to hear some sentences. Tell him one sentence will have a silly word in it, and that you are going to ask him to say the sentence, using a word that is not silly.
10. Say, "Bill rided his bicycle."
11. Say, "Rided is a silly word. Can you say the sentence and use a word besides rided?"
12. Give him an opportunity to create the new sentence, "Bill had ridden his bicycle."
13. Clap when he states the correct sentence.
14. Explain to him that he is going to hear another sentence.
15. Say, "I see-ed a pretty rainbow." (Sentence 4)
16. Say, "See-ed is a silly word. Can you say the sentence and use a word besides see-ed?"
17. Give him an opportunity to create the new sentence, "I had seen a pretty rainbow."
18. Clap when he states the correct sentence.

19. Continue the above procedure with sentences 5 through 6.
20. If he has difficulty with identifying the correct sentence structure (Part One above), do not ask him to restate the sentence (Part Two above).
21. Show him a picture of a boy riding a bicycle and say, "The boy's name is Bill. He rode his bicycle."
22. Ask the child, "What is the boy's name?" Prompt as necessary.
23. Ask him, "What had the boy done?" Prompt as necessary (he "had ridden").
24. Continue by showing him a picture of a girl running to a car.
25. Say, "The girl's name is Sue. She was in a hurry. Sue had run to the car."
26. Ask him, "What is the girl's name?" Prompt as necessary.
27. Ask him, "What did the girl do?" Prompt as necessary.
28. Explain to him that he is going to hear some sentences again. Tell him one sentence will sound silly, and the other one will sound right. Tell him to laugh if the sentence sounds silly and to clap if it sounds right.
29. Say, "Listen! Bill rided his bicycle."
30. Pause for him to laugh; if he is hesitant to respond, repeat the sentence, stressing the word "rided" and begin to laugh.
31. When he laughs, assure him that he is correct in doing so because "rided" is a funny word.
32. Say, "Listen again! Bill rode his bicycle."
33. Pause for him to clap; if he is hesitant to respond, repeat the sentence, stressing the word "rode" or "had ridden" and begin to clap.
34. When he starts to clap, assure him that he is correct in doing so because "rode' is the correct word.
35. Continue the above steps with sentences 2 through 3.

Level Two:
36. Observe the child when he is involved in a discussion or a conversation for appropriate verbalization of a past tense of verbs.

Credit: + Child correctly uses a past participle to form a past tense when involved in a verbal situation or presented with a visual.

Adaptations
See #2.129.

2.152 Uses verb "have" to form past tense
Strand: 2-3   **Age:** 49-54m 4.1-4.6y

Definition
When the child is involved in a verbal situation or presented with a visual, she will respond by using the verb "have" to form past tense. (e.g., We have a new kitten. She has run far.)

Assessment Materials
Five sets of two pictures per set. Picture 1 in each set should illustrate an activity going on, and picture 2 should show the conclusion of the activity. Example: Set One: Picture 1--Three children watching television. Picture 2--The television screen is dark, and the children are talking. Set Two: Picture 1--Two dogs eating out of a bowl. Picture 2--Two dogs sitting by the bowl, and the bowl is empty. Set Three: Picture 1--A girl sleeping. Picture 2--The girl waking up. Set Four: Picture 1--A man standing by a snow-covered sidewalk holding a shovel. Picture 2--The man standing by a clean sidewalk holding the shovel. Set Five: Picture 1--A boy and a girl blowing up balloons. Picture 2--The same boy and girl, except the balloons have popped.

Assessment Procedures
Grouping: This skill can be assessed one-on-one with the child. However, the most important assessment procedure is made by observing the child in a natural verbal situation and listening for sentence structure and word usage.

Level One:
1. Explain to the child that you are going to show her two pictures. Tell her that after she looks at the pictures, you are going to talk about them. Place Set One on the table in front of her. Make sure that Picture 1 precedes Picture 2.
2. Discuss the pictures with her, making sure to ask her what is happening in Picture 1 and in Picture 2.
3. Observe her response and her use of the verb "have" in past tense. Expected responses are: "They have turned off the TV," or "The children have stopped watching TV."
4. Continue the above procedure, using Set Two.
5. Place Set Three on the table in front of the child. Make sure that Picture 1 precedes Picture 2.
6. Discuss the pictures with her, making sure to ask her what is happening in Picture 1 and in Picture 2.

© 2010 VORT Corporation. All rights reserved. Do Not copy.

7. Observe her response and her use of the verb has in the past tense. Expected responses are: "She just got up," or "The girl has been asleep," or "The girl has just opened her eyes."
8. Continue the above procedure using Sets Four and Five.
9. If the child has difficulty with a response, involve her in the following steps: (1) Instruct her to look at Set One, Picture 1. Say, "The boys are watching television. What are the boys doing?" Pause for her response. Instruct her to look at Set One, Picture 2, and say, "The boys have turned the television off. What did the boys do?" Pause for her response.
10. Repeat the above correction procedure, if necessary.
11. Instruct her to look at Set Three, Picture 1. Say, "The girl is asleep in her bed. What is the girl doing?" Pause for her response.
12. Instruct her to look at Set Three, Picture 2, and say, "The girl has just woken up," or "The girl has been asleep. What has happened while she slept?" Pause for her response.
13. Explain to her that you are going to show her two pictures. Tell her that after she looks at the pictures, you will talk about them.
14. Place Set Two on the table in front of her. Make sure that Picture 1 precedes Picture 2.
15. Discuss the pictures with her, making sure to ask her what is happening in Picture 1 and in Picture 2.
16. Observe her response and her use of the verb have in past tense. Expected responses are: "The two dogs have eaten," or "The dogs have cleaned the bowls."
17. Continue with the other picture sets.

Level Two:
18. Observe the child when she is involved in a discussion or a conversation for appropriate verbalization of the verb "have."

Credit: + Child uses the verb "have" to form past tense while speaking or after looking at a visual.

Adaptations
See #2.129.

2.153 Repeats what happened in story previously read by another
Strand: 2-1A **Age:** 50-58m 4.2-4.10y

Definition
When the child is presented with a short story, he will be able to retell the story. The story will be read from beginning to end without pausing between pages or episodes to ask questions or to reinforce the actions. If the child has difficulty telling the story, the reader may break the story down to smaller units. The story selected should be within the child's experiences and interests. If needed, visuals may be used to assist him in story recall.

Assessment Materials
Level One:
A short story with content within the experience of the child and of interest to him. Suggested titles: *Doctor Dan, The Bandage Man, The Tawny, Scrawny Lion, The Saggy, Baggy Elephant, The Sailor Dog, My Puppy, The Shy Little Kitten.* (These are all Golden Book Classics.) Drawing paper, crayons.

Level Two:
A story the child has not heard before and one that is easy to dramatize. Puppets that match the characters in the selected story, for dramatization. Construct the puppets from foam balls. They are easy to make and also make an enjoyable art activity for the child. Directions for making foam ball puppets are:
(1) Gather the following materials: foam balls, either egg-shaped or round, nontoxic paint or markers, unsharpened pencil or small stick, scraps of yarn, ribbon, and felt, 12-inch felt squares, wiggle eyes, pipe cleaners, nontoxic glue, Popsicle sticks, toothpicks, collections of buttons, fringe balls, old jewelry, trim, sequins, and feathers.
(2) Use a spoon to scrape out a hole in the foam ball. Make it big enough to fit over the child's third finger. (For young children, push a stick up through the center of the ball, and if the head falls off or wobbles, dab some glue on the stick.) Place the ball on a pencil or stick and select markers to put on the facial features and hair. Use glue to add wiggle eyes, a fringe ball for a nose, and yarn for hair. If the character requires a hat or cap, make it out of scraps and felt. Remove the stick after the construction unless the stick is being used to move the puppet.
(3) While the face is drying, cut out the clothing (dress or cape) by folding the felt in half and cutting one-fourth of a circle, making sure that one side of the quarter of the circle is on the fold. After cutting, unfold the material, and you have a half circle for a dress, cape, shirt, or coat.
(4) Mark the center of the half circle and lay flat. Measure 1 inch on either side of the center mark. Measure down 2 inches from the 1-inch marks and draw a small circle on each side. The circles should not be larger than ½ inch circumference,

large enough to slip the child's index and fourth fingers through. Cut out the circles.
(5) Decorate the front of the dress or coat with the collection of scraps in keeping with the character in the story. Use glue, staples, needle, and thread to keep the decoration in place, provide supervision.
(6) Lay the felt right side up on a table. Fold one side edge down the center back line, and place glue down the outside edge of the felt. Take the opposite side edge of the felt and place it over the glue, and let it dry.
(7) To assemble the hand puppet, place the dress or jacket on one hand of the child. Slip the proper fingers through the arm holes, pushing the third finger in the scooped-out hole. If using a stick and the head wobbles, place some glue on the stick where it comes in contact with the foam ball.

Assessment Procedures
Grouping: This skill should be assessed in one-on-one with the child.

Level One:
1. Ask the child to join you at the story time center. Make sure he is comfortable and that distractions have been put away. Tell him you are going to read him a story, and show him the book.
2. Discuss the cover pictures and the title of the story. Read the story to him.
3. At the conclusion of the story, give him a sheet of drawing paper and the crayons.
4. Ask him to tell you whom the story was about; prompt if necessary.
5. Ask him to draw a picture of the character he named.
6. Allow him ample time to complete his drawing.
7. Using his illustration as the focal point, ask him to tell you the story.
8. Prompt as needed, and use the story pictures to assist him in recalling events.
9. As he retells the story, listen for the following: main idea, sequence of events, identification of characters, plot, and conclusion.

Level Two:
10. Allow the child an opportunity to manipulate the puppet before he dramatizes the story.
11. During story time, read the selected story. Discuss ways that the story could be acted out with the child. During the discussion, decide what method would be best for retelling the story. Besides puppets, the methods could include a playlet, flannel board pieces, creating a tape recording, or a video tape/CD/DVD presentation.
12. After the child has decided on the dramatization method, help him with planning, props, settings, and production.
13. As he performs the story dramatization, observe whether he is retelling the story in a meaningful manner.

Credit: + Child repeats what happened in a story read by another person using visuals to assist him, if necessary.

Adaptations
When the child is asked to retell a story of more than one event, sequential recall is required. The specific order in which the events of a story occurred are the base for the content, and he needs to recall the events accurately and in the correct order to retell. Often a child becomes confused, not as to what happened in a story, but when it happened. A child who begins to tell a story by telling the end first may be experiencing a problem in recalling item order. Teaching strategies that are helpful in working with memory problems are: (1) The learning of nursery rhymes, finger plays and action songs. Anytime the child is involved in a physical activity that includes associated words, there is a added modality linkage; (2) Before reading the child a story, ask him to listen and remember a certain thing. Say for example, "I am going to read the story of *The Three Bears*, and I want you to remember only one thing. I want you to remember what the Little Bear did when he saw his soup was all gone." Continue to increase the number of items for him to recall, making sure there is association between the items--"I want you to listen and remember what the Little Bear did when he saw his soup, his chair and his bed."; (3) State two words (chair, table) for him to remember. Say the two words and ask him to repeat them. Gradually add other words to the list. The first few words should be associated, and a visual reminder in the form of a picture may also be helpful.

2.154 Carries out 4 simple related successive commands in order
Strand: 2-2 **Age:** 50-58m 4.2-4.10y

Definition
When the child is presented with a four-step command in which the steps are logically related, she will correctly complete the required tasks in order.

Assessment Materials

At least four different activities each consisting of four steps which logically follow one another. These activities may commonly occur in the child's typical daily routine. Example: Activity One-(arriving at school) Hang up your backpack, take off your coat, go to the bathroom, and come to group time. Activity Two-(lunch time) Wash your hands, get your lunch box, find a seat at the table, and open your lunch box. Activity Three-(outside play) Put your toys away, put on your jacket, get a playground ball, and line up at the door. Activity Four-(end of the day) Put your lunch box in your backpack, put on your jacket, put on your backpack, and sit down until it's time to go.

Note: The sequence of steps for each activity might vary according to the particular classroom routine, but you should be able to find a number of four-step commands that naturally occur within the regular daily schedule. Make sure the motor skills and the vocabulary used are within the range of the child's ability.

Assessment

Note: It is important to consider the procedures for learning analysis when you ask a child to deal with multi-step tasks. The learning analysis is: (1) Tell the child what you want her to do and allow time for a response. If she does not respond: (2) Demonstrate what you want her to do and allow time for response. If she does not respond: (3) Tell and demonstrate what you want her to do and allow time for response. If she does not respond: (4) Tell her what to do and provide physical cueing as needed. If she does not respond (5) Tell her what to do and physically assist her through each step. Repeat any of the above as needed.

Grouping: This skill should be assessed one-on-one with the child.

1. Before giving the commands, explain that you are going to give the child some directions, and ask her to listen carefully. Tell her not to start until you say, "Begin now."
2. Say, "Hang up your backpack, take off your coat, go to the bathroom, and come to group time."
3. Say, "Begin now." Observe her response.
4. If she has a problem performing the task, repeat the directions very slowly.
5. If she continues to have a problem, break the sequences down by saying, "Hang up your backpack," pause for her to react, then say, "Take off your coat," pause, say, "Go to the bathroom," pause, say, "Come to group time," and pause for the child's response.
6. The next day, repeat the four-step command without pausing.
7. If she is successful, continue with the other activities at the appropriate times.
8. Observe her responses.

Credit: + Child correctly carries out a four-step command in which the steps are logically related.

Adaptations

See #2.106.

2.155 Points to or places object by, beside, behind

Strand: 2-1A **Age:** 36-54m 3.0-4.6y

Definition

The child will respond to one-part directions containing indefinite and instrumental prepositions. He will demonstrate an understanding of verbal directions such as: (1) Put the rock by the box; (2) Stand beside the chair; (3) Hide behind the tree.

Assessment Materials

A set of at least six directions using the prepositions "by," "beside," and "behind." Examples: (1) Put the ball by the box; (2) Place the pencil beside the box; (3) Sit by the door; (4) Lay the paper behind the box; (5) Hide behind the door; (6) Move the apple beside the orange. Gather the materials that are mentioned in the directions: box, ball, pencil, paper, apple, orange, door.

Assessment Procedures

Grouping: This skill can be assessed in a small group setting, no more than four children. Remind the children that they will need to listen and take turns during the activity.

1. Ask the child to come to the assessment table. Explain that you have several items on the table and that you are going to ask him to move the items around.
2. Tell him that he is to listen very carefully and that he is not to move the items until you say "Go."
3. Put aside all the items except the ball and the box.
4. Say, "Listen. Put the ball by the box. Go."
5. Pause, allowing him time to react to the directions.
6. Note his response.

© 2010 VORT Corporation. All rights reserved. Do Not copy.

7. If he exhibits any problems, provide the following assistance: (1) Point to the ball and say, "This is a ball." Point to the box and say, "This is a box"; (2) Pick up the ball and say, "I am going to put the ball by the box"; (3) Hand the child the ball; (4) Say, "Listen. Put the ball by the box. Go."
8. Observe the child after the task modification.
9. Continue the above procedure using the other directives (2) through (6).

Credit: + Child correctly points to or places an object by, beside, and behind.

Adaptations

Some children have a difficult time with prepositional modifiers and the multiple meanings often connected with them. As an example, a child has heard "by" used as a form of departure--"good-bye," to purchase things--"I will buy a drink," as a point of destination--"I am going by Mary's house," and as a behavior--"I am not going to stand by and do nothing." To be given a directive such as "Stand by the door," requires the child to sort through the various meanings of "by." This sorting process can create confusion and frustration. When dealing with the variations of word meaning, it is important that you demonstrate the concept before you ask the child to carry out a direction. Then phase out the demonstration step when he has comprehended the meaning.

2.156 Points to or places object in front, in back, around, through based on verbal cues

Strand: 2-1A **Age:** 36-54m 3.0-4.6y

Definition

When the child is given the prepositions "in front," "in back," "around," and "through" as verbal directions, she will respond correctly by completing the required actions. Example: (1) Place the pencil in front of the book; (2) Put the red block in back of the green block; (3) Move the box around the corner; (4) Push the string through the bead.

Assessment Materials

A set of at least eight directions using the prepositions "in front," "in back," "around" and "through". Examples: (1) Put the ball in front of the box; (2) Place the pencil in back of the box; (3) Move the toy car around the box; (4) Put the straw through the hole in the paper; (5) Place the box in front of the book; (6) The teddy bear should be in back of the doll; (7) Use a crayon to draw around the picture of the cat; (8) Push the toy car through the paper tunnel.

The necessary articles that are mentioned in the directions: a box, a ball, picture of a cat on paper, a pencil, a doll, a teddy bear, crayons, a straw, a toy car, a paper tunnel (paper towel tube).

Assessment Procedures

Grouping: This skill can be assessed in a small group setting, no more than four children. Remind the children that they will need to listen and take turns during the activity.

1. Ask the child to come to the assessment table. Explain that you have several items on the table and that you will be asking her to move the items around. Explain that she is to listen very carefully and that she is not to move the items until you say "Go."
2. Put aside all the items except the ball and the box.
3. Say, "Listen. Put the ball in front of the box. Go." Pause, allowing her time to react to the directions.
4. Note her response.
5. If she exhibits any problems, provide the following assistance: (1) Point to the ball and say, "This is a ball." Point to the box and say, "This is a box"; (2) Pick up the ball and say, "I am going to put the ball in front of the box"; (3) Hand the ball to the child; (4) Say, "Listen. Put the ball in front of the box. Go."
6. Observe her after the task modification.
7. Continue the above procedure, using the other directives (2 through 8).

Credit: + Child correctly points or places an object in front, in back, around, and through as verbally directed.

Adaptations

Some children have a difficult time with prepositional modifiers and the multiple meanings often connected with them. As an example, children have heard "around" used to mean "on all sides of a structure" (Go around the house three times), "somewhere in or near" (The ball is around the toy box), "approximate time" (We will do it around snack time), "present in or at some place" (I will be around when you call). A direction such as "Move the toy car around the box" requires the child to sort through the various meanings of "around" and to react. This sorting process can create confusion and frustration. When dealing with the variations of word meaning, it is important that you demonstrate the concept before you ask the child to carry out a direction. Phase out the demonstration step when she has comprehended the meaning.

2.157 Acts out at least two, but no more than five, commands in the same order they were presented

Strand: 2-2 **Age:** 42-60m 3.6-5.0y

Definition
The child will listen to at least two and not more than five commands. After the commands are issued, the child will act them out in the order in which they were presented.

Assessment Materials
A series of commands. Set One--should include two commands; Set Two--should include three commands; Set Three--should include four commands; Set Four--should have five commands. Note: Design commands to be acted out by the child. Examples: Set One--(1) March two steps forward; (2) Stop. Set Two--(1) Pretend to wash your hands; (2) Pretend to dry your hands; (3) Pretend to hang up the towel. Set Three--(1) Dance around the chair; (2) Sit down on the chair; (3) Kick your feet; (4) Jump up fast. Set Four--(1) Pretend to blow up a balloon; (2) Pretend to tie a string on your balloon; (3) Pretend your balloon flies away; (4) Pretend to run after your balloon; (5) Pretend to catch your balloon on a tree.
A chair.

Assessment Procedures
Note: In Set Two and Set Four, accept whatever creative dramatization the child performs.
Grouping: This skill should be assessed one-on-one with the child.
1. Explain to the child that you will give him some fun directions and ask him to listen carefully because you want him to act them out.
2. Say, "Listen carefully; I want you to march two steps forward and then I want you to stop. Do it now."
3. Pause to allow him time to perform the commands.
4. If he shows hesitancy, repeat the commands and demonstrate with him.
5. Repeat the command.
6. Continue with Set Two through Set Four as outlined above.
7. Stop the assessment when the child is unable to complete the commands in the sequence presented.
8. Observe him as he acts out the commands, looking for: correct sequencing, moving from one directive to another with ease, whether he uses any self-cueing, whether he requires approval for each step in the series, and whether he is comfortable in responding to the commands.

Credit: + Child acts out at least two and not more than five commands in the order they were presented.

Adaptations
Young children can develop insecurities, a desire to please, and fears of not being able to achieve. They often display fluctuations in behavior, and when they are asked to perform, they may exhibit rebellion, shyness, or become overly exuberant. Hence, although a child is able to act out the commands, he may choose not to react due to various reasons. To assist in overcoming these reasons, consider the following: (1) Encourage participation, and refrain from demanding; (2) Join him in the response mode; (3) Use immediate reinforcement, not just for achievement but also for effort; (4) Show genuine concern for his feelings, and provide security and assurance.

It is important to evaluate the reason for a child's lack of response to the commands. It could be a behavior concern as outlined above, or it could be a sequential recall problem. To perform a series of commands requires a child to have the ability to sequence. Children may become confused as to what order they are to do something. Helpful teaching strategies are: (1) Learning nursery rhymes, finger plays, and action songs. Any time a child is involved in a physical activity that includes associated words, he receives an added modality linkage; (2) Give him two actions (e.g., jump, clap) to hold in his mind. Say the two words and ask him to repeat them. Ask him to perform the two actions. Gradually add to the list. The actions should be associated first, and a visual reminder in the form of a picture or a prior demonstration may be helpful.

2.158 Names main idea after listening to a story

Strand: 2-1A **Age:** 53-60m 4.5-5.0y

Definition
When the child is read a short selection, she will identify the main idea when asked. Her response may be expressed verbally, illustrated, or selected from a multiple choice grouping.

Assessment Materials
Make up your own short story or use an original story that would be of interest to the child and within her environmental experiences. An example of a short story follows:

<u>The Cow Who Wanted to Fly</u>
Once upon a time, there was a black and white cow who wanted to fly. She jumped up on the shed and tied a sheet to her long tail. The cow took a big breath and jumped. A horse was standing nearby, and she saw the cow jumping up and down off the shed with this funny white thing on her tail. The horse finally asked the cow what she was trying to do. The cow said, "I am trying to fly." The horse began to laugh, and she said, "Fly! Cows can't fly, you silly thing!" The cow was very sad and about to cry, when she realized that she could have a lot of fun swishing her tail, walking, and running about. Besides, she didn't like that white thing on her tail, and she was tired of flying.

Also, a picture that shows action; however, it must communicate one main idea. Drawing paper, crayons.

Assessment Procedures
Note: Do not read the title of the story.
Grouping: This skill can be assessed in a small group setting, no more than four children. Remind the children that they will need to listen and take turns during the activity.

<u>Level One:</u>
1. Ask the child to join you at the assessment area. Tell her that you are going to read her a story and that she is to listen carefully because you will be asking her some questions about the story.
2. After you read the story, ask the child to tell you what the story was about.
3. If she responds with: "A cow who wanted to fly," "A silly cow," or "A cow who wanted to fly but couldn't," give her credit and say, "What would be a good title (or name) for this story?" Pause for her to give you a title.
4. If she has difficulty with the main thought response or answers the question with: "A cow and a horse," "A cow on a shed," "A cow," or "Something white," ask her to listen to the story again. After you reread the story ask, "Which of the following do you think best describes this story?" (1) Two animals talking about flying, (2) A cow who wanted to fly, (3) How a cow and a horse live.
5. Pause to allow the child to respond with one of the selections. The multiple-choice answers may need to be repeated.
6. If she still shows a problem locating the main idea in a story read to her, do the following: (1) Show her an action picture. Discuss the picture and what is happening. Make up a story about the picture. After the discussion and the story, ask the child to tell you what the picture is about. (2) Observe whether she uses the picture detail that was discussed to arrive at a main theme. Make a note that the task of "Naming main idea after a story has been read" had to be task-analyzed and the child skill level required had to be reduced.

<u>Level Two:</u>
7. After you read an unfamiliar story to the child, ask questions that will generate her knowledge of the main idea. Observe whether she was able to use the collective detail, to sort through for a common thread, and to state the main idea.

Credit: + Child identifies either verbally, illustratively, or by multiple choice selection, the main idea of a short story that has been read.

Adaptations
When a child is asked to listen, she is being asked not just to hear, but also to comprehend the communication message that is being sent. As she moves from the sensory stimulation (hearing only) of receptive language skills, to decoding skills (auditory understanding and recognition of sounds and words heard), to receptive comprehension (following directions, understanding sequence, recalling detail, getting the main idea, making inferences, drawing conclusions, and listening critically), she is expected to receive the information, make sense out of it, organize the auditory input into meaningful units, and apply specific thinking skills. If she has not experienced the prerequisites for listening comprehension such as listening for sounds without meaning, being able to localize sounds, recognizing sounds that are alike and different, and she has not experienced understanding and recognition of sounds and words heard, she may find listening

comprehension difficult. For the children who are unable to acquire functional listening skills by themselves, it is important that they receive specific instruction in how to focus on basic listening.

2.159 States the characteristics and attributes of an object or a place
Strand: 2-4B **Age:** 53-60m 4.5-5.0y

Definition
The child will name the characteristics of an object or place when the situation is stated (e.g., when he hears the word "zoo", he will name as many words as he can that describe a zoo). He will not be given a situation that represents a place where he has never been or an object with which he can not associate.

Assessment Materials
At least three different words that represent objects or places to which the child can relate in each of the following categories: (1) Associative thinking--place (bedroom), object (pet). Associative thinking refers to the ability to relate facts with concepts, because in the past, he must have clearly received the perceptions common to an object or event; (2) Convergent thinking--place (zoo), object (tree). Convergent thinking refers to the bringing together of known facts or associations that will result in one stated, predicted outcome; (3) Divergent thinking--place (birthday party), object (friend), (happy). Divergent thinking refers to the utilization of knowledge in different ways to produce unique or a variety of ideas.

Assessment Procedures
Grouping: This skill can be assessed one-on-one with the child. However, you can listen for the child to describe the characteristics of objects or places during an activity when the situation has been presented spontaneously.
Level One:
1. Explain to the child that you will mention a word (associative thinking) and when he hears the word, he is to name all the things that he would see, hear, or feel if he were at that place.
2. Say, "Bedroom."
3. Provide time for him to respond with characteristic words.
4. If he has a problem say, "Think about your bedroom and name all the things you can think of that are in your room." Provide time for him to respond.
5. If he continues to have difficulty, prompt by saying, "Does your bedroom have a bed?" Pause, then say, "Good, what kind of bed do you have?" Pause and say, "What is beside your bed?" Pause and say, "Tell me more."
6. Record his response, and whether he used single words or sentences and the level of assistance he needed.
7. Continue with the other focus words.
8. If he has difficulty with responses to words at the associative level, do not continue. If he has difficulty with responses to words at the convergent level, do not continue.
Level Two:
9. During conversations, discussions, "show and tell" times, dramatic play, or telephoning, observe the child's ability to describe the characteristics of objects, events, and situations.

Credit: + Child correctly names the characteristics of an object or place when the situation is stated and the situation or object is familiar to the child.

Adaptations
A child may not have a problem dealing with language, but he may have a problem with content. There can be a breakdown as the child moves from figural (information that can be seen, heard, or felt) to symbolic and semantic content (information that refers to the ideas or meanings), and finally to behavioral content (information that refers to one's own reactions and behaviors or to the reactions and behaviors of others). Each level is more complex, requiring a greater degree of conceptualization and a more sophisticated way of expressing information. Therefore, the child must have ample experience and practice dealing with figural content before he moves into semantic and behavioral expressive issues.

2.160 Describes attributes of objects or items in picture
Strand: 2-4B **Age:** 53-60m 4.5-5.0y

Definition
When the child is presented with a picture, she will describe an object or an item by telling about its properties, characteristics, or qualities, using at least three sentences. Example: She looks at a picture of an apple, and she may say, "The apple is red and round. It grows on a tree. Apples are good in pies." Begin the activity by using single-item pictures of objects (nouns) and then single-item pictures in which the

object is involved in an action (verbs). After she has successfully responded to single-item pictures, show her a multi-visual picture.

Assessment Materials

Three sets of at least five pictures per set. Set One: Pictures of single-item objects, such as an apple, a cat, a house, a sweater, a ball. Set Two: Pictures of objects or items involved in an action, such as a boy jumping, a balloon floating, an adult washing a car, a dog digging a hole, a girl riding on a merry-go-round. Set Three: Multi-item and/or multi-object, such as a scene of a playground, a parade, a group of children playing, a store, a library, a shopping mall.

Assessment Procedures

Note: If you want to limit the description time, ask her to tell you as many things as she can about the item in the picture until you tell her to stop. Although this is not intended to be a timed assessment item, it is a strategy to keep the overly verbal child on task.

Grouping: This skill can be assessed in a small group setting. However, observe the child when she is asked to describe an object or item in a picture during an activity with others.

<u>Level One:</u>

1. Explain to the child that you are going to show her a picture and that you want her to tell you as many things as she can about the item in the picture.
2. Show the child a picture from Set One and say, for example, "Look at the apple in this picture and tell me about it."
3. Observe her response, noting how many different descriptive elements she used, and whether her descriptors included a variety of different attributes and whether she extended her verbal description to information that was not visible. For example, when you show her a picture of a single apple and no tree, she may say, "Apples grow on trees."
4. If she has a difficult time describing the single-item object, prompt her by pointing to the object and saying, "This is an [apple]. What color is it?" After she responds, say, "What else can you tell me about the red apple?"
5. Provide only one verbal prompt.
6. Continue the above process with the other pictures in Set One.
7. Show her a picture from Set Two, and say, "Look at the [boy] in this picture and tell me what is happening."
8. Observe her response, noting how many different descriptive elements she used, and whether the descriptors included a variety of different attributes and whether she extended her verbal description to items that were not visible.
9. If she has a difficult time describing the single item object, prompt her by saying, "Look at the [boy] in the picture. What is he doing?" After she responds, say, "What else can you tell me about the boy," or "What else is he doing?"
10. Continue the above process with the other pictures in Set Two.
11. Show her a picture from Set Three, and say, "Look at this picture, and tell me about it."
12. Observe her response, and prompt one time only.

<u>Level Two:</u>

13. When the child participates in an activity that includes pictures, such as story time, language development, or picture reading, observe her when she is asked to describe an object or item in a picture.

Credit: + Child describes an object or an item by telling about its properties, characteristics, or qualities, using at least three sentences.

Adaptations

Even though a child may be able to identify an object or an action and may be able to demonstrate what can be done with the object or is able to dramatize the action, she is unable to describe it. She may have problems structuring her thoughts into grammatically correct units or sentences; she can often recognize sentence structure when she hears it, but she is not able to reproduce a meaningful sequence. To assist a child to verbalize descriptions, encourage her to verbalize her actions while she is playing. Using a picture, elicit a response from her by saying a sentence, leaving out a word, and then asking her to fill it in. Asking her to repeat a series of sentences about an object one at a time is helpful. Say, for example, "This is an apple. The apple is red. The apple is red and round. The round red apple is good to eat."

2.161 Uses four- to eight-word sentences

Strand: 2-4B **Age:** 48-72m 4.0-6.0y

Definition

The child will speak four- to eight-word sentences on the same subject. The sentences can be in response to a past experience, a present happening, a visual representation, participation in a conversation or a future expectation.

Assessment Materials
A developed list of at least six stimulus words that represent information or a happening in the child's experiences or environment. Examples: birthday, park, swimming, brother, baby, pet, ice cream. A group of pictures that represent a category. Examples: Pictures of things that hold things--a box, a present, a jar, a sack, a cupboard, a car, a trunk, a refrigerator, a garbage can, a backpack, a purse.

Assessment Procedures
Grouping: This skill can be assessed one-on-one with the child. However, listen to the child during various activities to see if he uses multi-word sentences to relate information or express a topic.

Level One:
1. Tell the child that you are going to say a word and that after he hears it, he is to tell you things about the word.
2. Say, "Birthday. Tell me about a birthday." Pause to allow him to express himself.
3. Observe whether he uses at least four-word sentences and whether they are relevant, descriptive, sequenced, and informative. If he includes creativity or originality, make a note of it.
4. If he has difficulty with this assessment, check to make sure that the stimulus word is within his realm of experience and that he has the vocabulary that can express the experience.
5. If he continues to have a problem relating sentences to a key word, assist him by asking questions, such as, "What is fun about having a birthday? What did you do on your birthday? Have you ever been to a birthday party? What did you do at the party?" Then repeat, "Tell me about a birthday."
6. If he demonstrates an inability to answer the questions or does not use the questions as a stem to expand the information, attempt to develop verbalization by comparison responses. Say, for example, "When I have a birthday, I want someone to sing the 'Happy Birthday' song. Can you sing that song with me?" (Sing the song.) "What do you like best about having a birthday?"
7. Continue with the other five words in the stimulus grouping.
8. Place the six pictures that represent a category face down on the table.
9. (Use the first drawn card as a teaching card.) Ask the child to draw a card and to tell something about the item on it.
10. Discuss some things that he may wish to tell such as what the item is, what it is used for, and what is kept inside the item pictured, or anything else he wants to express.
11. Encourage him to use complete sentences. If he has difficulty using sentences, model constructing sentences.
12. Observe whether he uses at least four sentences and whether they are relevant, descriptive, sequenced, and informative. If he includes creativity or originality make a note of it.

Level Two:
13. During story time, language time, or sharing time, observe whether the child uses sentences to express the topic, whether he relates information, and whether he sequence his content.

Credit: + Child uses four- to eight-word sentences to describe an experience, something that is happening, a visual representation or to participate in a conversation.

Adaptations
A child may have problems structuring his thoughts into grammatically correct units or sentences. Often he can recognize sentence structure when he hears it, but he is not able to reproduce a meaningful sequence. To assist him to verbalize descriptions, encourage him to verbalize his action while he is playing. Model complete sentences as he is engaged in play. Say, for example, "You just threw the ball. The ball went a long way." Using a picture, elicit a response from him by saying a sentence, leaving out a word, and asking him to fill it in. Asking him to repeat a series of sentences one at a time about an object is also helpful. For example: "This is an apple. The apple is red. The apple is red and round. The round red apple is good to eat."

2.162 Rephrases others' comments in a discussion
Strand: 2-1A **Age:** 55-60m 4.7-5.0y

Definition
The child will rephrase another's comments and will retain the original meaning. In rephrasing, she may use synonyms, reorganization of words, substitution of words, and expanded statements. She may be asked to fill in a different word in a sentence. Example: You

say, "The wind is howling." Ask the child to complete, "The wind is _____" by using another word for howling. Or she may be asked to reorganize words she heard. Example: Statement heard: "Sally put her doll, her stuffed rabbit, and her basket in the wagon. They took a ride." Rephrased: "The doll, the play rabbit, and the basket took a ride in Sally's wagon." The child may then be asked to substitute a word that has been heard. Example: Statement heard: "The girls and boys were playing." Rephrased: "The children were playing." The child may be asked to expand a heard statement. Example: Statement heard: "I could tell the boy was having a good time." Rephrased: "I could tell the boy was having a good time because he was laughing."

Assessment Materials
An object that is of interest to the child, for example: a piece of sports equipment, a new puzzle, a special toy, a glob of clay made into a funny form, or a toy dinosaur.

Assessment Procedures
Grouping: This skill can be assessed one-on-one with the child. However, look for opportunities during different activities to ask the child questions about a story that was read or to explain what they just heard someone else say.

Level One:
1. Ask the child to look at the toy dinosaur while you talk about it. In not more than six sentences, tell the child about the dinosaur. Say, for example, "This is a dinosaur. It is called a Triceratops. It lived many years ago. It ate plants. This horn helped it dig up plants. It had a big hard bone around its neck."
2. Repeat the description of the Triceratops.
3. Ask the child to tell in her own words what she just heard about the Triceratops.
4. Listen to her and note whether she included the facts, whether she used the terms, whether she kept the information in the sequence presented, whether she added or embellished any items, and whether she appeared to be confident in her response.
5. If she has difficulty, repeat in the following manner: Say, "This is a dinosaur. It is called a Triceratops. It lived many years ago."
6. Say to the child, "Tell me in your own words what you just heard about this dinosaur."
7. Continue with the remaining sentences.

Level Two:
8. When you are reading a story or are involved in a discussion with the child, pause often to ask her what a main character just said. Or after reading her a story, ask her to explain what the two friends talked about on the picnic, to tell you what the lady said in a different way, or to explain what the chicken said the day it rained, etc.

Credit: + Child rephrases another's comments and will retain the original meaning. The child may use synonyms, reorganization of words, substitution of words, and expanded statements when rephrasing the comment.

Adaptations
Many children are not willing to change what they have heard another person say, particularly if the person is an adult or if the verbalization has come from a book. A child feels that what an older person says is right and what comes from a book has to be correct. When she is asked to restate what she has heard, her attempt will be to repeat it exactly. As she gains confidence in her own abilities and realizes that rephrasing is not an attempt to be critical of a speaker, she begins to attempt the task without parroting.

2.163 Uses "will" to form future tense
Strand: 2-3 **Age:** 56-62m 4.8-5.2y

Definition
When the child is involved in a verbal situation or presented with a visual, he will respond by using "will" to form future tense. (e.g., He will run far.)

Assessment Materials
A prepared set of five pictures that illustrate a future happening. Example: (1) A girl standing under a dark rain cloud; (2) Two people planting small plants in a garden; (3) A car with a flat tire; (4) Sun shining on a snowman; (5) A boy walking with a ball and a bat.

Assessment Procedures
Grouping: This skill can be assessed one-on-one with the child. However, the most important assessment procedure is made by observing him in a natural verbal situation and listening for sentence structure and word usage.

Level One:
1. Explain to the child that you are going to show him a picture. Tell him that after he looks at it, you are going to talk about it.
2. Place Picture 1 on the table in front of him. Discuss the picture with him, making sure to ask him what is happening in Picture 1. (It is going to rain on the girl.)

3. Say, "It is going to rain. The girl. . ." Ask the child to complete the sentence.
4. Expected responses: "will get wet" or "will run for cover."
5. Observe his response and use of the word "will."
6. Continue the above procedure using Picture 2.
7. Place Picture 2 on the table in front of him. Discuss the picture with the child, making sure to ask him what is happening in Picture 2.
8. Say, "The people are planting a garden. Soon the plants. . ."
9. Observe his response and his use of the word "will."
10. Expected responses: "will grow" or "will be pretty."
11. Continue the above procedure using Pictures 3 through 5.
12. If he has difficulty with a response, involve him in the following steps: (1) Instruct him to look at Picture 1. Say, "It is going to rain. The girl will get wet." Ask him to repeat the two sentences.
13. Instruct him to look at Picture 2. Say, "The people are planting a garden. Soon the plants will grow big." Ask the child to repeat the two sentences.
14. Instruct him to look at Picture 3. Say, "The car has a flat tire. The man. . ."
15. Observe the child's response and his use of the word "will."
16. Expected responses: "will have to fix the tire" or "will have to put on a new tire."
17. If he is successful, continue with Pictures 4 and 5.

Level Two:
18. Observe the child when he is involved in a discussion or a conversation for appropriate verbalization of "will."

Credit: + Child uses "will" to form a future tense sentence when involved in a verbal situation or presented with a visual.

Adaptations
See #2.129.

2.164 Describes events of past and future experience in logical, sequential order
Strand: 2-3 **Age:** 59-64m 4.11-5.4y

Definition
After the child has heard a simple story with at least three occurrences, she will be given a set of pictures showing the story's sequence. When asked, the child will arrange the pictures in the correct order and tell the story. The set of pictures will clearly depict past and future events. The child may also describe events of past and future experiences they have personally had in a logical, sequential order.

Assessment Materials
A simple story based on the child's activities; however, the first and last part of the situation should be omitted.
Example:
Story One—A girl calls her dog. A dog runs to the child. The child pets her dog. The dog and the child are very happy. The following pictures to go with it: (1) The child calls her dog; (2) The dog comes running; (3) The child pets the dog; (4) The dog and the child are very happy.
A simple story with contents familiar to the child but not about her activities.
Story Two--It started to rain very hard. The girl ran to get out of the rain. The following pictures: (1) A swing still swinging, as if someone had been on it; (2) A dark cloud and rain; (3) The girl running to get under a cover.
A simple story that is not within the child's realm of experiences. Example: Story Three-- Once upon a time a little bear put on a heavy coat. The little bear went outside, and her feet got very cold. She had forgotten to put on her heavy boots. The little bear ran inside and put on her boots. The following picture: (1) A little bear putting on a heavy coat; (2) The little bear stepping outside the door; (3) The little bear stepping with her bare feet into a snowdrift; (4) the little bear inside the house, putting on her boots.

Assessment Procedures
Grouping: This skill can be assessed one-on-one with the child. Additionally, observe the child when she is involved in a discussion or conversation for listening for her verbalizations related to past, present, and future events.

Level One:
1. Tell the child that you are going to tell her a story and ask her to listen carefully. Tell her Story One.
2. Place Pictures 2 and 3 that accompany Story One face-up on the table. Ask the child to look at the pictures.
3. Explain that two pictures are missing, one picture that shows what happened before the dog came running to the girl and a picture that shows what happened after the dog and girl happily walked away.

4. Ask the child to tell what she thinks happened before the dog came running to the girl. Possible answers: "The girl called the dog," or "The girl whistled for the dog to come." Accept any reasonable answer.
5. Ask her to tell what she thinks happened after the girl petted the dog. Possible answers: "The girl and the dog started to play," or "The girl and the dog are happy." Accept any reasonable answer.
6. If Picture 1 and 4 match her response, give them to her and ask her to place them in the correct sequence. If the pictures are not appropriate, you may wish to have her draw her own Picture 1 and 4.
7. Ask the child to begin with Picture 1 and tell the story.
8. Continue the above instructional steps with Story Two and Story Three.
9. If she was unsuccessful in determining what occurred in the past or what will happen in the future, and was unable to retell the story, tell the story and hold up the picture that matches the sequential content.
10. Randomly place the pictures on the table, and ask her to put them in the correct order.
11. If she is unsuccessful, retell the story, moving the pictures to the correct positions as you are telling the story.
12. Shuffle the pictures and place them on the table, and then ask the child to put them in the correct order.
13. Ask her to tell the situation or story. Assist her as needed.

Level Two:
14. Observe the child when she is involved in a discussion or a conversation for appropriate verbalization of past, present, and future events.

Credit: + Child describes events of past and future experiences in logical and sequential order related to something they did or she arranges pictures from a story with at least three sequences in the correct order and tells the story.

Adaptations
Some children are overly influenced by irrelevant verbal information and have a difficult time focusing on that which is relevant. A child may often find a single event or word that triggers a totally new thought chain. For example, hearing the word "dog" in a spoken sentence or story may lead to a linkage of dog, bark, bite, hurt, cry, bandage, or bad dog. In this process of mind wandering, the comprehension of the spoken words was not retained by the child. Using visuals with the expressed words and stories is an effective way to center the child's concentration.

2.165 Distinguishes between spoken messages differing in tone
Strand: 2-1A **Age:** 60-63m 5.0-5.3y

Definition
The child will detect anger, joking, or calmness between two messages that are just alike except for the intonation (keep facial expression the same). He will identify the difference based on the voice tone. He will demonstrate the identification by using various response modes. Example: When he hears, "Put your sweater on now!" spoken in an angry voice, he will point to a pre-drawn angry face. When he hears, "Put your sweater on now," spoken in a calm manner, he will point to a pre-drawn calm face.

Assessment Materials
Four 3- by 5-inch index cards, each one illustrated with one of the following facial expressions: angry, joking, calm, tired. Five different statements that can be said with the following intonations and different word stress: angry, joking, calm, tired. Example: (1) It is time to put your toys away; (2) Don't you want to go to the party? (3) Put your sweater on now; (4) I have a good story to read to you; (5) Will you tell your sister to come downstairs with you?

Assessment Procedures
Grouping: This skill should be assessed one-on-one with the child.
1. Tell the child to join you at the table, and place the set of facial expression cards picture-side-up in front of the child.
2. Discuss each facial expression with him to be sure he understands the illustrated emotion.
3. Tell him that you will give him a sentence, and that after he hears it, he is to point to the card that represents how the speaker felt.
4. Do a practice sentence.
5. Say in an angry manner, "It is time to put your toys away."
6. Ask the child to point to the picture that represents how the speaker felt when he said the sentence.
7. Correct his response if needed, and discuss the answer.
8. Continue with another practice sentence.
9. Say in a calm manner, "It is time to put your toys away."

© 2010 VORT Corporation. All rights reserved. Do Not copy.

10. Ask him to point to the picture that represents how the speaker felt when he said the sentence.
11. Correct his response if needed, and discuss the answer.
12. Note his response.
13. Say in a tired manner, "It is time to put your toys away."
14. Ask him to point to the picture that represents how the speaker felt when he said the sentence.
15. Note his response.
16. Continue with the other sentences.

Credit: + Child distinguishes differences in intonation in a variety of spoken messages (angry, joking, calm or tired expressions).

Adaptations

Some children have a difficult time dealing with the pragmatics of receptive language. They acquire skills in mastering the content from what is heard, but they are unaware of how to respond effectively. They have a problem reacting behaviorally or socially to the affective manner in which language is spoken.

The way a speaker states a message may be quite different from the word content. Some children tend not to understand the double message of emotion and information/direction; to them the interpretation is only literal. The act of speaking usually involves a relationship between content, form, and what is to be communicated. Often a speaker selects an appropriate speech form according to the situation and the desired results. When a speaker makes a statement to a listener, he involves one of the following pragmatic processes: (1) Utterance--Simply saying words and sentences; (2) Prepositional--The production of a sentence that tells the listener about something; (3) Illocutionary--The speaker intends to have an effect on the situation: it could be in the form of a promise, a threat, a demand, or a commitment; (4) Perlocutionary-- This is how the listener comprehends what is being said and the reaction that occurs: it could be fright, enjoyment, intimidation, or persuasion.

To assist children in dealing with the affective in receptive language, it is important to set the stage before relaying the information. Example: If the statement to be interpreted is: "It is time to put your toys away," explain to the child before making the statement that John has been playing with his toys and they are scattered all around the room. Mary has asked John to put the toys away, and he asked for a little more time to play. Mary asked again, and John still wanted more time to play. Finally, Mary said (say in angry voice), "It is time to put your toys away."

Discuss how Mary felt when she said, "It is time to put your toys away."

Continue with another scenario that sets the stage for the statement, "It is time to put your toys away," to be said in a joking way.

2.166 Identifies differences in unlike speech sounds, m, g, t, p, when in isolation
Strand: 2-1A   **Age:** 60-65m 5.0-5.5y

Definition
When the child hears the m--"mummer sound," she will point to a picture that begins with the m sound. When she hears the g--"growner sound," she will point to a picture that begins with the g sound. When the child hears the t--"tippler sound," she will point to a picture that begins with the t sound. When she hears the p--"popper sound," she will point to a picture that begins with the p sound.

Assessment Materials
Pictures of items that begin with "m," "g," "t," and "p" cut from magazines, catalogs, and flyers, and mounted on index cards with glue. The collection should include at least four pictures for each letter; the illustrations should be within the child's experiences.

Assessment Procedures
Grouping: This skill should be assessed one-on-one with the child.
1. On the table place three pictures of items that begin with "m," two pictures of items that begin with "g," and one picture of an item that begins with "t" and one with p."
2. Tell the child that you will make a sound, and that after she hears the sound she is to find a picture that starts with the same sound.
3. Teaching item: Make the sound of m-m-m-m. Say, "Find a picture on the table that begins with this sound: m-m-m-m."
4. Pause, allowing her to locate a picture.
5. Assist and prompt if necessary.
6. Take the selected picture from her and place it facedown.
7. Say, "Find another picture on the table that begins with the m-m-m sound."
8. Pause, allowing her to locate a picture.
9. Assist and prompt if necessary.

10. Take the selected picture from the child and place it facedown.
11. If she understands the task, begin the assessment.
12. Say, "Find a picture on the table that begins with this sound: m-m-m-m."
13. Pause, allowing the child to locate a picture.
14. Take the selected picture and place it facedown.
15. Note the child's response.
16. Continue with the letter/sounds "g," "t" and "p," using the picture cards for the responses.

Credit: + Child identifies the difference in the sounds m, g, t, and p.

Adaptations

Some children experience a problem in discriminating auditory sounds when in isolation (m-m-m) versus the same sound blended with other sounds (mouse). Such a child has a need in auditory discrimination between the two sound settings. The sound appears to be distorted when it is blended. The child may even sense that mouth/throat positions are different in producing the variants. Hence, she is unable to locate a visual representation of an item that begins with the isolated sound. However, she may be able to reproduce the isolated sound and to say a word that begins with the sound, but she is unable to perceive the relationship. This child can be helped when she becomes aware of the symbol that represents the sound (sees the letter "m" as the single sound is produced and sees the letter "m" as the word "milk" is read). It is also helpful to emphasize the beginning sound of "m" when you say a word that begins with the sound (M-m-m-m ouse); this allows for closer auditory comparison.

2.167 Identifies differences in similar speech sounds, f, s, th, when in isolation

Strand: 2-1A **Age:** 60-65m 5.0-5.5y

Definition
When the child hears the f --"fuffer sound," he will point to a picture that begins with the f sound. When he hears the s --"sassy sound," he will point to a picture that begins with the s sound. When he hears the th --"thather sound," he will point to a picture that begins with the th sound.

Assessment Materials
Pictures of items that begin with "f," "s," and "th" cut from magazines, catalogs, and flyers, and mounted on index cards. It is recommended that the collection include at least four pictures for each letter and that the illustrations be within the child's environment and experiences.

Assessment Procedures
Grouping: This skill should be assessed one-on-one with the child.
1. On the table place three pictures of items that begin with "f," two pictures of items that begin with "s," one picture of an item that begins with "th."
2. Tell the child that you are going to make a sound, and that after he hears the sound, he is to find a picture that starts with that same sound.
3. Teaching item: Make the sound of f-f-f-f. Say "Find a picture on the table that begins with this sound: f-f-f-f."
4. Pause to allow him to locate a picture.
5. Assist and prompt if necessary.
6. Take the selected picture from him and place it facedown.
7. If he understands the task, begin the assessment: Say, "Find a picture on the table that begins with this sound: s-s-s-s."
8. Pause to allow him to locate a picture.
9. Take the selected picture and place it facedown.
10. Note his response.
11. Continue with the letter/sounds "th," using the picture cards for the responses.

Credit: + Child identifies the differences in the speech sounds f, s, and th when they are presented in isolation.

Adaptations
Some children experience a problem discriminating auditory sounds in isolation (f-f-f) versus the same sound blended with other sounds (funny). These children have a need in auditory discrimination between the two sound settings. The sound appears to be distorted when blended. The child may even sense that mouth/throat positions are different in producing the variants. Hence, he is unable to locate a visual representation of what an item begins with when the sound is presented in isolation. He may be able to reproduce the isolated sound and to say a word that begins with the sound, but he is unable to perceive the relationship. Often, this situation is aided when he becomes aware of the symbol that represents the sound (sees the letter "f" as the single sound is produced and sees the letter "f" as the word "fan" is read). It is also helpful to emphasize the

beginning sound of "f" when saying a word that begins with the sound--"F-f-f-f-a-n," since this allows for a closer auditory comparison.

2.168 Identifies where sound differences occur in words

Strand: 2-1A **Age:** 60-65m 5.0-5.5y

Definition

The child will identify the same sound when it appears either in the initial or in the final position of a word. She will be asked to listen for the sound, and she will be able to tell the sound position.

Assessment Materials

Two signs for the child, one of which has the word "First" written in green and the other with the word "Last" written in red. Directions to make signs: Cut two squares, write the word "first" in green on one of the squares, staple the squares together, and slip the stapled area over a ruler or a small dowel stick. Construct the second sign in the same manner, but write the word "last" in red. A list of words to read to the child: These words should have the same sound in first and the last positions. Example: M--Mat, Sam; P--Pat, Cap; T--Tap, Cat; G--Got, Bag; F--Fit, Off; S--Sat, Dress; etc.

Assessment Procedures

Note: If the sign raising becomes a concern to the child, and she focuses on that task rather than the sound placement, modify the response mode. The modification might be verbal response (saying "first" or "last"), pointing to the first position and the last position, or raising the left hand for first position and the right hand for the last position.

Grouping: This skill can be assessed in a small group setting, no more than four children. Remind the children that they will need to listen and take turns during the activity.

1. Invite the child to come to the table. Show her the two signs and explain the meaning of the words "first" and "last."
2. Place the two signs in front of her.
3. Tell her to listen and then say the sound, "M-m-m."
4. Tell her that you are going to say a word that has the sound of "m-m-m" (make the sound) as the first sound. Say "M-m-m-mat."
5. Ask the child to take the sign that says "First" and hold it up because the sound of "m-m-m" came first in the word "mat."
6. Encourage the child to say the word "M-m-mat."
7. Provide assistance as needed.
8. Tell her to listen and then say the sound "M-m-m."
9. Tell her that you are going to say a word that has the sound of "m-m-m" (make the sound) as the last sound. Say "Sam m-m-m."
10. Ask the child to take the sign that says "Last" and hold it up because the sound of "m-m-m" came last in the word "Sam."
11. Encourage the child to say the word "Sam-m-m."
12. Provide assistance as needed.
13. After these teaching examples, begin the assessment.
14. Repeat the above sequence, using the letter sound/word "p," "t," "g," "f," and "s."
15. Note the responses, making sure that the letter sound and the placement are recorded.

Credit: + Child identifies the same sound when it appears either in the "first" or "last" position of a word.

Adaptations

To distinguish auditory sound patterns in words requires the ability to distinguish letter sounds and to receive and repeat a series of sounds.

Often a child is unable to "hear" the similarities in words that begin or end with the same sound. She may have difficulty listening for a part of a word, and she thinks of another word with the same ending (bent, went). Due to this auditory reception need, she may encounter problems when she is asked to associate a visual symbol with a sound association (phonics approaches to learning to read). It is important for her to be exposed to a direct visual association when she is involved with identifying sound location. For example, show her a picture of a baby and bat for the beginning sound of "b," and show her a picture of a pan and a man for the final sound of "n." The beginning/final consonant sounds should be addressed from the easiest to the most difficult. A recommended sequence is: b, p, m, w, h, d, t, n, g, k, y, f, v, th (as in that), sh, l, s ,z, r, wh, ch and j.

2.169 Describes the outcome of a sequence of actions

Strand: 2-4B **Age:** 60-72m 5.0-6.0y

Definition
When the child is shown a picture that depicts sequential actions, he will identify the action, and he will answer questions relating to the effect of the sequence. The sequence will illustrate at least three actions. Allow him to tell about each sequence before he answers questions about the results of these actions.

Assessment Materials
A series of at least three single pictures that represent a single task. Example: Set One: Picture 1--A person getting out of bed in the morning. Picture 2--The same person in a shower. Picture 3--The same person dressed and putting on his shoes. Picture 4--The same person walking down the stairs.

A series of at least three single pictures that represent a scene in which a sequential action is shown. Example: Set Two: Picture 1--A group of people at a birthday party. Picture 2--A birthday cake being brought to the group. Picture 3--The cake beginning to slip off the plate. Picture 4--Several hands ready to catch the cake.

Assessment Procedures
Grouping: This skill should be assessed one-on-one with the child.

Level One:
1. Explain to the child that you are going to show him a series of pictures. Lay Pictures 1 through 4 from Set One on the table in the child's view. The pictures should be in the correct sequence.
2. Ask him to look at each picture and tell him when he gets to the last one, you will ask him a question.
3. Give him time to study the four pictures. When he reaches the last picture, say, "What do think will happen next?"
4. Accept any response that is within reason.
5. If he has difficulty accomplishing the task, point to each picture and ask him to tell what is happening. When he reaches Picture 4, ask him what he thinks will happen next.
6. Accept any response that is within reason.
7. If he has difficulty accomplishing the task, point to each picture and tell the story by the illustrated sequences. When you reach Picture 4, ask him to tell what he thinks will happen next.
8. Accept any response that is within reason.
9. Place Pictures 1 through 4 from Set Two on the table in the child's view. The pictures should be in the correct sequence.
10. Repeat the directions for Set Two that are provided above for Set One.

Level Two:
11. When the child is involved in a group activity such as story time and the story being read has accompanying pictures, show him a sequence of at least three pictures that go along with the story. Before you read the next part of the story or show him a picture that goes along with its content, ask him what he thinks the picture will show.

Credit: + Child describes the outcome of a sequence of actions and answers questions relating to the effect of the sequence.

Adaptations
A child may have a problem when he views a sequence of illustrations and is asked to generalize and categorize what the next action or activity will be. For example, when a child is presented with a series of pictures that portray getting up in the morning and he is asked to state what will happen next, he has to use the visual input to determine that they represent a specific time of day (cognitive categorization), specific routine activities (cognitive categorization), and then come up with a next activity (cognitive generalization). After this thought process occurs, he must then use the correct verbal terms to describe the next event. Many children form concepts and predictions spontaneously when they acquire the necessary verbal facility; however, some children need to be assisted in learning to match verbal expression with cognitive generalization. One method to assist a child in this area is to prompt thinking and verbal expression by asking questions. Example: Point to the boy getting out of bed and say, "The boy is getting out of bed, it must be. . . " Pause for the child's response. Or say, "Look at this picture: the boy is getting out of bed; in this picture he is putting on his shirt. What time of day do you think it is?"

2.170 Uses sentences that express logical relations between concepts

Strand: 2-4B **Age:** 60-72m 5.0-6.0y

Definition
The child will use sentences that express logical relations between concepts. These will include comparative and "if-then" sentence structures.

Examples of sentences using logical relations are: (1) Whole-part relationships--Sky is to airplane as water is to ship; (2) Part-whole relationship--Comb is to hair as toothbrush is to teeth; (3) Part-part relationship--Tires are to a steering wheel as pedals are to handle bars; (4) Object-to-action--A pencil is to writing as a scissors is to cutting; (5) Action-to-object relationship--Kicking is to soccer as batting is to baseball; (6) Cause-effect relationship--Sadness is to crying as happiness is to laughing; (7) Purpose relationship--A tail is to a kite as a string is to a balloon; (8) Antonym relationship--Hot is to cold as up is to down; (9) Synonym relationship--Jump is to leap as crawl is to creep; (10) Familial relationship--A sister is to a brother as a grandmother is to a grandfather; (11) Temporal relationship--Morning is to sunrise as evening is to sunset; (12) Sequential relationship--Monday is to Tuesday as first is to second. The child expresses the linguistic concepts in sentence format such as, "If it rains, I will wear my raincoat," "Smoke means there is a fire," or "Airplanes fly in the sky. Ships float on water." These are easier and more understandable formats than "Sky is to airplanes as water is to ships." These sentences require logical operations for interpretation and expression.

Assessment Materials

Three prepared sets of statements that require logical relationship responses. Set One: should contain at least four statements that require the child to determine whether they are correct or incorrect. Example: (1) A cat has whiskers. A girl has hair. (2) A boy can be an uncle. A girl can be a brother. (3) Jane bakes cookies. Jane fries an egg. (4) We can swim in the snow. We can ski in the winter. Set Two: should contain at least four statements that require the child to determine appropriate target words from sets of alternatives. Example: (1) A handle belongs on a cup. A doorknob belongs on a chair/door. (2) You can fly a kite. You can ride in a box/car. (3) John uses a ball to play soccer. John uses a bat to play tennis/baseball. (4) Breakfast comes before lunch. Lunch comes before breakfast/dinner. Set Three: should have at least four statements that require the child to say a word to complete a sentence. Example: (1) A cat says meow. A dog says _____ . (2) Orange juice is something we drink. A banana is something we _____ . (3) Ice comes from water. Smoke comes from _____ . (4) A cow is big but an elephant is bigger. A cricket is small but an ant is _____ .

Assessment Procedures

Grouping: This skill should be assessed one-on-one with the child.

1. Explain to the child that you will read her some sentences (Set One), and that some of them are correct and some are incorrect. Add that some may even sound silly.
2. Tell her to listen to each sentence and then to tell you if they are correct or incorrect.
3. Say, "A cat has whiskers. A girl has hair." Pause for her response.
4. Record her correct or incorrect answer.
5. If she has difficulty with the sentence relationships, draw a picture of a cat's face and then draw a picture of a girl's face. Discuss the two faces with her. Draw whiskers on the cat's face and put hair on the girl. Discuss the whiskers and hair with her; how each became part of the faces.
6. Tell her to listen to each of the sentences and then to tell you if they are correct or incorrect. Say "A cat has whiskers. A girl has hair."
7. Continue the above process with the other statements in Set One.
8. Explain to her that you are going to read her some sentences (Set Two) and that she must choose the correct word.
9. Say, "A handle belongs on a cup. A doorknob belongs on a chair or a door." Pause for her response.
10. Record her answer.
11. If she has difficulty with the sentence relationships, draw a picture of a cup with a handle. Discuss the illustration, and why cups have handles. Draw a picture of a chair with a doorknob and a door with a doorknob. Discuss which one is correct and why.
12. Explain to her that you are going to read her two sentences and that she must select the correct word. Say, "A handle belongs on a cup. A doorknob belongs on a chair or a door."
13. Continue, using the other sentences in Set Two.
14. Explain to her that you will read her some sentences (Set Three) and that she must add a word.
15. Say, "A cat says meow. A dog says _____ ." Pause for her response.
16. Record her answer.
17. If she has difficulty with the sentence relationship, draw a picture of a cat, point to the cat, and say, "meow." Then draw picture of a dog, point to the dog, and say, "What should I say?"

18. Continue using the other sentences in Set Three.

Credit: + Child correctly uses sentences that express logical relations between concepts. Child correctly uses at least two sentences from each of the three sets.

Adaptations

Processing sentences that express logical relationships between words or phrases can be a challenge for some children. These sentences require the processes of perceiving and interpreting. Example: Apple trees have apples. Rose bushes have roses. The child must understand the logical relationship between an apple tree and apples; she must discern a whole-part system. She must repeat the logical relationship to understand a rose bush and a rose. She must also know the composition of a bush, a tree, an apple, and a rose, have the words "apple," "tree," "rose," "bush" from her memory, and she must also have a firm verbal association between the word "apples" and "trees," plus "roses" and "bushes." To assist a child who is experiencing problems in this area, discuss the relationships, starting with whole-part analogies and then moving to part-whole analogies. Pictures of the subjects help to create an image. Also consider teaching antonyms before synonym analogies, and action-object relationships before object-action ones. Be sure the child is able to verbalize sentences that address logical relationships before you present any grammatical orders.

2.171 Names an object's parts and gives the function of the object

Strand: 2-4B **Age:** 60-72m 5.0-6.0y

Definition

When the child is presented with a picture of an object, he will name the parts of the object and tell what the object does. The first objects presented to him will have standard parts and have basically one function, such as a pan (to hold things), a chair (for sitting on), a stove (to heat things), or a sweater (to wear). The second objects presented to him will be items that have unique parts and varied functions; such as a plant (to eat, for decoration, to protect) or a building (to live in, for storing things).

Assessment Materials

Two sets of not less than five pictures per set. Set One--Single-item objects that have standard parts and have one major function. Examples: a pan, a comb, a chair, a sweater, a belt. Set Two--Single-item objects that have unique parts and varied functions. Examples: a tree, a plant, a car, a rope, a lake. Purchase pictures or make them out of cutouts from magazines mounted on large index cards.

Assessment Procedures

Note: Due to the nature of the pictures in Set Two, the child may identify and call the parts by different names. However, there are various correct answers.

Grouping: This skill should be assessed one-on-one with the child.

1. Invite the child to join you at the work area. Tell him that you will show him some pictures and then you will ask him some questions about them.
2. Show him a picture from Set One. Say, "This is a picture of a what?" Pause for his response.
3. Say, "Name its parts." Pause for his response.
4. Say, "Tell me what it does." Pause for his response.
5. Note his answers.
6. Continue the above with the other pictures in Set One.
7. If he has difficulty with this task, reduce the expected answers by: (1) Telling him the name of the object. Say, "This is a pan"; (2) Naming its parts, for example, say "handle," and ask the child to point to it; (3) Giving him hints as to the object's function, such as, "It has something to do with food. It is used in the kitchen." After he has identified the pan, pointed to its parts and determined its function, repeat the procedure outlined above, using the second picture from Set One.
8. If he continues to have difficulty, use a real object and repeat the remedial steps (name the object, point to its parts, and demonstrate its use.)
9. Continue with the other pictures in Set One; however, if he experiences failure, discontinue the assessment.
10. If he is successful, continue with Set Two.
11. Explain that you are going to show him some pictures and that you will ask him some questions about them.
12. Show him a picture from Set Two.
13. Say, "This is a picture of a _____ ?" Pause for his response.
14. Say, "Name the parts of the _____ ?" Pause for his response.
15. Say, "Tell me what this does." Pause for his response.

16. Observe and record his responses.

Credit: + Child names an object's parts and gives the function of the object in at least three of the five pictures for each set.

Adaptations

In order to describe an object, name its parts, and state its function, a child is required to give a variety of verbal/cognitive responses. Among the abilities he needs are: (1) Verbal fluency--words readily available; (2) Amenability--to move from one classification or set to another in terms of words; (3) Originality--responses that not only include the most obvious but also the unusual; (4) Amplification--expressed by the detail and description, and the embellishment of the verbal response.

Often a child will have a problem describing the attributes of an object such as its size or form, who has ownership of the object, or making object-action or action-agent connections. To assist this child, implement these suggestions: (1) The immediate description of an object may require the review of past descriptions, because divergent semantic production is dependent upon past experiences and information stored in memory. (Example: "This is a picture of a snowman, do you remember when we made a snowman? What did we use for his arms? I remember we had rocks; where did they go?"); (2) Begin child inquiry by asking general questions about an object (Example: "What can you tell me about this snowman?"); (3) Using the responses from Item 1 and 2, ask him specific descriptive and functional questions, moving from the general to the more specific.

2.172 (Moved to Cognitive, skill 1.298)

2.173 Describes parts of a movie, TV show, live event or other audio/visual presentations

Strand: 2-4B **Age:** 48-66m 4.0-5.6y

Definition

After the child views an audio/visual presentation or a live production, he will be able to describe the content, sequence of events, characters, and outcomes. He will respond to the presentation when he is asked questions (Examples: What is the story about? Who was the story about? What was the first thing that happened in the story?) or when he is prompted (Tell me about the movie you saw yesterday).

Assessment Materials

A story on TV or an audio/visual story presentation. Select one the child has not seen before and one within his attention span and interest.

Assessment Procedures

Note: Place earphones on him if he is in a setting where there are other auditory distractions.

Grouping: This skill can be presented in a small group setting, but the questions should be asked one-on-one with each child shortly after they have seen the presentation. Remind the children that they will need to listen and take turns during this activity.

Level One:
1. Explain to the child that he is going to watch a story on TV, video, or DVD. Do not tell him that you will ask him questions about the story after he has viewed it. Make sure he is comfortable and that all distractions have been removed. Allow him to watch the presentation without interruptions.
2. After he has viewed the story, encourage him to tell about it. Use noncommittal responses, ("oh," "really,") to vitalize his retelling.
3. Listen to the story for literal interruption, sequencing of events, analysis of happenings, descriptions, and critical evaluations.
4. Ask him questions about the story, beginning with who, what, when and where for literal translations, then moving to what happened first, next, and so on. Then question the child on interpretation by asking, "What do you think.?" or "Why do you think he did it?" and asking expanding questions such as, "What do think will happen next?" "If [suggest alternative] would have happened, how would that have changed the ending?"
5. If he has difficulty retelling the video/DVD presentation, allow him to see it again. If he continues to have a problem, divide the story into sections: show the first section and prompt or ask questions, show the next section and prompt or ask questions, and continue with the rest of the story.
6. If he demonstrates a problem, evaluate the selection as to its length, content, quality, the child's interest and prerequisite cognitive needs.

Level Two:
7. After the child has viewed an audio-visual story or a live show, ask him to tell you about

it. Observe the elements he includes in his retelling and whether he included different levels of comprehension (literal, sequential, interpretive, analytical, critical, and creative). Use prompts or questions as needed.

Credit: + Child correctly describes parts of a movie, television show, live event, or other audio/visual presentation when asked questions or prompted. His descriptions will relate to content, sequence of events, characters, and outcomes.

Adaptations

Some children have difficulty retelling an event or a story. Often such a child lacks the ability to store auditory or visual material over a few seconds or minutes. He may be influenced by an outside stimulus and finds staying on task troublesome. Distractions may occur when varied items intervene between the presentation and the recall. When you are dealing with a child who has a short-term memory or a retelling concern, consider the following: (1) The complexity of the material; (2) The amount of time between the presentation and when he is asked to respond; (3) Using prompts to keep him on task and to clarify the retelling; (4) The utilization of visual cues to assist in the recollection; (5) Allowing for multiple viewings.

2.174 Chooses previously specified details from spoken material

Strand: 2-1A **Age:** 63-70m 5.3-5.10y

Definition

The child will be told what details to listen for before she hears the spoken material. After hearing the spoken material, she will answer questions based on the details she was directed to note. The selected details will be those that require detailed/interpretive responses only and will answer who, when, where, what types of questions.

Assessment Materials

A short story to read to the child within her experiential base. (You may also write a short story or use the following example:

Two Pigs
Once upon a time two pigs went into the woods. They met a rabbit. The rabbit started to talk to the pigs. The two pigs and the rabbit decided to have a race. They got in a line. A bird in a tree nearby said, "Ready, set, go!" The two pigs and the rabbit started to run very fast. The rabbit just knew she would win, so when she got tired she found a nice shady tree and decided to take a nap. The two pigs ran past the sleeping rabbit. And when she woke up she saw that the two pigs were about to win the race, so the funny rabbit went back to sleep.

Assessment Procedures

Note: It is important that the "listen for" things begin with What, Where, Who or When.
Grouping: This skill should be assessed one-on-one with the child.

1. Ask the child to join you at the story-telling area. Tell her you will read her a story and ask her to listen for two things in the story. Listen for: (1) What did the pigs and the rabbit decide to do one day? (2) What did the rabbit do under the shady tree?
2. Secure her attention. Read the story.
3. Ask these questions: What did the pigs and the rabbit decide to do one day? What did the rabbit do under the shady tree?
4. Record the child's responses.
5. If she has difficulty responding, do the following in this sequence: (1) Provide prompts if she is having recall problems; (2) Reread the story segments that include the answers to the questions, and then re-ask the questions; (3) Offer her multiple choice responses, for example: What did the pigs and the rabbit decide to do one day? Did they decide to (a) have a picnic? (b) run a race? (c) eat a piece of pizza? (4) Tell her the answer.
6. Read the story again, asking the child to listen for a different detail.
7. Ask about the things she was prompted to listen for earlier.
8. Record her responses.
9. If she continues to have difficulty with this task, reduce the story facts presented by using a two- or three-line story and only one pre-designated detail for her to listen for.
Example: Joan and Anne
Joan had a new black cat.
Joan's new cat liked milk.
Joan's new cat was named Anne.
10. Ask the child to listen to the story about Joan and Anne. Ask her to listen for: "What did Joan have that was new?"
11. Continue as outlined above.

Credit: + Child correctly answers question based on the details she was directed to note before hearing a story. The selected details require detailed/interpretative responses and will be answered with who, when, where, and what-type questions.

Adaptations

Memory plays a key role in this activity. Not only does the child have to listen and hear, but she must also retain the auditory information and relate it when asked. If she is having problems retaining and retrieving information, she may experience some real learning problems. To assist her, consider the following: (1) Improving techniques of selective observation; (2) Organization of material; (3) Sufficient repetition; (4) Splintering the requested task into smaller segments; (5) Being sure the child is dealing with information that is relative to her.

2.175 Makes facial expressions appropriate to spoken material
Strand: 2-1A **Age:** 63-70m 5.3-5.10y

Definition
The child will make a facial expression that reflects what he has heard. For example, he will smile at another person's joke, will look awed when he is told something surprising, and will scowl after he is told something unpleasant.

Assessment Materials
A written selection about faces. Examples: *On Monday When It Rained* (book) by Cheryl Kachenmeister, *Faces* (book) by Barbara Brenner, *The Worth of a Smile*--an Uncle Arthur story, riddles about expressions or facial expression poems. If a written selection is difficult to locate, create a poem, a scene, or a paragraph dealing with facial expressions in response to different emotions. A set of facial expression cards, either purchased, drawn, or cutout faces from newspapers and magazines and mounted on index cards. The faces should include the following emotions: happy, frightened, proud, sleepy, sad, and angry. Other emotions may be included.
Example selection:
<u>The Look</u>
1. I created a face that was happy;
   I included a eye.
2. I created a face that was sad;
   I made it almost cry.
3. I created a face that was angry;
   I worked up a mouth with a frown.
4. I created a face that was frightening;
   I made eyes as round as a clown's.
5. I created a face that was proud;
   I included a smile big and wide.
6. I created a face that was sleepy;
   I made the eyes to look like a slide.

Assessment Procedures
Note: The first two lines should be used as an instructional procedure to the assessment.
Grouping: This skill should be assessed one-on-one with the child.
1. Tell the child that you are going to read a poem to him. Read the poem, "The Look."
2. Briefly talk about what your face looks like when you are angry, sad, or happy.
3. Place at least three different facial expression cards on the table in front of the child. Be sure that one of the cards is the happy expression.
4. Read the first two lines of the poem (1). Say, "Point to the picture on the table that shows the face that you just heard about."
5. If the child has difficulty or if he appears to be unclear of the directions when you have said, "Point to the picture on the table that shows the face that I just told you about," say instead, "Point to the picture on the table that shows a happy face."
6. Begin the assessment by reading the next two lines (2) of the poem.
7. Place at least three different facial expression cards on the table in front of the child, making sure one of them shows the sad expression. Say, "Point to the picture on the table that shows the face that you just heard about."
8. Pause to allow him time to respond.
9. If he is unable to respond, repeat the lines (2) and the directions.
10. Record the answer.
11. Read the next two lines (3) of the poem.
12. Place at least three different facial expression cards on the table in front of the child, making sure one of them shows the angry facial expression. Say, "Point to the picture on the table that shows the face that you just heard about."
13. Pause to give him time to respond.
14. Repeat the lines if needed.
15. Record the answer.
16. Continue the above procedure with poem lines 4, 5, and 6.
17. The concept of "proud" may not be within the child's listening comprehension; if this is a problem, do not administer lines 5 and 6.

Credit: + Child makes facial expressions, or chooses pictures of facial expressions, appropriate to the spoken information/material he has just heard.

Adaptations

Facial expression is very significant regarding the comprehension of nonverbal language. A child may be unable to interpret from appearances how a person feels because he has not related the facial changes to a feeling. For example, an upturned mouth indicates a happy feeling or wide-open eyes portray the feeling of fear. Because a child does not typically grasp experience vicariously, it is important to deal directly with the personal experience when it occurs. Some strategies for reflecting the child's expression: when he displays an excited face due to the setting, an unhappy face because of the situation, or a frightened face that is related to an incident, draw his attention to his reaction and his concomitant facial expression by using a mirror or a photograph. The camera is an excellent source for assisting him to recall the experience, including the expression on his face and its relationship to the situation.

2.176 Identifies order of sounds in a word and blends the sounds together to make meaningful words

Strand: 2-1A **Age:** 64-68m 5.4-5.8y

Definition

As soon as the child has learned some of the consonant sounds and the short sounds of two vowels (preferably short "a" and short "i"), she needs to receive instruction on how to blend these sounds into meaningful words. The blending must be done smoothly to prevent mispronunciation of words and distortions. It is helpful to begin with words composed of nasal consonants with a short "a" so there are no sound pauses between the letters (man, nap, map, mat, etc.) Once the child is able to sound blend a few words (man), consideration should be given to initial consonant substitution and the forming of other words by sound-blending (pan, fan, ran).

Assessment Materials

Twenty wooden blocks at least 1½ inches square made or purchased and marked as follows with a black marking pen. On five blocks, one letter per side, randomly place the consonants b, c, d, f, g, h. Both capital and lowercase letters may be used. On five blocks, one letter per side, randomly place the consonants m j, k, l, m, n, p. Both capital and lowercase letters may be used. On five blocks, one letter per side, randomly place the consonants r, s, t, v, w, z. Both capital and lowercase letters may be used. Please note the consonants q, x, y are not included. On five blocks, one letter per side, randomly place the vowels a, e, i, o, u. Use only lowercase. Select blocks that have the letters on them that will make the following words: map, man, mud, mit, nan, nat, nap, lot, got, rug, hug, jug, jet, vet, wet. It is suggested that you start with the list of words provided, but other consonant-vowel-consonant words may be used. It is best to present words with the short sound of "a" at the beginning of the assessment. Separate the presentation of the short sounds of "e" and "i," because the sounds are so similar. Prepare a score sheet with the list of words to be used.

Assessment Procedures

Grouping: This skill should be assessed one-on-one with the child.

1. Ask the child to join you at the table. Align three blocks to form the word "tan."
2. Ask the child to say the word.
3. If she has difficulty in sound-blending the word "tan," move the "t" block away from the "an," and ask her to sound the "t" as you quickly move it to meet the "a" and "n" blocks. As the "t" block connects with the stationary "a-n" blocks, ask her to sound the complete word. She needs to sound-blend at the following duration: t (half-second interval) an.
4. Continue the above procedure with the other letter blocks.
5. On the scoring sheet, indicate the words she could sound blend without any prompting, those she needed assistance with, those that took her longer than a half-second interval, and those that she sounded each letter ("M---a---n").

Credit: + Child first identifies the order of sounds and blends the sounds into a meaningful word. Child blends the nasal consonants with a short "a" and there is no pause between the letters. Next, the child is given words with initial consonant substitution and the forming of other words by sound-blending.

Adaptations

One of the concerns regarding sound-blending is the rate at which sounds are expressed. The closer they are presented in time, the more readily the child will be able to blend a word as a unit. When sounds are presented that require a decoding process for word recognition, some children need over two seconds to identify the letter and recall the sound associated with it. The child then must hold that sound, while moving on to the next letter(s) and recalling that sound(s). She must reach the level of proficiency in which she is only concentrating on recalling the sounds/symbols, instead of recalling each letter sound and having to focus on blending successive sounds. The first task in dealing with auditory sound-blending is time, the rate at which sounds are introduced. The closer they are presented, the more accurately they will be blended. Ask the child to repeat a word after you, then to repeat it when you say it slowly. For example, say, "What is this word: tr-(½ second) -ee?" If she cannot respond with the word tree, ask her to say "tree." Then say, "What is this? Tr-tr-tr-tr-ee-ee," holding each sound but blending them together. Ask her to say the word. Continue this practice until she can process sounds into words in at least two-second intervals.

2.177 Responds verbally and non-verbally to questions concerning abstract and factual concepts

Strand: 2-1A **Age:** 42-54m 3.6-4.6y

Definition
When the child is presented with questions, he will answer verbally or he will indicate an answer nonverbally (e.g., shaking his head no or nodding yes). Examples of questions are: How old are you? (factual), Do you like apples? (abstract,) Did you hear the dog bark? (may be answered by nodding or shaking his head), Where would you like to go in the car? (abstract), What color is the sweater you are wearing? (factual), Are you ready to go? (may be answered by nodding or shaking his head).

Assessment Materials
A set of questions to ask the child. The questions should include abstract (the answer exists only in child's mind and is usually an opinion), factual (an answer known to be true), and those that can be answered non-verbally. They should also use words the child comprehends and involve experiences to which he can relate.

Assessment Procedures
Grouping: This skill can be assessed one-on-one with the child. However, you can ask questions during group activities related to comments the child has made in order to assess their skills at responding verbally and non-verbally to questions concerning abstract or factual concepts.

Level One:
1. Place the child in a comfortable setting and tell him you are going to ask him some questions. Tell him to answer each question after he hears it.
2. Begin asking the questions. Note his responses, in particular, whether he has difficulty with questions that were abstract or those that were factual.
3. If he has difficulty responding, evaluate the questions to determine whether he was able to comprehend the message.
4. Reword or rewrite the questions to make sure that the words are within his knowledge bank and that he can relate to their content.

Level 2:
5. During child "talking time" in school, be sure to include questions. Let the child provide the initiative in the "talking time," then follow up with comments and questions to generate answers and further visiting. Consider this example: The child brings a spring tulip to school. The "talking time" may go something like this:
Child: "Look at what I brought for you today. It is a tulip."
Teacher: "It is a very pretty red tulip. Where did you get the tulip?" (factual).
Child: "Out of my grandma's garden."
Teacher: "Does your grandma have other flowers in her garden?" (may be answered nonverbally).
Child: (Nods head yes) "I found another flower in my grandma's garden."
Teacher: "What color was that flower?"(factual).
Child: "It was a white flower, and it had been picked."
Teacher: "Do you think your grandma picked it and put it on the ground?"
Child: "No, my grandma wouldn't throw a flower away." (abstract).
The above is an example of an informal assessment that could occur during the routine of a day.
6. Note the child's responses.

Credit: + Child responds correctly, either verbally and non-verbally, to questions concerning abstract and factual concepts.

Adaptations
Responding to questions is a thinking process that involves several steps. Questions focusing on memory (recalling information), translation (changing information into a different language form), and interpretation

(determining relationships among facts, generalizations, and definitions), correspond to beginning skills or concept development. The next level of questioning--application (requires the understanding of an issue and the choosing of an appropriate skill), analysis (solves problems by knowing the parts and the relationship of these parts to the action), and synthesis (addresses a problem by creative thinking), focuses on retention and the reinforcement of a concept or a skill already learned. The final level of questioning is evaluation--making a judgment of right or wrong according to the values individually identified, which is a level that focuses on constant review and the sustaining of concepts. Some children need to become involved with questioning in a very sequential, structured manner. Therefore, it is important that these children become skilled in memory-type questions before they attempt translation questions and then build to interpretive questions, application questions, etc. A technique that provides support for children who are having problems with receiving and responding to questions is to ask questions of a group, and to request unison answers. This provides the child with an opportunity to follow a model, and the technique is particularly helpful when concepts are first being learned.

2.178   Identifies initial sounds of words

Strand: 2-1A   **Age:** 65-72m 5.5-6.0y

Definition
When the child is asked to listen to a list of at least three words, of which two start with the same sound, she will be able to say the two that begin alike.

Assessment Materials
Four clusters of three words each, two that begin with the same sound and one that does not. Example: (1) baby, boy, mat; (2) pull, cat, pan; (3) fun, team, take; (4) Sam, sit, come. Four clusters of four words each, two that begin with the same sound and two that do not. Example: (5) gray, jump, grew, like; (6) water, win, from, sat; (7) fun, dog, drag, bite; (8) run, mind, lap, last. Select one sound (e.g., t) and a list of 10 words, six of which start with t. Example: (9) walk, toe, turn, hat, boy, take, Tom, table, put, top. Continue with two more sounds and a listing of 10 words.

Assessment Procedures
Grouping: This skill should be assessed one-on-one with the child.

<u>Level One:</u>
1. Explain to the child that you are going to say some words. Tell her that two of the words start with the same sound. Tell her to listen carefully and to say the two words that sound alike.
2. Say, "Let's practice; listen for the two words that start with the same sound." Say, "Cup, hat, come."
3. Say, "Say the two words that start with the same sound." Pause for her response.
4. Repeat if necessary.
5. If she understands the directions, begin the assessment with Word Cluster 1.
6. Say, "Listen for the two words that start with the same sound." Say, "Baby, boy, mat."
7. Say, "Say the two words that start with the same sound." Pause for her response.
8. Include the letter sound (b) when you record her answer.
9. Continue the above procedure with Word Clusters 2 through 8.

<u>Level Two:</u>
10. In presenting Word Clusters 9 through 11, proceed as follows.
11. Say, "This time I am going to say a sound first and then I will say some words.
12. Say, "Every time you hear a word that starts with the sound I gave first, I want you to raise your hand."
13. Say, "Let's practice, listen for the sound--m-m-m-m-m-m. Now, I am going to say the words, and remember to raise your hand if you hear a word that starts like m-m-m."
14. Say, "Man." If she does not raise her hand, remind her of the sound of m-m-m and that man starts like that sound, so therefore, she should raise her hand.
15. Continue the list of words for the m sound, "Dog, make, mother, put, fun, Mike, son, milk, mile."
16. Repeat if necessary.
17. If the child understands the directions for Level Two, begin the assessment with Word Cluster 9.
18. Say, "Listen for the sound of t-t-t-t. Now I am going to say some words, and you are to raise your hand if you hear a word that starts like t-t-t."
19. Say the words from Word Cluster 9.
20. Include the letter sound "t" when you record her answer.

Credit: + Child listens to a list of at least three words, of which two start with the same sound, and she is able to say the two words that begin alike.

Adaptations
Some children have a difficult time discriminating abstract sounds (m-m-m, t-t-t). A child may not have a problem discriminating environmental sounds, such as a barking dog or water running, due to the fact that she is able to place a visual image (a dog) with the environmental sound. Single phoneme sounds do not have a visual association; hence, the sound needs to be heard and cognitively processed based on auditory signal only. For a child who depends on a visual stimulus, single-sound association can be difficult. Because beginning stages of reading often depend on phoneme sound discrimination, it is important to provide her with various activities to enhance this skill. Using pictures of words that start with a given sound (t) or asking her to look through magazines and find pictures that start with a specific sound are effective techniques.

2.179 Uses compound sentences with more than one main clause
Strand: 2-3 **Age:** 65-78m 5.5-6.6y

Definition
When the child is involved in a verbal situation, he will respond by using a compound sentence. He will connect the main clauses using such words as "and", "but", and, "or." (e.g., "I ran to the store and came back in an hour." "Jane can bake some cookies or a chocolate cake.")

Assessment Materials
At least five sets of picture "pairs." Example: (1) A cow and a pig; (2) A spoon and a fork; (3) A pie and a cake; (4) A car and a truck; (5) A doll and a baseball bat.

Assessment Procedures
Grouping: This skill can be assessed one-on-one with the child. However, the most important assessment procedure is made by observing the child in a natural conversational setting and listening for his use of compound sentences.
Level One:
1. Explain to the child that you are going to place two pictures (Set 1) on the table. Tell him to look at the pictures and listen closely.
2. Say, "This is a _____ and this is a _____."
3. Ask him to complete the sentence (allow pauses for his answer).
4. Say, "This is a cow ___ this is a pig."
5. Ask him to complete the sentence (pause for his response).
6. Say, "Now, tell me about these animals."
7. Tell him that you are going to place two pictures (Set 1) on the table. Ask him to look at the pictures and listen.
8. Say, "Would you rather have a _____ or a _____?"
9. Ask him to complete the sentence (allow pauses for his answer).
10. Say, "Would you rather have a cow _____ a pig?"
11. Ask him to complete the sentence (pause).
12. Say, "Tell me about these animals."
13. Continue the above procedure with Picture Sets 2 through 5.
14. If he has a difficult time connecting the two main clauses with "or," "but," or "and," say the complete sentence instead of pausing when you state the model sentence.
15. For example, explain to him that you are going to place two pictures (Set 1) on the table. Tell him to look at the pictures and listen. Say, "This is a cow (point to the picture of the cow), and this is a pig (point to the picture of the pig)."
16. Ask him to repeat the sentence.
17. Say, "Would you rather have a cow or a pig?"
18. Ask him to repeat the sentence.
19. Explain to him that you are going to place two pictures (Set 1) on the table. Tell him to look at the pictures and listen. Say, "This is a _____ and this is a _____."
20. Ask him to complete the sentence (allow pauses for his answers).
21. Say, "This is a cow _____ this is a pig."
22. Ask him to complete the sentence (pause for his answer).
23. Say, "Please tell me about these animals."
24. Explain to him that you are going to place two pictures (Set 1) on the table. Tell him to look at the pictures and listen. Say, "Would you rather have a _____ or a _____?"
25. Ask him to complete the sentence (allow pauses for his answers).
26. Say, "Would you rather have a cow _____ a pig?"
27. Ask him to complete the sentence (pause).
28. Say, "Tell me about these animals."

29. Continue the above procedure with Picture Sets 2 through 5.

Level Two:

30. Observe the child when he is involved in a discussion or a conversation for appropriate use of compound and complex sentences.

Credit: + Child uses compound sentences with more than one main clause. The clauses are connected using words such as "and," "but," and "or."

Adaptations

A child may be able to use single words, short phrases, and simple sentences, but he is ineffective in generating longer syntactic sentences (compound or complex). He may have a problem internalizing sentence patterns so that they can create new sentences. To be able to internalize sentence patterns, the child needs to: (1) Understand language heard; (2) Recall word sequences; (3) Naturally formulate the different sentence structures. To assist a child to build more expansive sentences: (1) Start with the basic sentence patterns, and help him combine them. Example: The boy is running. The boy is jumping. Combine to say, "The boy is running and jumping"; (2) Create statements and then ask questions that correspond. Example: Children eat popcorn. Do children eat popcorn? Popcorn is eaten by children. Is popcorn eaten by children?; (3) Provide the child with a sentence that includes only key words and ask him to add the structure words. Example: Mr. Johnson is a kind _____ funny, old man; (4) Assist him to form new sentences by substituting a single word in a simple sentence. Example: The dog is barking. The dog is _____. The dog is barking and _____ ; (5) Provide him with conversational opportunities by using props such as puppets, play telephones, dramatic play, riddles and jokes, and story-telling.

2.180 Identifies initial and final sounds of words

Strand: 2-1A   **Age:** 66-72m 5.6-6.0y

Definition

When the child is presented with a list of words that have different beginning and ending sounds, she will identify the sounds. The following sequence is recommended for beginning and ending sound recognition: (1) Present words verbally that have the same beginning and ending sound (pip); (2) Begin initial sound identification by consonant substitution (nip, tip, lip, sip); (3) Deal with final sound identification by consonant substitution (pin, pit, pill, pic).

Assessment Materials

Four clusters of three words each, two words that begin or end with the same sound and one that does not. Example: (1) mom, pip, top; (2) tot, got, mum; (3) fun, son, bib; (4) tat, hot, pop. Four clusters of four words each, two that begin with the same sound and two that do not. Example: (5) nip, tip, nap, lap; (6) top, mop, tub, rub; (7) bell, fell, wall, ball; (8) run, sun, rake, make. Four clusters of four words each, two that end with the same sound and two that do not. Example: (9) pen, pat, hen, bell; (10) fat, cat, sum, rip; (11) row, pad, hut, mad; (12) cab, sat, dog, tab. Select one sound (e.g., r) and a list of 10 words, six of which start with the sound of "r." Example: (13) race, ride, turn, rat, boy, rake, rice table, rut, top. Select one sound (e.g., n) and a list of 10 words, six of which end with the sound of "n." Example: (14) sun, get, ran, pup, tin, gun, his, ton, hen, new.

Assessment Procedures

Grouping: This skill should be assessed one-on-one with the child.

Level One:

1. Explain to the child that you are going to say some words and that two of the words start and end with the same sound. Tell her that she is to listen carefully and say the two words that start and end alike.
2. Say, "Let's practice; listen for the two words." Say, "Mom, pip, top."
3. Say, "Say the two words that start and end with the same sound." Pause for her response.
4. Repeat if necessary.
5. If she understands the directions, begin the assessment with Word Cluster 2.
6. Say, "Listen for the two words that start and end with the same sound." Say, "Tot, got mum."
7. Say, "Say the two words that start and end with the same sound." Pause for her response.
8. Include the letter sounds when you record her answer.
9. Continue the above procedure with Word Clusters 3 and 4.

Level Two:

10. In presenting Word Clusters 5 through 8, proceed as follows.
11. Say, "This time I am going to say a sound first, and then I will say some words."

12. Say, "Every time you hear a word that starts with the sound I gave, I want you to raise your hand."
13. Say, "Let's practice; listen for the sound: n-n-n-n. Now I am going to say the words. Remember to raise your hand if you hear a word that starts like n-n-n."
14. Say, "Nip." If the child does not raise her hand, remind her of the sound of "n-n-n" and that nip starts like that sound, so therefore she should raise her hand. Continue the list: fun, nip, tip, nap, lap.
15. Repeat if necessary.
16. If she understands the directions for level two begin the assessment with Word Cluster 6.
17. Say, "Listen for the sound of t-t-t-t, and now I am going to say some words. Raise your hand if you hear a word that starts like t-t-t."
18. Say the words from Word Clusters 7 and 8.
19. Include the letter sound (t) when you record the child's responses.
20. Continue the above procedure with Word Clusters 9 through 14.
21. Be sure you clearly explain to the child that in Word Clusters 9 through 12, the she is to listen for the same final sounds. In Word Cluster 10, she is to listen for like beginning sounds in 10 words. In Word Cluster 11, she is to listen for like ending sounds in 10 words.

Credit: + Child identifies the initial and final sounds of words.

Adaptations

Some children have a difficult time discriminating abstract sounds (n-n-n, t-t-t). A child may not have a problem discriminating environmental sounds, such as a barking dog or water running, due to the fact that she is able to place a visual image (dog) with the environmental sound. Single phoneme sounds do not have a visual association; therefore, the sound must be heard and cognitively processed based on auditory signal only. For a child who depends on a visual stimulus, single sound association can be difficult. Because the beginning stages of reading often depend on phoneme sound discrimination, it is important to provide the child with various activities to enhance this skill: (1) Identification of words with the target sound from among randomly selected words (m) cat, dog, man; (2) Same or different decisions of word pairs containing the target sound (m) mat, fat; (3) Identification of the sound in word triplets (m) bad, pad, mad; (4) Identification of the position (initial or final) of the target sound in word pairs (m) drug, drum; (5) Re-auditorization and production of an omitted target sound (m) ____arbles. Using pictures of words that start like a given sound (t) or asking the child to look through magazines to find pictures that start with a sound are effective techniques.

2.181 Repeats story just heard maintaining original sequence

Strand: 2-1A **Age:** 68-72m 5.8-6.0y

Definition

When the child is told a short, simple story, he will be able to tell the story back and repeat the original sequence. He should tell at least four ordered events that were included in the story. The story will be one he has not heard before, but one within his experience level.

Assessment Materials

A short story with at least four sequenced events. (The story may be selected or written, or use the example.) At least four pictures that illustrate the events in the story. Example: (1) A fairy sitting on a white cloud; (2) The fairy being tossed by the wind on the darkened cloud; (3) The fairy being rained on and flying with a rain drop to earth; (4) The fairy under a big leaf staying dry during the rain storm.
Example:
<u>The Flying Fairy</u>
Once upon a time there was a special fairy.
She rode on clouds.
One day she flew up to a white cloud.
She sat down on the cloud and sank way down deep.
The cloud was so soft, so comfortable, and so quiet.
Suddenly the cloud turned dark, and the wind tossed the fairy upside down.
Soon the little fairy heard a big noise and a saw a bright light.
Then the special fairy felt rain on her face.
She quickly flew with a raindrop to earth.
She found a big leaf and crept under it until the rain stopped.

Assessment Procedures

Grouping: This skill can be assessed one-on-one with the child. However, after reading a story during a group activity call on a child to see if they can retell the story maintaining the original sequence.

Level One:
1. Explain to the child that you are going to read him a story. Tell him to listen carefully. Read the story.
2. Ask him to retell the story.
3. Observe whether he maintains the story sequence.
4. If he has difficulty repeating the story, reread it.
5. Then ask him to retell the story.
6. Observe whether he maintains the story sequence after the second reading.
7. If he has difficulty telling the story, reread it and show the pictures at the appropriate times.
8. Then ask him to retell the story.
9. If needed, use the visuals as prompts to help him.
10. Observe whether he maintains the story sequence after the third reading and with the support of the visuals.
11. Record how many times he heard the story (do not read more than three times), and if he needed the pictorial cues.

Level Two:
12. After class story time, discuss the story that was read and pay particular attention for the child's responses that deal with retelling and sequencing.

Credit: + Child repeats a story he has just heard maintaining the original sequence, without prompting. The story should have at least four ordered parts/sequences.

Adaptations

Some children have a difficult time separating the action sequence ("One day she flew up to a white cloud.") from descriptive narrative ("The cloud was so soft, so comfortable and so quiet"). When the child is asked to retell a story, he tries to recall every detail and every word. He treats retelling as more of a memorization task than a synopsis of the plot, action, and conclusion. He has a difficult time separating main ideas from single details and evaluating the key parts of a story that relate the whole. To assist him in developing the skill of determining the difference between narrative and sequential events: (1) Present stories that are total events that lead up to a conclusion. Example: Mary and Joe got into the car to visit their grandmother in the country. They had a flat tire. Mary and Joe helped Dad change the tire. They made it to Grandmother's house by dark; (2) When telling or reading a story, use numerical sequential words. Example: First, Mary and Joe got into the car to visit their grandmother in the country. Second--They had a flat tire. Third--Mary and Joe helped Dad change the tire. Fourth--They made it to Grandmother's house by dark; (3) Include pictures that illustrate the sequential events and any detail necessary to the story's content; (4) During the rereading of a story, whenever you read an action sequence, ask the child to repeat just the detailed sequence. Example: "Mary and Joe got into the car to visit their grandmother in the country." Say, "Donald, tell me what happened." Continue with the story, asking for a repeat of each detail; (5) Ask the child to dramatize the events as they occur in the story.

2.182 Repeats a poem when prompted by the title, a subject clue, or the first line

Strand: 2-1A **Age:** 68-78m 5.8-6.6y

Definition
The child will repeat a poem that she has learned when prompted by the title, a subject clue, or the first line. She may say the learned poem with another person. The poem should be no more than 20 words in length.

Assessment Materials
A poem of not more than 20 words that the child is familiar with and has learned. Examples: *Roses are Red*, and *Hickory, Dickory, Dock*.

Assessment Procedures
Grouping: This skill can be assessed one-on-one with the child. However, after a group activity in which a poem or finger play is shared, see if the child can repeat it back to you.

Level One:
1. Explain to the child that you will tell her the name of a poem that she knows, and then you want her to say the whole poem.
2. Say, "Roses are Red." Pause to allow her to say the known poem.
3. If she has difficulty with the verse, provide lead words in a strong voice, then phase your voice out to allow her to pick up the stanzas.
4. If she is unable to recall the poem, say it for her.
5. After she has heard the poem, say, "Your turn to say the poem, *Roses are Red*."
6. Observe her response.

Language

Level Two:
7. During a group activity in which children are to say a poem, do finger play, a chant, or any other rhyming selection that they have already learned, observe which children recall and say the selection.
8. If they have walked to school on a rainy day, teach them a new poem about rain; then observe which children can recall the poem correctly.

Credit: + Child repeats a poem that she has learned when prompted by the title, a subject clue, or the first line. The poem should be no more than 20 words in length. She may say the poem with another person.

Adaptations

It is important that poetry be presented in a manner where it means much more than just memorizing words or even ideas. A child who has a difficult time with memory skills will soon forget just learning words. She needs to understand the words and concepts of the poem before she memorizes them. Most children like the feel of poetry, and frequently, they will join in as a teacher reads or recites a poem. If a poem is really understood, enjoyed, and appreciated by the child, she will find the memorization process easy. After she has memorized a poem, review it with her often, either as a listening activity, a joining-in activity, or an activity when she says the poem.

2.183 Chooses main ideas from spoken material

Strand: 2-1A   **Age:** 70-78m   5.10-6.6y

Definition

When the child is questioned about spoken material, he can tell the main idea from it. The material should have only one central thought without any subplots.

Assessment Materials

A short story the child has not heard before and one with a single main idea. If a short story is not available, create one or use the example:
Once upon a time there was a squirrel high up in a tree.
The squirrel was looking and looking.
All of the sudden he saw a nut on the ground.
The squirrel ran down the tree and got the nut.
The squirrel kept the nut in his mouth and dug a hole by the tree.
He put the nut in the hole.
Mr. Squirrel had put one more nut away for the cold winter.

Assessment Procedures

Grouping: This skill can be assessed one-on-one with the child. However, after a group activity in which you have read a new story, see if the child can choose the main idea of the story.

Level One:
1. Read the story to the child. Discuss the details of the story.
2. Mention to him that the story did not have a title. Explain that a title tells in a few words what the story is all about.
3. Ask the child to give the story a title.
4. Record whether the title that he gave relates to the main idea.
5. If he was unable to state a main idea title, read the story again and give him options for a title. Say, for example, "Which of the following would be the best title for the story? Mr. Squirrel Digs a Hole, Mr. Squirrel Saves a Nut for Winter, or Mr. Squirrel Sits High in a Tree?
6. Pause for him to respond.
7. Make a notation of the title that he selected and include in the observation that the task level was lowered.

Level Two:
8. Before story time, select a story to read to the child but do not read the title of the story. After story time, discuss the facts and important details of the selection with the child. Discuss the sequence of events and ask what the main idea was or what a good title would be for the story.
9. Observe the responses to determine any child unable to state a title or the main idea.

Credit: + Child chooses the main idea from spoken material, such as a short story, with one central thought and no subplots.

Adaptations

Being able to state the main idea from spoken material is a more difficult skill than stating facts or details. Some children are unable to see through details to get the central thought. Listening for information is a continual change. With every sentence heard, the listener must take into account the context, the problems that are being expressed, and the perplexities of the material. When the child is asked what the main idea of the material was, he must assess the facts and details, the continuous flow of the information heard, then accept or reject thoughts, and finally come up with a conclusion. Assessing the details can be a very difficult task, and often the child will concur that the first or the last sentence is the main idea. To assist him to conceptualize the parts and to come up with a conclusion, read the material and ask detailed questions in the following manner: (1) "Who" questions (Who was sitting in the tree? Who saw a nut on the ground? Who put the nut in his mouth? Who dug the hole and put the nut in it?) (2) "Where" questions (Where was the squirrel sitting? Where did he see the nut? Where did he put the nut?) (3) "What" questions (What was the squirrel doing in the tree? What did he see on the ground? What did he do with the nut?) (4) "Why" questions. "Why" questions are very important, as they lead to the summarization of the Who, Where, and What questions that, when consolidated, determine the main idea. (Why was the squirrel looking? Why did he dig a hole? Why does the squirrel save nuts for the winter?). The "Why" questions should not require any author interpretation or expectations of the child to predict outcomes.

2.184 through 2.223—Note: Assessment procedures are not available for Skills 2.184 through 2.223. See the Curriculum Guide for suggested instructional activities.

2.224 Answers questions logically
Strand: 2-4B **Age:** 42-47m 3.6-3.11y

Definition
When asked a question, the child will respond by giving a logical answer.

Assessment Materials
A group of at least four pictures that show people engaged in everyday activities. Commercial sets of pictures are available to purchase or make them by cutting and mounting pictures from magazines, newspapers, or old workbooks. Example: (1) A child with dirty hands, (2) A child with a cut on their finger or knee, (3) A child standing outside in the rain without a coat or an umbrella, (4) A child watching other people eating, looking hungry.

Assessment Procedures
Grouping: This skill can be formally assessed one-on-one with the child or informally during a small group activity.

Level One:
1. Tell the child that you are going to ask him some questions about what he might do in different situations and you want him to answer the questions as best he can.
2. Begin by asking him a question related to an everyday occurrence at school, such as, "What would you do if your hands got dirty when you were painting?"
3. Note his response.
4. If he has difficulty with the response, repeat the question or provide a visual cue by showing the child the picture depicting the scene you are asking about.
5. Note the child's response and any prompt that was required.
6. Ask him another question, such as, "What would you do if you cut your finger?"
7. Record his response.

Level Two:
8. When you are engaged in an activity, ask the child questions pertaining to what he needs to do. Before eating snack or lunch ask the child, "What do you do when you are hungry?" Another example, when it is raining outside ask, "What do you do when you need to go outside, but it's raining?"
9. Provide cues if necessary, but note what help was needed.
10. Record the child's responses.

Credit: + Child answers questions logically.

Adaptations
Answering questions requires the child to listen and comprehend information he has heard. We can verify how well a child has been listening, and whether he accurately understood what was said, by asking him questions. Eliminate any auditory or visual distractions in the environment so that the child can focus on what you are saying. Once you have the child's attention, provide him with the information you want him to hear and then follow up by asking him specific questions to see if he answers the questions logically. If he is able to answer the questions, you know he was listening and comprehending the information. If he is unable to answer the questions, he may be having difficulty comprehending what is being said. Sometimes, it is helpful to provide the child with a visual to go along with what you are saying. Also, you may need to repeat the information more than once, as well as provide one piece of information at a time.

2.225 Responds appropriately to "where" questions

Strand: 2-4B **Age:** 48-54m 4.0-4.6y

Definition
When asked a question starting with "where", the child responds correctly.

Assessment Materials
Several specific questions related to everyday activities that can be answered correctly by the child.

Assessment Procedures
Grouping: This skill can be formally assessed one-on-one with the child or informally during a small group activity.
1. Tell the child that you are going to ask her some "where" questions and you want her to answer the questions as best she can.
2. Begin by asking her a question related to an everyday occurrence, such as, "Where do you play?"
3. Note her response. Keep in mind that there are multiple places where a child can play, so there is no one correct response.
4. If she has difficulty with the response, repeat the question.
5. If necessary, prompt her by saying, "Where to you go to swing and go down the slide?" Record any prompt given.
6. Again, note her response.
7. Ask another question, such as, "Where do you take a bath?"
8. Record her responses.

Credit: + Child answers "where" questions correctly.

Adaptations
Responding appropriately to a "where" question requires the child to identify the place where something occurs or the situation in which an event occurs. Children will need to interpret exactly what is being asked and respond accordingly. Answering questions requires the child to use their recall to reproduce what they have heard or seen previously. We can help a child with her ability to answer questions, by modeling how we answer questions. Encourage the child to use her words to express herself. She may be more comfortable pointing or gesturing to answer a "where" question, but we should hold out for her to use words to express herself. When necessary, we can verbally prompt the child, but we should provide her with ample opportunities to express herself with words. Playing as if you do not understand her pointing or gesturing can be helpful in getting her to use more words.

2.226 Answers "why" questions by giving a reason

Strand: 2-4B **Age:** 54-60m 4.6-5.0y

Definition
When asked a "why" question, the child will respond by stating a reason.

Assessment Materials
Several specific "why" questions related to everyday activities that the child has personally experienced many times before.

Assessment Procedures
Grouping: This skill can be formally assessed one-on-one with the child or informally during a small group activity.

Level One:
1. Tell the child that you are going to ask him some questions and you want him to tell you why we do some things.
2. Begin by asking him a question related to an everyday occurrence, such as, "Why do we wear shoes?"
3. Note his response.
4. If he has difficulty with the response, repeat the question making sure you emphasize your questioning inflection while showing an inquisitive facial expression.
5. Ask him another question, such as, "Why do we eat breakfast?"
6. Note his response.
7. Continue asking "why" questions.
8. If he is unable to answer, give him an opportunity to be the one who asks the questions and demonstrate answering.

Credit: + Child answers "why" questions by giving a correct reason.

Adaptations
"Why" questions require the child to think and problem-solve. The answer to a "why" question can vary from one child to another. For example, "Why do you like that toy?" Some children may be responding to the color of the toy, while other children may be responding to the creativity the toy provokes from them. "Why" questions can be open-ended, allowing the child to present their unique perspective on the topic. As we go through the day, we should stop and reflect on why we are doing

something, while at the same time sharing our thoughts with the child. For example, while cleaning up the toys, we might say out loud to ourselves, "Why am I cleaning up these toys when we are just going to play with them again after lunch?" We can then begin answering our question so the child can be privy to our thought process. For example, "Well, if I left the toys on the floor I might trip and fall as I go to get my lunch box." Let the child hear you respond to questions so they can learn for themselves.

3.147 Catches a large ball thrown from 5 feet using hands/arms

Strand: 3-7F **Age:** 30-42m 2.6-3.6y

Definition
The child will catch a ball at least 10 inches in diameter when it is thrown from a distance of 5 feet. The child will catch the ball using both hands and arms. The ball should be tossed gently, using an underhand motion. When the ball is tossed, it should be aimed in a curve peaking from above the child's head and following a downward path into the child's outstretched hands and arms at chest height.

Assessment Materials
A large ball at least 10 inches in diameter, masking tape.

Assessment Procedures
Grouping: This skill can be assessed one-on-one or in a small group setting. The most effective assessment is made by observing the child in a natural setting.

Level One:
1. Place a strip of masking tape on the ground or floor 5 feet from the person throwing the ball.
2. Demonstrate how to catch a ball. Have another person, or the child, throw the ball to you. Your demonstration catch should include: (1) Arms outstretched, close together, and bent; (2) A forward body motion as the ball approaches and is caught; (3) Outstretched arms to catch the ball away from the body; (4) The ball either drawn into or trapped against the body.
3. After the demonstration, ask the child to stand on the tape and explain that you are going to throw the ball to her.
4. Toss the ball gently, using an underhand motion. When you toss the ball, aim it in a curve peaking from above the child's head and then pursuing a downward path into her outstretched arms at chest height. As you toss the ball, say, "Catch the ball."
5. Allow the child two attempts to catch the ball.
6. Observe the child to determine whether she catches the ball with her arms outstretched and elbows bent, with her body demonstrating a forward motion as the ball approaches, and that her arms catch the ball away from her body and bring the ball into her body after the catch.
7. If the child has difficulty catching the ball, either by holding her arms stationary in front of her body, not moving her arms to where the ball is arriving, or not relaxing her arms as the ball touches them, try using a large, lightweight ball and aiming the throw so that the ball lands in her upper arms.
8. Give the child ample time to practice catching the ball; the art of catching a ball with both hands is a visual-motor skill that requires repetition.
9. Repeat the assessment as the child progresses.

Level Two:
10. Observe the child as she is involved in catching a ball during playtime.

Credit: + Child catches a large ball thrown from five feet using her hands/arms in at least one out of two attempts.

Adaptations
Some children lack the ability to integrate visual stimulus with motor action. A child must convert one type of information (visual--the ball approaching) to another type of information, (motor--catch the ball). If a child is delayed in converting one type of information to another, she may have difficulty responding with a motor action to a visual stimuli. Children may react only to one process and find visual-motor integration difficult.

To assist children in developing their catching skills: (1) Use a large, soft, easy-to-catch, textured ball; (2) Gently throw the ball to the child; (3) Provide verbal cues as the ball is approaching the child, for example, "Get your arms ready," "Bend your arms," or "Arms together; (4) Provide physical assistance as a ball is gently thrown to her.

3.148 Balances on each foot for 5 seconds, without support

Strand: 3-7A **Age:** 36-44m 3.0-3.8y

Definition
The child will stand on one foot holding onto a support for at least one second. He will then stand on the other foot holding onto a support for at least one second. He will stand on one foot for at least five seconds, with his eyes open and his arms outstretched for balance. He will then stand on the other foot for at least five seconds, with his eyes open and his arms outstretched for balance. He will stand on one foot for at least five seconds with his eyes open and his arms in any position except hanging onto a support or outstretched. He will then stand on the other foot for at least five seconds with his eyes open and his arms in any position except hanging onto a support or outstretched.

Assessment Materials

Masking tape; an object to use for support, such as a chair; a stopwatch or watch with a second hand.

Assessment Procedures

Grouping: This skill should be assessed one-on-one with the child.

1. Place a 3-foot piece of tape on the floor.
2. Ask the child to watch closely as you stand on the tape and lift one foot off the floor. Stand for at least five seconds. Place both feet on the tape. Then ask him to watch as you stand on the tape and lift the other foot off the floor. Stand for at least five seconds. Explain what you are doing as you demonstrate, saying, for example, "I have both my feet on the tape. I am going to lift one of my feet off the tape. Now I have both feet on the tape. Next, I am going to lift my other foot off the tape."
3. Tell the child to stand on the tape. Say, "When I say Go, I want you to lift one of your feet off the floor and stand like that until I say Stop."
4. Say, "Go."
5. After five seconds say, "Stop."
6. Record his performance.
7. Tell him to stand on the tape. Say, "When I say Go, I want you to lift your other foot off the floor and stand like that until I say Stop."
8. Say, "Go."
9. After five seconds say, "Stop."
10. Record his performance.
11. If he has a problem with this stationary balance task, repeat the procedure, demonstrating and allowing him to use his outstretched arms for balance. It is important that he sees you demonstrate the use of arms for balance. If he continues to display difficulty, provide some physical support to assist him in the one-foot stationary balance.

Credit: + Child stands on one foot for at least five seconds with his eyes open and his arms in any position except hanging on to something for support. He then repeats this skill on the other foot.

Adaptations

Some children have delayed gross motor development as shown by: (1) Overflow movements--If the right hand performs a movement, the left hand will also show some form of movement; (2) Poor coordination--Body movements act as parts, not whole; (3) Lack of directionality--He becomes confused or cannot operate in a particular direction; (4) Problems with laterality--Concerns about body sides and directions aimed at the side of the child's body; (5) Problems related to balance--One side of the body (left or right or front or back) may not be able to come to a position of equilibrium. This condition could be constant or periodic; (6) Lack of visual/motor integration--When the eyes and the body are expected to act simultaneously, one element is unable or untrained to perform the expected response; (7) Weak auditory/motor integration--When the auditory channel and the body are expected to act simultaneously, one is unable or untrained to perform the expected response; (8) Inadequate rhythmic movement-- Unable to move to a beat, tempo, or rhythm; (9) A lack of body awareness and body image--He is not conscious of his body as a whole or how the individual parts work, to include an awareness of body movements.

To assist this child in developing his gross motor skills, practice: (1) Walking activities and games; (2) Floor tasks and games; (3) Playing on playground equipment; (4) Imitation of movement such as pantomime games; (5) Exercises that are low entry, localized, non-competitive, and have a long or wide base of support.

3.149 Balances on one leg with hands on hips

Strand: 3-7A **Age:** 36-44m 3.0-3.8y

Definition

The child will balance on one leg for at least five seconds with her eyes open and her hands on her hips. She will then balance on the other leg for at least five seconds with eyes open and hands on hips.

Assessment Materials

Masking tape, a stopwatch or watch with a second hand.

Assessment Procedures

Grouping: This skill should be assessed one-on-one with the child.

1. Place a 3-foot piece of tape on the floor.
2. Ask the child to watch as you stand on the tape and lift one foot off the floor with your hands on your hips. Stand for at least five seconds. Place both feet on the tape. Then ask her to watch as you stand on the tape and lift the other foot off the floor with your hands on your hips. Stand for at least five seconds. Explain what you are doing as you demonstrate, being sure to point out hands on hips. Say, for example, "I have both my feet

on the tape, and I have my hands on my hips. I am going to lift one of my feet off the tape, and I still have my hands on my hips. Now I have both feet on the tape. I am going to lift my other foot off the tape, keeping my hands on my hips."

3. Tell her to stand on the tape. Say, "When I say Go, I want you to put your hands on your hips, lift one of your feet off the floor and stand like that until I say Stop."
4. Say, "Go."
5. After five seconds say, "Stop."
6. Record her performance.
7. Tell her to stand on the tape. Say, "When I say Go, I want you to put your hands on your hips, lift your other foot off the floor and stand like that until I say Stop."
8. Say, "Go."
9. After five seconds, say, "Stop."
10. Record her performance.
11. If she has a problem with this stationary balance task, repeat the procedure, demonstrating and allowing her to use a leaning prop for pre-balancing. If she continues to display difficulty, provide her support for one hand before she places that hand on her hip and balances on one foot.

Credit: + Child balances on one leg with her hands on her hips for at least five seconds. She then balances on the other leg for five seconds with her hands on her hips.

Adaptations
See #3.148.

3.150 (Removed, see page xviii)

3.151 (Removed, see page xviii)

3.152 Bounces and catches a large ball
Strand: 3-7F   **Age:** 36-44m 3.0-3.8y

Definition
The child will bounce a 10-inch ball at least once and catch it on the upward movement. She will begin the bounce-and-catch activity by standing in one spot and bouncing the ball; as she progresses, she may walk forward and bounce the ball.

Assessment Materials
Two 8- to 10-inch rubber balls, masking tape, chalk.

Assessment Procedures
Grouping: This skill can be assessed one-on-one with the child. However, you can make the most effective assessment by observing the child in a natural setting to determine her physical skills.

Level One:
1. Place a 3-foot strip of tape on the floor.
2. Stand next to the child on the tape, and demonstrate bouncing the ball once and catching it.
3. Give the child a ball and invite her to join you in the activity.
4. Bounce and catch the ball several times, explaining aloud what you are doing.
5. Ask the child to bounce the ball once and catch it.
6. Give her two attempts.
7. Observe the child, watching for such actions as: (1) Holding the ball comfortably; (2) Pushing the ball down with an exact motion, using her fingertips; (3) Receiving the ball as it ascends and either pushes the ball down with her fingertips or catches the ball; (4) Placing her feet slightly apart and solidly, establishing a stationary base.
8. If the child presents a stance of uncertainty and the ball is being captured instead of caught, or if she is pushing the ball down with her whole hand instead of her fingertips, you may wish to use the following strategies: (1) Give her a textured ball; (2) Place a chalk mark on the floor to guide her as she releases the ball; (3) Mark a place on the floor where the child should put her feet; (4) Model bouncing a ball several times for the child; (5) Standing in front of her, place your hands on his, and use this position to gently pull the ball away from her body. Tell her you are going to pull her hands away from the ball so it will bounce. Release the ball and catch it by pressing her hands on the ball as it rises.
9. Repeat the assessment by asking the child to stand on the tape, bounce and catch the ball one time.
10. Observe her as she performs the skill.

Level Two:
11. Observe the child as she bounces a ball during playtime or a physical exercise period.

Credit: + Child bounces and catches a large ball while standing in one spot. Credit if the child is successful in three out of four trials.

Adaptations

To assist a child in developing and improving her bouncing and catching skills: (1) Use a large, soft, easy-to-catch, textured ball; (2) Place the child's body in a comfortable position-- feet apart and stationary with knees bent, hands cupped, and fingers outstretched; (3) Provide verbal cues as the she prepares to bounce the ball; (4) Provide physical assistance by guiding the child's hands in the bounce-and-catch act. Standing behind the child when you assist may also help.

3.153 Walks down stairs using alternate feet without holding railing

Strand: 3-7B **Age:** 42-54m 3.6-4.6y

Definition
When the child approaches stairs, she will walk down at least five regular-size steps alternating her feet, without holding railing.

Assessment Materials
/*\Safety Note: Guide and supervise the child closely.
Stairway with at least five stairs and a handrail that the child can reach.

Assessment Procedures
Grouping: This skill can be assessed one-on-one with the child. However, the most effective assessment is made by observing the child and her physical skills of walking down the stairs in a natural setting.

Level One:
1. Ask the child to walk down the stairs. Observe whether she uses alternating feet as she descends at least five steps and whether she holds onto the handrail.
2. If she does not use alternating feet as she comes down the stairs and does not hold onto the handrail, show her how to use alternate feet and use the handrail for balance.
3. After you demonstrate this, ask her to walk down the stairs again.
4. Observe whether she uses alternating feet as she descends at least five stairs and whether she holds onto the handrail.
5. If she does not use alternating feet after the demonstration, hold the child's other hand and point to the foot to use as she moves down the stairs. Then gradually eliminate the pointing or giving any physical support.
6. After the physical cueing, ask the child to walk down the stairs.
7. Observe whether she uses alternating feet as she descends and whether she holds onto the handrail.

Level Two:
8. Observe the child as she walks down stairs and notice whether she uses alternating feet for at least five steps without holding onto the rail.

Credit: + Child walks down at least five regular-size steps alternating her feet without holding on to the railing.

Adaptations
When you assist a child who exhibits slow motor development in the area of walking, running or climbing stairs, remember the following sequence: (1) Explain the motor skill you want and let the child respond without any assistance or cueing; (2) Demonstrate the motor skill wanted and then let her respond without any further assistance or cueing; (3) Explain as you demonstrate the motor skill what is happening and then permit her to respond without any further assistance or cueing; (4) Demonstrate and talk the child through the motor skill, and then ask her to respond independently without any further assistance or cueing; (5) Physically assist the child with the motor skill desired.

3.154 (Removed, see page xviii)

3.155 Stands on tiptoe for 10 seconds

Strand: 3-7A **Age:** 38-42m 3.2-3.6y

Definition
The child will rise on her tiptoes when requested and will balance on her toes for 10 seconds. She may place her hands and arms in any position. If her heels touch the floor and she rises again on her toes, the timing must start over.

Assessment Materials
Masking tape, a stopwatch or watch with a second hand.

Assessment Procedures
Grouping: This skill should be assessed one-on-one with the child.
1. Place a 4-foot piece of tape on the floor.
2. Ask the child to watch you as you stand on your tiptoes on the tape. Stand on your tiptoes for 10 seconds. Explain what you are

doing as you demonstrate, saying, for example, "I am standing on my tiptoes."
3. Tell the child, "When I say Go, I want you to stand on your tiptoes. You may put your arms anywhere you wish. Stay on your tiptoes until I say Stop."
4. Ask the child to stand on the tape. When she appears ready, say, "Go."
5. After 10 seconds say, "Stop."
6. Record her performance.
7. If her heels touched the floor before 10 seconds, remind the child to stay on her toes until you tell her to stop.
8. Repeat the steps above.
9. If she has a problem with stationary balance, repeat the procedure, demonstrating and allowing her to use a leaning prop for pre-balancing. If she continues to display difficulty, provide support for one hand and then for the other hand before she maintains a tiptoe balance.

Credit: + Child stands on her tiptoes for at least 10 seconds with her arms in any position, but not allowing her heels to touch the floor.

Adaptations
See #3.148.

3.156 (Removed, see page xviii)

3.157 Walks 10 feet on 4-inch wide line
Strand: 3-7H   **Age:** 36-44m   3.0-3.8y

Definition
After a demonstration, the child will walk in a straight line on a 4-inch wide line of tape. The child may hold her arms and head in any position. (Prerequisite skill to walking on a balance beam.)

Assessment Materials
A 10-foot strip of 4-inch-width masking tape attached to the floor.

Assessment Procedures
Grouping: This skill should be assessed one-on-one with the child.

Level One:
1. Demonstrate walking on the tape. Explain to the child what you are doing as you are walking on the line.
2. Ask her to stand at one end of the tape. Say, "I want you to walk on the tape all the way to the end without stepping off the tape."
3. Observe her as she walks the 10 feet staying on the strip of tape. Watch for the following:

(1) Does she use her hands to balance or are her hands on her hips? (2) Is she walking naturally on the tape by touching the heel of her back foot to the toe of her front foot? (3) Is she looking at her feet in an effort to stay on the tape? (4) Does she have to stop to regain her balance before moving forward?

4. If the child is having difficulty walking on the 4-inch tape, assist her by modeling the heel-to-toe step and saying, "Step, heel-to-toe, Step, heel-to-toe, Step, heel-to-toe." Make sure the child is imitating your steps, and encourage her to say aloud, "Step, heel-to-toe," with the movements. If she needs assistance in balancing, give her physical support. Then gradually phase out the prompts, reduce the physical support, discontinue the heel-to-toe modeling and give the verbal direction (step, heel-to-toe) only when needed.
5. Ask the child to stand at the end of the tape. Say, "Walk on the tape until you get to the end."
6. Observe her as she walks the 10 feet staying on the tape.

Level Two:
7. Observe the child as she walks heel-to-toe when she is at play, during an organized play period, or when you take a walk with her. You may see her use this foot movement when she follows a crack in the sidewalk, walks along the border of a rug, walks on the edge of a shadow, or stays inside a line on a flat surface.

Credit: + Child walks a distance of 10 feet on a 4-inch wide piece of tape maintaining her balance. Her arms and head can be held in any position.

Adaptations
Children who have problems with heel-to-toe steps and walking within a specific area often exhibit: (1) Poor coordination--putting one foot in front of the other smoothly or when a child stands on one foot she will easily become off-balance; (2) Concerns with laterality--requires a child to associate placing one foot in front of the other with forward motion; (3) Problems with balance--if a child narrows her base by placing her feet in a row instead of in a parallel stance, her body's balance point is diminished; (4) Confusion when visual/motor integration is not within the normal viewing range--Disorientation often results when a child is unable to view her foot movements, because a

sense of visual imagery is required and it may interfere with her motor integration.

When you assist a child who exhibits slow motor development in the area of step, heel-toe-heel, use the following sequence: (1) Explain to the child the motor skill you want her to do and let her respond without any assistance or cueing; (2) Demonstrate the motor skill you want and then permit her to respond without any further assistance or cueing; (3) Explain as you demonstrate the motor skill what is occurring and then let her respond without any further assistance or cueing; (4) Demonstrate and "talk" the child through the motor skill and then ask her to respond independently without any further assistance or cueing; (5) Physically assist the child accomplish the motor skill.

3.158 Walks 20-foot diameter circle staying on path

Strand: 3-7B **Age:** 38-44m 3.2-3.8y

Definition
The child will walk on a line at least 4 inches wide in a circle 20 feet in diameter. The child's feet must touch the line, and he must use a heel-toe-heel-toe step alternating feet without physical assistance.

Assessment Materials
Chalk.

Assessment Procedures
Grouping: This skill should be assessed one-on-one with the child.

Level One:
1. With chalk, draw two parallel circles 4 inches apart to make a circular path 20 feet in diameter. Identify a starting place by marking an X.
2. Explain to the child that he is to walk between the lines around the circle, using alternate feet in a heel-toe-heel-toe step. Tell him his walk will start at the X and will end on the same X.
3. Observe him as he follows the directions and walks around the circle. Look for: (1) Staying within the lines, (2) Using alternate feet in a heel-toe-heel-toe step, (3) Maintaining balance and moving in the correct direction, (4) How he uses his hands and arms and whether he has to look each time he moves, (5) The speed in which he moves around the circle, (6) The smoothness of his motor movements.
4. If the child has difficulty walking between the lines, assist him by modeling the heel-to-toe step and saying, "Step, heel-to-toe, Step, heel-to-toe, Step, heel-to-toe." Make sure he is imitating your steps and encourage him to say aloud, "Step, heel-to-toe" with the movements. If he needs assistance in balancing, provide him with physical support. Then gradually phase out the prompts, reduce the physical support, discontinue the heel-to-toe modeling, and provide the verbal direction (step, heel-to-toe) only when needed.
5. Ask him to stand at the X and say, "I want you to walk between the lines until you come back to the X."
6. Observe him as he walks around the circle.

Level Two:
7. Observe the child as he walks heel-to-toe at play, during an organized play period, or when you see him taking a walk. You may also see him use this foot movement when he follows a crack in the sidewalk, stays within the border of a rug, walks on the edge of a shadow, or keeps within a line that has been drawn on a flat surface.

Credit: + Child walks within the lines of a circle 20-feet in diameter staying on the path using a heel-toe-heel-toe step, without assistance.

Adaptations
See #3.157.

3.159 Kicks a stationary ball using a 2-step start

Strand: 3-7A **Age:** 38-48m 3.2-4.0y

Definition
Place a stationary ball (soccer or rubber playground) on a flat surface approximately 2 to 4 feet away from the child (a distance of two steps for the child). The child will kick the ball, using a two-step start, any distance or any direction.

Assessment Materials
A 10-inch ball (soccer, rubber playground), masking tape.

Assessment Procedures
Note: The placement of the ball should allow the child to use a two-step start from the tape.

Grouping: This skill can be assessed one-on-one with the child. However, observe the child as she is spontaneously playing ball during playtime. Note how she kicks a ball and whether she uses a 2-step start.

Level One:
1. Place a 2-foot piece of tape on the ground or floor and set the ball about 3 feet in front of the tape.
2. Ask the child to watch closely as you demonstrate standing on the line, taking two steps and kicking the ball.
3. It is important not to count out loud as you take the steps.
4. How you kick the ball is important, not where you kick it.
5. Ask the child to stand on the tape, and place the ball at the appropriate distance in front of her.
6. Say, "Kick the ball."
7. Allow her two tries.
8. Observe her as she kicks the ball, watching for: (1) The two-step approach; (2) Whether she firmly places one foot near the ball and swings her other leg behind her; (3) That her kicking leg moves forward, kicks the ball, and the kicking leg follows through.
9. If the child demonstrates a problem in the basic kick, by pushing the ball instead of kicking it, bending her knees before straightening her leg for the kick, if her arms are inactive and not in opposition to her leg movement, if she loses balance after the kicking motion, or if she appears to be clumsy and out of synchronization, direct assistance is recommended. The following are some suggestions: (1) Increase the size of the ball; (2) Walk her through the movements of approaching the ball, kicking the ball, and the follow through; (3) Tell the child the steps to take, for example, "Stand, Ready, Step, Step and Hold, Foot Back, Swing Forward, Kick the Ball"; (4) Place footprints on the floor that are color-coded, left foot/right foot, and ask the child to follow the path before she kicks the ball; (5) Physically assist her by pointing to which leg or foot she should move and which arm to swing in opposition.
10. After you have provided assistance and allowed her to practice, repeat the assessment above.

Level Two:
11. Observe the child as she kicks a ball during playtime or a physical exercise period.

Credit: + Child kicks a stationary ball using a 2-step start, any distance or direction.

Adaptations

Some children lack the ability to integrate a visual stimulus with a motor action. A child must convert one type of information (visual--the stationary ball) to another type of information (motor--kick the ball). If the child's sensory system (converting one type of information to another) is delayed, she may exhibit difficulty responding with a motor action based on a visual stimuli. Often such a child reacts only to one process and finds visual-motor integration difficult. To assist a child with her kicking skills, the following is recommended: (1) Use a large, soft, easy-to-kick, textured ball; (2) Remind her to get ready to kick the ball; (3) Walk her through the kicking motion; (4) Provide physical assistance to her as she tries to kick the stationary ball.

3.160 Rides tricycle with pedals to maneuver around obstacles, turn, stop and start

Strand: 3-7G   **Age:** 42-52m 3.6-4.4y

Definition
The child will get on a tricycle and pedal forward without touching his feet to the ground, and negotiate a turn without bumping into any obstacles.

Assessment Materials
A tricycle in the right size for the child. The size criteria is: (1) When the child sits on the tricycle seat, his feet will touch the pedals and will stay on the pedals for the full circle; (2) The child's arms reach the handlebars when he is sitting straight up; (3) He can see over the front of the tricycle).
Cardboard boxes, cones, large balls, and other items to be used as obstacles.

Assessment Procedures
/***Safety Note:** For safety, children should always wear a helmet when riding a tricycle and know where they are permitted to ride. Supervise carefully

Grouping: This skill should be assessed one-on-one with the child. However, observing the child during a playtime when he is spontaneously riding a tricycle can provide you with the information needed to determine the child's ability related to this skill.

Level One:
1. Select an area with sufficient space for the child to ride the tricycle forward, to turn it, and to ride it back.
2. Place the tricycle in a position that will allow the child to cycle forward and turn it.
3. Ask the child to ride the tricycle.

4. Observe him as he rides the tricycle; watch for the following: (1) The ability to start and stop the tricycle independently; (2) The pressure put on the pedals to generate forward motion; (3) Guiding and steering the tricycle; (4) Smooth continuous pedaling; (5) slowing down the pedal motion.
5. Set obstacles in the path of the tricycle and tell the child to avoid hitting any of them.
6. If he appears to be unsure on the tricycle, help him by asking him to sit on the cycle. Ask him to put his feet on the pedals and his hands on the handlebars. Push him slowly, allowing his feet to ride along, and keep one hand on the handlebars to steer the machine. Gradually remove your steering assistance, and allow the child to assume the guiding; however, be prepared to regain the steering if he becomes unsure. When you sense he is generating enough pressure to move the tricycle, stop pushing.
7. Be prepared to keep pushing if necessary. Allow the child time to practice, and give him encouragement and assistance.

Level Two:

8. You can make the most effective assessment by observing the child when he rides a tricycle during free time or during a structured play period.

Credit: + Child rides a tricycle and pedals forward without touching his feet to the ground while maneuvering around obstacles, making turns, and starting and stopping the tricycle without bumping into any obstacles.

Adaptations

Some children find riding a tricycle a difficult task to learn. A tricycle with pedals requires the child to put foot pressure on the pedal when it begins the downward clockwise motion. If he places the foot pressure before the downward motion, he will stop the machine and the coordinated motion. Often he will put his foot under the pedal to pull it up, creating a stall or a pull to the left or right. To learn to put an equal amount of pressure on the pedals requires practice and a natural sense of timing. Besides being difficult, learning to ride a tricycle is frustrating to many children because riding a tricycle is the first step to mobility, and mobility means independence--being grownup. In wanting to be successful, some children become anxious, frustrated and angry when learning to ride is not an immediate success. It is important to provide the child with the following assistance: (1) Make sure the tricycle is adjusted to the correct size for him; (2) Place the child on the tricycle, push the tricycle, press his thighs to indicate timing and movement, and guide the handlebars. Reduce the support when he indicates assurance, timing and movement; (3) Limit the amount of cycle time when the child is first learning; doing this may avoid feelings of inadequacy; (4) Have another child model riding a tricycle and point out the various movements as he does them; (5) Reinforce and praise him for every step of achievement and also for trying; (6) Arrange for practice times when the child will not be observed by others; (7) Place a large plastic hoop over the handlebars at the neck of the tricycle. Seat the child on the tricycle. Place his feet on the pedals. Stand in front of the tricycle and face him. Pull the tricycle with the hoop. Be careful to avoid the child tipping over as you pull him. Tell the child to pedal as you pull. Allow him to take over the movement of the tricycle by pedaling as he is able. Slacken or withdraw the use of the hoop as appropriate. Learning to ride a tricycle is an important milestone in the child's physical development so it should be presented when he has demonstrated he has the physical skills necessary to successfully perform the task.

3.161 Jumps forward 2-foot distance, feet together

Strand: 3-7C **Age:** 42-52m 3.6-4.4y

Definition

The child will jump forward at least 2 feet and will land with her feet together. She may take as many consecutive jumps as she wants. She will complete this jump without physical assistance and without falling.

Assessment Materials

Masking tape in two colors (red and green), small floor mat (mat can be made from a piece of foam covered with a washable material).

Assessment Procedures

Grouping: This skill can be assessed one-on-one with the child. However, you can make the most effective assessment by observing the child in a natural setting to consider her physical skill of jumping.

Level One:

1. Attach two 2-foot strips of tape to the floor 2 feet apart. Use green for the starting line tape and red for the ending tape. Set a mat in front

of the green tape, but do not let it go over 2 feet to the red tape.
2. Stand on the green tape facing the mat and tell the child that you will jump to the red tape.
3. Demonstrate the jump.
4. Ask the child to stand on the red tape facing the mat and to jump to the green tape.
5. Allow her at least two attempts to jump to the tape.
6. Observe the child, watching for: (1) Beginning the jump with feet parallel; (2) Swinging her arms back, then forward and upward; (3) Bending her knees and then straightening her legs before leaving the floor and landing with her feet ahead of her body; (4) A forward body movement and extension.
7. If the child has difficulty with the jumping motion, do the steps that follow before making another assessment: (1) Model a jump for the child and encourage her to imitate each step. For example, stand with feet parallel, making sure the child is in the same position. Bend your knees, asking her to bend her knees. Ask her to swing her arms back the way you are doing. (2) Provide verbal cues to assist the child in her arm movements--"Swinging your arms, move them forward, put them above your head"--and leg positions--"Bend your knees, get ready to jump, straighten your legs, land on both feet." (3) Physically guide the child's arms and legs as she jumps. (4) Allow her ample practice time.
8. Repeat the assessment above with the child jumping from the green to the red tape.

Level Two:
9. Observe the child as she jumps distances during play periods and other informal physical activities.

Credit: + Child jumps forward a 2-foot distance with her feet together, without assistance or falling.

Adaptations
Some children have a problem when they are involved in the horizontal jump. The problem could be related to body movement or to acquiring distance. A horizontal distance jump requires timed power, strength in the legs, balance, coordination, bravery, awareness of body movement, direction and flexibility. Locomotion, which requires an understanding of the relationship between one item and another in space may be difficult for these children. The locomotion act of jumping requires a child move through space to investigate the properties surrounding them and the relationships between these objects. To physically move a body in space means that the child is coordinating her motor skills and also that she is attempting to move in an unexplored area (space). When you work with children, it is important that you simplify each step in jumping and teach each step as an isolated skill before you coordinate the movement. Provide ample time for practice and the encourage the child to perfect her jumping abilities.

3.162 Step-hops for five feet
Strand: 3-7C **Age:** 40-50m 3.4-4.2y

Definition
After a demonstration the child will step-hop for 5 feet. He will step-hop-stand on one foot, maintaining balance without assistance for at least three seconds. Then he will step-hop-stand on the other foot for at least three seconds.

Assessment Materials
Masking tape in different colors.

Assessment Procedures
Grouping: This skill should be assessed one-on-one with the child.

Level One:
1. Place two 1-foot tape strips in different colors on the floor 10 feet apart, the starting strip green and the ending strip red.
2. Ask the child to watch as you demonstrate several step-hop steps. Explain what you are doing as you model the step-hop movement. Repeat this demonstration several times.
3. Ask the child to stand on the green line and step-hop to the red line, doing exactly what you just demonstrated.
4. Observe him, checking for a smooth forward step, a bent opposition knee, and a hop with the stationary foot. Also, his elbow should be bent, swinging slightly at his side.
5. If he is successful, ask him to repeat the step-hop step from the green line to the red line. This time, however, tell him that when you say "Stop," he is to stop all movement until he hears the word "Go." (Say "Stop" when the child is on one foot, and say "Go" immediately after he has demonstrated balancing ability.)
6. Observe him, watching in particular to see if he is able to balance on one foot.
7. If he has difficulty with the step-hop movement, the following are recommended:

(1) Provide support for him (standing between two tables and holding onto the edge or holding onto two people); (2) Ask the child to hop in place several times while he holds onto some support; (3) Have him step-hop while he holds onto a moving object (grocery cart, wheelchair, portable pushcart); (4) Place patterned footprints on the floor that represent the step-hop pattern; (5) Introduce him to a musical accompaniment that enhances a step-hop-step (*Bunny Hop, Glow Worm, Little Brown Jug, Salto Mortale, Ramenes tes Moutons*); (6) Physically place the child's legs, feet, and arms in the correct position and guide the limbs during the movements.

8. After the additional assistance, repeat the assessment as described above.

Level Two:

9. Observe the child as he performs a step-hop movement or various modifications of the step during playtime or other physical and musical activities.

Credit: + Child step-hops for 5 feet alternating feet. He step-hops landing on one foot, maintaining balance without assistance for at least three seconds, before alternating to the other foot, maintaining balance without assistance for at least three seconds.

Adaptations

A step-hop will be difficult for some children because it requires them to move while a foot is off the floor. These children may tend to lose their balance when they are expected to equalize body stance. The step-hop requires a child to move in rhythm and coordination, which requires locomotion skills and coordination. Such a child is often slow in responding to a set motor pattern; he knows what he should do, but he cannot relate the patterns to his motor system. He may begin the specific task of hopping by using the upper part of his body and trying to balance on only one foot. As a child increases his awareness of balance, he has a tendency to swing his arms; this is positive because it lends itself to learning to balance.

To assist a child to learn the step-hop action: (1) Use a rhythmic beat to accompany the step (a loud drumbeat), hop (a tap on the drum), and repeat; (2) Lead him through the steps, verbalizing what you expect; (3) Allow him to hang onto something as he begins to balance on one foot; (4) Draw footprints on the floor to establish the pattern; (5) Eliminate unnecessary steps and simplify the procedure.

© 2010 VORT Corporation. All rights reserved. Do Not copy.

3.163 Kicks a large ball when the ball has been rolled directly to him

Strand: 3-7A **Age:** 36-42m 3.0-3.6y

Definition

The child will kick a moving ball as it is rolled directly to him.

Assessment Materials

A 10-inch ball (soccer, rubber, plastic or utility), masking tape.

Assessment Procedures

Grouping: This skill should be assessed one-on-one with the child.

1. Place a 12-inch strip of tape on the floor, and set the ball about 5 feet in front of the tape.
2. Ask the child to watch closely as you demonstrate kicking the ball. Stand on the tape and ask another person to roll the ball to you. As the ball approaches, kick the ball by placing one foot stationary and moving the other foot back with a swing forward to meet the rolling ball. How the rolling ball is kicked is important, not where it goes.
3. Ask the child to stand on the tape, and roll the ball from the appropriate distance in front of the child as you say, "Kick the ball."
4. Allow him two attempts.
5. Observe him as he kicks the rolling ball, looking for: (1) The step-swing approach; (2) Placement of one foot firmly near the ball and swings the other leg behind him; (3) Kicking leg moving forward to kick the moving ball, and the kicking leg follows through.
6. If the child demonstrates a problem by missing the rolling ball, by pushing the ball rather than kicking it, by bending his knees before straightening his leg for the kick, by keeping his arms inactive and not in opposition to his leg movement, by losing balance after the kicking motion, or if he appears to be clumsy and out of synchronization, direct assistance is recommended. The following are some suggestions: (1) Roll the ball very slowly and closer to the child; (2) Walk him through the movements of approaching the kick, kicking the ball and the follow through; (3) Tell him the steps to take, making sure that the directions are timed with the approaching ball, for example, "Stand, Ready, Step, Step and Hold, Foot Back, Swing Forward, Kick Ball"; (4) Place footprints on the floor that are color-coded for the left and right feet, and ask the child to follow the pattern before he kicks

the ball; (5) Physically assist him by pointing to the leg and foot to move and help swing his arm in opposition.
7. After you have provided assistance and allowed time for practice, repeat the assessment above.

Credit: + Child kicks a large ball when the ball has been rolled directly to him.

Adaptations

The activity of kicking a rolling ball adds another dimension to the visual-motor integration process; the dimension of timing. The child has to use judgment to begin his initial movements, to prepare to make contact, and finally, to connect with the ball.

To assist a child in developing and improving his kicking skills: (1) Roll the ball very slowly and give a verbal cue when he needs to prepare to kick the ball; (2) Roll the ball very slowly and give a verbal cue--"Ready"--as well as a visual cue--wave a scarf--when he needs to prepare to kick the ball; (3) Use a textured or foam ball that will roll slowly and maintain a true path; (4) Provide physical assistance as a ball is gently thrown to him.

3.164 Runs and changes direction without stopping, avoiding obstacles

Strand: 3-7B **Age:** 44-55m 3.8-4.7y

Definition
When the child is running, she will change directions without coming to a complete stop, and she will dodge obstacles and corners.

Assessment Materials
Masking tape, green marker.

Assessment Procedures
Note: Do this activity in a large room or outdoors.
Grouping: This skill can be assessed one-on-one with the child. However, you can observe her during a play period to see if she runs and changes direction without stopping or pausing.

Level One:
1. Tape two strips of 2-foot-long masking tape to the floor at least 20 feet apart. With a green marking pen, color each strip green (down the center).
2. Stand on one of the taped strips and explain to the child that you plan to run to other taped strip, and then without stopping, you will run back. Demonstrate.
3. Tell the child that you want her to stand on the green tape, and when given the direction to start she will run to the other green tape and back without stopping.
4. Say, "Run to the other green tape and back."
5. Observe her as she performs the running task. Look for a smooth running style, arms swinging in opposition, long strides, running with a heel-toe step, and bending the front leg at nearly a right angle. Also, look for a continuous running pattern at the turn and return.
6. If the child has difficulty with the motion of running, the following are recommendations for correction: (1) Ask her to practice running at a slow speed, actually a fast walk, and assist her with moving her arms with each step; (2) Put a piece of tape on the floor and ask her to step on the tape with a running step (to encourage longer strides, place the tape strips farther apart; to encourage a more controlled stride, place the tape strips closer together). (3) Give her an object to hold in her hands to increase her awareness of opposition arm swing.
7. If the child has difficulty with the continuous run, tell her to walk around a planned area and when she hears you say the word "run," she is to run until she hears the word "walk." (At first, use short intervals of walk and run; then as the child becomes comfortable with the changing pattern, reduce the walking sequences and increase the running ones.)
8. Repeat steps 2 through 4.
9. Observe her as she performs the running task.

Level Two:
10. Watch the child as she is running during playtime or other physical activities to see if she changes direction without stopping and avoids obstacles in her path.

Credit: + Child runs with changes in her direction without stopping and avoiding obstacles.

Adaptations

The child with gross motor delays may need to be taught how to maintain balance without running flat-footed, how to lower and swing arms in opposition to the lead foot, how to manipulate the heel-toe step process, and how to maintain the rhythmic stride movement and posture necessary for a coordinated run. If a child has difficulty learning motor patterns, natural movements may seem difficult. She knows what she should do, but she cannot relate the patterns to her own motor system.

© 2010 VORT Corporation. All rights reserved. Do Not copy.

She will need concentration and extra practice. Simplify the activity for the child by playing simple, fun chase games that incorporate running.

3.165 Runs a 20-foot distance, breaking stride/rhythm

Strand: 3-7B **Age:** 44-55m 3.8-4.7y

Definition
The child will run 10 feet in one direction, stop, and then turn around and run 10 feet back.

Assessment Materials
Masking tape in two colors (green and red).

Assessment Procedures
Grouping: This skill can be assessed in a small group setting, no more than four children running together at a time. If you have a child who is easily distracted by other children, assess the skill one-on-one with them.

1. Tape two strips of 2-foot-long masking tape (one of each color) to the floor at least 10 feet apart.
2. Stand on the green tape and explain to the child that you plan to run to the red tape, stop and run back to the green tape.
3. Demonstrate the running and stopping movement.
4. Explain that you want him to stand on the green tape, run to the red tape, stop and run back to the green tape.
5. Say, "Run to the red tape, stop and run back."
6. Observe him as he performs the running task.
7. If the child has difficulty with the stop and return run, tell him to walk and when he hears you say "stop," he is to stop until he hears you say the word "walk." (At first, use short intervals of walk and stop; as he becomes comfortable with the changing pattern, reduce the walking and stopping sequences.)
8. Repeat the above assessment.
9. Observe him as he performs the running task.

Credit: + Child runs 10 feet in one direction, stops, and then turns around and runs back 10 feet to where he started.

Adaptations
See #3.164.

3.166 Performs a complete forward roll (somersault)

Strand: 3-7G **Age:** 45-60m 3.9-5.0y

Definition
The child will do a forward somersault without assistance and without falling to either side. She will place her hands, palms down, on the floor. Her hands will be placed on either side of her knees. She will lower her chin to her chest and put the back of her neck and her shoulders on the floor. She will give her body a forward push, roll over and land sitting up on the floor. She may also do a forward roll by beginning in a squat position, placing her arms in front of her body in a start position and her right foot in front of her left foot. She should then lean forward, tucking her head between her feet, roll and land sitting up.

Assessment Materials
Mat large enough for the child to roll forward on.

Assessment Procedures
/*\Safety Note: The forward roll should be done on a mat or a soft, carpeted surface.

Grouping: This skill can be assessed one-on-one with the child. However, you can make the most effective assessment by observing the child in a natural setting and determining her physical skills of performing a forward somersault spontaneously during a gross motor play period.

Level One:
1. Ask the child to sit on the mat. Tell her to watch while you or another child do a forward somersault. As the somersault is demonstrated, explain what is happening.
2. Give her an opportunity to practice the movement.
3. Ask the child to do a forward somersault on the mat.
4. If she needs beginning assistance, do the following: Place your hands on the child's back and give her a slight push to begin the somersault.
5. Observe her as she turns a somersault, watching for the following: (1) Hands palms down by her knees (not appropriate for a squat forward roll); (2) Chin against her chest; (3) Back of neck and shoulders placed on the mat; (4) A slight forward thrust movement and landing sitting up (if her front momentum is strong enough, the child may land standing up); (5) A total front action without falling to either side.

6. If the child has difficulty in performing the forward somersault, the following is recommended: (1) Ask her to sit on the mat and place her chin against her chest and simply act like a rocking chair; (2) Ask her to sit on the mat, place her chin against her chest, hold her legs close to her chest with her arms (she will look like a rolled-up ball), and rock back and forth; (3) When the child is in the ball position, gently push the rocking motion, and when she has the physical momentum and feels comfortable, gently push her forward for the complete roll. If she falls to either side, begin the ball position once again. Increase your physical support by placing one hand on one side of her curled body and your other hand on the other side, using enough pressure for her to feel protected. With your hands in place, begin the rocking motion and finally the forward roll; (4) Since one of the most important aspects of doing a somersault is courage, assure the child that you are there to support her and the mat will act as a pillow in case she falls; (5) Allow ample time for her to practice before you repeat the assessment.
7. When she has received additional assistance and is confident, repeat steps 1 through 4.
8. Observe for position, completion of the somersault, and doing the roll without assistance and without falling to either side.

Level Two:

9. Observe the child when she is doing somersaults during playtime or other physical activities.

Credit: + Child completes a forward somersault without assistance and without falling to either side.

Adaptations

Note: Remember that support, practice, and reinforcement are the keys to motor skill development, and particularly when dealing with an activity such as a somersault.

Most children have problems when they first try somersaults, and they often fail. Doing a somersault requires controlling body weight as it moves around an axis. A child may feel hesitant to put her body in the position necessary to do a forward roll, since this position requires a tucked-in head and the loss of visual contact with the floor. The position also requires the child to time a forward push. To help develop somersault skills and reduce apprehension: (1) Ask the child to sit on the floor and rock back and forth; (2) As she is sitting on the floor, ask her to put her hands on the floor in front of her and to put her head on the floor, and then to rock back and forth; (3) Encourage her to continue her rocking motion until she rolls forward or falls to one side; (4) Repeat suggestions 1 through 3, verbalizing what is happening with each step; (5) Repeat suggestions 1 through 3, providing physical assistance if needed. Some children achieve a forward somersault from a squat position instead of from a sitting/rolled position. To attempt a forward roll from a squat position, ask the child to put her arms in front of her body in a start position and her right foot in front of her left foot. She should then lean forward, tuck her head to her chest close to her feet, roll and land sitting up.

3.167 Maintains momentum on swing
Strand: 3-7G **Age:** 46-54m 3.10-4.6y

Definition
When placed on a regular swing in a sitting position, the child will swing by himself. He may be started by someone giving a backward or forward push. He should maintain momentum on the swing by doing a pumping motion, which consists of knees bent, feet under the seat, elbows bent and body forward in a pushed-back position while moving backwards in the swinging arc; and knees straight, feet pointed forward, arms straight and body in a pulled-out position while moving forward in the swinging arc. The child should keep the swing in motion for at least 30 seconds.

Assessment Materials
An outdoor swing.

Assessment Procedures
/*\ **Safety Note:** Attempt this task only if the child shows interest, has experience sitting on a swing, and is stable sitting on and making the swing move. Supervise carefully.

Grouping: This skill should be assessed one-on-one with the child.

Level One:
1. Tell the child that you are going to sit in the swing and swing. Ask him to watch as you do the motions that keep the swing in momentum. (See the definition for the specific motions for swinging.) Describe the motions as you perform the actions.
2. Invite the child to sit in the swing and swing. If needed, start him by giving a backward or forward push.

3. Allow him to take some practice time.
4. Observe him as he swings. Use your judgment and knowledge of the child to determine the number of seconds or minutes that is appropriate for him to maintain swinging. Thirty seconds is a base recommendation.
5. If he has difficulty swinging: (1) Place him in the swing, making sure he is holding on, stable and secure (supervise closely); (2) Begin pushing the swing gently and in a narrow arc. Let the child know he is swinging; (3) During the gentle swinging, physically manipulate the child's legs at the different arc positions; (4) Physically manipulate his arms at the different arc positions during the gentle swinging; (5) Finally, during the gentle swing, physically manipulate his body at the different arc positions; (6) Coordinate the use of his arms and legs, using physical assistance if needed; (7) Gradually remove the physical assistance and apply it only when needed; (8) Verbal support is often helpful.
6. Observe the child as he swings, watching for continuous momentum and body movements.

Level Two:

7. Observe the child as he swings at playtime, on a visit to the park or at other outdoor play activities.

Credit: + Child maintains his momentum on a swing. The recommended baseline is 30 seconds.

Adaptations

Some children have a difficult time maintaining their momentum on a swing. This is often related to coordination and timing of the required push/pull motor skills. The knees are the key body movement; generally, when they are timed to bend at the back of the arc and straighten out at the sweep and top of the arc, the rest of the body will harmonize. It is important that you provide physical prompting and verbal instruction to help the child with timing. Also make sure that the swing is the right height and that the child's feet touch the ground. A child will gain confidence from a small swinging arc to begin with and your verbal encouragement. He will need a starting push to be able to assume the swinging action.

3.168 Walks 10 feet carrying object blocking view of floor

Strand: 3-7B   **Age:** 48-54m   4.0-4.6y

Definition

The child will walk at least 10 feet carrying a large ball or empty box in her arms/against her chest, preventing her from seeing her feet.

Assessment Materials

A stop-and-go sign made by drawing a large red circle on one side of a stick (ruler or dowel) and a large green circle on the other side. Staple the circles together around the edges, leaving an opening to be taped to the stick. Also, a ball or a box large enough to block the view of the floor when the child holds it within her arms and chest. Masking tape.

Assessment Procedures

Grouping: This skill should be assessed one-on-one with the child. However, the most effective assessment made is by observing the child in a natural setting and determining her physical skills of spontaneously walking while carrying a large object.

Level One:

1. Determine an approximate 10-foot floor length, and mark a beginning point and an ending point with masking tape.
2. Show the child the stop sign, and explain that when she sees the red side she is to stop and when she sees green she is to go. Using the sign, let the child practice the stop and go movement.
3. Ask her to stand on the beginning mark, hand her a ball or an empty box that restricts her downward view, and tell her to watch the sign. Turn the sign to green; do not turn to the red side until the child reaches the ending marker.
4. Observe whether the child walked comfortably and with confidence when she was unable to see the floor. Look for such items as: (1) Looking around or over the obstacle in an effort to see the floor; (2) Moving the obstacle forward to observe the floor; (3) Hesitant stepping or foot-groping before taking a step; (4) Using a side-shuffle step with a slight forward motion instead of a front forward step; (5) Standing on tiptoes and moving forward in tiny staccato-like steps.
5. If the child has a problem with stepping forward when she is unable to see the floor, the following is recommended: (1) Give her

the ball or the box, place your hands on her hands, and use a gentle forward "nudge" to cue her to take a step. Release your hands gradually, when she displays a sense of confidence; (2) Allow her to take a step forward without the object, then a step forward with the object; continue this alternating procedure; (3) Give her an object that allows some view of the floor and then increase the size of the object little by little to build confidence and visual imagery.

6. Show the child the stop sign, and explain that when she sees red she is to stop and when she sees green she is to go.
7. Using the sign, allow her to practice the stop-and-go movement.
8. Ask her to stand on the beginning mark; then hand her a ball or a box that restricts her downward view, and tell her to watch the sign.
9. Turn the sign to green; do not turn to the red side until she has reached the ending marker.
10. Observe whether the child walked comfortably and with confidence when she was unable to see the floor.

Level Two:
11. Observe the child carrying an object that obstructs her view of the floor during a play or physical activity.

Credit: + Child walks a distance of at least 10 feet carrying a large object (large ball or empty box) that blocks her view of the floor.

Adaptations

Some children have difficulty learning non-visual motor patterns. Their non-visual motor development has lagged so they have difficulty with natural movement. In evaluating these children, observe whether they can imitate verbal motor patterns and how they learn to manipulate in a non-visual setting. Reacting to a non-visual pattern may be difficult for them. This is often related to a child's inability to learn motor patterns; the child knows what she should do, but she cannot relate to the motor patterns because she doesn't see to her own motor activities. To assist this child: (1) Ask her to perform a known movement, such as tapping a foot or swinging an arm. Ask her to close her eyes and perform the same movements; (2) Ask the child to close her eyes and physically guide her arm in a swinging motion; verbalize the action as it is being performed; (3) Present a concise visual pattern, including a detailed verbal description of the motor skill you want her to do; (4) Request the child to observe the area of motion visually and to describe her actions ("I will put one foot in front of the other one and take a step," or "I will pick up my back foot and move it ahead of my other foot.") Then ask her to close her eyes and describe the movement without directly viewing it.

3.169 Gallops forward
Strand: 3-7B **Age:** 48-60m 4.0-5.0y

Definition
The child will gallop for at least 10 feet. A gallop is a movement in which the same foot is always the lead foot, and the trailing foot comes up to meet but never passes the lead foot. The lead foot strides forward, and the body weight is on the lead foot. When the trailing foot meets the heel of the lead foot, the weight is shifted to the trailing foot, enabling the lead foot to repeat the action.

Assessment Materials
Masking tape strips in red and green.

Assessment Procedures
Grouping: This skill can be introduced and assessed during a small group activity, no more than three or four children.

1. Place two 3-foot masking tape lines on the floor 10 feet apart, one in red and one green.
2. Ask the child to watch as you demonstrate and explain a gallop while you stand on the green piece of tape and gallop to the red piece of tape.
3. Tell the child to stand on the green piece of tape and to gallop to the red piece of tape when he hears the word "Go."
4. Say, "Go."
5. Observe him as he gallops; watch for a long, smooth gallop, leading with one foot and transferring the weight smoothly.
6. If the child has a problem with the gallop action, demonstrate the walk step, stop and back foot up stop motion. Tell the child to imitate you by taking a step and stopping, then bringing his back foot up to meet his front foot. Repeat the walk step, stop and back foot up stop motion several times. Demonstrate the walk step, stop and back foot up stop motion, and add a hopping action; encourage the child to model the step with the hop added. Continue the walking step with a forward step, with the same foot leading each step only increase the hopping speed until it becomes a gallop. Ask the child to watch closely as you demonstrate and explain the

gallop while you stand on the green piece of tape and gallop to the red piece of tape.
7. Allow the child time to practice.
8. Repeat items 3 through 5.

Credit: + Child gallops forward at least 10 feet in a smooth and coordinated fashion.

Adaptations

A child having difficulty with galloping needs to be taught how to maintain balance without spreading his feet too far apart, how to swing his arms as part of a timed gallop, how to manipulate the lead foot forward and rear foot moving to meet the lead foot and how to present the rhythmic movement and posture necessary for a smooth gallop.

3.170 Stands up without losing balance after lying on back

Strand: 3-7A **Age:** 48-66m 4.0-5.6y

Definition

The child will rise from a horizontal (prone) position to a vertical position, by sitting up, placing his feet flat on the floor, pushing his body up with his hands while maintaining his balance as he comes to an upright stance.

Assessment Materials

A carpeted area or a mat is desirable but not necessary.

Assessment Procedures

Grouping: This skill should be assessed one-on-one with the child.
1. Ask the child to lie down on his back in the designated area. Explain that when you say "Go," you want him to sit up and then stand up. Encourage him not to lose his balance.
2. Say, "Go."
3. If he exhibits difficulty doing this assessment, assist him by working with the sub-skills that lead to standing up without losing his balance. For example, (1) Ask the child to lie down on his back; (2) Say "Sit up" and provide physical assistance if it is needed; (3) Say, "Put your feet on the floor," and provide physical assistance if it is needed; (4) Say, "Use your hands to help yourself get up," and provide physical assistance if it is needed; (5) Say "Stand up," and provide stabilizing assistance if it is needed.
4. Ask the child to lie down on his back in the designated area.
5. Explain that when you say "Go," you want him to stand up just as you showed him. Encourage him by verbalizing each step.
6. Say, "Go."
7. Repeat until the motor patterns are integrated and he can accomplish the task in five to 10 seconds.

Credit: + Child stands up after lying on his back without losing his balance.

Adaptations

Motor patterns provide the groundwork for motor development. Balance is one of the first generalizations of motor patterns. Balance is an internal process; it is the awareness that the body can maintain a position by adjusting weight in space or laterality in space. Because laterality is an internal process between left and right, some children have not decided directionality. Directionality becomes the basis for a child's concept of his position in space. Until motor and perceptual information become synonymous, the child will react to two separate elements: motor and perceptual, and he will display confusion, clumsiness and the inability to balance. To assist a child who is experiencing motor pattern inconsistency and laterality confusion, the following are recommended: (1) Imitate movement--The child imitates the actions of another; (2) Use obstacles courses--He moves around and/or over objects in varied directions; (3) Moving to music or chanting--"Forward - one, two (loud) three, four (softly)"; (4) Acting out directions--"Tall as the sky," "Stand like a stork," "Sway like the wind"; (5) Games--"Follow the Leader," "Chain Tag"; (6) Physical equipment use--balance beams, balance boards, stilts.

3.171 Walks 4 feet on 4-inch wide beam without stepping off

Strand: 3-7H **Age:** 52-64m 4.4-5.4y

Definition

After your demonstration, the child will walk at least 4 feet on a 4-inch wide balance beam without stepping off or holding onto another person or object. The balance beam should be placed securely on the floor.

Assessment Materials

A 4-inch wide floor balance beam. The beam should be at least 4 feet long. (If a 4-inch wide balance beam is not available, a 2-inch by 4-inch piece of lumber will also work). The beam should be secure/stable (does not rock or twist), and should not be more than 6 inches off the floor. Mat to place under the balance beam. Dowel or short broomstick.

Assessment Procedures

Grouping: This skill should be assessed one-on-one with the child.

Level One:

1. Place the balance beam on a mat. Demonstrate walking on the balance beam, and explain what you are doing during the demonstration.
2. Ask the child to stand at the end of the beam. Say, "I want you to walk on the balance beam as far as you can go. Stay on the beam, and do not touch anything or anyone."
3. Observe the child as she walks the beam, staying on the board. Check for the following: (1) Does she use her hands to balance, or are her hands on her hips? (2) Is she looking at her feet in an effort not to step off? (3) Does she stop to regain her balance before moving forward?
4. If the child has difficulty walking on the balance beam, help her by modeling a walking step and saying, "Step, hold, step, hold, step. Step, hold, step." Make sure she imitates your steps and encourage her to say, "Step, hold, step," with the movements.
5. Give her a dowel, such as a short broomstick, minus the broom. Show her how to hold the stick (across the front of her body, with an equal length on the left and right side of the body).
6. If she needs additional assistance in balancing, give her physical support or allow her to take one step on the beam and another step on the floor. Gradually phase out the prompts, reduce the physical support, and provide verbal direction (step, hold, step, hold, step) only when needed.
7. Ask the child to stand at the end of the board.
8. Say, "I want you to walk on the beam as far as you can go without touching the floor."
9. Observe her as she walks the balance board, staying on the beam.

Level Two:

10. Observe the child as she walks heel-to-toe at play, during an organized play period, or when taking a walk. She may use this foot movement when she is walking on a balance beam.

Credit: + Child walks a distance of 4 feet on a 4-inch wide balance beam without stepping off and without physical assistance.

Adaptations
See #3.157.

3.172 Throws a ball ten feet overhand

Strand: 3-7F **Age:** 53-65m 4.5-5.5y

Definition
When the child is provided with a ball that is easily held and manipulated with one hand, he will throw the ball overhand, not aiming at any specific target.

Assessment Materials
A ball that is easily handled by the child. Masking tape.

Assessment Procedures

Grouping: This skill should be assessed one-on-one with the child.

Level One:

1. Place a strip of tape about 14 inches long on the floor.
2. Invite the child to stand with you behind the tape. Ask him to watch as you throw the ball across the tape.
3. Demonstrate throwing the ball by: (1) Placing the ball in the throwing arm and pulling the arm back; (2) Stepping forward with the foot that is opposite of the throwing arm; (3) Throwing the ball by moving the arm above the shoulder and following through.
4. Repeat the demonstration and explain what you are doing. Say, for example, "The ball is in my hand, and my arm is behind me."
5. Give the child the ball and ask him to stand on the line and throw it.
6. Give him two additional attempts to throw the ball.
7. Observe him, watching for such actions as: (1) Placing the ball in the throwing arm and pulling the arm back; (2) Stepping forward with the foot that is opposite of the throwing arm; (3) Throwing the ball by moving the arm above the shoulder and following through. (It may often seem natural to the child to step forward on the same side as his throwing arm.)
8. If he has difficulty with the overhand throw, consider the following: (1) Give him a beanbag to throw; (2) Place a footprint on the floor and ask the child to throw the ball or beanbag by stepping forward on the footprint while he throws; (3) Physically assist him by moving his throwing arm, body and extended foot.

9. After you have assisted him and allowed time for him to practice, repeat the assessment above.

Level Two:
10. Observe the child as he catches a ball during playtime.

Credit: + Child throws a ball overhand a distance of ten feet, not aiming at any specific target.

Adaptations

Some children experience difficulty coordinating their bodies when they attempt an overhand throw. The overhand throw requires strength in the arm and hand. It also requires left and right orientation, balance, torso flexibility, and awareness of directionality. Throwing a ball adds another dimension, timing. The child has to use timing and judgment to begin his initial movements, prepare to throw, and finally, release the ball. This judgment is based on speed, direction, and location.

To assist a child in developing and improving his throwing skills: (1) Give him verbal cues for throwing; (2) Use different objects; beanbags, for example, are excellent because of the weight; (3) Guide the child through the throwing process.

3.173 Hangs from bar using overhand grip

Strand: 3-7G **Age:** 54-66m 4.6-5.6y

Definition

The child will hang from an overhead bar using an overhand grip for at least five seconds. An overhand grip is one in which the child's knuckles are on top of the bar and her fingers are wrapped down around the bar. Her feet should be off the ground, and her mount could be assisted.

Assessment Materials

/***Safety Note:** Mats should be placed under the climbing apparatus. Supervise carefully.
An overhead bar: usually located at a playground, park or gym. Mat to place under the bar.

Assessment Procedures

Grouping: This skill can be assessed one-on-one with the child. However, the most effective assessment is made by observing the child in a natural setting to determine her physical skills for hanging from a bar using an overhand grip.

Level One:
1. Demonstrate an overhand grip on a hanging bar for the child. Make sure that your arms are straight, feet are off the ground, and hands are directly above your shoulders. Make sure the child sees that your knuckles are on top of the bar and fingers are wrapped down around the bar. (If the equipment is not high enough for an adult to demonstration, ask another child to model.)
2. Point out the position of your hands, feet and arms to the child.
3. Ask her to hang from the bar with her hands over the top of it. She may need assistance to mount the bar.
4. Give her ample time to practice.
5. Observe her as she maintains a hanging position, looking for the following: (1) Her knuckles should be on top of the bar, with her fingers and thumb wrapped around the bar; (2) Hands perpendicular to her shoulders; (3) Arms straight; (4) Body straight. It is important for the child to maintain the hanging position for at least five seconds; however, timing should be based on the developmental level of the child, her physical skills, and other entry behaviors. The point of the activity is for her to hang for a period of time, not just to jump up, grasp the bar and let loose.
6. If she has difficulty hanging onto the bar with an overhand grip, the following is recommended: (1) Provide assistance for her to reach the bar; (2) Focus should be placed on the grip on the bar: the thumb should go around the bar, and the back of the hands should face the child. If this grip makes her apprehensive, have her try a mixed grip with the back of one hand facing the child and the fingers of the other hand facing the child. This grip often acts as a stabilizing base; (3) Encourage the child to just hang and not to attempt swinging or climbing; (4) Assure her that you will assist her to get off the bar; (5) If she has a fear of heights, she may need verbal and physical reassurance. Be sure she sees your hands close to her body as she performs the overhand grip hang.
7. Allow her ample time to practice the hang, and observe her response as outlined in the assessment above.

Level Two:
8. Observe the child's bar grip, mount, hanging posture and dismount as she plays on climbing frames and horizontal ladders.

Credit: + Child hangs from a bar using an overhand grip with her feet off the floor. The child can receive assistance mounting the bar.

Adaptations

Some children have a problem with the non-locomotive skill of hanging because it requires strength in the arms and continuous grasping skills. If a child's muscles have not developed sufficiently, they will not contract when strength is needed. As children mature, more load will be placed on their muscles (to carry more, lift heavier objects, etc.) and their strength increases. If a child whose strength is not fully developed tries to hang from an overhead bar, both the maintenance of body weight and the amount of hanging time will be affected. To assist a child and provide her with a successful experience, encourage any amount of hang time. Place a secure platform under the bar and ask her to stand on it. Have her place her hands on the bar and lift her feet off the platform when she feels ready. To help her with a tight continuous grasp, place your hands over hers with a gentle firmness. Provide assurance to her if she seems unsure of her position when her body is free of ground support; both verbal and physical assistance are vital. Do not force a physical situation on any child who is not developmentally ready or who exhibits apprehension.

3.174 Hops forward ten feet on either foot without assistance

Strand: 3-7C **Age:** 54-68m 4.6-5.8y

Definition
The child will stand on her right or left leg and maintain her balance without support or help. She will hop forward ten feet on either leg, the other foot suspended without assistance. The child does not have to hop in a straight line.

Assessment Materials
Masking tape in two colors.

Assessment Procedures
Grouping: This skill can be introduced and assessed in a small group setting, no more than four children. However, one of the most effective assessments can be made by observing the child spontaneously hopping in a natural setting.

Level One:
1. Place two 1-foot tape strips on the floor 7 feet apart. Use green tape for the start and red tape to indicate the finish line.
2. Ask the child to watch as you demonstrate standing on one foot and hopping forward. Describe what you are doing as you model the hopping movement. It is not important that you hop to the red tape.
3. Repeat the modeling several times.
4. Ask the child to stand on the green line, to stand on one foot and then to hop forward. Explain to her that it is not important for her to reach the red line.
5. Observe her, watching for: (1) A stable balance when on one foot; (2) That the knee of the leg that is suspended be at a right angle; (3) A smooth forward hop; (4) A bent elbow, swinging slightly at her side.
6. If she is successful, ask her to repeat the hopping, moving from the green line to the red line.
7. Observe her, checking in particular to be sure she is able to balance while she hops.
8. If she has difficulty with the hopping movement, the following steps are recommended: (1) Provide the child with support, such as having her stand between two tables and hold onto the edge, or having her hold onto two people. Tell her to stand on one foot first. Ask her to hop in place several times while holding onto the support; (3) Have her hop while she holds onto a moving object such as a grocery cart or stroller; (4) Ask her to hold onto a broomstick that you hold in front of her and to hop forward. Then replace the broomstick by lightly holding her hand; (5) Physically place the child's legs, feet, and arms in the correct position and guide her limbs during the hopping movements.
9. After this additional assistance, repeat the assessment as described above.

Level Two:
10. Observe the child as she performs a hopping movement during playtime or other regular physical activities.

Credit: + Child hops forward ten feet on either foot maintaining her balance without support of help.

Adaptations
Hopping can be difficult for some children because it requires them to take a foot off the floor. These children have a tendency to lose their balance when they are expected to equalize body stance. Hopping also requires that a child

move in coordination, which is demanding of locomotion skills. She may begin the specific task of hopping by using the upper part of her body and trying to balance on one foot. As she increases her awareness of balance, she may have a tendency to swing her arms many times; this excessive arm movement is positive because it aids in learning to balance.

To assist the child in learning to hop, using either foot: (1) Demonstrate hopping movements, addressing one skill at a time. Referring back to the verbal prompt of feet-together "hop-jump" is often helpful before you start working on the step-hop step skill. Referring back to a step-hop step is often helpful in regaining balance and support before you move to the hopping skill. Say, for example, "Step-hop, hop, step-hop, hop. Step-hop, hop, hop, step-hop, hop, hop"; (2) Lead the child through the steps, verbalizing what you want her to do; (3) Allow her to hang on to something as she begins to balance on one foot and hop.

3.175 Walks up and down stairs carrying an object, without support

Strand: 3-7B **Age:** 60-65m 5.0-5.5y

Definition
The child will walk down the stairs carrying an object in one hand and using his other hand for support. He will walk up the stairs carrying an object in one hand and using the other hand for support. He will then walk up and down the stairs carrying an object by using one or two hands and no support.

Assessment Materials
/*\ **Safety Note:** Guide and supervise the child closely.
A stairway with at least five stairs and a handrail that is reachable by the child. A few objects to carry -- two categories: (1) Objects that can be carried easily with one hand, for example, a small, soft, stuffed toy; an lightweight item with a handle; a small article of clothing, such as a cap; (2) Objects that require both hands to carry, for example, a large ball, a toy with handles on both sides, a shoe box, a bowl with dry cereal or popcorn in it.

Assessment Procedures
Grouping: This skill should be assessed one-on-one with the child. However, the most effective assessment is made by observing the child walking up and down stairs while carrying an object in a natural setting to determine his physical skills.

Level One:
1. Ask the child to walk up and down the stairs carrying an object that requires only one hand.
2. Observe whether he uses one hand for support while carrying the object.
3. Ask him to walk up and down the stairs carrying an object that requires him to hold with both hands.
4. Observe whether he is able to manipulate the stairs carrying an object that requires both hands.
5. If he is unable to hold an object with both hands while walking up and down the stairs, point out some other strategies he may use to be successful. Caution him to avoid over-watching the object he is carrying with two hands. Remind him to be confident and maintain his momentum as he is moving. Also, comment that when he hesitates he might lose his balance. Encourage him to use slow, steady steps, while keeping his eyes focused on where is going, not on the item he is holding.
6. After the child has had an opportunity to practice, repeat the assessment procedures described in steps 1 through 4.

Level Two:
7. Observe the child as he walks up and down stairs carrying an object with one hand, and note whether he is successful and at ease. Observe him as he walks up and down stairs carrying an object that requires both hands.

Credit: + Child walks up and down stairs carrying an object, without support.

Adaptations
Note: Because some children are not as proficient as others in motor development and integrated movements, carefully evaluate the importance of each task you assign, and also plan some activities that are not as demanding.

Walking up and down stairs carrying an object requires unique integrated motor skills. These include: (1) Grasping; (2) Balancing; (3) Directionality; (4) Visual/motor interaction. Some children have difficulty with this activity: their coordination of vision, motion and grasping may be fragmented and not sequenced.

To assist a child: (1) Explain the motor skill you want him to do and let him respond without any assistance or cueing; (2) Demonstrate the motor skill you want while explaining what is happening and then let him respond without any further assistance or cueing; (3) Demonstrate and talk the child through the motor skill and then ask him to respond independently without any further assistance or cueing; (4) Assist the child physically with the motor skill you want.

3.176 Runs through obstacle course avoiding objects
Strand: 3-7B **Age:** 60-68m 5.0-5.8y

Definition
The child will run a 20-foot course between two lines, 5 feet apart. Obstacles are placed at varied intervals (large box, cone, chair, foam blocks, etc.) The child will stay between the two lines and avoid making any contact with any obstacle.

Assessment Materials
Five to eight obstacles, such as cones, large boxes, inner tubes, masking tape.

Assessment Procedures
Note: Conduct this assessment in a large room or outdoors.
Grouping: This skill can be assessed in a small group setting, no more than four children. Remind the children that they will need to listen and take turns during the activity.
1. Place two strips of tape 20 feet long and at least 5 feet apart on the floor or outdoor surface. Scatter the obstacles between the two pieces of tape, beginning with a clear running pattern.
2. Discuss the obstacle course with the child, showing her where to start and stop. Explain that she must avoid the obstacles.
3. Demonstrate the task by walking through the course and not making any contact with the obstacles. Then demonstrate running through the obstacle course without touching any of the obstacles.
4. Ask the child to stand on the starting line, and when you say "Go," to run to the end of the course and to avoid touching the obstacles.
5. Say, "Go."
6. Observe the child as she runs through the course, watching for: (1) General running movements; (2) Mobility skills that enable her to avoid the obstacles; (3) Effort exhibited; (4) Consistency in motion.
7. If she has difficulty with the motion of running, ask her to practice running through the course at a slower speed, actually a fast walk.
8. If the child has a problem with touching the obstacles, take one or two away and rearrange them so they are easier to avoid. Ask the child to walk through the course without touching the obstacles. Then gradually add obstacles and arrange them in easy-to-difficult patterns.
9. Replace the obstacles between the tape as described in step 1 and repeat steps 3 through 6.

Credit: + Child runs a 20-foot obstacle course between two lines, 5 feet apart, avoiding the obstacles (five to eight obstacles) placed in the path avoiding contact with any of the obstacles.

Adaptations
Some children may need to be taught running skills that involve avoidance and how to present the rhythmic stride movement and posture necessary for a coordinated run. These children may know what they should do, but they cannot relate the motor patterns they see to their own motor system. Natural movement is difficult. A child may feel embarrassed that her motor development lags or is inferior to what she sees others do.

When you work with a child who has a problem relating motor patterns to her motor system, remember that it will take longer for her, as she will need both physical demonstrations and verbal explanations from you, and making progress will demand absolute concentration and additional practice on her part. It may also be necessary for you to simplify the activity.

3.177 Skips forward
Strand: 3-7C **Age:** 60-72m 5.0-6.0y

Definition
After the child has seen a demonstration, she will skip forward, using alternate feet, leading with the left or right foot at least four times. Example: Skip left-skip right, Skip left-skip right, Skip left-skip right, Skip left-skip right. Distance is not important.

Assessment Materials
Masking tape in two different colors.

Assessment Procedures
Note: It is not important if she does not reach the red line; rather, the form of skipping she demonstrates is what is important in this activity.
Grouping: This skill can be assessed one-on-one with the child. However, observe the child

during outside play or during a motor activity to see if she spontaneously skips forward.

Level One:
1. Place two 1-foot strips of tape on the floor 25 feet apart. Use green for the starting tape and red for the ending tape.
2. Standing on the green tape, explain to the child that you will skip to the red tape. Skip to the tape, describing the skipping movement as you do it.
3. Ask the child to stand on the green tape and to skip forward when you say go.
4. Give her several attempts to skip forward.
5. Observe the child as she skips forward, watching for: (1) Body erect and flowing; (2) Moves her feet in a step-hop pattern; (3) Moving her weight from one side of her body to the other; (4) Swinging arms in opposition to foot movement; (5) Direction determined by body weight transfer.
6. If the child has difficulty skipping forward, review the step-hop rhythmic patterns and encourage her to say "step-hop" as she attempts the skipping motions. Skipping with her may also help; explain how to move her arms and when to change feet as you skip with her. Skipping is a difficult motor skill for many children. Provide ample practice time and try to limit distractions for the child, as skipping requires not only coordination but also concentration.
7. After she has received additional direction and practice time, administer the assessment as outlined above.

Level Two:
8. Observe the child as she skips during playtime or other physical activities.

Credit: + Child skips forward using alternate feet, leading with the left or right foot, at least four times.

Adaptations
Skipping is probably the most difficult of the locomotion skills.

Some children find skipping complicated because the child must use both sides of her body in a cross pattern. The left arm must swing forward as the right leg swings up, and the right arm must swing forward as the left leg swings up. This left to right orientation is often a delayed developmental action and involves laterality and directionality. Because skipping involves a variety of actions, a child may be unable to learn to skip by imitation from simple observation. She may use a galloping pattern until she is ready or has internalized the skipping process. If the child is having difficulty ask her to focus on the leg movements as you demonstrate for her; ask her next to focus on the arm movements as you demonstrate again. Then ask her to join you in using her legs in a skipping action. Next ask her to join you in using her arms in a skipping action. Finally, ask her to use her arms and legs and to skip with you. (Encourage her to transfer her weight evenly by over-exaggerating a rocking motion.) It is important to provide sufficient space and practice time to the child so she can feel the natural rhythmic pattern.

3.178 Maintains balance on a movable platform (balance disc, etc.)
Strand: 3-7G **Age:** 60-78m 5.0-6.6y

Definition
The child will stand (both feet) on a movable platform holding on to a support (both hands) for at least 30 seconds. The child will stand (both feet) on a movable platform holding on to a support (one hand) for at least 30 seconds. The child will stand (both feet) on a movable platform holding on to a support when needed for at least 30 seconds. The child will balance on a movable platform for at least 30 seconds, arms in any position. The child will balance on a movable platform for at least 1 minute. (In extending the time, the child may need to repeat the support steps as outlined above.)

Assessment Materials
Secure a movable platform, such as a balance disc. If a movable platform is not available, one is easily made by securing a truck-size inner tube and tightly attaching a canvas jumping surface to the tube. The truck-size inner tube should inflate to about 4' in diameter and 12 inches high. For some children it is helpful to place an outline of foot positions on the canvas.

Assessment Procedures
/***Safety Note:** Supervise carefully so the child does not fall off the platform.
Grouping: This skill should be assessed one-on-one with the child.
1. Explain to the child that he is to stand on the platform without losing his balance. Allow the child the opportunity to place one foot on the platform and the other foot on the floor, to gain a "feel" for the movement. Tell the child that he will have time to become comfortable on the stand before you say "Go".

2. Allow the child time to experiment and become familiar with the movable item.
3. When the child appears comfortable, say, "Go".
4. Time the child and record the seconds or minutes.
5. Encourage the child to repeat the moving balance activity to increase his time.
6. If the child has a problem with this balancing task, demonstrate some techniques for balancing, such as outstretched arms, using a balancing stick, moving the body in the opposite direction of a falling sensation and keeping feet apart. If the child continues to demonstrate a concern with this balancing task, provide him with physical support or an object to hold on to.

Credit: + Child maintains balance on a balance platform or disc, with their arms in any position for at least one minute without support.

Adaptations

Some children have difficulty in becoming aware of the force of gravity and how to maintain their relationship with it. Children learn to deal with gravitational forces in almost all situations, such as: a baby lifts its head against a pull, a toddler stands to an erect position; or a young child keeps his balance in walking. But when a variable such as movement is added, the child has to deal with an inconsistent gravitational pull, such as jumping from a soft surface, swinging while standing up, skating, riding a bicycle, etc.

3.179 Completes a backward roll (somersault)

Strand: 3-7G   **Age:** 70-72m 5.10-6.0y

Definition

The child will do a backward somersault without assistance and without falling to either side. He will begin by lying on his back, clasping his fingers behind his neck with elbows out to his sides, with his knees next to his chest and his chin on his chest. He will appear to be in a tucked-in position. He will rock back and forth until he achieves momentum and then will push out with his arms on the floor and roll completely over backwards, taking the weight of his roll on his forearms.

Assessment Materials

A padded floor mat large enough for the child to roll backward.

Assessment Procedures

/*\Safety Note: The backward roll must be done on a padded floor mat.

Grouping: This skill can be assessed one-on-one with the child. However, you can make the most effective assessment by observing him in a natural setting and determining his physical skills when he spontaneously does a backward roll.

<u>Level One:</u>
1. Ask the child to kneel on the mat. Explain to the child that he is to watch while you (or another child) do a backward somersault. During the somersault, explain what is happening.
2. Ask the child to do a backward somersault on the mat. Make sure the child places his hands on the back of his neck with his elbows out to the side as he rolls over (to protect his neck).
3. If he needs any beginning assistance, the following is recommended: Place your hands on his buttock and give him a slight push to begin the somersault.
4. Give him an opportunity to practice the movement.
5. Observe him as he performs the somersault, watching for the following: (1) His fingers should be clasped behind his head with elbows at his side; (2) His knees and chin should be on his chest; (3) A rocking movement with his legs doing the push and his head tucked into the chest; (4) The backward thrust should move him to a squatting position. (If the back momentum is strong enough, he may land with a slight hop or standing up); (5) A total backward action without falling to either side.
6. If the child has difficulty doing the backward somersault, the following is recommended: (1) Ask him to lie on the mat, clasp his fingers behind his head and place his elbows at his side; (2) Ask him to place his knees and chin on to his chest. He should be in a tucked-in position; (3) When he is in the tucked-in position, gently begin the rocking motion, and when he has the physical momentum and feels comfortable, gently push him backward for the complete roll. If he falls to either side, begin the tucked-in position once again. Increase your physical support by placing one of your hands on one side of the child's curled body and your other hand on the other side, using enough pressure for him to feel protected. With your hands in place, begin the rocking motion and finally the backward roll;

(4) One of the most important aspects of doing a somersault is courage; assure the child that you are there for support and that the mat will act as a pillow in case he tumbles; (5) Give him ample time to practice before you repeat the assessment.
7. When he has received additional assistance and feels confident, repeat the assessment following steps 2 through 5.

Level Two:
8. Observe the child if he does a somersault during playtime or other physical activities.

Credit: + Child completes a backward roll without assistance and without falling to either side.

Adaptations

Note: Remember that support, practice, and reinforcement are the keys to motor skill involvement, but particularly for a locomotion activity such as a somersault.

A child may be hesitant to put his body in the position necessary to do a backward roll; this position requires a tucked-in head and the loss of visual contact. It also requires the child to time a backward push. Unless a child has been able to do a somersault with success, he may feel apprehensive about having his head down, no vision, the backward push and suspension in the roll. Suggested activities to develop somersault skills include: (1) Ask the child to sit on the floor and rock back and forth; (2) Ask him to lie on the floor with his knees bent and his feet placed on the floor, and to put his hands behind his head, fingers clasped in, and head and shoulders on the floor, and then to rock back and forth; (3) Encourage him to continue his rocking motion until he rolls backward or falls to one side; (4) Repeat items 1 through 3, verbalizing what is happening with each step; (5) Repeat items 1 through 3, providing physical assistance as needed.

3.180 Lifts torso from ground to complete one sit-up

Strand: 3-7G **Age:** 70-78m 5.10-6.6y

Definition

The child will lie on her back with feet flat and knees bent at a 45-degree angle, arms crossed on her chest, hands on opposite shoulders. Her feet may be held, if needed. The sit-up is done to a two-count pattern. A two-count pattern is up on one and down on two.

Assessment Materials

A padded floor mat.

Assessment Procedures

Grouping: This skill should be assessed one-on-one with the child.
1. Ask the child to lie on the mat with her knees bent at 45-degree angle to the floor. Her feet should be flat on the floor, and her arms should be crossed on her chest.
2. Sit beside the child, and physically move her through the sit-up actions. Example: Place her feet on the floor, making sure her knees are bent, and place her hands across her chest. Ask her to sit up on the count of one; if necessary, assist her by putting your arm around her shoulders and pushing her up.
3. If she sits up, but her feet rise off the floor, repeat the above procedure, only hold her feet.
4. Allow her to practice the procedure several times.
5. After she has had sufficient time to copy the demonstration and to practice, say, "When I say go, do as many sit-ups as you can." If needed, remind her of the correct procedures as she performs the fitness exercise.
6. Observe her, watching for: (1) Sitting up in less than a right angle; (2) Attempting to sit up by moving from one side to another to gain balance; (3) Achieving upward movement by stretching her arms forward instead of keeping them crossed; (4) Being unable to do more than one sit-up. The number of sit-ups the child does depends on variables such as the child's size, her abdominal strength, agility, and aptitude for physical exercise. How many sit-ups she is expected to do is up to the discretion of the assessor.
7. For future planning, keep a record of how many sit-ups she completes in a given period of time.
8. If the child has difficulty accomplishing a sit-up, perhaps abdominal strength is lacking, or the stomach and abdominal muscles are unable to move against resistance. She may need to strengthen her abdominal muscles to react in resistance. Because this strengthening process cannot be accomplished in one or two exercise periods, the assessment should be given after an organized exercise program is implemented.
9. If the child has difficulty accomplishing a sit-up because she is unable to coordinate the movements, practice doing some curl-ups, before you ask her to do a sit-up. The following are suggestions to improve

coordination: (1) Provide the child with directions as she attempts a sit-up, for example, "Lie down, put your arms across your chest, bend your knees, and on the count of three, sit up... One, two, three, sit up!"; (2) Physically assist her through the steps to do a sit-up. You may need another person to hold the child's feet as you give other physical assistance.
10. After proceeding with the specific steps in coordination, repeat the assessment following steps 5 and 7.

Credit: + Child lifts torso from the ground to complete at least one sit-up.

Adaptations

   Note: If maturation is a concern, postpone the sit-ups until her muscles are ready developmentally.

   Some children find sit-ups difficult; often the reason is the lack of abdominal strength. To assist children to do sit-ups, first establish a series of exercises that will develop abdominal strength. The following are suggested exercises: (1) Ask her to lie on her back with her legs straight. Ask her to bring one of her knees up to her chest, straighten it out, and bring it back to the floor. Repeat with the other leg. Continue alternating the knees in the knee-to-chest and back to the floor, making sure the back is flat; (2) Tell her to lie on her back and bring her legs up to her chest. Ask her to use her legs and pretend to ride a bicycle; her back must be straight; (3) Tell the child to lie on her back and use her hands to support her buttocks. Then ask her to raise both her legs a few inches off the floor, hold them suspended, and then drop them back to the floor. This exercise requires fairly strong abdominal muscles, so adjust steps and timing according to the child's abilities -- do not have the child over-exert herself.

   After she has successfully completed the abdominal exercise program, encourage her to try a sit-up.

3.181 Lifts body off the floor to complete one push-up

Strand: 3-7G   **Age:** 70-78m   5.10-6.6y

Definition

After a demonstration, the child will lie flat on the floor, face down, with his palms flat on the floor. He will push his body straight up once, his toes on the floor and his arms extended (girls should start push-ups with their knees staying on the floor). He will then lower his body until his chest is 3 inches from the ground, straighten his elbows, and then raise his body once again. The child's head should be up and his eyes should be forward as he raises himself.

Assessment Materials

A padded floor mat large enough for the child to lie on face down.

Assessment Procedures

Note: The form of the body while doing the exercise, not the number of push-ups, is the goal of this skill.

Grouping: This skill should be assessed one-on-one with the child.

1. Demonstrate a push-up and ask the child to watch your movements carefully. Repeat the demonstration, explaining the different body positions and motions.
2. Ask the child to lie on his stomach on the mat, and place his hands, palms down, even with his shoulders. Describe the various body placements and movements as he performs the motions step-by-step.
3. Allow him ample time to practice the push-ups.
4. Ask him to do as many push-ups as he can when you say go. Say, "Go."
5. As the child does the push-ups, observe for: (1) Body straight on the upward movement, hips not raised higher than the rest of the body; (2) Pushing up with the arms and shoulders, not using his knees to assist in the rise (girls will should start on knees); (3) Lowering the body with the chest barely touching the floor, avoiding a fall-down drop; (4) Straightening the elbows for the rise and bending the elbows for the drop; (5) Head and eyes forward.
6. If the child has difficulty accomplishing a push-up, perhaps arm-shoulder strength is lacking. An effort to strengthen the arm-shoulder muscles may be needed. Because this strengthening process cannot be accomplished with one or two exercise periods, the assessment should be given after an organized exercise program is implemented.
7. However, if he has difficulty accomplishing a push-up because he is unable to coordinate the movements, practice using other parts of his body for support before working on a body straight lift with the weight on the arms and shoulders. The following suggestions are intended to improve coordination: (1) Provide the child with directions as he attempts a

push-up, for example, "Lie down, put your hands flat on the floor by your shoulders, straighten your arms to lift up, keep your body straight, lower your body, touch the floor with your chest, and lift your body again as you keep it straight."; (2) Physically assist the child through the steps to do a push-up. Place your arms under his waist and on the count of three, ask him to lift as you provide coordination by gently lifting him up; on the count of two, lower his body. Be sure to use your physical assistance to keep his body straight.

8. After he has covered the specific steps in coordination, repeat the assessment identified above.
9. Observe him as he performs the push-ups, and if appropriate, record how many he accomplishes.

Credit: + Child lifts body off the floor to complete one push-up without assistance. The child uses correct form to complete the push-up.

Adaptations

/***Safety Note:** If maturation is a concern, delay push-ups until the child's muscular structure indicates developmental readiness.

Note: This exercise requires sufficiently strong arm and shoulder muscles, so adjust steps and timing according to the child's abilities -- do not have the child over-exert himself.

Some children find push-ups difficult due to lack of arm and shoulder strength. To assist a child in doing push-ups, instruct him to do a modified version. The modified version includes: (1) Pushing up from the knees instead of the toes; (2) Asking the child to stand facing a wall, his feet against the wall, and hands, palms flat, against the wall. Tell him to push away gradually from the wall. This perpendicular push-up is effective in enhancing body coordination.

The following are suggested exercises to develop arm and shoulder strength: (1) Tell the child to put his hands on a table, palms down. At the count of three, tell him to push against the table, elbows bent; (2) Attach a rope to a hook on a wall, and place the child on a scooter (a square board with four wheels); ask him to pull himself forward, hand over hand.

3.182 through 3.228—Note: Assessment procedures are not available for Skills 3.182 through 3.228. See the Curriculum Guide for suggested instructional activities.

4.94 Puts together simple inset puzzles
Strand: 4-6B **Age:** 30-40m 2.6-3.4y

Definition
When the child is presented with a four to six-piece inset puzzle, he will put it together.

Assessment Materials
Four to six-piece inset puzzles. These puzzles are available from commercial sources.

Assessment Procedures
Grouping: This skill may be assessed one-on-one with the child. The best way to assess this skill is to observe the child during an activity time when puzzles are readily available and the child has chosen to work on puzzles.

Level One:
1. Place one of the inset puzzles on the table in view of the child. Ask him to help you remove the puzzle pieces.
2. Mix up the pieces and ask him to put the puzzle pieces back together in the puzzle board.
3. Observe him as he puts the puzzle together.
4. If he has difficulty with this task, his eye-hand coordination may not be functioning in such a manner that he can place the puzzle pieces together. He may also have a problem with organization skills. To assist him, (1) Allow ample time for him to process the visual stimulus; (2) Hand him one puzzle piece at a time; (3) Use auditory cues to support the visual placement.
5. Reassess him after he has been involved in some of the assisted learning skills.
6. Place the pieces of another puzzle on the table and ask the child to put this puzzle together. See if he can complete the puzzle without auditory or visual cues.
7. Observe him as he completes the puzzle.

Level Two:
8. Observe the child as he works on a puzzle during an independent activity time or at a learning center.

Credit: + Child completes a simple inset puzzle with four to six-pieces, independently.

Adaptations
Some children have difficulty in putting a puzzle together due to visual-motor coordination or motor planning. To assist these children: (1) Include verbal description and direction as he is putting the puzzle together; (2) Make sure he has plenty of time to visually explore the puzzles before he is asked to put them together; (3) Have him begin putting puzzles together using knob pieces in a single piece inset puzzle board; (4) Make sure the puzzle object is something he is familiar with in order to have a visual image; (5) Make sure the child has ample time to apply a trial-and-error approach to piece placement.

4.95 (Removed, see page xviii)

4.96 Cuts across paper following a straight line 6 inches long and then a curved line 6 inches long
Strand: 4-7D **Age:** 36-48m 3.0-4.0y

Definition
When she is shown how to cut across a paper following a line, the child will cut along a straight line 6 inches long and not more than ¼ inch wide. She will then cut along a curved line 6 inches long and not more than ¼ inch wide. She will cut with appropriately sized scissors, and she will hold the paper correctly, not deviating from the line more than ¼ inch. She will do this cutting task without assistance.

Assessment Materials
/*\Safety Note: Provide scissors appropriate for the child. Remind the child of safety regarding scissors.

Scissors in the correct size for the child. Four sheets of paper marked with a straight black line 6 inches long and not more than ¼ inch wide drawn across the page, four sheets of paper marked with a curved black line 6 inches long and not more than ¼ inch wide drawn across the page.

Assessment Procedures
Grouping: This skill may be assessed one-on-one with the child. During an art activity, you can observe the child as she cuts on a straight and a curved line to assess her skills.

Level One:
1. Ask the child to watch as you use one of the sheets of paper to demonstrate cutting the straight line.
2. Give the scissors and a sheet of paper to the child for her to practice cutting a straight line.
3. After she has practiced, give her another paper with a straight line and ask her to cut the line.
4. Observe as she cuts the paper, looking for: (1) Her finger positions on the scissors (thumb in

top hole, index finger in bottom hole); (2) The manner in which she holds the paper; (3) Whether the position of the scissors is perpendicular to the paper; (4) Whether she cuts on the line without deviating more than a ¼ inch; (5) Whether she used a forward pushing movement.

5. If she does not respond or demonstrates a concern, the following is recommended: (1) Model how to hold the paper and the scissors; (2) Guide her fingers into the holes of the scissors, with your hand over hers to show her how to open the blades, how to put the paper between the blades, and how to apply the necessary pressure to cut; (3) Secure adaptive scissors, either double-blunt with two sets of handles or self-opening scissors with cushioned handles that spring back after each cut.

6. After she has experienced the above assistance and has demonstrated improvement, repeat the assessment above.

7. Ask her to watch as you use one of the sheets of paper and model cutting the curved line.

8. Give her the scissors and the paper, and give her an opportunity to practice cutting a curved line.

9. After she has practiced, give her the other sheet of paper with the curved line and ask her to cut the line.

10. Observe for the points outlined in step 4 above. In addition, look at whether she uses any stop and starting motions when she cuts on the curved line.

11. If she does not respond or demonstrates a concern, follow the recommendations from step 5. Include modeling how to hold and turn the paper and the scissors while cutting a curved line.

12. After you have given her assistance, if she has demonstrated improvement, repeat the assessment above.

Level Two:

13. Observe the child as she uses scissors to cut during an independent working time or during an instructional activity.

Credit: + Child cuts across a straight line and a curved line, each 6 inches long and not more than ¼ inch wide, without assistance. She holds the paper correctly and does not deviate from the drawn line more than ¼ inch.

Adaptations

Some children have difficulty cutting on a line. She may be able to perform the act of holding the scissors and manipulating them to cut; however, when she is asked to incorporate a visual-motor pattern of cutting on a line to the task, she may become frustrated and have difficulty with the task. Because she is expected to cut on a line, she must view the line, move the scissors in a specific manner, and continue her thinking/motor coordination until the task is completed. She may need additional assistance to achieve this visual-motor activity. When she first begins to cut on a line: (1) Make sure the line is short, yet long enough for a cutting stroke; (2) Draw the line 1 inch wide and in black; (3) Draw a large red dot to indicate where she is to stop cutting; (4) Instead of using plain paper, use corrugated paper and draw the line between the rows of the corrugation; (5) Use adaptive scissors with loop handles that automatically open after each cut and are adaptable to either left- or right-handed cutters; (6) Have her snip plastic straws into small pieces (approximately 1 inch pieces) to get comfortable with the cutting motion; (7) Set up an art activity that calls for fringe by cutting short lines along the edge of a piece of paper.

4.97 Builds tower of more than nine blocks without assistance

Strand: 4-6B **Age:** 36-48m 3.0-4.0y

Definition

The child will build a tower of at least ten blocks without assistance. The child will make continued attempts on his own even if the tower topples over.

Assessment Materials

Fifteen 1-inch blocks of different colors.

Assessment Procedures

Grouping: This skill may be assessed one-on-one with the child. You can make the most effective assessment by observing him in a natural setting to determine his coordination in building a tower of at least 10 blocks.

Level One:

1. Place the blocks on a table and invite the child to sit across from you. Explain to him that you are going to stack some blocks. Demonstrate how to stack ten blocks.

2. After you demonstrate, remove the blocks from the stack and give him the blocks to build a tower.

3. Observe him as he builds the tower, watching for movements such as: (1) Picking up the blocks with a pincer hold; (2) Aligning the blocks one on top of the other; (3) Using a

motion that assures a balanced position of the blocks.
4. If he demonstrates a problem stacking the blocks, the following steps are recommended: (1) Limit the number of blocks to stack; (2) Mark the sides of the block that indicate where the child is to place his thumb and forefinger; (3) Give him larger blocks to stack; (4) Give him blocks that are soft or have a distinct texture, such as foam blocks, to provide a griping surface; (5) Tell him to build stacks next to each other for support.
5. After he has had an opportunity to practice the prerequisite skills to building a block tower, reassess him following the steps outlined above.

Level Two:
6. Observe the child as he is involved in block play or is in an instructional setting.

Credit: + Child builds a tower of at least 10 blocks, without assistance.

Adaptations

A child may need help in: (1) Using her pincer (thumb and forefinger) grasp; (2) Judging distance and direction; (3) Transferring visual information to a motor response (she sees what she wants to move, but she cannot imagine the motor plan); (4) Understanding the motor movement necessary to align one block on top of another and then being able to transfer the information to the motor system. To assist her: (1) Give her larger sized blocks to make a tower; (2) Have her use textured blocks to build a tower; (3) Add verbal directions to the construction process, for example: "Place another block on top," or "Be careful, the blocks might fall. Make sure to stack them as straight as you can." (4) Physically assist her in building a block tower. Remember, the joy of building with blocks should be the main goal, and if you expect too much structure and use too many instructional procedures, the pleasure and spontaneity may diminish.

4.98 Strings small beads, cubes, cylinders (based on a simple shape pattern)

Strand: 4-7C   **Age:** 36-48m   3.0-4.0y

Definition

When presented with a pattern/model, the child will string at least five small beads. The beads should be ½-inch to 1-inch wooden spheres, cubes, and cylinders in different colors; the string should have a hard-tip or use a shoelace.

Assessment Materials

Two hard-tipped strings or shoelaces and ten small beads, two identical sets of five beads. Make sure there is a knot at the end of each string.

Assessment Procedures

Grouping: This skill can be assessed one-on-one with the child. You can also observe the child during an activity time when she is stringing beads to see if she can reproduce a presented model.

Level One:
1. Place the beads in a shallow container and lay the string on the table. Explain to the child that you are going to place a bead on the string.
2. Very deliberately pick up a bead, look at the hole, place the hard-tipped end of the string through the bead hole, and let the bead fall to the knot at the end of the string.
3. String four more beads in a specific pattern, e.g., cube followed by a sphere, then another cube, etc.
4. Tell the child to string the beads in the same pattern that you made. Allow ample time for her to respond. Observe her as she strings the beads.
5. If she is unable to string the beads or has a difficult time, the following is recommended: (1) Demonstrate stringing a bead; (2) Tell the child to hold a bead as you place the hard-tipped end through the hole in the bead and then ask her to push the bead to the end. If she is having a difficult time grasping objects, reverse the situation: you hold the bead and ask the child to string it; (3) Gently hold one bead in the child's hand and hold the string in the her other hand, then push the string through the bead, pull the string through, and let the bead drop to the knot.
6. Repeat the assessment as outlined above.

Level Two:
7. Observe the child when she plays with beads and pattern cards during an independent time or at an interest center.

Credit: + Child strings at least five small beads following a presented pattern/model, using a string with a hard tip or a shoelace.

Adaptations

When doing a task such as stringing beads, when the motor skill is the principal skill, the child will have to use more than her visual modality to do the activity. She needs grasping skills to pick up the bead, dexterity to turn the bead to thread, motor directionality to place the string through the hole, and pressure to guide the bead to the bottom of the string. Provide the child with an opportunity to first practice grasping an object in the palm of her hand and then trying a pincer grasp. Placing a small ball (with an X written on it) in her hand and having her move the ball so the X goes from the top to the bottom of the ball, will improve not only her strength but also her dexterity. Tracing also aids the improvement of directionality and space awareness. Her visual and motor skills will begin to react together; when visual perception is required, the motor skill will respond.

4.99 Folds paper three times
Strand: 4-6D **Age:** 36-48m 3.0-4.0y

Definition
When the child is given a demonstration of how to fold a piece of 8 ½ by 11 inch paper in half, in half again, and in half again, he will fold his paper in the very same way. The edges of the paper will be nearly even.

Assessment Materials
Several 8 ½ by 11-inch sheets of easy-to-fold paper, other size sheets of easy-to-fold paper, a black marker, dot or sticker, small ruler.

Assessment Procedures
Note: Make sure the child understands the concept of half.
Grouping: This skill should be assessed one-on-one with the child.

1. Invite the child to join you at the table. Tell him to watch as you fold a sheet of paper in half, emphasizing the alignment and the creasing of the fold. Fold the paper in half again, emphasizing the alignment and the creasing of the fold, and then fold it in half again, emphasizing the alignment and the creasing of each fold.
2. Give him a sheet of paper and ask him to fold it in half, in half again, and in half again.
3. Give him several opportunities to practice folding the paper.
4. Observe him as he folds the paper, watching for: (1) How he began the task; (2) How even the edges of the paper were and whether he attempted to even up the edges before he creased the paper; (3) The number of attempts made; (4) The manner in which he coordinated his hand movements. For example, did he use his predominant hand to guide the paper from the centerfold before creasing it, in an attempt to make the edges even? Did he use his non-dominant hand to align the edges? To see that the edges were even, did he use his predominant hand to crease the fold, holding the paper steady with his non-predominant hand; (5) The number of folds he made.
5. After he has successfully folded the 8 ½ by 11-inch sheet of paper, repeat the steps outlined above using a another sheet of 8 ½ by 11-inch paper in half the other direction.
6. If he demonstrates a problem in folding the paper in half, in half again and in half again, the following sub-tasks may help: (1) Model how to fold the paper, emphasizing the alignment, then crease the folds and verbally count them. For example, say, "One" as you make the first fold, "Two" as you make the next fold, and "Three" as you fold the last fold; (2) Provide physical assistance by placing your hands below his wrists and guiding them through the folding process; (3) Mark a wide creased line down the middle of the paper where the folds should be, and assist him to fold on those lines. Mark the middle of the other folds; (4) Place a dot or sticker at the bottom left-hand corner of the paper and at the bottom right-hand corner of the paper. Ask the child to put his first finger on top of the dot or sticker and his thumb under the dot or sticker. Tell him to fold the paper to the top and cover the dot or sticker; (5) Give him another sheet of paper with a reduced marked line down the middle and ask him to fold the paper. Provide no assistance; (6) Place the edge of a ruler at the halfway point on the paper, hold the ruler in place, and ask him to fold the paper, using the ruler edge as a guide; (7) Place the edge of a ruler at the halfway point on the paper, and ask him to use one hand to hold the ruler in place and to use the other hand to match the top or side edges. (If needed, provide assistance to help the child put enough pressure on the ruler so it will stay in place.)
7. Give him ample time to practice prior to reassessment.
8. Tell him to watch as you fold a sheet of paper in half, in half again, and in half again and crease the fold.
9. Give him a sheet of paper and ask him to fold just like you did.
10. Give him several opportunities to fold the paper.

Credit: + Child folds paper three times after the task has been demonstrated. Look for the alignment and creasing of the paper to be close to that of the model.

Adaptations

Some children have a difficult time when they are asked to add a motor component to a visual task. As long as the activity involves visual control of movement--moving the paper, the child is fine, but when the motor skill--creasing the fold--becomes a major part of the task, he may have a problem. When he performs an action that feels unnatural to him, he tends to focus on the motor requirement and not the visual aspect. For example, to crease the paper, he will use both hands, which may cause the paper to open. For a child who uses visual control over movement and finds motor control difficult, being asked to fold a sheet of paper without any directives may create frustration. Instead, follow these recommendations: (1) Provide visual guidelines, such as drawing a line on the paper to indicate where to fold; (2) Use a kinesthetic approach, such as gluing a strip of sandpaper indicating where to fold the paper; (3) Use a stable guide such as a ruler to assist in the paper fold.

4.100   Matches or chooses through tactile cues like objects: hot/cold; wet/dry

Strand: 4-8   **Age:** 40-43m 3.4-3.7y

Definition

The child will use his tactile sense to match objects that are hot and cold or wet and dry only by touching or handling them. He will not use his sense of sight to differentiate the objects or forms.

Assessment Materials

"Feel Box": locate a cardboard box with a lid, cut a hole in the side of the box large enough for the child to put his hand inside, and decorate it on the outside. Four identical plastic jars that will hold at least 4 ounces of water with identical lids, four identically textured and sized washcloths. Just before the assessment, pour warm water in two of the jars and cold water in the other, making certain the lids are tightly fastened. Rinse two of the washcloths in water and squeeze. A blindfold.

Assessment Procedures

Grouping: This skill should be assessed one-on-one with the child.

1. Before you introduce the Feel Box, place a small surprise inside, for example, a new pencil, a box of animal cookies, a small toy, or a ticket for special time. Place the Feel Box on a table and invite the child to join you. Talk about the Feel Box, what it is for, how to use it, and what surprises may be hidden inside. Stress that it is for feeling, not for seeing. Put on a blindfold and put your hand inside the box; exaggerate feeling around the inside of it. Pull your hand out and take off the blindfold. Tell the child that you felt something in the box.
2. Put the blindfold on the child, and ask him to put his hand inside the Feel Box to see if he can find the special treat. After he has found the surprise, see if he can guess what he found without looking.
3. Whether he can accurately identify what he found or not, take off his blindfold so he can enjoy the surprise.
4. Place a jar that is warm and a jar that is cold inside the Feel Box.
5. Set the other jar that is warm and the other jar that is cold on the table.
6. Discuss what "hot" and "cold" mean. (Remind him of the dangers of hot items.)
7. Ask the child to feel the jars on the table and to tell you which one is warm and which one is cold.
8. Ask him to point to the warm jar. Then, ask him to point to the cold jar.
9. After he has identified the jars, tell him there is a warm jar and also a cold jar in the Feel Box.
10. Place the blindfold on the child.
11. Tell him to put his hand inside the box, and to carefully feel for a jar. Once he gets a jar, have him take the jar out of the box, and set it next to the jar that feels the same on the table.
12. Mix up the jars that are now on the table.
13. After he has selected and matched a warm or cold jar, ask him to put his hand into the box, to carefully feel for the other jar in it, and to use his other hand to feel for a jar on the table that feels the same.
14. Observe him as he selects the jar from the box and matches each with one like it on the table.
15. If he has a problem matching temperatures, review the directions, making sure he understands the concepts of warm and cold. It is important not to change terminology--if you use the term "cold" when discussing the different temperatures, continue to use "cold" and do not interchange "cold" with "cool." To

help him feel, match and choose without a blindfold, set the four jars on the table, ask him to feel a jar and tell you if it is warm or cold; when he has responded set the like jars together.
16. After reviewing the directions, terms, and procedures with him, repeat the above assessment.
17. Place a wet washcloth (folded like the dry ones) and a dry washcloth in the Feel Box. Lay the other wet washcloth and the dry washcloth on the table.
18. Discuss what "wet" and "dry" mean.
19. Ask the child to feel the washcloths on the table and tell you which is wet and which is dry.
20. After he has identified the washcloths, explain that there is a wet washcloth and also a dry washcloth in the Feel Box.
21. Place the blindfold on him. Tell him to put his hand into the box, feel for a washcloth, take it out of the box and lay it next to the washcloth on the table that feels like it.
22. Repeat the directions to make sure he understands what he is to do.
23. After he has selected and matched a wet or dry washcloth, ask him to put his hand into the box, feel the cloth still there, and use his other hand to feel the like cloth on the table.
24. Observe him as he selects a washcloth from the box and matches it with the one like it on the table.
25. If he has a problem matching wet and dry, review the directions, making sure that he understands the concepts of "wet" and "dry." Do not change terms; if you use the term "wet" when discussing the different conditions, continue to use "wet," and do not interchange "wet" with "damp." To help him feel and match without a blindfold, lay the four cloths on the table folded alike, and ask him to feel a cloth and tell you whether it is wet or dry. After he responds, place the like cloths together. After reviewing the directions, terms, and procedures with him, repeat the above assessment.

Credit: + Child matches like tactile objects without looking (hot/cold and wet/dry). He is blindfolded during this activity to insure he does not use his vision in making his decisions.

Adaptations

Some children are not able to establish a classification scheme because they have not totally involved their sense of touch (be aware of a child's sensitivity to items; check with his parents first). As an example, when he is asked to understand the shape of a wooden block, he may refrain from touching its lines and corners to really comprehend the shape, or if he does touch the block, the concept of "blockness" is not transmitted. Touching items is natural for most children, and learning occurs through these tactile experiences, but some children often are cautioned not to touch things. As a result learning becomes limited to the visual and auditory channels. Without tactile activities, children find classifying a challenge. For example, if a child must arrange rocks without understanding how some can be smooth and others can be rough, or some round and others flat, it can be hard for him He needs to have many touching opportunities. To assist him, the following are suggested activities: (1) Provide him with various feeling tasks, such as a Feeling Bag (place items in a bag and have him identify or match items by feeling only); (2) Have him make a "Feely Picture": a textured picture made from materials such as cotton, velvet, seeds, and sandpaper; (3) Introduce "Feel and Draw"-- Place various objects in a feeling box, and ask the child to reach into the box to feel an object, describe how it feels and draw a picture of it; (4) Attach various textured materials, such as satin, corrugated cardboard, beans, and fur, to cards, then give him the cards and ask him to feel them, walk on them barefooted, and rub them on his legs and arms.

4.101 Places small pegs in holes on board
Strand: 4-6A **Age:** 42-50m 3.6-4.2y

Definition
The child will place at least six small pegs in a pegboard without assistance.

Assessment Materials
A large board (16 ½ inches by 16 ½ inches with 100 holes, or 8 5/8 inches by 8 5/8 inches with 25 holes and 3/8 inches thick); pegs (2 ½ inches long and 3/8 inches in diameter). Bell. Small snack foods like popcorn or raisins. Piggy bank and coins.

Assessment Procedures
Grouping: This skill may be assessed one-on-one with the child. However, the most effective assessment is made by observing the child in a natural setting to determine his visual-motor skills.

Level One:
1. Place the pegboard and 10 pegs on a table. Model how to place a peg in the pegboard.
2. Ask the child to put a peg in the pegboard.
3. Model how to place several pegs in the pegboard.
4. Give the child six pegs and ask him to put them in the pegboard.
5. Observe him as he places the pegs, watching for: (1) Picking the peg up and grasping the peg with his thumb and forefinger in a pincer hold; (2) Placing the peg in a hole; (3) Holding the board with his other hand for support; (4) Securing the peg in the hole.
6. If he demonstrates grasping problems, the following procedure is recommended: (1) Place a bell with a handle on the table and ask the child to reach for, grasp, and ring the bell; (2) Place a handful of a small snack food item, such as popcorn or raisins, on the table and ask the child to pick up each piece one at a time as he eats the food, (3) Have the child pick up coins and place them in the slot of a piggy bank; (4) Physically assist by placing your hand just below his wrist, and guide him through the grasping task.
7. Invite the child to the table. Repeat the steps outlined above.
8. Observe him as he places the pegs.

Level Two:
9. Observe the child as he manipulates pegs in a pegboard during an independent activity time or an instructional activity.

Credit: + Child places at least six small pegs in a pegboard, independently.

Adaptations

Some children have a difficult time with visual-motor skills, including: using a neat pincer (index finger- and thumb-closing) movement/grasp, judging distance and direction, transferring visual information to motor response (he sees what he wants to pick up but cannot conceive the motor plan), or of transferring information (he is unable to associate various movements to accomplish a task). Some activities to help him include: (1) Ask him to pick up several large items that are soft (large stuffed animals) and to put them into a large box. Gradually reduce the size of the items, for example, having him move inch-size cubes into a basket or pegs into an empty egg carton; (2) Ask him to tell you what he did when he picked up the soft stuffed animals and put them in the big box; (3) Provide verbal direction as he attempts to grasp an object and move it to another location.

4.102 Reproduces a two-dimensional block design

Strand: 4-6B **Age:** 42-50m 3.6-4.2y

Definition
The child will view a demonstration, and use blocks to reproduce a block design card. When she is presented with a two-dimensional block design card involving not more than seven blocks, she will copy the pattern with the blocks directly below or near the pattern card. She may also refer to the card when she is involved in manipulating the blocks to match the design.

Assessment Materials
At least four different two-dimensional block design cards (available from commercial sources), 10 1-inch cube blocks. If block design cards and blocks are not accessible, make block design cards by following these directions: On 8 ½ inch by 11 inch heavy white paper, trace around 1-inch blocks to draw not more than seven block squares in various patterns. Color the drawn blocks the same colors as the real blocks.

Examples:

Card 1: Draw around four blocks, one on top of another vertically; next to the four vertical blocks, draw two blocks, one on top of the other; and finally, draw one block next to the two vertical blocks. Color in the blocks.

Card 2: Draw around four blocks in horizontal positions; draw around a block on top of the far right block in the horizontal position; then draw around a block on top of the next to the far right block in the horizontal position; and finally, draw around a block on top of the far right block. Color the blocks.

Card 3: Draw around four blocks in horizontal positions; draw around a block on top of the first block in the horizontal row; draw around a block on top of the second block in the horizontal row, and finally; draw around a block on top of the last block in the horizontal row. Color the blocks.

Card 4: Draw around three blocks in a horizontal row; draw around a block on top of the first block in the horizontal row; and draw around three blocks one on top of the other on top of the last block in the horizontal row. Color the blocks.

One-inch cube blocks are available from commercial sources; 1-inch by 1-inch cubes can be cut from lumber scraps. Sand the cubes well and place in several pots of nontoxic dye, mixed to the colors desired.

Assessment Procedures

Grouping: This skill can be assessed one-on-one with the child. However, the most effective assessment is made by observing the child in a natural setting to determine his ability to reproduce a block design from a two-dimensional model.

Level One:
1. Place the blocks on a table, and invite the child to the working area. Place the two-dimensional Block Design Card 1 showing seven blocks on the work area in front of her. Ask her to watch as you use the cubes and reproduce the pattern on Card 1.
2. Make comparisons as you reconstruct the pattern.
3. Mix up the blocks.
4. Give the child Card 2 and the blocks. Ask her to copy the pattern with the blocks directly below or just to the right of the card.
5. Observe her as she reproduces the design, watching for: (1) The manipulation of the cubes; (2) The process by which she approached the task; (3) The accuracy of the reproduction; (4) The need for placing the cube on the card before recreating the pattern; (5) If she placed by blocks by color or followed some other strategy for placement; (6) The speed with which the task was accomplished.
6. If she is successful, repeat the above process using Card 3, Card 4 and Card 1.
7. If she has difficulty in the reconstruction, the following suggestions are for addressing the prerequisite skills necessary before reproducing a two-dimensional design: (1) Demonstrate by pointing to a cube on the pattern card, naming the color of the cube, pointing to a block of the same color, and naming the block color. Then place the block on the table in the same position as it is on the pattern card. Continue with the other blocks; (2) Show her how to place a block on the pattern card, then slide the block off, place it in position, and continue with other blocks; (3) Take turns with the child in placing blocks. Example: You place a block, ask her to place a block, you place another, then she places another block, and so on; (4) Make a two-dimensional pattern card with two blocks side-by-side. Give the child two blocks in the same colors as those on the pattern card, and ask her to produce the design. Gradually increase the number of blocks on the cards and the number of blocks she manipulates; (5) Physically assist her in the reconstruction of the pattern cards.
8. Once she has had an opportunity to practice the prerequisite skills, repeat the assessment process outlined above.

Level Two:
9. Observe the child as she works with block pattern cards and blocks as an independent activity or in small groups.

Credit: + Child reproduces a two-dimensional block design with up to seven blocks, placing her blocks directly below or near the pattern card, without assistance.

Adaptations

Some children have difficulty when they are asked to repeat a design, particularly when it requires the manipulation of an object. The problem can be related to visual-motor coordination or the ability to analyze patterns into component parts and recognize the way the parts fit together. If a child has a problem with visual-motor integration, she should practice grasping items that are larger, that have different textures, and that are marked for finger placement. The child should practice picking up objects and placing them in a container along with squeezing a soft ball for strength. If the problem is associated with conceptualization of a whole-to-a-part or the part-to-the-whole, involve the child with concrete items such as blocks or beads before having her work with semi-abstract items such as pattern cards. For example, build a block design from blocks, then take the design apart block by block, and allow the child to view how the parts went together. Replace the block design and ask the child to reproduce the model.

4.103 Matches or chooses through tactile cues like objects that are rough and smooth
Strand: 4-8 **Age:** 45-48m 3.9-4.0y

Definition

The child will use his tactile sense to match objects that are rough or smooth only by touching or handling them. He will not use his sense of sight to differentiate the objects or forms.

Assessment Materials

"Feel Box": locate a cardboard box with a lid, cut a hole in the side of the box large enough for the child to put his hand inside, and decorate it on the outside. Two rough objects (piece of sandpaper, a scouring pad), two smooth objects (plastic dish, polished paperweight). A blindfold.

Assessment Procedures

Grouping: This skill should be assessed one-on-one with the child.
1. Before you introduce the Feel Box, place a small surprise inside the box, such as a new pencil, a wrapped snack, a small toy, or a ticket for special time. Place the Feel Box on a table and invite the child to join you. Talk about the Feel Box, what it is for, how to use it, surprises that may be hidden in it. Stress that it is for feeling, not for seeing. Put on a blindfold and put your hand in the box; exaggerate feeling around the inside the box. Pull your hand out and take off the blindfold. Tell him that you felt something in the box.
2. Put the blindfold on him, put his hand in the Feel Box, and ask him if he can find the special treat inside the box.
3. After he has found the surprise, take off his blindfold and let him enjoy it.
4. Place a rough and a smooth object inside the Feel Box.
5. Place a rough object and a smooth object on the table.
6. Discuss what "rough" and "smooth" mean.
7. Ask the child to feel the rough object and the smooth object on the table.
8. Ask the child to point to the rough object. Ask the child to point to the smooth object.
9. Explain that there is an object in the Feel Box.
10. Place the blindfold on the child.
11. Tell him to put his hand in the box, feel for an object, taking one item out of the box, and put it next to the object on the table that feels the same.
12. Mix up the items on the table.
13. After he has selected and matched a rough or smooth item, ask him to put his hand into the box, to carefully feel for other items, and to use his other hand to feel for the item on the table that feels the same.
14. Observe him as he selects the object from the box and matches it with the like one on the table.
15. If he has a problem matching objects that are rough and smooth, review the directions, making sure that he understands the concepts of rough. It is important that you do not change terms; if you use the word "smooth" when discussing that condition, continue to use "smooth," and do not interchange "smooth" with "slick," or the word "scratchy" for "rough." To help him feel, match, and choose, do not blindfold him; instead, place the four objects on the table, and ask him to feel an item, choose it, and match it with another object of the same texture.
16. After reviewing the directions, terms and procedures with him, repeat the above assessment.
17. Observe him as he selects an object from the box and matches it with the like one on the table.

Credit: + Child matches with like tactile objects without looking (smooth and rough). He is blindfolded during this activity to insure he does not use his vision in making his decisions.

Adaptations
See #4.100.

4.104 Matches or chooses through tactile cues like objects that are sticky and nonsticky

Strand: 4-8 **Age:** 45-48m 3.9-4.0y

Definition
The child will use her tactile sense to match objects that are sticky or non-sticky only by touching or handling them. She will not use her sense of sight to differentiate between the objects or forms.

Assessment Materials
"Feel Box": locate a cardboard box with a lid, cut a hole in the side of the box large enough for the child to put her hand inside, and decorate it on the outside. Two objects that are sticky, such as tape, marshmallow creme, sugar dissolved in water; two objects that are non-sticky, such as paper, marshmallow, sugar. Small containers. A blindfold.

Assessment Procedures

Grouping: this skill should be assessed one-on-one with the child.
1. Before you introduce the Feel Box, place a small surprise inside it, such as a new pencil, a wrapped snack, a small toy, or a ticket for special time. Place the Feel Box on a table and invite the child to join you. Talk about the

Feel Box--what it is for, how to use it, and surprises that may be hidden inside. Stress that it is for feeling, not seeing. Put on a blindfold and put your hand in the box; exaggerate feeling around the inside of the box. Pull your hand out and take off the blindfold. Tell the child that you felt something inside the box.
2. Place the blindfold on her, and ask her to put her hand into the Feel Box to see if she can find the special treat.
3. After she has found the surprise, take off her blindfold and let her enjoy it.
4. Place a sticky object inside the Feel Box.
5. Place a sticky object and a non-sticky object in individual small containers on the table.
6. Discuss what "sticky" and "non-sticky" mean.
7. Ask the child to feel the sticky object and the non-sticky object on the table.
8. Ask her to point to the sticky object. Ask her to point to the non-sticky object.
9. Tell her there is an object in the Feel Box.
10. Place the blindfold on her.
11. Tell her to put her hand into the box, feel for the object, take it out of the box and put it next to a like object on the table.
12. Observe her as she selects the object from the box and matches it with the like one on the table.
13. Place the non-sticky item inside the Feel Box, and repeat the process.
14. If she has a problem matching objects that are sticky and non-sticky, review the directions, making sure she understands the concepts of sticky and non-sticky. It is important not to change terms; if you use the word "sticky" when discussing that condition, continue to use "sticky," do not interchange "sticky" with "gooey." To help her feel, match, and choose, do not put the blindfold on her, but instead, place the four containers on the table, ask her to feel one of the items and to match it with another like item.
15. After reviewing the directions, terms, and procedures with her, repeat the above assessment.
16. Observe her as she selects an object from the box and matches it with the like one on the table.

Credit: + Child matches like tactile objects without looking (sticky and nonsticky). She is blindfolded during this activity to insure she does not use her vision in making her decisions.

Adaptations
See #4.100.

4.105 Matches or chooses through tactile cues like objects that are long and short
Strand: 4-8 **Age:** 45-48m 3.9-4.0y

Definition
When he is presented with five objects that vary in length from a few inches to 10 inches, the child will sort the objects as long or short based only on tactile cues.

Assessment Materials
Four 6-inch, three-dimensional, safe, stick-like objects. One 4-inch, three-dimensional object. Four 4-inch, three-dimensional objects. One 6-inch, three-dimensional object. (Use objects such as unsharpened pencils, dowels, drinking straws.) Paper strips of different lengths: one strip 5 inches long, four strips 10 inches long, one strip 10 inches long and another strip 4 inches long. Two boxes such as shoe boxes, two balloons, string, tape, a blindfold.

Assessment Procedures
Grouping: This skill should be assessed one-on-one with the child.
1. Place the four 6-inch sticks and the one 4-inch stick on the table.
2. Invite the child to the work area, and show him the two boxes, then blow up the two balloons and tie a long string to one balloon and a short string to the other balloon.
3. With transparent tape, attach the balloon with the long string to one box and the balloon with the short string to another box.
4. Show the child the sticks and ask him to point to a long stick.
5. Ask him to point to the short stick.
6. After the child has identified the long stick, ask him to put the long stick in the box with the balloon on the long string.
7. After he has identified the short stick, ask him to put the short stick in the box with the balloon on the short string.
8. Blindfold the child.
9. Explain that you are going to put the five sticks on the table and that he is to feel the sticks with his fingers, pick one of the sticks, and identify whether it is long or short.
10. After he makes an identification, ask him to place it in the correct box. It is helpful if he is familiar with the position of the box with the

balloon on the long string and the box with the balloon on the short string. If he needs assistance to locate the correct box, guide his hand along the string to the balloon.

11. Observe him as he feels the sticks, identifies long or short, and places the sticks in the correct box.
12. If he is successful, continue the above procedure using the four short sticks and the one long stick.
13. Observe him as he feels, identifies, and places these sticks.
14. If he is successful, continue the above procedure using the long and short paper strips. (Additional practice in feeling the paper strips is recommended because paper is a flat dimension that makes it more difficult to identify tactually.)
15. If he has difficulty with this task, the following suggestions address the prerequisite skills needed to accomplish the assessment: (1) Make sure that he understands the concepts of long and short; (2) Allow him to feel, identify, and place the sticks and paper strips in the correct category without a blindfold; (3) Before he uses tactile skills for identification, ask him to put the long objects together on the table and the short objects together on the table; (4) Put nontoxic glue on all the short objects, and before the glue dries, place something with texture on them, such as salt, cotton tuffs, or sand. This gives him an additional tactile cue; (5) Ask him to identify the object by saying "long" or "short" instead of placing the item in the correct box.
16. After he has received instruction and practice in the prerequisite skills, reassess him as outlined above.
17. Observe him as he feels, identifies, and places these sticks.

Credit: + Child matches with like objects without looking (long and short). He is blindfolded during this activity to insure he does not use his vision in making his decisions.

Adaptations
See #4.100.

4.106 Matches or chooses through tactile cues like objects that are hard and soft
Strand: 4-8 **Age:** 48-51m 4.0-4.3y

Definition
The child will use his tactile sense to match objects that are hard and soft only by touching or handling them. He will not use his sense of sight to differentiate the objects or forms.

Assessment Materials
A "Feel Box": Locate a cardboard box with a lid, cut a hole in the side of the box large enough for the child to put his hand in, and decorate it on the outside. Two objects that are hard (wood, plastic, or rock), two objects that are soft (cotton, sponge, foam). A blindfold.

Assessment Procedures
Grouping: This skill should be assessed one-on-one with the child.
1. Before introducing the Feel Box place a surprise inside the box, for example, a new pencil, a wrapped snack, a small toy, or a ticket for special time. Place the Feel Box on a table and invite the child to join you. Talk about the Feel Box, what it is for, how to use it, surprises that may be hidden inside. Stress that it is for feeling, not for seeing. Put on a blindfold, and put your hand in the box; exaggerate feeling around the inside the box. Pull your hand out, take off the blindfold. Tell the child that you felt something in the box.
2. Place the blindfold on him, put his hand into the Feel Box and ask him to try to find the special treat.
3. After he finds the surprise, take off his blindfold, and let him enjoy it.
4. Place a hard and a soft object inside the Feel Box.
5. Place a hard object and a soft object on the table.
6. Discuss what "hard" and "soft" mean.
7. Ask him to feel the hard object and the soft object on the table.
8. Ask him to point to the hard object. Ask him to point to the soft object.
9. Tell him there is an object in the Feel Box.
10. Place the blindfold on him.
11. After he has identified the texture, explain that there is another item in the box. Tell him to put his hand in the box, feel for the item, use his other hand to select an object on the table that has the same feel.
12. Repeat the directions to make sure he understands what to do.

13. Observe him as he selects the other object from the box and matches it with the like one on the table.
14. If he has a problem matching objects that are hard and soft, review the directions, making sure that he understands the concepts of hard and soft. Do not change the terms, if you use the term "soft" when discussing that condition, continue to use "soft," do not interchange "soft" with "puffy," or "hard" with "solid." To help him feel, match and choose, do not have him use a blindfold; instead, place the four objects on the table, ask him to feel an item, choose it and match it with another object that feels the same, hard or soft.
15. After reviewing the directions, terms and procedures with him, repeat the above assessment.
16. Observe the child as he selects an object from the box and matches it with the like one on the table.
17. After reviewing the directions, terms and procedures with him, repeat the above assessment.

Credit: + Child matches like objects without looking (hard and soft). He is blindfolded during this activity to insure he does not use his vision in making his decisions.

Adaptations
See #4.100.

4.107 (Removed, see page xviii)

4.108 Matches or chooses through tactile cues like objects that are thin and fat
Strand: 4-8 **Age:** 48-53m 4.0-4.5y

Definition
The child will use his tactile sense to match objects that are thin or fat by only touching or handling them. He will not use his sense of sight to differentiate the objects or forms.

Assessment Materials
"Feel Box": Locate a cardboard box with a lid, cut a hole in the side of the box large enough for the child to put his hand inside, and decorate it on the outside. Two thin objects, for example, a comb and a key; two fat objects, for example, a lemon and a ball of yarn). A blindfold.

Assessment Procedures
Grouping: This skill should be assessed one-on-one with the child.
1. Before you introduce the "Feel Box," place a surprise inside the box, such as a new pencil, a box of animal cookies, a small toy, or a ticket for special time. Place the Feel Box on a table, and invite the child to join you. Talk about the Feel Box, what it is for, how to use it, surprises that may be hidden inside. Stress that it is for feeling, not for seeing. Put on a blindfold, and put your hand in the box; exaggerate feeling around the inside of the box. Pull your hand out and take off the blindfold, and tell the child that you felt something inside the box.
2. Help the child put on the blindfold, and ask him to put his hand inside the Feel Box and find the special treat.
3. After he has found the surprise, take off his blindfold and let him enjoy it.
4. Place a thin and a fat object in the Feel Box.
5. Place a thin object and a fat object on the table.
6. Discuss what "thin" and "fat" mean.
7. Ask the child to feel the thin object and then the fat object on the table.
8. Ask him to point to the thin object. Ask him to point to the fat object.
9. Tell him there is an object inside the Feel Box.
10. Place the blindfold on the child.
11. Tell him to put his hand into the box, feel for an object, taking one item out of the box, and put it next to a like object on the table.
12. Repeat the directions to make sure that he understands what to do.
13. Observe him as he selects the object from the box and matches it with the like one on the table.
14. If he has a problem matching objects that are thin and fat, review the directions, making sure that he understands the concepts of thin and fat. Be careful not to change terms, if you use the term "thin" when you talk about that condition, continue to use "thin," do not interchange "thin" with "flat." To help the child feel, match and choose, do not have him use a blindfold; instead, place the four objects on the table, ask him to feel an item, and to choose and match it with another object of the same dimensions.
15. After reviewing the directions, terms and procedures with him, repeat the above assessment.

16. Observe him as he selects an object from the box and matches it with the like one on the table.

Credit: + Child matches like objects (thin and fat) through tactile cues. He is blindfolded during this activity to insure he does not use his vision in making his decisions.

Adaptations
See #4.100.

4.109 (Removed, see page xviii)

4.110 Spreads paste/glue on one side of paper and turns over to stick it to another paper
Strand: 4-6D **Age:** 30-40m 2.6-3.4y

Definition
When she is asked, the child will spread paste or glue on one side of a sheet paper that is at least 4 inches by 6 inches in size, and then she will attach the glued sheet to another sheet of paper. It is not important that she align the two sheets of paper. She will turn the glued side over to adhere it to another sheet.

Assessment Materials
Several sheets of paper at least 4 inches by 6 inches, nontoxic paste or glue, paper towels, clip clothespin.

Assessment Procedures
Grouping: This skill can be assessed in a small group, no more than four children. Remind the children that they will need to listen and take turns during the activity. However, the most effective assessment is made by observing her in a natural setting while engaged in an art activity.

Level One:
1. Ask the child to watch as you model putting paste or glue on a sheet of paper and then turning the paper over and attaching it to another sheet of paper.
2. Give her two sheets of paper and the paste or glue, and ask her to glue a sheet of paper and turn it over so it will stick to the other sheet.
3. Observe her as she spreads the paste or glue, turns the paper over, and applies enough pressure to assure that the two papers adhere.
4. Watch for the following: (1) The amount of paste or glue she used and the manner in which she spread it; (2) Whether she turned the pasted sheet over to attach it to the other or reversed the process; (3) The manner in which she made certain the two sheets of paper were attached. (Did she allow the paper to adhere without using any pressure or did she press the papers with her fingers, use a pounding approach, or use the heel of her hand, rotating it around the area?)
5. If she had a difficult time applying the glue or paste, the following strategies are recommended: (1) If she used an excess amount of paste or glue, limit the amount you give her, either by dispenser or by bulk; (2) Provide a spreading tool and demonstrate how to apply the glue or paste, for example, a plastic spoon or brush; (3) To absorb some of the excess substance, give her a paper towel for blotting; (4) Model how to put on drops of glue or paste and spread it around. If she has a difficult time in attaching the two sheets of paper, the following suggestions are recommended: (1) Model how to pick up the glued sheet of paper and turn it over to attach it to the other sheet. As you demonstrate, give a verbal description of what you are doing; (2) Give her a clip clothespin to attach to one side of the sheet of paper to act as a flipping handle; (3) Bring up the two sheets, perpendicular to the table, and gently push them together before laying them down.
6. After she has practiced the sub-task skills, reassess her according to the directions above. Remember that the objective is to attach two sheets of paper, and the exact method of attachment can be achieved in many different ways. To insist that she do it a certain way may interfere with her accomplishment and the objective.

Level Two:
7. Observe the child as she is gluing paper during an art experience or when she is involved in an independent activity.

Credit: + Child spreads paste on one side of piece of paper and then turns it over to attach it to another sheet of paper making sure the two sheets adhere together.

Adaptations
Some children take extra time to become familiar with an adhesive. When a child first uses glue or paste, she may: (1) Use more than is needed or not enough; (2) Over-spread the substance and make holes in the paper; (3) Be apprehensive about touching and spreading the adhesive (or have tactile sensitivity); (4) Allow the glue or paste to dry up because she didn't manipulate it right away; (5) Place the two items

to be attached together without spreading or moving the glue or paste to the correct place, with the result being the glue leaks out, doesn't adhere, or creates bumps.

To assist her: (1) Introduce her to a glue stick so she becomes familiar with the volume of glue that is needed; (2) Gradually let her become familiar with the substance; (3) Give her a tool such as tongue depressor for spreading if she seems apprehensive about touching the glue; (4) Use a dispenser to drop a few drops of glue on a sheet of paper for spreading; (5) Have paper towels available so she can wipe her hands often; (6) Before using glue or paste, let her spread a similar substance, such as shaving cream or flour mixed in water. Remember that the goal of using an adhesive is to attach things together and that it is important to let her discover her own method before you make suggestions to her.

4.111 Draws a picture of a person
Strand: 4-6A **Age:** 48-60m 4.0-5.0y

Definition
When asked to draw a person, the child will draw her own person, which will include at least eight of the following recognizable body parts: a head, body, eyes, nose, mouth, hair, arms, shoulders, legs, hands, and feet. She will draw her person using a pencil, a marker or a crayon. If she wishes, she may add additional features to her person.

Assessment Materials
Paper, pencils, markers, and crayons.

Assessment Procedures
Grouping: This skill should be assessed one-on-one with the child. However, you can make the most effective assessment by observing the child in a natural setting to see if they can draw a person.

Level One:
1. Give the child a sheet of paper and her choice of writing tools.
2. Ask her to draw a person.
3. Do not allow her more than two practice sheets.
4. Observe her as she draws and completes her stick person.
5. Make note of the following: (1) Whether she held and used the writing tool effectively; (2) Whether she adjusted and held the paper effectively; (3) Whether she applied pressure on the pencil or marker sufficiently to control her movements; (4) Whether she drew a body, head, arms and legs, and whether they were located in the correct positions; (5) Whether she added to the picture.
6. If she has difficulty drawing a person, it is important to determine whether the problem is with the mechanics of the task or with the visual representation.
7. If she demonstrated a problem with the mechanics, the following are recommendations: (1) Demonstrate how to hold the pencil and paper; (2) Tape the paper to the table and adjust the writing tool by adding a grip or providing adaptive writing instruments; (3) Physically assist her with hand-over-hand assistance and guiding her drawing; then gradually withdraw the assistance, and assist only when needed.
8. If the child demonstrated a problem with the visual representation, the following are recommendations: (1) Show the child the pre-drawn figure of a person and discuss the body, head, arms, and legs; (2) Tell her to draw the different parts with you; draw a head and ask the child to draw the head, draw a body and ask her to draw a body, draw an arm and ask her to draw an arm, and so on; (3) Draw a body and ask the child to put a head on the body you drew; draw an arm and ask her to draw the other arm, and so on.
9. Repeat the assessment outlined above.
10. Give her no more than two practice sheets.
11. Observe her as she draws and completes the person.

Level Two:
12. Observe the child as she draws pictures during her independent period or during an art activity.

Credit: + Child draws a person, which includes at least eight body parts. Other body parts may also be included.

Adaptations
Some children need help when they try to perform a visual-motor task that requires placement and precision. To reproduce an object that has definite perimeters requires a child to demonstrate precision, dexterity, visual recall, motor control and skill transfer. A child must have been involved in a sequential visual-motor program, beginning with grasping, small-object control, physical control of a writing tool, scribbling, line formation, shape development, copying from a model, and finally, image representation from real things and experiences.

To help a child, provide a variety of activities that reinforce the same task and encourage creativity as a valid experience.

4.112 Strings small beads reproducing color and shape sequence/pattern

Strand: 4-7C   **Age:** 48-60m 4.0-5.0y

Definition
When the child is presented with a bead-stringing set and a bead pattern for him to copy, he will demonstrate his ability to reproduce the bead pattern by stringing the beads to match the visual model. The bead pattern will represent different colors and bead shapes, and will include at least ten beads.

Assessment Materials
Set of 24 beads for stringing in five different colors and five different shapes, hard-tipped strings or shoelaces with knot at end, bead pattern cards. Purchase bead pattern cards at a school supply store or use the following directions to make them: Card 1--On a 4 ¼-inch by 11-inch card draw eight beads on a string that are distinguishable from each other in color and shape. Make sure the card shows the knotted end of the string. Card 2--On a 4 ¼-inch by 11-inch card draw ten beads that are distinguishable from each other in color and shape. Make sure the card shows the knotted end of the string.

Assessment Procedures
Note: Stringing beads is usually a fascinating experience for young children and testing them on this skill should not interfere with their enjoyment of the activity.

Grouping: This skill should be assessed one-on-one with the child. However, you can make the most effective assessment by observing the child in a natural setting to see if they can string small beads to match a visual sequence/pattern.

<u>Level One:</u>
1. Give the child the box of 24 beads and Bead Pattern Card 1. Ask him to string the beads, matching the pattern on Card 1. He must select the correct beads from the box and put them on the string.
2. Observe him as he strings the beads.
3. If he is successful in stringing eight beads, give him Card 2 and a box of 16 beads that contain different colors and different shapes. Ask him to string the beads, matching the pattern. He must select the correct beads from the box and put them on the string.
4. Observe him as he strings the beads.
5. If he has difficulty stringing the beads, he may be exhibiting a problem in controlling small objects or in pincer hold. If the concern is with his control, assist him by: (1) Increasing the size of the beads to help with pattern-matching; (2) Replacing the string with a dowel stick or pipe cleaner to add stability and control to the motion of placing the bead; (3) Allowing him ample time to handle the beads without stringing them. Ask him to pick up a bead and place it in a container; expand this task by asking him to pick up a bead and hold it over a container until he hears you say "Drop." If the concern is with pincer hold, assist him by: (1) Increasing the size of the beads, making marks on the side of the larger beads where his thumb and forefinger should be placed; (2) Placing your thumb and forefinger over his and using pressure for bead pick-up; (3) Allowing ample time for him to handle the beads without stringing them; (4) Changing from wooden beads to soft foam beads, due to the texture and griping effect of the foam. After the child has been involved in some of these less demanding and lower task levels of bead-stringing activities, consider making a reassessment.
6. If he is having difficulty stringing the beads because of the pattern matching, recommended ways to assist him include: (1) Reduce the number of beads on the Bead Pattern Card to a single bead, then add one bead at a time. This gradual pattern of increasing beads allows him to look and match a single bead at a time; (2) Limit the number of beads for him to select from; (3) Join him in the stringing experience to create a model. For example, follow this sequence: Point to a bead on your Bead Pattern Card and ask him to point to the same bead on his card; point to the matching bead in your box and ask him to point to the bead in his box; pick up the bead from your box and ask him to pick up the bead from his box; and finally, place the bead on your string and ask him to place the bead on his string. Continue with the other beads on the pattern cards.
7. Assess him as outlined above.

<u>Level Two:</u>
8. Observe the child as he is stringing beads during an independent period, at an interest

center or when he is involved in an instructional period.

Credit: + Child strings at least five small beads reproducing the color and shape from a sequence/pattern card.

Adaptations

See #4.98.

To assist a child with control and pincer grasp, (1) Give him larger objects to pick up and place in a container, physically helping him if necessary; (2) Provide him with soft-textured items to let him have a kinesthetic grip; (3) Give him a soft ball to hold in his palm and squeeze to encourage strength and finger control.

Visually matching what is seen with a motor reaction is difficult for some children. This sequence of looking, matching, motor reaction, and checking, often creates confusion and frustration. Allow the child to hold each bead next to the pattern before he decides on the match and then have him place the bead on the string. By limiting the number of beads to choose from and limiting the number of options on the pattern card, you can diminish much of the confusion, stress and anxiety this task created for him.

4.113 Cuts out small square/triangle with scissors

Strand: 4-7D **Age:** 48-62m 4.0-5.2y

Definition

When he is given a sheet of paper with a square at least 3 inches on each side, the child will use scissors to cut the square out without assistance, staying within ½ inch of the lines. When he is given a sheet of paper with a triangle at least 3 inches on each side, he will cut the triangle out without assistance, within ½ inch of the lines.

Assessment Materials

/*\Safety Note: Provide scissors appropriate for the child. Remind the child of safety regarding scissors.

Child-size safety scissors. Twelve sheets of 8 ½-inch by 11-inch paper prepared as follows: four sheets with a 3-inch diameter circle drawn on each, four sheets with a 3-inch square drawn on each, four sheets with a 3-inch triangle drawn on each side. Black marker.

Assessment Procedures

Grouping: This skill should be assessed one-on-one with the child.

1. Start with a circle to remind the child how to cut. Ask the child to watch as you cut out the circle. Exaggerate the turning of the paper to cut the different line directions.
2. Give him the scissors and a sheet of paper with a circle drawn on it, and give him an opportunity to practice cutting out the shape.
3. After he has practiced, give him a sheet of paper with a shape (square, then triangle) drawn on it and ask him to cut it out.
4. Observe as he cuts out the shapes, looking for: (1) The manner in which he holds the paper; (2) The position of the scissors--should be perpendicular to the paper; (3) The way he turns the paper in order to cut in a different direction, such as corners or curves; (4) His accuracy of cutting on the line without deviating more than a ½ inch; (5) His use of a forward pushing movement; (6) The way he begins to cut--whether he starts from the edge of the paper to the line or pokes a hole on or near the line; (7) His starting and ending spots--whether he starts cutting at a single point and ends at that spot or whether he makes several different starting and ending places.
5. If the child does not respond, or demonstrates a concern, the following is recommended: (1) Model how to hold and turn the paper; (2) Demonstrate how to start at the edge of the paper and cut until reaching the outline of the object; (3) Provide him with practice in cutting curves, corners, and straight lines by drawing these figures on a sheet of paper and asking him to cut the lines before he cuts out an object; (4) Draw a single-line figure including curves, straight lines, gradual corners, and then exact corners for him to cut; (5) If his problem is manipulating the scissors, provide adaptive scissors, either double-blunt with two sets of handles, self-opening scissors with cushioned handles that spring back after each cut., or wrap a pipe cleaner around the finger holes to provide a more snug fit of the scissors on fingers.
6. After giving the above assistance, repeat the assessment above if he has shown improvement.

Credit: + Child cuts out a small square and a small triangle with scissors, staying within ½ inch of the line, without assistance.

Adaptations

If a child needs assistance, follow these recommendations when he first begins to cut on a line: (1) Have him begin with a straight line;

make sure the line is short, yet long enough for a cutting stroke; (2) Have him move to a curved line; make sure the line is drawn with a 1-inch-wide black marker; (3) Draw a straight line, then curve the line, and include a scissors turn; (4) Demonstrate how to use the non-dominant hand to guide the paper and tell him to watch how the scissors move with the paper; (5) Begin by having him cut out shapes that have straight lines with not more than two scissor turns (triangle), then an object that is curved with a gradual arc (a circle), and finally a shape that has straight lines with not more than three scissor turns (square); (6) Adaptive scissors, particularly those with loop handles that automatically open after each cutting and are adaptable to either left- or right-handed cutters. As he begins cutting out shapes, do not emphasize "staying on the line," as much as the important skill of having the two hands working together, one guiding the paper and the other directing the scissors. Be sure to allow him enough practice time and to encourage him for trying.

4.114 (Moved to Cognitive, skill 1.308)

4.115 Matches or chooses through tactile cues like objects that are circular, triangular, rectangular, and square

Strand: 4-8 **Age:** 53-60m 4.5-5.0y

Definition
The child will use his tactile sense to match or choose two-dimensional and three-dimensional shapes that are square, circular, triangular, and rectangular, only by touching or handling them. He will not use his sense of sight to differentiate the various shapes.

Assessment Materials
"Feel Box": locate a cardboard box with a lid, cut a hole in the side of the box large enough for the child to put his hand inside, and decorate it on the outside. Two circular templates; two triangular templates; two rectangular templates; two square templates. A blindfold.

Assessment Procedures
Grouping: This skill should be assessed one-on-one with the child.

1. Before you introduce the "Feel Box," place a surprise inside the box, such as a new pencil, a box of animal cookies, a small toy, or a ticket for special time. Place the Feel Box on a table, and invite the child to join you. Talk about the Feel Box, what it is for, how to use it, surprises that may be hidden inside. Stress that it is for feeling, not for seeing. Put on a blindfold, and put your hand in the box; exaggerate feeling around the inside of the box. Pull your hand out and take off the blindfold, and tell the child that you felt something inside the box.
2. Help the child put on the blindfold, and ask him to put his hand inside the Feel Box and find the special treat.
3. After he has found the surprise, take off his blindfold and let him enjoy it.
4. Place the square template in the Feel Box. Place the other templates--square, rectangle, triangle and circle--on the table.
5. Discuss the different shapes.
6. Ask the child to feel the templates on the table.
7. Ask him to point to the square, then the rectangle, the triangle, and the circle.
8. After he has felt the templates on the table, explain that there is a shape in the Feel Box like one of the shapes on the table.
9. Place the blindfold on the child.
10. Place the following shapes in the box: a circle, square, a triangle, and a rectangle.
11. Ask him to put his hand into the box, to feel for a shape, and to use his other hand to select a like shape on the table.
12. Observe him as he selects the shape from the box and matches it with the like one on the table.
13. Repeat the above using the other shapes.
14. Ask him to remove his blindfold to do a self-check.
15. If he has a problem matching the flat shapes, review the directions, making sure that he understands the concepts of rectangle, square, triangle, and circle. To help him, ask him to feel, match, and choose without a blindfold: place the shapes on a table, give him a circular shape to feel, and then ask him to find another object on the table that is the same shape. After he has one shape in one hand and the other shape in the other hand, ask him to compare the two shapes. Correct him, if needed.
16. After reviewing the directions, terms and procedures with him, repeat the above assessment.
17. Observe him as he selects a shape from the box and matches it with a like one on the table.

Credit: + Child matches like geometric objects (circle, triangle, rectangle, and square) through tactile cues. He is blindfolded during this activity to insure he does not use his vision in making his decisions.

Adaptations
See #4.100.

4.116 Traces around own hand
Strand: 4-6A **Age:** 53-62m 4.5-5.2y

Definition
The child will trace around her own hand. She will trace her non-dominant hand. Her first drawing will be an outline with fingers closed, thumb extended. Her second drawing will be with thumb extended and fingers apart.

Assessment Materials
Drawing paper and a pencil or a thin-line marker.

Assessment Procedures
Note: It is important not to insist that she draw around her hand or draw what you suggest. Developmentally, she may not be ready, and forcing her could affect her enjoyment of being creative and expressive.
Grouping: This skill should be assessed one-on-one with the child.
1. Ask the child to join you at the table. Place your hand (fingers closed, thumb extended) on a sheet of paper and draw around it.
2. Give the child a sheet of paper and ask her to draw around her hand.
3. Observe her as she outlines her hand.
4. Place your hand (thumb extended, fingers apart) on a sheet of paper and draw around it.
5. Give her a sheet of paper and ask her to draw around her open hand.
6. If she has difficulty completing this task; ask her to put her hand on the drawing paper so that you can draw around it, holding the hand steady with slight pressure. After the modeling, invite her to draw around her hand. If she continues to demonstrate problems, place your hand over her hand and guide it through the outlining.

Credit: + Child traces around her own hand, with her non-dominant hand. The child makes two tracings. The first tracing is an outline with the fingers closed, with the thumb extended. The second tracing is an outline of the thumb extended and the fingers apart.

Adaptations
At a beginning developmental level, some children have a difficult time using only one hand in a visual-motor activity. Generally the two hands work together, with one hand acting as a stabilizer and the other as the action leader. For example, one hand holds the paper and the other hand does the writing or drawing. When the stabilizer hand is assigned another role (palm down on a sheet of paper), it may be unsteady, unable to lay flat, turn over, etc. A child may encounter a problem with the stability of her wrist when she is asked to draw around her hand. When drawing or writing, the wrist is usually in a controlled position and resting on a flat surface. The wrist provides the support needed for finger control of the writing instrument. As variations of drawing occur, the wrist needs to move into and out of a stable position and must often be raised from the flat surface. When a child traces around an object, the wrist is definitely in a raised and non-stable configuration; to some children this feels unnatural and uncomfortable or they are unable to maintain the varied position. Remember not to sacrifice the child's self-image, her enjoyment of drawing, and her appreciation of creative expression by forcing her to draw around her hand.

4.117 Matches or chooses through tactile cues like objects that are light and heavy
Strand: 4-8 **Age:** 57-60m 4.9-5.0y

Definition
The child will use her tactile sense to match objects that are light or heavy only by handling them. She will not use her sense of sight to differentiate the objects or forms.

Assessment Materials
/*\Safety Note: Supervise the child closely regarding use of the hammer.
Four balls of different weights, textures, and sizes, such as a golf ball, tennis ball, steel ball, fleece ball, yarn ball, jacks ball. Fill four small brown paper bags with materials of varying weights. Examples: Bag 1--cotton, Bag 2--nails (large/not sharp) wrapped in paper, Bag 3--sand in a tied plastic bag, Bag 4--jelly beans in a tied plastic bag. A scale. Hanger, two pieces of string 12 inches in length, two plastic cups. A hammer and a straw.

Assessment Procedures

Grouping: This skill should be assessed one-on-one with the child.

1. Place four balls of different sizes and weights on the table.
2. Without touching the balls, discuss their different sizes with the child.
3. Place the blindfold on the child.
4. Ask her to pick up one of the balls and decide whether it is heavy or light. If it is heavy, tell her to set the ball at one end of the table, and if it is light, tell her to set it at the other end of the table.
5. Ask her to continue picking up the balls and placing them with the heavy ore light balls.
6. Remove the balls.
7. Place the four different bags on the table.
8. Ask the child to pick up two of the bags and decide which is the heaviest and to place it at one end of the table.
9. Have her place the other bag back on the table.
10. Ask her to pick up two more bags and decide if they are heavy or light. Lights bags go at the other end of the table.
11. Have her put the other bag back on the table.
12. Ask her to continue until she has "hand-weighed" all the bags and placed them in the correct location.
13. Observe her as she makes the weight comparisons and judgments.
14. If she had a difficult time determining heavy versus light, the following suggestions address these decisions, comparisons and judgments, based on the sense of touch: (1) Limit the containers to two; one very heavy and the other very light; (2) Allow her to participate in filling the bags; (3) Place the weighted material in plastic bags instead of brown paper bags to let her see the contents; (4) Provide a scale to weigh the items after she has made the weighted comparison. If a scale is not available, make a hanger scale from a clothes hanger: tie two strings the same length on each side of the hanger, attach a plastic cup to each string, and allow the scale to hang freely. Place an object in each cup; if the object is heavier, the cup will go down and the cup holding the lighter of the two objects will go up. Give the child two objects, and ask her which she thinks is the heaviest, and then place the object in the cups to verify her response; (5) Add verbal support to her decisions by giving her a hammer and saying, "This is a heavy hammer," and then giving her a plastic straw and saying, "This straw is not heavy; it is light." Give her a heavy object, and ask her to tell you if the item is heavy or light.

Credit: + Child chooses through tactile cues only (holding the objects while blindfolded) which objects are heavy and which are light.

Adaptations

When some children are asked to estimate differences in weight, they will make this determination by a single variable, especially if the items are the same size, texture, and degree of smoothness, even though blocks are made of different woods, and thus are different weights. To assist her: (1) Ask her to participate, using tactile and not visual input; (2) Allow her to utilize a trial-and-error method, and demonstrate this approach if necessary; (3) Limit the number of items involved in her determining weight; (4) Begin the comparison tasks with objects that vary in appearance; (5) Provide a method by which she can verify her conclusions.

4.118 Identifies objects through the sense of touch

Strand: 4-8 **Age:** 57-60m 4.9-5.0y

Definition

When he is presented with objects of different properties, the child will identify the objects by touching them. He will not use his visual sense to identify the objects.

Assessment Materials

At least five different objects, such as a block of wood, a foam ball, a walnut, a plastic bottle, and a potato. It is important for these objects to have a distinct texture, such as hard, soft, smooth, slick, bumpy, and rough. Be sure the child is familiar with the selected objects. A blindfold.

Assessment Procedures

Grouping: This skill should be assessed one-on-one with the child.

1. Ask the child to join you. Explain that you want him to identify an object only by feeling it.
2. Place a blindfold on him, and ask him to hold out his hands. Place one of the objects in his hand.
3. Ask him to feel the object and tell you what it is.

4. If he responds correctly, ask him to describe how the object felt and if he can think of anything else that feels the same way.
5. If he is successful, continue with the other objects.
6. If he has a problem identifying the objects, provide the following recommended activities related to the sub-skills: (1) Make sure he is familiar with and can name the selected objects; (2) Allow him to see all the objects before putting the blindfold on him; (3) Provide verbal help by asking questions such as: Does it feel hard? smooth? soft? (4) Place the objects on a table, ask the child to point to each item, feel it, and then name it before you put the blindfold on him and ask him to feel the item; (5) Take him on a "feeling trip" around the room or in a drawer. For this feeling trip, he should close his eyes and feel different objects in his immediate environment, then tell you what they are and how they feel.
7. After he has reviewed the sub-skills, repeat the assessment procedure as outlined above.

Credit: + Child identifies at least four out of five familiar objects by touching them, he will not use his visual sense during the identification.

Adaptations
See #4.100.

4.119 Cuts out pictures following general shape

Strand: 4-7D **Age:** 58-61m 4.10-5.1y

Definition
When she is shown how to cut out a general shape that is not less than 6 inches in length and width and is outlined with a line not more than ¼ inch wide, the child will cut out the general shape of the picture without physical assistance.

Assessment Materials
/*\Safety Note: Provide scissors appropriate for the child. Remind the child of safety regarding scissors.
Note: The objects on the four sheets of paper may be the same or each different.
Scissors that are the correct size for the child. Four sheets of paper with an object drawn on each sheet. Each object should consist of a combination of straight and curved lines, for example, a drinking glass, a loaf of bread, a tent, a ghost, or a rag doll. The objects should be not less than 6 inches in length and width and should be drawn with a black marker line not more than ¼ inch wide. Blank sheets of paper.

Assessment Procedures
Grouping: This skill should be assessed one-on-one with the child.
Level One:
1. Ask the child to watch as you use one of the sheets of paper and model cutting out the object. Exaggerate the turning of the paper to cut the different straight and curved lines.
2. Give her the scissors and a sheet of paper, and allow her an opportunity to practice cutting.
3. After she has practiced, give her a paper with an object drawn on it and ask her to cut it out.
4. Observe her as she cuts out the object, looking for: (1) The manner in which she holds the paper; (2) The position of the scissors--should be perpendicular to the paper; (3) The way she turns the paper in order to cut in a different direction, such as corners and curves; (4) Her accuracy of cutting on the line without deviating more than a ¼ inch; (5) The use of a forward pushing movement; (6) The way she begins to cut, whether she starts from the edge of the paper, cutting to the line, or pokes a hole on or near the line; (7) Her starting and ending points, whether she starts cutting at a single point and ends at that spot, or whether she makes several different starting and ending places.
5. If she does not respond or demonstrates a problem, the following is recommended: (1) Model how to hold and turn the paper; (2) Demonstrate how to start at the edge of the paper and cut until reaching the outline of the object; (3) Allow her practice time to cut curves, corners, and straight lines by drawing these figures on a sheet of paper and asking her to cut the lines before cutting an object; (4) Draw a single-line figure that includes curves, straight lines, gradual corners, and then exact corners; (5) If her difficulty is manipulating the scissors, provide her with adaptive scissors, either double-blunt with two sets of handles or self-opening scissors with cushioned handles that spring back after each cut. You can try wrapping pipe cleaners around the finger holes so the scissors fit more precisely. After she has experienced the above assistance and has demonstrated improvement, repeat the assessment above.
Level Two:
6. Observe the child as she uses scissors to cut an object during an independent work time or during an instructional activity.

Credit: + Child cuts out general shapes that are at least 6 inches in length and width, independently. The child stays within ¼ inch of the line and turns the paper to cut in different directions depending on the outline.

Adaptations
See #4.113.

4.120 Cuts cloth with scissors
Strand: 4-7D   **Age:** 66-72m 5.6-6.0y

Definition
When the child is presented with a cotton flat-weave cloth, she will use sufficiently sharp scissors to make a cut at least 6 inches long.

Assessment Materials
/*\Safety Note: Provide scissors appropriate for the child. Remind the child of safety regarding scissors.

Three pieces of cotton flat-weave cloth, scissors, a black marker, black dot stickers, masking tape.

Assessment Procedures
Grouping: This skill should be assessed one-on-one with the child.

1. On each piece of cloth, draw a black line 6 inches long and place a large black dot at the end of the 6-inch line.
2. Ask the child to watch as you cut on the black line, stopping at the dot.
3. Demonstrate how to cut the fabric by keeping the cloth on the table and a blade of the scissors anchored on the table.
4. Allow her to practice cutting the fabric by giving her a piece of fabric and asking her to use the scissors to cut the line.
5. After the practice cut, provide her with another piece of fabric, and ask her to cut it on the line.
6. Observe her as she cuts the fabric, watching for: (1) The manner in which she positions the scissors; (2) Whether she uses a forward motion when she cuts; (3) How she begins and ends the task; (4) Whether her cutting motion is continuous or made up of stopping and starting over; (5) The position of the fabric as she made the cut.
7. If the child demonstrated a problem with cutting the fabric, the following sub-skills are recommended: (1) If her strength to cut is an issue, use a lighter weight fabric or a sheet of paper; (2) Reduce the distance of the line but allow for at least two forward thrust cuts; (3) Place two pieces of masking tape on either side of the drawn line to provide guidelines for the cut; (4) Demonstrate and verbalize a cutting chant ("thumb up, push forward, thumb down, thumb up, push forward, thumb down"). Make sure the position of the scissors is perpendicular to the table and the fabric is between the blades; (5) Demonstrate the position of the non-dominant hand in holding the fabric during the cutting process; (6) Give her enough time to practice; (7) Provide her with adaptive scissors if needed.
8. After she has been involved with these sub-skills, reassess her as described above.
9. Remember that the goal is for her to cut the material, and insisting on certain procedures, positions and the concept of only one correct way is dangerous. For the child, this insistence can result in negative feelings of pressure to doing it right instead of the joy of creating.

Credit: + Child cuts at least a 6 inch line on a piece of cloth, independently.

Adaptations
Some children find cutting fabric difficult. Although they are able to perform the motor action of cutting paper, when asked to cut fabric, its loose texture creates a different cutting challenge. The visual-motor task involves anchoring the scissors and stabilizing the fabric. The child is expected to cut the fabric by modifying the process of cutting paper. However, in cutting fabric, her manipulation of the scissors is different and the control of the fabric with the non-dominant hand is a new experience. It may be difficult for a child to "unlearn" a visual-motor procedure, to "relearn or adapt" a motor process when the medium changes. You may need to provide additional assistance for her to achieve this visual motor activity. If so, follow these recommendations: (1) Demonstrate, and make sure the child is aware of the anchored perpendicular scissors position and how the non-cutting hand should hold the fabric; (2) Place one of your hands over her hand as she learns to hold and manipulate the scissors to cut the fabric; (3) Provide her with adaptive scissors, particularly the loop handle type that automatically open after each cutting and are adaptable to either left- or right-handed cutters; (4) Replace the fabric with paper, making sure she keeps the paper on the flat surface and she holds the scissors upright with the side of her hand stabilized on the table; (5) Draw a line on the fabric long enough for at least two forward cuts.

4.121 Makes fine visual discriminations, matches letters that look very similar

Strand: 4-6A **Age:** 60-72m 5.0-6.0y

Definition
The child will recognize all the letters in a row that are the same. The sequence of letters for him to match will be: 1) Uppercase open letters; 2) Uppercase round letters; 3) Lowercase open letters; 4) Lowercase round letters. The child does not need to provide the letter name or the letter sound.

Assessment Materials
Six paper strips 3 inches by 10 inches. With a marking pen, make lines to divide each strip into sections measuring 3 inches by 2 inches. Mark the first section off with a double line to designate its importance from the other sections. In Strip 1, first section, write the letter M; in the other sections write the letters O, M, V, P. In Strip 2, first section, write the letter L, and in the other sections write the following letters: T, A, L, B. In Strip 3, first section, write the letter D, and in the other sections write the letters C, N, R, D. In Strip 4, first section, write the letter t, and in the other sections place the letters a, t, b, h. In Strip 5, first section, write the letter g, and in the other sections write the following letters: j, e, r, g. In Strip 6, first section, write the letters Ss, and in the other sections write the following letters: Kk, Ss, Ww, Yy. These letters can also be printed on colored paper, cut out and then glued on the paper strips. Letter stamps also work very well.

Assessment Procedures
Grouping: This skill should be assessed one-on-one with the child.
1. Place the first strip on a table in front of the child. The first strip is an instructional strip. Point to the first letter, and ask the child to look at the other letters in the sections. Then ask him to point to another letter that looks just like the first one (M).
2. Continue this process with the other five strips.
3. Record the number of letters the child answered correctly and record any forms or configuration he had problems with (uppercase--open, uppercase--closed, lowercase--open, lowercase--closed).

Credit: + Child recognizes letters in a row that are the same from each of the following groupings: uppercase open letters; uppercase round letters; lowercase open letters; and lowercase round letters.

Adaptations
Some children may have difficulty because they can not discriminate the constancy of form. The letters may appear in various positions to the child, such as reversed, rotated, elongated, or incomplete. Strategies should include activities prior to letter-matching. Matching should begin with shapes in this order: level one--matching shapes that are solid, level two--matching shapes that are outlines, level three--open shapes. When the child has passed level three, a gradual introduction of letters can be made.

4.122 Draws a picture of at least three objects

Strand: 4-6A **Age:** 60-72m 5.0-6.0y

Definition
The child will draw a recognizable picture that includes at least three different objects. She will be prompted only if the objects she draws are not recognizable or if she does not respond.

Assessment Materials
Several sheets of paper, pencils, markers, crayons, nontoxic paint or any other drawing material. Several sample pictures with at least three objects on them.

Assessment Procedures
Note: It is important not to insist that the child draw a picture or draw what you suggest. Developmentally, she may not be ready and to force her could affect her enjoyment of being creative and expressive.

Grouping: This skill should be assessed one-on-one with the child.

Level One:
1. Give the child a sheet of paper and the drawing material. Say, "Draw a picture."
2. Allow for a practice drawing.
3. Give her sufficient time to complete the illustration.
4. When she finishes the picture, discuss it, and praise her efforts.
5. If she has a problem, show her a sample picture, discuss it, then remove it and ask her to draw a picture.
6. Give her sufficient time to complete her illustration.
7. If she has a problem drawing a picture of at least three objects, say, for example, "Draw a [house]."

8. Pause to allow her time to draw the item.
9. Say, "Now draw [smoke coming out of the chimney]" or "Draw [a cloud in the sky]." The second drawing suggestion should relate in some way with the first.
10. Say, "Now draw a [tree]." The third drawing suggestion should relate in some with the first and second.
11. If the child continues to have difficulty, provide physical assistance by placing your hand over her hand, and gently put pressure on her hand and guide it to draw a simple but recognizable drawing.

Level Two:
12. Observe the child as she draws a picture during free time or an art experience.

Credit: + Child draws a recognizable picture that includes at least three different objects. Prompts are used only when the objects drawn are not recognizable of if she does not respond.

Adaptations
Some children have a difficult time drawing a picture from memory. They may be unable to re-visualize what they want to draw; they simply cannot "see" it in their minds to reproduce the object. Often they may be able to draw part of the object, but they are either unable to complete it or they get the visual image mixed up with another object. These children need to move from image recognition to partial image recall to total image recall. However, drawing a picture has other benefits besides visualization; therefore, be sure the child approaches art as an enjoyable and creative activity. To address concerns regarding visual memory and visual-motor skills through the drawing experience may cause damage to the child's enjoyment of artistic creativity. You should work on the process of correction through shapes, lines, and letters, and allow the art experience to be an outgrowth of the remedial process, not the vehicle. A child with an inability to draw a picture often has a desire to create a picture like her peers. Show this child some patterns of various familiar objects and allow her to choose the patterns she wants, to place them on a sheet of paper and then to draw around them. It is important to remove the patterns as soon as she is able to illustrate recognizable objects.

4.123 Cuts out complex pictures following outlines
Strand: 4-7D **Age:** 64-78m 5.4-6.6y

Definition
The child will cut out a complex picture, conforming to the edges of the picture. He will cut out the complex picture without any assistance.

Assessment Materials
/*\Safety Note: Provide scissors appropriate for the child. Remind the child of safety regarding scissors.
Note: Coloring books are an excellent source of simple to complex pictures.
At least four pictures composed of more than one object that have straight lines, curved lines, and corners. Scissors that are appropriate for the child.

Assessment Procedures
Grouping: This skill should be assessed one-on-one with the child.

Level One:
1. Ask the child to watch as you take one of the pictures and demonstrate cutting it out.
2. Give him the scissors, one of the pictures, and give him an opportunity to practice cutting.
3. After he has practiced, give him another picture and ask him to cut it out.
4. Observe him as he cuts out the picture, looking for the following: (1) The manner in which he holds the paper; (2) The position of the scissors, which should be perpendicular to the paper; (3) The way he turns the paper in order to cut in a different direction, such as corners or curves; (4) His accuracy in cutting on the lines; (5) His use of a forward "pushing" movement; (6) The way he begins to cut, starting from the edge of the paper to the line, or by poking a hole on or near the line; (7) The starting and the ending points of his cutting--starting at a single point and ending at that spot or several different starting and ending places.
5. If he does not respond or demonstrates a concern, the following is recommended: (1) Demonstrate how to start at the edge of the paper and to cut until reaching the outline of the objects; (2) Draw a very heavy line around the objects in the picture, and ask him to cut on these lines; (3) Give him a sheet of paper and ask him to cut a slash, turn the paper, cut down, turn the paper, cut down again, and so on. Help him with turning the paper, if necessary. Give him another sheet of paper

and ask him to cut the paper in curves and corners. Assist him as needed; (4) Provide him with practice in cutting curves, corners, and straight lines by drawing these figures on a sheet of paper and then asking him to cut on the lines. After he has received the above assistance and has demonstrated improvement, repeat the assessment above. When the child is asked to cut out a complex picture and his developmental visual motor skills are not adequate, it is important to remember that he should not be expected to accomplish the task. Give him adequate practice in cutting different directional lines and simple objects to increase his developmental level prior to complex cutting.

6. When he exhibits the ability to cut on various lines, assess him as outlined above.

Level Two:

7. Observe the child as he uses scissors to cut an object during an independent work time or during an instructional activity.

Credit: + Child cuts out a complex picture, conforming to the edges of the picture, independently.

Adaptations

Some children have difficulty when they are asked to cut out a picture that involves complex curves, corners, and turns. The following activities are recommended: (1) Begin with a straight line, making sure the line is short, yet long enough for a full cutting stroke; (2) Move to a curved line, making sure the line is drawn with a 1-inch wide black marker; (3) Draw straight lines and curved lines that include the child needing to turn the scissors; (4) Locate a simple picture that has varied lines and ask the child to cut it out; (5) Provide him with adaptive scissors if needed, and model how to turn the paper to change directions. Concentrate on his two hands working together, one guiding the paper and the other directing the scissors, rather than emphasizing "staying on the line."

4.124 Puts together complex/interlocking puzzle

Strand: 4-6B **Age:** 64-78m 5.4-6.6y

Definition

When the child is presented with at least a 12+-piece interlocking puzzle, she will put it together.

Assessment Materials

At least a 12+ piece interlocking puzzles. Purchase these puzzles or make a puzzle by following these directions: (1) Locate a single-item picture such as an animal, a face, or a toy, or a multi-item picture such as a plate and a glass, a ball and a bat, a group of dinosaurs, or a nursery rhyme illustration; (2) Glue the picture on heavy paper that can be cut; (3) Cut the picture into 12 pieces.

Assessment Procedures

Note: Do not interfere in the fun of playing with puzzles and manipulating the pieces of the puzzle. Interference can lead to the child losing interest and not completing the project.

Grouping: This skill can be assessed one-on-one with the child. However, look for opportunities to observe the child putting a multi-piece interlocking puzzle together spontaneously during an independent activity time.

Level One:

1. Place the interlocking puzzles on the table in view of the child. Ask her to help remove the puzzle pieces.
2. Mix up the pieces and ask her to put the puzzle pieces back together.
3. Observe her as she puts the puzzle together.
4. If she has difficulty in this task, it may be because her eye-hand coordination skills are not functioning in a manner to enable her to place the puzzle pieces together, or she is experiencing a problem in interpreting a visual object when she can view only a part. She may also be demonstrating a concern in organization skills and is not familiar with a trial-and-error process.
5. To assist her: (1) Allow ample time for her to process the visual stimulus; (2) Use auditory cues to support the visual placement; (3) Place several pieces together, talking about them as you place them, and then ask the child to complete the puzzle and put the pieces in place, with physical assistance.
6. Reassess her after she has been involved in some of the assisted learning skills described above.

Level Two:

7. Observe the child as she completes a puzzle during work time at a learning center or while she is involved in an group instructional period.

Credit: + Child puts together a complex interlocking puzzle with at least 12-pieces, independently.

Adaptations

A child may have difficulty putting a puzzle together due to a developmental delay in visual motor coordination, a problem dealing with parts creating a whole, a need for organizational structure, not understanding the process of trial-and-error, and a lack of visual association when only a segment is exposed.

To assist this child, it is important to: (1) Include verbal description and direction when she is putting the puzzle together; (2) Make sure she is aware of what the total object looks like before the parts are exposed; (3) Make sure she has plenty of time to visually assimilate the parts and put them together; (4) Make sure the puzzle pictures something she is familiar with and possesses a visual image of it; (5) When selecting a puzzle to address the concern of parts relative to a whole, choose one that pictures an object that has identifiable parts; (6) Expose her to giant floor puzzles, which are often effective, not only because of their size, but also because they are more easily manipulated and lend themselves to the support of a group activity; (7) Make sure she has ample time to apply a trial-and-error approach to piece placement.

4.125 Identifies look-alike words correctly

Strand: 4-6A **Age:** 65-72m 5.5-6.0y

Definition

Note: *He does not have to read the words.*
The child will match words that are visually alike. He will match words that are very different in configuration. Next he will match words that are similar in configuration. Finally, he will be asked to match words that are identical from a field of four words.

Assessment Materials

Six paper strips 3 inches by 10 inches. With a marking pen, make lines to divide the strips into sections measuring 3 inches by 2 inches. Mark the first section off with a double line to designate its importance from the other sections. In Strip 1, first section, print the word "ball;" in the other sections print the words "pat," "him," "ball," "sun." In Strip 2, first section, print the word "make;" in the other sections print the words "tape," "make," "seat," "play." In Strip 3, first section, print the word "little;" in the other sections print the words "matter," "apple," "dollar," "little." In Strip 4, first section, print the word "cat;" in the other sections print the words "cat," "rat," "car" "cot." In Strip 5, first section, print the word "ride," in the other sections print the words "hide," "rode," "ride," "side." In Strip 6, first section, print the word "funny ;" in the other sections print the words "sunny," "funny," "fuzzy," "runner." The words should be printed in the same color.

Assessment Procedures

Grouping: This skill should be assessed one-on-one with the child.
1. Place Strip 1 on the table in front of the child. Use the first strip as an instructional strip.
2. Point to the first word and ask the child to look at the other words in the squares.
3. Then ask him to point to another word that looks just like the first one.
4. Continue with the other five strips
5. Record the number of correct words he got. Also note if he had difficulty with Strips 1 to 3 (grossly different) or 4 to 6 (close visual representation). Record if he had difficulty with Strip 3 or 6 (two-syllable words).

Credit: + Child identifies words that are identical from a field of four.

Adaptations

Some children may have difficulty with this activity because they cannot interpret what is seen-- the ability to comprehend the visual representation of words. They may need additional time to process what they see and to learn to look for the details. The following examples may help: (1) Ask the child to trace the outside shape of a word; (2) Make a word puzzle for him to put together (write a word on heavy cardboard and then cut it into two or three parts); (3) Allow him to use color-coding to emphasis word shapes.

4.126 Builds 5-block bridge

Strand: 4-6B **Age:** 66-72m 5.6-6.0y

Definition

The child will make a five-block bridge after viewing a demonstration. The bridge will have an opening between the bottom blocks of no less than ¼ inch.

Assessment Materials

Five one-inch blocks, crayon or pencil, small ruler.

Assessment Procedures

Grouping: This skill should be assessed one-on-one with the child.

Level One:
1. Invite the child to come to the table and sit across from you. Explain that you are going to build a bridge with five blocks.
2. Build the bridge, placing three blocks in a line for the supports. Make sure that the openings between the bottom three blocks is at least ¼ inch. Cover the two openings with the last two blocks.
3. After the bridge is built, push a crayon or pencil through the two openings.
4. Dismantle the bridge.
5. Give the child the five blocks and tell her to build a bridge.
6. Observe her as she builds the bridge, watching for: (1) The way she proceeds to build the bridge; (2) The fine motor skills that are required to push the blocks on the table or to pick up any blocks for placement; (3) The manner in which she makes sure there is a space between the bottom blocks; (4) Whether her eye and hand coordinated to accomplish the task.
7. If the child had difficulty building the bridge, the following are suggestions to assist her in the assessment process: (1) Tell her that both of you are going to build a block bridge. Give her five blocks and ask her to place her blocks in the same way you place yours; (2) Draw three square outlines the size of the blocks on a paper on the table, and instruct the child to put a block in each outline; (3) Have an object available for her to use to put between the bottom blocks; (4) Place a small ruler on top of the base blocks to act as a support for the top blocks; (5) Physically assist her in block placement.
8. After the child has had an opportunity to be involved with these assisted skills, reassess as outlined above.
9. It is important to observe the assessment process, and if it takes away from the joy of playing with blocks in any way, the child should not be involved in the assessment process.

Level Two:
10. Observe the child as she plays with blocks independently or in a group situation.

Credit: + Child builds a 5-block bridge after viewing a demonstration. The bridge does not have less than a ¼ inch opening between the bottom blocks.

Adaptations

A child may experience problems when she picks up small objects and replaces them because she needs help in: (1) Using the pincer (thumb and forefinger) grasp; (2) Judging distance and direction; (3) Transferring visual information; (4) Understanding the motor movement necessary to align blocks on top of another.

Some activities to help include: (1) Ask her to use larger blocks to make a bridge; (2) Ask her to use textured blocks to build a bridge; (3) On a flat surface, draw an outline of the base blocks on a sheet of paper. Instruct the child to place the blocks within the drawn square; (4) Use interlocking blocks to build a bridge; (5) Put a ruler across the top of the base blocks, then put a block on top of the ruler, and adjust the top blocks to create a bridge; (6) Reverse the process: Place the block bridge in front of the child and ask her to take the bridge apart one block at a time. Encourage her to rebuild the bridge; (7) Add verbal directions to the construction process. Say, for example, "Place the red blocks next to each other, but not touching. The green blocks go on top in between the red blocks"; (8) Physically assist her in building a block bridge. Remember that the joy of building with blocks should be the main goal.

4.127 (Removed, see page xviii)

4.128 Holds paper with one hand while drawing with the other hand

Strand: 4-6A **Age:** 36-48m 3.0-4.0y

Definition
When given a piece of paper and a crayon to draw with, the child will take the crayon in her dominant hand and will use her non-dominant hand to hold the paper while drawing.

Assessment Materials
Paper and crayons.

Assessment Procedures
Grouping: This skill can be assessed one-on-one with the child or in a small group.

Level One:
1. Give the child a sheet of paper and his choice of a crayon.
2. Ask him to draw a picture.

3. Observe him as he draws.
4. Make note of the following: (1) Whether he held and used the crayon effectively; (2) Whether he adjusted and held the paper with his other hand; (3) Whether he applied sufficient pressure on the crayon to control his movements; (4) Whether the paper moved as he was drawing because he did not maintain control and stabilize the paper properly.
5. If he had difficulty holding the paper still, the following suggestions are recommended: (1) Demonstrate how he can hold the paper to keep it from moving; (2) Tape the paper to the table top so he can experience how much easier it is to color when the paper does not move; (3) Provide hand-over-hand support to position his hands correctly if he is having difficulty doing so on his own.
6. Repeat the assessment outlined above.
7. Give him another sheet of paper and a crayon.
8. Observe him as he draws to see if he uses both hands efficiently, one to hold the crayon and the other to hold the paper.

Level Two:
9. Observe the child as he draws pictures during an art activity.

Credit: + Child holds the paper with one hand while he draws with the other.

Adaptations

Bilateral coordination may not come naturally to all children. Through demonstration and practice they can learn to develop bilateral skills and begin to use their hands together more spontaneously. If the child does not typically use his hand together provide him with opportunities to perform tasks which require this skill, such as pulling a toy apart using two hands or holding a balloon in one hand while he hits it with his other hand. When it comes to drawing and writing, learning to hold the paper steady with one hand while you draw or write is a very important pre-writing skill. If necessary, tape the paper to the table or on an easel to demonstrate how to stabilize the paper. Demonstrate how you perform this skill yourself. You may want to ask the child to hold the paper for you when you have something else in your "helper" hand, using the opportunity to explain how holding the paper made the act of writing or drawing so much easier.

4.129 Cuts out a circle with scissors
Strand: 4-7D **Age:** 42-48m 3.6-4.0y

Definition
When she is given a sheet of paper with a circle, at least 6 inches in diameter, the child will use scissors to cut the circle out without assistance, staying within ½ inch of the lines.

Assessment Materials
/***Safety Note:** Provide scissors appropriate for the child. Remind the child of safety regarding scissors.

Four sheets of paper with a circle that is six inches in diameter and drawn with a line not more than ¼ inch wide drawn on each piece of paper.

Assessment Procedures
Grouping: This skill may be assessed one-on-one with the child. During an art activity, you can observe the child as she cuts out a circle.
1. Ask the child to watch as you use one of the sheets of paper to demonstrate cutting out a circle. Exaggerate the turning of the paper as you cut out the circle.
2. Give her the scissors and a sheet of paper with a circle drawn on it, and give her an opportunity to practice cutting out the shape.
3. After she has practiced, give her another paper with a circle and ask her to cut it out.
4. Observe as she cuts the paper, looking for: (1) The manner in which she holds the paper; (2) The position of the scissors, they should be perpendicular to the paper; (3) The way she turns the paper in order to cut out the circle; (4) Her accuracy of cutting on the line without deviating more than ½ inch; (5) Her use of a forward pushing movement with the scissors; (6) The way she begins to cut, whether she starts from the edge of the paper to the line or she pokes a hole on or near the lie; (7) Her starting and ending points, whether she starts cutting at a single point and ends at that spot or whether she makes several different starting and ending places.
5. If she does not respond, or demonstrates a concern, the following is recommended: (1) Model how to hold and turn the paper; (2) Demonstrate how to start at the edge of the paper and cut until reaching the outline of the circle; (3) Provide her with practice in cutting curves and straight lines by drawing these figures on a sheet of paper and asking her to cut the lines before she cuts out the curved lines; (4) If she has difficulty manipulating the

scissors, provide adaptive scissors such as double-blunt with two sets of handles, self-opening scissors with cushioned handles that spring back after each cut, or scissors with a pipe cleaner wrapped around each finger hole to provide a more snug fit on her fingers.
6. After giving assistance, repeat the assessment above if she has shown improvement.

Credit: + Child cuts out a circle with scissors staying within ½ inch of the line, without assistance.

Adaptations
See #4.96.

If a child needs assistance, follow these recommendations when she first begins cutting on lines: (1) Have her begin with a straight line; make sure the line is short, yet long enough for a cutting stroke versus a snip with the scissors; (2) Have her move to curved lines; make sure the line is drawn with a ¼-inch-wide black marker; (3) Draw a straight line, then curve the line, and include a scissor turn; (4) Demonstrate how she should use her non-dominant hand to guide the paper and tell her to watch how the scissors move the paper; (5) Provide adaptive scissors, particularly those with loop handles that automatically open after each cutting are adaptable to either a left-or right-handed child. As she begins cutting out shapes, do not emphasize, "staying on the line." Focus on the important skill of having two hands working together, one guiding the paper and the other directing the scissors. Be sure to give her practice time and encourage her to continue trying.

4.130 Places a paper clip on paper
Strand: 4-6D **Age:** 48-60m 4.0-5.0y

Definition
When provided with paper and paperclips, the child will place a paperclip on a single sheet of paper, or a few sheets of paper, without tearing the paper.

Assessment Materials
Paper and paper clips.

Assessment Procedures
Grouping: This skill may be assessed one-on-one with the child. During an art activity, you can observe the child as he manipulates a paper clip on to a sheet of paper.
1. Invite the child to join you at the table. Tell him to watch as you place the paper clip on a sheet of paper.
2. Give him a sheet of paper and a paper clip and ask him to put the paper clip on the paper.
3. Give him several opportunities to practice putting the paper clip on a single sheet of paper or several sheets of paper.
4. Observe him as he manipulates the paper clip and paper, watching for: (1) How he began the task; (2) The manner in which he coordinated his hand movements; (3) The number of attempts he made at placing the paper clip on the paper; (4) How challenging the task was to complete.
5. If he demonstrates difficulty placing the paper clip on the paper, the following sub-tasks may help: (1) Model how to take the paper clip in one hand while holding the paper in the other hand; (2) Then verbally talk him through your movements while you slowly perform the task. For example, say, "First, I take the paper clip in this hand (your dominant hand) and the paper in my other hand. Then I carefully slide the round end that has two half circles onto the paper, making the smaller half circle slide under the paper while the bigger half circle slides on top of the paper. Finally, I push the paper clip all the way onto the paper." (3) Demonstrate the movement a few times; (4) Place the paper clip partially on the paper and then ask the child to finishing pushing the clip onto the paper.
6. Give the child the paper and paper clips and allow him ample time to practice prior to reassessment.

Credit: + Child places a paper clip onto a sheet of paper, or papers, without tearing the paper.

Adaptations
Placing a paper clip onto a sheet of paper requires eye-hand coordination, motor planning, and patience. When first teaching this skill, provide the child with heavy paper or a thin sheet of cardboard and a larger paper clip. If necessary, help him with the task by providing hand-over-hand support. To make the task more interesting, give him different colored and sized paper clips and a variety of paper to practice with. As he becomes more proficient, give him a special job of paper clipping his art work together so he can take it home. Allow him to cut or tear pictures out of a toy catalog and have him paper clip them together. Give him a glue stick and paper to make a collage with the pictures he paper clipped together.

4.131 Holds pencil/crayon using a static tripod grasp

Strand: 4-6A **Age:** 42-48m 3.6-4.0y

Definition
The child will hold the pencil/crayon near the sharpened part using a static tripod grasp. The fingers make a rough approximation of a more mature, adult-like grasp. The sharpened part of the pencil is positioned with the thumb on the side and the middle, ring, and index fingers resting on top of the pencil. The child's wrist is straight and the hand moves as a unit.

Assessment Materials
Primary-size pencils, large crayons, and a large sheet of paper.

Assessment Procedures
Note: A child needs to be stable when sitting at a table, with their feet resting flat on the floor or placed on a footrest.
Grouping: This skill should be assessed one-on-one with the child.
1. Invite the child to a table.
2. Place the crayon in the center of the paper and say, "Please take the crayon and draw me a picture." (This allows you to see which hand the child uses to pick up the crayon and how she grasps the crayon.)
3. Observe and record the child's grasp on the crayon.

Credit: + The pencil is positioned with the thumb on the side and the middle, ring, and index fingers resting on top of the pencil. The child's wrist is straight and the hand moves as a unit.

Adaptations
Writing skills start with the proper grasp of the writing marker/tool (crayon/pencil, etc.) If holding the marker is a concern, the following are suggestions for remediation: (1) Make sure the marker is wide enough, as manipulation of a wider marker is easier for young children; (2) Allow the child to draw on a chalkboard with chalk or introduce an easel. It is often easier to draw on a vertical surface using large movements versus small movements. An easel would allow you the opportunity to secure a large piece of paper for the child to draw on; (3) If the child is having difficulty remember the correct position, there are aids available, such as a pencil grip.

4.132 Holds pencil/crayon using a dynamic tripod grasp to draw

Strand: 4-6A **Age:** 54-72m 4.6-6.0y

Definition
The child will hold the pencil/crayon at the sharpened end using a dynamic tripod grasp. The fingers have a more precise position like that of a mature, adult-like writing grasp. The sharpened end of the pencil is between the pads of the thumb and the middle finger with the index finger resting on top of the pencil. The ring and little fingers are flexed, forming a stable arch. The child's wrist is slightly extended and moves as the child draws.

Assessment Materials
Primary-size pencils, large crayons, and sheets of paper.

Assessment Procedures
Note: A child needs to be stable when sitting at a table, with their feet resting flat on the floor or placed on a footrest.
Grouping: This skill should be assessed one-on-one with the child.
1. Invite the child to a table.
2. Place a crayon or pencil in the center of the paper and say, "Please take the crayon (pencil) and draw me a picture." (This allows you to see which hand the child uses to pick up and grasp the writing tool.)
3. Observe and record the child's grasp pattern.

Credit: + Child grasps the crayon/pencil with a mature, adult-like grasp, holding it at the sharpened end between the pads of the thumb and the middle finger with the index finger resting on top of the pencil. The ring and little fingers are flexed, forming a stable arch. The child's wrist is slightly extended and moves as the child draws.

Adaptations
See #4.131.

5.95 Tells own age
Strand: 5-2 **Age:** 30-36m 2.6-3.0y

Definition
When the child is asked, "How old are you?" she will answer by stating her age. She may indicate how old she is by holding up the appropriate number of fingers as she tells the number.

Assessment Materials
A large sheet of chart paper, with four birthday cakes drawn on it with markers. On cake one draw one candle, on cake two draw two candles, on cake three draw three candles, on cake four draw four candles.

Assessment Procedures
Grouping: This skill should be assessed one-on-one with the child.
1. Invite the child to the sharing area. Show her the birthday cake chart. Talk about the birthday cakes, how many candles are on the cake, and how old a child would be if she had Cake One for her birthday. Ask her how old she would be if she had Cake Two. Continue with the rest of the cakes.
2. Ask the child how old she is.
3. Point to the cake that represents how old the child is at present.
4. If she has difficulty telling her age, observe whether her problem is because of shyness or lack of knowledge. If she appears to be shy in responding, try the following approach: Ask her if she is six. Pause for a response. Ask her if she is one. Pause for a response. (This questioning game should be fun and enjoyable for the child.) Ask her if she is three. When she says yes, respond with a positive approach, such as," I can just tell you are becoming a big three year old girl."
5. Later in the interaction, ask her how old she is. If she appears not to know how old she is, find out her age and say, "You are three." Show her Cake Three and discuss the three candles on the cake. Count the candles on the cake, saying, "One, two, three." Show her three fingers, counting them one, two, three. Say, "You are three years old." Ask the child, "How old are you?" Note her response. Repeat the fact and then the question, if necessary.
6. After she has responded correctly, ask her randomly how old she is.
7. Teach her that birthdays are important events, so she must be able to tell her age and begin to calculate birthdays with years.

Credit: + Child verbally states her own age correctly when asked. She tells her age, but can also hold up the correct number of fingers as she answers the question.

Adaptations
To assist the child, talk about how old the child is, how old their siblings are, and how old their friends are. When someone the child knows has a birthday, talk about the fact that, "They were two years old, but now they will be three." Talk about upcoming birthdays and the change in the child's age. When you discuss the child's age or birthday, do it in respect to events. Say, for example, "You are three years old now. You turned three years old on your birthday. Your birthday is close to Halloween and when we start to rake the leaves."

5.96 Plays with one or two other children
Strand: 5-5 **Age:** 30-38m 2.6-3.2y

Definition
The child will begin to exhibit adaptive behaviors and to play with other children by beginning to share and engage in a simple conversation while playing, but their play agendas may differ.

Assessment Materials
Two or three identical toys, collection of various small toys.

Assessment Procedures
Grouping: When you assess a child's ability to play with others, the most effective procedure is play-based observation. An observational assessment can either be spontaneous or occur in a semi-structured situation.
1. If the choice is semi-structured, provide the children with the same toys and observe the interaction.
2. During the observation, determine the number of times the child did the following: (1) Started an interaction; (2) Accepted an interaction; (3) Ended an interaction. Often noting the specific behaviors used can be helpful.
3. Determining what specific types of interactions to watch for leads to specific intervention techniques. Some suggestions for specific behaviors are: (1) The child started an interaction by: (a) greeting the other person(s), (b) asking for an object from other person(s), (c) beginning a conversation, (d) wanting approval, (e) helping the other person(s), (f) seeking affiliation; (2) The child

accepted an interaction by: (a) returning affection (touch), (b) returning a greeting (verbal), (c) returning a positive facial expression (smile), (d) answering back, (e) demonstrating approval, (f) giving an object when asked; (3) The child continued and ended an interaction by: (a) contributing to the conversation or terminating conversation, (b) continuing play or concluded play.
4. Analyzing to whom the interactions are directed is helpful in the assessment process, as the child may react differently when he engages in play with an adult, a sibling, a new child, or a special friend. Analyzing the situation in which the play is occurring is also important to the observations, as the child may react differently in a familiar setting, when a family member is present, when the environmental stimulus is active, in front of strangers, or in a structured situation. These suggested observational assessments address social behaviors only. Considerations for skill development such as expressive/receptive language and visual-motor integration are not included, but these do have an effect on any changes in emotional and social interactions.

Credit: + Child plays with other children (one or two) by beginning to share and engage in simple conversations during the play. The agendas of the children may differ.

Adaptations

Provide the child with opportunities to interact and engage with other children. When needed, facilitate the interactions by modeling appropriate behavior and setting up opportunities for the child to interact with one or two peers. Engage with the child, using toys that are of interest to him and invite the other children to join you in play. Also, provide the child with play opportunities with an adult that encourage the child to interact and help build the scaffolding that is necessary for the child to move from parallel play associative play level.

5.97 Exchanges items with another child during play

Strand: 5-5 **Age:** 32-38m 2.8-3.2y

Definition

The child will trade a toy with another child. They do not have to talk, and the other child should go along with the trade. The children may engage in independent play with the exchanged toys. They may or may not play together with the exchanged toys.

© 2010 VORT Corporation. All rights reserved. Do Not copy.

Assessment Materials

Two similar toys that are liked by the children, a timer.

Assessment Procedures

Grouping: Informal observation is effective because it is done in a natural setting without some of the variables that accompany a formal assessment procedure. However, if necessary this skill can be formally assessed in a small group setting.

Level One:
1. Give two children similar toys. Allow them time to play with the toys.
2. Set the timer for a short length of time. Explain that when the timer goes off, they are to trade toys.
3. As a teaching item, allow the timer to go off and say, "Trade your toys." If necessary, demonstrate the concept of trading.
4. Reset the timer and explain to them that when the buzzer goes off, they are to trade toys.
5. Observe the actions of the children.
6. Watch for actions such as: (1) The toy exchange happened without any unusual behaviors; (2) One child refused to exchange his toy; (3) Neither of them would exchange toys; (4) They lost interest in the toys; (5) They were busy playing and chose not to be interrupted to exchange; (6) Aggressive behavior occurred.
7. If the children had a difficult time trading toys, consider lowering the task levels in this manner: (1) Make sure they understand the concept of trading; (2) Compare the two toys by verbally and visually showing them how each toy works; (3) Role-play with one of them the act of trading the toy; (4) Assist them in the art of parallel play (two children using the same or similar toys or materials, but each is playing independently); (5) Help the child who is unwilling or unable to share by showing him how sharing brings approval and allows friends to enjoy playing together.
8. After they have an opportunity to deal with the lowered task activities, repeat the assessment.

Level Two:
9. Observe the children as they engage in a trading activity, and listen as they discuss the activity.

Credit: + Child trades a toy with another child. The children do not have to talk to each other or play together after exchange. However, the other child should be a willing participant in the exchange.

Adaptations

A child may be naturally quite self-centered; he hoards his belongings and often grabs those belonging to other children as well. When he is asked to share, he does not understand the concept, and if he does comply, he is probably just obeying, not being unselfish. He is often so absorbed in himself and his things that sharing is not a consideration. His self-centeredness may be caused by being forced to act unselfishly before he felt secure. When such a child feels a sense of security and develops an independent self-image, he will tend to become less selfish. To help him share, make sure he understands that his possessions are under his control. Once he understands the concept of "mine," help him comprehend terms such as "not" mine, yours, his, hers. The idea of sharing and trading is more difficult because it is the concept of "sometimes mine, sometimes yours," and that concept involves the idea of time (How long is sometimes?). When you are addressing this concept, it is important for you to control the time an item is shared or traded; this helps the child realize that his possession will be returned. However, avoid letting the child become too charitable, allowing himself to be imposed upon (often an attempt to win acceptance by using material objects).

5.98 Engages in cooperative play with other children

Strand: 5-5 **Age:** 36-48m 3.0-4.0y

Definition
When a child is playing cooperatively with other children, she should be involved with the two essential elements of cooperative play which include: (1) The goals should be similar; (2) There should be positive interdependence among the children.

Assessment Materials
An area that has adequate floor space for crawling.

Assessment Procedures
Note: In trying to develop the ability to play cooperatively, a child may make several short-lived attempts to be part of a group. If she is unsuccessful, she will likely return to parallel play for comfort unless she is provided with support to be more successful in her attempts to engage in cooperative play.

Grouping: When you are assessing a child's ability to play with another, the most effective procedure is observation of the child at play. An observational assessment can be either spontaneous or occur in a semi-structured situation.

1. If your choice is semi-structured, provide them with a collection of toys and observe the interaction.
2. During your observation, determine the number of times the child does the following: (1) Starts an interaction; (2) Accepts an interaction; (3) Ended an interaction. Often, watching for some specific behaviors during specific types of interactions helps you in determining specific intervention techniques. Some suggestions for specific behaviors are: (1) The child started an interaction by (a) greeting the other person, (b) asking for an object from other person, (c) beginning a conversation, (d) wanting approval, (e) helping the other person, (f) seeking affiliation, (g) initiating cooperative play; (2) The child accepted an interaction by (a) returning affection (touch), (b) returning a greeting (verbal), (c) returning a positive facial expression (smile), (d) answering back, (e) demonstrating approval, (f) giving an object when asked, (g) accepting cooperative play, (h) being selective about the situation and being selective about the place before she will accept an interaction; (3) The child continued and ended an interaction by (a) contributing to conversation or terminating conversation, (b) continuing cooperative play or concluding cooperative play.
3. Analyzing to whom the child directs her interactions helps you in the assessment process; for example, she may react differently when she is engaged in play with an adult, a sibling, a new child, or a special friend. Analyzing the situation in which the play is occurring is also important to the observations; for example, the child may react differently in a familiar setting, when a family member is present, in front of strangers, or in a structured situation. These suggested observational assessments address social behaviors only; considerations for skill development such as expressive/receptive language and visual-motor integration are not included, but they do have an effect on any changes in emotional and social interactions.

Credit: + Child plays cooperatively with another child.

Adaptations

Some children find that learning to get along with others can be difficult. A child who has not had experiences with peers may lack play skills. If she has played with older children, she may exhibit passive interaction with others because she is used to having others make decisions. Steps that a child generally goes through to move from immature to mature cooperative play are: (1) Solitary play--She chooses to play alone. She does not want to play with others; however, she will play in the same general area with little contact: (2) Observational play--She simply watches others while they play; (3) Parallel play--She plays with her own toys near another child who is playing with her own things. Little contact is made, and when they do visit, it is more "at" each other instead of "to" each other. The children take turns talking but do not necessarily talk about the same subject or respond to each other; (4) Associative play--Children play together, sometimes happily and sometimes otherwise. The child's attitude is that there is only one way and that everyone views things in the same way. These children have a very difficult time participating in any cooperative activity. They need to begin to relate to the views and actions of others; (5) Cooperative play--Children play together, sharing items, ideas, and goals. It is important for them to have many opportunities for play interaction to develop communication and planning skills, which leads to successful cooperative play.

5.99 Avoids hazards and common dangers

Strand: 5-8 **Age:** 34-41m 2.10-3.5y

Definition

/*\Safety Note: *This definition offers examples only; local program/family safety procedures should be reviewed to prepare a comprehensive list of dangerous situations/objects.*

When the child is shown items that are dangerous, such as matches, knives, medicine bottles, sharp-pointed instruments, or cleaning materials, he will demonstrate his understanding of the item's potential danger. He may express this by saying, "Bad," "No," "Hurt," "An ouch," "Stay away," or he may respond by non-verbal behavior such as backing away or shaking his head.

Assessment Materials

/*\Safety Note: Remind the child of safety regarding scissors, knives, cutters, sharp objects, as well as other items used to assess this skill.

Note: It is important to put each item in a secure package such as a heavy plastic container with the top taped shut so they are safer to handle/show.

A collection of potentially dangerous items, such as matches, a knife, a medicine bottle, cleaning materials, a sharp-pointed instrument, a bottle of something dangerous other than medicine. A group of non-dangerous items, such as a paintbrush, a thimble, a cotton ball, an eraser. Place the non-dangerous items in the same type plastic bags as the dangerous items. A large box to hold all the items.

Assessment Procedures

Note: It is important to explain to the child what dangerous means, using one or two objects as teaching items.

Grouping: This skill can be assessed one-on-one with the child.

1. Place all the containers in a box. Invite the child to the table.
2. Explain to him that you are going to place some things on the table and that you want him to tell you if they are dangerous or not.
3. If they are dangerous, he should say "bad" or "No," and if they are not dangerous, he should say "good" or "okay."
4. Show the child a bag with matches in it. Say, "What is this? Is it dangerous?" Pause for his response.
5. Repeat the above using a non-dangerous object.
6. Continue with the remaining objects.
7. Note his response and knowledge of common dangers.

Credit: + Child recognizes and avoids hazards and common dangers.

Adaptations

Some children have a problem with the concept of dangerous and not dangerous. A child may be unaware of good safety practices in his home because he is too well protected or not exposed to proper safety precautions. He needs to understand what is dangerous and what is not. He may also be overly and continuously warned of dangers, or he may think he will not be hurt by identified dangers so he begins to disregard warnings. Use a matter-of-fact manner, especially if you are dealing with a sensitive child, because scaring him about outcomes and gruesome details is ineffective. Such a child should be taught not only to keep safe within his usual surroundings and activities, but also to develop the habit of approaching the unfamiliar with reasonable caution. Caution can be developed without creating fear by making a children competent to recognize and deal with dangerous situations.

5.100 (Removed, see page xviii)

5.101 Sits quietly when listening to stories, music, television, movies, etc.

Strand: 5-4 **Age:** 36-40m 3.0-3.4y

Definition
The child will quietly listen to an audio, visual, or audio/visual presentation. During the presentation he will remain seated and quiet, except to answer questions or to make comments pertinent to the presentation and at appropriate times. The length of attending time will depend on different variables such as (1) The child's age; (2) His interest in the presentation; (3) The time of day; (4) Others involved in the activity; (5) Peer acceptance; (6) The antecedent that occurred to prompt the presentation; (7) The reward offered for attending.

Assessment Materials
Note: Musical selections are available from your local library.
An instrumental musical selection, (march, ballet, rainstorm sounds, dancing music, lullaby) and the necessary play-back equipment; some recommended titles are Prokofiev's *The Ugly Duckling*, Saint-Saens' *Carnival of The Animals* or *A Gathering of Great Poetry for Children*. A soft chair, pillows, or blanket, or a listening carrel, earphones, stuffed animals, a table tent. Books. Play dough or clay.

Assessment Procedures
Grouping: Informal observation is effective because it is done in a natural setting without some of the variables that accompany a formal assessment procedure. However, if necessary this skill can formally be assessed one-on-one or occur in a small group setting.

Level One:
1. Explain to the child that you are going to play a musical selection and that you want him to listen to it. Invite him to select a chair, a pillow, or blanket to sit on, and allow him to use a listening carrel or earphones if he wishes or to hold a stuffed animal if he chooses.
2. Play the selection and observe his behavior as he listens to the music.
3. Look for: (1) The child's attending behavior; (2) How long did he stay on the listening task? (3) Did he remain seated? (4) Did he demonstrate any aggressive behaviors? If so, what? (5) Did he move, sing, dance, sway, or hum to the music? (6) Did he become lethargic or fall asleep? (7) Did he exhibit any mind-wandering actions?
4. After the musical selection is completed, ask him how the music made him feel and what he was thinking about while he was listening.
5. If he did not stay on task during the musical selection, invite him to select his favorite book. Invite him to choose a chair, pillow, or blanket to sit on while you read the book to him.
6. Observe his behavior as he listens to the story.
7. If he does not stay on task during the story, give him a mound of clay or play-dough and encourage him to play with the clay as he listens to the story. Observe whether having something to manipulate with his hands helps him focus and attend better.
8. Noting his behavior during this listening time is not for ranking or grading, but for management and intervention strategies.

Level Two:
9. Informally observe the child as he listens to a musical selection or story, and observe his behaviors.

Credit: + Child sits quietly when listening to a story, music, television, movies, etc.

Adaptations
To sit still and listen to a presentation is very difficult for some children. There may be several reasons for this inattention: (1) Lack of interest in the presentation--His interest has not been developed, he has insufficient background information to create an interest, he does not view it as personal to him, or other subjects in the same category seem more interesting (e.g., action songs enjoyed more than lullabies); (2) Unawareness of the purpose of the task and what is expected of him--He was not told what to listen for, how to attend, and what to ignore.

He should be given specific instructions on how to act during the listening experience; (3) Overly active--This refers to children who have a high activity/energy level. Standardization of "normal" activity level of a child at a given age is difficult. The highly-active child needs clear and consistently enforced rules, as well as a structured environment; (4) Affected by group behavior--A child may often behave a certain way because of group reaction. He may assume a role that can create behavior problems, may be the group's natural leader, the clown, the one who takes the blame in order to gain group acceptance, or the instigator; (5) Short attention span--He is limited in the amount of information he can receive before he tunes out and seeks another activity. This time varies from child to child.

To assist a child with on-task behavior: (1) Create motivation prior to his involvement; (2) Explain the acceptable behaviors; (3) Provide a clear structure for actions; (4) Adjust the time to his attention level; (5) Modify the activity to include listening, physical activity, and discussion; (6) Allow him to assist in the activity selection process; (7) Permit him to listen in a selected environment (sitting in a quiet area) and/or include a fine motor experience (listening to music and painting a picture) or props (hold a favorite toy or enjoy a popcorn treat).

5.102 (Removed, see page xviii)

5.103 Requests aid for spills

Strand: 5-6   **Age:** 36-40m 3.0-3.4y

Definition
When the child spills, he will ask for help to clean up the spilled material using the proper sponge/towel, etc. An adult will provide assistance as needed.

Assessment Materials
A small plastic glass filled with ¼ cup of sand or cornstarch.

Assessment Procedures
Grouping: This skill can be assessed in a semi-structured activity or it can be assessed through observation during daily activities that occur spontaneously.

Level One:
1. Invite the child to come to a table. Place the plastic glass of sand or cornstarch on the table.
2. Tell him to pretend that the cornstarch or sand is water. Ask him to dramatize a scene in which he accidentally spills the water on the table.
3. Ask him what happened to the glass of water, saying, "What do you need to do now?"
4. Tell him to request help to clean up the spill.
5. Observe the child, watching for: (1) The words he uses when he asks for help; (2) The manner in which he deals with the problem (e.g., asks for help, walks away, blames others, cries); (3) The words he uses after the spill is cleaned up; (4) An independent attempt to clean up the spill. It is important to remember that social interaction and manners are closely associated with the cognitive dimensions of the desired behavior. He must be able to identify the need in order to select the appropriate social manners.

Level Two:
6. Observe this skill during the child's everyday activities, such as eating a snack or at lunch, painting with water colors, etc.

Credit: + Child requests help to clean up spilled materials.

Adaptations
A child may be reluctant or not know when he needs to ask for assistance. Possible reasons for this include: (1) He lacks the necessary expressive language to make a request; (2) He does not realize that he has a responsibility for his actions; (3) He chooses to try to correct his own actions, even if he is not successful; (4) He is apprehensive to ask for assistance because of past experiences. To assist him: (1) Provide him with experiences that increase his knowledge and expand his thinking; add words to these experiences to enhance his vocabulary. Remember to emphasize his development of cognition, which is the source from which verbal competence occurs; (2) Give him every opportunity to be responsible, starting with small matters and increasing them as fast as his development allows. Realize that you don't address teaching a child to be responsible by doing a task for him, even though at times you can do it faster and better for him. However, he needs to know that it is okay to ask for help. When he demonstrates responsibility and reliability, let him know that he is appreciated; (3) Allow him to do what he can, and not only what he can do well. Making mistakes is part of learning and becoming independent. The key is to let him try and to provide encouragement. However, he needs to know that when a

problem is too much for him, someone is there to help; (4) Make sure to give him positive feedback for effort and for trying. If he thinks the only time he will be rewarded is when he has done the task correctly according to someone else's values and standards, he may refrain from subjecting himself to any criticisms. When a child asks for assistance, give him support that helps him find his own solution.

5.104 Names a friend or a pet
Strand: 5-2 **Age:** 36-42m 3.0-3.6y

Definition
The child is presented with the question, "Do you have a friend [or pet]? What kind of pet is it?" and then, "What is the name of your friend [or pet]?" She will be given ample time to respond, and if she has more than one friend [or pet], she will be encouraged to tell the names of each one.

Assessment Materials
Pictures of the following: (1) Two children playing together; (2) At least four children playing together. Pictures can be located in magazines, catalogs, calendars, photographs; (3) Child with a pet

Assessment Procedures
Note: Be sure that she understands the meaning of the word "friend."
Grouping: This skill can be assessed one-on-one with the child.
1. Show the child the picture of two children playing together.
2. Discuss what they are playing, that they appear to be having a good time, and that they are friends.
3. Explain that friends are wonderful to have and are very important.
4. Ask the child to tell you about her friends, the games they play together, where they go. Encourage her to name her friends in the discussion. If she doesn't, ask her to tell you her friends' names.
5. If she has difficulty naming her friend, cue her by saying, for example, "You have a friend, and his name is Kent. What is the name of your other friend?"
6. Talk about pets with the child--how to care for pets, the fun of having pets, how pets help, and so on.
7. Ask her whether she has a pet. Talk about the kind of pet she has, a pet she knows of, or one that she wishes she had.
8. Ask her the name of her pet(s).
9. If she has difficulty naming her pets, cue her by saying, for example, "You have a pet golden retriever, and her name is Penny. What is the name of your pet cat?"

Credit: + Child names a friend or pet when asked for their names. Give the child time to respond.

Adaptations
When she is asked to name a friend, first explain what a friend is. Say, for example, "A friend is a someone you like to play with. Can you tell me the name of someone you like to play with?" If she needs additional prompting, say, "Your name is Andrea, and the friend who you like to play with is named ..." (pause for a response). Provide additional assistance by using visual cues. Explain the meaning of friendship by showing a picture of two children playing happily together or a child playing with a pet. Discuss the picture with the child, making sure that she understands the meaning of "friend." Show her a picture of one of her friends, point to the picture, and name her friend, saying, "This is your friend, his name is Dale. Now you point to your friend in the picture and tell me his name."

5.105 Responds to simple questions
Strand: 5-7 **Age:** 36-42m 3.0-3.6y

Definition
When the child is presented with a question, he will answer/respond correctly.

Assessment Materials
Several concrete questions that can be answered correctly by the child.

Assessment Procedures
Grouping: This skill can be formally assessed one-on-one with the child or informally during a cooperative activity or game.
<u>Level One:</u>
1. Examples: (1) Do you like to play outside? (2) Do you like ice cream? (3) Do you like puppies? (Questions 1 through 3 can be answered by saying "yes" or "no.") (4) What color do you like the best? (5) Where would you like to go on a picnic? (6) What is your favorite toy? Why? (The questions 4 through 6 must be answered with at least one word, phrase or sentence.)

2. Tell the child that you are going to ask him some questions and that you want him to answer them any way he chooses.
3. Begin by asking the yes- or no-type questions (1-3), and then move to the questions that require single word, or short phrase, answers (4-6).
4. Note his responses.
5. If he has difficulty with the responses, evaluate the questions to be sure they are within the child's experiential level so that he is capable of answering.
6. If the questions are within the realm of his information, provide cues to assist in the response. Examples: How old are you? Ask him to hold up his hand and count out the fingers that show his age. Repeat the question. Count his fingers if necessary. Repeat the question.

Level Two:

7. When you are doing a cooperative activity or playing a game, ask the child questions pertaining to the concepts. Examples: As he is putting a puzzle together with you, ask questions such as, "Where does this piece go?" "Have you ever put this puzzle together?" or "What do you think the picture will be when we are finished?"
8. During game time, give the child an item to hide. After he hides the object, try to find it. Ask him questions such as, "What did you hide?" "Did you hide it by the book?" or "Am I getting close?"
9. During the more informal assessment, note his responses to the questions that are integrated into the activity.

Credit: + Child responds correctly to simple questions (yes/no questions and questions that require at least a one word response, phrase or sentence).

Adaptations

If a child has a misconception about his world, this misconception is often related to experience and cognitive development. Without basic knowledge, he may not be able to answer specific questions. For example: Question-- "How old are you?" Answer--"I'm not old; I am little." (inability to comprehend the meaning of the question) or "I don't have to tell you." (inadequate social language behaviors); Question--"Do you have a brother?" Answer-- "Yes"; Question--"And does he have a brother?" Answer--"No, I am my brother." (inability to apply associations) or Answer--"Yes, but he hits me all the time." (inadequate social responses).

These type of answers often indicate a need for the child to be offered broader experiences. And during these experiences, it is important to talk, to describe, to model, to link, and to provide him with a process of using information so he is able to sequence events into thought classification patterns and to understand the importance of acceptable social language.

5.106 (Removed, see page xviii)

5.107 Practices safe procedures when riding in a car

Strand: 5-8 **Age:** 36-48m 3.0-4.0y

Definition

/**Important Safety Note:* This definition is not exhaustive. Be sure to check your state's motor vehicle safety code for complete car-safety procedures. Also, prior to the child independently demonstrating this skill, remind parents and all drivers of their responsibility to properly place infants/young children in approved car seats (based on age and weight).

When he is riding in a car, the child will always properly be in a car seat (based on age and weight) or wear a seat belt, refrain from putting his arms or hands out of car windows, not play with an object that can be dangerous or is distracting to the driver, not play with the car door locks or windows, and will follow directions he is given.

Assessment Materials

Two pictures of children riding in a car. In Picture One the children and driver are wearing seat belts and sitting quietly. In Picture Two the children and driver are not wearing seat belts; one child is playing with a balloon that obstructs the driver's view, another child has his hand out the window, and child three is hitting the dashboard with a sharp stick. (Such pictures are available from auto clubs, highway patrol offices, your state motor vehicle or transportation department, police department, or you may sketch them.)

Assessment Procedures

Note: The child who has been provided very specific and consistently enforced rules about riding in a car will assume that these safe behaviors are a way of life and something that everyone does. A child who has not been exposed to car-riding rules or who has not had the rules enforced will be at a disadvantage when he discusses these two pictures.

Grouping: This skill can be assessed in a semi-structured activity with the child. It will be important to learn from the family whether the child actually practices safe procedures while riding in a car.

1. Invite the child to the table, and place the "riding safely" picture on the table.
2. Point to the children riding in the car. Ask, "What are these children wearing that shows they are practicing safe car-riding?"
3. Pause for the child's response.
4. Ask, "Why should we wear seat belts?"
5. Pause for his response.
6. Ask, "When should we wear seat belts?"
7. Pause for his response.
8. Point to the children who are riding in the car. Ask, "Are the children riding in this car sitting quietly or are they jumping around?"
9. Pause for his response.
10. Ask, "Why should the children be seated?"
11. Pause for his response.
12. Ask, "Look carefully; where are the children's hands?"
13. Pause for his response.
14. Ask, "What are safe places for hands and arms in a car?"
15. Remove the safe riding picture and replace it with the unsafe riding picture.
16. Point to the children who are riding in the car. Ask, "What are these children doing that is not safe?"
17. Pause for the response (e.g., "not wearing seat belts," "hands and arms out of windows," "not sitting still," "playing with dangerous toys," "distracting the driver").
18. Observe the child's responses, and if possible, encourage him to summarize--(1) Wear seat belts; (2) Sit quietly; (3) Keep hands and arms inside the car; (4) It is dangerous to distract the driver.

Credit: + Child demonstrates knowledge of appropriate safety procedures when riding in a car. Family confirms that the child practices safety procedures when riding in the car.

Adaptations

There are strict rules regarding safety measures when children ride in cars. A very simple procedure to enforce auto safety riding rules is to refuse to start the car until everyone is buckled in. The child will learn that the car does not move until everyone has cooperated with the safety rules. It is also important to let the child know that if he unbuckles while the car is in motion, the driver will pull over to the side of the road and sit until the seat belt is fastened. If there are exact rules when riding in a car, and if these rules are enforced and rewards are provided when the rules are obeyed, the use of seat belts and other car-riding safety rules will be learned. It is important to provide the parents with information on the importance of proper car safety procedures and how to enforce the rules.

5.108 Names siblings
Strand: 5-2 **Age:** 32-42m 2.8-3.6y

Definition
The child names her siblings when she is presented with the question, "Do you have any brothers? How many brothers do you have?" and then "What are your brothers' names?" Then she is presented with the following questions, "Do you have any sisters? How many sisters do you have?" and then, "What are your sisters' names?" She is allowed ample time to respond. If the child has multiple siblings, accept the names in any order.

Assessment Materials
At least two pictures of a family, to include at least one adult in each and several children, both girls and boys. These pictures may be secured from magazines, photographs, picture books, catalogs. Large sheet of paper, markers.

Assessment Procedures
Grouping: This skill should be assessed one-on-one with the child.
1. Explain to the child that you have some pictures to show her. Tell her they are pictures of families. Show her the family picture.
2. Point to the adult and say, "He is the father of these children."
3. Point to the girls in the picture and say, "These girls are sisters."
4. Point to the boys in the picture and say, "These boys are brothers."
5. Pick out one child in the picture and say, "I am going to name her Megan." Ask the child to point to Megan.
6. After the child has pointed to Megan, ask her to point to one of Megan's sisters.
7. Ask the child to give Megan's sister a name.
8. Continue with the other girls in the picture.
9. Ask the child to point to Megan.
10. Ask the child to point to one of Megan's brothers and to give Megan's brother a name.

11. Continue with the other boys in the picture.
12. Using the picture, name Megan, the father, the brothers, and the sisters.
13. Ask her if she has any brothers.
14. If she says "yes," ask her to name them.
15. Pause while she names her brothers.
16. Ask her if she has any sisters.
17. If she says "yes," ask her to name them.
18. Pause while she names her sisters.
19. Note her responses.
20. If she has difficulty naming her siblings, obtain their names from her records.
21. On a sheet of paper, draw a stick figure to represent the child. Draw stick figures to represent her brothers and sisters. If her brothers and sisters are older, draw them larger and if they are younger, draw them smaller.
22. Point to the stick figure that represents the child and say, "This is you, your name is [child's name]."
23. Point to a stick figure brother and say, "This is your brother; his name is Bill." Ask the child to point to the same stick figure and say, "This is my brother; his name is Bill."
24. Point to a stick figure sister and say, "This is your sister; her name is Jenny." Ask the child to point to the same stick figure and say, "This is my sister; her name is Jenny."
25. Continue with the other brother and sister figures.
26. Remove the picture and ask her to name her brothers.
27. Ask her to name her sisters.
28. Note her responses.

Credit: + Child correctly names siblings.

Adaptations

Learning the names of brothers and sisters who live in the home and have grown up with the child is normally a natural and simple task. The child hears the names of her siblings daily, and she probably was taught to say the names of her brothers and sisters at an early age. However, if her brother or sisters are much older and are in and out of her environment, she may easily become confused about the relationship, especially if her peers have siblings closer in age. If there are stepbrothers or stepsisters, again the relationship becomes difficult to comprehend, and the child cannot decide whether she should claim them as brothers and sisters. If there are non-relatives who are referred to as, "She is just like a sister," she feels unsure about the meaning of "real sister" and the meaning of "just like a sister."

Therefore, when she is asked to name her brothers and sisters, she may: (1) Refrain from responding due to the fact that she is not sure who is or is not a brother or sister; (2) Begin to name them and then hesitate, retract, or try to explain a relationship. Help her understand the various meanings of brother and sister. Children's books about sibling relationships may provide a catalyst for a clarification discussion. Remember that children come from varied environments and home situations, and that their home terminology may have different meanings. Consider the child's background, heritage, value system, and the language of the home.

5.109 Categorizes children/adults in correct sex group
Strand: 5-2 **Age:** 36-44m 3.0-3.8y

Definition
When the child is asked, he will be able to identify members of his family, and other familiar people, by sex. For example, he will be able to tell that his mother and sisters are girls and that his father and brothers are boys.

Assessment Materials
Note: Pictures may be cut from magazines, catalogs, calendars, or photographs and mounted on poster board.
At least four single pictures of young girls and four single pictures of young boys. Collect at least four single pictures of adult females and four single pictures of adult males. These adult females and males may range in ages from teenagers to senior citizens.

Assessment Procedures
Grouping: This skill should be assessed one-on-one with the child.
1. Randomly place the four single pictures of the young girls and the four single pictures of the young boys on a table face-up.
2. Invite the child to the table, and tell him that there are pictures of girls and boys on the table.
3. Ask him to put the pictures of the girls together and the pictures of the boys together.
4. Give him ample time to sort. Note his response.
5. If he has difficulty sorting the groups, place a picture of a girl at the top of the table, and next to that picture, place the picture of the boy.

6. Point to the picture of the girl and say, "This is a picture of a girl. Can you find any other pictures of girls?"
7. Ask him to place the girl pictures below the one at the top of the table.
8. Repeat this process with the pictures of the boys.
9. Randomly place the four single pictures of the adult females and adult males on the table face-up.
10. Ask him to put the pictures of the girls together and the pictures of the boys together.
11. Give him ample time to sort. Note his response.
12. If he has difficulty sorting the groups, place a picture of an adult female at the top of the table, and next to that picture, place a picture of an adult male.
13. Point to the picture of the female and say, "This is a picture of a girl. Can you find any other pictures of girls?"
14. Ask him to place the girl pictures below the one at the top of the table.
15. Repeat this process with the pictures of the boys.
16. Mix up the pictures of the children and the adults, and then repeat the above procedure.

Credit: + Child correctly identifies family members and friends, or categorizes photographs of people, by sex (girls and boys).

Adaptations

When talking to the child about another person, take advantage of the opportunity to state whether the person is a boy or a girl. When the child is sharing an experience about another person, ask him whether that person is a boy or a girl. Allowing the child to learn and practice this skill with you will only enhance his ability to categorize children and adults by the correct sex group.

5.110 Looks at person when speaking/spoken to

Strand: 5-5 **Age:** 36-44m 3.0-3.8y

Definition

In either a group situation or a one-to-one conversation, the child will look at the person who is speaking. When greeting someone, she will look at their face at least part of the time. She may or may not make direct eye contact.

Assessment Materials
A short story the child would enjoy.

Assessment Procedures

Note: It is important to be aware that some cultures teach children to lower their eyes when they are spoken to, and to counter this would be inappropriate.

Grouping: This skill can be assessed during an exchange the child is having with a classmate or adult. You may do this observation either in a group setting or in a one-on-one situation.

Level One:
1. Invite the child to the listening/story area. Show her the book, read the title, discuss the pictures, and ask the child questions such as what she thinks the story is about and who is in it.
2. During this discussion time, watch to see if the child looks at you.
3. Read the story, and observe if she looks at you when you ask questions about the story.
4. If she has a problem looking at you when you are talking, the following is recommended: (1) Before you talk, say her first name; (2) Before you talk, say, "Look at me"; (3) Reinforce her when she is looking at you; (4) Gently turn her face in your direction.

Level Two:
5. Observe the child as she is listening to another person to determine if she is looking at the speaker.

Credit: + Child looks at the person who is speaking to them. Direct eye contact does not need to be made, but the child should look at the persons' face at least part of the time.

Adaptations

A child may refrain from making eye contact because of shyness or cultural issues. A shy child may refrain from practicing social interactions; and therefore, she does not receive feedback to help her learn interaction skills. The result is that a child who has limited opportunities often becomes even more withdrawn and shy. When you assist her, it is important to provide her with positive, fun-filled experiences with others. One of the most effective strategies is to role-play different ways of behaving around others. Learning to say "hello," to smile, and to make eye contact are important behaviors to rehearse. Using a companion approach is often very helpful, for a companion can act as a model and can communicate behaviors to her. Once she feels comfortable, the child will begin to risk, knowing that her companion is close at hand, and she will finally transfer the support skills to other social interactions.

5.111 Remains calm if goals cannot be reached
Strand: 5-5 **Age:** 36-44m 3.0-3.8y

Definition
The child will accept a situation when the goals cannot be reached. He will accept this disappointment in a calm manner. If the goals change, he will accept the new situation, begin an activity to achieve the new goal, and display an adaptive attitude.

Assessment Materials
/*\Safety Note: Be aware of special diets and allergies before doing this assessment. Baking utensils and kitchen area with equipment for making rolled cookies.

Assessment Procedures
Grouping: When you assess a child's ability to accept that a goal cannot be reached, the most effective procedure is play-based observation. An observational assessment can either be spontaneous or occur in a semi-structured situation.

1. If your choice is semi-structured, invite him to help you make cookies.
2. Explain enthusiastically to him that he will make dinosaur and kitten cookies, by using cookie cutters.
3. Allow him to assist in mixing, stirring, and rolling the dough.
4. Remember to take special precautions when the child is around heat or handling hot pans.
5. When it is time to use the cookie cutters, tell him they are gone. Discuss the situation with him, and observe how he handles the change.
6. Continue the discussion by leading him into some problem-solving strategies. For example, cut the dough with other tools (water glass, jar lids), use a dull-bladed knife to cut the dough into different designs, or make cookie cutters out of heavy cardboard.
7. Assist him to accept the lost cookie cutters and move to a newly established goal.
8. Complete the baking experience.
9. During the observational assessment, it is important for the process to involve some structure, not for grading, but for developing a program or assisting the child with an identified behavior. Some suggestions to consider during the observation are: (1) When the child realized there was a problem in the event or activity, what type of reaction did he demonstrate? (2) Did he change his reaction when he was assured that there was a solution? (3) Did he assure others that the change/disappointment was all right and things would work out? (4) Did it appear that he needed continued assurance and reinforcement from another person before he could accept the fact that an alternative was planned? (5) Did he retain his enthusiasm when the new goal was established and implemented?
10. Observed behaviors are based on social interaction, but consideration should also be given to his cognitive level, receptive language skills, and attention levels. Another consideration should include the way he views the person(s) dealing with the problem, the setting in which the change/disappointment is happening, others involved in the activity, and any antecedents that occurred before, and any behavior that occurred during or after the situation.

Credit: +Child remains calm, and accepts a disappointment in a calm manner, when his goals cannot be reached. He accepts a new situation if the goals are changed and proceeds with a positive attitude.

Adaptations
Some children have difficulty understanding and accepting disappointment or change, and they exhibit varied behaviors in response. A child may approach daily activities methodically, limiting himself to what he is comfortable and familiar with. Therefore, when he operates within a structure, any deviation from that structure is upsetting to him; a change or disappointment creates an upsetting environment. He will likely withdraw, become overwhelmed with the unusual happening, and will have no idea how to deal with the disappointment. A young child, in particular, finds satisfaction in doing an activity himself and in his ability to perform, so when that is interrupted by change, his self-motivation may also be affected. To help a child deal with changing situations/unmet goals: (1) Provide him with different options to accomplish an activity; (2) Warn him in advance when you know there might be a change. Discuss various options that he might choose from; (3) Interrupt him when he is involved with a spontaneous fun activity, and assure him that he can return to

his task; (4) Let him have "acceptance/planning time" when he is confronted with change or a disappointment.

5.112 Shares toys/equipment with another

Strand: 5-5 **Age:** 36-44m 3.0-3.8y

Definition

The child will share her toys/equipment with another when asked. She will share her toy/equipment with another without being asked. When she has shared her toy/equipment, she will also establish ownership, limit sharing time, and display the ability to request the toy or equipment back.

Assessment Materials

At least two items belonging to each child.

Assessment Procedures

Grouping: When you assess a child's ability to share on request, the most effective procedure is play-based observation. An observational assessment can either be spontaneous or occur in a semi-structured situation.

1. If your choice is semi-structured, ask at least two children each to bring at least two things to the table that belong to them that they are willing to share. Ask each child to describe the items that she brought to share with someone else. After the sharing time, encourage them to play with the shared items.
2. Observe each child's behavior, watching for: (1) Inconsistent or unpredictable behavior: she selected the items to be shared, then changed her mind, and became unwilling to share; (2) Oversensitive or overreacts: she reacts when the other person does not "play with her toys right." She retrieves her belongings when they are not used according to her way; (3) Worried or anxious about the toys that she is playing with because they belong to someone else, and she is anxious about her things. This child may totally withdraw from the activity; (4) Over-generous: she uses her things to buy friends. When a friend enjoys playing with one of her belongings, she gives it to him, not realizing that this kind of behavior (bribe) does not really win friends. After the children have had ample time to play with the shared toys, ask each child to collect her own belongings. Repeat this assessment, noting any change in sharing behaviors.
3. It is important to remember that a child needs to reach a developmental level of social development before asking her to share belongings. She needs time to understand the feeling of ownership and possession, for she cannot share what she does not have. Requiring her to "be nice and share" may go against her own need to have something that is just for her. Respecting her right to share what and when she is ready shows you recognize her rights and gives her the security she needs to begin the experience of sharing.

Credit: + Child shares her toys/equipment with someone else when asked and also without being asked.

Adaptations

Some children have a concern about sharing. This is often based on the fact that "owning" comes before "sharing." A child needs to get the feel of ownership worked into her activities before she can let anything go. She is usually only generous once she knows that the others in her life regard special possessions as important. A wish to share with others can only be achieved in a situation in which the child's needs are understood and valued. Until she feels respected, self-centeredness easily becomes her social behavior, and she never enjoys the pleasure of sharing. To assist her: (1) Model ownership and sharing, such as saying, "You may use my blue crayon, but please do not use my green one"; (2) Before a sharing experience, tell her to select the items she wants to share and put away those that are not for sharing; (3) Explain to her that she has a right to say, "You cannot play with my new truck, but you can play with my red car"; (4) Allow her many opportunities to understand that sharing toys and equipment is much more fun than playing alone. For example, show her how playing with building blocks is twice the fun when she does it with someone else. Forcing her to share before she understands the full impact of ownership can invite self-centered behavior. Precious possessions are very important to a child, so sharing is often difficult to comprehend.

5.113 Shows independence from an adult

Strand: 5-5 **Age:** 42-54m 3.6-4.6y

Definition

The child will independently engage in an activity/task without adult assistance. He does not need to complete the activity but must demonstrate a comprehensive independent skill level. Example: Puts on his sweater correctly, but does not zip it up. Puts his toys in his toy box, but does not put the toy box away. Plays pretend with a friend, without asking an adult how to do it.

Assessment Materials
Collection of props for pretend play, such as dress-up clothes, empty boxes; play items such as toy dishes, dolls, pans, spoons; larger set-building props such as pillows, chairs, tables, curtains.

Assessment Procedures
Grouping: The most effective procedure when you are assessing a child's level of independence is a play-based observation. An observational assessment can either be spontaneous or occur in a semi-structured situation.

1. If the choice is semi-structured, the following is recommended: (1) Assemble the various props and play items in one area; (2) Invite the children to the prop area and leave.
2. Observe them as they engage in pretend play, watching for the use of props, establishing of a plot, and identification of roles. When a child moves from the protective environment of his immediate family, to the adults in another environment, he encounters new experiences and situations that require independent reactions. He may deal with this new sense of independence through pretend play, and he often pretends to be one of his own parents. He independently acts out scenes he has viewed and participated in--he cooks, cleans, takes care of children, goes to work, drives a car, talks on the telephone, shops, etc.
3. Pretend play helps him feel capable and independent, and through it he is able to work out unsure feelings. Also observe him as he independently engages in skill-oriented activities, an important individual achievement. However, these activities are often related to developmental growth, not on social/emotional growth.

Credit: + Child shows independence from an adult by engaging in an activity/task without the assistance of an adult.

Adaptations
A child may have a difficult time separating himself from his secure environment. He may be overprotected, often lacking knowledge, motor skills, and an understanding of social complexities. If every time he attempts an independent activity, he meets with failure, he is not allowed to try to complete the task, or he is met with negative reactions, he may soon determine that becoming independent is not a good choice. To assist him, provide as many experiences as possible that assure success, adjust the environment that facilitates independence (material at reachable levels, substantial educational/play materials, ample space for work and play activities, equipment and furniture scaled to his size, etc.), resist the urge to complete a task for him, accept signs of initiative, reinforce for effort, provide tips that will assist him to accomplish a new task and maintain a high expectancy level. It is important to remember that each child may demonstrate a different level of independence, depending on what skills are required. For example, a child with memory skills can be successful when he is asked to color a picture: he will get the crayons, paper, and pencil, draw a picture, and color it. A child with underdeveloped fine motor skills may find putting on a jacket, buttoning it, and putting on gloves to be a slow, time-consuming, and difficult activity.

5.114 Stays with group during an activity
Strand: 5-5 **Age:** 36-44m 3.0-3.8y

Definition
The child will stay with her designated group during an activity, until told otherwise. When she is involved in an outside activity (visiting a museum, attending a presentation, going to a park, etc.), she will stay with the group to which she was assigned, unless told otherwise. When asked to select a group, she will remain with that group until she is reassigned or is given an opportunity to re-select.

Assessment Materials
Pictures of a child not staying with a group. Examples: (1) A group of children visiting a zoo and one child is leaving the group. An adult is motioning for her to return to the group. (2) A child has a paper circle pinned to her shirt that indicates that she is to be with other children who have circles. She is taking off her circle, leaving the other children with circles and walking to another group. (3) A group of children are sitting on a rug listening to a story, but one child is leaving the group to play alone. (4) Two children are involved in a race (wheelbarrow, one-leg sack, arms linked) against two other children. One child of a team has stopped in the middle of the race and is walking away. If pictures are difficult to find, make simple drawings.

Assessment Procedures

Grouping: When you are assessing a child's ability to stay with a group during an activity, the most effective procedure is play-based observation. An observational assessment can either be spontaneous or occur in a semi-structured situation.

Level One:
1. If the choice is semi-structured, invite the child to look at one of the pictures. Discuss with her what is happening in the picture.
2. Ask her lead questions such as: What could happen to the person who is leaving the group? Why do you think she is leaving? What would you do if you were there? Have you ever been told to stay with a group? What did you do?
3. Continue by showing her the other pictures and using the same procedure.
4. Observe her responses, realizing that there are many variables that affect responses when you are using visuals and lead questions.

Level Two:
5. Observe the child as she is involved in an activity that requires her to stay with a group. Record any inappropriate behaviors that were exhibited, particularly those related to not participating with the group, leaving the group, causing trouble in the group, etc. This observational recording is not for grading or ranking, but to determine intervention strategies.

Credit: + Child stays with her designated group during an activity until she is told the activity is completed and she can go elsewhere.

Adaptations

Note: It is important to make sure that the child understands that staying with a group is the safe and secure thing to do.

A child may feel that staying with a group is confining, or she may be unaccustomed to it, especially if she has been playing independently or lacks skills in cooperation. She needs to understand there are specific skills and strategies to participate with a group. These are: (1) There are reasons for being assigned to a group; (2) Children in a group should have similar goals; (3) Children in a group should have positive interdependence. If she has not had enough group experiences, she may lack these skills. To assist her: (1) Take ample time to prepare her for an activity that requires belonging to a group; (2) Make sure that she understands the goal of the group activity and why it is important to stay with the group. For example, groups are formed so that: (a) everyone can participate on the tour, (b) no one gets lost, (c) everyone gets a turn, (d) members have a chance to share, (3) Make sure the child has a role in the group. For example: (a) first in line, (b) helps another child stay with the group, (c) passes out name tags, etc.

5.115 Speaks clearly without mumbling
Strand: 5-7 **Age:** 36-48m 3.0-4.0y

Definition
When he is speaking, the child will speak clearly and distinctly so others can understand him.

Assessment Materials
A tape recorder/blank tape or CD player, an object familiar to the child.

Assessment Procedures
Note: If he seems apprehensive about the tape recorder, remove it from view.

Grouping: Informal observation is effective because it is done in a natural setting without some of the variables that accompany a structured assessment procedure. If necessary, this skill can be formally assessed one-on-one or in a small group setting.

Level One:
1. Prepare the tape recorder for recording, and invite the child to come the table.
2. Place a familiar object (e.g., toy car) on the table.
3. Turn on the tape recorder.
4. Say, "What is this?" Pause for his response.
5. Say, "What color is it?" Pause for his response.
6. Say, "What is it made of?" Pause for his response.
7. Say, "Where do you find cars?" Pause for his response.
8. Say, "Where do cars go?" Pause for his response.
9. Say, "What can a car be used for?" Pause for his response.
10. Say, "Who has a car in your family?" Pause for his response.
11. Say, "Where do you like to go in a car?" Pause for his response.
12. You may stop asking questions as soon as you obtain a large enough sample of the child's responses to assess.
13. If he hesitates to answer the questions, lower the task level by reciting a series of words and

asking him to repeat them. Make sure the tape recorder is activated. For example say:
Slithery, slimy, squirmy worm.
Funny, fast, firm frog.
Cuddly, furry, fluffy cat.
Mangled, mushy, muddy mop.
Tingly, touchy, tickly toe.

14. If he has difficulty repeating the total series of four words, break them down to two (e.g., funny, fast--pause for repeat), then say two more (firm, frog--pause for repeat).
15. After his responses, play the tape recorder and listen for clear speech without mumbling.

Level Two:
16. When the child is involved in verbal interaction, listen for clear speech without mumbling.

Credit: + Child speaks clearly and distinctly so he can be understood by others.

Adaptations

Note: If you find a child persists in using varied speech patterns, consider a referral for a speech and language evaluation.

To assist a child who does not speak clearly: (1) Ignore his unusual speech patterns; (2) Use an "I" message. Say, for example, "Allen, when you mumble, I am sorry because I cannot understand you, and I know you have something interesting to tell me. Please speak clearly"; (3) Make a lesson out of the mumbling. For example, mumble to the child, making sure what is non-understandable would be important and rewarding to him if he could understand it; (4) Reward children who articulate clearly. Letting them hold a microphone and speak into a tape recorder, and then hear themselves back is an envied activity. Prior to any intervention, be sure the speech patterns are not related to an articulation concern.

The reason for mumbling may also be that the child is afraid his answer will be wrong. Rather than risk being wrong, he speaks so others cannot understand him. To assist him: (1) Be aware of his instructional level and his frustration level when you are expecting him to respond to questions or verbal presentations; (2) Expand on the words that are understandable. Say, for example: "You said _____ ; that was a good answer. Now let me help you with the rest of that question." (3) Make sure he understands that being wrong and not knowing is okay. Help him become aware that everyone makes mistakes and that everyone has to learn new things; (4) Refrain from criticizing him for his responses, and reward him for trying. If he

has been exposed to models that do not articulate clearly, his speech patterns may be an imitation of his environment.

5.116 Transitions from one activity to another at the request of an adult

Strand: 5-1 **Age:** 36-48m 3.0-4.0y

Definition

When the child is actively engaged in an activity of her own choosing, she can transition to another activity at the direction of an adult. She will maintain focus on the new activity and complete the activity before moving on to something else.

Assessment Materials
A set of blocks or a simple puzzle.

Assessment Procedures

Note: The typical school day has many transitions built into the classroom schedule. You can use these logically occurring transitions to assess for this skill.

Grouping: This skill can be observed naturally during the course of play by seeing if the child can follow the classroom routine or schedule and transition from one activity to another at the direction of an adult.

Level One:
1. During a play period, encourage the child to play with blocks in the block area or put a puzzle together at the manipulative table.
2. Observe her as she works. When you see that she is engrossed in her work, call her to circle time, story time, or snack time.
3. Watch to see if she transitions easily without additional verbal reminders, whether she physically needs to be prompted to stop what she is doing and join in the new activity, or if she comes to the new activity but has difficulty shifting her focus to the new activity and attempts to go back to what she was previously doing.
4. Note whether the child was able to participate in the new activity or if her focus was on what she was doing before.
5. When the activity ends, observe how she transitions to the next activity.

Level Two:
6. Observe the child as she engages in an activity with another child. Call the children to a new activity and see whether she can transition to the new activity without adult assistance.

Credit: + Child transitions from one activity to another at the request of an adult. The child transitions willingly and does not need the support of an adult to help her with the transition.

Adaptations

A child may have a difficult time learning to transition from one activity to another at the request of an adult. This is an important skill to learn because it incorporates the child learning to follow a classroom schedule or routine, as well as an established routine at home. There will be times when a child has to stop an activity they are enjoying because it is time to move on to another activity. Ways to help a child learn to transition to a new activity are: (1) Let the child know two to three minutes before the transition will be occurring. Pre-stressing her prior to a change gives her an opportunity to finish what she is doing so she can move on more easily; (2) If you see a child is actively engaged in building something or drawing a picture and there will not be enough time for her to finish, you can suggest that she put her building or drawing in a safe place so she can finish it later; (3) Develop a routine or schedule and try to adhere to it, knowing that changes will occur. When a change does need to occur, again pre-stress the child so she knows in advance that there will be a change.

5.117 Performs or attempts new activity

Strand: 5-1 **Age:** 37-42m 3.1-3.6y

Definition

When the child is asked he will attempt an activity he has not previously performed; however, the new task will involve motor, cognitive, and behavioral skills that he has. He will demonstrate adaptive behaviors that indicate an effort to try the new activity, and he will attend to it for a reasonable length of time; he will also demonstrate a trial-and-error approach, will ask questions to aid in doing the activity, and will seek support or help with the material, if needed.

Assessment Materials

An easy-to-roll ball, a box large enough for the ball to roll into.

Assessment Procedures

Grouping: Informal observation is effective because it is done in a natural setting without some of the variables that accompany a formal assessment procedure. If necessary, this skill can formally be assessed one-on-one or in a small group setting.

Level One:
1. Place the box on the floor or on a table.
2. Invite the child to come to the table.
3. Show him the ball and the box. Bounce the ball, toss it in the air, and throw it on the floor. Ask him to roll the ball into the box. Do not demonstrate rolling the ball into the box.
4. Observe him as he attempts the task.
5. Watch for behaviors such as: (1) Handles and looks at the ball; imitates bouncing, tossing, and throwing it, but he makes no attempt to roll it into the box; (2) Begins to roll the ball, but the ball stops or goes in another direction, and he does not go after it; (3) Begins to roll the ball, but he is distracted and loses focus; (4) Becomes frustrated and punches or hits the ball; (5) Is very careful to slowly roll the ball on a path to the box, displaying patience in moving the ball to the box; (6) Asks for help; (7) Begins to roll the ball; it stops, and he picks it up and starts over; (8) Tries to get attention by diverting your attention from rolling the ball to another subject.
6. It is important to remove the ball before the child becomes overly frustrated and aggravated.
7. Annotate the observed behaviors as he attempts a new activity. This observation is not for ranking, but for planning behavior change, management, and intervention strategies.
8. Model how to roll the ball into the box, and assist him to get started.
9. Note the observed behaviors as he attempts the new activity with directions and assistance. Determine whether the previously observed behaviors are demonstrated. This comparison is not for ranking, but for planning behavior change, management, and intervention strategies.

Level Two:
10. Informally observe the child as he is presented with a new task and a limited amount of directions to complete.

Credit: + Child performs or attempts a new activity when asked. He demonstrates that he at least attempted or tried to perform the new activity, for a reasonable length of time, using a trial-and-error approach. He asks for help when needed.

Adaptations

When a child is asked to attempt a new activity, he must be ready to understand that there is not just one way of doing things. He must understand that trial-and-error is a way of learning and that when a single trial is made and it is unsuccessful, another attempt should be made. A child may have a difficult time with problem solving. His thinking process is often limited to reacting to only one alternative to the exclusion of another. Therefore, when he is asked to attempt a new task without direction and demonstration, he tends to try just one way, and if he is not successful, he gives up. Or he will try the one way over and over, hoping that at some point his way will work. To assist a child to deal with trial-and-error and with learning to try another way: (1) Review a skill with him that he knows and can do in different ways. For example, toss a ball with a two-handed overhead throw, an underhanded flip throw, a front hand/back hand throw, and a side throw. Make sure to mention the fact that the ball can be thrown in different ways. Stating the various "throw" names often assists him in understanding the concept of "more than one way." For example, tossing a ball with a two-handed overhead throw could be called an "Uppie," or an underhanded flip throw could be called a "Flippy." Limit the number of tosses to which you give names, because too many names to remember may confuse him; (2) Demonstrate different ways to accomplish a task. For example, roll a ball into a box, starting near the box to make sure that the ball makes its mark. Invite the child to try rolling the ball in different ways; (3) Reinforce his efforts for attempting a new task, making sure that he is reinforced for trying, even if he was not totally successful; (4) Give him directions for how to do the new task; (5) A child may prefer to try a new activity when no one is around to avoid known failure; therefore, leave him alone to make the effort; (6) Sometimes problem-solving is more effective to do with another child. Let him work with another child, particularly if they are comfortable playing together. Remember that if he chooses not to attempt a new task, he may not be developmentally ready to do it. If you insist that he complete the activity, it may create frustration, inappropriate behaviors, and a diminished feeling of self-worth.

5.118 Takes turns

Strand: 5-5   **Age:** 37-42m 3.1-3.6y

Definition

The child will respond to a demonstration or verbal reminder to take turns during a structured game, when playing with others, or while waiting to use material. While she waits for her turn, she will demonstrate appropriate behavior and refrain from such behaviors as aggression, poor sportsmanship, pouting, or seeking attention.

Assessment Materials

A large sheet of white poster board, plain paper, markers, tape to attach to the floor, and five different colored sponges, each at least 3 ½ inches by 5 inches. Draw a scary creature on the poster board and cut a hole for a mouth large enough for a sponge to go through. Prop the Scary Creature up and place a tape marker on the floor at least 3 feet from the creature. (This distance may vary depending on the physical ability of the children.)

Assessment Procedures

Grouping: When you assess a child's ability to take turns, the most effective procedure is play-based observation. An observational assessment can either be spontaneous or occur in a semi-structured situation.

Level One:
1. If the choice is semi-structured, invite at least four children to play the Scary Creature game. Tell the children that the Scary Creature is very strange because it only eats sponges and since it does not have any hands, sponges must be thrown to it.
2. Give each child a sponge and tell them they will have to take turns standing in line to "feed" the Scary Creature. If a child throws the sponge into the Scary Creature's mouth, she gets her name added to the list of people who fed the Scary Creature, and if she misses she goes to the end of the line.
3. Demonstrate standing on the taped line and throwing the sponge.
4. Line up the children, and tell the first child to come to the line and begin the game.
5. Explain that the Scary Creature gets angry when a crowd gathers around, so everyone must wait for their turn.
6. Observe each child as she plays the game, focusing on how she takes turns. Watch for behaviors such as: (1) Being aggressive, such as pushing to get ahead in the line, throwing the sponge at another child; (2) Makes excuses for missing the mouth and takes another turn; (3) Pretends not to understand what it means to take turns; (4) When told to take her turn, she stops playing and pouts; (5) Tells the others how to play the game, how to throw the sponge, and how to take turns.

7. These observational behaviors and needs are based on social interactions, but consideration should also be given to the child's cognitive level, receptive language skills, physical development and attention levels. Another consideration should include the way she views the other children involved in the structured play, the environment in which the game is being played and variables that might occur before, during, or after the game.

Level Two:

8. Observe children as they play in an organized game that requires them to take turns. Record any inappropriate behaviors that were exhibited, particularly those that relate to taking turns. This observational recording is not for grading or ranking, but to determine program planning and any intervention strategies.

Credit: + Child takes turns during a structured activity or game and can wait for her turn in an activity or game.

Adaptations

At this age, it usually takes a child some extra time to learn to see things from another child's point of view. Taking turns is not a natural reaction for many children. A child who has been playing independently or lacks skills in cooperative play is especially unaccustomed to taking turns. The specific skills and strategies that a child must learn to play successfully and cooperatively include: (1) Learning to really listen to others; (2) Coordinating her movements, directions, and energies with others; (3) Adapting social actions that facilitate and prolong interaction with others in a play setting. She needs skills and ways to apply techniques to keep other children interacting and playing with her instead of driving others away. The most important of these skills or techniques are: (1) Talking nicely to others and commenting on another person's strengths, not weaknesses; (2) Sharing and taking turns cheerfully; (3) Including children who have not been accepted and finding a part in the playtime for all; (4) Helping other children when they are experiencing problems. Playing games is one of the best methods for a child to gain experience with turn taking skills; however, games do not have to be competitive, resulting in winners and losers. When learning to take turns it is helpful to avoid having winners and losers, but instead work together as a group toward a common end.

Often a child expects her wants to be met instantly, so that the concept of "wait till your turn" is meaningless. She is unable to see wholeness, because she gets so caught up in the details and is unaware of the total activity. A child who is at an early age of social development is not ready for any delay or waiting. Her view of the environment is composed only of her wants, demands, and impulses. She is unaware of others or their needs. To assist her: (1) Take ample time to prepare her for a new activity that requires a change in behaviors (taking turns); (2) Limit the time (few seconds) she needs to wait for her turn. Extend the waiting period as she adjusts; (3) Play team games that require the team members to take turns to enable her to view a unit working together; (4) Provide a reward for a predetermined waiting period.

5.119 Eats most foods in a tidy manner
Strand: 5-6 **Age:** 37-46m 3.1-3.10y

Definition
When the child is given food in a bowl or a small plate, he will use a spoon, a fork (regular or child size), and a cup (with a handle) with little spilling.

Assessment Materials
Note: Be aware of any diet or food restrictions before you select food for the assessment. A soft food (e.g., apple sauce, pudding, oatmeal), a hard food (sliced apples, cheese, pretzels), a liquid (milk, juice, water), a small plate, a bowl, a cup, a spoon and a fork.

Assessment Procedures
Grouping: When you assess a child's ability to eat foods in a tidy manner, the most effective procedure is play-based observation. An observation can either be spontaneous or occur in a semi-structured situation.

1. Put the soft food in a bowl, the hard food on the plate, and the liquid in the cup.
2. Give the child the prepared food and the utensils. (Make sure he is seated so he can spear and scoop the foods with his utensils.)
3. Tell him he may eat the food and drink the milk or juice.
4. Observe him as he eats the food and drinks the liquid, watching for spilling, mixing food, use of utensils, and wiping his mouth.
5. Remember that the objective should be that the child does not need to be reminded what to do.

Credit: + Child eats most foods given to him independently using a spoon, a fork, or a cup with little spilling.

Adaptations
Some children are not skilled in using spoons and forks without assistance and they will not be able to eat in a tidy manner. A child may not know how to manipulate the food against the dish to get it on the silverware. He may not know how to scoop the right amount of food onto a spoon, and he may not know how to spear or scoop with a fork. Not being able to handle utensils leads to spills, drips, misses, and dribbles. To assist him: (1) Demonstrate the use of utensils; (2) Provide him with child-oriented silverware; (3) Allow him to use a short, flat-handled spoon or an adapted spoon if needed; (4) Place the food in a dish that has a lip around the edge; (5) Select foods that are easy to scoop and spear; (6) If he has delays in his fine motor (grasp) development, provide physical assistance by using a hand-over-hand technique as you help him use utensils.

5.120 Performs new activities voluntarily
Strand: 5-1 **Age:** 40-46m 3.4-3.10y

Definition
When the child is presented with, "Who wants to [name of a new activity]," she will volunteer to do it, or when she is presented with a new activity, she will want to do it. When she is presented with a group of new activities, she will explore and perform at least one of them, as well as exhibit behaviors that adapt to the new task.

Assessment Materials
A variety of new activities, such as clay, finger-painting, building blocks, puzzles, games, stencils, pegs, beads for lacing, log builders, stacking toys.

Assessment Procedures
Grouping: Informal observation is effective because it is done in a natural setting without some of the variables that accompany a formal assessment procedure. If necessary, this skill can be formally assessed one-on-one or in a small group setting.

Level One:
1. Place no more than three new activities on a table.
2. Explain to the child that there are three new activities on the table.
3. Tell her she may choose to play any of them.
4. Observe her as she explores the activities, selects an activity, and plays with her selection. Watch for the following: (1) Explores the different activities; (2) Tries out the activities; (3) Selects only one activity; (4) The length of her attention span; (5) Use of the trial-and-error approach to the activity; (6) Becomes bored or discouraged with the selected activity; (7) Seeks help doing the task; (8) Withdraws from the situation. Record the behaviors that occurred, not for ranking or grading, but for program planning and determining intervention strategies.
5. When the child has reacted to the provided activities, remove them and replace them with three additional new activities.
6. Tell her you have placed three new activities on the table, and tell her she may choose one of them.
7. Observe her as she explores the new activities. Watch for the same behaviors you identified in the first experience. Compare the behaviors between the two experiences to determine similarities, consistency, reactions to new activities, and attention span. This comparison can provide valuable information for determining whether modifications of behaviors are necessary. It is important to remember that young children continue to grow developmentally and their skills across domains can vary.

Level Two:
8. Informally observe the child as she explores, selects, and performs a new activity voluntarily.

Credit: + Child performs at least one new activity voluntarily.

Adaptations
A child may have a difficult time voluntarily performing a new activity because she is either used to a structured situation, has not developed the cognitive abilities, lacks experience, or has limited experiences. If in the past, she had many things done for her, she may not feel a need to develop new skills because she knows things will be done for her. When a child is asked to attempt something for which she lacks background information, she may display different behaviors such as: (1) Makes other choices that can be accomplished based on her past experiences, including applying or altering her knowledge to the new task; (2) Becomes frustrated and withdraws from the situation; (3) Becomes angry; (4) Seeks a way to learn how to do the new activity. To assist a child in building

a "bank of experience" and to avoid frustrating behaviors: (1) When she is involved in an experience, discuss and clarify the concepts. For example, during a block-building activity, talk with her about how to pick up blocks, how to stack them, what she must do to move them; (2) When she is involved in an experience, be sure to put names and labels with the actions or the items. Labels assist her to apply information to a new setting; (3) Helping her try new ways based on what she already knows is a way to develop cognitive growth, as well as a way to avoid frustrating behaviors and to build her self-esteem.

5.121 Says "Thank You" when appropriate. Says "Please" with requests

Strand: 5-7 **Age:** 40-52m 3.4-4.4y

Definition
When the child is given an object he requested, or receives a compliment or a service, he will say "thank you" voluntarily. When he requests an object or a service, he will say "please" without being prompted.

Assessment Materials
Paper plates, napkins, snacks and drinks.

Assessment Procedures
Note: The observational process is intended to provide information for modification of an inappropriate behavior or for program planning. This observational process considers social interactions only; other skills such as conceptual understanding, expressive/receptive levels, and motor responses should also be considered.

Grouping: When you are assessing a child's ability to understand when "thank you" and "please" should be used, the most effective procedure is observation. An observational assessment can be either spontaneous or occur in a semi-structured situation.

Level One:
1. If the choice is semi-structured, have the bowls of snacks and drinks available at the table.
2. Invite the child to the table, and place the napkins and the small paper plates in stacks on the table.
3. Ask him if he would like a paper plate; model the request by using the word "please" to indicate a desire for the item.
4. Say, "Arthur, would you ask for a paper plate and use the word 'please'?"
5. Observe him as he makes the request, watching for such behaviors as: (1) Uses the word "please" appropriately; (2) Does not include the word "please;" (3) Refuses to request the item; (4) Verbally indicates he does not want the object; (5) Leaves the table.
6. If he uses the word "please," repeat the request by saying, "Arthur, would you please ask for a paper plate?" (no cueing).
7. If he does not use the word "please" in his request, repeat the modeling and the request statement by saying, "Arthur, would you ask for a paper plate and use the word 'please'?"
8. After he has requested the paper plate using the word "please," give him the paper plate; model receiving the object by using the words "thank you."
9. Say, "Arthur, would you say 'thank you' when you receive the paper plate?"
10. Observe him as he makes the request, watching for such behaviors as: (1) Uses the words "thank you" appropriately; (2) Does not use the words "thank you;" (3) Refuses to receive the item; (4) Verbally indicates he does not want the item; (5) Leaves the activity.
11. If the child uses the words "thank you," when receiving the item, pass him another item, and pause for him to say "thank you."
12. If he did not say "thank you," cue him once again.
13. Place the three bowls of treats on the table out of reach of the child.
14. Select a child to request one of the bowls.
15. Cue him to say the word "please" if he does not.
16. Cue him to say the words "thank you" if he does not.
17. Select another child to request one of the snacks.
18. Continue with the other children, observing their responses and encouraging them to use the words "please" and "thank you."

Level Two:
19. When the child is involved in an activity, informally observe whether he uses the word "please" to indicate a desire for an item or service and "thank you" upon receiving an item or service.

Credit: + Child says "thank you" when appropriate and "please" with requests, without being prompted.

Adaptations

Some children have not been given an opportunity to learn manners that involve social language. A child needs to learn the socially appropriate words to say, but these expressions are not always learned quickly. Most children learn social manners and verbal skills gradually, usually as the need arises. A child should reach a level of wanting to tell others that he appreciates what they are doing for him and to make others feel good. Probably the most important process for learning good manners is to be in surroundings where good manners are a way of life, not used just once in awhile. If a child is use to angry, raised voices, unreasonable demands, interruptions, and being told what to do without a "please" or a "thank you," he does not have an opportunity to view positive social manners. To assist him: (1) Set positive good examples; use manners with consistency, and make effective social manners a habit; (2) Good social manners should be practiced daily, not just as "when-company-is-here manners." When you practice good manners daily, they become a habit, and the child feels comfortable using them; (3) Provide a time to teach good manners through role-playing, dramatization, and discussions, and give the child opportunities to practice each newly learned manner. Address only a few manners at a time.

5.122 Assists with simple adult tasks

Strand: 5-5 **Age:** 41-48m 3.5-4.0y

Definition

The child will assist with simple adult chores. Her involvement will depend on her cognitive abilities, motor skills, attention span, interest, and her level of responsible behaviors. She will be allowed to select a simple adult task that she wishes to do; however, the options presented to her should be within her capabilities and at the discretion of the adult.

Assessment Materials

An adult activity based on the ability level of the child. Examples: (1) Clean the tabletops; (2) Pass out papers; (3) Clean the paint brushes and jars; (4) Rearrange the furniture for an activity; (5) Place material (books) back on the shelves, cases, or in boxes; (6) Pass out juice or milk; (7) Manipulate electronic material (recorders, computers, cameras); (8) Prepare material for rest time; (9) Distribute toys, playground equipment; (10) Water plants; (11) Simple cooking.

Assessment Procedures

Grouping: Informal observation can be an effective tool because it is done in a natural setting without some of the variables that accompany a formal assessment procedure. If necessary, this skill can formally be assessed one-on-one or in a small group setting.

Level One:
1. Ask the child to assist you in the selected adult task. As an example, the child prepares a pan of water and the sponges to wash off tabletops. After the adult washes the tables, she uses a towel and dries them. She cleans up the materials, and returns the pan and sponges to the proper locations. Observe her as she participates with an adult in the selected task. Watch for such behaviors as: (1) Shows initiative and does tasks without being told; (2) Needs to be told what to do and how to do it; (3) Stops before the task is completed; (4) Is distracted while doing the task; (5) Needs consistent reinforcement and reassurance; (6) Prolongs the task.

Level Two:
2. Informally observe the child as she assists with an adult task.

Credit: + Child assists with a simple adult task that she selects from a group of tasks presented by the adult. The options presented are within her capabilities and are at the discretion of the adult.

Adaptations

A child who feels incapable or uncomfortable doing adult tasks may feel this way because she has not been allowed to help. Not being allowed to help can give her a sense of inadequacy and affects her self-esteem. This is often caused by adults who find it easier to do a task themselves rather than letting the child do it for herself. When you ask such a child to participate, she needs to have: (1) Specific directions and demonstrations; (2) Ample time to do the task; (3) The opportunity to use a trial-and-error approach; (4) Reinforcement, not only for accomplishment but for effort; (5) Practice and opportunities to repeat the task. A child may view "helping" as a chance to seek adult attention. This is not necessarily a concern; however, the intent of helping should include the desire to contribute, the understanding of responsibility, and the learning of skills that will benefit her as she matures.

5.123 Comes to an activity when asked by a responsible person

Strand: 5-5   **Age:** 41-48m   3.5-4.0y

Definition
The child will come to an activity when he is asked; however, if he chooses to not be involved, he will decline appropriately. If the activity is in his best interest (his safety or health), he will be instructed to come to it (e.g., fire drill) immediately.

Assessment Materials
An activity the child enjoys doing, such as a puzzles, block-building, listening to a story, drawing, pretend play. An activity unfamiliar to him, such as a new game, an art experience, new block construction.

Assessment Procedures
Grouping: Informal observation can be an effective tool because it is done in a natural setting without some of the variables that accompany a formal assessment procedure. If necessary, this skill can formally be assessed one-on-one or in a small group setting.

Level One:
1. Place the enjoyable activity on a table, and say, for example, "Larry, will you come to the table and play 'Go Fish,'" or "Ian, will you come to the table, I am going to read a book."
2. Pause to enable the child to respond.
3. If he does not come, repeat the request.
4. Pause for a response, and repeat once more.
5. Observe whether he comes to the activity when he is asked, watching for behaviors such as: (1) He hears but ignores the request; (2) He explains the conditions he wants if he comes (e.g., "I'll come if I can be first," "If Ross is going to be there, I will come."); (3) He comes reluctantly; (4) He seeks additional information to gain attention (e.g., "Where do you want me to come?" "How long do I have to stay?" "Is it the same game as we played before?") (5) He hears but refuses to come, either by stating his refusal verbally or he does not act physically. If you observe any of the above behaviors, rather than addressing the action, the following is recommended: (1) Use "I" messages such as "I can tell you would rather do something else; we will miss you," or "I can tell you are not very excited about this puzzle; that is too bad, because you are so good at putting puzzles together"; (2) Ignore him, and continue the activity; (3) Ignore the attention-seeking behavior; however, be sure to reinforce appropriate behavior during the activity.
6. Have an unfamiliar activity on the table and say, "Daryl, will you come to the table and play a new game?" or "Christopher, will you come to the table and listen to a new book?" or "George, I have a new puzzle and I want you to enjoy it with me."
7. Pause to enable him to respond.
8. If he does not come, repeat the request.
9. Pause to enable him to respond.
10. Repeat only once more.
11. Repeat step 5.
12. It is important to understand that responding to verbal directions involves other developmental areas; the child must also have receptive language skills, auditory memory, and conceptual understanding. His reactions may be related to other than social interaction abilities.

Level Two:
13. Informally observe the child when he is asked to come to an activity. Observe any variables, such as the nature of the activity, the people involved, the setting, and who makes the request.

Credit: + Child comes to an activity when asked by a responsible person and he is interested in participating or when it is necessary for his safety or health that he come to the activity.

Adaptations
Some children are consistently disobedient. A certain amount of refusal to obey can be healthy since it suggests a degree of independence. However, when a child disobeys too frequently and with a high degree of intensity, it may be a time to address this issue. A child who enjoys disobeying may find being negative a habit and a way to get attention. He usually refuses to respond by being: (1) Passively resistant (whines, withdraws, reacts negatively, pouts); (2) Defiant (abusive, temper outbursts); (3) Power noncompliance (does the opposite on purpose with an "I'll show you" attitude).

Assist this child before he resists every request: (1) Make sure that when you make a request, he knows exactly what to do and when to do it. (e.g., "I want you to come to the table right away."); (2) Make sure he knows why he is being asked to respond (e.g., "We need you to help make clay pots."); (3) Give the directive in such a manner that he realizes that he is expected to respond (e.g., "Aaron, please come to the table and work with the clay."), and say it in a firm no-nonsense presentation; (4) When he arrives at the table, reinforce his obedience; (5) As he begins to respond positively, give him an opportunity to demonstrate positive social reactions.

5.124 Waits for turn at least two times
Strand: 5-5 **Age:** 42-54m 3.6-4.6y

Definition
The child will respond to a demonstration or verbal reminder to take turns during a structured game, when playing with others, or waiting to use material. While waiting for her turn, she will demonstrate appropriate behavior and refrain from behaviors such as aggression, poor sportsmanship, pouting, seeking attention, wanting power. She will wait at least two times before having her turn.

Assessment Procedures
See #5.118 for assessment materials and procedures, as well as suggested adaptations. This skill is almost identical to #5.118 except the child has to wait at least two times before having her turn.

5.125 Says "Hello" and "Good-Bye" at correct times
Strand: 5-7 **Age:** 36-48m 3.0-4.0y

Definition
When the child arrives at a location, he will respond to and will give the correct verbal greeting (e.g., "Hello," "Hi," or "Hi, how are you?") to the persons in attendance. When he leaves a location, he will respond to and make the correct verbal farewell (e.g., "Good-Bye," "Bye," "Good-Bye, it was good to see you.") to those in attendance. Prompting may be necessary; however, it should be faded as early as possible. Likewise, if others arrive at or leave his location, the child will say "hello" or "good-bye" appropriately.

Assessment Materials
At least four pictures, two of them illustrating someone saying "hello," and these two pictures should depict different settings. The other two pictures illustrating someone saying "good-bye," with each of the two depicting a different setting. Cut pictures from magazines, newspapers, or photographs or make line drawings.

Assessment Procedures
Note: This assessment is designed to address social language; consideration for skill development such as expressive/receptive levels, conceptual understanding, and motor responses are not included but needs to be taken into consideration.

Grouping: Informal observation is a very effective assessment tool because it is done in a natural setting without some of the variables that accompany formal assessment procedure. If necessary, this skill can formally be assessed one-on-one or in a small group setting.

Level One:
1. Invite the child to join you at the table. Explain to him that you are going to show him a picture and that you want him to look at it carefully.
2. After he has a chance to look at it, point to the person(s) who is probably saying "hello" or "hi" and say, "What do you think this person is saying?"
3. Pause for him to respond.
4. Observe his response, watching for: (1) Correct response (e.g., "Hello," "Hi," "Hi there," "Hi, how are you?", or "hello" in the language spoken in the child's home); (2) Made no verbal response; (3) An inappropriate response; (4) Appeared not to understand what was expected.
5. Explain to the child that you are going to show him another picture and that you want him to look at it carefully.
6. After he has a chance to look at it, point to the person(s) who is probably saying "good-bye" and say, "What do you think this person is saying?"
7. Pause for him to respond.
8. Observe his response, watching for: (1) Correct response ("Good-bye," "Bye," "So Long," or "good-bye" in the language spoken in the child's home); (2) Made no verbal response; (3) An inappropriate response; (4) Appeared not to understand what was expected.
9. Continue with the other two pictures.

Level Two:
10. Observe the child when he is in a position to say good-bye or hello at the appropriate time.

Credit: + Child says "Hello" and "Good-Bye" at the correct times. Prompting may be necessary, but should be faded as soon as possible.

Adaptations

Some children may not be aware of the specific language courtesies involved with greeting behaviors. (Also, some children are hesitant to express themselves due to shyness.) If the child is unaware of the appropriate language, provide her with models and many opportunities to hear other people using words relative to greetings. Remember that requiring her to respond one certain way is not appropriate. Instead, she should be exposed to different verbal greetings and non-verbal reactions, and then be encouraged to use them. A child who is hesitant to express herself may lack self-confidence and not feel comfortable enough to extend a greeting. It is important to explain and demonstrate verbal greetings and nonverbal actions. This explanation should be done in an accepting, caring manner, by encouraging a response but not expecting more than she is ready for. Role-playing and walking her through an upcoming situation are effective techniques for helping her feel confident and secure.

5.126 Tries again when a change or disappointment occurs

Strand: 5-1   **Age:** 42-46m 3.6-3.10y

Definition
The child will try an activity again after a proper length of time has lapsed. During this recovery period, she will be reassured and reinforced for her efforts, ability, approximation, and patience.

Assessment Materials
Block stacking set, building blocks, balloons, puzzles.

Assessment Procedures
Grouping: The most effective procedure when you assess a child's ability to continue an activity when there has been a change or a disappointment in that activity, is observation. This informal assessment can either be spontaneously or occur in a semi-structured situation.

1. If your choice is semi-structured, some suggestions are: (1) Give her a stacking set, but keep out one of the tiers; (2) Encourage her to build with blocks, using a limited supply; (3) Set up a balloon game for her, such as volleyball balloon. If a balloon breaks, she will need to stop playing and wait for you to blow up another balloon, tie it at the end, and put it into play.

2. It is important for your observation process to involve some structure, not for grading, but for program planning and individual intervention strategies. Some suggestions to consider during the observation are: (1) Did the child go back to the activity after the change or disappointment?; (2) After she went back to the activity, did she adjust to the change or disappointment by attempting a new technique?; (3) If her first attempt did not work, did she give up or try another approach?; (4) If she did not go back to the activity, what behaviors did she exhibit?; (5) When the change or disappointment occurred, how did she react?; (6) Did she seek another activity rather than return to the disappointing task?

3. Some suggestions for dealing with the observed behaviors are: (1) Verbally encourage her to return to the task; (2) Give her some suggestions on how to deal with the change and disappointment; (3) If she reacts aggressively, provide her with a cooling-off period, an opportunity to return to the task with some suggestions for action, and be prepared to offer an alternative if she becomes upset again; (4) If she reacts by destroying or affecting the materials for the activity, collect the material, and use an "I" message with her. The "I" message should have four parts: (a) describe the disruptive behavior; (b) tell how it makes you feel; (c) tell the effect her behavior has on others; (d) state a firm, descriptive request. For example, say, "When you poke your neighbor, I become upset because we all forget what we are doing. Please stop poking your neighbor right now;" (e) if she blames herself for the change or disappointment, discuss what occurred and the cause, making sure she understands, and then provide her with an experience you know will be successful.

4. Analyzing to whom the interactions are directed is helpful in the assessment process, because the child may react differently when she is engaged in play with an adult, a sibling, a new child, or a special friend. Analyzing the situation in which the play is occurring may also be important to the observations, because the child may react differently in a familiar setting, when a family member is present, when the environment is active, in front of strangers, or in a structured situation.

Credit: + Child tries an activity again when a change or disappointment has occurred. The length of time to wait is determined by the assessor. Reassure the child for her efforts and patience, and reinforce her for trying.

Adaptations

A child may have a short attention span and be overly affected by surrounding stimuli. She has the ability to stay on task if she is motivated, if she is successful, and if she does not have a lot of distractions. As she matures, her attention span increases and she is less affected by other factors; however, if she is unmotivated or is not successful at the task, her attention is reduced. She may also have a tendency to stop an activity if there is an interruption, and she may not return to it because the motivation is gone and the success level is diminished. To assist her, help her maintain a feeling of success when challenges occur and determine ways to begin an activity again. The following are recommended: (1) Break the accomplishment of the activity into steps, and help her achieve each step; (2) Allow her to take breaks, and when she resumes the task, review what she did and what she needs to do next; (3) Assist her in determining different ways to do the activity; (4) Assist her in determining which of the various ways to do the activity she will choose; (5) Reinforce her when she attempts to complete or completes each step of the task and reinforce her when she renews her motivation to accomplish the activity after an interruption.

5.127 Quiets down after active period

Strand: 5-4 **Age:** 42-46m 3.6-3.10y

Definition

After active play, the child will sit down, remain seated, stop talking loudly, refrain from physical play, keep his hands and feet to himself, and present a relaxed manner.

Assessment Procedures

Grouping: The most effective procedure when you assess a child's ability to modulate his behavior and quiet down after an active period is through observation. This informal assessment can either be spontaneous or occur in a semi-structured situation.

1. If your choice is semi-structured, discuss the difference between active play and quiet time with the child.
2. Ask him to tell you what he does during playtime and during quiet time.
3. Ask him to demonstrate what he does during playtime and during quiet time.
4. Provide any clarification of the two different situations.
5. After a child has been involved in active play, ask him to go to his seat or select a location and begin a quiet time.
6. Observe him as he moves from an active period to a quiet time.
7. The process of the observational assessment should involve some structure, not for grading or ranking, but for developing a program or for assisting the child with a social behavior.
8. Some suggestions for observation are: (1) Did the child sit down after the playtime? If not, what did he do? (2) Did he talk quietly after playtime? If not, how did he talk? (3) Did he leave others alone during the quiet period? If not, what did he do to others? (4) Did he alternate quiet with active behaviors? Explain. (5) Did he become lethargic or go to sleep? (6) Did he maintain quiet time without participating in another activity (listening to a story, looking at a book, listening to music, etc.)? If so, for how long? (7) Did he maintain a quiet posture only while he participated in an activity (listening to a story, looking at a book, listening to music)? If so, how long? (8) Did he need to be reminded that it was quiet time? If so, how often? These observational behaviors are based on social interactions only, and consideration should also be given to his cognitive level, receptive language skills, and attention levels. Other variables need to be considered, such as: (1) How active the child was during playtime; (2) The time of day; (3) Children and adults involved in the playtime and the quiet time; (4) The visual or auditory stimulus that was part of the environment during the quiet time; (5) The type of activity that the child was involved in during quiet time; (6) Any reinforcements that were involved in playtime or quiet time.

Credit: + Child quiets down after an active period. During the quiet down, he sits down, remains seated, stops talking loudly, refrains from physical play, keeps his hands and feet to himself, and presents in a relaxed manner.

Adaptations

Some children shift their attention very quickly from one activity to the next. He simply makes a quick decision before obtaining or reviewing information he needs to make a successful decision. He often makes decisions about how to behave before he fully considers what is expected of him and what the alternatives are. He tends not to consider how to get along with others, so he hurries around exhibiting bursts of poorly considered behavior. To assist a child who overreacts or has difficulty quieting down: (1) Provide him with praise and rewards for desired behaviors; (2) Ignore inappropriate behaviors; (3) Use a brief "time-away" from others as an opportunity for him to think things over; (4) Place him in a visually and auditorially free situation; (5) Provide a firm structure and a firm limit-setting environment; (6) Communicate the behaviors expected clearly, concisely, and repeat if necessary. After telling him the expected behaviors, ask him to repeat them. Say, for example, "Fred, quiet time means to sit down. Fred, can you tell me what quiet time means?" Repeat if necessary, and ask him to repeat the desired behaviors several times; (7) Remove any objects or items that act as distractions; (8) Challenge him to enjoy quiet time until the timer goes off; (five minutes, then seven minutes, etc.) Verbally reward him for staying focused; (9) Use relaxation techniques.

5.128 Claims ownership of own possessions

Strand: 5-4   **Age:** 36-48m 3.0-4.0y

Definition
The child will declare ownership of items and will defend her own possessions. If an adult or peer tries to take away a possession that belongs to her, she will resist. She will physically resist by holding onto the item or grabbing it back. She will verbally resist by saying such things as, "It is mine," "It belongs to me," or "Give my ball back."

Assessment Materials
Child should bring her own toy or clothing.

Assessment Procedures
Note: Your effort to take away the possession should be done in the spirit of determining whether she will defend her ownership. Take care that you do not present the procedure as teasing or only a temporary "let me have a look," or as a replacement offer.

Grouping: When you assess a child's ability to claim and defend ownership of her possessions, use play-based observation as the most effective procedure. An observational assessment can either be spontaneous or occur in a semi-structured situation.

1. If your choice is semi-structured, invite the child to bring her favorite toy or her favorite item of clothing to you.
2. Make sure she understands that the toy or the article of clothing is her possession. As she holds onto the article, puts on the clothing article or plays with her toy, take it away from her in a manner that, for example, feigns a mistake. Such as, take her coat and say to another child, "Bob, please come get your coat."
3. Some suggestions to consider during the observation are: (1) Did she make an attempt to get the possession back? (2) Was her only reaction to cry or whimper? (3) Did she seek assistance from someone else to get her possession back? (4) Did she offer to give the article to you rather than admit it was hers and request it back? (5) Did she offer you an alternative, such as, "Give me my sweater, and you can wear this one," or "You may play with my truck for a little while, and then I want it back." (6) Was her response overly aggressive?
4. Remember that the observational assessment is not for grading, but for developing a program to assist a child with behavioral concerns or to plan intervention strategies. This suggested observational process addresses behavioral issues only, and consideration for skill development such as expressive/receptive levels, conceptual understanding, and motor responses is not included but needs to be appraised.

Credit: + Child defends her own possessions when an adult or peer tries to take away something that belongs to her.

Adaptations
Some children feel that they cannot or should not stand up for their rights. To a child, a possession is an extension of herself. If someone takes it away, she loses a sense of security. Others telling her to get it back only adds to her problem since she does not know how and she is probably confused. If she has been told she should not fight, her frustration increases, making it difficult for her. It is important for her to understand the difference between fighting and defending herself or her property. She should be encouraged to respond with words when others take advantage of her. A child may also be overly generous and when someone

takes property from her, instead of defending her possession, she may even give it away. When you deal with a child who would rather give her things away than defend ownership or create a problem, be careful not to change the behavior in a totally different direction of selfishness.

5.129 Shows an emerging sense of humor by laughing at the appropriate time

Strand: 5-7 **Age:** 42-54m 3.6-4.6y

Definition

When the child is involved with a humorous story, a comment, an event, a caper, or a funny trick, he will laugh at the appropriate time. The appropriate time will most likely be at the end or during the humorous presentation.

Assessment Materials

(Items that can involve you in an obvious silly mistake.) An available drinking glass, a pitcher, and a cereal bowl. Shoes with shoestrings. A shirt that buttons up the front.

Assessment Procedures

Grouping: When you assess a child's emerging sense of humor, use play-based observation as the most effective procedure. An observational assessment can either be spontaneous or occur in a semi-structured situation.

Level One:
1. If your choice is semi-structured, invite the child to join you at the table. Place the bowl and the drinking glass on the table in front of the child.
2. Tell him you want to give him a glass of water.
3. Using the pitcher, pour the water into the bowl, not the glass.
4. Observe whether the child finds this obvious, silly mistake funny and laughs appropriately.
5. Watch for such behaviors as: (1) Pauses to determine what is going on and then laughs; (2) Does not see the humor in the silly mistake; (3) Becomes upset and verbally reacts; (4) Enjoys the role reversal (thinks, "Even you can make a mistake, and 'little' me recognizes it."); (5) Demonstrates a sensitive reaction (cries, verbally indicates a disaster).
6. Using the shoes with shoestring, attach your left shoe string to your right shoe string and then trying to walk or using the shirt with buttons up the front, button your shirt incorrectly. These are some other ways to make obvious, silly mistakes.

Level Two:
7. When the child is involved in a humorous activity, informally observe whether he laughs at the appropriate time.

Credit: + Child demonstrates an emerging sense of humor by laughing at a funny story, comment, event, or trick at the appropriate time.

Adaptations

Some children are unable to summon humor on their own. Children display vast differences when they respond to a funny situation, often because they are so busy trying to understand what is going on around them and to determine what is expected of them that not everything seems humorous. The education in humor can come from suggestions, experiences, and environment. To help a child use and develop his own sense of humor, and appreciate the humor of others: (1) Expose him to silly mistakes made by others (without being negative towards others); (2) Help him to enjoy the silly mistakes he makes; (3) Encourage him to deal with the normal feelings of give-and-take by enjoying silliness, clowning around, rough-housing, and pretending to be angry; (4) Accept his silly humor and what appears to be uncontrollable laughter, and address any necessary modification by modeling. Providing an atmosphere of cheerful give-and-take is the best setting for developing natural humor.

5.130 Sits without moving when involved in an activity

Strand: 5-4 **Age:** 43-46m 3.7-3.10y

Definition

The child will sit in a seat, on a bench, or on the floor without excessive moving or fidgeting when she is participating in or observing an activity. The time she sits without moving excessively will be determined by the entry behavior of the child, the amount of time the activity takes, the group participating, the child's interest in the activity, her background information and skill level relative to the activity. Excessive moving and fidgeting behaviors are viewed as: (1) Getting out her seat, (2) Standing on the seat, (3) Lying on the table, (4) Poking, hitting and kicking, (5) Interfering with the activity by swinging or swaying arms, (6) Stamping feet, (7) Overtly grabbing or hugging other participants, (8) Tipping over in the chair, (9) Rolling, if on the floor,

(10) Any excessive motions that interfere with the activity or others who are involved in it.

Assessment Materials

Several pictures from a category of interest that are familiar to the child. Example: Pictures of animals that live in the zoo, of trees, bushes, and flowers, or of toys. A large sheet of paper, nontoxic glue, scissors, markers.

Assessment Procedures

Grouping: Informal observation is very effective is assessing the child's ability to sit still during an activity because it is done in a natural setting. An observational assessment can either be spontaneous or occur in a semi-structured situation.

Level One:
1. If your choice is semi-structured, invite the children to the worktable and explain that they are to sit quietly. Demonstrate what sitting quietly means.
2. Discuss with them the selected category, show the pictures and talk about them.
3. Use a quiet, soothing voice during the discussion, and observe whether each child sits quietly.
4. This observation is not intended to determine any level, ranking, or achievement, but is intended to be used for social skill improvement and behavioral change.
5. Invite the children to help make a big picture of "Animals in the Zoo."
6. Tell them that the first thing for them to do is to choose one of the pictures and cut it out. (The selected pictures should be simple to cut out and if some of the fine edges of the animal are cut off, it is not an important issue.)
7. While each child is cutting out her picture, draw several walkways on the sheet of paper to indicate paths at the zoo. Also write "The Zoo" on the large sheet of paper.
8. During this independent cutting activity, observe whether each child sits quietly.
9. Compare this observational information with the observational information collected during the picture discussion.
10. These observations are not intended to determine any level, ranking, or achievement, but for social skill improvement and behavioral change.
11. After each child finishes cutting out her animal, show her the large sheet of paper that represents the zoo. Talk about which animals must be in cages, which ones need to be near water, which ones can walk about.
12. Have each child take turns to select a spot for her zoo animal along the walkways.
13. Ask the others to sit quietly, watch, and wait their turns.
14. Ask one child to place her animal, name it, talk about it, and glue it in place.
15. Continue with the other children until all the animals are in place and the zoo picture is complete.
16. Observe whether each child sits quietly as she places her animal and waits her turn.
17. Compare this observation information with the information collected during the picture discussion, the independent cutting experience, and the group activity of creating a picture. This comparison can be most helpful in determining under what conditions, or what catalyst, the child behavior is acceptable, changes, or is modified.
18. You may add other things to the zoo picture, such as cages, trees, water, people.

Level Two:
19. When the child is involved in an activity, informally observe whether she sits quietly without excessive and inappropriate movement.

Credit: + Child sits without excessive moving or fidgeting when she is participating in or observing an activity.

Adaptations

Young children are often very active and their actions can be purposeful, directed to the task, and productive. However, some children rarely sit still and are in constant motion. Their movements are usually undirected and inappropriate to the task at hand; in fact, they often prohibit completion of an activity or even being able to join in. A child who is rarely still adopts movement as a way of life. To assist a child to deal with her activity level, use the following techniques: (1) Avoid excessive stimulation, such as high noise levels or an unstructured, messy environment; (2) Provide her with stimulation (play material) and experiences; however, keep the presentation of the toy or the experience organized;. (3) Avoid constant verbal directions, as it often acts as a movement stimulus; (4) Reinforce productive behavior, making sure that when she does sits still and completes a task she is verbally praised; (5) Make sure she understands clearly what is expected of her. Modeling is an effective way to explain procedures; (6) Prepare her before an event is to take place. It can be helpful to tell her what is going to happen and to model the desired behavior.

To encourage the overactive child to sit down and quietly interact with a task, consider motor inhibition. For example, (1) Have the child participate in a gross motor skill that allows her to move around, jump, run, etc. before asking her to participate in an activity that will require her to sit still and focus on an activity; (2) Show her how to string beads in a slow, diligent manner. Tell her that success is measured by being gradual and correct. Keep in mind that the child has a high energy level, so that sitting still is often difficult, especially if the activity is not of interest or within her experience level.

5.131 Follows directions and obeys an authority figure

Strand: 5-1 **Age:** 43-48m 3.7-4.0y

Definition

The child will follow directions given by an authority figure. (An authority figure is a person such as a parent, a teacher, a teacher's adult helper, a baby-sitter, community figures such as police officers or firefighters, persons involved in the education, safety, and health of the child.) The response time will depend on the child's cognitive and language development, his adaptive behaviors, experiences, and association with the authority figure.

Assessment Materials
Another teacher of supervising adult.

Assessment Procedures

Grouping: When assessing a child's ability to follow directions given by an authority figure, the most effective procedure is observation. An observational assessment can either be spontaneous or occur in a semi-structured situation.

1. If your choice is semi-structured, invite the child to join you in a school assembly or in another classroom in which another teacher or supervising adult asks the child to join them in various activities. The other teacher/adult will give the child directions in ways so he can participate. During your observational assessment, it is important that the process involve some structure, not for grading, but for developing a program or assisting a child with an identified behavior.
2. Some suggestions to consider during the observation are: (1) Did the child respond to the directions given by the authority figure? If not, how did he respond? (2) Did he follow all the directions or did he respond to only part? (3) Did he exhibit any inappropriate behaviors when he responded? If so, what were they? (4) Did he appear to respect the fact that the person giving the directions was a person of authority? (5) Did it appear that he needed reinforcement from another person before he reacted to the directions given? For example, when the other teacher/adult provided directions, did he look to his teacher, or friend to receive positive feedback that it was all right to follow the directions?

Credit: + Child follows directions given by an authority figure.

Adaptations

A child may have a problem responding to any person giving directions. If he is expected to listen and follow directions, but has not developed the maturity to be attentive, he may display various behaviors. Some of these behaviors include: (1) Withdrawal-- He completely ignores the directions given. (2) Dependency--He demands help to understand the directions and respond to them; (3) Impulsiveness--He becomes impatient because he does not understand what he is supposed to do, so he does whatever comes to mind; (4) Disassociated--He removes himself from the action and the task. (This does not necessarily mean that he physically leaves the setting.) In dealing with a person of authority, a 3- or 4-year-old may experience uncertainty that may cause him to be jealous and at times belligerent toward parents, teachers, and others who give him directions. When you are dealing with someone this age, remember that the child has emotional extremes and can be insecure; therefore, patience and understanding are the key. Letting him know that he is understood and appreciated are the first steps to helping him deal with conforming to an authority figure.

5.132 Identifies dangerous situations/objects verbally or with gestures

Strand: 5-8 **Age:** 43-48m 3.7-4.0y

Definition

The child will identify dangerous situations such as sharp objects, hot appliances, toys on a stair-step, cleaning-fluid bottles, broken glass, medicine bottles.

The child will either tell another that the identified object is dangerous, or she will point to the situation. She may or may not take action to remedy the dangerous situation.

/\Safety Note: This definition offers examples only; local program/family safety procedures should be reviewed to prepare a comprehensive list of dangerous situations/objects.*

Assessment Materials

Picture cards of contrasting pairs, such as a glass jar and a broken glass; a red hot burner and a cool burner; a ball in a toy box and a ball in the middle of a stair step; a book of matches closed and a book of matches open; a lighted candle standing straight and a lighted candle tipped over; a sharp knife laying on the floor and a sharp knife in a drawer; some pills laying on a counter and a pill bottle tightly closed. These pictures are available from commercial sources, or cut them from magazines or make line drawings.

Assessment Procedures

Note: This assessment is not meant to grade or to rank a child. The intent is to determine what, if any, intervention teaching techniques need to be considered, and for curriculum planning.

Grouping: Informal observation is effective because it is done in a natural setting without some of the variables that accompany a formal assessment procedure. If necessary, this skill can formally be assessed one-on-one or in a small group setting.

Level One:
1. Invite the child to the table. Discuss with the child some dangerous things and how safe things can become dangerous.
2. Show her a picture of a glass jar, and ask her to tell you what is in the picture.
3. Show her the picture of the broken glass, and ask her to tell you what is in the picture.
4. Ask her to point to the picture that is dangerous. Ask her to tell you why she thinks the selected picture is dangerous. Ask her to tell you what she would do if she found broken glass.
5. Observe her as she: (1) Identifies the dangerous situation; (2) Tells why it is dangerous; (3) Tells what she will do if she encounters this danger.
6. Show her the picture of the heated (red) stove burner, and ask her to tell you what is in the picture.
7. Show her the picture of the cool stove burner, and ask her to tell you what is in the picture.
8. Ask her to point to the picture that is dangerous. Ask her to tell you why she thinks the selected picture is dangerous. Ask her to tell you what she would do if she sees a hot burner.
9. Observe her as she: (1) Identifies the dangerous situation; (2) Tells why it is dangerous; (3) Tells what she will do if she encounters this danger.
10. Continue the above procedure using the other pictures.

Level Two:
11. Observe the child when she encounters a dangerous object or situation to determine whether she verbally reacts or makes a gesture to indicate she is aware of the concern.

Credit: + Child correctly identifies dangerous situations either verbally or with gestures.

Adaptations

Some children have a problem with the concept of "dangerous" and "not dangerous." A child may not be aware of good safety practices in the home because she is well protected in that environment. However, she soon will encounter things that can hurt her, and she needs to understand what is dangerous and what is not. She also needs to know what to do when she is involved with a dangerous situation or object. Direct instruction is the best educational procedure. Sometimes a child has been overly warned of dangers, or she finds out that she is not hurt by the threatened dangers so she begins to disregard warnings. She often becomes reckless and unable to recognize danger and how to deal with it. To assist her, discuss the concept of dangers in a matter-of-fact mode. She should be taught not only to keep safe within her usual activities, but also to develop the habit of approaching unfamiliar situations with reasonable caution. Caution can be developed without creating fear by making children competent to recognize and deal with dangerous situations. However, she must understand that there are certain dangerous situations she needs to stay away from without asking any questions.

5.133 Cleans up spills independently
Strand: 5-6 **Age:** 44-52m 3.8-4.4y

Definition
When the child spills, he will clean it up using the proper material.

Assessment Materials
A small glass filled with a ¼ cup sand or cornstarch.

Assessment Procedures
Grouping: Informal observation is very effective because it is done in a natural setting. An observational assessment can either be spontaneous or occur in a semi-structured situation.
1. If your choice is semi-structured, invite the child to come to a table. Place the glass filled with the sand or cornstarch on the table.
2. Tell him to pretend that the cornstarch or sand is water. Ask him to dramatize a scene in which he accidentally spills the water on the table.
3. After he tips over the glass filled with cornstarch or sand say, "What do you need to do?"
4. If he does not know what to do, tell him to clean up the spill.
5. Observe the child, watching for: (1) The way he accepts the fact that he needs to clean up his spill; (2) The manner in which he deals with the problem (e.g., asks for help, walks away, blames others, cries); (3) The words he uses after the spill is cleaned up; (4) If he appears to be more careful so that the glass will not spill again. It is important to remember that social interaction and manners are closely associated with the cognitive dimensions of the desired behavior. The child must be able to identify the need in order to select the appropriate social manners.

Credit: + Child cleans up a spill independently using the appropriate materials.

Adaptations
See #5.103.

A child does not always act independently because: (1) He feels inadequate to do the task; (2) He does not realize that he has a responsibility for his actions; (3) He has always had someone else to clean up after him. To assist him: (1) Tell him the necessary steps to clean up the spill; (2) Show him how to clean up the spill; (3) Physically assist him in cleaning up the spill by doing these steps: Step 1--Get the towel. Step 2--Tell the child to take the towel and wipe the spill. Step 3--Using a hand-over-hand technique, help wipe up; Step 4--Tell him to bring the towel to the sink. Give the child every opportunity to be responsible, starting with small matters and increasing them as fast as his development allows. You will not help him to be responsible by doing tasks for him, even though at times you could do it faster and better than him. When a child demonstrates responsibility and reliability, let him know he is appreciated; (4) Allow him to do what he can, not only what he can do well. Making mistakes is part of learning and independence. The key is to let him try and to provide encouragement. However, he needs to know that when a problem is too much for him, someone is there not only for him, but also to assist; (5) Make sure he receives positive feedback for effort and for trying. If a child feels that the only time he will be rewarded is when a task has been done correctly by someone else's standards, he may refrain from subjecting himself to any criticisms.

5.134 Tells name of city in address
Strand: 5-2 **Age:** 44-54m 3.8-4.6y

Definition
When the child is asked, "In what city do you live?" or "In what town do you live?", she will respond correctly. If she lives in a rural area, her response will probably be the town or city where she goes for shopping and services. When asking the question, say, "In what city or town do you live?" instead of, "What town or city is in your address?" If she responds by giving her name and complete address, accept this because she has probably learned by rote memory how to respond to a question about where she lives.

Assessment Materials
Three sheets of 18-inch by 24-inch drawing paper, markers.

Assessment Procedures
Note: Ask the adult to use the term "city" or "town," based on the acceptable term in the area.
Grouping: This skill should be assessed one-on-one with the child.
1. Recruit the assistance of another adult.
2. Ask the adult to go to the child and say, "In what city or town do you live?"
3. If the child has difficulty responding with her city or town, observe whether her problem is

because of shyness or because of a lack of knowledge. If she appears to be shy in responding, the following is recommended: Talk with her about her house, the neighborhood, and the park. Make sure that she feels comfortable talking about her environment. Ask her questions about her home and community. Later in the interaction, ask her the name of the town or city where she lives. If she appears not to know the town or city where she lives, the following is recommended: (1) Show her a sheet of paper and ask her questions about her home. As she responds to the questions, draw a picture of her home (house, apartment house, mobile home); (2) Show her the second sheet of paper and draw her home (from sheet one) on this paper. Ask her questions about her neighborhood, stores, parks, and schools. As she responds to the questions, draw the neighborhood landmarks she mentions, making sure that they are within the proximity of the child's home. Tell her to point to her home, the park, the school, the store; (3) Show her the next sheet of paper, and draw in her home and neighborhood landmarks, and add other elements that make up the town or city where she lives, for example, tall buildings downtown, a lake, farms, mountains, small town main street.

4. Ask the child to point to her home, park, school, and store and explain that her home, park, school, and store are all part of a bigger town or city called Glendale, for example. Review the three sheets of paper, emphasizing the name of her town or city. Later in the interaction, ask her in which town or city she lives. Note her response and ask her randomly the name of the town or city where she lives.

Credit: + Child correctly names the city or town where she lives when asked.

Adaptations

Some children have problems making intuitive judgments about relationships. They may lack the ability to understand how one element of a concept relates to another. A child may understand that her bedroom is part of her home and that the yard is part of her home; however, for her to conceptualize that her home is part of a neighborhood, and that the neighborhood is part of a community, a town, or a city is beyond her understanding. The ability to view a category from its parts to the whole can be a difficult task. As long as the parts are represented in the child's concrete environment (bedroom, yard), she can understand it, but once the parts leading to the whole are a symbolic concept (home to neighborhood, neighborhood to city, city to state), she is confused. Hence, when she is asked to name the city or town where she lives, she is lost, because she lives in "a bedroom, a yard, a house," which is her understanding of a part to a whole. To assist her, present relationships in as concrete a manner as possible. When the actual touch and feel is not possible, present the concepts by visual representation. For example, illustrate the relationship from the child's bedroom to her home to her neighborhood to her town or city. Maturation plays an important role in the development of logical reasoning.

5.135 Plays with group of 3 or more children

Strand: 5-5 **Age:** 42-54m 3.6-4.6y

Definition

The child will participate in a group game with other children. The group activity may be played inside or outside, and the activity maybe active (ball or circle games) or passive (table games). At least three other children will be involved in the game/activity. The child may or may not follow all the rules.

Assessment Materials

Outdoor group game such as *Mother (Father), May I?* or *Kitty Wants a Corner*. Chalk.

Assessment Procedures

Note: The following are the different kinds of steps for "Mother (Father) May I?": Giant Step--as big a step as possible, Backward Step--a step backwards, Frog Step--crouch and jump like a frog, Baby Step--a step forward the length of the child's foot, Solider Step--stiff-legged step, Slide Step--Slides one foot forward and brings the other foot up, Rabbit Step--Hop with feet together.

Grouping: When you assess a child's ability to play a group game with other children (three or more), the most effective procedure is observation. An observational assessment can either be spontaneous or occur in a semi-structured situation.

1. If your choice is semi-structured, select a group outdoor game such as, "Mother (Father), May I?" Two lines are drawn at least 36 feet apart. One child is chosen to be Mother (or Father), and the other children stand on

one of the lines facing her. Mother starts the game by saying a child's first name and the kind of step she may take. She might say, for example, "Victor, you may take two baby steps." Before Victor moves, he must say "Mother, May I?" Mother will answer by saying, "Yes, you may," or "No, you may not." If the player forgets to ask permission from Mother/Father, she must go back to the starting line. The first child to cross the end line wins and becomes the next Mother/Father.

2. Another good outdoor game is "Kitty Wants A Corner." One child is named Kitty, and she stands in the center of the designated area of the yard (gym). The other children stand in a corner or in another spot. The Kitty (child who is "it") goes from one child to another asking for a corner or spot. The Kitty is always told, "No go find another corner (or spot)." While the Kitty is moving from child to child, the children are calling to each other to exchange corners or spots. When two children agree, they try to exchange corners before Kitty can reach an empty corner. The child who does not have a corner becomes the Kitty. Kitty may also stand in the middle of the area and say "Everybody change." All the children must change corners, which gives Kitty a chance to move to one of them.

3. Indoor games such as Concentration or Tic-Tac-Toe may also be used. During the observational assessment, it is important for the process to involve some structure, not for grading, but for developing a program or assisting the child with an identified behavior.

4. Some suggestions to consider during the observation are: (1) Did she play by the rules? (2) Did she try to change the rules to suit her needs? (3) Was she a good sport? (4) Did she want to play another game when she did not win? (5) Did she indicate that she did not understand the rules? (6) Did it appear that she needed continued assurance and reinforcement from another person before accepting the activity?

5. Analyze the list of players who were involved in the game to help with the assessment process, because a child may react differently when she engages in play with an adult, a sibling, a new child, or a special friend. Also analyze the situation in which the play was occurring when making the observations, because she may react differently in a familiar setting, when a family member is present, when environmental stimulus is active, in front of strangers, or in a structured situation.

6. These suggested observational assessments address social behaviors only. Considerations are not included for gross motor and receptive language skills that do have an effect on any changes in emotional and social interactions.

Credit: + Child participates in a group game with three or more children. The game takes place inside or outside and may be active or passive.

Adaptations

For some children, playing group games may require too much concentration and too many things to remember, may last too long, and may be too competitive. A child may prefer to play independently or with one or two other children. She may want an adult around during playtime. Sometimes the competition of group play is too much for her because it introduces an element she has not directly dealt with before. When she plays independently or with only one other child, winning occurs often; however, when she plays a game with a group of children, winning does not come as often. Learning to wait for success and winning can be difficult. The more she participates in group play, the more skilled she becomes at adapting her behavior. Group play may also require motor skills (running), memory skills (concentration), and other developmental skills. If any of these are lacking, the group becomes aware, and the child's self-esteem can be affected.

5.136 Shares toys with other children
Strand: 5-5 **Age:** 46-52m 3.10-4.4y

Definition
The child will share her toy or equipment with several other children when asked. She will also share her toy/equipment with others without being asked. When she has shared her toy or equipment she will establish ownership, limit sharing time, and display the ability to request the toy or equipment back.

Assessment Procedures
See #5.112 for assessment materials and procedures, as well as suggested adaptations. This skill is almost identical to #5.112 except the child has to share with several other children.

5.137 Uses appropriate manners to request an object

Strand: 5-7 **Age:** 40-53m 3.4-4.5y

Definition
When the child is requesting an object or service, he will say "please" and word his request in a polite manner using acceptable language.

Assessment Materials
Three small bowls with snacks, at least three cartons of different drinks, paper plates and napkins.

Assessment Procedures
Note: The observational process is not intended to rank the child, but rather, to provide information for modification of an inappropriate behavior or for program planning. This observational process considers social interactions only; other skills such as conceptual understanding, expressive/receptive levels, and motor responses should also be considered.

Grouping: When you are assessing a child's ability to use correct manner/words to request something, the most effective procedure is observation. An observational assessment can be either spontaneous or occur in a semi-structured situation.

1. If the choice is semi-structured, set out at least three small bowls with snacks, at least three cartons of different drinks, small paper plates, and napkins on the table.
2. Invite the child to the table. Place the napkins and the paper plates in separate stacks on the table.
3. Ask the child if he would like a paper plate. If he does not use the word "please" in his request, model the correct response by saying, "please" to indicate a desire for the item.
4. Ask the child again if he would like a paper plate. Observe him as he makes the request.
5. Watch for such behaviors as: (1) Uses the word "please" appropriately; (2) Does not include the word "please;" (3) Refuses to request the item; (4) Verbally indicates he does not want the object; (5) Leaves the table.
6. If the child used the word "please," give him a paper plate?"
7. If he does not use the word "please" in his request, repeat the modeling and the request statement ("Peter, would you ask for a paper plate and use the word 'please'?")
8. After he requests the paper plate using the word "please," continue with the other children, observing their responses and encouraging them to use the words "please" and "thank you."

Level Two:
9. When the child is involved in an activity, informally observe whether he uses the word "please" to indicate a desire for an item or a service.

Credit: + Child uses correct manners/words to request an object by saying "please" and states his request in a polite manner.

Adaptations
See #5.121.

5.138 Behaves according to desires of others

Strand: 5-4 **Age:** 48-60m 4.0-5.0y

Definition
The child will comply with an appropriate behavior when the desire of others is expressed. Examples: "Please be quiet," "Sit down," "Stand in line." She will comply with the accepted, implied behavior, in varied settings. Example: She is quiet when she is in a place where others are reading. She sits on a chair at a table when she is eating in a restaurant, or she stands in line when she is ordering food in a restaurant.

Assessment Materials
On a table place two activities the child enjoys, such as a coloring book, puzzle, etc.

Assessment Procedures
Grouping: When you are assessing a child's ability to comply with an appropriate behavior when she is asked or when the correct behavior is implied, the most effective procedure is play-based observation. An observational assessment can either be spontaneous or occur in a semi-structured situation.

1. If your choice is semi-structured, place the two child-oriented activities on a table.
2. Say, for example, "Ashley, come to the table."
3. Observe whether she comes to the table.
4. If she comes to the table, say, "Here is a coloring book and crayons, and here is a puzzle. Select the one you want to do."
5. Observe whether she selects an activity.
6. If she selects an activity, say, "Please do not talk while you are doing the puzzle."
7. Observe whether she refrains from talking while she does the activity. When she

completes it, say, "Now, you may try out the new coloring book and crayons."
8. Observe whether she begins this other activity.
9. If she begins the other activity, say, "Please do not talk while you are coloring."
10. Observe whether she refrains from talking while she does it.
11. If she does not respond to the behavioral directions, the following are suggestions for emphasizing the requests: (1) Make sure she understood the directions you gave, for example, does she understand the word "select?" Should it be changed to "choose," or should you explain and demonstrate what "select" means? (2) Repeat each direction twice; (3) Ask her to repeat the behavioral request after you say it once; (4) If she does not respond to a direction you give, record the response, but correction is not recommended. It is important for this observational process to involve some structure, not for grading, but for developing a program or for assisting her with an identified behavior. Observe her when she is asked to behave a certain way or when she is in a situation in which she needs to read the environment and determine the appropriate behavior.

Credit: + Child behaves/complies with the desires of others.

Adaptations

A child who is not consistent in complying with a request may be used to discipline that is unduly demanding or inconsistent. The non-complying child will usually react in one of the following ways. She will: (1) Become defiant either verbally and/or physically, (2) React with hostility often exhibited by doing the opposite of what is asked, (3) Respond by being passively resistant--slow, complaining, or sullen. To assist a child who, for whatever reason, chooses not to comply with a behavioral request, consider these recommendations: (1) Establish behavior rules and enforce them in such a manner that she has no choice but to respond. In establishing rules remember: (a) develop rules that are in the best interest of the situation and the child; (b) as you develop the rules, state them in a positive way; (c) when you explain the rules to her, include the reason the rule is needed; (d) be consistent in enforcing the rules and expect the child to obey; (e) if the child breaks a rule, apply reasonable consequences such as loss of privileges. (2) When requesting a behavior, try to give the child a choice. For example, say, "Either sit at the table to do the activity, or sit by yourself in the quiet center"; (3) Make sure to praise her each time she does obey a request; (4) Let her know that her noncompliance has created a problem for you and/or other children. For example, say, "Barbara, when you do not sit down and do the puzzle, it means the rest of us have to wait for story time, and that makes us unhappy."

It is important to remember that all children will be unresponsive at times and will refuse to obey a request at times. A certain amount of non-complying is viewed as positive, because it is an expression of independence.

5.139 Passes food/drink on request
Strand: 5-6 **Age:** 48-54m 4.0-4.6y

Definition
The child will pass food or drink, when requested. He will pass food without spilling.

Assessment Materials
/*\Safety Note: Be aware of special diets and allergies before doing this assessment.
A plate, a cup or glass, silverware, a small pitcher, a bowl. Pour a small amount of a liquid (water, milk, juice) into the pitcher. Put some cookies on a plate.

Assessment Procedures
Grouping: When you are assessing a child's ability to pass food or drink on request, the most effective procedure is play-based observation. An observational assessment can either be spontaneous or occur in a semi-structured procedure.
1. If your choice is semi-structured, place a placemat on the table, and on the placemat, put a plate, a cup or glass, and silverware. Place the pitcher and the plate of cookies on the table within child's reach.
2. Explain to the child that he is to pass the pitcher of juice when he is asked.
3. Say, "Please pass the pitcher of juice."
4. Observe the child, watching for: (1) Passes the pitcher; (2) Ignores the request; (3) Verbally refuses; (4) Spills and does not clean up the accident; (5) Spills and cleans up the accident.
5. Explain to him that he is to pass the plate of cookies when he is asked.
6. Say, "Please pass the cookies."

7. Observe the child, watching for: (1) Passes the plate of cookies; (2) Ignores the request; (3) Verbally refuses; (4) Spills and does not clean up the crumbs; (5) Spills and cleans up the accident.
8. Children mature at different levels and become independent at some tasks at one time and some at other times. Any assessment should consider the developmental level of the child, his experiences, attention span, and objectiveness. This assessment is not meant to rank a child or grade him in any way; instead, it is meant to determine intervention strategies and curriculum planning.

Credit: + Child passes food/drink, when requested, without spilling.

Adaptations

A child may not have been exposed to the table manner of passing dishes when asked. The reason are: (1) That particular table manner has not been identified as important in his home situation; (2) Whenever anyone is out of food, someone else refills it; (3) To get another helping, the acceptable procedure is to get up and get it; (4) He lacks the receptive skills to respond. To assist him: (1) Model passing food and drink at the table; (2) Make sure he is aware of the meaning of the words, "please pass." Give him ample time to practice this table manner, and provide cueing as necessary. It is important to remember not to expect more of him than he can do; conversely, let him do what he can do.

5.140 Performs assigned task

Strand: 5-4   **Age:** 48-55m 4.0-4.7y

Definition

When the child is presented with a task to do, she will perform the assignment to the best of her ability. She will perform the task by following directions, asking questions, requesting assistance if needed, accepting help when provided, and persisting in accomplishing the task.

Assessment Materials

An activity within the child's ability level and interests. A work area that is free of distractions.

Assessment Procedures

Grouping: When you are assessing a child's ability to perform an assigned task, the most effective procedure is play-based observation. An observational procedure can either be spontaneous or occur in a semi-structured situation.

1. If your choice is semi-structured, select a task that is within the child's ability level and interests. When you set up the activity, avoid a work area that has visual and auditory distractions.
2. Invite the child to the work area and explain the task. Observe her as she performs the assigned task, watching for behaviors such as: (1) Distractibility--She becomes involved with activities around her; (2) Loses interest in the task--It appears that her mind is wandering or she is day-dreaming; (3) Wastes time--She plays around and appears to be spending time loafing around; (4) Helplessness--She keeps asking for help to do the task even though she is capable of doing the work; (5) Lack of confidence that she can do the task correctly--She may be concerned about her ability or wants to do a perfect job, so rather than risk not being successful or doing less than a perfect job, she does not attempt the activity.
3. Informally observe the child when she has been assigned a task, watching for behaviors such as: (1) Distractibility, (2) Loss of interest, (3) Wastes time, (4) Overly dependent, (5) Lack of self-confidence. Remember that all children do not mature at the same rate. A child may be deficient in a certain area and excel in another. Physical health, environmental issues, people involved also contribute to social/behavioral actions.

Credit: + Child performs an assigned task to the best of her ability. She follows the directions given, asks questions when necessary, requests help if needed, accepts help when it is provided, and shows persistence in accomplishing the task.

Adaptations

A child may not have acquired the patience necessary to stick with an activity until completed. If any complications or problems occur while she is doing the task, often they will show up as aggressive or withdrawn behaviors. When she lacks the understanding of what will happen because of her actions, her responses are not based on outcomes. For example, the outcome of not getting to work is that the project does not get done. Cause and effect are not clear concepts to some children and are not viewed as important. To assist a child to perform a given task, give her positive reinforcement for staying on the task, for trying, for accomplishing a portion of the activity, and for continuing an activity after a distraction. Another idea would be to divide the activity into small segments, making sure that she understands how to do each part and reinforce her for doing or attempting each small part. If the child requests help, provide assistance in the following manner: (1) First request for help--Ignore it; (2) Second request for help--Say, "I know how you feel; sometimes [e.g., putting a puzzle together] is hard work, but you can do it"; (3) Third request for help--Say, "I have time to help you with [just one piece of the puzzle]." Give help and then reinforce non-verbally, for example, give her a reassuring pat on the back or smile; (4) Fourth request for help--Say, "You are having a lot of trouble doing that [puzzle]; you watch while I do it, and then you can do it." After she observes you doing the task (putting the puzzle together), prepare the activity (take the pieces out, place them face-up on the table), tell the child it is her turn, and leave. Repeat if necessary. She may need assistance in sequential thinking if she becomes frustrated and does not understand what to do first, second, third, and so on. Tell her what to do first, reinforce her for accomplishing that step, then tell her what to do next, and reinforce her for accomplishing each step; (5) Fifth request for help--Remove/stop the task, without any explanation.

5.141 Returns objects or materials to their assigned/appropriate place

Strand: 5-4 **Age:** 48-55m 4.0-4.7y

Definition
When he is asked, the child will return objects or materials to their assigned places without any verbal prompting or physical assistance.

Assessment Materials
Crayons, clay, puzzle, blocks, books, etc.

Assessment Procedures
Note: Informal observation is very effective because it is done in a natural setting, without the child's being aware and not restricted by some of the variables that accompany assessment procedures.

Grouping: When you assess a child's ability to return objects or materials to their assigned places, the most effective procedure is observation. An observational assessment can either be spontaneous or occur in a semi-structured situation.

1. If your choice is semi-structured, invite the child to the work area. After he arrives, from an assigned place, take down an activity (crayons, clay, puzzle, blocks, books, sewing cards, pegboard and pegs, parquetry cards and parquetry blocks), making sure he sees you take down the activities.
2. Place the activities/toys on the table, and tell him he may play with them.
3. After he has completed an activity or time is up, ask him to put the activities back where they belong.
4. Observe him as he puts the activities away, watching for the following behaviors: (1) Verbally refuses to put the items away ("I don't want to."); (2) Puts the activities away carelessly and disorderly; (3) Demonstrates a lack of organizational skills; (4) Becomes destructive with the materials; (5) Leaves the area without putting the items away.
5. The intention of the observational assessment is for planning behavioral intervention strategies and curriculum direction. The observational assessment should be objective, not subjective. Record the behaviors that you observe as they happen in behavioral terms. For example, record: The child threw the puzzle on the floor (Destructive behavior). The child put the crayons in with the blocks and some of blocks were mixed up with the crayons (Careless). The child put all the items on one shelf rather than on the designated shelf (Disorganization). The child said, "I do not want to." (Disobedience).
6. Informally observe the child when he asked to put away items or material after an activity.

Credit: + Child returns objects or materials to their assigned places without verbal prompting or physical assistance.

Adaptations
Some children lack motivation or interest in being organized and tidy. A child may not feel a need to pick up things and put them away. A child like this needs a lot of understanding and patience. Forcing him to pick up and put away his things will not make him neater or better organized. What he does need are clear directions, concrete experiences, practice, and lots of encouragement. He is much more interested in going to another activity than in cleaning up after the last one. He does not understand the effect of not putting things away--being able to find things again, keeping his material in good condition, not losing items-- these thoughts are not part of his conceptualization. An unmotivated child may become angry and aggressive when he is firmly

instructed to put things away. He may exhibit his anger and aggression in the form of a tantrum, or he destroys the materials in a deliberate manner. To assist him in learning to put items away: (1) Make sure he knows where the items belong. Show him the box, shelf, or carton, and model putting it in its correct place. Ask him to place an item in the correct location while you are observing. Make sure he is reinforced for putting an item away in the correct spot; (2) Explain to him what might happen if he does not put away materials (consequences), and let him add other consequences that might occur; (3) Allow him to experience natural consequences. Example: He mixes the red crayon with the blocks at the end of play, so the next time he needs a red crayon, it is not in the crayon box; (4) When giving a command, look at the child, use his first name, and give clear directions, telling the child what you want him to do instead of telling him what he cannot/should not do. Example: "Tim, place the blocks carefully in the box." (5) Require the child to clean up any mess he creates by being destructive. One of the most important elements of training children to be organized and for them to understand the importance of putting things away is for them to see the correct behaviors. If the child views you putting things in their proper place, he will be more inclined to model this behavior and learn the benefits of being organized.

5.142 Quiets down after active period and waits for instructions

Strand: 5-4 **Age:** 48-60m 4.0-5.0y

Definition
After active play, the child will sit down, remain seated, stop talking loudly, refrain from physical play, keep her hands and feet to herself, and present herself in a relaxed manner. She will remain quiet, waiting for further instructions.

Assessment Procedures
See #5.127 for assessment materials and procedures, as well as suggested adaptations.

5.143 Verbalizes feelings to another prior to physical expression

Strand: 5-5 **Age:** 48-60m 4.0-5.0y

Definition
The child controls his temper by verbalizing his feelings rather than exhibiting behaviors such as aggression, tantrums, or withdrawal. He will find less reason to exhibit anger, frustration, or aggressive behaviors, because expressing himself with words more effectively communicates his feelings and needs.

Assessment Materials
At least four feeling situational or behavioral types of pictures either obtained commercially, cut from magazines and mounted on poster board cards, or line drawn on large index cards. Examples: Card One--A group of children standing together all looking at a child standing alone but away from the group. The group of children are pointing and laughing at the lone child. The lone child looks angry. Card Two-- Two children playing in a sand box; one building sand houses and roads. The other child destroying the houses and roads, and throwing sand at his playmate. The child whose work is being destroyed looks very angry. Card Three-- A group of children standing in a line, getting ready to go outside to play. One child has pushed down the child who is first in line. The child who was pushed down has an angry look on his face. Card Four--An adult standing over a child who has a mean expression on his face as he stomps on a sweater. The adult has her hands on her hips and is talking at the angry child.

Assessment Procedures
Note: It is important to accept his comments, evaluations, and judgments about the pictured happenings. If you lead his responses, he may modify his comments in an effort to be right or receive your approval. As he comments about the picture, use effective noncommittal comments such as "Oh," "Really," and "That's interesting."

Grouping: When you assess a child's ability to verbalize his feeling rather than exhibit physical behaviors, the most effective procedure is observation. An observational assessment can either be spontaneous or occur in a semi-structured situation.

1. If your choice is semi-structured, invite the child to join you at the worktable. Explain to him that you are going to show him some pictures and you want him to look at them very carefully.

© 2010 VORT Corporation. All rights reserved. Do Not copy.

2. Show him Card One. Set the stage by pointing to the group of children and saying, "What do you think these children are saying and doing?"
3. Allow him time to respond, and if necessary, prompt him to share what the group might be saying.
4. Point to the child standing alone and say, "What do you think this child is going to do?"
5. Give him time to respond and encourage him to state as many optional behaviors as he can think of, for example: they are fighting, he ran away because he was mad, they are teasing the boy, etc.
6. From the options that he shares, ask him how he thinks the child should control his temper and what he should do so he does not get so angry.
7. Observe whether he suggests that the child should talk about how he feels and whether he gives examples or words or statements the child might use.
8. Accept his comments without making any judgmental remarks.
9. Discuss what might happen next.
10. Show him Card Two. Set the stage by pointing to the two children and saying, "What do you think these children are saying and doing?"
11. Follow the steps outlined above in steps 3 through 9.
12. Show him Picture Cards Three and Four, and discuss the happenings, what might occur, some ways to control anger, and what words the picture characters might use. Observe and note whether he suggests a way to control anger is to talk about how one feels in a tense situation.
13. This behavioral pictorial assessment is meant to assist in the developing of curriculum goals or some individual social intervention strategies.

Credit: + Child controls his temper by verbalizing his feelings rather than exhibiting behaviors such as aggression, tantrums, or withdrawals.

Adaptations

When a child becomes angry, he may not have the words to express his feelings, or if he has the words, he has some reservations about saying them. With all children, it is important to avoid arousing their anger, but it is necessary to realize that when their anger is aroused, it must have an outlet, since anger is difficult to suppress. When a child does not know the words or chooses not to express himself verbally, he will find another way to vent his feelings. If he has difficulty controlling his anger, he may resort to aggressive actions, temper tantrums, or withdrawing. Once he knows and feels comfortable discussing his anger, he realizes that he has a way to control outbursts. To assist him: (1) Increase his vocabulary by matching feelings with words. As he develops a vocabulary of expressive "feeling" words and as he comprehends what the words mean, assist him to use them in phrases and sentences; (2) Help him organize his thoughts. In striving for adequate expression of feelings, he learns to emphasize the more significant parts of his frustrating experience. As he shares his feelings with others, he is also interpreting the thoughts and feelings of others in the light of what he shares. This allows him to modify his behavior and his verbal expression; (3) Encourage him to feel free to express his feelings, making sure that what is said is acceptable and no judgments are made. He should feel that he is expressing his concern to interested listeners. He should also be led to feel that he is being encouraged to share and communicate his feelings. It can be devastating for a child who finally is willing to share his feelings if he is presented with a non-listener, a listener who passes judgment, with someone who ridicules him, tells him to wait a minute with his story, or tells him that "little boys and girls do not say things like that." He will be very hesitant to express his feeling again.

5.144 Asks for assistance when needed
Strand: 5-5   **Age:** 48-56m 4.0-4.8y

Definition
The child will ask for assistance from another person when she needs help. The child can request the assistance of an adult or another child. When she asks for assistance, she will use courteous language.

Assessment Materials
Large, white handkerchief or piece of sheeting, crayons, paper towels and iron. These materials will be used to make a crayon batik.

Assessment Procedures
/⚠\Safety Note: Carefully supervise the child with the iron. Make sure she understands that she is to ask for assistance when she is ready to iron her picture.
Grouping: When you are assessing a child's ability to ask for assistance when needed, the most

effective procedure is observation. An observational procedure can either be spontaneous or occur in a semi-structured situation.

Level One:
1. If the choice is semi-structured, select a task the child is capable of doing up to a point. If you selected the crayoned batik, use the directions that follow.
2. Place the large white handkerchief or the piece of sheeting, crayons, paper towels and an iron on a table.
3. Explain to the child that she is to use the crayons to draw a design on the white material. Encourage her to press hard when she uses the crayon, in order to push the crayon wax into the material. Demonstrate the pressure needed to leave the wax residue.
4. Tell her when she completes her drawing, she must lay the material between dampened paper towels and iron it until they are dry. Let her know she will need help completing this step.
5. Observe her as she creates her picture, waiting for the time when she is ready to ask for assistance with ironing (Supervise very carefully). Watch for behaviors such as: (1) Requests assistance using appropriate words; (2) Tries to do the task without assistance; (3) Requests assistance in a demanding mode; (4) Leaves the task before or when she needs assistance; (5) Insists on doing it herself; (6) Is not satisfied with her finished product and wants to start over. When she asks for assistance, make sure the following occurs: (1) Positively reinforce her for requesting assistance; (2) Explain to her why your assistance is needed (hot iron), and that eventually she will learn how to use a hot iron; (3) She understands that it is okay to ask for assistance when it is needed.
6. When you provide the ironing assistance, it is important to ask her to help you do the following: (1) Place the fabric between the dampened paper towels; (2) Iron the paper until it is dry and the melted wax is set. As you assist her, verbally discuss what you are doing, why the need to be careful when using a hot iron.

Level Two:
7. Informally observe the child while she is working on a task and realizes she needs assistance, and the manner in which she asks for it.

Credit: + Child asks for assistance when needed, using courteous language, and accepts the assistance.

Adaptations

A child may judge her performances according to the expectations and standards established by others. When she reaches a difficult point in completing a task and discovers that she needs assistance, she may view it as a failure based on established expectations. She would rather fail than to let her inadequacies be known, so she modifies her behavior to cover up her need for assistance, withdraws, or loses any motivation for achievement. Perhaps when she has asked for assistance, she has been told, "You are a big girl; you can do it yourself," "You are old enough to do it," "You should try harder," or "Is there anything you do for yourself?" Dealing with those types of attitudes becomes discouraging and leads to a refusal to ask for any assistance. To assist her, make sure that the task she takes on is within her ability level, and that she is aware of the area in which she will need assistance. It is important to encourage her to achieve, but also to help her realize that tolerance for frustration comes from feeling good about herself, even though she needed assistance. Asking for help or changing tasks should not affect her self-image.

However, some children can take advantage of asking for assistance by over-requesting, often as a way to get attention rather than a real need for help to do a task.

5.145 Obeys rules
Strand: 5-5   **Age:** 48-60m 4.0-5.0y

Definition
The child will participate in a group activity with other children and he will follow the rules. The group activity may be played inside or outside and the activity may be active (ball or circle games) or passive (table games). The rules of the game will be clearly defined prior to any action.

Assessment Procedures
See #5.135 for assessment materials and procedures, as well as suggested adaptations.

5.146   (Removed, see page xviii)

5.147 Requests food/drink be passed at the table

Strand: 5-6 **Age:** 48-60m 4.0-5.0y

Definition
The child will ask for food or drink that is out of reach to be passed to him.

Assessment Procedures
See #5.139 for assessment methods/activities. This skill is similar to #5.139, however, the child now needs to request that the food/drink be passed to him at the table.

Adaptations
Some children have not been exposed to the table manner of saying, "Please pass the salad," waiting for the dish to be passed, taking the dish, serving themselves, and passing the dish on or putting it back on the table. Reasons for this include: (1) That particular table manner has not been emphasized in their home; (2) Whenever they are out of food on their plate or water in their glass, someone refills it for them; (3) To get another helping, the acceptable procedure is to get up and get it; (4) They lack the verbal skills and the vocabulary to respond; (5) They are unaware of when to ask for something to be passed. To assist this child: (1) Model asking for food and drink to be passed at the table; (2) Make sure he is aware of the meaning of the words, "please, pass," and "thank you"; (3) Make sure he is aware of when to use the words, "please," "pass," and "thank you." Allow him ample time to practice this table manner, and provide cueing as necessary. It is important to remember not to expect more of him than he can do; conversely, let him do what he can do. For instance, filling his plate and passing the bowl to him without his asking will not lead to his independent request for things at the table.

5.148 (Removed, see page xviii)

5.149 Participates in conversation/discussion

Strand: 5-7 **Age:** 48-60m 4.0-5.0y

Definition
The child will participate in a discussion, both as a listener and as a contributor. He will contribute to the discussion in a polite and constructive manner.

Assessment Materials
Select topics, one at a time, making sure the child has information and experience on that topic.

Assessment Procedures
Grouping: Informal observation is very effective in assessing a child's ability to participate in a conversation because it is done in a natural setting without some of the variables that accompany any assessment procedure. If necessary, the skill can be assessed during a semi-structured activity.

<u>Level One:</u>
1. Invite the children to the communication area. Initiate a discussion with them based on likes and dislikes.
2. The topic of this discussion should focus on likes/dislikes relevant to foods, clothing, games, activities, toys, or trips.
3. After selecting a topic, begin with a lead statement or two, such as, Which do you like better, an apple or a banana? Why? Are there other things you would rather eat than an apple or a banana? Why? If you were going to pack a lunch, what would you put in it, potato chips or an apple? What else?
4. Encourage each child to participate in a shared constructive manner, and explain that we must listen and take turns during the conversation, remembering to be polite.
5. Observe the child as he interacts in the discussion, watching for such behaviors as: (1) Monopolizing the discussion; (2) Not participating or contributing; (3) Being argumentative; (4) Being a positive, active listener; (5) Sharing information in a caring manner, as well as making significant contributions; (6) Attempting to change the subject; (7) Interrupting others often. It is important to understand that children are usually very open-minded, willing to consider another person's opinion and point of view.

<u>Level Two:</u>
6. Observe the child when he is involved in a conversation or discussion to determine whether he participates in a positive manner, contributes to the topic, accepts others, and displays social manners in the setting.

Credit: + Child participates as both a listener and a contributor during a conversation in a polite and constructive manner.

Adaptations

Some children are not willing to listen to others' opinions impartially. They either will not or cannot judge a topic fairly nor contribute to a discussion based on relevant facts. When a child is not willing to listen and participate, he often exhibits behaviors that reflect impatience and a lack of self-control. His opinions are often based on prejudice and environmental points of view. This child may use a conversation or a discussion to seek attention. He considers contributing and participating in the discussion only if his primary needs are satisfied. To assist him, be patient and reasonable, since he may not have the background or experience to conceptualize things in a logical, fact-based manner. Helping him understand the skills necessary to participate in a verbal interchange are very important; this training should include role-playing and suggestions to develop specific skills, including: (1) Knowing how to be an active listener (looking at the person, rewarding the speaker by smiling, and not interrupting when another is talking); (2) Accepting what others say and feeling comfortable to share opinions and ideas; (3) Refraining from seeking group attention by finding a non-acceptable position such as the group clown or the agitator; (4) Addressing the discussion topic and avoiding trying to change the subject; (5) Understanding it is alright to ask questions to clarify opinions and facts. Providing him with numerous opportunities to participate in conversations and discussion groups will enhance his ability to become a caring contributor to group dynamics.

5.150 Keeps safe distance from matches, stove, and open flame

Strand: 5-8 **Age:** 48-60m 4.0-5.0y

Definition

When the child is shown fire hazards, such as matches, a hot burner, or an open flame and candles, she will demonstrate her understanding of the danger of fire and hot items. She may exhibit this understanding by keeping a safe distance, going for help, calling an emergency telephone number, or by following procedures for a fire drill.

Assessment Materials

At least six pictures that illustrate a fire hazard. Examples: (1) A book of matches that are burning; (2) Burners left on that are very hot; (3) A fire burning out of control; (4) A fire that is flaming up and burning the food; (5) Fire burning in a closet; (6) A candle tipped over and the flame is still burning. Pictures may be available commercially or you can cut pictures from magazines and newspapers, or make line art drawings.

Assessment Procedures

Grouping: This skill can be assessed one-on-one with the child.
1. Place the pictures face down on a table and invite the child to join you.
2. Discuss with her the danger of fire and what a person should do when she sees a fire. Encourage her to contribute to the discussion to be certain she understands the danger of fires.
3. Tell her you are going to show her some pictures of fires. Tell her that you want her to tell you what she would do if she were around the fire as illustrated.
4. Turn over a picture. Discuss what is happening in the picture together.
5. Say, "What would you do if you were there?"
6. Continue the above process with the other pictures.
7. Note her responses to determine whether she is aware of the dangers of fire and what action is appropriate.
8. This assessment is meant to determine her conceptual understanding of the dangers of fire and the correct response to make when exposed to this danger. The process should consider the child's cognitive, perceptual, language, and motor levels.

Credit: + Child demonstrates an understanding of the danger of fire and hot items.

Adaptations

Some children have a problem with the concept of "dangerous" and "not dangerous." Such a child may be unconscious of good safety practices in the home because she is well protected in that environment. However, her external protection can last only so long, for she soon encounters things that hurt her and she needs to understand what is dangerous and what is not. Sometimes a child has been overly and continuously warned of dangers until she realizes she is not hurt by the threatened dangers, and she begins to disregard warnings. Often she becomes reckless and unable to recognize danger or how to deal with it. A child may also seek attention from her peers by disregarding the dangers involved with the misconception that dealing with the dangerous situation will make others look on them as a hero or Superman instead of smart. To help her, discuss with her the concept of danger in a matter-of-fact manner. Especially if you are dealing with a sensitive child, scaring her about outcomes and gruesome details is ineffective. She should also be taught to keep safe within her usual activities, and to develop the habit of approaching a tenuous situation with caution. Caution can be developed in a meaningful manner if the child understands that being a real hero is being smart. She needs to be taught how to recognize a safety hazard and made aware of the alternatives that are available when she deals with a dangerous situation.

5.151 Comforts playmates in distress
Strand: 5-5 **Age:** 48-60m 4.0-5.0y

Definition
The child will comfort a peer who is in distress, either physically or emotionally. He will show his caring by either a gesture or verbal comments.

Assessment Materials
At least four pictures that show a child comforting another child who is hurt, sick, crying, or distressed. Obtain pictures from commercial sources or make simple line drawings on large-size index cards. Examples of pictures: (1) A child who has fallen down on the playground with two other children comforting him; (2) A child sitting in a chair crying, with another child sitting next to him comforting him; (3) A sick child lying in bed, with another child sitting on a chair next to the bed showing him a book; (4) A child standing and looking down at a broken toy on the floor. He is crying and looks distressed. Another child has his arm around the crying child, as another child picks up the pieces.

Assessment Procedures
Grouping: Informal observation is very effective in assessing a child's ability to comfort a peer because it is done in a natural setting without some of the variables that accompany a formal assessment procedure. If necessary, the skill can be assessed during a semi-structured activity.
1. Invite the child to the work area. Show him Picture One, and ask him what is happening in the picture.
2. If he does not respond, prompt him by asking questions such as, "What do you think happened to the boy lying on the ground?" and "What do you think the two other children are doing to help the boy who is hurt?"
3. Observe him as he responds, noting statements such as, "They want to help him," "The poor little boy is hurt," "They should get help for him," or "I think they are telling him not to cry."
4. Repeat the above procedure using Pictures Two, Three and Four.
5. Most children behave in thoughtful and helpful ways when a peer is in distress. Many are just reaching the stage when they realize that others do not feel just as they do (egocentrism), but yet they understand when someone else is hurt or feels sad. This positive social understanding (altruism), which demonstrates behaviors that are supportive and sympathetic, certainly indicates a comprehension of another's feelings.

Credit: + Child comforts a peer who is in distress, either physically (a gesture) or emotionally (a verbal comment).

Adaptations
Some children feel apprehensive when someone else is sick, hurt, or unhappy. They prefer to stay away from the situation or they remain silent because they do not know what to say or do. A child may appear to be afraid of unhappiness or a crisis. However, he may not have been allowed to share his feelings or to demonstrate personal concerns. He may have been told, "You are brave, you are not hurt," "Big boys do not cry," or "If you cannot be pleasant, maybe you should play by yourself for a while." When he wants to share feelings, disappointments, or hurts, he has been told these are signs of weakness. As a result, when someone else is in distress, he may feel that if he expresses concern, he will be demonstrating character inadequacy. To assist him: (1) Create a supportive, secure, and encouraging environment; (2) Explain clearly what the rules and standards are in the situation; (3) Allow him to do very helpful things in the setting; (4) Model being thoughtful, generous, and helpful; (5) Encourage him to talk about his feelings, using reflective listening skills (non-judgmental responses). Help him understand that it is okay to have different feelings and to talk about them. Also, share your feelings with the child. Children naturally vary a great deal in the

amount of altruistic behavior they demonstrate and that they react differently, depending on their relationship with the person who is hurting.

5.152 Uses basic playground equipment safely

Strand: 5-8 **Age:** 48-60m 4.0-5.0y

Definition
The child will demonstrate using playground equipment safely, not only for herself, but without endangering others. The playground equipment involved should be the basic items available to most children on a playground.

Assessment Materials
Playground equipment on an available playground. Child to demonstrate safe use.

Assessment Procedures
Grouping: Whenever the skill to be assessed relates to real-life functioning, it is best to conduct the assessment in the setting in which it will be performed. Often this requires changing environments and modifying the educational atmosphere. Informal observation is effective in assessing a child's skill of using basic playground equipment safely because it is done in a natural setting without some of the variables that accompany any assessment procedure. If necessary, the skill can be assessed during a semi-structured activity.

1. Accompany the child to the playground, specifically the playground equipment. Prearrange with another child to demonstrate safe procedures, using the various equipment.
2. Proceed as follows: Discuss the various safety procedures for the different pieces of playground equipment. For example: (1) Slide—Sit down, go down the slide alone, and keep your feet in front of you; (2) Swing--Sit in the seat, watch for others who might be in the pathway of the swing; (3) Bars--One person may be crossing the bar at a time. Watch out for others walking under the bars; (4) Ladders--One person climbs at a time.
3. Ask the child your assessing to demonstrate safe procedures while sliding down a slide.
4. Ask the child to name all the safe things the child-model did when she played on the slide.
5. Note her responses.
6. Ask the child-model to swing on the swing.
7. Ask the child to name all the safe things that the child-model did while she was swinging.
8. Note her responses.
9. Continue with the other playground equipment.

Level Two:

10. Observe her during regularly scheduled playground time, noting the safe and unsafe things she does. These notations are to help plan teaching strategies for any unsafe behaviors.

Credit: + Child uses basic playground equipment safely, without prompting.

Adaptations
A child may not have received instruction on the proper safety rules for playing on playground equipment or she may choose to ignore the rules. If she opts to ignore the rules, she may be acting impulsively, seeking attention, or uninhibited. If she is not aware of the proper rules, she should be instructed until she can demonstrate the safety procedures necessary and until she has a full understanding of the playground rules. If she exhibits inappropriate behavior, it is important for her to understand the rules and the consequences that will occur if she continues her inappropriate actions. Typical playground equipment rules include: (1) When going down the slide, sit down with feet in front and only one person at a time; (2) One person at a time when moving across the bars or going up the ladder; (3) When swinging, watch for others crossing the path; (4) Pushing and pulling others will not be tolerated; (4) Take turns on the equipment; (5) Tricks that endanger yourself and others are not allowed. Each child who plays on the playground equipment must understand and practice good safety procedures at all times. These are safety issue and are not negotiable because they are in the best interest of all involved.

5.153 Avoids or maintains distance from dangerous situations/objects

Strand: 5-8 **Age:** 49-54m 4.1-4.6y

Definition
When the child encounters a dangerous situation or object, he will avoid or immediately move away from the setting or item. He will also report the situation to a responsible adult. He will also point out dangers that confront others.

Assessment Materials
At least three pairs of pictures. Each pair should represent two dangerous situations, one in

which the child stays in the setting, and the other in which he moves away from the situation. Examples: (1) Picture One--A dog growling and showing his teeth and a child walking away. Picture Two--A dog growling and showing his teeth and the child is about to touch the animal. (2) Picture One--Two children playing with a ball that has rolled into the street; one child running into the street after the ball. Picture Two--Two children playing with a ball that has rolled into the street; the children wait while an adult gets the ball. (3) Picture One--A glass bowl broken with the sharp pieces on the floor, and a child is picking up the sharp pieces. Picture Two--A glass bowl broken with the sharp pieces on the floor; a child is standing back and calling for help. These pictures can be obtained from commercial sources, or made by the illustrating the situations on large index cards.

Assessment Procedures

Grouping: When you are assessing a child's ability to avoid or move away from a dangerous situation, the most effective procedure is observation. An observational procedure can either be spontaneous or occur in a semi-structured situation.

1. If the choice is semi-structured, place the pictures face down on the table. Invite the child to the table. Discuss with him the meaning of the word "dangerous," what we should do when we see something dangerous, what we should do when we are not sure if something is dangerous or not. Name situations that are dangerous, and discuss the ramifications of what may happen if a person does not avoid a dangerous situation.
2. Encourage him to contribute to the discussion to be certain he understands the meaning of "dangerous."
3. Tell him you are going to show him some pictures of dangerous happenings.
4. Turn over the first pair of pictures on the table.
5. Discuss what is happening in the pictures.
6. Say, "Point to the picture that shows what you should do if you see a strange, angry dog."
7. Point to the other picture and say, "What is this child doing that is dangerous?"
8. Pause to give him an opportunity to respond.
9. Say, "What should he do?"
10. Pause to give him an opportunity to respond.
11. Continue the above process with the other picture pairs.
12. Note his responses and knowledge of dangerous situations.
13. This assessment is not meant to grade or to rank children, but instead, to determine intervention techniques and curriculum planning.

Credit: + Child avoids or maintains a distance from a dangerous situation or object, or reports the situation to a responsible adult.

Adaptations
See #5.132.

5.154 Remains calm in changing/disappointing situation
Strand: 5-1   **Age:** 49-55m 4.1-4.7y

Definition
The child will accept a situation that is disappointing or has caused a change. When the situation changes due to circumstances beyond her control (e.g., because of rain, the trip to the park was canceled), and the child is told the reason, she will remain calm, accept that the situation will be altered or modified, and display adaptive behaviors.

Assessment Materials
Ingredients for making a treat, for example, chocolate chip cookies, banana bread, peanut cookies, with one ingredient missing, such as a banana for banana bread. Utensils for baking and kitchen area for cooking.

Assessment Procedures

/*\Safety Note: Be extremely careful when the child is around heat. Do not let her handle hot pans. Be aware of special diets and allergies before doing this assessment.

Grouping: When you are assessing a child's ability to accept a change or a disappointment, the most effective procedure is observation. An observational assessment can either be spontaneous or occur in a semi-structured situation.

1. If your choice is semi-structured, invite the child to help you make a treat (e.g., cookies, muffins). Explain to her specifically what the treat will be, for example, chocolate chip cookies, banana muffins, or peanut cookies.
2. Let her assist you in the mixing, stirring, and dropping the mix on a pan.
3. Bring to her attention that a particular ingredient called for is not available (e.g., chocolate chips, bananas, peanuts, etc.)

4. Discuss the situation with her, and observe how she handles the change.
5. Assure her that an available substitute can be used (for example: butterscotch chips, dates, walnuts).
6. Complete the cooking experience.
7. During the observational assessment, be sure the process involves some structure, not for grading, but for developing a program or for assisting a child with an identified behavior. Some suggestions to consider during the observation are: (1) When the child realized that there was a change in the event or activity, what type of reaction did she demonstrate? (2) Did she change her reaction when she was assured that there was a solution? (3) Did she assure others that the change or disappointment was all right and that things would work out? (4) Did she regain her enthusiasm when the modification was implemented? (5) Did it appear that she needed continued assurance and reinforcement from another person before she could accept the fact that an alternative was planned?

Credit: + Child remains calm in a disappointing situation or when a change needs to be implemented.

Adaptations
See #5.111.

5.155 Volunteers for tasks
Strand: 5-4   **Age:** 49-56m 4.1-4.8y

Definition
When the child is presented with, "Who wants to (do a specific task)?", he will volunteer, or when he presented with a new activity, he will want to do it. When he is presented with a group of activities, he will volunteer to perform at least one of them, and will exhibit behaviors that adapt to the new task.

Assessment Materials
Materials for a variety of activities for the child, such as clay, finger-paints, building blocks, puzzles, games, stencils, pegs, beads for lacing, log builders, stackers. (Three of the materials should be new activities to the child.)

Assessment Procedures
See #5.120 for assessment procedures.

Adaptations
See #5.120.

To help a child to volunteer: (1) Let him observe the assistance another child receives when he volunteers for a task; (2) Encourage him to volunteer by presenting a task that he has the skills to do; (3) Provide a reinforcement for those who volunteer. Helping a child want to volunteer begins by presenting him with a task that he is capable of doing successfully. Then, when you present him with an unfamiliar task, make him aware that support will be available. Also, make sure that the volunteering child receives plenty of positive reinforcement.

5.156 Cooperates with request for quiet
Strand: 5-4   **Age:** 49-58m 4.1-4.10y

Definition
When the child is requested to be quiet, she will become quiet. "Quiet" is defined as sitting still, waiting to talk, or using a quiet voice (whisper), refraining from tapping, pounding, or thumping, and keeping her hands and feet to herself. The request to be quiet is made verbally or with a predetermined visual or auditory signal.

Assessment Materials
A song the child is familiar with, such as *Farmer in the Dell*, or *Jingle Bells*.

Assessment Procedures
Note: / = one clap for each beat or syllable.
Grouping: When you assess a child's ability to be quiet on request, the most effective procedure is observation. An observational assessment can either be spontaneous or occur in a semi-structured situation.

1. If your choice is semi-structured, ask the child to sing a song (e.g., *Farmer in the Dell*, *Jingle Bells*, or *Twinkle Twinkle*) and to clap while she sings. After she has sung the song a few times and reaches the end of the verse or chorus, ask her to be quiet.
2. Observe her quieting behaviors, watching for the following: (1) Continued to sing and clap; (2) Verbally said she did not want to be quiet; (3) Sat down for a few minutes and then started to sing and clap again; (4) Rejected the idea of being quiet by pretending she did not know how; (5) Put her head down and tuned out the world; daydreamed; (6) Stayed sitting down but acted silly.
3. Explain to her that she was singing a nice tune, but that now she must be quiet because you are going to draw the claps on the board. For example, "Farmer in the Dell" would be:

The (one slash / on the board)
farmer (two slashes // on the board)
in the (two slashes // on the board)
dell (one slash / on the board)
Heigh (one slash / on the board)
ho (one slash / on the board)
the derry o (four slashes //// on the board).

4. Ask the child to sing the song quietly without clapping while you point to the clap marks. Ask her to sing quietly and clap the song quietly while you point to the clap marks. Ask her to sing and clap the song quietly, without your pointing to the marks. Observe if she sang and clapped the song quietly, or if she disregarded the quiet approach and sang and clapped loudly. Observe her behaviors, and compare them to your earlier observations.
5. The intent of the observation is to identify any social skills that need addressing and to decide what intervention strategies to use, not to be a ranking or grading procedure. This suggested observational process addresses behavioral issues only; developmental levels, conceptual understanding, language skills, and motor reactions are not included, but should be considered.
6. Informally observe the child when she is asked to be quiet, noting her behaviors and reactions.

Credit: + Child cooperates with the request to be quiet, made verbally or with a predetermined visual or auditory signal.

Adaptations

When a child is asked to shift from one behavior to another, she may find it difficult because just when she finally understands how to behave in one setting, she is thrust into another situation. Each transition requires her to prepare herself for the change. It also requires her to anticipate what is going to happen and to bring experience from her past behavioral patterns. She may become impulsive, which leads to a mixed behaviors or even total withdrawal. Her sense of uncertainty, her concern about the change and the unknown, all contribute to a fear of making a mistake, so she exhibits a behavior that is familiar to her. Often this known behavior is not appropriate for the change in activities. To help her, use these recommendations: (1) When you ask her to be quiet, make sure she understands in behavioral terms what "being quiet" means. For example, say, "Sit down in your seat." Demonstrate what sitting in a seat means. Ask her to sit in her seat. After she sits down, ask her to tell you what she is doing, and prompt if necessary. Say, "Do not move while you are sitting in the seat." Demonstrate what "not moving" means in a seated position. Ask her to show you how to sit in a seat without moving. Ask her to tell you what she is doing, and prompt if necessary. Reinforce her after each behavior step; (2) When you ask her to be quiet, tell her why. By telling her why, she will be able to anticipate, adjust, and prepare for the change, and she will have time to determine what social behavior is accepted; (3) Rather than telling her to be quiet, use a signal that means "sit down, stop talking, and no touching." As an example, turn the lights off, wait till everyone is quiet, and turn them back on. Or hold up a pillow, a stuffed animal, or a sign to indicate "be quiet." Or do a limp body exercise before you ask her to be quiet. Children develop their attending skills at different times. Provide them with the support of knowing exactly what you mean, and why you are asking them to do something. Providing a variety of ways to accomplish a request is motivating and helpful for all children.

5.157 Conforms to group decisions
Strand: 5-4   **Age:** 49-58m   4.1-4.10y

Definition
In a group of at least three children, all the group members, except for the child, decide that something should be done a certain way. The one child may initially protest the decision, but he does what the other group members do (as long as it does not conflict with health/safety rules he has been taught).

Assessment Materials
At least three different table games or activities the children enjoy.

Assessment Procedures
Grouping: When you assess a child's ability to conform to a group decision, the most effective procedure is observation. An observational assessment can either be spontaneous or occur in a semi-structured situation. Observe a group of at least three children in a decision-making process. Note the individual and group behaviors.
1. If the observational assessment is semi-structured, the following is a suggested procedure. Invite at least three children to the game area, and present them with the three different games or activities.

2. Explain that the group may do only one of the activities.
3. Tell them that they must decide as a group which one to do.
4. Allow the group to discuss the options.
5. Observe how the group determined the game or activity to do and if there was a dissenting child.
6. In observing, note whether the children: (1) Discussed the different options; (2) Argued about the options; (3) Sought outside help to decide; (4) Agreed on one activity; (5) Never came to a collective decision. In observing a single child, check for these reactions: (1) Pouted, withdrew, or cried when he did not get his own way; (2) Became verbally abusive to the others when he did not get his own way; (3) Became destructive when he did not get his own way; (4) Carried over his upset feelings when he participated in the activity with the others; (5) Pretended he did not want to play any of the games and left the scene; (6) Became unreasonable and resentful. These observational suggestions are based on social skills only, but consideration should be given to the child's entry level in language receptive/expressive, thinking and reasoning skills, and length of attending. Other considerations are: (1) The membership of the group; (2) Which child assumed the leadership role? (3) Did one child act as the instigator? (4) Did the group react to a weaker child as a scapegoat? (5) Did the group disintegrate and have to be coerced to participate? Remember that children behave differently when they are part of a group than they do as individuals. This is particularly true when the group is involved in decision-making. Group expectations influence a child's individual behavior, and a single child's behavior influences the group. Outcomes decided by a group are often a combination of what the group wants and the exhibited behaviors.

Credit: + Child conforms to the group decision, in a group of at least three children.

Adaptations

It can be very difficult for a child to deal socially with group dynamics. Even if a child has learned to exhibit acceptable behavior as an individual when he is involved in parallel and associative play, he may not have had experiences in group involvement. When he is involved in a group, the group expectations strongly influence his behavior. Individually, a child behaves to meet a need, to belong, and to contribute; however, when the child finds himself part of a group, his individual concerns and behaviors change to the needs of the group--how to belong to the group and how to contribute to it. Because group expectations can be unknown, a child may attempt to be the leader, not realizing he could be viewed as bossy by the group members. He may find himself in a position of making the group laugh to hide his feelings of uncertainty. The group may select a child as the one to blame for misbehavior, and the inexperienced child does not understand how to deal with the group's manipulation. He may choose to cause trouble knowingly and then to make his behaviors appear to be innocent. A child selects a role to play in a group because he thinks he is doing what is expected and others will enjoy it. To assist a child to understand how to be part of a group that plans and makes good decisions: (1) Provide guidance in group interaction and decision-making; (2) Be sure the group assignments are within his ability and of interest to him; (3) Support the child who needs help in self-control when he is in a group, in ways such as: (a) send a signal--shake your head or raise eyebrows to say. "I know what you are doing, and I do not approve"; (b) move close to him physically as a way of saying "do you want to help?"; (c) show interest in every person in the group; (d) use humor to modify and redirect the group; (e) help the child over a behavioral problem; (f) redirect him within the group structure; (g) reinforce appropriate group behavior; (4) Provide various opportunities for him to experience cooperative group action.

5.158 Treats other's property with respect
Strand: 5-4 **Age:** 49-58m 4.1-4.10y

Definition
When she handles property that belongs to someone else, the child will take proper care of it so that it is not damaged, destroyed, or unusable. She will treat property that belongs to others as if it were her own.

Assessment Materials
At least three toys or activities that belong to someone else that the child would enjoy playing with.

Assessment Procedures

Grouping: When you are assessing a child's ability to treat another child's property with respect, the most effective procedure is observation. An observational procedure can either be spontaneous or occur in a semi-structured situation.

Level One:
1. If the choice is semi-structured, place the collected toys or activities on a table and invite the child to the area.
2. Show her one of the items and tell her to whom it belongs and that she wants it back in good shape.
3. Show her another item and tell her to whom it belongs and that she wants it back in good shape.
4. Continue until you have shown her all the items and made the explanation for each.
5. Tell her she may choose one of the toys or activities and that she may play with it. Remind her to whom it belongs, emphasizing that she wants it back in good shape, so she must be careful when she plays with it.
6. Observe her as she plays with one of the items, paying particular attention to the way she handles the toy since she knows that it belongs to someone else. Watch for such behaviors as: (1) Is she destructive with the item? If so, how? (2) Did she refrain from playing with it? (3) Does she do things that will keep the item well taken care of? For example, does she take off the lid and set it in a clean place? Wipe off the ball when it rolls into a puddle? Put the crayons back in the box after using them? (4) Did she put all the parts together when she was finished playing with the toy or activity? (5) If an accident happened to the item, did she explain how it happened or did she make up a story about the damage? This observation process is intended to provide information on any behaviors that need to be addressed and for curriculum planning.

Level Two:
7. When the child is involved in playing with someone else's possessions, informally observe how the takes care of other person's property.

Credit: + Child handles the property of someone else with respect, making sure not to damage, destroy, or make unusable.

Adaptations

When a child is entrusted to do certain tasks, such as taking care of someone else's property, the results of the task is the child's responsibility. She should be told that once she accepts this task, the consequences are also hers. A child may forget her responsibility because she becomes distracted or finds something more interesting to do. If she simply forgets, it is important not to make her feel guilty or to feel that anyone has lost faith in her. Allow her to start over, and give her a chance to prove that she can be depended on. On the other hand, a trusted child may fail to assume her responsibility because she is defiant or she willfully neglects her task. When she is asked why she has been negligent, she may become defensive and resentful instead of admitting that she does not know how, she does not want to take the time, or she forgot about it. The sooner a child learns to be dependable and to develop good work habits, the sooner she will acquire the skills essential to good adjustment and responsibility It is also important to remember that as a child matures, she learns more about being responsible and what actions demonstrate reliability.

5.159 Sits in seat, stands in a line without excess moving during an activity

Strand: 5-4 **Age:** 49-60m 4.1-5.0y

Definition

The child will sit in a seat or stand in a line without excessive moving or fidgeting when he is observing or participating in an activity. The time he sits or stands without moving excessively will be determined by his entry behavior, the amount of time the activity takes, the group participating, the child's interest in the activity, his background information and skill level relative to the activity. Excessive moving and fidgeting behaviors are viewed as: (1) Getting out of his seat; (2) Standing on the seat; (3) Sitting on the floor; (4) Poking, hitting and kicking; (5) Interfering with the activity by swinging or swaying arms; (6) Stamping feet; (7) Overtly grabbing or hugging other participants; (8) Tipping over in the chair; (9) Rolling on the floor; (10) Any excessive motions that interfere with the activity or with the others involved.

Assessment Procedures

See #5.130 for assessment materials and procedures, as well as suggested adaptations.

5.160 Tells or gestures to adult about any danger/injury

Strand: 5-8 **Age:** 49-60m 4.1-5.0y

Definition
When the child witnesses another person involved in a dangerous setting or injured in some way, she will quickly report the incident to an appropriate person, or she will motion to someone to indicate that assistance is needed.

Assessment Materials
At least six pictures that represent dangerous situations or someone being injured. Examples: (1) Picture One: A child who has fallen off playground equipment and is lying on the ground; (2) Picture Two: Two children playing with a ball that has rolled into the street; (3) Picture Three: A child who has fallen down the stairs and is lying at the bottom of the stairs; (4) Picture Four: Two children walking down the street near a fire burning in a vacant lot; (5) Picture Five: Two bicycles that have crashed and one of the riders is hurt; (6) Picture Six: Two children standing in the kitchen, where the sink faucet is on and water is beginning to flood the area. You can obtain these pictures from commercial sources or make line art illustrations.

Assessment Procedures
Grouping: When you are assessing a child's ability to quickly report a dangerous situation they have witnessed, the most effective procedure is observation. An observational procedure can either be spontaneous or occur in a semi-structured situation.

Level One:
1. If the choice is semi-structured, place three pictures face-down on the table. Invite the child to the table. Discuss with her the meaning of the word "dangerous," what she should do when she see something dangerous, what she should do when she is not sure if something is dangerous or not, name situations that are dangerous, and discuss the ramifications of what can happen if a person does not seek help.
2. Encourage the child to contribute to the discussion to be certain she understands the meaning of dangerous.
3. Tell her you are going to show her some pictures of dangerous happenings. Explain that you want her to tell you what is happening in each picture.
4. Turn over Picture One. Discuss what is happening in the picture and prompt her as necessary.
5. Say, "What do you think is going to happen next?"
6. Give her an opportunity to respond.
7. Say, "What would you do if you were there?"
8. Pause for her response.
9. Turn over Picture Two. Discuss what is happening in the picture, and prompt as necessary.
10. Say, "What do you think is going to happen next?"
11. Give her an opportunity to respond.
12. Say, "What would you do if you were there?"
13. Pause for her response.
14. Continue with the remaining pictures.
15. Note her responses and knowledge of dangerous situations.
16. This assessment is not meant to grade or to rank children, but the intent is to determine intervention techniques and curriculum planning.

Credit: + Child tells or gestures to an adult, to let them know about a dangerous situation they have witnessed or someone who has fallen and injured themselves.

Adaptations
See #5.132.

5.161 Performs activities in presence of or when led by new person

Strand: 5-1 **Age:** 50-55m 4.2-4.7y

Definition
The child will demonstrate confidence and will perform an activity in front of or in conjunction with a new person. He will adapt his actions and behaviors when he is involved with the new person. A new person may be defined either as an observer or as a participant in the environment.

Assessment Materials
A person not familiar to the child. A song the child knows.

Assessment Procedures
Grouping: When you assess a child's ability to perform in the presence of a new person, the most effective procedure is play-based observation. An observational assessment can either be spontaneous or occur in a semi-structured situation.

1. If your choice is semi-structured, invite a person not familiar to the child to his environment, and when the person arrives, ask the child to sing his favorite song, do a special dance, perform a finger-play, say a rhyme, or show and tell about a picture he painted. Make sure the child feels comfortable, is successful, and enjoys doing whatever you ask him to do. Observe him as he performs for those in attendance, including the stranger.
2. This observational process should involve some structure, not for grading, but for developing a program or assisting the child with an identified behavior. Some suggestions to consider during the observation are: (1) Did he demonstrate confidence when he performed the activity in front of both know and unknown persons? If not, what behavior did he display? (2) Did he monopolize the new person and strive to establish an overt relationship? (3) Did he need prompting and verbal assurance during his presentation while the new person was in attendance? (4) Did he pause to "read" the new person before interacting with him?

Credit: + Child performs an activity in the presence or a new person. The child responds appropriately to the new person when interacting.

Adaptations

Some young children have not identified the difference between actions and intentions, and they still react based on what they see people do. So when a child is asked to perform before a new individual, he may decline, withdraw, or exhibit behaviors that will eliminate his need to perform. He is waiting for the new person to do something or to act, so he can decide on the possible consequences rather than intent. He is not sure whether the stranger will respond/react to his performance.

It is important to stress the importance of not having anything to do with strangers in certain situations. Make sure the child understands the difference between meeting new people in a controlled or planned situation, and contact with a stranger. If he seems confused or he has any questions about the difference between the two types of contacts, place the emphasis on (safety/security) how the child should react if he is approached by a stranger.

5.162 Uses napkin to wipe hands, mouth during and after meal
Strand: 5-6 **Age:** 50-57m 4.2-4.9y

Definition
The child will use a napkin to wipe her hands and mouth during and after the meal. She may need to be reminded.

Assessment Materials
/*\ **Safety Note:** Be aware of special diets and allergies before doing this assessment.
At least two different colors of food coloring, a mirror, silverware, two bowls, soft foods in which food coloring will mix well (e.g., applesauce, oatmeal, soft cereal), a napkin.

Assessment Procedures
Grouping: When you assess a child's ability to use a napkin to wipe her hands and mouth during and after meals, the most effective procedure is play-based observation. An observational assessment can either be spontaneous or occur in a semi-structured situation.

Level One:
1. If your choice is semi-structured, mix one food coloring into one of the soft foods, and mix the other food coloring into the other soft food.
2. Place the mirror in view of the child. Place the food, utensils, and napkin on the table.
3. Explain to the child that she is to eat a spoonful of the green-colored applesauce, look in the mirror, and use her napkin to wipe the green off her face.
4. Observe her as she uses her napkin to wipe off the green.
5. Ask her to eat a spoonful of the purple-colored applesauce, look in the mirror, and use her napkin to wipe the purple off her face.
6. Observe her as she uses her napkin to wipe off the purple.
7. Tell her to continue eating the different colored applesauce and to use her napkin to wipe off the colors.
8. Watch how and when she uses her napkin, looking for: (1) Wiping after each bite, (2) Not using the napkin, (3) Using the napkin inappropriately, (4) Playing with the color, (5) Destroying the paper napkin, (6) Playing with the napkin, instead of using it to wipe face and hands.
9. Provide the necessary cueing. Remember to allow her to do as much as she can independently, and assist by first giving

verbal clues, then modeling, and finally using physical prompting if necessary.

Level Two:

10. Informally observe the child during snack or lunch to see if they use their napkin to wipe their mouth and hands.

Credit: + Child uses a napkin to wipe hands and mouth appropriately, both during and after a meal. She may need to be reminded.

Adaptations

A child may not have been expected to use a napkin to the point where it has become a habit. Most table manners are matters of information and habit. These habits are learned largely by imitation. A child needs to practice good manners until they are habitual and natural. Even if she forgets, when she does remember or is reminded, she will feel comfortable in the action and not inept. To assist her: (1) Model using a napkin to wipe mouth and hands; (2) Reward her for demonstrating good manners. Give her ample time to practice this table manner, and provide cueing as necessary. It is important to remember not to expect more of the child than she can do; conversely, let her do what she can do. Filling her plate, passing the bowl for her, and telling her to wipe her mouth and hands will not lead to an independent level of table manners.

5.163 Bargains with other children

Strand: 5-5 **Age:** 50-66m 4.2-5.6y

Definition

The child will exchange items after a discussion of the exchange. Example: "If you let me swing, you may ride my bike." The agreement may include the following elements: (1) Items to be exchanged or activities to exchange, (2) Criteria involved (time, location, person).

Assessment Materials

At least two items that belong to each child.

Assessment Procedures

See # 5.112 and #5.136 for assessment materials and procedures, as well as suggested adaptations. Respecting a child's right to bargain with his own items when he is ready acknowledges his rights and gives him the security he needs to begin this experience.

5.164 Tells month of birth

Strand: 5-2 **Age:** 48-58m 4.0-4.10y

Definition

When the child is asked, she will tell the month of her birthday. Some prompting may be necessary. Examples: "Halloween is in the same month," "Remember, it is in the same month when we build snowmen," or "January, February ..." (pause to allow her to say March.)

Assessment Materials

A calendar that has a visual representation of each month. Examples: valentines for February, kites for March, spring flowers for April. If such a calendar is not available, locate monthly stickers or stamps that represent months of the year.

Assessment Procedures

Grouping: This skill can be assessed one-on-one with the child, or in a small group setting.

1. Invite the child to join you at a table. Ask her how old she is.
2. Discuss with her how old she will be on her next birthday.
3. Talk about special things that happen on her birthday.
4. Say, "What month is your birthday?"
5. Give her time to respond. Note her response.
6. If she has difficulty remembering or knowing the month of her birthday, follow these recommendations: (1) Say, "Is it in January? Is it in December? Is it in May?" (2) Show her a calendar, say the months, and when you come to the month of her birthday, draw a circle around the correct day; (3) Place a sticker on a piece of paper that represents the month of her birthday. Discuss what the sticker represents (February--Valentine's Day) and then talk about another special day in the same month, her birthday. Say, "There is a special day in the month of February, and that day is your birthday." Point to the symbol of February and say, "What month is your birthday?" Randomly ask her the month of her birthday.
7. Since her birthday is such an important event, even if she has a problem remembering or saying the month of her birthday, she will soon make the association and be able to respond.

Credit: + Child correctly tells the month of her birthday, some prompting may be used.

Adaptations

Some children will have more difficulty telling how old they are, the month of their birthday, and the date. A child will probably be able to learn her birthday by rote but often without complete comprehension. To assist her to learn the month and date of her birthday, make her birthday a special event. Make her important that day by giving her the title of being the "Girl of the Day," "The Birthday Girl," and let her to do special tasks, pick out the game of the day or the story of that day. Provide her with a special treat to share with her friends. Be sure to remind her of her birthday frequently after the special day.

5.165 Tells street name and town in address

Strand: 5-2 **Age:** 48-66m 4.0-5.6y

Definition

When the child is presented with the question, "In what city do you live?" or "In what town do you live?" he will respond correctly. If he lives in a rural area, his response will probably be the town or city where he goes for shopping and services. When you asking the question, it is important to ask, "In what city or town do you live?" instead of "In what town or city is your address?" When he is presented with the verbal question, "On what street do you live?" he will respond correctly. After he has named the street and city or town where he lives ask, "On what street and in what city/town do you live?" If he responds by stating his name and complete address, accept this because he has probably learned to respond to a question about where he lives by rote memory.

Assessment Procedures

See #5.134 for assessment materials and procedures, as well as suggested adaptations.

5.166 (Removed, see page xviii)

5.167 Uses appropriate pitch/volume when speaking

Strand: 5-7 **Age:** 48-60m 4.0-5.0y

Definition

When he is speaking, the child will use appropriate intonation, inflection, and volume. He may increase or decrease voice pitch to emphasize a part of a verbal description, or he may increase or decrease the volume to be heard or for effect.

Assessment Materials

A short story that leads up to an exciting ending. Once the story is told up to a climatic part, the ending is to be left to the child. Look for a story in the local public library or use the example that follows. Example: Story One--Bill went to visit his grandmother in a strange city. When the plane landed and Bill got off he looked for his grandmother. She was not there, so he was all alone. Bill said... Story Two--Sue took her float into the ocean. She was lying on it and floating far away from shore. Suddenly Sue saw a big fish jump out of the water. Sue cried.

Assessment Procedures

Note: It is important to become an enthusiastic listener as the child becomes excited about telling his story.

Grouping: When you assess a child's ability to use appropriate pitch/volume when speaking, the most effective procedure is play-based observation. An observational assessment can either be spontaneous or occur in a semi-structured situation.

<u>Level One:</u>
1. If your choice is semi-structured, explain to the child that you are going to tell him a story without an ending. Tell him that he is to make up the ending.
2. Read or tell Story One to him, stopping after you read, "Bill said." Pause to let the child finish the story.
3. Note the pitch and volume the child uses to complete the story.
4. If he speaks too loudly, too softly or with a too high or too low a pitch, repeat his ending to the story, using a comfortable volume and pitch. Ask the child to repeat the ending, saying it as you did.
5. Continue in the same manner with Story Two.

<u>Level Two:</u>
6. During conversation time, show-and-tell, or "chat and chuckle," observe the child's voice volume and pitch as he relates an experience or an event.

Credit: + Child uses appropriate intonation, inflection, and volume with speaking.

Adaptations

The three aspects of voice response are: (1) Pitch-- usually in a monotone; (2) Intensity-- talking too loudly or too softly; (3) Quality-- hyper nasality (talking through the nose), hypo-nasality (sounds like the nose is plugged up, often referred to as the "head cold sound"), and others, such as a metallic voice (sounds like cartoon character) or raspy (sounds like there is gravel in the throat). If the child's voice reflects a problem with pitch, intensity, or quality, it is recommended that he see a qualified speech/language pathologist. Some voice concerns are related to a structural abnormality and others are related to hearing losses; the child cannot hear himself speak and is therefore not aware that he should be changing his pitch to make the normal intonation patterns. Other causes are abuse or misuse of the voice or an emotional condition. Some children do not have voice problems, but still lack inflection in their speech. A child who does not show voice enthusiasm when describing the witches visit on Halloween may not understand that a witch is scary, especially on Halloween. A child who does not use a whisper when he puts his teddy bear to sleep may not understand that there is a need to be quiet when someone is sleeping. If a medical evaluation reveals there is no physical condition, the child may be directed to voice therapy with special emphasis placed on the understanding of words and the setting that represents different moods.

5.168 Stays on topic during a conversation

Strand: 5-7 **Age:** 53-60m 4.5-5.0y

Definition
The child will participate in a topic or discussion, using appropriate vocabulary, allowing others to contribute, and maintaining the topic for a reasonable length of time or until closure.

Assessment Materials
At least three topics familiar to the children that they enjoy talking about and feel they can contribute to. Pictures of the selected topics to help stimulate discussion.

Assessment Procedures
Grouping: Informal observation is very effective because it is done in a natural setting without some of the variables that accompany formal assessment procedures.

Level One:
1. Invite the children to the visiting area, and encourage them to get comfortable. Introduce the selected topic as follows: (1) Show the picture and ask the children to talk about the picture and what is happening in it; (2) Ask a lead question, for example, "What do you like to do on your birthday?" or "If you could have a pet, what would it be? Why?"; (3) Read a poem on a very specific topic, and after reading it, ask "what," "when," and "where" questions to initiate the conversation; (4) Show the children something new and ask them to discuss it. Observe each child as she participates in the conversation, watching for: (1) Levels of participation; (2) Staying on the subject; (3) Appropriate listening skills; (4) Quality of contributions; (5) Encouraging others to interact. Remember that if the children are to contribute to the discussion, they must have some knowledge or experience relative to the topic. It is also important to make the child feel capable of contributing and to feel accepted by the other group members.

Level Two:
2. When the child is involved in a conversation, observe whether she stays on the subject during the interchange.

Credit: + Child stays on topic during a conversation, using appropriate vocabulary, allowing others to contribute, and maintaining the topic for a reasonable length of time or until closure.

Adaptations
A child may find it difficult to stay on the subject during a conversation because of the following: (1) A short attention span; (2) Sensitivity to criticism; (3) Lacks background information; (4) Low self-esteem so feels incapable of contributing; (5) Seeks attention. A child who experiences a short attention span may shift from one topic to another, and because of this scatter, she soon forgets her intended subject. To assist her, provide her with structure, select a topic she enjoys, remind her often of the selected subject (e.g., "Erica, we would like to hear about the circus some other time, but right now we are talking about farm animals"), reward her attending behaviors, and explain expected behaviors thoroughly. A child may choose not to contribute to a conversation because she is concerned that what she says will be criticized or laughed at. To assist her, make sure that the environment is supportive rather than challenging and disapproving. Also, explain to her that not all situations are alike so her responses must also be different. Often she may change the subject in order to gain attention from the group leader or her peers. She may use this negative approach to seek attention in an

aggressive manner or in a passive-aggressive style. The best approach for dealing with this behavior is to ignore it, to use an "I" message (e.g., "I get upset when we are talking about something and you change the subject, please stay on the topic we are talking about.") Remember that if the child does not have the necessary knowledge of the topic or an experience dealing with it, she will undoubtedly want to change the subject during a discussion. Being selective of the topic is important to enable her to be motivated and involved in the conservation.

5.169 Tells father's and mother's first and last names

Strand: 5-2 **Age:** 54-62m 4.6-5.2y

Definition
When the child is asked, "What is your father's first and last name?" he will be able to respond. When he is asked, "What is your mother's first and last name?" he will be able to respond. The person who asks the questions will be aware of the proper names used by the child's parents and of his family situation (e.g., single-parent family), and will respond accordingly. Any discussion about the use of different names, acceptable nicknames, names of endearment, and names of identification (Daddy Paul) will be avoided.

Assessment Materials
Check of records to find child's parents' first and last names.

Assessment Procedures
Grouping: This skill should be assessed one-on-one with the child.
1. Ask an adult to assist you in the assessment process.
2. Tell the adult to ask the child the question, "What is your father's first name?"
3. After the child responds, have the adult ask, "What is your father's last name?"
4. After the child responds, have the adult ask, "What is your father's first and last name?"
5. Note the child's responses.
6. After he responds, have the adult ask him, "What is your mother's first name?"
7. After he responds, have the adult ask him, "What is your mother's last name?"
8. After he responds, have the adult ask him, "What is your mother's first and last name?"
9. Note his response.
10. If he has difficulty responding, determine whether he understands the concept of "first" and "last." For example, say to him, "Your first name is William. What is your father's first name?" Pause for a response. Then, say, "Your first name is William. What is your mother's first name?" Pause for a response. Continue the same procedure with last names. If he is unsure of his mother or father's names, say, "Your father's first name is Steve. What is your father's first name?" After he responds, say, "Your father's last name is Hall. What is your father's last name?" Ask the child to say his father's first and last name. Continue the same procedure with the mother's first and last name. Remember, it is important that you know his father's and mother's first and last names, and that you are sensitive in the questioning process as well as accepting of the child's responses.

Credit: + Child correctly tells his father's and mother's first and last names when asked.

Adaptations
A child may exhibit difficulty saying his mother's and father's names because of name changes, nicknames, dual names used, association with the terms Mother and Father, professional titles, etc. As a result, he may not be able to respond, not because of lack of information, but because of confusion caused by terminology and situations. The best way to help is to accept his responses. However, make sure the child understands the ordinal meaning of names (first and last), and if necessary, clarify these position names. Use the child's own names to help him comprehend ordinal relationships.

5.170 Recites emergency telephone number (911) and when to use it

Strand: 5-8 **Age:** 54-66m 4.6-5.6y

Definition
When asked, the child will state the universal emergency telephone number (911) and will demonstrate an understanding of when to use the number. She will understand the number is not to be used falsely.

Assessment Materials
/*\ **Safety Note:** Check and confirm the emergency number or numbers used in your area.
At least six pictures, three of them showing a situation in which the universal emergency

telephone number should be used and three of them showing a situation in which the emergency telephone number would be inappropriate. Purchase these illustrations commercially, cut and glue them from magazines, or make simple line drawings. Examples: Picture One--A person has collapsed on the floor and no one else is around except a child. Picture Two--A masked person is crawling over a fence in a backyard. Picture Three--A child is walking out the back door and sees the barn on fire. Picture Four--Two children are arguing over the use of a swing, and another child is trying to break up the confrontation. Picture Five--A person is taking a cookie sheet full of cookies out of the oven, and the cookies have burned. Picture Six--A car parked in a driveway has two flat tires.

Assessment Procedures

Grouping: This skill should be assessed one-on-one with the child.

1. Ask the child to tell you the emergency telephone number.
2. If she is unable to tell you the number, ask her to repeat it after you.
3. Repeat the number several times, and ask her to say it after you.
4. Say, "Tell me the emergency telephone number."
5. Pause to allow her to respond.
6. Reinforce her for giving the correct answer.
7. Discuss with her the importance of the number, what will happen if she calls it, and that it is only to be used in an emergency.
8. Make sure she understands the concept of situations that are considered emergencies.
9. Tell her you are going to show her some pictures of situations in which the emergency number should be called and some situations in which the number should not be called.
10. Say, "Look at the picture, and tell me if you would call the emergency number if you were there."
11. Show her one of the pictures, and ask her to tell you what is happening.
12. Prompt her if necessary.
13. Ask her if she had would have called the emergency number if she were there.
14. If her answer is "yes," ask her what the number is.
15. Record her response.
16. Continue the above sequence with the other pictures.
17. It is extremely important for the child to be able to recite the emergency telephone number, but also for her to understand when the number should be used.
18. This assessment is not meant to rank or grade a child, but to determine instructional needs and assist in curriculum planning.

Credit: + Child recites your local emergency telephone number and the universal 911 number, and knows when she should use it.

Adaptations

A child needs to move developmentally through a cognitive process to reach the level of making sound, logical judgments. When she is asked to determine emergencies versus non-emergencies, if she has not reached competency for thinking judgmentally, the task could be overwhelming. To assist her: (1) Provide her with real experiences using real objects and hands-on activities; (2) Use pictures to depict real-life experiences, new situations, objects, and expanded predictions. She can learn all concepts best through considering real-life experiences to which she attaches words. If she by-passes this step, she misses the foundation for making logical judgments. As a result, she will have a difficult time determining what is an emergency and what is not.

5.171 Accepts an altered routine when requested

Strand: 5-1 **Age:** 48-72m 4.0-6.0y

Definition

When the child is presented with a change in his schedule or routine, he will accept the modification by displaying adaptable behavior. The change in the schedule or routine may be permanent or temporary.

Assessment Materials

A short story about a child who was used to a certain schedule and something happened to change that schedule. Example: Every Monday afternoon Donny goes to the park to play; however, this Monday he could not go because there was an emergency.

There are reference books at your local library that match storybooks with a specific behavior you may be addressing. As an example, if you look up "Acceptance," there will be a listing of books by title that address this issue. However, if a short story is not available, make up a story or use the example:

<u>The Puppets Came</u>
Mary Lou could hardly go to sleep.
Tomorrow was her birthday.

Mary Lou was going to be 5 years old.
She was going to have a party, and all her friends were coming.
But when Mary Lou woke up the next morning, she felt sneezy and wheezy.
Mother came to say a big "Happy Birthday."
Mother looked at Mary Lou and felt her head.
Mother said, "Oh my, it looks like a sneezy-wheezy cold."
Mary Lou began to cry, and she said, "My birthday, my birthday party!"
Mother said, "I am afraid we will have to call the party off. I will call your friends and tell them not to come."
Mary Lou was very disappointed. Big tears fell from her eyes.
How could she celebrate her birthday?
What would they do with all the balloons, the streamers, the games, the cake, and the ice cream?
All of the sudden, Mother said, "We will still have a birthday party, except that the guests will be puppets."
Mary Lou stopped crying for a minute and she said, "Puppets?"
"Yes, puppets, they will not catch your sneezy-wheezy cold," said Mother.
Mother and Mary Lou got busy and began to make puppets for the party.
Mary Lou forgot how disappointed she felt, and she stopped crying.
They made the puppets look like the friends who could not come to the party.
After they finished making the puppets, they blew up the balloons, hung the streamers, and set the table.
Mary Lou and the puppets played games until it was time for ice cream and cake.
Mary Lou had a grand time.
It was a wonderful birthday, and the best part was that the puppet friends did not have to go home.

Assessment Procedures

Grouping: The most effective assessment is made by observing the child in a natural setting to determine how he accepts changes in his schedule or routine. An observational assessment can either be spontaneous or occur in a semi-structured situation.

Level One:
1. If your choice is semi-structured, explain to the child that you are going to read him a story and ask him to listen carefully.
2. After you have read the story, ask him general interpretive questions about it. Ask, for example: What was the little girl's name? What special day was it? What was going to happen on her birthday? What did her mother have to do?
3. After you have established the factual information, ask affective questions, for example: How did Mary Lou feel when her birthday party had to be called off? What did she do to help forget about her disappointment? How did the puppet party make Mary Lou feel?
4. When the child has responded to the affective questions, ask him the following questions? Examples: Have you ever been disappointed? How did it make you feel? What did you do?
5. Evaluate his responses, and if appropriate, extend the discussion for clarification.

Level Two:
6. Observe the child when he is confronted with a change in his routine. Observe: (1) Whether he accepts the alternative presented; (2) His feelings; (3) His behaviors; (4) Any indication of adapting to the change.

Credit: + Child accepts a change in the routine when requested due to a modification to the planned schedule.

Adaptations

When a child is confronted with an alteration in a routine, he may exhibit impulsive reactions and demonstrate a lack of self-control. These behaviors may take the form of acting out, reacting too quickly, or retreating from the situation. He may be unsure, even frightened when his routine is disrupted. His uncertainty is based on his not knowing what the alternative is, being unsure what he should do, questions as to whether he can be successful, and general fear about the change. To assist him: (1) Help him understand that certain situations are negotiable and other are not; (2) Make sure that he is aware of the altered routine, including when it will happen, what will occur, who will be there, and what he will need to do. To deal with his uncertainty, start a step-by-step description or role-playing; (3) If possible, let him be part of the alternative planning; (4) Help him problem-solve by giving him a series of options, expectations for each option, his role in each option, and the outcomes of each option; (5) Explain the support system he will have during the alternative.

5.172 Independently tries out new activities

Strand: 5-1 **Age:** 48-60m 4.0-5.0y

Definition
When the child is asked, she will attempt a task she has not previously performed; however, the new task should involve motor, cognitive, and behavioral components that are familiar to her. She will adapt her behaviors and demonstrate an effort to try the new task, will attend to the task for a reasonable length of time, will demonstrate a trial-and-error approach, will ask questions to aid her in doing the activity, and will seek support and help with the materials, if needed.

Assessment Materials
At least three new activities that the child has not done before. (She may have been involved with some of the elements of the new activity; for instance, if it is a picture to color, she probably has used crayons before; if it is building with new interlocking blocks, she has probably built with blocks before; or if it is a new lotto game, she has no doubt matched pictures before.)

Assessment Procedures
Grouping: Informal observation is very effective because it is done in a natural setting without some of the variables that accompany a formal assessment procedure. However, if necessary a semi-structured assessment may be used.

Level One:
1. If a semi-structured approach necessary, place the new activities on a table. Invite the child to the table and explain that there are some new and different things for her to do.
2. Tell her she may play with any of the new activities. Leave the table, but stay within an observable location.
3. Observe her as she explores, selects, and interacts with the new activity. Watch for the following behaviors: (1) Handles and looks at each of the new activities; (2) Selects one of the new tasks and begins to explore how to play with it (lays the pieces out, manipulates parts), and then attempts the new activity; (3) Stays with the selected task, even if her first attempt to play with it does not yield results or satisfaction; (4) Becomes frustrated when the selected activity does not bring results or satisfaction; (5) Moves from one new activity to another, not staying with any activity for any length of time; (6) Becomes frustrated when she cannot figure out how to interact with a new activity and reacts by being destructive with the activities, cries, leaves the table, whines; (6) Asks for help; (7) Tries all the new activities, selects the one that interests her the most, and plays with it; (8) Tries to get attention by diverting attention from the new activities. (It is important to remove the new activities before the child becomes overly frustrated and aggravated.)
4. Note her behaviors as she attempts the new activities. This observation is not for ranking, but for planning behavior change, management, and intervention strategies.

Level Two:
5. Informally observe the child as she independently attempts a new activity.

Credit: + Child independently tries out new activities that involve developmental components that are familiar to her. She tries the new task, attends for a reasonable length of time, demonstrates a trial-and-error approach, asks question to help her with the activity, and seeks support, if needed.

Adaptations
When you ask a child to attempt a new activity, she should be ready to understand that there is not just one way to do things. She needs to understand that trial-and-error is a way of learning; when she makes a single trial and is unsuccessful, she should try again. A child may have a difficult time realizing that there are different ways and alternatives. Her thinking process is often limited to reacting to only one alternative to the exclusion of another. Hence, when she is asked to attempt a new task without direction and demonstration, she tends to try one way and if she is not successful, she gives up. Or she will try the one way again and again, hoping that at some point her way will work. To assist a child to deal with trial-and-error and to teach her to try another way, the following is recommended: (1) Review a skill with her that she knows and can do different ways. For example, show her how to interlock the new and different blocks. Make sure you mention the fact that these blocks are very much like the blocks that she used to build a [bridge]; (2) Demonstrate different ways to accomplish a task. For example, place lotto cards picture side-up for matching on a playing board, or place the deck of picture cards face-down, and draw one card at a time for board matching; or deal the cards to each child who is playing and match the cards with the playing board; (3) Reinforce the

child for attempting a new task, making sure that she is reinforced for trying, even if she is not totally successful; (4) Provide her with a general description of the new activity, including references to activities that she is familiar with and suggestions for ways to begin the new task; (5) Because a child may prefer to try a new activity when no one is around to avoid public failure, leave her alone with the new effort; (6) Because problem-solving with another child is sometimes more effective, allow the child to work with another child, particularly if the children are comfortable with cooperative play. Remember that if she chooses not to attempt a new task, she may not be developmentally ready to do it. To insist she try may create frustration, inappropriate behaviors, and a diminished feeling of self-worth.

5.173 Remains in designated play areas
Strand: 5-8 **Age:** 55-60m 4.7-5.0y

Definition
When the child is made aware of the boundaries of the play area, he will remain in that area without supervision.

Assessment Materials
A large play area, such as a recreation room, a gym, or exercise area. Mark or rope off a section large enough for active play.

Assessment Procedures
Grouping: The most effective assessment is made by observing the child in a natural setting to determine whether he will stay in the designated play area. An observational assessment can either be spontaneous or occur in a semi-structured situation.

Level One:
1. Inform the child of the selected area, and tell him he may not go into any other part of the room. Make sure he understands the restricted space.
2. Give him several options of activities he can play.
3. Place yourself in a position where you can observe him, but not be obvious to the child that you are watching.
4. Observe him to determine whether he follows the directions and remains in the designated play area.
5. If he ventures out of the restricted area, remind him of the rule and tell him to return.
6. Continue observing his behavior.
7. During this observation, it is important to note not only whether the child left, but also the reason for his departure.

Level Two:
8. Observe the child when he is playing outside to determine if he remains in the designated play area. During this observation, again it is important to note not only whether he left, but the reason for his departure.

Credit: + Child remains in designated play areas without supervision.

Adaptations
Some children become disoriented about space and directions, which may be accompanied by a fear of getting lost and feelings of confusion when restricted to a specific area. To assist the child: (1) Make sure he understands words that indicate spatial relationships (e.g., "around," "behind," "beside," "next to"); (2) It is also important to walk the child around the boundaries of the area, pointing out landmarks and discussing them; (3) Using color signals as cues (e.g., red means you may not go, green means it is approved) may be helpful; (4) Remind him of the restrictions often. A child may demonstrate disobedient behavior just to be contrary, often to gain attention or to show independence. He learns that he can successfully refuse to do things that are demanded of him and then sits back to enjoy the commotion, attention, and concerns his refusal causes. He needs to understand that certain restrictions are necessary for his safety on which there will be no compromise or modification. To help him understand the safety issues, a complete explanation of why the rule is enforced is mandatory as well as positive modeling. It is important to let him know there is no negotiating when it comes to issues related to safety.

5.174 Stays with the group and refrains from following unknown people
Strand: 5-8 **Age:** 55-60m 4.7-5.0y

Definition
When the child is involved in an outside activity (visiting a museum, attending a presentation, going to a park), she will stay with the group to which she

was assigned. She will refrain from following an unknown person or group of people.

Assessment Materials

Pictures of a child not staying with a group. Examples: (1) A group of children visiting a zoo and one child is leaving the group. The child who is leaving her group is following two adults; (2) A child has a paper circle pinned to her shirt that indicates that she is to be with other children who have circles. She is taking off her circle, leaving the other children with circles and walking to another group; (3) A group of children sitting on a rug listening to a story, and one child is leaving the group to play alone; (4) Four children walking to the playground, and one is waving to her friends as she follows a group of teenagers. If pictures are difficult to find, make simple line drawings.

Assessment Procedures

Grouping: When you assess a child's ability to stay with the group and not follow strangers, the most effective procedure is play-based observation. An observational assessment can either be spontaneous or a semi-structured situation.

Level One:
1. If the choice is semi-structured, invite the child to look at one of the pictures. Discuss with her what is happening in the picture.
2. Begin asking her questions such as: What could happen to the person who leaves the group and follows strangers? Why do you think she is leaving? What would you do if you were there? Have you ever been told to stay with a group? What did you do? Have your ever followed a stranger? What could happen?
3. Continue by showing her the other pictures and using the same procedure.
4. Observe her responses, realizing that there are many variables that affect responses when you are using visuals and are asking questions.

Level Two:
5. Observe the child as she is involved in an activity that requires her to stay with a group. Record any inappropriate behaviors she exhibited, particularly those related to not participating with the group, leaving the group, following strangers rather than staying with her friends, and causing trouble in the group. This observational recording is not for grading or ranking, but to determine intervention strategies.

Credit: + Child stays with the group she has been assigned to during an outside activity. She refrains from following strangers.

Adaptations

/***Safety Note:** It is important to make sure the child understands that staying with a group is the safe and secure thing to do.

She must understand the reason for staying with her assigned group and not becoming involved with strangers. These strategies are: (1) Give her the reason for being assigned to a group (e.g., the group needs your help, to avoid getting lost, being safe, keeping an equal number in each group, etc.); (2) Children in a group need to have similar goals; (3) Children in a group should have positive interdependence. If a child has not had ample group experiences, these skills are not part of normal assimilation. To assist her: (1) Take ample time to prepare the child for an activity that requires belonging to a group; (2) Make sure she is aware of the dangers of leaving a group and following strangers; (3) Make sure she understands the goal of the group activity and why it is important to stay with the group. For example, groups are formed so that: (1) Everyone can participate on the tour; (2) No one gets lost; (3) Groups are safe from outside hazards; (4) Everyone gets a turn; (5) Members can have a chance to share. Make sure the child has a role in the group. Roles to assign might include being first in line, helping another child stay with the group, making sure that everyone is together, or passing out name tags.

5.175 Performs undesirable task when changed to be viewed as desirable

Strand: 5-4 **Age:** 55-62m 4.7-5.2y

Definition

When the child is presented with a task to do that he does not want to do, he will change his attitude once the same task is presented in a motivating way that makes it seem more desirable/like a game. Example: The child is asked to pick up the paper from the floor. He reacts with one of the following behaviors: (1) Picks up the paper on the floor; (2) Picks up one piece of paper and quits; (3) Shoves the paper on the floor under another child's seat; (4) Picks up the paper only when verbally prompted; (5) Puts his head down and ignores the request; (6) Verbally refuses to pick up the paper. But when the request to pick up the paper on the floor is presented in a game format, he views the task as fun and something he would like to do. Example: He is asked to pick up the paper from

© 2010 VORT Corporation. All rights reserved. Do Not copy.

the floor, wad it into a ball, and shoot it into the wastebasket. And for every wad that hits the basket from 2 feet away, he gets a point. The child with the most points wins.

Assessment Materials
Shaving cream, sponge, water, and towels.

Assessment Procedures
Grouping: You can assess how a child will perform an undesirable task once it is changed to be more desirable, most effectively by play-based observation. An observational assessment can either be spontaneous or occur in a structured situation.
1. If your choice is a structured situation, assign the child to scrub the top of the table with a wet sponge.
2. Observe his reaction. If he rejects the task, restate the activity. Example: Tell him you want him to clean off the top of the table. Tell him how you want him to do it by saying, "First, I want you to spray the top of the table with shaving cream. You may play with the shaving cream, and make pictures or designs. When you are finished playing, wash the shaving cream off with a sponge and water, and then dry the tabletop."
3. Observe his reaction to the same task except for being presented in a more motivating manner. Compare his first reaction with his reaction to the second presentation.
4. The intent of this observational assessment is to determine whether he would perform an undesirable task if it is presented as fun and desirable and how his behaviors changed when he viewed the request as a game or an enjoyable activity.

Credit: + Child performs a task that he did not want to do originally, when it was presented in a motivating way that made it seem more desirable, or like a game.

Adaptations
Some children do not realize that when they finish playing they have an additional responsibility. That responsibility is to clean up after playing. He needs to put his toys away, clean up after himself when he has engaged in a messy art activity, or clean up after having a snack or eating a meal. It is important to help him understand that even though clean-up might be viewed as undesirable, it will help him out when he is ready to play again or begin another activity. He will know where his possessions are and he will have a clean area to play in. The following strategies can be used; (1) Help him understand that he has duties and responsibilities that are the result of his actions. When he accepts this premise, he will also experience maximum enjoyment from play; (2) When an undesirable task needs to be presented as a desirable task, make him aware that he can also find a way to make unappealing jobs enjoyable. However, making a task enjoyable is not the same thing as having fun or playing games all the time.

5.176 Refuses ride and/or gifts presented by stranger
Strand: 5-8 **Age:** 55-62m 4.7-5.2y

Definition
/*\Caution Alert: *Because of important family and community concerns regarding this issue, there are materials available and professional groups that make presentations It is recommended that these groups be contacted. They should provide prevention and follow-up techniques. Contact your local PTA, School District Office, Police Department, State Educational Agency, etc.*

5.177 Follows defined rules whether or not an authority figure is present
Strand: 5-4 **Age:** 56-62m 4.8-5.2y

Definition
The child will follow at least two rules that were given to him earlier without any verbal prompting in the present situation. The authority figure is either not present or is present but may or may not be aware of the child's actions. The intent is for the child to follow predefined rules because he is developing behaviors that involve self-discipline, responsibility, and cooperation, rather than behaviors based on consequences (pleasure or pain).

Assessment Procedures
Grouping: When you assess a child's ability to follow defined rules whether an authority figure is present or not, the most effective procedure is play-based observation. An observational assessment can either be spontaneous or occur in a semi-structured situation.
1. An essential aspect of a child's behavior involves his comprehending rules and understanding that rules are established in his best interest or in the best interest of the group. Rules will allow others to evaluate

how well he can follow directions, even when an authority figure is not present.

2. Assessing the child's intent of following rules is best conducted by delayed observation. Some suggestions are: (1) Tell the child that when he is finished playing with the blocks he must put them away. When it is time for him to put the blocks away, observe whether he followed the rule of putting the blocks away without any prompting. If he did not put away the blocks, remind him, and observe if the single verbal prompt was the needed reminder; (2) Tell him that sitting is the best way to listen to a story, and while you read the story, observe if he remains seated. Pause while you read the story to restate the rule, and observe whether he remains seated after the reviewing of the rule; (3) Tell him he may talk to his painting partner, but ask him to use his regular, inside voice. Then observe by listening for a voice louder than an inside voice. Use a general statement such as, "Someone is forgetting the rule about using an inside voice. I'm having a difficult time thinking, because a voice is too loud."

3. Observe whether the general statement deterred the behavior. If other children are involved during this assessment, reinforce them for following the rules, and then observe if the target child modified his behavior after the directed positive response. During the observational process, determine whether the child: (1) Disregarded the rule; (2) Obeyed the known rule only when the authority was looking; (3) Reacted by giving excuses for not obeying the rules; (4) Retreated from the situation by withdrawing or crying; (5) Pleaded guilty and then repeated breaking the rule. The observational assessment is an important procedure to determine what behavioral or social skills the child needs.

4. Intervention strategies should be implemented.

Credit: + Child follows at least two rules that were given to him earlier without any verbal prompting used, and whether an authority figure is present or not.

Adaptations

Some children depend on others to determine how they should or should not behave. If this dependency becomes too strong it can create many problems for a young child. This dependency might be because many of the people in his life are constantly telling him what to do, when to do it, and how to do it. This dependent behavior may also be due to his inability to determine correct social responses and a concern about being able to transfer a behavior from one situation to another. The child reacts by becoming lethargic, indecisive, and may even be resentful and hostile. To assist in reducing behavioral dependency, provide him with many opportunities to select his behavior independently. It is also helpful for you to present him with several solutions and then let him decide on one. If he is allowed some self-selection, he is more likely to live up to the standards of behavior since he has a sense of "ownership." When you establish rules for behavior, it is important to invite cooperation rather than to demand it. To initiate this approach, decide with the child before an activity what kind of behavior is going to be required. And if these decided-on behaviors are disregarded during the activity, stop the task and provide him with behavioral choices. For example, say, "We can sit quietly and listen to this story, or we can go to our tables and put our heads down. You decide." Remember, if the child selects being quiet and listening to the story, and he is disruptive again, it is essential to follow through with the alternative. The child needs to learn that there are consequences to his behavior, both negative and positive, and that the adult will consistently follow through with the expectations and consequences. Learning to abide by rules whether an adult is present or not is the result of giving the child an opportunity to cooperate and be responsible.

5.178 Identifies fire drill signal and follows teacher's directions during the fire drill

Strand: 5-8   **Age:** 36-60m   3.0-5.0y

Definition

The child will practice following the teacher's directions during a fire drill. By following the directions, the child will get out of the building when the fire alarm sounds.

Assessment Materials

/*\Safety Note: It is important to prepare the child before a fire drill so that when the alarm sounds, she will not be frightened, disoriented or panicky. A brief demonstration of the sound of the alarm and letting the child know when the first few fire drills will happen is recommended. After the child is aware of the sound and routine, it is recommended that you conduct unannounced drills.

A prepared fire drill plan.

Assessment Procedures

Grouping: The most effective assessment is made by observing the child in a natural setting to determine his behaviors. In this case, the observation would take place during a fire drill.

Level One:
1. Discuss with the children the importance of knowing what to do in case of a fire.
2. Explain that a fire drill is a time to practice how to get out of the building safely in case of a fire.
3. Tell them they are going to practice a fire drill, so they must listen carefully to your directions. The directions should include, for example: (1) Line up at the door; (2) Follow me and no running; (3) Stay in the line and walk briskly, and quietly, to the outside; (4) Stay in line and follow me to a safe place outdoors; (5) Raise your hand and say, "Hi" or "Here" when I call your name; (6) I will tell you when it is safe; the group will stay in line and follow me back into the building.
4. When the group is back in the building, discuss the fire drill steps.
5. Repeat the steps several times.
6. Encourage the children to demonstrate the steps of the fire drill.
7. Observe their responses.

Level Two:
8. During a fire drill, observe the children's actions, and immediately correct any inappropriate behaviors.
9. There are no exceptions for not following the rules of a fire drill. All rules must be enforced with no excuses.

Credit: + Child identifies the fire drill signal and follows the teacher's directions during the drill.

Adaptations

Some children may panic or become frightened when they hear the fire alarm. This reaction can lead to erratic behaviors, such as confusion, hysteria, or being "frozen" in place. To assist the children, give them an opportunity to hear the alarm sound prior to the drill, and to make sure they understand what the sound means and what procedures they are to follow. If the alarm continues to frighten a child, make sure you are close by her to give support. It is important to remember which children overreact when the fire alarm rings to make sure they get safely out of the building with the others. Be sure to give the child an opportunity to practice the rules of a fire drill over and over. He should know exactly what to do as soon as a fire alarm rings.

5.179 Recites telephone number
Strand: 5-2 **Age:** 48-66m 4.0-5.6y

Definition

When the child is asked, "What is your telephone number?" he will respond with the correct numbers. It is necessary for him to include only the local numbers (not necessarily the area code). Example: He should respond by saying the numbers in order (e.g., 8364932).

Assessment Materials

A telephone book, a large piece of poster board on which to write the child's telephone number, a marker. Adjust appropriately if the child's family has only a cell phone.

Assessment Procedures

Grouping: This skill should be assessed one-on-one with the child.
1. Open the telephone book to the child's home phone number. Show him his number in the book, and explain that people use this number to call his house.
2. Ask him to tell you his telephone number.
3. Record his response.
4. If he has difficulty recalling his telephone number, write his phone number in large numbers on the poster board.
5. Point to and say each number, and then ask him to repeat the number after you.
6. Repeat this rote learning process several times.
7. Point to each number, and ask him to say it. Prompt as necessary, and repeat the process several times.
8. Cover up the first number and ask him to say it.
9. Cover up the first two numbers and ask him to say them.
10. Continue covering up the numbers until he can give his number in sequence. If the child exhibits a concern saying the numbers, uncover the numbers as a cue.
11. Ask him to tell you his telephone number.
12. On random occasions, ask him to repeat his telephone number.

13. Record his response.

Credit: + Child recites his telephone number correctly. The seven digit telephone number is what is being assessed, he does not have to provide the area code.

Adaptations

Even though the technology exists for a child to call home on a cell phone with the push of one number, it is important for a child to learn their home telephone number, or a parent's cell phone number, so they can contact someone in an emergency or when they do not have a programmed cell phone available. Learning a telephone number or any sequence of numbers can be difficult for some children. This task can create the following problems: (1) Mixing up the order of the numbers; (2) Reversing the numbers; (3) Being unable to retain the information; (4) Needing a visual cue before being able to recall the numbers; (5) Being asked to learn more than one telephone number (e.g., a parent's work number) easily causes confusion. To assist a child, follow these recommendations: (1) Teach him his telephone number by rote (say the first number, and ask him to say that number; say the first number and the second number, and ask him to say the two numbers; say the first three numbers, and ask him to say those numbers; continue with the other numbers); (2) Write the child's telephone number, then point to numbers, and ask him to say each number; (3) Create a telephone number song, much like singing the ABCs; (4) Provide an opportunity for rehearsing and repeating the telephone number. Review the number often, and allow the child to say it, write it, and find it. Be sure to help him understand the importance of knowing his number.

5.180 Creates own activities

Strand: 5-1 **Age:** 58-64m 4.10-5.4y

Definition

When the child is presented with a topic, material, resources, games, or presentations, she will create her own activity. These activities may be for an individual child or for a group. The child will demonstrate appropriate and adaptive behavior when she is involved with her created activity.

Assessment Materials

A collection of dress-up clothes for men and women: hats, helmets, bridal veils, capes, jewelry, handbags, scarves, neckties, shoes, luggage, aprons, sportswear, robes.

Assessment Procedures

Grouping: Informal observation is very effective because it is done in a natural setting without some of the variables that accompany formal assessment procedures.

Level One:
1. Place the dress-up clothes and props in an easily accessible spot. Tell the child that she may use anything in the dress-up and prop box she wishes and that she can play anything she wants.
2. Observe her as she creates a play scene, and note her behaviors.
3. If she involves other children in her creative play, observe her behavior, not for grading but for program planning. Watch for such interactions as being dogmatic, bossy, possessive, or blaming others. Also observe whether she develops a plot for a play scene, refuses to yield to others' wishes, is realistic in her creative play, has a good time, or is sympathetic.
4. It is important not to interfere with her creative play unless she or others are in a position to be hurt. Creative play occurs when the child is free to create, and she is free only when she is comfortable in her behavior. In addition, she is then able to adapt her actions to a situation.

Level Two:
5. Informally observe the child as she creates her own activity or playtime.

Credit: + Child creates her own activities when presented with a topic, materials, resources, games, or presentation. Her activity may be for herself or for a group. She demonstrates appropriate behavior when engaged in her creative play.

Adaptations

A child may find it difficult to formulate new processes or activities; to modify normal ways to reach solutions and address problems. She tends to look at an activity and see only one solution. Then when she is asked to create a new activity, a new solution, a new direction or a new product, dissatisfaction often sets in, and as a result, her behavior changes. One of the best ways to encourage creative thinking is to begin with the known solution and build new possible solutions from that point.

5.181 Tells house number, street, and town

Strand: 5-2 **Age:** 54-66m 4.6-5.6y

Definition
When the child is presented with the question, "In what city do you live?" or "In what town do you live?" he will respond correctly. If he lives in a rural area, his response will probably be the town/city where he goes for shopping and services. When you ask the question, it is important to say "In what city/town do you live?" instead of "In what town/city is your address?" When the child is presented with the question, "On what street do you live?" he will respond correctly. After he has named the street and city/town where he lives, ask, "On what street and in what city/town do you live?" When he is presented with the verbal question, "What is your house number?" he will respond correctly. After he has named his house number ask, "What is your house number, the name of the street on which you live, and the city/town where you live?" If he responds by stating his name and complete address, accept this because he has probably learned where he lives by rote. Make sure he understands that his house number, street address, and city/town make up his address.

Assessment Materials
Three sheets of 18-inch by 24-inch drawing paper, markers.

Assessment Procedures
Grouping: This skill should be assessed one-on-one with the child.
1. Recruit the assistance of another adult.
2. Ask the adult to go to the child and say, "In what city/town do you live?" Ask the adult to use either the term "city" or "town," based on the acceptable term in the child's area.
3. Tell the adult to ask, "What is the name of the street where you live?"
4. Note the response.
5. Say to the child, "Name the street and town/city where you live."
6. Ask an adult to go to the child and say, "What is your house number?"
7. Note the response.
8. Say to the child, "What is your house number, street name and the town/city where you live."
9. If he has difficulty responding to his house number, observe whether his problem is because of lack of knowledge. If it appears that he does not know his house number, the following is recommended: (1) Show him a sheet of paper, and ask him questions about his home. As he responds to the questions, draw a picture of his home (house, apartment house, mobile home, etc.) Make sure to include the house number in the drawing; (2) Show him the second sheet of paper, and draw his home (from sheet one) on this paper. Ask him questions about his street, making sure to include the street sign in the picture. As he responds to the questions, draw any street landmarks he describes, making sure that they are within the proximity of his home. Tell him to point to his home, his house number, the house next door, the street sign; (3) Show him the third sheet of paper, and from the second sheet, draw his home with the house number, the street with the street sign, and landmarks. Ask him to point to his home, different places on the street, and explain that his home and his street are all part of the town/city called [Omaha]. Review the three sheets of paper, emphasizing his house number, the street sign, and the name of the town/city. Stress that the house number, the street name, and city/town make up his address. Later in the interaction, ask him again to give his house number, the street where he lives, and the town/city where he lives. Note his responses.

Credit: + Child correctly states his house number, street name, and the city/town where he lives when asked.

Adaptations
A child usually learns to repeat his address by rote memory. When he is learning his address, it is easy for him to confuse numbers and names. Much of this confusion is caused because of his limited attending skills, numbers and words that have no meaning to him, concerns with recall, and problems storing information. It is difficult for him to receive information that is not clearly understandable, or information that has little meaning. It is also a concern if a child has problems in attending and storing the messages. If he lacks attending skills, he may receive and store only part of his address, the part he was able to focus on. Once he stores the selected information, he still needs to retrieve it when he is asked. Because he stored only the part that had meaning to him or the part to which he paid attention, the results will probably be incomplete and confused. To assist him: (1) Present the material in small segments, with many opportunities for repetition; (2) Encourage him to attend by

saying his name before you present the material, making comments such as, "Listen to me"; (3) Ask him to look at you when he is learning the information; (4) Provide as many visuals as possible for memory support; (5) Present the material in a variety of activities, games, stories, and pictures, so the effort of over-learning will be motivational.

5.182 Displays good sportsmanship, win or lose

Strand: 5-5   **Age:** 54-66m 4.6-5.6y

Definition
The child will demonstrate being a good loser and a gracious winner.

Assessment Materials
A selected story that addresses sportsmanship. Check your local public library for references that are available that identify stories dealing with behaviors such as sportsmanship.
If a sportsmanship story is not available, use the example that follows:
The Ball Game
It had been raining all day.
Sam, Tim, and Steve had to stay inside.
They really wanted to play ball.
Finally the rain stopped.
The boys were so happy.
They took the ball and went to the field.
Sam said he would pitch.
Tim wanted to catch.
Sam said he would throw the ball to Steve four times.
If Steve did not hit the ball after four tries, he would be out.
Sam threw ball one, and Steve missed it.
Sam threw ball two; Steve missed it.
Sam threw ball three; Steve missed it.
Sam threw ball four; Steve missed it.
Tim said, "You are out!"
Steve laughed and said, "I am out. I hope I hit the ball next time I am up to bat."
Then it was Tim's turn to bat, and Steve became the catcher.
Sam threw ball one, and Tim missed it.
Sam threw ball two; Tim missed it.
Sam threw ball three; Tim missed it.
Sam threw ball four; Tim missed it.
Tim was very unhappy and said, "I want another turn. I had only three turns."
"No," said Sam. "I threw the ball four times."
Tim was so angry that he threw the bat on the ground and ran away.
Sam called to Tim, but Tim kept on running.
Steve said, "Sam, I will pitch to you. Can you bat and catch?"
"Sure," said Sam.
Steve threw ball one; Sam hit it, and guess who caught it?
Steve laughed and said, "You are such a good hitter that I became the pitcher and the catcher both."
Steve and Sam had a good time playing ball.

Assessment Procedures
Grouping: When you assess a child's ability to display good sportsmanship, the most effective procedure is play-based observation. An observational assessment can either be spontaneous or occur in a semi-structured situation.

Level One:
1. If the choice is semi-structured, invite the child to join you at the listening area. Explain to her that the story she is about to hear is about being a good and a bad sport. Discuss what sportsmanship means, giving examples of being a good and bad sport.
2. Read the story and afterwards, ask the child the following questions: (1) Which boy was the good sport? Why? (2) Which boy was the bad sport? Why? (3) What did Steve say and do that made him a good sport? (4) What did Tim say and do that made him a poor sport? (5) What would you have done if you had been playing ball with Steve, Sam, and Tim?
3. Observe the child's responses, listening for evidence that she understands the concepts of good and bad sportsmanship.

Level Two:
4. Informally observe the child as she participates in an activity in which she demonstrates good sportsmanship.

Credit: + Child demonstrates being a good loser and a gracious winner when participating in a group game.

Adaptations
A child may have a difficult time realizing that to be accepted means that she must be at least a reasonably good sport. Often she does not understand that being a good sport is an admired trait and makes you someone whom others enjoy being around. Instead, she may think if she blames others, changes the rules to benefit herself and brags, she will be looked up to as important. When she realizes that others want to win too and learns that when someone complains in defeat, she is not liked, she may be

© 2010 VORT Corporation. All rights reserved. Do Not copy.

inclined to modify her sportsmanship behavior. She then learns that the element of uncertainty is part of the enjoyment in games and contests. "Getting the breaks," "being lucky," and "It will be different next time" are all reactions to defeat, but more important is the challenge of playing the game to the best of your ability. To help a child to become a good sport: (1) Try to make sure that she wins and loses; winning all the time leads to being unable to accept losing, and losing all the time leads to excuses or attempts to manipulate the activity; (2) Make sure she has good sportsmanship models to follow; (3) Assist her to accept failure and to be ready to try again, but not to be discouraged; (4) Help her learn that she should continue to play her best, even if she is behind while a chance to win remains and not to become overconfident or obnoxious in success.

5.183 Expresses feelings in controlled manner

Strand: 5-5 **Age:** 60-72m 5.0-6.0y

Definition

The child controls his temper by verbalizing his feelings rather than exhibiting behaviors such as aggression, tantrums, withdrawal. Maturity and increased vocabulary are the vehicles for talking about feelings that control tempers that often lead to inappropriate behaviors. When he has a bank of words he can use to express his feelings and feels comfortable using these terms, he will find less reason to exhibit unusual behaviors because words will work for him. He will also find he is more acceptable in his social interaction.

Assessment Procedures

See #5.143 for assessment materials and procedures, as well as suggested adaptations.

5.184 Waits appropriately for attention in group situation

Strand: 5-5 **Age:** 60-66m 5.0-5.6y

Definition

In a group situation, the child will request assistance not more than twice, and after she is recognized, she will wait quietly for attention. She will follow the established rules for seeking attention or help, such as raising her hand and waiting to be called on.

Assessment Materials

/*\\Safety Note: Use with close supervision and caution and make sure the child has no allergies or health conditions related to a spray, and spray in a well-ventilated area. Plans for a task the child can achieve except for one step for which she will need to ask assistance. For example, placemats that are unwoven and made with a loosely woven fabric such as burlap cut into 12 inch by 15 inch pieces, a can of plastic spray, child-safe scissors.

Assessment Procedures

Grouping: Informal observation is effective because it is done in a natural setting without some of the variables that accompany assessment procedures. When you are assessing a child's ability to wait for attention in a group setting, an observational procedure can be either spontaneous or occur a semi-structured situation.

Level One:
1. If the choice is semi-structured, select a task that she can achieve, except for one step for which she will need to ask for assistance.
2. Lay a piece of burlap on the worktable. Demonstrate how to make an unwoven placemat: Take a piece of burlap, select two threads on the edge of the material. Wrap the two threads around your finger, and pull them out, being careful not to break them. Continue pulling out the threads until you create a symmetrical design. (It is impossible to make two placemats look alike, due to the unique weave and the threads that are pulled.) When the design is completed, lay the burlap piece on a sheet of paper and spray it with the plastic spray, moving evenly across the placemat. Turn it over and spray the other side. Hang the placemat up to dry immediately after spraying.
3. Provide each child with the burlap material to create a placemat. (Keep the plastic spray out of reach of the children, so each child will need to let you know when they are ready to complete the final step with the spray.)
4. Review the steps with them: (1) Select two threads; (2) Wrap the threads around your fingers and pull; (3) Select two more threads; (4) Pull the threads; (5) Tell the child that when she is pleased with her design to raise her hand and that you will help her with the plastic spray, supervising her using it; (6) Spray both sides of the placemat; (7) Hang it up to dry.

5. Allow the children to begin the project, and when a child raises her hand for your assistance, respond non-verbally (nod head, smile, hand up as if to say, "I see you and will be with you"), showing that you have noticed her.
6. Observe her as she waits for you to assist her with the next step of her project (spraying the placemat).
7. Watch for such behaviors as: (1) Sits without asking again for several minutes; (2) Waves hand frantically and speaks out to get you to pay attention to her; (3) Leaves seat, brings project to you; (4) Causes disturbances to get attention; (5) Gives up and withdraws (puts head down) from the project.
8. It is important to tell the child who waits appropriately how much you appreciate her waiting and following directions.

Level Two:
9. Informally observe the child as she is involved in a group situation and requests assistance, watching for such behaviors as: (1) Raises hand and waits patiently; (2) Creates disturbances when attention is not immediate; (3) Causes problems for her group; (4) Verbally demands to be recognized; (5) Leaves the group.

Credit: + Child waits for attention in a group situation. She requests assistance no more than two times following the established rules, such as raising her hand and waiting to be called on, and she waits quietly.

Adaptations
A child may feel that she belongs only when someone is paying attention to her or when she is the center of attention. All children want and need attention. However, a child who already demonstrates inappropriate behaviors in order to seek attention is probably going to seek more and more. Hence, inappropriate behavior is part of her social interaction. At first, she seeks attention from adults, but soon she realizes that attention-seeking behaviors such as being silly, teasing, and taunting others attract peers. Often she is rewarded for her behavior with what she is seeking--attention--and sometimes she is unaware of how to ask for positive attention. To assist her: (1) Reinforce appropriate behavior, making sure that she is aware of the message, "Appropriate behavior is rewarded"; (2) Establish a signal with her that means "stop and wait"; (3) Use an "I" message--a verbal statement that identifies the inappropriate behavior, tells how it affects others, and asks her to stop it; (4) Ignore the behavior when it occurs, but only for the number of times that has been pre-established with the child and with the understanding that the number of occurrences will decrease; (5) Focus her attention on something different; (6) Refuse to react to the overt attention-seeking actions. It is very important for you to remember to give ample attention for good behavior and to work with children on how to ask for attention when they need it.

5.185 Acts upon helpful criticism presented by authority
Strand: 5-4 **Age:** 60-66m 5.0-5.6y

Definition
The child will modify his performance so that it is more like what the authority figure has in mind/suggested. The authority figure will communicate to the child ways to change his behavior by demonstration, explanation, suggestion, and modeling. The modification of his behavior may occur immediately after the recommendations or the next time he has an opportunity to react.

Assessment Materials
A packet of at least 10 cards with a picture on each card of something that would be included when going on a picnic. Example: (1) Sandwiches; (2) Cookies; (3) Fruit; (4) Blanket or cloth; (5) Picnic basket; (6) Bat and ball; (7) Drinks; (8) Paper plates and cups; (9) Umbrella; (10) Chicken.

Assessment Procedures
Note: Make sure when you criticize or correct the misbehavior, avoid attacking the child's character and over-verbalizing what you dislike about his actions.
Grouping: When you are assessing a child's ability to act on helpful criticism, the most effective procedure is unstructured observation. An observational assessment can either be spontaneous or occur in a semi-structured situation. If your choice is semi-structured, establish a circumstance in which the child will be open to criticism.
1. Ask the children to come to the group table, show them the 10 picture cards, and explain that they are going on a pretend picnic. Tell them they may take only five items along on the picnic, so they must choose which of the 10 items they will take.

2. Make sure they understand that they must agree on the five items. Give them an opportunity to decide on the selected items. If one of the children becomes impulsive, tries to take over, or becomes argumentative, tell him that he must stop arguing and help the other child choose the items.
3. Direct the corrective statements at what you saw and then give the suggestion of acceptable alternatives. In this way the child knows how the authority feels about his behavior and exactly how he is supposed to behave differently.
4. Observe the child's response to the direction to stop arguing and to help the other child. Suggestions for what to watch for in observation are: (1) Blames the other child for getting him into trouble; (2) Complains that he is always treated unfairly; (3) Leaves the group table; (4) Becomes very aggressive; (5) Withdraws, puts head down or cries; (6) Destroys the cards and appears to be satisfied with the destruction; (7) Is verbally abusive.
5. The intent of the observation is to determine behavioral concerns and intervention strategies, not to label a child. Consideration should also be given to the following: (1) The involvement that the child has in the presented task, (2) The experience that he has in reacting to the situation (Has he worked with this child before? Has he worked in a cooperative assignment prior to this one?); (3) Is he familiar with the person in authority? (4) Is the assignment something that he feels strongly about or cares about? (5) The environment in which the criticism was expressed? (6) Was there a group involved in the activity, behavioral reaction, or the criticism?
6. Observe the child as he acts upon helpful criticism when it is provided by an authority figure. Observe the types of reactions that he displays.

Credit: + Child modifies his performance to match what the authority figure has suggested. The change in behavior can occur immediately or the next time the child is in a similar situation.

Adaptations
A child may be insecure in his own abilities or social interactions and have many self-doubts so he is sure that whatever he does will be criticized. A child may have experienced so much criticism from others that he has ceased to attempt anything. He will often be very anxious when he is asked to do a task, perform a skill, play a game, or in any way risk the reaction of criticism from others. When he feels the criticism is putting him down, he moves to a defensive behavior. This defensive behavior may be aggressive or passive, and usually, the child shows disappointment. To help him feel secure about his abilities and to realize that criticism can be constructive and helpful: (1) When communicating with him, do it in such a manner that the message is expressed on an equal basis, not as from an authority. Exception: If child safety or health is an issue, the message must be clear and direct. "Fire! Get out of this room now!" (2) The communication should be expressed in the spirit of cooperation. Say, for example, "I would be really pleased if you would go back to the art table and put away the crayons. When you put the crayons away after you use them, the crayons are ready for the next person"; (3) The communication should be expressed in such a manner that it conveys mutual respect. Say, for example, "Greg, I think you forgot to put the crayons away. I know that you want to have them ready for the next person, so would you please put them away?" (4) After he acts on the helpful criticism, be sure to reinforce him for accepting the criticism and reacting to it in a positive way.

5.186 Remains quiet when others are talking
Strand: 5-7 **Age:** 54-72m 4.6-6.0y

Definition
The child will remain quiet when other people are talking. If it is necessary for her to interrupt, she will first excuse herself.

Assessment Materials
A short story with ample visual imagery. Stories with action (e.g., attending a circus, riding a horse, walking in the woods) or stories with surprises (e.g., a birthday present that moves, a basket left by the door, toys that move in the dark) present many opportunities for visual imagery. If stories are not available, write a short visual imagery story or use the example:
<u>The Basket That Moves</u>
I heard a knock at the door.
There was another knock at the door.
I opened the door, and no one was there.
But a basket was sitting in front of the door.
The basket had a big towel on top of it.
The towel was moving.
There was something alive inside the basket.

Suddenly I saw a paw.
It was a black paw, and it looked soft.
It was a black kitten.
The kitten jumped out of the basket.
I heard the kitten say, "Mew-mew-mew."
The basket moved again, and another kitten jumped out.
This one was black and white with a white tail.
The two kittens started to play beside the basket.
Whoops! The basket toppled over, and another kitten fell out.
This kitten wanted to play.
The three kittens chased each other in and out of the basket.
I was about to look inside the basket, when I heard a purr.
And inside I saw one more kitten, fast asleep.
Now there were four kittens.
I love my four new kittens.
I watch them play and sleep.
I listen to them say, "Mew-mew-mew," and I listen to them purr.
Can you help me name my new kittens?

Assessment Procedures

Grouping: When you are assessing a child's ability to remain quiet when others are talking, the most effective procedure is observing the child. An observational assessment can either be spontaneous or occur in a semi-structured situation.

1. If your choice is semi-structured, remember this activity is for more than one child. Ask the children to come to the listening area, and encourage the child you are observing to feel comfortable by sitting on pillows or lying on the rug.
2. Tell her to close her eyes and be ready to make pictures in her mind while you read her a story.
3. Be sure she understands that she is to listen and not talk during the story.
4. Read the selected story.
5. Observe her as she listens, watching for such behaviors as: (1) Listens and does not talk; (2) Talks to the person reading the story; (3) Talks to others while the story is being read; (4) Leaves the area; (5) Becomes verbally aggressive; (6) Withdraws and becomes lethargic.
6. After reading the story, explain that you are going to ask her some questions about the story.
7. Be sure she understands that only one person is to talk at a time and that the others are to listen.
8. Ask questions such as: How many kittens were there? How did the kittens get to their new home? What sounds would you have heard if you had been there? What would you have named the kittens? What do kittens eat and drink?
9. Observe the child to determine if she remains quiet while others are answering the questions and talking about the story.
10. This assessment is not meant to be a procedure for ranking or grading, but for developing intervention techniques and curriculum planning.

Credit: + Child remains quiet when one or more other people are talking. If she needs to interrupt, she will excuse herself first.

Adaptations

A child may have a difficult time remaining quiet when others are talking because: (1) She cannot wait to say what she has to say; (2) She is seeking the attention someone else is getting; (3) The social manner of not interrupting has not been a focus in her home environment; (4) She may often respond without thinking, react on impulse, and be unable to wait her turn or delay a desire, so her first reaction may be inappropriate. She may have been rewarded for behaving spontaneously and impulsively, because the adult in charge felt a need to respond to the interrupting child, the loud talker, the verbally aggressive child or the child who could not wait to be heard. To assist her, address her need to have patience and teach her to wait for gratification. Using self-talk and self-reinforcement are effective techniques. Teach her to say to herself, "Wait while others are talking," "Think and listen before talking," or "I must wait for my turn to talk" as ways to remember not to interrupt. Whenever she pauses after she reminds herself to pause, she should give herself a quiet compliment. Whenever you catch her being quiet while others are talking, reward her immediately. Using a non-verbal cue is also effective: whenever she is talking while others are talking, place your index finger over your mouth to remind her to be quiet. As she becomes aware of her interrupting behavior, she should learn to consider the cause and the effect, for example, "What will likely happen if I keep talking while others are talking?" This approach is most effective when you use it not as a criticism, but as a way to help her understand her behavior and solve her problem.

5.187 Understands and practices good safety procedures when boarding a bus, riding on a bus and leaving a bus

Strand: 5-8 **Age:** 60-66m 5.0-5.6y

Definition
The child will demonstrate safe procedures when entering a bus that includes using the bus steps and handrail. He will demonstrate safe procedures when riding on the bus, that include sitting in a seat at all times, keeping his hands to himself, not throwing objects, keeping hands and objects inside the bus, and following directions from the bus driver or any other person in charge. He will demonstrate safe procedures when disembarking from the bus, which includes using the bus steps, handrail, and moving away from the bus immediately.

Assessment Materials
/*\Safety Note: Many young children, except possibly those with special needs, will not have the opportunity of riding a bus to preschool. But this is an important readiness skill for attending elementary school.

Access to a school bus not being used during school time.

Assessment Procedures
Note: If taking the child on a bus is not possible, simulate boarding, riding, and leaving a bus in the classroom using classroom chairs as seats and a foot stool as the boarding area.

Grouping: When you are assessing a child's ability to understand and practice good safety procedures when boarding, riding and leaving a bus, the most effective procedure is observing the child's skills in a natural setting.

1. Have the child line up at the appropriate boarding location.
2. Ask him to walk from the boarding area to the bus steps.
3. Ask him to walk to an unoccupied seat and sit down.
4. Ask him to walk from his seat to the disembarking area and exit the bus using the bus steps.
5. Observe him as he goes through the steps, watching for his use of the handrail, walking on the bus, stepping clear of the bus when he leaves the bus, securing his seat belt, if the bus has them.
6. Allow each child to perform the assessment.

Credit: + Child understands and practice good safety procedures when boarding, riding and leaving a bus.

Adaptations
/*\Safety Note: Each school, school district, or program will have their own rules regarding bus safety. Be sure to check with them to determine and follow appropriate policies.

A child may not have received instruction on proper safety rules when boarding, riding, and exiting a bus, or he may choose to ignore the rules. If he opts to ignore the rules, he may be impulsive, seeking attention, awkward, or uninhibited. If he is not aware of the proper bus-riding rules, he should be instructed until he can demonstrate the physical actions necessary and until he fully understands the established bus rules. If he exhibits inappropriate behavior to get attention from being impulsive or uninhibited, he must understand the rules and the consequences that will occur if he continues his inappropriate actions. Typical bus-riding rules are: (1) Remain in your seat when riding a bus; (2) Keep your hands and feet to yourself and inside the bus at all times; (3) Fighting will not be tolerated; (4) Keep the noise level low so it will not be distracting to the driver; (5) Keep your seat belt fastened at all times. Consequences for breaking bus rules range from: (1) A verbal signal (e.g., bell, whistle, toy horn) from the driver or bus monitor as a warning; (2) Bus monitor moves to physical proximity; (3) Driver stops the bus; (4) Referral is made through the educational system; (5) The school informs the parents that the child may no longer ride the bus for a given period of time. Each child who rides a bus must understand and practice good bus safety procedures at all times. This is a safety issue that is not negotiable in the best interest of all involved.

5.188 Looks both ways before crossing a street/road in which there is no traffic light and there may or may not be a stop sign

Strand: 5-8 **Age:** 60-66m 5.0-5.6y

Definition
The child will look both ways before she crosses a street or a road where there is no traffic light. These streets and roads are found in neighborhoods, rural communities, apartment complexes, retail and office areas, and educational campuses. Crosswalks and

stop signs may or may not be available. She will go to a corner or a crosswalk to cross, if available.

Assessment Materials
/*\Safety Note: Because you are assessing the child, you do not know if the child will succeed or fail. Have an explicit safety plan ready to use if the child does not succeed.
A street or road where there is no traffic signal.

Assessment Procedures
Note: If taking her to a real-life setting is not possible, simulate a street or road setting on the playground.
Grouping: When you are assessing a child's ability to look both ways before crossing a street/road, an observational procedure can be either spontaneous or occur in a semi-structured situation.
1. Accompany the child to a street or road where there is no traffic signal.
2. Procedure: (1) Walk with the child to the corner of the street, or if there is not a corner, select a logical crossing area; (2) Explain to her that you are going to cross the street; (3) Ask her to walk with you; (4) Stop and look both ways before crossing the street, as you explain your actions to the child; (5) Walk rapidly across the street or road.
3. Repeat the procedure by walking back across the street or road.
4. Ask the child to cross the street or road.
5. Observe her as she goes through the steps, watching to see whether she stops, looks both directions, and walks briskly across the street.
6. Allow each child to perform the assessment.

Credit: + Child goes to the crosswalk or corner to cross, if available. The child looks both ways before crossing a street or road when there is no traffic light or stop sign.

Adaptations
See #5.132.

5.189 Apologizes when reminded
Strand: 5-5 **Age:** 42-54m 3.6-4.6y

Definition
When it is appropriate (e.g., the child accidentally breaks something, bumps into someone, hurts another), he will apologize by saying at least, "I am sorry." He may need to be reminded to apologize and what to say.

Assessment Materials
At least two puppets.

Assessment Procedures
Note: If the child is not aware of how or when to apologize, or lacks experience in apologizing, learning episodes should be implemented. A good beginning learning strategy is to set the stage, model an apology several times, and allow him a chance to imitate the presentation.
Grouping: When you are assessing a child's ability to apologize when reminded, the most effective procedure is unstructured observation. An observational assessment can either be spontaneous or occur in a semi-structured situation.

Level One:
1. Place a puppet on your hand. Introduce the puppet to the child. Talk as the puppet, and allow the child and the puppet time to visit.
2. While the puppet and the child are visiting, make the puppet accidentally bump the child.
3. Have the puppet turn to the child and say, "I'm sorry I bumped you. I didn't mean to."
4. Ask the child how he felt when the puppet accidentally bumped him and then apologized.
5. Observe his responses, listening for comments that indicate he understands the concept of apologizing, he knows when apologizing is appropriate, and he has command of words that are used to apologize.
6. Give him an opportunity to apologize by the following: (1) Give the child a puppet; (2) Decide on names for the puppets; (3) Use the two puppets and begin creative and imaginary play; (4) Set the stage in which the child's puppet will bump into your puppet; (5) Observe whether his "puppet" apologizes; (6) If his "puppet" does not apologize, prompt by saying, for example, "Smoky is sorry he bumped you, right Smoky?" (7) Create another situation in which the child's puppet needs to apologize and observe the response.

Level Two:
7. Observe the child when he has an occasion to apologize for an action, such as when he accidentally pushes someone, knocks something over, breaks something. During the observation, listen for comments that indicate he understands the meaning of apologizing, is aware when to use it, and uses the right words.

Credit: + Child apologizes when appropriate, he may need to be reminded to apologize and what to say.

Adaptations

Some children are not aware of what an apology is; they have not been exposed to the concept and are unaware of how to give or to receive an apology. When such a child receives an apology, he responds with either aggressive reactions (e.g., "You meant to push me," " You are not sorry."), or he appears to be confused (e.g., "What do you mean?" "Sorry, excuse?"). When he is in a position when he should apologize, either he is not aware that an apology is in order, or he is reluctant, does not know how to say it, or is afraid of the response he may receive. It is possible that he experienced situations when an apology was viewed as a character weakness and negatively reinforced. To assist this child to understand what an apology is, when to use it, how to say it, and how to receive an apology: (1) When an opportunity arises when an apology from him would be appropriate, explain to him the importance of saying words such as, "I'm sorry," "Please excuse me," or "I didn't mean to." Model an apology, and ask him to imitate the model; (2) Role-play a situation in which an apology is needed or is extended. Props, such as puppets, are excellent for role-playing; (3) When an apology is in order, and he does not respond, state the apology (e.g., "LeBron is sorry he dropped your crayons, right LeBron?") for the child, and prompt him to answer the question (e.g., "right LeBron, you're sorry?"). Sincere apologies come with practice, learning to be perceptive, an increase in vocabulary, and a concern for others and their feelings.

5.190 Plays group games following rules

Strand: 5-1 **Age:** 60-72m 5.0-6.0y

Definition

The child will participate in a group game with other children and she will follow the game rules. The group activity may be played inside or outside, and the activity may be active (ball or circle game) or passive (table game). The rules of the game will be clearly defined prior to any action.

Assessment Procedures

See #5.135 for assessment materials and procedures, as well as suggested adaptations.

5.191 Plays simple competitive table games

Strand: 5-5 **Age:** 60-72m 5.0-6.0y

Definition

The child will participate in a competitive table game with other children, and he will follow the game rules. The rules of the game will be clearly defined prior to any action.

Assessment Materials

Competitive table game such as *Bingo, Lotto, Dominoes, Memory Game*. Purchase table game from commercial source or make. Directions to make a Memory Game: Select six pairs of stickers in which the pairs are identical. Put one sticker on one 3- by 5-inch card, and put the match on another 3- by 5-inch card. Continue with different sticker pairs to make a deck of 12 cards containing six pairs. If stickers are not available, use stamps or line drawings.

Assessment Procedures

Grouping: When you assess a child's ability to play a competitive table game and to follow the rules, the most effective procedure is observation. An observational assessment can be either spontaneous or occur in a semi-structured situation.

Level One:
1. If the choice is semi-structured, select a simple table game, such as the Memory Game you made.
2. Place the deck of cards on the table, and show the children the pairs. After the pairs have been exposed, shuffle the deck of cards and place the cards face-down, four cards in three rows.
3. Explain that each child will take a turn, turning over two cards. If the cards are a matching pair, he gets to keep the cards. If the cards are not a matching pair, he must turn them over and wait for his next turn.
4. Demonstrate how to turn two cards over, and if they match, take the pair; if they don't match, turn the cards over.
5. Select a child to begin the table game.
6. During the observational assessment, it is important for the process to involve some structure, not for grading, but for developing a program or for assisting the child with an identified behavior. Some suggestions to consider during the observation are: (1) Did he play by the rules? (2) Did he try to change the rules to suit his needs? (3) Was he a good sport? (4) Did he want to play another game

when he did not win? (5) Did he indicate that he did not understand the rules? (6) Did it appear that he needed continued assurance and reinforcement from another person before accepting the activity? Analyzing who was involved in the game setting is helpful to the assessment process because he may react differently when he is engaged in play with an adult, a sibling, a new child, or a special friend. Analyzing the situation in which the play occurs is also important because he may react differently in a familiar setting, when a family member is present, when an environmental stimulus is active, in front of strangers, or in a structured situation. These suggested observational assessments address social behaviors only. Considerations for skill development such as gross motor skills and receptive language are not included, but they do have an effect on any changes in emotional and social interactions.

Level Two:
7. Informally observe the child when he is playing a competitive table game, watching for behaviors such as taking turns, playing by the rules, accepting others, being a good sport.

Credit: + Child participates in a group game with other children following the rules that were clearly defined prior to the game beginning.

Adaptations
See #5.135.

5.192 Maintains appropriate distance when talking to another
Strand: 5-7 **Age:** 60-72m 5.0-6.0y

Definition
When the child speaks to another person, she will maintain an appropriate social distance (at least 1 to 2 feet). She will sense when she is too close from cues, such as the listener's backing away, turning her head, pushing the talker, or leaving the situation.

Assessment Materials
A hand-mirror.

Assessment Procedures
Grouping: When you assess a child's ability to maintain an appropriate social distance when talking to another person, the most effective procedure is play-based observation. An observational assessment can either be spontaneous or occur in a semi-structured situation.

Level One:
1. Invite the child to sit down across from you at the table. Lean over the table and get very close to her face and talk to her. Observe whether she seems uncomfortable that you are in her sphere. Note this by observing whether she backs away from the table, lays her head down, or exhibits concerned facial expressions. If she appears to be distressed, gradually back off, and observe her reaction.
2. Explain to her that you will hold a mirror so she will be able to see her face in it.
3. Ask her to begin talking or singing.
4. Gradually, move the mirror closer and closer to her.
5. Observe her reactions.
6. Give the child the mirror, and ask her to move the mirror closer to her, but tell her to keep talking.
7. Watch her as she manipulates the mirror, looking for her stopping point, whether she continues to talk as the mirror moves closer, if she lays the mirror down, or if she makes any motion to indicate the image is too close.

Level Two:
8. When the child is involved in a conversation with another person, informally observe whether she keeps an appropriate distance when she converses.

Credit: + Child maintains an appropriate distance when talking to someone else. She picks up on the social cues given by the other person when she is too close.

Adaptations
Some children are unable to make non-verbal social adjustments. Such a child does not learn to perceive the feelings of others naturally; therefore she needs direct intervention on how to judge non-verbal behavior. She is often unable to size up a situation and to make necessary adjustments. Gradually, she must acquire tact and learn to anticipate the consequences of her own behavior. Once guided by these observations, she acquires the ability to react and empathize on a non-verbal basis. To assist a child in non-verbal social perception, verbalize the observational behavior and then interpret the social response. Pictorial representations are helpful. Dramatizations, charades and role-playing are also effective techniques. The important issue is that the child must be instructed in different, meaningful

5.193 (Moved to Cognitive, skill 1.309)

5.194 (Removed, see page xviii)

5.195 Recognizes items described as dangerous
Strand: 5-8 **Age:** 61-72m 5.1-6.0y

Definition
When she is asked, the child will identify dangerous items. When she is asked, she will tell the results of mishandling or playing with dangerous items.

Assessment Materials
At least eight pictures, four of them representing items that are dangerous (broken glass, knives, chain saw, burning candle) and four that represent items that are not dangerous. These pictures may be available through commercial resources. If not, you can find these pictures in magazines, catalogs, or newspapers, and mount them on poster board or cardboard to make them more durable.

Assessment Procedures
Grouping: This should be assessed one-on-one with the child.
1. Ask the child to come to the table. Explain to her that you want her to look at a picture. Show the child a picture and say, "What do you see in the picture?"
2. Pause to allow her to respond.
3. Say, "Do you think the broken glass is dangerous?"
4. Pause to allow her to respond.
5. If she correctly identifies the item as dangerous say, "What might happen if you played with, went too near, or put your hand on the broken glass?"
6. Pause to allow her to respond and note her answers.
7. Continue with the other pictures in the same procedure.
8. A child may have limited exposure to dangerous materials so that her responses may be varied and based on a lack of experience.

Credit: + Child recognizes items that are dangerous and can tell what might happen if she were to handle or play with the dangerous items.

experiences and auditory verbalization so she will react properly to non-verbal behaviors.

Adaptations
See #5.132.

5.196 (Removed, see page xviii)

5.197 Adjusts behavior to fit rules and routines of different situations
Strand: 5-1 **Age:** 48-60m 4.0-5.0y

Definition
When the child is in a different situation (an assembly at school, a friend's house, a restaurant, a cafeteria, a store, a library, a museum, a church service), she will exhibit behaviors that are appropriate to that setting. She will learn the appropriate behaviors in the setting by observation or by being told the rules and routines.

Assessment Procedures
Grouping: When you are assessing a child's ability to adjust her behaviors in a different situation, the most effective procedure is activity-based observation. An observational assessment can either be spontaneous or occur in a semi-structured situation.
1. If your choice is semi-structured, explain to the child that she is going to an assembly in the school auditorium. Tell her about the assembly, and explain to her how she should act (role-play correct behaviors if necessary). It is important to select only a few important behaviors to explain to her rather than requiring her to understand and recall too many.
2. If she is going to a assembly, important behaviors might be: (1) Stay in your seat unless instructed otherwise; (2) Follow the rules pertaining to clapping and cheering; (3) Stay with the person who brings you or with your group; (4) Follow the directions given by the adult in charge. During the assembly, observe her to determine if she is able to adjust her behavior to fit the rules and routine of the different situation.
3. This observational process should include some structure, not for grading, but for developing a program or for assisting her with an identified behavior. Some suggestions to consider during the observation are: (1) Did she stay with the group? (2) Did she observe the setting/behaviors of others and model her behavior after this observation? (3) Did she follow the directions of the person in charge? (4) Was she a role model for others in the

group? These suggested observational assessments address social behaviors only; considerations for skill development, such as gross motor skills and receptive language, are not included, but they do have an effect on any changes in emotional and social interactions.

Credit: + Child recognizes and adjusts her behavior to fit the rules and routines in different situations and settings. She learns appropriate behavior in different settings by observing or being told the rules and routines.

Adaptations

Some children need to be consistently reminded on how to behave. They have difficulty transferring a direction from one setting to another. They ignore following the rules, they desire attention, or past experience was not efficient to learn what was required. Ideally, to help the child reach a proper level of adaptive behavior, you should provide control and directives for every inappropriate action. Your training will be most effective if you permit no bad habits to develop and no instances of misunderstood directions. Thus, allowing a child to modify her behavioral responsibilities, to dodge the natural consequences of a mistake, to ignore stated requirements, or to receive a reward without earning it, may diminish, however slightly, her development of adaptive behaviors. Children of all ages and ability levels become confused in too permissive an atmosphere, and as a consequence, come to feel unsure, helpless, passive, or depend on others to follow. They can adjust to a variety of rules and routines if they are provided with directions for dealing with new situations or unfamiliar settings. These directions should assist a child to apply past acceptable behaviors, and teach her how to "read" the unfamiliar environment, how to ask questions, and to recall previously stated behavioral guidelines.

5.198 (Removed, see page xviii)

5.199 Leaves provoking situation
Strand: 5-4 **Age:** 60-78m 5.0-6.6y

Definition
The child will voluntarily remove himself from a provoking situation. The irritating situation could be caused by a single person, a group action, an activity, an interruption, or an unexpected event.

Assessment Materials
At least four prepared short stories that deal with inappropriate behaviors. Short stories pertaining to child conflict, aggression, fighting, and disobeying are available from local public libraries. The librarian will usually have a behavior subject index to assist in story selection. You may also write the short stories, or use the following examples:

Story One--<u>Cake is for Eating</u> (Seeking Attention via Aggressive Actions)
It was a special day in Room 6.
It was party day, and the treat was a chocolate cake.
John, Megan, Brian, and Tim were sitting at a table.
John passed out the plates, napkins, and forks.
Miss Turner put a piece of cake on everyone's plate.
Megan said, "This is the best cake."
Brian said, "I really like chocolate cake."
Tim picked up a piece of his cake, and he threw it at Brian.
Tim picked up another piece of his cake, and he threw it at Megan.
Megan said, "Tim, stop throwing your cake."
Brian made a ball out of his napkin and threw it at Tim.
John took his plate and moved to another table.
Miss Turner took Tim's plate and asked him to leave the table.
Story Two--<u>The Captain</u> (Power-Seeking via Bossy Actions)
Tom, Susan, Kelly, and Pete decided to play a game about a space ship.
Pete said, "I will be the captain, and because the captain is the boss, everyone must do what I say."
"But you were the captain last time," said Susan. "I think it would be fair if someone else got a chance."
"No, I am the captain," said Pete. "Now you do what I tell you."
Tom, Kelly, and Susan decided it was not any fun to play with Pete. He was too bossy.
"I'll see you later," said Tom, and he left.
"I'm going home," said Susan, as she ran away.
Kelly said, "Wait for me, Susan. We can play Space Ship at your house."
Pete yelled at his friends to come back and play.
The friends were all gone and Pete was alone.
Story Three--<u>The Winner</u> (Over-Competitiveness via Winning Is the Only Way)

One day Steve, Derrick, and Brook were sitting on Steve's front porch.
They were talking about what to play that day.
Steve said, "We can play bat and ball."
"I do not want to play bat and ball with you," said Derrick, "You always win."
Brook said, "No, Steve always has to win, or he goes home."
Derrick said, "We can have a race."
"Not me," said Steve. "You always win; that is why you want to have a race."
"I lose every time I race," said Brook.
"I know," said Steve. "How about we see who can kick the big ball the farthest?"
Derrick said, "You just want to do that because you can kick it the farthest."
"That's no fun, I can't kick the ball very far." said Steve.
Suddenly Derrick and Brook got up to leave.
Derrick and Brook both said, "We are going home. We are tired of trying to be a winner. We just wanted to play."

Story Four--<u>The Block Village</u> (Inability to Play Cooperatively via Selfishness and Withdrawing)
Charles, Howard, Anne, and Marguerite decided to use the big blocks and build a town.
They decided that the town would have streets.
It would have four tall buildings and one bridge.
The town would have a park and a wall all around the town.
Charles and Anne started to build the bridge.
Howard went to work on the buildings.
Marguerite was busy with the park.
Anne decided that she and Charles needed some of the blocks that Marguerite was using.
Anne took the blocks from Marguerite.
Marguerite started to cry.
Howard took the blocks away from Anne and gave them back to Marguerite.
An argument started about the blocks.
Marguerite started to cry again, and Howard took all the blocks.
Charles gave his blocks to Howard and walked away.

Assessment Procedures

Grouping: When you are assessing a child's ability to leave a provoking situation, the most effective procedure is unstructured observation. An unstructured observational assessment allows for individual consideration, such as the child's developmental level, her learning style, motivation, disposition, and interaction patterns. But there may also be a need for a semi-structured observational situation.

Level One:
1. In a semi-structured situation, the following is recommended. Invite the child to the storytelling area. Tell her that you are going to read a story, and ask her to listen carefully.
2. Read Story One.
3. After you read the story, ask her questions such as: Why did John move from the table? What do you think will happen next? What would you have done?
4. During the discussion, observe if her responses indicated that leaving a situation is an acceptable alternative and one she would use. As long as she is attending, continue using Stories Two, Three, and Four, or use Stories Two, Three and Four at a different time. Compare her responses to the four stories; these could be important in program planning, since each story deals with a different social interaction and an individual in a group behavior.

Level Two:
5. When the child is playing with others and a conflict arises, how does she resolve the concern? Does she leave the situation as a solution to the provoking setting?

Credit: + Child voluntarily leaves a provoking situation.

Adaptations

Sometimes a child has not yet learned to apply standards of fairness and justice. She may have developed some ideas of being fair to others as well as a sense of justice and of the rights of others; however, having these ideas and implementing them are at two different social levels. As she plays with others, and experiences that everyone should be treated with equal consideration, she begins to understand that others have rights too. She learns there are certain things that must not be done: Jane may not take her blocks nor may she take Jane's. An appreciation that there are rules that apply equally to all is the basis of a sense of justice. However, when the child is confronted with a provoking situation and realizes that the sense of justice is not prevailing, she is confused as to what to do. Often she sides with someone else, stops any interaction, or she walks away. As she begins to play organized games, she becomes more conscious of what is fair, and she learns how to react to those who do not play fairly. Children learn how to implement fairness and justice best from each other; however, their impulses can be strong and selfish. When you are dealing with a child who has difficulty carrying out what is "right," remember to be impartial when you are settling disputes. When you correct her arbitrarily, to her it may seem like punishment for having disobeyed, not justice. Arrange encounters so she will learn that uncomfortable consequences are the natural result of doing something wrong. Provide her with many experiences, because experience will help her understand the esteem that fairness brings, and that the rewards of unjust behavior are mistrust and contempt. Once she understands ways to implement being fair and just, she will select the most appropriate reaction when she is involved in a disturbing setting or a provoking situation.

5.200 Tells month and day of birth
Strand: 5-2 **Age:** 64-72m 5.4-6.0y

Definition
When the child is asked, he will tell the date and month of his birthday. Some prompting may be necessary.

Assessment Materials
A marker, a calendar with a visual representation of each month. Examples: Valentine for February, kites for March, spring flowers for April. If such a calendar is not available, have monthly stickers or stamps that represent each month.

Assessment Procedures
Grouping: This skill should be assessed one-on-one with the child
1. If the child has difficulty remembering the date of his birthday, the following is recommended: Point to and say the dates in the month, and when you reach his birthday, emphasize the date. If he does not react, say, for example: "This is your birthday, the date is the [8th]. Your birthday is [point to and say the month], [point to and say the date]."
2. Draw a picture of a birthday cake on the child's birthday. Ask him why there is a birthday cake on the [birthday date].
3. Using a blank calendar, write in the month of his birthday and then the date of his birthday. Leave the other days of that month blank. Ask the child to tell you the month and the date of his birthday. If he has a problem remembering or saying the date and month of his birthday, he will soon make the association and be able to respond because his birthday is such an important event.

Credit: + Child states the month and day of his birthday. Some prompting may be necessary.

Adaptations
See #5.164.

5.201 Keeps napkin in lap
Strand: 5-6 **Age:** 64-72m 5.4-6.0y

Definition
The child will keep her napkin in her lap except when in use.

Assessment Materials
/*\Safety Note: Be aware of special diets and allergies before doing this assessment.
A drink (milk, juice), a tray of snacks foods (crackers, cheese, cut fruit, cookies, etc.), a dish, a glass or cup, a placemat, utensil, and napkin for each child.

Assessment Procedures
Grouping: Informal observation is effective because it is done in a natural setting without some of the variables that accompany a formal assessment procedure. However, if necessary this skill can formally be assessed one-on-one or in a small group setting.
1. On a table, place a placemat, and on it put the dishes, a glass or cup, silverware, and a napkin. Place the drinks and the tray of snack foods on the table.
2. Invite the child to sit down at a placemat.
3. Point to the plate and ask her what she will do with it
4. Point to the glass, and ask her what she will do with it.
5. Point to the silverware and ask her what she will do with them.
6. Point to the napkin and ask her what she will do with it.
7. If she says, "I will wipe my mouth and hands with it," ask her to demonstrate.
8. Ask her, "Where do you put it when you are not wiping with it?"
9. Ask her to demonstrate.
10. Observe her as she responds to that question and demonstrates.
11. Remember that if she has not been involved in this table manner, placing a napkin in her lap when it is not in use will probably not be a responding behavior.
12. The child's response will depend on her experiences, value system, training, and exposure to models. This assessment is not meant to be a procedure for ranking or

grading, but for developing instructional techniques and curriculum planning.

Credit: + Child keeps her napkin in her lap, except when it is in use.

Adaptations

Some children have not been expected to use a napkin to the point where it has become a habit. Most table manners are matters of information and habit and these habits are learned largely by imitation. A child needs to practice good manners until they are habitual and natural. Even if she forgets, when she does remember or is reminded, she will feel more comfortable. Do not expect more of the child than she can do; conversely, let her do what she can do. Telling her to wipe her mouth and hands with a napkin, or placing the napkin in her lap for her will not lead to independent table manners.

5.202 (Removed, see page xviii)

5.203 Makes appropriate request for food items in public

Strand: 5-6 **Age:** 64-72m 5.4-6.0y

Definition

The child will order (request) food appropriately when she is in public. She may make her request of a family member, a waitress, or a friend. She may need to ask for help if she does not have the necessary reading skills.

Assessment Materials

/*\Safety Note: Be aware of special diets and allergies before doing this assessment.
At least two choices of drinks; two choices of snacks such as raw vegetables, crackers, cheeses, dried fruit; two choices of cookies, or cupcakes. A plate, napkins, a cup or glass, and appropriate silverware for each child.

Assessment Procedures

Grouping: Informal observation is effective because it its done in a natural setting without some of the variables that accompany a formal assessment procedure. However, if necessary this skill can formally be assessed one-on-one or in a small group setting.

1. Place the dishes, napkin, silverware, and the food choices on the table.
2. Invite the child to the table.
3. Point to each of the drink choices and name them.
4. Point to each of the drinks, and ask her to name them.
5. Point to each of the snack choices and name them.
6. Point to each of the snacks, and ask her to name them.
7. Repeat if she is unsure of the names.
8. Tell her she may choose one of the drinks, and ask her which drink she wants.
9. Observe as she responds, watching for behaviors such as: (1) Points to the juice without naming it; (2) Asks for one juice, using the words "please" and "thank you"; (3) Cannot decide, changes her mind several times; (4) Says just the name of the juice, not using any sentence structure; (5) Grabs the juice without making any verbal request.
10. Tell her she may choose [one or two] of the snacks, and ask her which of the snacks she wants.
11. Observe as she responds, watching for the same behaviors outlined in step #9.
12. Show the child the desserts.
13. Point to each of the choices of desserts, and name them.
14. Point to each of the choices of desserts, and ask her to name them.
15. Repeat if she is not sure of the names.
16. Tell her she may choose one dessert, and ask her which one she wants.
17. Observe her responses as outlined above.

Credit: + Child requests/orders food appropriately when she in public.

Adaptations

A child may have never experienced requesting food in public. Either she has not been taken to a restaurant or someone else always orders for her. The ability to request/order food at a restaurant is learned mostly through modeling. When a child is not allowed to request foods or is told what she will receive, she does not learn the process, what is acceptable behavior, or the appropriate manners involved. To assist her: (1) Role-play ordering from a menu before actually having the experience; (2) Read stories about requesting food from various food outlets; (3) Review each specific behavior before you go out to a restaurant. For example, show her a menu, discuss the reason for the menu, point to and read the different items on the menu, explain to her how to order from the menu, explain the role of the waitress, talk about condiments and how to request them. Different food services will require modified behavior reviews; (4)

Provide the child with experiences in which she will need to request food in public. Give her ample time to practice requesting food in public, prompting as needed. It is important to remember not to expect more of a child than she can do; conversely, let her do what she can. Ordering for her, putting words into her mouth, and interrupting her while she is requesting food, will not lead to independent social manners.

5.204 Says "Excuse me" appropriately
Strand: 5-7   **Age:** 64-72m 5.4-6.0y

Definition
When it is important for him to interrupt an ongoing conversation, the child will say, "Excuse me," before he begins any verbal interaction. When he accidentally bumps into someone, needs to get around someone, or must walk in front of someone, he will say, "Excuse me."

Assessment Materials
At least five pictures that depict the use of social manners in which the child has to say, "Excuse me." Obtain pictures from school supply stores or educational publishers. However, you may also draw effective line art as follows. Examples: Picture One--A person being accidentally bumped by another. Picture Two--An adult talking on a telephone and beside the adult stands a child with a ball and a bat as if he is in a hurry to go to a ball game. The child is trying to interrupt the telephone conversation. Picture Three--A theater-type row of seats with people sitting in the seats. Two children are walking in front of the seated people to get to two empty seats in the middle of a row. Picture Four-- Several children sitting around a table drawing pictures; one child is reaching in front of another to get a can of paint. Picture Five--A child who tried to throw a rubber ball to a friend, but the ball accidentally hits another child.

Assessment Procedures
Grouping: Informal observation is effective because it is done in a natural setting without some of the variables that accompany a formal assessment procedure. However, if necessary this skill can formally be assessed one-on-one with the child or in a small group setting.
1. Place Picture One face-up on the table, and invite the child to the table. Ask him to look at the picture and tell you what he sees.
2. If necessary, ask questions to be certain he understands what is happening in the illustration.
3. Point to the person in the picture who accidentally bumped into another person and say, "What do you think this person said when he accidentally bumped into this person (point to the person being bumped)?"
4. Observe his response, listening for suggestions such as: (1) "Excuse me"; (2) "I am sorry"; (3) "Whoops, I did not mean to bump you"; (4) "Why did you move in my way?" or other negative remarks.
5. Place Picture Two face-up on the table. Ask the child to look at the picture and tell you what he sees.
6. If necessary, ask questions to be sure he understands what is happening in the picture.
7. Point to the person in the picture who needs to talk to the other person and say, "What do you think the boy is saying to the lady on the telephone?"
8. Observe his response.
9. Continue the above procedure with Pictures Three, Four, and Five.
10. Remember if the child has not been expected to say, "Excuse me" or has not been exposed to this social manner, he may be unaware of the response. This assessment is not meant to grade or rank children, but it is meant to determine intervention strategies and to plan curriculum techniques.

Credit: + Child says, "Excuse me" appropriately when interrupting a conversation, bumping into someone, going around someone, or walking in front of someone.

Adaptations
See #5.121.

5.205 Waits to be acknowledged before speaking
Strand: 5-7   **Age:** 64-72m 5.4-6.0y

Definition
When part of a group, the child will wait to be acknowledged before she speaks. She may request recognition by a non-verbal signal such as raising her hand, or she may need to wait for her turn to speak.

Assessment Materials
A list of several questions the child is able to answer, such as: (1) How old are you? (2) What is your favorite game? (3) What is your favorite color? (4) Where do you like to go and what do

you do when you get there? (5) Tell me about your pet or a pet you would like to have. If questions are not appropriate, select a story to read and prepare questions to ask after reading the story.

Assessment Procedures
Grouping: Observe the child in a group-sharing experience to determine whether she raises her hand and waits to be acknowledged before speaking. In this informal situation, observe whether she is consistent in this action or if it is just an occasional behavior. If necessary, this skill can formally be assessed one-on-one or in a small group setting.

1. Invite the children to the communication area, and explain to them that you are going to ask some questions.
2. Explain to the child that when they are part of a group activity, there is a hand-raising rule. The rule is: Raise your hand to get permission to speak before talking. Wait quietly until you are called on to speak.
3. Ask the children the questions. If any child speaks without waiting for permission to speak, remind her of the rule. Use the reminder only two times.
4. Observe the child as she waits to be acknowledged before she speaks, watching for: (1) Raises her hand and waits quietly to be called on; (2) Raises her hand and talks aloud at the same time; (3) Demonstrates withdrawn behavior by choosing not to participate; (4) Raises and waves her hand in exaggerated motions, appears to be seeking attention non-verbally; (5) When she is called on, the child refrains from responding, either because she forgot, does not know the answer, seems unsure, and does not want to risk a response; (6) Waits until another child has been called on and interrupts before the acknowledged child responds.
5. It is important to remember that some children are so anxious to tell what is on their mind, that waiting is very difficult. The important issue is to give them the assurance that they will have a turn to respond and will not be ignored.

Credit: + Child waits to be acknowledged before speaking, by raising her hand or waiting her turn to speak.

Adaptations
See #5.186.

5.206 Answers telephone and carries on simple conversation
Strand: 5-7 **Age:** 64-72m 5.4-6.0y

Definition
The child will answer the telephone when it rings, and he will say, "Hello." If the person calling asks to speak to another person, the child will call the correct person to the telephone. If the caller asks the child how he is, he will respond appropriately.

Assessment Materials
/*\\Caution Note: The child should be taught not to speak to someone he doesn't already know.
Two play telephones, making sure that one of the phones rings.

Assessment Procedures
Grouping: This skill is assessed one-on-one with the child.

1. Place the telephones on a table and invite the child to join you. Tell him he is to answer his phone when it rings.
2. Call him. Pause for him to answer the ringing phone.
3. Pause for him to say, "Hello."
4. Say, "Who am I talking to?" Pause for him to say his name.
5. Say, "Steve, may I speak to your mother?" Pause to allow him to say, "Yes," "Just a minute," "I'll get her," or "I will call her." (If he lays the telephone down and calls his mother, accept the role-playing.)
6. Observe the child as he answers the telephone, watching for behaviors such as: (1) Says "hello" and carries on a simple conversation; (2) Picks up the receiver and does not speak; (3) Ignores the ring; (4) Only mumbles, "Hello;" (5) Appears to be embarrassed and laughs; (6) Looks at another person and asks for help.
7. A child learns how to answer a telephone and talk to the caller from observation, role-playing, and experience. This assessment is based on the fact that the child has had an opportunity to observe this behavior or has had experience in telephone talking.

Credit: + Child answers the telephone appropriately and carries on a simple conversation.

Adaptations
Most children are fascinated by telephones and cell phones, they enjoy talking on them and enjoy listening to others talk on them. Play telephones have always been a very popular toy,

and two-way telephones are a favorite pastime; however, some children enjoy listening on a telephone, but when they are asked to talk they become unsure, cautious, and refuse to speak. For a child, talking on a play telephone and being in control of what is being said is comfortable, but when he is expected to respond to a real voice, he can become apprehensive and withdrawn. Some children may find fantasy difficult to deal with, because they react best to what they can actually see, hear and touch. To assist a child in this situation, make sure he understands that the voice on the telephone is a real person and that talking on the phone is only a different way of talking directly to a person. Once he accepts that concept, the child should be given very specific directions for how to answer the telephone appropriately. For example, using toy telephones (one for the child and one for you), make the child's telephone ring and when it does, say, "Mike, your telephone is ringing; answer it." If he is unsure of how to pick up the receiver, physically assist him. Before providing further instructions, make sure he will pick up the receiver correctly when it rings. Once that step has been mastered and the child is holding the receiver to his ear and mouth, say "Hello." If he does not respond by saying "hello," prompt him and reward his effort. Before providing further instructions, review the telephone ringing, the child picking up the receiver, and the child saying, "Hello." Continue these steps until the responses appear to be habitual and automatic. After the child says, "Hello," say, "Hello, who is this?" If the child does not say his name, prompt him, and reward his effort. Review this procedure by saying, "Hello, who is this?" and give him time to answer. After he becomes comfortable answering the telephone, saying, "Hello," and responding when the caller asks for him, begin a simple telephone conversation. Make sure the conversation is short, and at the end, tell the child to say "good-bye." Each time the child has an opportunity to answer the telephone, extend the conversation. It is important for the child to understand that talking to a person on the telephone is as real as talking to a person face-to-face, and he needs ample time to practice telephone skills.

5.207 Walks on sidewalk, does not go into street

Strand: 5-8 **Age:** 64-78m 5.4-6.6y

Definition
The child will not go into a street, unless she is in the crosswalk to cross the street or walking from one corner of the street to the other corner.

Assessment Materials
/*\Safety Note: Because you are assessing the child, you do not know if the child will succeed or fail. Have an explicit safety plan ready to use if the child does not succeed. Supervise closely.
A sidewalk that parallels a street.

Assessment Procedures
Grouping: When assessing a child's ability to walk on the sidewalk, the most effective procedure is observation. An observational assessment can either be spontaneous or occur in a semi-structured situation.

1. Take the child to a sidewalk that parallels a street.
2. Follow these steps: (1) Ask the child to walk on the sidewalk; (2) Stop the child and say, "I want to cross the street; what should I do?" Pause to give her an opportunity to respond; (3) Ask her to show the group where to go to cross the street. Pause to allow her to direct the group; (4) Ask a child to explain to the group what they should do before they cross the street. Pause to allow her to give directions; (5) After the child has crossed the street, guide her to the sidewalk, and repeat assessment items 1 through 4.
3. Observe the child as she reacts and responds.
4. If the child has a difficult time understanding the rationale for having to stay on sidewalks and not being able to play in the street, remember that in some communities playing in the street is often used instead of a playground; in some rural communities where automobile traffic is limited, playing in the street is a way of life, and in some communities, the street is a designated play area. If these experiences are relative to the child, the concept of staying on the sidewalk and not going in the street will need to be thoroughly explained and the various environments will have to be taken into consideration.

Credit: + Child walks on the sidewalk, does not go into the street, unless she is in the crosswalk or walking from one corner of the street to the opposite corner of the street.

Adaptations
Some children have not been instructed to stay out of streets other than to cross them. These children may come from environments where the streets are often used for other purposes than traffic. Examples include a non-busy rural location, a street that is blocked off, a cultural way of life, or a community where the streets are only open certain hours. If a child has a different definition of street than the usual one, she needs instruction in safety rules for streets and the various different uses discussed. If a child exhibits inappropriate behavior for attention, or because she is impulsive or uninhibited, it is important for her to understand the rules and the consequences that will occur if she continues her actions. Staying on sidewalks and not going into the streets is a safety issue that is not negotiable because it is in the best interest of all involved.

5.208 Sacrifices immediate desires for delayed reward
Strand: 5-4 **Age:** 65-72m 5.5-6.0y

Definition
The child is given the choice of being given an immediate smaller reward (e.g., one pencil, a short story read to him, five minutes free time of his choice) or a later larger reward (e.g., a package of pencils, a longer story read to him, 15 minutes of free time of his choice), and he selects the later reward.

Assessment Materials
Several selected rewards of interest to the child that he will work to earn. The rewards may range from tangible reinforcers (e.g., stickers, stamps, stars, pencils, badges, popcorn, toys, books) to activity reinforcers (e.g., sitting near the teacher, caring for a pet, sharing a toy, a party, free time).

Assessment Procedures
Grouping: This skill should be assessed one-on-one with the child.

Level One:
1. Young children initially respond well to tangible reinforcers such as food, toys, stickers and to external social rewards such as praise or special privileges. The child who waits patiently for his turn on the bars should be rewarded each time he waits, and then intermittently until his behavior becomes habit. The reward should occur as he is actually waiting and not as an afterthought when he is ready to go home. However, to reinforce the habit of waiting for a turn, provide him with the option of receiving a single reward each time he waits his turn or of waiting until the end of play to receive a cumulative reward for each time he waited his turn. To assess whether he chooses to sacrifice an immediate reward to wait for the delayed reward, select a behavior that has become a habit or that will complete a total desired behavior. A total desired behavior is one that was formally reinforced at each task level. Example: If you ask him to clean up the art area, reward him for putting the lids on the jars, reward him for washing out the brushes, reward him for picking up the paper, and reward him for washing off the tabletop. Gradually move to giving him a single reward when all the clean-up tasks have been finished.
2. Select a task that needs to be done in the setting, and tell the child, for example, that he needs to clean up the art area.
3. Explain to him that he will receive three pieces of popcorn each time he does one cleanup job such as putting the lids on the paint jars, or else he may wait until he has cleaned up the whole area and then he may have a whole bag of popcorn.
4. Place three pieces of popcorn on a paper plate so he can visually see the amount. Next to the paper plate place a filled bag of popcorn.
5. Ask him which reward he wants.
6. If he chooses the three-pieces method, make sure to reward each step with the agreed upon amount. If he chooses the bag, make sure he has cleaned the area before giving him the bag.
7. After he has selected his reward choice, observe his behaviors, looking for such things as: (1) Did he try to re-negotiate the reward? If so, how? (2) Did he leave the area before the job was done and sacrifice his reward? Did he say or do anything before he left? (3) Did he try to convince someone else to do his job? If so, how? (4) Did he do an adequate cleanup job, or did he have to do certain parts over? How did he react to having to do parts over? (5) What did he do with his earned popcorn? Did he save it, share it, or eat it? The assessment procedure recommended is designed to deal with behaviors only but consideration should be given to the child's

entry levels in thinking skills, receptive/expressive communication, motor development, and attending abilities.

Level Two:

8. When the child is participating in an activity that has reached the habit stage or that involves steps of accomplishments, observe whether he will sacrifice an immediate reward for a delayed reinforcement.

Credit: + Child sacrifices immediate small reward for a delayed larger reward.

Adaptations

A child may have a difficult time reacting to any form of reinforcement. For example, his focus may have been, "If I don't do something right I will be corrected by being told I am wrong, and if I do something right I will not be corrected or told I am wrong." Praise and appreciation have probably not been an integral part of his social interaction. Hence, he may be hesitant to respond, so he is reluctant to appear pleased or accepting. He is so used to having his behavior shaped by negative consequences that positive responses are nearly an unknown. To assist him, remember that a positive reinforcer is a stimulus that will increase the likelihood that he will repeat the act. Also, that behavior is weakened if it is not followed by reinforcement. The following are sequential steps for introducing positive reinforcement: (1) Begin by using constant reinforcement strategies; a desired behavior is reinforced every time it occurs. Reinforce the actual behavior ("You earned a star by your name for cleaning up the art area so well."), not the child ("You earned a star by your name for being good."); (2) Once the behavior has been learned, it is best maintained through intermittent reinforcement, which is provided only occasionally on an unpredictable schedule; (3) Select a reinforcer that he will enjoy receiving and work for. Reinforcers are verbal comments, tangible rewards (stickers, stars, marks, food prizes and tickets to be accumulated and traded in for a prize), activity reinforcers (free time, sit with the teacher, visit with a friend, story time), and tangible items; (4) Apply the reinforcement system in two ways: (a) the child is observed performing a desired act; he receives a reward and will tend to do the desired act again, (b) the observer observes him performing an undesired act; the observer either ignores it or corrects the child, then praises another child who is demonstrating correct behavior. Do not direct rewards toward the child himself, but reward what he does. He is not to be evaluated as good or bad; what he did is being evaluated. When the product or specific behavior and not the child himself receives the reward, the child directs his attention toward the value of what he is doing.

5.209 Displays behavior appropriate for the situation/place

Strand: 5-4   **Age:** 65-72m 5.5-6.0y

Definition

When the child is in a particular situation or place, she will act appropriately. Examples: (1) If she is at the park, she will take turns, play with the others, play fair, stay with her group, and be ready to leave when the group leaves; (2) If the child is in a school setting, she will follow directions, listen carefully, work cooperatively, stand up for her own rights, and try her best. Appropriate behavior is behavior that does not interfere with others or their property, and is also such that the child has a good time and cooperates with others to help them have a good time. Appropriate behavior helps the child and others contribute to the situation, connect with the happenings, and demonstrate capability. In evaluating a child's behavior, remember that value systems differ, and criteria for appropriate behavior varies with individuals, backgrounds, and experiences.

Assessment Materials

At least six pictures of different behaviors in different situations and places, obtained commercially, cut from magazines and mounted on 5 x 8-inch cards or illustrated as line drawings on 5 x 8-inch cards. Examples: Card One--Three children of various ages and an adult washing a car. One of the children holding a hose so it will squirt all over one of the others. Card Two--Several girls playing and having a good time. One girl is standing off to one side crying. Card Three--Several children at a birthday party sitting around a table. One child is putting both her hands in the middle of the birthday cake and smashing it. Card Four--One child about to go down a slide and another child climbing over him. Card Five--Two children and an adult in a grocery store. One child is about to throw an orange. Card Six--A classroom scene in which a child with a paintbrush is painting all over another child's picture book.

Assessment Procedures

Grouping: When you assess a child's ability to act appropriately, the most effective procedure is play-based observation. An observational assessment can either be spontaneous or occur in a semi-structured situation.

Level One:

1. If the choice is semi-structured, invite the child to join you at the worktable. Explain to her that you are going to show her some pictures and ask her to look at them very carefully.
2. Show her Card One. Set the stage for looking at it by saying, "It looks as if this group is washing a car. Washing a car can be hard work."
3. Ask the child to tell you what is happening in the picture.
4. Accept her comments without making any judgmental remarks.
5. Ask her to identify any inappropriate behavior (squirting someone with the hose).
6. Discuss what might happen next and what would happen if she decides to get someone wet.
7. Observe if she comes to a conclusion about the inappropriate behavior and reaches a solution.
8. Show her Card Two.
9. Set the stage for looking at it by saying, "These girls (point to the girls playing) are having lots of fun playing. But this girl (point to the crying girl) is not having a good time."
10. Ask the child to tell you what is happening in the picture.
11. Accept her comments without making any judgmental remarks.
12. Ask her to identify any inappropriate behavior.
13. Discuss what might happen next and what would happen if she were the child playing or the child crying.
14. Observe if the child comes to a conclusion about any inappropriate behavior and reaches a solution.
15. Show her Cards Three, Four, Five and Six, following the same discussion and questioning procedure as outlined above.
16. It is important to accept her comments, evaluations, and judgments about the pictured happenings. If you lead her responses, she may modify her comments in an effort to be right or to receive approval.
17. After your initial comments about the picture, the use of "oh," "really," or "that is interesting," are effective noncommittal comments.
18. This behavioral pictorial assessment is meant to assist in the development of curriculum goals or some individual social intervention strategies. The observational data should not be used to classify a child in any developmental sequence or category.

Level Two:

19. When the child is involved in a specific structured situation, such as playing a group game in which taking turns is required, observe and note her behavior. When she is involved in an unstructured situation (free play), observe and note her behavior. Observe her when she is in a one-on-one peer interaction and note her behavior. Observe her when she is involved in a situation that she has not been in before and note her behavior. When you are involved in observational assessment, remember that each child will construct her own reality rather than be a passive recipient.

Credit: + Child displays appropriate behavior given the situation or place.

Adaptations

A child may require a structured approach to behavior. She needs to know precisely what is expected of her in every situation. When something occurs that was not planned on, she becomes frustrated and exhibits unusual behavior. Her behavior may include: (1) Does inappropriate actions or says inappropriate things; (2) Acts belligerent when she does not understand what to do; (3) Forces herself into the situation and upsets what is going on or is planned; (4) Bosses others around and tries to organize the action because she is so disorganized herself; (5) Overreacts to the slightest criticism or teasing; (6) Acts silly or leaves when she realizes she is reacting differently; (7) Cheats and shows poor sportsmanship when winning is a must.

As a result, each new encounter should include the following: (1) Pre-planning social interactions; (2) Helping her deal with possible outcomes; (3) Providing her skills that will hopefully help her avoid problems; (4) Suggesting things to do when she needs to get out of the setting. Example: If she is going with a group to a puppet show, review with her the sequence of events that will occur ("We will walk to the theater, locate a seat, sit down, and wait for the show to start, be quiet during the show, clap when the curtain goes down or the show is over").

Discuss with her what she should do if someone gets ahead of her in line, pokes her, or tries to take her seat. Provide her with some behavior suggestions in case the situation is too much: (1) Close your eyes and relax, pretending to be a rag doll; (2) Say your name three times; (3) Go to the adult and tell her you feel stressed and need to leave; (4) Stop any action and think about your favorite thing; (5) Close your eyes and put your hands over your ears.

5.210 Acts according to social rules in work and play situations
Strand: 5-4 **Age:** 65-72m 5.5-6.0y

Definition
When the child is working or playing, he will act according to acceptable social rules. Examples: (1) If he is at the park, he will take turns, play with others, play fair, stay with his group, be ready to leave when the group leaves; (2) If he is in a school setting, he will follow the identified rules; (3) If he is a public restaurant, he will behave according to social rules of the place; for instance, if he should sit down and wait to give his order, then wait to be served; he will adhere to this socially acceptable behavior. Appropriate social behavior is behavior that does not interfere with others or their property. This behavior should help the child and others contribute to the situation, connect with the happenings, and demonstrate capability. In evaluating a child's social behavior, remember that value systems differ, and criteria for appropriate behavior varies with individuals, backgrounds, and experiences.

Assessment Materials
At least six pictures of different behavioral actions in different situations and places purchased commercially, cut from magazines and mounted on 5- by 8-inch cards or illustrated as line drawings on 5- by 8-inch cards. Examples: Card One--Three children and an adult visiting an art museum. One of the children and the adult are looking at the painting. The other two children are wrestling on the floor. Card Two--Two girls at side-by-side easels, painting. One girl has all the paintbrushes in both hands, the pocket of her dress, and is even standing on one. The other girl is holding her hand out as if to ask for a brush so she can paint. Card Three--A boy is sitting on a pillow trying to look at a book. Another boy is trying to grab the book away. Both boys are holding on to the book. Card Four--Two children and two adults in a restaurant. One child and the adults are sitting at the restaurant table, and the other child is lying on the floor under the table. Card Five--Two children and an adult in a grocery store. One child is about to throw an orange. Card Six--Two adults talking to each other, standing on the front lawn. One adult has a rake in her hand as if she is about to rake leaves. The other adult has a child with her, and the child is hanging on her arm, kicking his feet and yelling.

Assessment Procedures
Grouping: When you assess a child's ability to act according to social rules in both a work and play situation, the most effective procedure is play-based observation. An observational assessment can either be spontaneous or occur in a semi-structured situation.

<u>Level One:</u>
1. If the choice is semi-structured, invite the child to join you at the worktable. Explain to him that you are going to show him some pictures and ask him to look at them very carefully.
2. Show him Card One. Set the stage for looking at the picture by saying, "Have you ever been to a museum?"
3. Discuss what you do at a museum and how you should behave at a museum.
4. Ask him to tell you what is happening in the picture.
5. Accept his comments without making any judgmental remarks.
6. Ask him to identify any inappropriate behavior (play-wrestling on the floor).
7. Discuss what might happen next.
8. Observe if he comes to a conclusion about the inappropriate social behavior and reaches a solution.
9. Show him Card Two. Set the stage for looking at the picture by saying, "It is fun to paint pictures, and you are a good picture painter. I know because I have seen some of your work."
10. Ask him what is needed to paint a picture.
11. Show him the picture, and say, "These girls (point to the girls) are working at the easel. But this girl (point to the girl without the brushes) is not having such a good time."
12. Ask the child to tell you what is happening in the picture.
13. Accept his comments without making any judgmental remarks.

© 2010 VORT Corporation. All rights reserved. Do Not copy.

14. Ask him to identify any inappropriate behavior.
15. Discuss what might happen next.
16. Observe if he comes to a conclusion about any inappropriate social behavior and reaches a solution.
17. Show him Cards Three, Four, Five and Six, following the same discussion or questioning procedure as outlined above.
18. It is important to accept his comments, evaluations, and judgments about the pictured happenings. Do not lead his responses, or he may modify his comments in an effort to be right or to receive approval.
19. After your initial comments about the picture, the use of "oh," "really," or "that's interesting" are effective noncommittal comments.
20. This behavioral pictorial assessment is meant to assist in the development of curriculum goals or some individual social intervention strategies. The observational data should not be used to classify a child in any developmental sequence or category.

Level Two:
21. When the child is involved in a structured situation (playing an organized game) in which there are some identified or understood social rules, observe and note his behavior. When he is involved in an unstructured situation (free play) in which there are some identified or understood social rules, observe and note his behavior. Observe him when he is in a one-on-one peer interaction in which there are some identified or understood social rules, and note his behavior. When you are involved in observational assessment, remember that each child constructs his own reality rather than being a passive recipient.

Credit: + Child acts according to acceptable social rules in both work and play situations.

Adaptations
See #5.209.

5.211 Controls temper well, verbalizes feelings in appropriate manner
Strand: 5-4   **Age:** 40-72m 3.4-6.0y

Definition
The child controls her temper by verbalizing her feelings instead of exhibiting behaviors such as aggression, tantrums, and withdrawal. Maturity and increased vocabulary become the vehicles for talking about feelings that control her temper that otherwise leads to inappropriate behaviors. When the child has a vocabulary that she can use to express her feelings and when she feels comfortable in using these terms, she will find less reason to exhibit unusual behaviors because words will work for her. She will also find she is more acceptable in her social interactions.

Assessment Procedures
See #5.143 for assessment materials and procedures, as well as suggested adaptations.

5.212 Contributes to ideas of group
Strand: 5-5   **Age:** 65-72m 5.5-6.0y

Definition
The child contributes suggestions, recommendations, ideas, and direction to a group. This group may be peers, adults, or a combination of both. The subject of the group may vary from playing a game, to making plans to go on a trip, to choosing a gift for a family member.

Assessment Materials
A selected discussion topic, such as (1) What game would you like to play if it were a rainy day? (2) If you were going to plan a birthday party, where would you go and what would you do? (3) How would we write a story about a little bear? How shall we start it? More than one child.

Assessment Procedures
Grouping: When you assess a child's ability to contribute ideas to the group, the most effective procedure is play-based observation. An observational assessment can either be spontaneous or occur in a semi-structured situation.
1. Invite the children to the group area. Present them with the discussion topic. Begin the discussion by asking lead questions, example: "What name should we give our little bear? Where shall our little bear live? What kind of friends does our little bear have?"
2. Observe the children as they discuss the story about the little bear. Listen for: (1) Constructive sharing of ideas; (2) Good listening skills; (3) Staying on task; (4) Taking turns; (5) Accepting others' ideas; (6) Willing to compromise.
3. After the children have shared ideas about the topic, translate it to a written document titled, *The Story about Little Bear*. Write the story on chart paper or a chalkboard.

4. Encourage the children to draw pictures to enhance the topic.

Credit: + Child contributes suggestions, recommendations, ideas and directions to the group.

Adaptations

A child may be reluctant to participate in discussions for three basic reasons: (1) He lacks the necessary techniques for oral expression; (2) He is unable to organize his thoughts in a meaningful way; (3) He has not been encouraged to express himself.

To assist him: (1) Provide him with many experiences to speak spontaneously, making sure he puts his thought into words. If he describes an experience in a disjointed, unorganized manner, ask him questions that will combine his expressed ideas in a sequence of events and bring closure; (2) Exposure to correct grammar. By exposing him to correct grammar, he will acquire knowledge and learn how to organize his thought in a sequential manner; (3) Adding dramatized non-verbal gestures to help fix and clarify an idea so it can be more easily accompanied with oral language; (4) Drawing is often very helpful for verbal expression, and it can easily be used in conjunction with language to aid in thought organization.

As the child matures and has expanded experiences, his vocabulary will increase and his ideas will become better organized.

5.213 Explains outcomes/consequences of not following rules

Strand: 5-5 **Age:** 65-72m 5.5-6.0y

Definition

The child will be able to explain to another child what will happen if a rule is broken. If there are sequences to what occurs when a rule is broken (e.g., warning first, a second chance, put head down, go to your room), she will be able to relate the correct order.

Assessment Materials

Three sets of two pictures per set that illustrate a child breaking a rule and then the same child involved in the consequence related to the rule. Situation pictures are available from commercial sources; however, line drawing are just as effective. Examples: (1) Set One: Picture 1--A child pushes another child out of a line. Picture 2--A child sitting on the sidelines while the others are playing a fun game (loss of a preferred activity); (2) Set Two: Picture 1--A child throwing her crayons. Picture 2--A child on the floor picking up her crayons (logical consequences). Logical consequences set by an adult are effective in most situations, except when addressing a power-seeking behavior; (3) Set Three: Picture 1--A child is talking while others are listening or have hands up waiting to be called on. Picture 2--The child is sitting away from the group with her head down (time out or thinking time).

Assessment Procedures

Grouping: This skill can be assessed in a small group setting.

1. Explain to the child that she is going to look at some pictures and then talk about them.
2. Show her Picture 1 from Set One, and ask her what the child in the picture is doing.
3. After she discusses the action in the picture, ask her what rule she thinks the child broke. Expected answers may be: "Keep your hands to yourself," "Stand quietly in line," or "Pushing and shoving is not accepted."
4. Show her Picture 2 from Set One, making sure she realizes the child in Picture 2 is the same as in Picture 1.
5. Ask her what happened to the child because he broke the rule in Picture 1. Expected answers may be: "He was not allowed to play with the others," or "He really wanted to play, but he broke a rule, and not playing is what happens when you break a rule."
6. Continue the above procedure with Picture Sets Two and Three.
7. Observe the responses the child makes, listening for such things as: (1) She is not clear when giving an explanation of the rules or the outcomes; (2) She makes up things that happen to children when rules are broken. These made-up consequences often are quite severe; (3) She has a difficult time separating the rules from the consequences; (4) She changes the subject; (5) She does not respond.
8. The vocabulary in this assessment may need to be adjusted, particularly if the child is not accustomed to the terms "rules," "outcomes," "consequences."

Credit: + Child explains the outcomes, or consequences, of what will happen if a rule is broken.

Adaptations

A child may find it difficult to explain what will happen when a rule is broken. Lack of recall may explain this; however, if the rules and consequences have not been explained to her clearly and in understandable behavioral terms, she will not be able to tell anyone else. Reasons for the rules and consequences are also necessary for her complete understanding. If she has experienced inconsistency of the consequences being enforced, the outcomes will become "sometimes, maybe, not always" and will lose not only effectiveness, but also meaning.

To help her: (1) Create rules and consequences that are short, clear, and stated positively. For example, say, "Take turns when talking," rather than, "No talking out of turn"; (2) Explain clearly the consequences for abiding by the rules and for breaking them; role-playing is helpful for explaining; (3) Review the rules and consequences often; bring any changes to the attention of the child before implementing them; (4) Present the rules and consequences in such a way that she understands she is expected to follow the rules, and that if she chooses to break a rule, she also selects the consequence. Remember that a child is often totally accepting of adult authority; she also feels that the meaning of being "bad" is to not please an adult, and also, she is very imitative; (5) Rules and consequences are useless if they are not enforced consistently. Penalties for breaking the rules should be applied immediately, impartially, and without malice.

5.214 (Removed, see page xviii)

5.215 Makes own decision concerning activities with minimal adult supervision

Strand: 5-4 **Age:** 65-78m 5.5-6.6y

Definition

When the child is involved with an activity and has at least two alternatives, he will independently select one of the alternatives with minimal adult supervision. If the selected alternative is not appropriate or is not effective, he may change to another choice with only minimal adult supervision. Example: The child has been asked to make a colored sand painting. He has a mixture of colored sand on a large sheet of newspaper. With white glue, he has made a design on a sheet of construction paper and he begins sprinkling the colored sand on top of his glue drawing. Before he completes his first sand picture, he takes another sheet of paper and starts drawing another picture with the glue because he has decided he wants to use different colors of sand. He controls the colors he wants to use in his sand painting.

Assessment Materials

An assortment of construction manipulatives, such as interlocking cubes, snap shapes, wooden connecting pieces, pattern snap blocks, etc. (If commercial construction manipulatives are not available, make manipulatives for the activity as follows: Collect different size straws including fat straws, thin straws, long ones, and short ones, paper clips. Open some of the paper clips, bend some of the clips, twist them and pinch them.)

Assessment Procedures

Grouping: Informal observation is effective because it is done in a natural setting without some of the variables that accompany a formal assessment procedure. However, if necessary this skill can formally be assessed one-on-one or in a small group setting.

Level One:
1. Place the construction manipulatives on a table, and invite the child to the work area.
2. Tell him that the construction materials are on the table and that he may make anything he wishes with them. If he has not used the materials before, demonstrate how to attach and form different shapes and sizes. If he is using the straws and paper clips, put the paper clips into one end of a straw and then into the end of another straw for him. Connect two or three straws together to show him how a shape begins to take a form. After the demonstration, tell the child that he may make his own decision about what he wants to make and how he does it.
3. Observe him as he begins his construction project, watching for such things as his decision-making skills, trial-and-error approaches, patience, persistence, discouragement, anger, need for perfection, and so on. Note the need for adult interaction or supervision. The intent of this observational assessment is to determine whether the child can or will make his own decisions concerning an activity. The observational data is intended to be used for curriculum planning and intervention strategies, not for classifying or ranking children.

Level Two:
4. As the child is involved in an activity, observe if he makes his own decisions about the activity regarding how to do it, changes he wants to make, and how he goes about the different steps of the activity. Also observe other behaviors that are a direct result of the decision-making process.

Credit: + Child makes his own decisions, with minimal adult supervision, regarding what activity he wants to participate in and he has at least two activities to choose from.

Adaptations

A child may have low self-confidence and think that the outcome of whatever he does will be wrong. He gives up and becomes discouraged easily. When he is asked to think on his own, to make decisions, or to take responsibility for outcomes, he exhibits frustration, anger, and withdrawal. He may be overprotected, so he does not respect his own judgment and does not feel able to operate independently. This overprotection comes from others doing everything for him and not allowing him to experience trial-and-error, to adjust to failure and to learn ways to make independent decisions. If he lives in an environment where he is expected to be perfect in all things, he cannot measure up and he will feel inadequate. Knowing he cannot meet the established standards, he will give up, procrastinate, or only partially apply himself. Therefore, when he is asked to make his own decisions about a task, his low self-confidence stands in the way of any independent action.

To assist him: (1) Help him understand that trying his best and doing his best is the most important definition of happiness and success; (2) Help him understand that there is more than one way to interact with a task, and he should consider various methods, pick one to implement, and if it does not work, choose another. Give him choices rather than a direction; (3) Help him to look at himself positively. This may be a slow process, because he may need to learn to compensate; (4) Plan experiences so that he is assured of success. You can achieve this by breaking the experience into small steps, using immediate reinforcement, making sure the tasks are productive, and if possible, one that contributes to another; (5) Determine what rewards he will work for and use them in the following manner: (a) give the reward as soon as he accomplishes an established task, (b) give the reward intermittently, (c) let him accumulate tokens to trade in for a prize when he wishes.

5.216 Understands the dangers of streets/roads and moving vehicles
Strand: 5-8 **Age:** 65-78m 5.5-6.6y

Definition
When she is asked, the child will be able to tell the dangers related to streets or roads and vehicles. She will describe safety rules relating to crossing streets, not running into streets, traffic lights, cars backing out of driveways, buses pulling away from curbs, riding tricycles or bicycles in the proper places, playing in alleys, playing on rural roads, understanding universal signs, and walking safely in parking lots and around cars.

Assessment Materials
/*\ **Safety Note:** Because you are assessing the child, you do not know if the child will succeed or fail. Have an explicit safety plan ready to use if the child does not succeed.

A series of safety questions that require the child to give answers that demonstrate an understanding of safe behaviors around streets and vehicles. Examples: What would you do if: (1) You wanted to go from one side of the street to the other? (2) Your ball rolled into the street? (3) Your friend started to ride her bike in the street? (4) You needed to get into a car that was parked on a busy street? (5) Your friend wanted to play in the alley? (6) You were standing on a street curb when the street light turned green? Several universal signs such as: (1) A stop sign; (2) A walking sign; (3) A "no walking" sign.

Assessment Procedures
Note: If the child has not been exposed to the dangers of the streets and cars, she will probably have a difficult time answering the questions. This assessment is designed to discover which children require instruction in personal safety.

Grouping: Informal observation is effective because it is done in a natural setting without some of the variables that accompany a formal assessment procedure. However, if necessary this skill can formally be assessed one-on-one or in a small group setting.

Level One:
1. Explain to the child that you are going to ask her some questions.
2. Ask, "What would you do if you wanted to go from one side of the street to the other?"

3. Pause for her answer.
4. Observe her response to determine whether she has an understanding of the correct procedure of crossing the street, as well as of the dangers of busy streets and rural roads.
5. Ask, "What would you do if your ball rolled into the street?"
6. Pause for her answer.
7. Observe her response to determine whether she has an understanding of the safest way to retrieve a ball from a busy street.
8. Continue with the rest of the questions following the procedure outlined above.

Level Two:

9. Observe the child when she is involved with crossing streets or roads or cars to determine whether she understands the dangers of streets and vehicles.

Credit: + Child demonstrates an understanding of the dangers associated with streets/roads and moving vehicles, either by answering questions or through demonstration when out in public.

Adaptations
See #5.132.

5.217 Waits until the designated time to leave the table

Strand: 5-6   **Age:** 66-72m 5.6-6.0y

Definition
The child will remain at the table until the identified time to leave. This time could be when he is excused, when others are finished, or at a designated time.

Assessment Materials
Note: It is important to be aware of special diets and health needs.

At least three different food treats (e.g., raisins, nuts, popcorn, small mints, miniature marshmallows, chopped dates, small dried fruits, cereal, wheat snacks), three paper cups per child to hold the treats, three serving trays, napkins, three index cards, a marker. On one of the index cards, write the number 1, on index card two write the number 2, and on the last card write the number 3.

Assessment Procedures
Grouping: This skill can be assessed in a group setting.

1. Make sure you have three paper cups per child. Divide the cups into three equal groups, placing each group on a separate tray. Fill the first group of cups with one treat, the second group of cups with another treat, and the third group of cups with yet another treat.
2. Place the index card signs at three different tables; index sign one at table one, index sign two at table two, and index sign three at table three. Place one tray of treats near the sign at each table.
3. Invite the children to sit down at table one.
4. Tell them that you are going to give each of them a cup of food treats. Tell them they are to eat (or at least taste) the food in the cup. When they finish, they must wait till everyone at the table is finished, and they are told they can move to table two.
5. After everyone has eaten (tasted) the treat, say, "You are excused to go to table two."
6. When the children have seated themselves at table two, give each of them cup number two. Tell them they are to eat (at least taste) the food in the cup. When they finish they are to say, "Please, may I be excused?" and wait until they receive permission to move to table three.
7. Observe them as they ask to be excused, watching for behaviors such as: (1) Using the modeled phrase; (2) Leaving the table without asking to be excused; (3) Treating the activity as a game rather than a social manner; (4) Exhibiting aggressive behaviors; (5) Choosing not to participate.
8. After everyone has been excused to move to table three and are seated at table three, give each of them cup number three. Tell them they are to eat (at least taste) the food in the cup. When they finish, they are to ask to be excused (no prompting).
9. Observe the children as they ask to be excused, watching for behaviors such as: (1) Using a sentence such as, "May I please be excused?" or "I would like to be excused, please," or "Please, may I be excused?" (2) Leaving the table without asking to be excused; (3) Treating the activity as a game; (4) Exhibiting aggressive behaviors; (5) Withdrawing and choosing not to participate.
10. This assessment is not meant to grade or rank the children; rather, it is meant to observe their ability to use an accepted social manner. The intent of the assessment is to plan intervention techniques and curriculum direction.

Credit: + Child waits until he is excused, is given permission, or until the identified time to leave the table.

Adaptations

Some children have not been expected to ask permission before they leave the table. Most table manners are matters of habit, and these habits are learned largely by imitation. A child needs to practice good manners until they are habitual and natural. Even if a child forgets, when he does remember or is reminded, he will feel comfortable having learned proper manners. Some of the reasons a child may have a problem is: (1) This particular table manner is not identified in his home situation as important; (2) Busy schedules create problems for eating together and waiting till everyone has finished; (3) He is not sure what the acceptable procedures are for being excused after eating; (4) He treats the situation as if it is a game; (5) Meeting the criteria for being excused is more important than enjoying the food or meal time.

To assist the child: (1) A decision should be made as to the criteria for leaving the table (e.g., verbally ask to be excused, wait till everyone has finished eating, leave at a specified time); (2) Model the selected decision; (3) Consistency is important; however, situations will arise when flexibility is needed; (4) Reward the child for waiting for the designated time to leave the table and for following the accepted procedure. Allow him ample time to practice this table manner, and provide cueing as necessary. It is important to remember not to expect more of him than he can do.

5.218 Initiates topics in conversation appropriate for the situation

Strand: 5-7 **Age:** 66-72m 5.6-6.0y

Definition

The child will initiate a topic or a discussion, using vocabulary and content appropriate for the situation. She will allow others to contribute and will maintain the topic for a reasonable length of time or until closure.

Assessment Materials

At least three selected situations the children will want to discuss and to which they can contribute. Examples: (1) Selecting a game to play during outside playtime; (2) Planning a class party; (3) Preparing a dramatization.

Assessment Procedures

Grouping: Informal observation is effective because it is done in a natural setting without some of the variables that accompany formal assessment procedures. However, if necessary this skill can formally be assessed one-on-one or in a small group setting.

Level One:
1. Invite the children to the group area, and encourage them to become comfortable.
2. Present the three selected situations, and ask them which one they would like to discuss.
3. After the group decides, select a child to initiate the conversation. Observe the child as she participates in the discussion, watching for: (1) Levels of participation; (2) Staying on the subject; (3) Appropriate listening skills; (4) Quality of contributions; (5) Positive support of convictions; (6) Encouraging others to interact. Because you expect the children to contribute to the discussion, it is important that they have information or experience relative to the topic. It is also important to make each child feel capable of contributing and comfortable with group interaction.

Level Two:
4. When the child is involved in a conversation, observe whether she initiates a topic into a conversational interchange.

Credit: The child initiates a topic in conversation, using vocabulary and content appropriate for the situation. She allows other people to contribute to the conversation and stays on topic.

Adaptations

See #5.168.

5.219 Accepts friendly teasing

Strand: 5-4 **Age:** 66-78m 5.6-6.6y

Definition

When the child is being teased, he will accept it without becoming angry or displaying any emotional outbursts. His response may be verbal or non-verbal. He should have the ability to determine if the teasing is friendly or if it is done with malice. Accepting friendly teasing will also depend on other variables, such as who is doing the teasing, what the teasing topic is, when, and where it is occurring.

Assessment Materials

At least two hand puppets, one for the child and one for you.

Assessment Procedures

Grouping: When you are assessing a child's ability to accept friendly teasing, the most effective procedure is observation. An observational assessment can either be spontaneous or occur in semi-structured situation.

Level One:
1. If the assessment is to be semi-structured, the following is a recommended procedure. Invite the child to the table and show him the finger puppets. Discuss with him the age of the finger puppets, whether the puppet is a girl or boy, and the facial expressions on the puppets' faces.
2. Show him how to put the puppet on his finger. Let him select one of the puppets and put it on his hand.
3. Provide him time to play with the puppet, talk for it, move its head, and become familiar with the manipulation.
4. Place the other puppet on your hand, and begin to tease the child's puppet. The teasing should be friendly teasing.
5. Observe how the child (through his puppet) reacts to your friendly teasing. Watch for reactions such as: becomes angry, decides he does not want to play puppets, pretends that his puppet cries, uses his puppet to strike out physically toward the other puppet, tells your puppet to stop teasing, puts the puppet down and leaves.
6. This observational assessment process is for behavioral interactions and is not intended to grade or rank children. The information gathered will be helpful in planning intervention techniques and curriculum approaches.

Level Two:
7. Observe the child in an unstructured setting when he is being teased. Note the type of teasing, who is doing it, the subject of the teasing, and any other pertinent information. Record his reaction.

Credit: + Child accepts friendly teasing without becoming angry or having an emotional outburst.

Adaptations

If a child has a low frustration tolerance, he may over react to teasing, even if it is done in the friendliest of manners. He may react to any teasing in a defensive fashion. He may have a difficult time relating to others, and in his attempts to interact, he is teased and ridiculed by others. In response to teasing, he becomes angry and aggressive or he withdraws. The angry, aggressive reactions are his attempt to get revenge at those who tease him, and the withdrawal is his way to avoid being criticized, rejected or embarrassed. The withdrawal approach is his way of rationalizing, "If I am not involved in any social contact, then I will not be teased." The aggressive behavior is often his way of retaliating for being hurt, because he feels hurting someone is another means of protecting himself from hurt. Interestingly, the child who shows aggressive responses in dealing with teasing is easier to work with than the child who makes no effort to respond.

To help this child: (1) Help him understand friendly teasing; (2) Help him understand that the more he lets teasing bother him, the more he will be teased; (3) Suggest some things for him to do and say when he is being teased: (a) agree with the teaser, (b) laugh and enjoy the teasing, (c) ask the person doing the teasing to stop by letting him know you do not like it, (d) gracefully leave the scene, (e) ignore the teasing and continue whatever you were doing, (f) if you become very frustrated by the teasing, find an activity to relieve your frustration, such as, run around outside, pound clay, tear and crumple up paper, (g) use self-talk to tell yourself they are teasing, but that you are okay and can do things. Tell yourself they are having a bad day, they really do not mean what they are saying, that it is okay if others think you are silly. Remember, self-talk takes practice. When you are teaching the child to use it, do it in a natural setting. Example: Select a negative comment that the child uses about himself, "I am stupid," and share a positive statement to make him feel better, which will eventually improve his social interactions. Say, "I am okay, I can do a lot of things really well." Discuss with him the things that he can do well, and encourage him to add to the list. Challenge him to think about the words, "I am okay," every time he starts to think about how stupid or how wrong he is. Each child will react to teasing differently, depending upon the persons doing the teasing, what the teasing is about, the antecedent that occurred before the teasing, the frequency of the teasing and perhaps most of all, how important the people doing the teasing are to the child.

5.220 Plays and works without disrupting work of others
Strand: 5-4 **Age:** 66-78m 5.6-6.6y

Definition
The child will play or work without disrupting others. She will not disrupt by talking, touching,

doing non-verbal antics, or making unnecessary noises.

Assessment Materials

A selected short story that deals with a child who is always interrupting and disrupting others. Example:

Nuisance Nancy

My name is Tim.
I am in Room Three.
One of my favorite things to do in Room Three is Book Time.
Mrs. Rubin puts out books we have never seen before.
She lets us pick out the one that we want to look at or read.
We may sit anywhere we want, even on the floor.
I have a special place in a big basket chair.
The chair is a basket, and it is big and round.
The chair has a big pillow in it.
I like to curl up and bury myself in the big chair.
A fun part is when Mrs. Rubin picks out a book to read.
She likes to sit on the floor during Book Time.
We are all supposed to be quiet during Book Time.
Almost everyone is busy looking at the new books, except for Nuisance Nancy.
We call her that because she is always bothering people.
Nuisance Nancy will sit right beside you and start to talk really loud.
If you do not pay attention to Nuisance Nancy, she will try to move your chin and face to make you listen to her.
If you still ignore her, she will poke and push you.
Sometimes Mrs. Rubin has to send Nuisance Nancy out of the book area.
I know what to do when she starts to come toward me.
I jump out of my big basket chair.
I quickly put the big pillow on the floor.
Then I turn the basket upside down on top of the pillow.
Guess where I am.
Under the basket reading my wonderful book, and I am away from Nuisance Nancy.

Assessment Procedures

Grouping: When you assess a child's ability to play or work without disrupting the work of others, the most effective procedure is play-based observation. An observational assessment can either be spontaneous or occur in a semi-structured situation.

Level One:
1. Invite the child to the listening area. Explain to her that you are going to read her a story. Ask her to listen carefully, especially to the part about Nuisance Nancy.
2. Read the story.
3. Ask her questions about the story. Begin with literal questions such as, "What is Book Time? Where did Tim sit during Book Time? Who sat on the floor? What did the others call Nancy? What does 'nuisance' mean? When Tim saw Nancy coming toward him, what did he do?"
4. After the facts of the story are clarified, ask her questions related to Nancy's behaviors, such as, "What did Nancy do that upset the others? What would you have done if she kept bothering you? How do you think others can help Nancy not be a Nuisance? Do you know anyone who bothers others when they are working or playing? What do you do about it? Why do you think people like Nancy disrupt others when they are working or playing?"
5. Allow the child to verbalize her responses without any value-weighted comments.
6. Note her answers to the behavior-oriented questions, listening for: (1) Identifying the problem (Nancy is disruptive. Others cannot read or look at their books.); (2) Collecting information (She talks loudly. She tries to force them to listen by moving their heads. Sometimes she has to leave.); (3) Selecting a solution (Put Nancy under the basket. Tell Nancy to leave during Book Time. Tell Nancy she has to stay in her seat and read a book for two minutes, then three minutes, then five minutes. Give Nancy a tape recorder and ask her talk into the recorder instead of to others. Explain to Nancy that she is bothering others.); (4) Selecting the best solution; (5) Deciding how others will know if the selected solution is working. You can assist the child by prompting them with questions to guide them through the problem-solving process.

Level Two:
7. Observe the child as she is involved in a work project or is playing to determine whether she stays on task and does not disrupt others. Also, observe her as she is working or playing and how she handles a disruption that takes her off the task.

Credit: + Child plays and works without disrupting the work of others by talking, touching, engaging in antics, or making noises.

Adaptations

When a child who has a short attention span is involved with a task or is playing a game, it can come to an early end. When her attention lapses or wanders from the activity, she may engage in disruptive behaviors. These disruptive behaviors often include bothering others and consequently getting into trouble. Short attention spans are due to various causes: (1) Environmental stimulus, just too many things to listen to and too many things to see; (2) Bored because the activity is too easy; (3) Frustrated because the activity is too difficult; (4) The activity is not at the child's developmental level; (5) Mind-wandering or day-dreaming; (6) Some children disrupt others because they are seeking attention.

To assist a child who has a short attention span: (1) Make sure the task she is asked to do is within her ability and interest levels; (2) Make sure she has a complete understanding of the assignment; (3) Remove environmental distractions or place her in an area that is free of visual and auditory stimuli; (4) Proportion the amount of the activity she is to do in a given length of time. Say, for example, "Color the sky and then raise your hand, because I want to look at your pretty picture." (5) Reinforce her for staying on task. To assist an attention-seeking child who is disrupting others, use the following recommendations: (1) Ignore the behavior to take away the reason for it; (2) Let her know that her behavior is not acceptable by establishing a signal. For example, make the baseball sign for "you are out." Be sure to make her aware of the meaning of the private signal; (3) Tell her to stop because you do not like what she is doing. Use the "I" message: first describe the disruptive behavior ("When you talk to Tim while he is reading"), how it makes you feel ("I become upset"), how it affects the situation ("because we forget what we are reading"), then the direction ("stop talking, please"); (4) Ask her to do another activity, explaining that it is apparent that she does not want to read a book during Book Time. Make the new assignment one she is not really pleased to do and one that will place her in a more isolated setting; (5) Reinforce appropriate behavior in other children in hopes that the attention-seeking child will stop in an effort to get the same positive reinforcement; (6) Remove her to an area where she has a chance to evaluate her behaviors. When you are determining strategies to deal with a child who disrupts others, consideration should be given to the other variables such as the group's focus, the child's peer acceptance, any interaction that occurred before the disruptive action, and the child's ability level.

5.221 Offers help to others voluntarily
Strand: 5-5 **Age:** 66-78m 5.6-6.6y

Definition
Without being asked, the child will offer help to others. His assistance may be in the area of academic work, physical help, behavioral support for peers, or he may volunteer to help an adult.

Assessment Materials
A selected task that can be facilitated by assistance. Examples: (1) Planting a bedding plant in a pot, which requires one hand to hold the plant upright and the other hand to put in the dirt; (2) Sorting puzzle pieces, from several puzzles that have become mixed up. In order to sort, each piece must be identified and then placed in the correct location; (3) Making a sign, which requires placing a ruler on the paper and drawing lines.

Assessment Procedures
Grouping: When you assess a child's willingness to offer help to another person, you can conduct the assessment most effectively by observation. An observational assessment can be either spontaneous or occur in a structured situation.
1. If the choice is structured, select a task to do that can obviously be accomplished more effectively and efficiently with help.
2. Refrain from making any verbal or non-verbal requests for assistance. Observe whether the child voluntarily offers to help you. If he does volunteer, watch for the following behaviors: (1) Stays with the task; (2) Encourages others to help; (3) Demonstrates a pleasant attitude about volunteering; (4) Makes helpful suggestions; (5) Exhibits a desire to be the only volunteer and seeks an abundance of attention; (6) Needs to be reinforced often.
3. It is important to remember that this assessment is not meant to rank or grade a child, but is intended to be used for social intervention and curriculum planning.

Credit: + Child offers help to others voluntarily, without being asked.

Adaptations

Some children have a difficult time working with others, so when they volunteer to help another person, it usually ends up in aggressive actions or in their withdrawing from the situation. This child generally has the least chance to learn the social skills he needs to get along with someone else because he plays or works alone either by choice or by request. When he continuously experiences social isolation and rejection, low self-esteem and negative self-image emerge. He takes his low level of social acceptance for granted, and thus, he stays caught between limited experience and low self-image.

To assist him: (1) Provide positive social experiences with another peer. These experiences should bring success and should be non-threatening; (2) Include him in groups in which there is positive social interaction for him to model; (3) Invite him to become a volunteer, providing him with a great deal of structure as he begins the effort. When he completes a volunteer task, be sure he is reinforced for his help. Remember, not all children who prefer to work and play alone have difficulty working with others; they simply find individualism more satisfying and successful.

5.222 Plays difficult games requiring knowledge of rules

Strand: 5-5   **Age:** 66-78m 5.6-6.6y

Definition

The child will participate in a group game that requires attention and knowledge of the rules. The group activity may be played inside or outside, and the activity may be active (ball or circle games) or passive (table games). The rules of the game will be clearly defined prior to any action.

Assessment Materials

Deck of playing cards.

Assessment Procedures

Grouping: When you are assessing a child's ability to play an involved group game and follow the rules, the most effective procedure is observation. An observational assessment can be either spontaneous or occur in a semi-structured situation.

1. If the choice is semi-structured, select a group card game such as *Crazy Eight*.
2. Using regular playing cards, deal each player seven cards. Place the rest of the deck face down in a pile and turn over the top card.
3. Explain the rules of the game and how to play.
4. The child left of the dealer begins the game. She tries to match a card in her hand with the card that is face up. The children may match or cover their cards in the following ways: (1) Cover the face-up card with any card of the same suit. For example, if the face-up card is a heart, the child may cover it with any heart; (2) Cover the face-up card with a card of the same value, even if the suit is different. For example, if the face-up card is a 2 of hearts, the player may cover it with any card that is a 2; (3) Cover any face-up card with an 8. When she covers it with an 8, she must also tell the next child which suit she may play. If a child cannot make one of these three plays, she must take the top card from the pile. If she cannot play that top card, she must keep the card. The child keeps taking cards from the pile until she can cover. When she covers, the play goes on to the next child. The game of Crazy Eight goes on until one child does not have any cards, making her the winner. If the pile is used up before there is a winner, the pile is reshuffled, placed face down, and the game continues.
5. During the observational assessment, it is important for the process to involve some structure, not for grading, but for developing a program or for assisting a child with an identified behavior.
6. Some suggestions to consider during the observation are: (1) Did the child understand the rules? (2) Did she play by the rules? (3) Did she try to change the rules to suit her needs? (4) Was she a good sport? (5) Did she want to play another game when she did not win? (6) Did she indicate that she did not understand the rules? (7) Did it appear that she needed continued assurance and reinforcement from another before playing the game? Analyzing who is involved in the game setting is helpful to the assessment process, because a child may react differently when she engages in play with an adult, a sibling, a new child, or a special friend. Analyzing the situation in which the play occurs is also important to the observations, as she may react differently in a familiar setting, when a family member is present, when environmental stimulus is active, in front of strangers, or in a structured situation.

These suggested observational assessments address social behaviors only. Considerations for skill development such as gross motor skills and receptive language are not included, but they do have an effect on any changes in emotional and social interactions.

Credit: + Child plays a game that requires attention and knowledge of the rules.

Adaptations
See #5.135.

5.223 Behaves in a courteous manner towards others
Strand: 5-5 **Age:** 60-78m 5.0-6.6y

Definition
The child will demonstrate behaviors that are courteous to his peers and to adults. The manners he exhibits must have meaning to himself as a person. They should relate to a sense of self-assurance that will make him feel comfortable with others. If his manners are not related to this self-assurance, he will be viewed as awkward, clumsy, and insincere.

Assessment Materials
A story about the importance of manners, such as saying "please" and "thank you." Your local library can assist you in locating a book dealing with manners; check several reference books that match titles with behavioral concepts. If a book about manners is not available write a story about manners or use the example:

The Magic Word
Once upon a time a man and his donkey were on their way to town.
The donkey was pulling a wagon crammed full of potatoes.
The man was going to sell his potatoes in town.
Everyone liked the man's potatoes.
Suddenly a rabbit ran across the road right in front of the donkey.
The rabbit scared the donkey.
In fact, the donkey was so frightened he would not move.
The man tried and tried to coax the donkey to move.
But the donkey would not move.
The man sat down on a rock and began to cry because he was afraid he would not get to town to sell his potatoes.
Soon a boy came down the road.
The boy asked the man why he was crying.
The man explained that a rabbit had frightened his donkey so he would not move.
The man told the boy that he needed to get to town to sell his potatoes.
The boy asked the man if he might try to coax the donkey to move.
The man said, "Please try, please try!"
The boy walked up to the donkey.
The boy took the donkey's ear and he whispered something into it.
Suddenly the donkey held his head up high and started down the road.
The man jumped up and said to the boy, "Oh thank you, thank you! What did you say to my donkey to make him move?"
The boy smiled at the man said, "I said, 'Plee-eeas-sse."
When the man got to town, he told his friend about the wonderful boy and the magic word "pleeeeassse."
His friend said, "Yes, that is a magic word, and it also tickled your donkey's ear."
The two men laughed and laughed.
After the man sold all his potatoes, he and his donkey went home very happy, thanks to the magic word "Pleeeeassse."

Assessment Procedures
Grouping: When you assess a child's ability to use courteous manners toward others, the most effective procedure is observation. An observational assessment can be either spontaneous or occur in a semi-structured situation.

Level One:
1. If the choice is semi-structured, tell the child he is going to hear a story about good manners.
2. Read him the story.
3. After reading the story, ask him whether he can talk about the good manners that were in the story ("Please try," "Thank you," and the magic word "Pleeeeassse").
4. Ask him to tell you when he uses the words "please" and "thank you." Discuss good manners with him and what they mean.
5. Observe him as he responds to the questions about the story, tells about when he uses "thank you" and "please" and other good manner issues. Listen for such things as: (1) An understanding of good manners; (2) A feeling or attitude that social behaviors are important to make people comfortable; (3) Whether he is sincere about expressing his behaviors and feelings; (4) If his expressed behaviors sound automatic.

Level Two:
6. Observe the child as he exhibits good manners in an informal, natural setting. This observation should include both verbal and non-verbal responses.

Credit: + Child behaves in a courteous manner toward his peers and adults, and his manners have meaning to himself.

Adaptations

Some children do not comprehend the real meaning of being courteous to others; their actions seem automatic and do not reflect an attitude of caring. Such a child has discovered that behaving in a courteous manner toward others is a way to receive adult approval or a way to avoid trouble. He has often been put through a "course" in manners, in the sense that an adult says to him, "Say thank you." He responds as requested, and the adult rewards him. Or the adult says to him, "Say thank you," the child does not say thank you, and he does not receive approval, and he may even be reprimanded. He likely learns to respond as expected to seek adult approval; however, when the rewards or reprimands are removed, it is questionable whether the manners are a learned skill. He does not understand that manners are a way to express gratitude, consideration, and caring about someone else. Instead, he will probably continue to be subjected to correction because someone wants him to be courteous and polite.

To assist him: (1) Decide on the manners that are essential for him in his environment; (2) Model good manners in a positive atmosphere, minus training and constant correction; (3) Help him realize that consideration for others and good manners are rewards enough; (4) Prepare him for new situations, and if possible, allow him to participate in the preparation. When you teach manners, remember that there are two major goals: (1) The manners being taught must have real meaning for the child, not just rote learning; (2) When a child hears a verbal courtesy extended, presented in an overly sweet voice that is covering up hostility, he sees through it. The same is true when he hears a verbal presentation done in a frightening, harsh way over a kind heart. Teaching manners by rote is quick, but the results are not lasting. Teaching the concepts of courteous manners takes longer, but a child will use these manners because he genuinely feels gratitude, consideration, or friendliness toward others.

5.224 Chews and swallows to empty mouth before speaking

Strand: 5-6 **Age:** 66-78m 5.6-6.6y

Definition

When eating, the child will not speak until she has chewed and swallowed her food.

Assessment Materials

/*\Safety Note: Be aware of special diets and allergies before doing this assessment.

A small amount of food that requires chewing (e.g., crackers, cheese, dried fruit, cookie, apples), small treat.

Assessment Procedures

Grouping: Informal observation is effective because it is done in a natural setting without some of the variables that accompany a formal assessment procedure. However, if necessary this skill can formally be assessed one-on-one or in a small group setting.

1. Explain to the child that you are going to ask her a question
2. Tell her you are going to offer her a treat before she answers the question.
3. Say, "What is the thing you like to do best?"
4. Offer her something to eat.
5. Encourage her to eat the food.
6. Repeat the question.
7. Observe her, watching for her to chew and swallow her food before answering the question.
8. If she talks with her mouth full, say, "Finish chewing your food before you tell me what you like to do best."
9. Observe her to see if she chews and swallows before she talks.
10. Repeat with another question, another treat, and a reminder, if necessary.
11. If she has not been expected to refrain from talking with her mouth full, this social manner will require a lot of reminding and reinforcement. This behavior--talking with mouth full--may have become habitual and natural; therefore, she will have to go through an unlearning and relearning process.
12. The child's response will depend on experiences, value systems, training, and exposure to models. This assessment is not meant to be a procedure for ranking or grading, but for developing instructional techniques and curriculum planning.

Credit: + Child chews and swallows food before speaking.

Adaptations

Some children have not been expected to chew and swallow food before talking. Most table manners are matters of information and habit, and these habits are learned mainly by imitation. A child needs to practice good manners, until they become habitual and natural. Even if she forgets, when she does remember or is reminded, she will feel comfortable in the action. Some of the reasons a child has a problem with certain manners is: (1) That particular table manner is not identified as important in her home situation; (2) Chewing food and trying to talk is often a way to seek attention; (3) She is so anxious to talk that she does not think about any other behavior; (4) This table manner can easily become a game. To assist such a child, follow these recommendations: (1) Model chewing and swallowing before talking; (2) Reward her for waiting to talk until she has swallowed her food; (3) Remind her that when she takes a bite, she needs to swallow before she talks; (4) If her inappropriate behavior is an attempt to seek attention, ignore the behavior and remind her of the correct behavior. If the behavior continues, explain to her that she is not to talk with food in her mouth, and warn her what will happen if she continues this behavior. Give her ample time to practice this table manner, and provide cueing as necessary. Remember not to expect more of her than she can do; conversely, let her do what she can do.

5.225 Pauses to allow others to speak
Strand: 5-7 **Age:** 60-78m 5.0-6.6y

Definition
The child will pause when one or more other persons are talking. If it is necessary for him to interrupt, he will excuse himself.

Assessment Procedures
See #5.186 for assessment materials and procedures, as well as suggested adaptations.

5.226 (Removed, see page xviii)

5.227 (Moved to Cognitive, skill 1.310)

5.228 Tells birthplace by state and town
Strand: 5-2 **Age:** 68-78m 5.8-6.6y

Definition
When the child is asked, he will say the town where he was born. When he is asked, he will say the state where he was born. He may say the town and state together when he is asked in what town he was born.

Assessment Materials
Check of records to be aware of the town and state where the child was born.

Assessment Procedures
Grouping: This skill should be assessed one-on-one with the child.
1. Recruit the help of another adult. Request the adult to ask the child two questions. The first question is: "In what town were you born?" and the next questions is: "In what state were you born?"
2. Invite the child to meet the adult, and allow time for them to become acquainted.
3. Observe the child's response when he is asked in what town he was born.
4. Observe his response when he is asked in what state he was born.
5. If he has difficulty responding, make sure the child understands the terms "town" and "state." Prompt him by saying "You were born in the town of (pause for response) _____," and "You were born in the state of (pause for response) _____." Showing him a map, pointing to and saying the name of the state where he now lives, and pointing to and saying the name of the state where he was born is helpful. Showing him a map of the town where he was born, pointing to, and saying the name of the town where he now lives (if applicable), pointing to and saying the name of the town where he was born is also helpful. Ask him to point to the state where he was born. Ask him to name the state. Ask him to point to the town where he was born. Ask him to name the town. If he becomes frustrated trying to recall the state and town where he was born, refrain from any required learning. At some point he will become interested in this data, and then he will recall the information easily.

Credit: + Child tells the state and town where he was born.

Adaptations
A child may have a difficult time with memory, particularly when the information he

must retrieve is not part of his current experiences. He must also see the relevancy of the information and link it to past knowledge. A child is typically very interested in hearing what he was like when he was a baby, if he cried, his favorite toy, or his first words; however, the town and state of his birth may not be as meaningful to him, particularly if his present residence is different. The reference is not as handy, as, for example, "We are driving past the hospital where you were born." To recall information requires him to assimilate and then retrieve upon request. To assist the child, use of visuals, over-learning, frequency of recall, and memory cues, are effective techniques.

5.229 Takes dirty dishes to designated area

Strand: 5-6 **Age:** 68-78m 5.8-6.6y

Definition
When the child is finished with her meal or has been excused, she will take her plate, silverware, glass, and bowl from the table to the designated place for dirty dishes. She will deliver the soiled eating utensils, when reminded, and then without verbal prompting or physical assistance.

Assessment Materials
/*\Safety Note: Be aware of special diets and allergies before doing this assessment.
Juice (small cartons or a pitcher), a glass, small paper plates, napkins, a snack tray (carrot sticks, raisins, crackers, dried fruit).

Assessment Procedures
Grouping: Informal observation is effective because it is done in a natural setting without some of the variables that accompany a formal assessment procedure. However, if necessary this skill can formally be assessed one-on-one or in a small group setting.

1. Place the paper plates, glasses, and napkins on the table.
2. Invite the child to the table.
3. Tell her that it is juice and snack time.
4. Have the child pour her juice into her glass and pass the pitcher to the child next to her.
5. Tell her that when she finishes her juice she is to bring her glass to the rolling cart.
6. Pass the snack tray, instructing her to take one of each snack.
7. Tell her that when she finishes with her paper plate and napkin she is to bring them to the trashcan.
8. Observe the child as she enjoys her snack time and takes her juice container, plate and napkin to the designated area.
9. Watch for behaviors such as: (1) Places the used containers in the designated area; (2) Leaves her eating dishes on the table and leaves the area; (3) Forgets where the designated areas are and so disposes of the material in other than the correct locations; (4) Tries to get someone else to clean up for her; (5) Needs to be reminded verbally; (6) Needs to be reminded physically; (7) Overreacts by cleaning up the entire table, including other child's dishes; (8) Expects others to clean up for her.
10. It is important to remember that if a child has not been expected to clean up after herself in her home environment, she may have difficulty assuming this responsibility in another setting. Also, this assessment is dealing with a social manner; other developmental levels are not considered, such as a receptive language concern or a short-term memory lag. Make sure that she is rewarded for her accomplishment and that verbal prompting occurs before you provided physical assistance.

Credit: + Child takes dirty dishes to the designated area, without verbal or physical prompting.

Adaptations
A child needs to practice good manners until they are habitual and natural. Even if they forget, when they do remember or are reminded, they will feel comfortable completing the manner/action. Some of the reasons a child has a problem with certain manners are: (1) That particular table manner was not identified as important in her home situation; (2) Someone else in her home setting cleaned up after a meal; (3) Remembering directions is difficult for her; (4) She has met with negative reactions when she took her dishes from the table; (5) There have been inconsistencies in the home environment; sometimes it has been appropriate to clear the table, and other times it has not been expected with no explanation why.

To assist her: (1) Model and give specific directions for placing soiled plates, silverware, and glasses; (2) Reward her for following the directions; (3) Remind her to remove her eating utensils to the designated location; (4) Physically assist her, putting your hand over hers and the glass, and take it to the designated area. Be consistent with your directions and expectations. It is important to remember not to expect more of the child than she can do; conversely, let her do what she can do. Cleaning up after her, picking up her dirty dishes, or telling her to wipe her mouth and hands with a napkin will not lead to independent table manners.

5.230 Chews and swallows quietly with lips closed

Strand: 5-6   **Age:** 68-78m 5.8-6.6y

Definition
When he is eating, the child will put the proper amount of food in his mouth and will chew and swallow with his lips closed.

Assessment Materials
/*\Safety Note: Be aware of special diets and allergies before doing this assessment.
A small amount of food that requires chewing (crackers, cheese, dried fruit, cookie, apples) and gum.

Assessment Procedures
Grouping: Informal observation is effective because it is done in a natural setting without some of the variables that accompany a formal assessment procedure. However, if necessary this skill can formally be assessed one-on-one or in a small group setting.

1. Invite the child to sit in a chair facing you.
2. Direct his attention to your mouth.
3. Move your mouth as if quietly chewing and keeping your lips closed.
4. Play a game having the child imitate the ways you move your mouth.
5. Vary by reversing the roles.
6. Put a piece of cheese or dried fruit in your mouth and chew quietly with your mouth closed.
7. Give the child a piece of food and encourage him to imitate you.
8. Verbalize his actions by saying, "You are chewing with your mouth closed. Good work!"
9. Model appropriate chewing for a child who fails to chew with his mouth closed and saying, "Watch me chew with my mouth closed."
10. If the child has not been expected to chew with his lips closed, this social manner will require a lot of reminding and reinforcement. This behavior (chewing loudly and with mouth open and closed) may have become habit; therefore, he will need to go through both an unlearning and a relearning process.
11. The child's response will depend on his experiences, value systems, training, and exposure to models. This assessment is not meant to be a procedure for ranking or grading, but for developing instructional techniques and curriculum planning.

Credit: + Child puts the proper amount of food in his mouth, then chews and swallows with his lips closed.

Adaptations
See #5.224.

5.231 Uses appropriate/non-vulgar language

Strand: 5-7   **Age:** 68-78m 5.8-6.6y

Definition
The child will use appropriate language for a given situation, based on his age, developmental vocabulary, and culture. He will not use vulgar language or exhibit obscene gestures.

Assessment Procedures
Grouping: When you assess a child's ability to use appropriate language, the most effective procedure is play-based observation. An observational assessment can either be spontaneous or occur in a semi-structured situation.

1. At various times, observe the child as he interacts with others, listening for his selection and use of words.
2. During this observation listen for the following: (1) Use of vulgar language, such as profanity (words that are disrespectful), obscenity (words that refer to sex or elimination used in a facetious manner), or cursing/swearing (words that refer to a desire to harm someone else); (2) Use of expressive slang in place of vulgar language; (3) Use of vulgar language, not just for effect, but with comprehension; (4) Repeating vulgar words, without comprehending their meanings; (5) Use of appropriate language based on the developmental age, experiential level, cultural background, and environmental situation; (6) Modifies the use of words, depending on the group involved.
3. This observational assessment is not meant to rank children or to grade them; the intent is to determine intervention strategies and curriculum planning. Remember that

overreacting to vulgar language often serves as a catalyst for continued use.

Credit: + Child uses appropriate language for a given situation, based on his age, developmental vocabulary, and culture, without using vulgar language or obscene gestures.

Adaptations

Some children use vulgar language because: (1) It is a way to be recognized and to belong; (2) A way of releasing anger or frustration; (3) It is a way of declaring independence from a very controlled setting; (4) The child heard others use these words and thinks such expressions indicate being "grown up;" (5) It is a means to create an air of superiority by shocking. Often a child does not understand the meaning or contextual use of the words, just the reactions.

To help a child to refrain from vulgar language: (1) Act ignorant, not shocked (e.g., "Tell me what that word means. I don't understand it."); (2) Ignore the child who uses the inappropriate language; (3) Explain to him that he is forbidden to use vulgarity by saying, for example, "Richard, you may not use that word in this classroom," or "I know that you want others to pay attention to you, but please find another way besides using inappropriate words." (4) Use an "I" message, for example, "When you use that word, I feel very upset because it affects others who are working. Please stop." (5) Instruct him in finding more acceptable ways of expressing himself. A child often reflects the language he hears in his environment; this language may have varied and had different connotations. For example, the use of swear words may be used as a form of endearment. Hence, when you correct him, there may be personal implications, for example, the implication that he is wrong and his family is wrong. Setting a good example and not overreacting are very effective procedures for dealing with inappropriate language.

5.232 Reads and follows directions on safety signs

Strand: 5-8 **Age:** 70-78m 5.10-6.6y

Definition

The child will recognize and understand the universal safety signs that are appropriate for his group and environment. These universal safety signs include but are not limited to: telling where to cross the street, where to exit, school crossing signs, when to stop, where restrooms are located, where a railroad crossing is, that danger is ahead, and where a telephone is located.

Assessment Materials

A set of universal safety signs. These signs are available from state safety departments, automobile agencies, and police departments, etc.

Assessment Procedures

Grouping: This skill can be assessed one-on-one with the child.

1. Place no more than four signs face-up on a table.
2. Explain to the child that you will show him some signs that help keep him safe. Tell him some of the signs give directions and that others are warning signs.
3. Ask him to look at the displayed pictures very carefully, because you will ask him some questions about them.
4. Say, "Point to the sign that tells you how to get out of a building."
5. Pause to give him time to point to the exit sign. Note the child's responses. If he is correct say, "Good!" and if he makes an error say, "No, try again" (allow for only one "try again."). If he continues making errors, move on with the assessment.
6. Say, "Point to the sign that tells you where to cross the street."
7. Pause to give him time to point to the yellow diamond with the black figure walking. Note his responses, and if he is correct say, "Good!" If he makes an error say, "No, try again" (allow for only one "try again."). If he continues to make an error, move on with the assessment.
8. Continue with the rest of the pictures.
9. This assessment is not designed to use as a child ranking or for grading. The intent is to determine intervention strategies and for curriculum planning.

Credit: + Child reads and follows the directions on universal safety signs.

Adaptations

Some children may not have been exposed to the universal safety signs often enough to be able to recognize and define them when they see them. Other children may only be able to recognize and define the signs when they see them in the intended environment. Hence, when the child is asked to identify the signs out of context, he may have difficulty.

To assist him, group the signs based on the safety category in which they are designed. For example: (1) The Exit sign shows where to get out of a building or a room in case of an emergency; (2) A Stop sign, a School Crossing sign and a Pedestrian Crossing sign tell people to stop, look, and listen before crossing the street; (3) A Walk sign or a visual representation of a person walking (usually found on traffic signals) indicates that it is safe to walk across the street; (4) Danger, Poison, RR (railroad) indicates to stay away; (5) A handicapped sign (wheelchair) indicates that the area is accessible to wheelchairs, crutches, walkers; (6) Restroom signs and Telephone signs provide directions to those facilities.

Once the signs have been classified, ask the child not only to tell what the sign means, but also where he would find the sign. Show him a sign, and ask these suggested questions: (1) How many of you have seen this sign before? (2) Where did you see it? (3) Why do you think it was there? (4) What does it tell you to do? or, Is it telling you not to do something? If so, what? (5) In what ways does this sign keep you safe?

If at all possible, teach the meanings of the signs in the environment in which they are placed. Teaching this real-life skill in its natural setting will facilitate comprehension and allow the children an opportunity to demonstrate their understanding of these safety signals.

5.233 Engages in rough-and-tumble play
Strand: 5-5   **Age:** 48-60m 4.0-5.0y

Definition
The child engages with a small group of children, interacting in a playful manner. The play is physical and fast, and the children may be loud.

Assessment Materials
/*\Caution Note: Supervise the children closely, making sure they tumble and play safely, and making sure they abide by the rules of play and care for the other children.

Tumbling mats, enough pillows or other soft toys for each child to have one. The book, *The Napping House*, by Audrey Wood.

Assessment Procedures
Grouping: When you assess the child's ability to engage in rough and tumble play with other children, the most effective procedure is observation. An observational assessment can either be spontaneous or occur in a semi-structured situation.

1. If your choice is semi-structured, invite a small group of children to the tumbling mats.
2. Have each child pick out a pillow or soft toy to sit on or hold during story time.
3. Have the children face you so they can all see the book.
4. Read the story *The Napping House* by Audrey Wood.
5. After you are finished reading the book, ask the children questions about the story.
6. Talk about everyone falling off the bed.
7. Ask the children to pretend they are all on a bed (the tumbling mat) and that the flea lands on top of them and everyone falls and bumps into each other with their pillows or soft toys.
8. Allow them to engage in some rough and tumble play, but caution them about being gentle.
9. Ask them to act out the scene, watch for: (1) Did the child engage in the rough and tumble play? (2) Did she seem to enjoy herself or was she more comfortable watching the other children play? (3) Was she able to modulate her play and activity level on her own, or did she need adult reminders to be careful? (4) How did she respond to the physical contact with the other children?
10. If the child had difficulty participating in the rough and tumble play, ask her parents if she engages in any similar type play at home.
11. Observe the child during recess or outdoor play to see if she spontaneously engages in any physical play with other children.

Credit: + Child engages in rough and tumble play with a group of children. The play is physical and fast, and the children may be loud.

Adaptations
Some children do not like to be touched by other people. It may be that they have a preference for light touch (such as a gentle tickle on the arms) or deep pressure (a firm touch that applies steady pressure). Ask the child's family about what type of touch the child prefers. Some children prefer quiet activities and avoid loud, physical games. Additionally, some children prefer activities that move slowly versus those that are performed quickly. All of these differences are related to the child's sensorimotor preferences. Exposing the child to different sensations may be something that you have to explore carefully with the child. Follow their lead as to what they are comfortable with and able to tolerate. As they have more

exposure, they may begin initiating more physical play. It is often helpful to solicit the help of the family when attempting to get a child to engage in rough and tumble play. A key factor with rough-and-tumble play is the child's beginning ability to modulate the intensity of their play, either by initiating actions that are louder, stronger, faster, longer, or by inhibiting actions on the same dimensions.

6.94 Pulls shoes off completely, including undoing laces, straps (*Velcro*), and buckles

Strand: 6-2B **Age:** 30-42m 2.6-3.6y

Definition
The child will take off both of her shoes, including undoing laces, straps (Velcro) and buckles (when asked or voluntarily - children should be urged to keep their shoes on, unless otherwise instructed/asked).

Assessment Materials
Locate the following poem, *Choosing Shoes* by Frida Wolf; this poem is available at your local library. If it is not easily obtainable the following is a poem that could be used:

<u>Shoes</u>
My shoes, shoes, shoes
I have new ones and old ones
White ones and brown ones
Some with strings and some with straps
I have play ones and dress-up ones
Easy to put on ones and hard to put on ones
Some are for work, but none are for naps
I have flat ones and tall ones
Quiet ones and squeaky ones
Some are just plain, others have flaps
My shoes, shoes, shoes.

Assessment Procedures
Grouping: Informal observation is effective because it is done in a natural setting without some of the variables that accompany a formal assessment procedure. However, if necessary this skill can formally be assessed one-on-one.

<u>Level One:</u>
1. Invite the child to a comfortable area that lends itself to removing her shoes (pillow on the floor, stool, low chair, etc.)
2. Ask the child to take off her shoes.
3. Observe the child as she is taking off her shoes, watching for such motions as untying the laces, losing the straps, removing the shoe heel first then toe, etc. If the child decides she would rather not remove her shoes, it is important not to insist.
4. Read the selected shoe poem.
5. Ask the child to look at her shoes and relate them to the poem just read. Ask questions about color, laces, work or play shoes, noises the shoes might make, etc.

<u>Level Two:</u>
6. Informally observe the child as she takes off her shoes.

Credit: + Child takes off both shoes, including undoing the laces, straps, and buckles when asked or voluntarily.

Adaptations
A child may have a difficult time removing her shoes, because: (1) The shoes do not fit correctly; (2) Her fine motor skills have not developed to allow her to coordinate push and pull motions; (3) She prefers to keep her shoes on; (4) She is unsure on how to put her shoes back on. If her shoes do not fit properly it is important to work with her family on acquiring shoes that are the correct size. Remember the child will have more opportunities to remove her shoes at home than she will as school, so seek the support of her parents on teaching this skill. If the child has not developed the necessary fine motor skills, assist her by using shoes that are too large as a beginning step. For the child who prefers to keep her shoes on, do not insist. Observe the child as she puts her shoes on to determine if she is capable of this task, if not, model by putting on her shoe for her. Provide the child with verbal step-by-step directions, gradually phasing out and using only physical/verbal cues when needed. Allow the child ample time to practice taking her shoes off and putting them on.

6.95 Indicates by words or gestures a need to go to the toilet

Strand: 6-6 **Age:** 30-42m 2.6-3.6y

Definition
The child will indicate by using words or gestures that he needs to be excused to use the bathroom.

Assessment Materials
A child will signal an adult that he needs to use the bathroom by: (1) Using appropriate words to indicate his need, such as, "toilet," "pee-pee," "poop," or "potty." (2) He will use a hand signal or sign that the adult knows as meaning he needs to go to the bathroom; (3) He will point or touch the front of his pants to demonstrate he needs to go to the bathroom.

Assessment Procedures
Grouping: When you assess a child's ability to indicate a need to go to the bathroom, the most effective procedure is informal observation.

1. Observe the child as he uses words or gestures to indicate he needs to leave the room to go to the bathroom.
2. Watch to determine if he uses the bathroom permission process correctly.
3. Watch to determine how many times he leaves the room.
4. Watch to see if he leaves the room without using the procedure.

Credit: + Child indicates through words or gestures the need to be excused to use the bathroom.

Adaptations

Some children will be comfortable using words to express their need to go to the bathroom, while others will use hand signals or gestures. Be clear on the signals and gestures different children use to excuse themselves to go to the bathroom. Some children may forget the permission process if it is too complex. It is important to make sure that the child understands the classroom process to leave the room to go to the bathroom; "walk" him through the steps several times, asking him to independently demonstrate the procedure. Also remember that emergencies do occur and that accepting these situations is important.

6.96 Unzips and unsnaps clothing

Strand: 6-2B **Age:** 32-40m 2.8-3.4y

Definition

The child will unzip or unsnap clothing that she is wearing. The child will pull the zipper completely down to release the item of clothing. The child will gently pull the snaps to open the article of clothing.

Assessment Materials

A jacket/coat that has a zipper and a jacket/coat that has snaps on it.

Assessment Procedures

Grouping: When you assess a child's ability to unzip and unsnap clothing, the most effective procedure is informal observation. An observational assessment can either be spontaneous or a semi-structured situation.

Level One:
1. Ask the child to put on the jacket/coat and help her zip up the piece of clothing.
2. Request that the child unzip her jacket/coat.
3. Observe her motions and task completion.
4. If the child has difficulty, zip up the jacket/coat and stand behind the child placing your arms around her and begin to help her unzip.
5. Stop and ask the child to complete the unzipping.
6. Observe her motions and task completion.
7. Note the cueing that was needed.
8. Ask the child to put on the jacket/coat, and help her snap the snaps on the piece of clothing.
9. Request that the child unsnap her jacket/coat.
10. Observe her motions and task completion.
11. If the child has difficulty, place her hands in the appropriate position on the material to unsnap. Provide physical help if needed.
12. Stop and ask the child to complete the unsnapping.
13. Observe her motions and task completion.
14. Note the cueing that was needed.

Level Two:
15. Informal assessment is preferred when dealing with unzipping and unsnapping; hence observe the child as she takes off her outer garments after playing outside.

Credit: + Child unzips clothing she is wearing by pulling the zipper completely down to release the item of clothing. Child unsnaps clothing she is wearing by gently pulling the snaps to open the garment.

Adaptations

Unfastening is easier than zipping up and snapping up. The child's fine motor skills may not be developed well enough for her to coordinate the movements necessary to unzip or unsnap. Provide her with physical support and many opportunities to practice unzipping and unsnapping.

6.97 Pulls pants up completely from floor to waist

Strand: 6-2A **Age:** 30-38m 2.6-3.2y

Definition

Note: *Training in dressing/undressing is a real-life skill experience that occurs more frequently in a home setting, rather than an educational setting. However, certain aspects could and should be reinforced in the child's educational setting. It is important when addressing dressing/undressing skills in the educational situation that program policies be adhered to.*

The child will pull up a pair of large pants. He will pull these pants up from his ankles to his waist.

Assessment Materials
A pair of pants that are too large for the child, to be used over his regular clothing.

Assessment Procedures
Grouping: Informal observation is effective because it is done in a natural setting without some of the variables that accompany a formal assessment procedure. However, if necessary this skill can formally be assessed one-on-one.

Level One:
1. Place the oversized pants on the floor. Invite the child to the area and ask him to put the pants on.
2. Observe his performance, noting his decision-making process and movements.
3. If he is unsuccessful, allow him several opportunities to attempt the task.

Level Two:
4. During dress-up dramatization time, observe the child as he puts on the costume pants.

Credit: + Child pulls his pants up completely from his ankles to his waist, without assistance.

Adaptations
Some children may find dressing requires coordination and conceptual skills too advanced for their fine motor development. Practice and verbal directions are important in developing the steps to dressing. Example: "Put one hand on one side of the pants and put the other hand on the other side of the pants. Step into one leg of the pants, and with the other foot step into the other leg of the pants. Pull the pants up until they reach your waist." Make sure that the legs of the pants he is putting on are clearly open to allow him to place his feet inside each leg on the floor. Often the child will become tangled up if his feet become "stuck" in the material.

6.98 Wipes around nose using tissue if reminded
Strand: 6-9 **Age:** 36-38m 3.0-3.2y

Definition
The child will wipe around her nose when asked-- using a tissue. The child may voluntarily get a tissue or the tissue may be given to her.

Assessment Materials
A box of tissue.

Assessment Procedures
Grouping: When you assess a child's ability to wipe her nose, the most effective procedure is an assessment in a natural setting.
1. Observe the child (informally) when she needs to wipe her nose.
2. If the child does not secure a tissue to wipe her nose, remind her that she needs to wipe her nose.
3. She can get herself a tissue, or you may provide her with one.
4. Observe her response.

Credit: + Child wipes her nose using a tissue when reminded.

Adaptations
Some children neglect to wipe their noses when they need to because: (1) They feel they can sniff and take care of the problem; (2) They do not have a tissue conveniently available; (3) They are unaware that their nose needs attention. Children often need to be reminded to wipe their noses, as well as being taught the correct nose blowing procedures.

6.99 Swallows food in mouth before taking another bite
Strand: 6-3A **Age:** 36-41m 3.0-3.5y

Definition
When he is eating, the child will place the proper amount of food into his mouth and will chew and swallow it before taking another bite.

Assessment Procedures
/*\Safety Note: Be aware of special diets and allergies before doing this assessment.

Grouping: When you are evaluating a child's ability that involves a real-life experience, if possible, conduct the assessment in the natural setting. Whenever the skill to be assessed relates to real-life functioning, it is best conducted in the setting where it will be performed. This often requires support and communication from the parents or caregivers in order to determine the child's level of achievement in their home environment.
1. Observe the child when he is involved in eating a snack or lunch. Note whether he swallows his food before he takes another bite of food.
2. If he demonstrates a consistent concern in this area, individualized instruction is

recommended as well as relating suggestions to the parents to support the child at home.

Credit: + Child swallows food when eating, placing the proper amount in his mouth, then chewing and swallowing before taking another bite.

Adaptations

Most eating habits are learned largely by imitation. Some children have not been expected to chew and swallow food before they take another bite. These children need to practice good eating habits until they become natural. Some reasons a child has a problem with certain eating skills are: (1) That particular eating habit was not identified in his home situation; (2) Chewing and swallowing food before taking another bite may be a way to seek attention; (3) He is anxious to finish eating and carry on with another activity; (4) This eating habit can easily become a game.

It is recommended that a child who demonstrates this eating style be given individual instruction. The following instruction is recommended: (1) Model chewing and swallowing before taking another bite; (2) Reward him for waiting until he has swallowed his food; (3) Remind him that when he takes a bite he needs to chew his food and swallow before taking another bite; (4) If the inappropriate behavior is an attempt to seek attention, ignore the behavior and remind him of the correct behavior. It is important to remember that this could be a learned eating habit and has become a natural behavior. Give him ample time to practice, and provide cueing as necessary.

Some suggested instructional intervention include these steps: (1) Begin the eating instruction by demonstrating the procedure; (2) Continue by asking the child to model the demonstration. Use physical prompts if necessary; (3) Fade out the physical prompts, and use verbal directions; (4) Reward him for success at each level of the task, for making an effort and for accomplishing the task. Because self-help skills are learned predominately in the home, it is important to share observational methods and strategies with the child's family.

6.100 Puts on appropriate clothing depending on the weather

Strand: 6-2A **Age:** 42-54m 3.6-4.6y

Definition

When the child is getting ready to go outside (depending on the weather) she will put on her jacket or coat without being asked.

Assessment Materials

Coat, jacket, hat.

Assessment Procedures

Grouping: When you assess a child's ability to dress appropriately depending on the weather, the most effective procedure is an observation during a naturally occurring activity.

1. Watch the child as she prepares to go outside, watching to make sure she obtains the correct garment.
2. Observe whether she puts the clothing on correctly.
3. If she does not remember to get her jacket or coat, prompt her and remind her why she needs to wear additional clothing when going outside because of the weather.

Credit: + Child puts on the appropriate clothing, depending on the weather, without being asked.

Adaptations

Sometimes children get so excited about going outside that they forget about putting on a jacket or coat, even if it is chilly or cold. A way to help a child learn to be independent with dressing for the weather is to engage her in regular conversations about the weather. Ask her what the weather is like outside. Follow up with questions about what she needs to wear in order to be comfortable outside, such as wearing a sweater if it is chilly, or a coat if it is cold. You can even broaden the conversation by discussing the accessories she may need, such as gloves, boots, a hat, a scarf, or an umbrella. By encouraging a conversation about the weather before going outside, the child is learning to care for her own needs by evaluating what she needs to wear. Eventually, she will take on the responsibility of getting her own jacket or coat and will not have to rely on someone prompting her.

6.101 Puts toothpaste on toothbrush and wets

Strand: 6-8 **Age:** 36-48m 3.0-4.0y

Definition
The program-based components for this skill are not covered because oral hygiene is a skill usually dealt with at home - rather than in an educational setting. If oral hygiene is dealt with in the educational program, it is important to check with local agencies to determine appropriate policies.

Assessment Materials
Toothbrush and toothpaste.

Assessment Procedures
Grouping: When you assess a child's ability to put toothpaste on a toothbrush, the most effective procedure is an observation. An observational assessment can be a semi-structured activity one-on-one or occur in a small group setting.
1. Provide each child with a toothbrush. Be sure to label the toothbrush with the child's name.
2. Have a discussion about appropriate hygiene, such as never sharing or using another person's toothbrush.
3. Demonstrate how to squeeze a small amount of toothpaste on the toothbrush.
4. Allow each child to place toothpaste on their own toothbrush.
5. Provide assistance, if necessary.
6. Tell her to put her toothbrush under slow running water to wet the brush and toothpaste.
7. If necessary, provide assistance.

Credit: + Child puts toothpaste on a toothbrush and adds some water, independently.

Adaptations
Squeeze the toothpaste on the child's toothbrush.
Have the child hold the toothbrush in their hand.
Take the child's hand and help to twist the water faucet on slowly. Tell child to put her toothbrush under the running water. Aid the child by physically grasping her hand and holding the toothbrush under the faucet, if needed. Repeat and gradually delete the physical assistance.

6.102 (Removed, see page xviii)

6.103 (Removed, see page xviii)

6.104 Cleans up spilled liquid

Strand: 6-3B **Age:** 36-48m 3.0-4.0y

Definition
When the child spills, she will clean it up with the proper material, with someone else providing assistance as needed.
See #5.103 and #5.133.

Assessment Materials
A small glass filled with a ¼ cup water.

Assessment Procedures
Grouping: When you are assessing a child's ability to clean up a spill, the most effective procedure is an observation during a naturally occurring activity. An observations assessment can either be spontaneous or occur in a semi-structured situation.
1. Invite the child to come to a table. Place a glass filled with water on the table.
2. Ask her to dramatize a scene in which she accidentally spills the water on the table.
3. Prompt her dramatization by asking her what happened to the glass of water and what she needs to do.
4. Tell her she can request help in cleaning up the spill.
5. Observe her, watching for: (1) The words she used when she asked for help; (2) The manner in which she dealt with the problem (e.g., asked for help, walked away, blamed others, cried); (3) The words she used after the spill was cleaned up; (4) An independent attempt to clean up the spill. Remember that social interaction and self-help skills are closely associated with the cognitive dimensions of the desired behavior. She must be able to identify the need in order to select the appropriate reaction.

Credit: + Child cleans up a spill with the proper materials by herself or with assistance.

Adaptations
Some children may exhibit considerable difficulty controlling movements, and they may rely on their vision for fine motor manipulation. Spilling and dropping become a way of life when a child depends on her visual abilities because the result is often erratic motor movements. When she performs a task such as picking up a glass to take a drink, the motor skill is the predominant aspect of the activity. Because she needs to use more than her visual modality, spilling often results. For a child who uses visual control over movement, but finds it

necessary to use motor control, training in eye-hand operation through the following activities should be helpful: (1) Give her a ball of clay or a soft rubber ball, and ask her to hold the ball in her hand and squeeze it to build strength; (2) Using a marker, make fingerprints on a liquid container (e.g., large milk carton) as a model for where the child should put her fingers. Ask her to take hold of the container as she places her fingers in the correct positions; (3) Let her pick up a liquid container using both hands for the raise, and encourage her to return it to the table with one hand; (4) It is helpful to place a non-slip mat under a liquid container for lifting off and setting purposes. These activities require her to learn to grip the container, balance it, as well as lift and return the glass or cup without spillage. Provide her with enough practice time, so that soon her visual and motor functions will begin to react as an equal team. When visual perception is required, the motor skill will respond, and when the motor movement becomes the predominant action, the visual perception will support.

6.105 Puts hands through both armholes of front-opening clothing

Strand: 6-2A **Age:** 36-42m 3.0-3.6y

Definition

The child will put his hands through both armholes of a front-opening blouse/shirt/jacket/etc. The garment should be opened, not requiring the child to open the item before putting it on. The child should put one arm through an armhole at a time.

Assessment Materials

Clothing that includes two front-buttoning shirts, a front-buttoning sweater or jacket. A container to hold the clothing.

Assessment Procedures

Grouping: Informally observe the child as he puts on an article of clothing watching for the procedures identified in the definition above. Informal observation is very effective as it is done in the environment in which the task is typically performed.

1. Place the selected clothing in the container. Ask the child to open the container, remove one of the articles of clothing and put it on.
2. Observe the child as he selects an item and puts it on. Watch for the manner in which he puts on the front-opened garment and the ease in which he does it.

Credit: + Child puts his hands through both armholes of a front-opening garment (i.e., blouse, shirt, jacket, etc).

Adaptations

Some children find that putting an arm behind their back and aiming a hand into an armhole is difficult. If the child has a problem with a back-arm movement, modify the task by placing the open garment on the floor, a chair or a low table with the top of the garment, or the neck or the garment, facing the child. Instruct the child to place his arms in the armholes while lifting and flipping the garment over his head. After he shows success with this approach, have him place his hands on his hips and twist from the waist up while moving his trunk from side to side. Once the child can imitate the trunk motion, instruct him to remove his arms from his waist and place them in front of his body, elbows bent and repeat the waist-twisting motion. Encourage the child to straighten his elbows while doing the twist. To assist the child in aiming at the armhole, hold the garment for him while he twists and extends one arm into a armhole and then his other arm into the armhole.

6.106 Pushes arm into second sleeve and pulls clothing to shoulders

Strand: 6-2A **Age:** 36-42m 3.0-3.6y

Definition

The child will put her hands through both armholes of a front-opening blouse/shirt/jacket/etc. and pull the garment to her shoulders. The garment should be opened, not requiring the child to open the item before putting it on. The child should put one arm through an armhole and then the other arm through the other armhole before pulling the sweater/shirt to her shoulders. The child may or may not use her predominate hand first in putting on the piece of clothing.

Assessment Materials

Clothing that includes two front-buttoning shirts, a front-buttoning sweater or jacket. A container to hold the clothing.

Assessment Procedures

Grouping: Informally observe the child as she puts on an article of clothing watching for the procedures identified in the definition above. Informal observation is very effective as it is

done in the environment in which the task is needed.
1. Place the selected clothing in the container. Ask the child to open the container, remove one of the articles of clothing and put it on.
2. Observe the child as she selects an item and puts it on. Watch for the manner in which she puts on the front-opened garment and the ease in which it does it.

Credit: + Child pushes her hands through both arm holes of a font-opening garment and pulls the garment to her shoulders.

Adaptations
See #6.105.

6.107 Assists in washing body when bathed by an adult
Strand: 6-5 **Age:** 40-54m 3.4-4.6y

Definition
The program-based components for this skill are not covered because bathing is a skill usually dealt with at home - rather than in an educational setting. If bathing is dealt with in the educational program, it is important to check with local agencies to determine appropriate policies.

6.108 Assists in drying body when finished with bath
Strand: 6-5 **Age:** 36-43m 3.0-3.7y

Definition
The program-based components for this skill are not covered because bathing is a skill usually dealt with at home - rather than in an educational setting. If bathing is dealt with in the educational program, it is important to check with local agencies to determine appropriate policies.

6.109 Turns water off when requested/on own
Strand: 6-5 **Age:** 36-44m 3.0-3.8y

Definition
The child will turn off running water when he is through using it (classroom sink, drinking fountain, sink in restrooms, etc.) He will turn if off when asked to or on his own.

Assessment Materials
Conduct the observation where there is a sink or a water fountain.

Assessment Procedures
Grouping: Informally observe the child as he turns water off spontaneously or on request watching for the procedures identified in the definition above. Informal observation is very effective as it is done in the environment in which the task is typically performed.
1. Observe the child as he washes his hands, fills a container, gets a drink, washes out a glass, etc. During the observation, determine if the child automatically turned the water off or if he needed to be reminded. If the child left the water running, tell him to return and turn it off; observe the child as he responds.
2. Continue the observation and determine if the child is developing the automatic habit of turning water off.
3. If the child is having difficulty, place the child and yourself at the sink with the faucet handle within easy reach. Physically assist him by using a hand-over-hand approach (placing your hand over the child's hand to gently guide and direct).

Credit: + Child turns off running water when he is done using it, when asked or on his own.

Adaptations
Some children do not realize that they need to turn off the water after using it. This is usually caused by: (1) Not being reminded in his home environment; (2) He is in too big a hurry; (3) Does not comprehend the sequence of events; (4) He is used to faucets/drinking fountains that automatically turn off. To assist him, it is important to make sure he understands why it is necessary to turn the water off, he knows how to turn it off, and he realizes the sequence of events: (1) Turn the water on; (2) Fill the glass, get a drink, wash hands, etc.; (3) Turn the water off; (4) Dry hands, put soap back, replace toothbrush, etc.

6.110 Puts comb/brush in hair
Strand: 6-5 **Age:** 36-44m 3.0-3.8y

Definition
The child places a comb or a brush in her hair; the comb/brush does not necessarily have to be used to actually "comb or brush" the hair.

Assessment Materials
Child comb or brush and a mirror.

Assessment Procedures

Grouping: Informally observe the child as she places a comb or brush in her hair, watching for the procedures identified in the definition above. Informal observation is very effective as it is done in the environment in which the task is typically performed.

1. Observe the child as she uses her comb or brush to "comb" her hair.
2. Watch for placement, replacement, combing/brushing motions, position of the hair care tools, etc.
3. If the child is having difficulty, physically assist her by using a hand-over-hand approach (placing your hand over the child's hand to gently guide and direct).

Credit: + Child places a comb or brush in her hair. She does not have to "comb or brush" her hair.

Adaptations

Some children find "sinking" a comb/brush in the hair difficult, the comb/brush often just "lays" on top of the hair rather than "sinking" into the hair to the scalp. Assist these children using physical guidance, such as placing your hand over her hand and gently guiding the motions. Combing/brushing a doll's hair is effective for hair combing/brushing practice.

6.111 Puts on T-shirt with front/back in correct position

Strand: 6-2A **Age:** 36-44m 3.0-3.8y

Definition

The child will put on a T-shirt making sure that the front and back are in the correct position.

Assessment Materials

A "dress-up box" with several T-shirt's; preferably those that have a design on the front (not a plain colored T-shirt).

Assessment Procedures

Grouping: Informally observe the child as he puts on a T-shirt, watching for the procedures identified in the definition above. Informal observation is very effective as it is done in the environment in which the task is needed.

1. Ask the child to go to the "dress-up box," find a T-shirt, and put it on.
2. If the child has difficulty finding the correct clothing item, provide him with a T-shirt.
3. Ask the child to put on the T-shirt.
4. Observe the child as he puts on the T-shirt, paying special attention to the fact that the child has the front and back in the correct positions.
5. During the observation, note how the child determined which was front and back of the T-shirt (looked at the front design, determined where the label was located, used a trial and error method, did not pay any attention, etc.)

Credit: + Child puts on a T-shirt making sure the front and back are in the correct position.

Adaptations

Some children find determining front and back either difficult or unimportant. Often these children will decide which is the front and the back of a garment, but putting it on the correct way is another level of achievement. For example, once they decide which is the front and the back they will often lay the T-shirt with the front facing up, hence when they go to put the shirt on they will put their arms and head in the way the garment is laying, which means that the shirt will wind up backwards. To assist these children, use a visual cue, such as a T-shirt typically has a pattern on the front and is plain in the back. If a patterned T-shirt is not available, taping a visual item (colored ribbon) on the front is effective. To assist these children in putting on the T-shirt, begin with a hanging shirt rather than one that is folded or lying down. If the shirt is on a hanger, the front and back can be positioned so it coincides with the front and back of the child.

6.112 Puts sock on completely

Strand: 6-2A **Age:** 36-44m 3.0-3.8y

Definition

The child will put on her sock and pull it on completely from the toe, to heel, to ankle.

Assessment Materials

Make sure there are several large socks in the dress-up box. The sock should be big enough to put on over shoes.

Assessment Procedures

Grouping: Informally observe the child as she pulls up her socks watching for the procedures identified in the definition.

1. Observe the child when she is involved with the dress-up clothing to determine if she is able to put on a sock, pull it over the toe, to the heel, and then to the ankle.

2. Watch for: (1) An understanding of the toe, heel and sock opening; (2) Holding the sock in a manner in which it will easily slide over the toe, heel and to be pulled up to the ankle; (3) Manipulating the sock without twisting or turning it; (4) Adjusting the sock, as needed.

Credit: + Child puts on her sock and pulls it on completely from the toe, to the heel, to the ankle.

Adaptations

Some children have difficulty putting on their socks due to lack of coordination, confusion about a sock's beginning position, sequence of movements, or their eye-hand coordination is limited. To assist these children, model folding the sock from the ankle to the toe, allowing the child to gradually unfold the sock moving from toe to ankle. Allow ample time for practice while the child uses a larger sock than they typically wear.

6.113 Directs spoon/fork into mouth without spilling

Strand: 6-3A **Age:** 30-42m 2.6-3.6y

Definition

The child will grasp a spoon or a fork, fill it, move the spoon or fork to his mouth and insert it with no spilling. He may grasp the utensil with either a supinate (palm of hand directly forward and thumb away from body) or palmar (grip controlled by palm down, fingers direct). He generally loads the spoon/fork with the right amount of food.

Assessment Materials

/*\Safety Note: Be aware of special diets and allergies before doing this assessment. Conduct the assessment during snack or lunch time, when the child will be using utensils to eat.

Assessment Procedures

See #6.99.

Adaptations

Some children have a difficult time when the world of spoons, forks, glasses, plates, napkins, and spills replaces finger food. To such a child, the ability to grasp a utensil, scoop or spear food, and to move the spoon/fork to their mouths without spilling may seem overwhelming, as well as senseless since his fingers work very well. Any problems with motor skills and visual-motor integration certainly will affect the success level of this basic eating process. The skill of using a spoon or fork to eat entails doing a task analysis of the activity. For example, the prerequisite skills needed to use a spoon or fork include: (1) Ability to grasp the handle of the utensil, either using a whole hand closure or using a thumb and forefinger closure; (2) Ability to direct arm to mouth; (3) Ability to close mouth and remove food from the utensil; (4) Ability to follow directions. The task analysis in using eating utensils includes: (1) Picks up utensil with hand; (2) Grasps utensil; (3) Moves utensil toward plate or bowl; (4) Maneuvers spoon under food (yogurt or ice cream are good to begin with, liquids are not) or uses fork to spear or lift (apple slices, pieces of bread, marshmallows, cheese); (5) Lifts food with the utensil; (6) Steadily moves utensil and hand toward mouth; (7) Inserts utensil with food into mouth; (8) Closes mouth with lips over the spoon or fork to remove food while withdrawing the utensil; (9) Repeats tasks until eating has been completed; (10) Places spoon or fork on table and releases the hold. Various adaptive materials are available to assist children to grip the spoon or fork and to manipulate the food. For example, a foam adapter fits over the spoon handle to increase grips, and built up handles and section plates provide a lip for easier scooping.

6.114 Serves self at table, pouring and scooping with no spilling

Strand: 6-3A **Age:** 36-48m 3.0-4.0y

Definition

The child will serve herself at the table. She will pour liquid into a glass or cup, use a spoon to scoop food from a serving dish, and take a finger food (e.g., slice of bread) from a plate. She will ask for food and drink to be passed to her.

Assessment Materials

/*\Safety Note: Be aware of special diets and allergies before doing this assessment.
A plate, a cup or a glass, silverware, a small pitcher, a bowl. A small amount of a liquid (water, milk, or juice) in the pitcher. A small amount of soft food (applesauce or pudding) in the bowl. Several slices of bread, crackers, or rolls on a plate. A placemat.

Assessment Procedures

Grouping: Informally observe the child as she serves herself at the table watching for the procedures identified in the definition above.

Informal observation is very effective as it is done in the environment in which the task is typically performed.
1. Lay a placemat on the table, and on it set a plate, a cup or a glass, and silverware. Set the pitcher, the bowl, and the plate on the table.
2. Ask the child to use the pitcher to fill her glass or cup.
3. Observe her as she handles the pitcher and fills her glass. Watch for her motor movements, eye-hand coordination, use of utensils, and body position when she serves herself at the table.
4. Ask the child to serve herself some of the food presented at the table.
5. Observe her as she uses the spoon to scoop food from the serving dish, pours liquid into her cup or glass, and takes a finger food from a serving tray.
6. Observe her to see if she asks for the food or beverage to be passed to her.
7. Note your observations.
8. Children mature at different levels; they become independent at some skills at one time and other tasks at other times. Any assessment should consider the developmental level of the child, her experiences, attention span and objectiveness. This assessment is not meant to compare a child to another child, but instead, to determine intervention strategies and for curriculum planning.

Credit: + Child serves herself at the table, pouring and scooping without spilling, and asking for items to be passed to her.

Adaptations

Some children have a difficult time serving themselves food or liquid at a table. Grasping a utensil to scoop or spear food from a serving dish, grasping a carton or pitcher, raising it and pouring it into a glass or cup, and holding a plate while selecting food from it are challenging tasks for such a child. These various movements require strength, agility, eye-hand manipulation, directionality, and coordination.

Serving oneself at the table requires the following skills: (1) Grasp the handle of the utensil, either using a whole hand closure or using a thumb and forefinger closure; (2) Scoop the food from the serving dish onto the spoon, or pierce the food from the serving dish with a fork; (3) Lift the utensil from the serving dish to a plate; (4) Place the food on the plate, and return the utensil to the serving dish; (5) Grasp a container that holds liquid. For example, grasp a pitcher by its handle, a carton of liquid, or a can of liquid; (6) Lift the liquid container to a height that will determine the flow of the contents into a glass; (7) Judge the amount to pour, and then tilt the liquid container upright; (8) Grasp and balance a plate long enough to remove a finger food.

6.115 Puts shoes on the correct feet
Strand: 6-2A **Age:** 30-42m 2.6-3.6y

Definition
Note: *It is not necessary that the child understand the concepts of right and left.*
The child will put on his shoes by matching the right shoe to his right foot and his left shoe to his left foot.

Assessment Procedures
Grouping: Informally observe the child as he puts on his shoes watching for the procedures identified in the definition above. Informal observation is very effective as it is done in the environment in which the task is typically performed, such as after naptime, after playing dress-up's etc.
1. Ask the child to take off his shoes.
2. Then, as the child is putting his shoes back on, watch for: (1) The manner in which the child picks up a shoe; (2) How he makes the shoe opening as large as possible; (3) Places toe of correct foot into the shoe; (4) Pulls the shoe on, over the heel, using a pulling plus pushing motion; (5) Adjusts the shoe/sock as needed.

Credit: + Child puts his shoes on the correct feet, without assistance.

Adaptations
To assist him: (1) Allow him to do what he can without help; (2) Use visual cues to alert the child which shoe goes on which foot; (3) Model putting on your shoe, verbally describing the steps.

6.116 Places outer-wear clothing in assigned location
Strand: 6-2B **Age:** 36-58m 3.0-4.10y

Definition
The child will hang her jacket/coat/sweater/head-gear (hat/scarf, etc.) on a designated hook or in a designated place.

Assessment Materials

Name tags, stickers or any other appropriate identification material to be used to designate the individual child's clothing hook. If shelves/bins/lockers/etc. are used, the same individual identification should be implemented.

Assessment Procedures

Note: It is important that the child is aware of her designated area and why she should use it rather than just any hook.

Grouping: Informally observe the child as he hangs his jacket on a designated hook. Informal observation is very effective as it is done in the environment in which the task is typically performed.

1. Observe the child as she hangs up her outdoor clothing on her designated hook.
2. Watch for: (1) How she hangs up her clothing and outdoor accessories, such as a hat; (2) If she uses her designated hook/bin/locker/etc.; (3) If she checks to make sure her coat/hat remain on the hook after placement; (5) If she hands the items to another child to hang up.

Credit: + Child puts her jacket, as well as any other outdoor accessories in her designated place (hook, shelf, bin, locker).

Adaptations

Some children find hanging up their outer garments an unnecessary task. These children may react this way due to: (1) Not being taught that care of objects is important; (2) Problems in recalling where to hang her garments; (3) Expecting others to do things for her; (4) Unsure of how to hang up the item and may become frustrated when the sweater/coat does not stay on the hook due to the way it is placed; (5) Wanting to wear the item rather than hang it up; (6) Having a fear of losing her outdoor clothing. To assist these children, clearly inform them where their hook is by having them place their name/sticker on the designated area. It is also recommended that the child identify her hook several times by walking to it, pointing to it, hanging up an item, etc. To help the child know how to hang up her sweater/jacket/coat, demonstrate how to take the back of the collar and place it over the hook. Allow the child numerous opportunities to find the back of the collar and then place the collar over the hook. If the child is concerned about her clothing being taken or losing it (so she chooses not to let it out of sight), allow the child to keep the items

6.117 Drinks from water fountain when turned on by adult

Strand: 6-3B **Age:** 37-42m 3.1-3.6y

Definition

The child will drink from a water fountain when it is turned on by an adult. He must be able to reach the fountain independently; however, steps may be provided.

Assessment Materials

Available drinking fountain.

Assessment Procedures

Grouping: Informally observe the child as he gets a drink of water from a water fountain watching for the procedures identified in the definition above. Informal observation is very effective as it is done in the environment in which the task is typically performed.

1. At break time, ask the children to line up for a drink at the water fountain. Explain to them that the fountain will be turned on for them, and all they have to do is drink.
2. Observe each child as he takes a turn to get a drink from the fountain, watching for such behaviors as: (1) Drinking the water successfully; (2) Taking the water into the mouth but not swallowing it; (3) Not opening his mouth; hence, the water sprays; (4) Places his whole mouth on the fountain; (5) Plays in the water with his hands; (6) Does not drink the water; (7) Spits the water out.
3. Note the type of drinking behavior each child exhibits.

Credit: + Child drinks from a water fountain when an adult turns it on.

Adaptations

Drinking from something other than a cup/glass may be difficult for a child because when he uses a cup or a glass, he can close his lips around the edge, which helps keep the liquid in his mouth. Drinking from a fountain involves a very different process since the amount of liquid intake and the swallowing of that liquid is not based on what is in a container. Also, the amount of liquid can be controlled in a container, so a child does not have to tip his head backward to drink it. Swallowing is usually easier with the head tipped slightly forward. To drink from a fountain, you must modify the normal swallowing behavior, because the head is tipped totally forward and swallowing occurs when the head is moved upright. It is helpful to teach him to take a mouthful of water, close his mouth, and then swallow the water. When he swallows, encourage him to move his head to an upright position. Once he masters drinking from a water fountain, every fountain he sees will create an immediate thirst.

6.118 Pulls off front-opening clothing over wrist, forearm and elbow with assistance

Strand: 6-2B **Age:** 28-38m 2.4-3.2y

Definition
The child will take off her front-opening clothing (sweater, shirt, jacket) by pulling it over her wrist, forearm and elbow with assistance, if needed.

Assessment Materials
Clothing that includes two front-buttoning shirts, a front-buttoning sweater or jacket. A container to hold the clothing.

Assessment Procedures
Grouping: Informally observe the child as removes an article of clothing watching for the procedures identified in the definition above. Informal observation is very effective as it is done in the environment in which the task is needed.
1. Place the selected clothing in the container. Ask the child to open the container, remove one of the articles of clothing and put it on.
2. After the child has put on the garment, ask her to remove it.
3. Observe the child as she removes the item. Watch the sequence the child performs when removing the sweater/shirt/jacket/etc.
4. The sequence should include pulling the clothing over her wrist, forearm and elbow. Provide assistance if necessary.

Credit: + Child takes off her front-opening clothing by pulling if over her wrist, forearm and elbow, with assistance if necessary.

Adaptations
Some children find it difficult to put one hand behind their back to pull a sleeve off. This may be due to the fact that when putting hands behind the back, fine motor skills have to be coordinated without the aid of visual support. Once the child understands that she is to join her hands and then tug at a sleeve, the lack of being able to see is compensated for. To assist her, plan a clapping activity, such as: instruct the child to clap in front of her body then immediately clap behind her body. Explain to the child that you are going to tell her when to clap and then to hold her hands together.

Example: "Front, clap --- Back, clap---Front, clap clap-----Back, clap clap---Front, clap and hold hands together--Back clap and hold hands together---Front, clap clap and hold hands---Back, clap clap and hold hands."

It is important that the child be given time to develop the ability to coordinate moving her hands behind her back.

6.119 Pulls pants down from waist to feet

Strand: 6-2B **Age:** 30-40m 2.6-3.4y

Definition
Note: *Training in dressing or undressing is a real-life skill experience that occurs in a non-educational setting. However, certain aspects could and should be reinforced in the child's educational setting. It is important that program policies be adhered to when teaching dressing/undressing skills in the educational setting.*
The child will pull his pants down from waist to floor.

Assessment Materials
Two pairs of pants that are too large for the child.

Assessment Procedures
Grouping: Informal observation is effective because it is done in a natural setting without some of the variables that accompany a formal assessment procedure. However, if necessary this skill can formally be assessed one-on-one.
1. Place the two pairs of oversized pants on the floor.
2. Invite the child to the area, ask him to select one of the pairs of pants and to put the "baggy" pants on.
3. Observe his performance, focusing on such movements as: (1) Used both hands on the waist band to move the garment down; (2) Pulled the pant legs down simultaneously; (3) Used body motion to assist in taking the pants off; (4) Used hands to move the pants over the feet and totally off.

Credit: + Child pulls pants down from his waist to his feet, independently.

Adaptations
Some children may find undressing too advanced for their motor development. Practice

and verbal directions are important in developing the steps to undressing. Example: "Put one hand on one side of the pants and put the other hand on the other side of the pants. Begin to pull the pants down, moving the two hands together until the pants reach your ankles. When the pants are at your ankles, step out of one leg of the pants, and then step out of the other leg of the pants. Pick up the pants."

6.120 (Removed, see page xviii)

6.121 Removes pull-over clothing from both arms and starts over head

Strand: 6-2B **Age:** 38-42m 3.2-3.6y

Definition

Note: *Training in dressing or undressing is a real-life skill experience that occurs in a non-educational setting. However, certain aspects could and should be reinforced in the child's educational setting. It is important that program policies be adhered to when teaching dressing/undressing skills in the educational setting.*

The child will take-off a piece of clothing that is not a front-opening garment. The child will take the pull-over clothing (sweater, T-shirt, etc.) off his arms and begin to pull the article over his head.

Assessment Materials

Two pull-over items (sweater, shirt, T-shirt). A container to hold the clothing.

Assessment Procedures

Grouping: Informally observe the child as he removes an article of clothing watching for the procedures identified in the definition above. Informal observation is very effective as it is done in the environment in which the task is needed.

1. Place the selected clothing in the container.
2. Ask the child to open the container, remove one of the articles of clothing and put it on.
3. Observe the child as he selects an item and puts it on.
4. After the child has put on the pull-over piece of clothing, ask him to take the garment off.
5. Observe the child as he removes the sweater/T-shirt, watching for: (1) First step of using both hands to take a hold of the bottom of the garment and begin pulling up; (2) The gradual straightening of the arms as the garment begins to go over the head and off; (3) The continued placement of the hands through the process; (4) Any adjustment that needed to be made as the item approached the chin.

- **Credit:** + Child removes a pull-over garment off his arms and begins to pull the article over his head.

Adaptations

Some children have a problem with the continuous motion of taking hold of the bottom of a pull-over garment, bending the elbows and gradually straightening the arms without moving their hands. If one hand lets go during the pull off motion, the garment has a tendency to stay on the child on one side and come off the child on the other side. If both hands are released the garment will not move. If the motion is not continuous, one arm may come out and not the other, the garment might become twisted, tangled arms occur, etc. To assist these children, it is helpful if they do an exercise involving the arms following the body and moving above the head, such as: ask the child to place his hands on his hips (demonstrate), request that he move his arms along his body under his arm pits, up to his shoulders and then leave the body and move upward until both arms are straight up in the air. Continue this exercise until the child becomes proficient with a smooth, even movement. Ask the child to put a pull-over garment on and do the exercise with it on. After several practice motions, modify the activity by asking the child to take hold of the bottom of the item and repeat the movement; only this time take the sweater/T-shirt off.

6.122 Refills a glass using a container with a handle and a spout

Strand: 6-3B **Age:** 38-46m 3.2-3.10y

Definition

Using a container with handle and a pouring spout that holds less than 8 ounces of a liquid (water, juice, milk), the child will refill a glass. Some spilling may occur at first.

Assessment Materials

A plastic container/pitcher with a handle and a spout, a plastic glass that will hold 8 ounces or less, a sponge, paper towels. Small amount of a liquid (e.g., water, milk, juice) in the container.

Assessment Procedures

Grouping: Informally observe the child as she refills a glass using a container with a handle and a spout watching for the procedures identified in the definition above. Informal observation is very effective as it is done in the environment in which the task is typically performed.

1. Set the container and the glass on the table.
2. Tell the child to use the container to fill her glass or cup.
3. She should grasp the container with one or two hands and pour the liquid into the glass about half full. Some spilling may occur.
4. Observe her as she handles the pitcher and fills her glass, watching for her motor movements, eye-hand coordination, use of utensils, and body position when she serves herself.
5. Children mature at different rates. Any assessment should consider the developmental level of the child, her experiences, attention span, and objectiveness. This assessment is not meant to rank a child or to grade her in any way, but instead, to determine intervention strategies and for curriculum planning.

Credit: + Child refills a glass using a container with a handle and spout, some spilling may occur.

Adaptations

A child may have a difficult time pouring liquid. She needs the ability to grasp a liquid container (e.g., carton or pitcher), raise it, and pour into a glass or a cup. Pouring movements require strength, agility, eye-hand manipulation, directionality, and coordination. Any of these motor-related problems will certainly affect her success in learning how to pour. To assist such a child, consider the following activities: (1) Provide the child with an opportunity to water outdoor plants with a small pitcher where spills will not be a big issue; (2) Allow the child to use pitchers and cups during water play to practice pouring; (3) During outdoor play in a sandbox, have the child pour sand from a pitcher into a cup; (4) Have a tea party and practice pouring water into the tea cups.

6.123 Blows into tissue with some assistance

Strand: 6-9   **Age:** 38-46m 3.2-3.10y

Definition

The child will blow his nose into a tissue. The child may voluntarily get a tissue or have the tissue given to him. He may need assistance holding or positioning the tissue.

Assessment Materials

A box of tissue.

Assessment Procedures

Grouping: Informally observe the child as he blows his nose into a tissue.

1. Observe the child when he needs to blow his nose.
2. If the child does not secure a tissue and blow his nose, remind him he needs to blow and provide him with a tissue.
3. If necessary, give assistance holding or positioning the tissue.
4. Observe his response.

Credit: + Child blows his nose into a tissue with some assistance.

Adaptations

Some children neglect to blow their noses when they need to because: (1) They feel they can sniff and take care of the problem; (2) They do not have a tissue; (3) They ignore the need to blow the nose. These children need to be reminded that they should blow their nose. They need to observe the correct modeling of blowing ones' nose.

6.124 (Removed, see page xviii)

6.125 (Removed, see page xviii)

6.126 (Removed, see page xviii)

6.127 Closes the front snap on an article of clothing

Strand: 6-2A   **Age:** 36-48m 3.0-4.0y

Definition

The child will close the front snaps to an article of clothing. The child will grasp the clothing that surrounds one of the snaps, match the two parts and press until the snaps interlock.

Assessment Materials

Have available clothing that has snaps on it or use a snapping board. A snapping board may be made by taking a section of clothing that has snaps on it (at least 3 snaps) and securing it firmly (nail it) to a piece of board that is larger than the material. It is important to allow some slack in the material prior to attaching it to the board.

Assessment Procedures

Grouping: Informally observe the child as she closes the snaps on an article of clothing watching for the procedures identified in the definition above.
1. Unsnap the snaps on either the clothing or the snapping board.
2. Give the child the article of clothing or the snapping board and ask him to snap the snaps.
3. Observe the child as she works with the snaps, watching for: (1) Eye-hand coordination, particularly when it comes to placing one snap over the other; (2) Pressure needed to close the snaps; (3) Using a trial and error approach; (4) Placing the material close to their eye to "line-up" the snaps, rather than using a visual/tactile approach; (5) Being able to match the snaps in alignment with the clothing when there is more than one snap.

Credit: + Child closes the front snaps to an article of clothing by matching the two parts and presses until the snaps lock.

Adaptations

Some children have difficulty in snapping snap-type devices. This may be related to: (1) Lacking the necessary strength to close the snaps; (2) Developmental delays in eye-hand coordination; (3) Lacking the patience to continue until the task is complete; (4) Lacking an understanding of the need to close the snaps (for warmth, cover-up, secure items, etc.); (5) Lacking the ability to close the snaps when the article of clothing is on the child. This requires the child to "crinkle" the material around each snap, match the two parts together and press.

To assist these children the following is recommended: (1) Model the snapping procedures; (2) Use physical assistance (hand-over-hand) support to perform the task; (3) Make sure that the learning experience is as directly related to where the snapping will occur as possible; (4) Allow for ample practice with support as needed, however the support should be gradually phased out.

If the child finds snapping a big problem, then other closures should be considered. The child's fine motor and eye-hand coordination may be delayed, hence snapping needs to be introduced at a later time.

6.128 (Removed, see page xviii)

6.129 Takes pull-over clothing off completely

Strand: 6-2B   **Age:** 40-48m 3.4-4.0y

Definition

Note: *Training in dressing or undressing is a real-life skill experience that occurs in a non-educational setting. However, certain aspects could and should be reinforced in the child's educational setting. It is important that program policies be adhered to when teaching dressing/undressing skills in the educational setting.*

The child will take-off a piece of clothing that is not a front-opening garment. The child will take the pull-over clothing (sweater, T-shirt, etc.) off completely. Some assistance may be needed, however the goal is to strive for independence.

Assessment Materials

Clothing that includes two pull-over items (sweater, T-shirt, etc.) A container to hold the clothing.

Assessment Procedures

Grouping: Informally observe the child as she removes an article of clothing watching for the procedures identified in the definition above.
1. Place the selected clothing in the container.
2. Ask the child to open the container, remove one of the articles of clothing and put it on.
3. Observe the child as she selects an item and puts it on.
4. After the child has put on the pull-over piece of clothing, ask her to take the garment off.
5. Observe the child as she removes the sweater/T-shirt, watching for: (1) Using both hands to take a hold of the bottom of the garment and begin pulling up; (2) The gradual straighten of the arms as the garment begins to go over the head and off; (3) The continued placement of the hands through the process; (4) Any adjustment that needed to be made as the item passed over the chin; (5) What the child did with the piece of clothing after it was taken off.

© 2010 VORT Corporation. All rights reserved. Do Not copy.

Credit: + Child takes pull-over clothing off completely, some assistance may be needed, but the goal is for the child to achieve independence.

Adaptations
See #6.121.

6.130 Takes front-opening clothing off completely
Strand: 6-2B **Age:** 40-48m 3.4-4.0y

Definition
The child will completely takeoff his front-open clothing (sweater, shirt, jacket), with assistance if needed. The assistance needs to be phased out as soon as possible.

Assessment Procedures
See #6.118 for assessment materials and procedures, as well as suggest adaptations.

6.131 Goes to toilet at regular intervals without asking
Strand: 6-6 **Age:** 30-44m 2.6-3.8y

Definition
The child will go to the bathroom at the scheduled classroom times.

Assessment Materials
A regular schedule for going to the bathroom.

Assessment Procedures
Grouping: Informally observe the child as she goes to the toilet at the scheduled classroom times.
1. Observe the child during the scheduled bathroom periods.
2. Watch to determine if she used the scheduled bathroom periods to attend to toilet needs, including: (1) She entered the bathroom; (2) She spent sufficient time to accomplish her toileting needs; (3) She asked to go to the restroom immediately after the scheduled time; (4) She used the restroom period for play time.

Credit: + Child goes to the bathroom at the scheduled times.

Adaptations
Some children neglect to go to the bathroom at the designated time, often due to: (1) Being in too big a hurry to do the next activity; (2) Does not feel a need to use the toilet at the scheduled time; (3) Have a concern about using the toilet while others are there; (4) Makes a habit of going to the bathroom just prior to the scheduled time. To assist these children, explain thoroughly why there are scheduled bathroom breaks. Be sensitive to those children who prefer to go to the bathroom in private. After evaluating any concerns, consider the possibility of increasing the number of breaks or allowing groups of children to go at different times.

6.132 Brushes teeth with horizontal and vertical motion
Strand: 6-8 **Age:** 40-52m 3.4-4.4y

Definition
The program-based components for this skill are not covered because oral hygiene is a skill usually dealt with at home - rather than in an educational setting. If oral hygiene is dealt with in the educational program, it is important to check with local agencies to determine appropriate policies.
Most communities have people who work in the dental care field who are available to visit educational settings.
These resource people bring materials for demonstration on correct ways to brush teeth, and kits that include toothbrushes, toothpaste, dental floss and parent information packets.
These dental visitors are also prepared to talk about proper care of teeth, preventive dental care, the importance of a good diet, and visiting a dentist. Often they will bring models of teeth for the children to practice on, and they will leave a dental educational unit for further exploration and practice.

6.133 Unbuttons clothing
Strand: 6-2B **Age:** 40-52m 3.4-4.4y

Definition
Note: *Training in dressing or undressing is a real-life skill experience that occurs in a non-educational setting. However, certain aspects could and should be reinforced in the child's educational setting. It is important that program policies be adhered to when teaching dressing/undressing skills in the educational setting.*
The child will unbutton her clothing. The clothing, to begin with, should be front-opening.

Assessment Materials
Clothes with large buttons on the front or a buttoning board. These boards can be commercially bought in school supply stores. If a buttoning board is not available, one can easily

be made by stapling or nailing a partial shirt with buttons to the front of a board. It is best to select a shirt that has large buttons and buttonholes and as the child becomes efficient in buttoning the larger buttons, remove the shirt and replace it with a shirt with smaller buttons and buttonholes.

Assessment Procedures

Grouping: Informally observe the child as she unbuttons an article of clothing watching for the procedures identified in the definition above.
1. Provide the child with the front-opening clothing with buttons.
2. Ask the child to unbutton the shirt/sweater/blouse/etc.
3. Observe the child as she performs the task, watching for the way the child: (1) Holds the material around the buttonhole; (2) Holds the button with the other hand; (3) Pushes the button through the buttonhole.

Credit: + Child unbuttons her clothing, independently.

Adaptations

Some children have difficulty in buttoning and unbuttoning. This may be related to: (1) Developmental delays in eye-hand coordination; (2) The necessary strength to push the button through the buttonhole; (3) The patience to continue until the task is complete; (4) The understanding of the need for buttoning and unbuttoning (for warmth, cover-up, secure items, etc.) To assist these children: (1) Model the unbuttoning procedures; (2) Use physical assistance (hand-over-hand) to perform the task; (3) Make sure that the learning experience is as directly related to where the unbuttoning will occur as possible; (4) Allow for ample practice with support as needed, however this should be gradually phased out. If the child finds unbuttoning a big problem, then other closures should be considered. The child's fine motor and eye-hand coordination may be delayed, hence snapping needs to be introduced at a later time.

6.134 Hangs/disposes of towel after using

Strand: 6-5 **Age:** 42-48m 3.6-4.0y

Definition

The child will hang the towel on the appropriate hook or bar. The child will throw the disposal towel in the appropriate waste container.

Assessment Materials

A hand towel or disposal towels, whichever are available in the setting.

Assessment Procedures

Grouping: Informally observe the child as he hangs or disposes of a towel after use, watching for the procedures identified in the definition above. Informal observation is very effective as it is done in the environment in which the task is typically performed.
1. After the child washes his hands, observe what he does with the towel after he has dried his hands.
2. Watch for such issues as: (1) Hangs the towel up; (2) Throws a disposable towel away in the garbage can; (3) Throws the towel on the floor; (4) Leaves the towel in the sink or around the sink area; (5) Does not use a towel; (6) Uses the towel as a toy; (7) Uses too many disposable towels.
3. It is important for the child to understand where to put the towel after using it; this needs to be modeled for him.

Credit: + Child properly hangs or disposes of a towel after using it.

Adaptations

Children will learn how to wash their hands and take care of the towel used to dry their hands by watching others and experiencing the skill first hand. Model the appropriate behavior. If the child still has difficulty, verbally walk them through the process of drying their hands. Remind them that a cloth towel should be hung back where they got it and a paper towel is thrown in the garbage can. Discuss the difference between the two different types of towels and why they are treated differently.

6.135 Spits toothpaste out
Strand: 6-8 **Age:** 36-48m 3.0-4.0y

Definition
The program-based components for this skill are not covered because oral hygiene is a skill usually dealt with at home - rather than in an educational setting. If oral hygiene is dealt with in the educational program, it is important to check with local agencies to determine appropriate policies.

Most communities have people who work in the dental care field who are available to visit educational settings.

These resource people bring materials for demonstration on correct ways to brush teeth, and kits that include toothbrushes, toothpaste, dental floss and parent information packets.

These dental visitors are also prepared to talk about proper care of teeth, preventive dental care, the importance of a good diet, and visiting a dentist. Often they will bring models of teeth for the children to practice on, and they will leave a dental educational unit for further exploration and practice.

6.136 Rinses toothbrush
Strand: 6-8 **Age:** 42-48m 3.6-4.0y

Definition
The program-based components for this skill are not covered because oral hygiene is a skill usually dealt with at home - rather than in an educational setting. If oral hygiene is dealt with in the educational program, it is important to check with local agencies to determine appropriate policies.

Most communities have people who work in the dental care field who are available to visit educational settings.

These resource people bring materials for demonstration on correct ways to brush teeth, and kits that include toothbrushes, toothpaste, dental floss and parent information packets.

These dental visitors are also prepared to talk about proper care of teeth, preventive dental care, the importance of a good diet, and visiting a dentist. Often they will bring models of teeth for the children to practice on, and they will leave a dental educational unit for further exploration and practice.

6.137 Wipes mouth and hands dry after brushing teeth
Strand: 6-8 **Age:** 42-48m 3.6-4.0y

Definition
The program-based components for this skill are not covered because oral hygiene is a skill usually dealt with at home - rather than in an educational setting. If oral hygiene is dealt with in the educational program, it is important to check with local agencies to determine appropriate policies.

Most communities have people who work in the dental care field who are available to visit educational settings.

These resource people bring materials for demonstration on correct ways to brush teeth, and kits that include toothbrushes, toothpaste, dental floss and parent information packets.

These dental visitors are also prepared to talk about proper care of teeth, preventive dental care, the importance of a good diet, and visiting a dentist. Often they will bring models of teeth for the children to practice on, and they will leave a dental educational unit for further exploration and practice.

6.138 Allows hair to be washed
Strand: 6-5 **Age:** 42-50m 3.6-4.2y

Definition
The program-based components for this skill are not covered because hair washing is a skill usually dealt with at home - rather than in an educational setting. If hair washing is dealt with in the educational program, it is important to check with local agencies to determine appropriate policies.

6.139 Washes and dries hands without assistance
Strand: 6-5 **Age:** 30-42m 2.6-3.6y

Definition
The child will wash her hands by rubbing soap all over her wet hands. She will rinse the soap off by placing her hands under running water. Finally, she will get a towel and dry her hands thoroughly, both the palms and the tops of her hands. She completes the task independently.

Assessment Materials
Faucet, soap, and disposable towels.

Assessment Procedures

Grouping: Informally observe the child as she washes and dries her hands without assistance, watching for the procedures identified in the definition above. Informal observation is very effective as it is done in the environment in which the task is typically performed

1. Observe the child as she washes and dries her hands.
2. During the observation, focus on the following steps: (1) The child automatically turns the water on and wets her hands; (2) Applies soap; (3) Rubs her hands well together; (4) Rinses; (5) Turns the water off; (6) Dries her hands (palms and tops), independently.
2. If necessary, verbally prompt the child through the washing and drying process, but phase out the prompts as soon as possible.

Credit: + Child washes and dries her hands without assistance.

Adaptations

If a child has difficulty washing and drying her hands independently, use hand-over-hand support to help her learn the process. Once she seems to have a clear understanding of what is expected of her, allow her to wash and dry her hands on her own. If necessary, verbally prompt her through the process if she has difficulty following the sequence.

6.140 Puts on clothing in the correct front and back position

Strand: 6-2A **Age:** 44-50m 3.8-4.2y

Definition

The child will put on clothing (like a T-shirt) making sure that the front and back are in the correct position.

Assessment Materials

Have available, in the "dress-up box", several pieces of clothing. Some of the pieces of clothing should have designs on the front and some pieces should have back position labels.

Assessment Procedures

Grouping: Informally observe the child as she puts on the piece of clothing watching for the procedures identified above.

1. Ask the child to go to the "dress-up box" and find a piece of clothing, they would like to put it on.
2. Ask the child to put on the selected garment.
3. Observe the child as she puts on the item, paying special attention to whether the child has the front and back in the correct positions.
4. During the observation, note how the child determined which was front and back (looked at the front design, determined where the label was located, used a trial and error method, did not pay any attention, etc.)

Credit: + Child puts on clothing in the correct front and back position, without assistance.

Adaptations

See #6.111.

6.141 Pinches tissue off end of nose

Strand: 6-9 **Age:** 44-52m 3.8-4.4y

Definition

The child will wipe around his nose using a tissue. The child will pinch the tissue when he reaches the end of his nose. The child may voluntarily get a tissue or the tissue will be given to him.

Assessment Materials

A box of tissue.

Assessment Procedures

Grouping: Informally observe the child as he blows his nose watching for the procedures identified in the definition above. Informal observation is very effective as it is done in the environment in which the task is typically performed.

1. Observe the child when he needs to wipe his nose.
2. If the child does not secure a tissue to wipe his nose, remind him he needs to wipe his nose and provide him with a tissue or direct him to the box of tissues.
3. Observe his response.

Credit: + Child uses a tissue to wipe his nose and pinches the tissue off when he reaches the end of his nose.

Adaptations

See #6.123.

6.142 Tears toilet tissue appropriately and flushes toilet after use

Strand: 6-6 **Age:** 44-56m 3.8-4.8y

Definition
The program-based components for this skill are not covered because toileting is a skill usually dealt with at home - rather than in an educational setting. If toileting is dealt with in the educational program, it is important to check with local agencies to determine appropriate policies.

6.143 Tightens shoelaces with a vertical or horizontal pull

Strand: 6-2A **Age:** 45-50m 3.9-4.2y

Definition
The child will tighten his shoelaces by pulling the laces. The child needs to pull both laces at the same time and can use a vertical or horizontal pull.

Assessment Materials
A shoe with laces, a lacing frame.

Assessment Procedures
Note: The child need only tighten the laces, not go through the entire process of tying his shoes.

Grouping: Informally observe the child as he puts his shoes on watching for the procedures identified in the definition above. Informal observation is very effective as it is done in the environment in which the task is typically performed.

1. Give the child the shoe or the lacing board.
2. Ask him to tie the shoelaces.
3. Observe him as he tightens the laces.
4. Watch for tightening the laces simultaneously.

Credit: + Child tightens his shoelaces by pulling the laces at the same time, either vertically or horizontally.

Adaptations
   Note: When the child displays evidence of physical agility, it is best to begin the training with a shoe with laces on the child's foot.

   Learning to tie one's shoes is a very difficult task for some children. Tying shoelaces requires well developed fine motor skills, the ability to use a pincer grasp, the need to hold the loops while moving them through the intersections, effective eye-hand coordination and on-task patience. If the child is experiencing any developmental lag in fine motor skills, visual coordination, strength, sequencing concerns, task attending, it is best to delay the shoe tying activity.

6.144 Tucks in or straightens front-opening clothing

Strand: 6-2A **Age:** 54-66m 4.6-5.6y

Definition
The child will push a front-opening shirt/blouse into pants/skirt and straighten the front of the garment.

Assessment Materials
Various dress-up clothes to be used for dramatization, creative dance, role-playing, etc. Make sure that there are front-opening clothing in the group.

Assessment Procedures
Grouping: Informally observe the child as he puts on clothing watching for the procedures identified in the definition above. Informal observation is very effective as it is done in the environment in which the task is needed.

1. Observe the child as he puts on a front-opening garment during dress-up time.
2. Watch for the child to tuck in the blouse/shirt after he has it on and do any straightening that is necessary (button flap straight).
3. The blouse/shirt should not be "crammed" in the pants/skirt, and the child might want to loosen a belt if they have one on.

Credit: + Child tucks/pushes in a front-opening shirt/blouse into pants/skirt and straightens the front of the garment.

Adaptations
   Some children do not feel a need to tuck a shirt/blouse. They are pleased if they get the shirt/blouse on and let the "tail" hang over pants/skirts. These children may have not been encouraged to learn any final dressing manners. To assist these children, model neatness of front-opening clothing, encourage the child to tuck in his "tail." But be sensitive to the family's preferences. When requiring a child to "tidy" up his shirt/blouse appearance and his family has opposite feelings (Dad always has his shirt out), you may be saying to the child, "You do not look your best and your family (dad) is not right." This may reflect values that are not within the child's culture and experiences. Hence the child may view himself as unworthy and rejected.

6.145 Dries face with towel when requested/on own
Strand: 6-5   **Age:** 36-48m   3.0-4.0y

Definition
The program-based components for this skill are not covered because washing/bathing involve skills usually dealt with at home - rather than in an educational setting. If washing/bathing is dealt with in the educational program, it is important to check with local agencies to determine appropriate policies.

6.146 Applies soap to cloth
Strand: 6-5   **Age:** 46-54m   3.10-4.6y

Definition
The program-based components for this skill are not covered because washing/bathing involve skills usually dealt with at home - rather than in an educational setting. If washing/bathing is dealt with in the educational program, it is important to check with local agencies to determine appropriate policies.

6.147 Prepares simple foods for eating
Strand: 6-3A   **Age:** 42-56m   3.6-4.8y

Definition
When she is presented with appropriate food, the child will demonstrate the skills necessary to prepare it for consumption. The preparation required could include peeling a banana, pouring a liquid, spreading a soft spread, cracking and peeling an egg, or inserting a straw. With the proper selection of foods for her to prepare, she will be exposed to sensory experiences. Example: Sensory--See how food changes (e.g., hard-boiled egg), the smell of food, how food feels (e.g., banana with the peel on it and after peel is removed), and the sounds of food (e.g., crunchy pretzels dipped in peanut butter).

Assessment Materials
/*\Safety Note: Be aware of special diets and allergies before doing this assessment.
Assortment of foods that need some preparation before eating, such as bananas, oranges, foods that are wrapped (e.g., cheese, crackers, bars), bread and soft spreads (e.g., butter, cream cheese), hard-boiled eggs, box of dry cereal and milk. Paper plates or bowls, plastic silverware, napkins, sponges, paper toweling.

Assessment Procedures
Note: It is important to remember that some children may not have been exposed to the foods presented or they may have no experience in preparing foods.

Grouping: An informal observation is very effective because it can be done in a natural setting without some of the variables that accompany a more formal assessment procedure.

<u>Level One:</u>
1. Place a container of the selected foods and the other eating materials on the table.
2. At snack time, invite the child to the table, and tell her you have a variety of different foods she can help you prepare.
3. Show her the eating utensils (plates, bowls, silverware).
4. Tell her she may choose any of the foods she wishes to eat.
5. Continue by explaining to her that before she eats the food, she must do something, such as peel the banana, pour milk on the cereal, unwrap the cheese and cookie snacks, crack and peel the egg, or spread the bread with the soft spreads.
6. Let her select a food and help her determine the necessary materials needed for preparing the food.
7. Observe her as she prepares the food for eating, watching for: (1) Use of fine motor skills to handle and prepare the food; (2) Uncertainty of what she is suppose to do; (3) Gives up and changes her mind as to the selection of the food; (4) Spills or mutilates the food; (5) Gives up and leaves the snack table.
8. If the observation indicates she is unsure of what she is supposed to do, stop the assessment, and model the preparation that is needed.
9. After the demonstration, ask the child to select a food and the necessary eating materials for preparing and eating the snack.
10. Observe her as she prepares the food for eating.

<u>Level Two:</u>
11. When the child is involved in an eating activity (e.g., lunch, snack time, party) that requires some simple food preparation before the food can be eaten (peeling, spreading, cracking), observe her as she takes the necessary steps prior to consuming the food.

Credit: + Child prepares simple foods for eating, without assistance.

Adaptations
A child may have difficulty with the needed manipulation to prepare food for eating. This difficulty could be a problem of adding the motor aspect to visual control. As long as the

activity is related to visual control of movement, she is fine, but when a motor skill becomes the predominant aspect of the task, she may have a problem. When she does a task such as peeling a banana—with the motor planning and coordination being the principal skills—she will have to use more than her visual modality to do the task. To peel it, she must grasp the banana with one hand, use the other hand to begin at the top of the fruit to peel, move the peel down the banana, and while still grasping the banana, repeat the peeling process. For a child who is using visual control over movement and for whom motor control is an unnatural element, training in kinesthetic operations is recommended. Providing her with an opportunity to practice grasping an object and using a pincer movement at the same time would be a very helpful activity. For example, give her a ball of clay, ask her to hold the clay in her hand, and squeeze it. As she squeezes it, tell her to use her other hand to pinch pieces of clay off the ball. Demonstrate this pincer grasp task, and assist her as needed. As you provide her with adequate practice, her visual and motor skills will soon begin to react as a team, or when the visual perception is required, the motor skill will respond, and then the motor movement becomes the predominant action that the visual will support.

6.148 Returns toothbrush, paste to designated container/location
Strand: 6-8 **Age:** 46-56m 3.10-4.8y

Definition
The program-based components for this skill are not covered because oral hygiene is a skill usually dealt with at home - rather than in an educational setting. If oral hygiene is dealt with in the educational program, it is important to check with local agencies to determine appropriate policies.

Most communities have people who work in the dental care field who are available to visit educational settings.

These resource people bring materials for demonstration on correct ways to brush teeth, and kits that include toothbrushes, toothpaste, dental floss and parent information packets.

These dental visitors are also prepared to talk about proper care of teeth, preventive dental care, the importance of a good diet, and visiting a dentist.

Often they will bring models of teeth for the children to practice on, and they will leave a dental educational unit for further exploration and practice.

6.149 Eats different types of foods
Strand: 6-3A **Age:** 48-54m 4.0-4.6y

Definition
When he is presented with different types of foods, the child will eat them appropriately. The foods should include foods that are crispy, sticky, chewy, liquid and solid.

Assessment Materials
/*\Safety Note: Be aware of special diets and allergies before doing this assessment. Remind the child of safety regarding scissors, knives, cutters, sharp objects.

Different types of foods (crispy, slippery, sticky, chewy, foods with liquid and solids), a tray to put them on, paper plates, paper placemats, plastic spoons, forks, knives, napkins.

Assessment Procedures
Grouping: An informal observation is very effective because it can be done in a natural setting without some of the variables that accompany a more formal assessment procedure.

1. For each child, place a paper placemat, a paper plate, plastic utensils, and a napkin on a table.
2. Invite the children to the table, and ask them to sit at one of the settings.
3. Explain to them that you are going to pass a plate of different foods, and that some are crispy, slippery, sticky, etc.
4. Tell them to select one of the foods on the tray to eat.
5. Pass the tray, and observe them as they eat their selected foods, watching for such things as (1) Use of utensils; (2) Use of hands; (3) Use of napkin; (4) Size of bites; (5) Taking food out of mouth; (6) Spitting; (7) Making negative/positive remarks about the food.
6. Pass the tray again and observe as they select and eat the foods, noting any preferences or avoidance of foods and any changes in eating behaviors after the first experience.

Credit: + Child eats a variety of foods with different tastes and textures (i.e., crispy, sticky, chewy, liquid, and solid).

Adaptations
Most children express a dislike for certain foods; some children reject foods due to texture,

taste, smell, experience, or a combination of these elements. Such a child often rejects another food because it looks or feels like a food he does not like. He also rejects food that looks hard to chew, too mushy, smells strange (burned), or generates an unpleasant sensory appearance or experience. Often these unfortunate experiences are: (1) Related to what others like or dislike; (2) The situation in which the eating occurred; (3) A strategy to be excused from eating; (4) To avoid some foods to get to a well-liked one (e.g., "Carrots taste awful; is it time for ice cream?"); (5) Tasting the food when he was not feeling well; (6) Feeling under pressure when he was asked to eat a certain food. Assist him by trying to get him to eat a variety of foods, to expand an awareness of different foods, and to try once disliked foods. This "trying experience" should be presented as an adventure, an activity that is fun and a part of growing up. In a group situation (family or school), generally, this child will try new foods, especially when he sees others trying them and when they are presented in a relaxed, motivating manner. Also remember that if the foods are presented in an attractive way, as well as in small proportions, the children will be more likely to try a taste. Tasting activities, creating new food mixes, and challenging the child to name a food by tasting it are exciting for a child and will help him appreciate new tastes and textures.

6.150 Puts proper amount of food in mouth and chews with lips closed

Strand: 6-3A   **Age:** 48-54m 4.0-4.6y

Definition
When eating, the child will place the proper amount of food into her mouth and will chew and swallow with her lips closed.

Assessment Materials
Note: Be aware of diets or allergies.
A small amount of food that requires chewing (crackers, cheese, dried fruit, cookie, apples).

Assessment Procedures
Grouping: Informally observe the child as she eats watching for the procedures identified in the definition above. Informal observation is very effective as it is done in the environment in which the skill is typically performed.
1. Invite the child to sit in a chair facing you.
2. Direct her attention to your mouth. Move your mouth as if you are quietly chewing and keep your lips closed.
3. Play a game, by asking the child to imitate the ways you move your mouth.
4. Vary the activity by reversing the roles.
5. Put (the food) in your mouth, and chew quietly with your mouth closed.
6. Give the child some food and encourage her to imitate you.
7. Verbalize her actions by saying, "You are chewing with your mouth closed. Good work!"
8. Model appropriate chewing for a child who fails to chew with her mouth closed, and say, "Watch me chew with my mouth closed."
9. If she has not been expected to refrain from chewing with her lips open, this social manner will require a lot of reminding and reinforcement. This behavior (chewing loudly and with mouth open and closed) may have become a habit and natural to him. Therefore, she will need to go through an unlearning and a relearning process.
10. The child's response will depend on her experiences, value systems, training, and exposure to models. This assessment is not meant to be a procedure for ranking or grading, but for developing instructional techniques and curriculum planning.

Credit: + Child puts the proper amount of food into her mouth, chewing and swallowing the food with her lips closed.

Adaptations
Some children have not been expected to chew quietly with their lips closed. Most eating behaviors are matters of information and habit, and habits are learned mostly by imitation. A child must practice good eating behaviors until they are habitual and natural. Some reasons a child has a problem with certain manners are: (1) That particular behavior was not identified as important in her home situation; (2) Chewing food and trying to talk at the same time is often a way to seek attention; (3) She is so anxious to talk that she does not think about any other behavior; (4) Filling one's mouth full of food can easily become a game. To assist such a child, follow these recommendations: (1) Model chewing with your lips closed; (2) Reward the child for chewing quietly with her lips closed; (3) Remind her when she takes a bite that she must close her mouth while she chews; (4) If her inappropriate behavior is an attempt to seek attention, ignore the behavior and remind her of

the correct behavior. If the behavior continues, explain to her that she is not to chew with her mouth open and alert her of what will happen if she continues this behavior. It is important to remember that this may be a learned eating behavior and has become natural. Give her ample time to practice, and provide cueing as necessary. Remember not to expect more of her than she can do, and conversely, let her do what she can do.

6.151 Buttons front-opening clothing
Strand: 6-2A **Age:** 36-54m 3.0-4.6y

Definition
Note: *Training in dressing or undressing is a real-life skill experience that occurs in a non-educational setting. However certain aspects could and should be reinforced in the child's educational setting. It is important that local policies be adhered to when teaching dressing/undressing skills in the educational setting. The child will button front-opening clothing.*

6.152 Replaces top on toothpaste
Strand: 6-8 **Age:** 48-54m 4.0-4.6y

Definition
The program-based components for this skill are not covered because oral hygiene is a skill usually dealt with at home - rather than in an educational setting. If oral hygiene is dealt with in the educational program, it is important to check with local agencies to determine appropriate policies.

6.153 Holds container with one hand while sucking liquid through a straw
Strand: 6-3B **Age:** 38-48m 3.2-4.0y

Definition
When the child is given a straw in a container, she will suck the liquid through the straw. She will need to hold the container with one hand and the straw with her other hand.

Assessment Materials
Straws, a drink container that can accommodate a straw (e.g., milk carton, juice box, glass of juice).

Assessment Procedures
Grouping: Informally observe the child as she sucks through a straw watching for the procedures identified in the definition above. Informal observation is very effective as it is done in the environment in which the skill is typically performed.
1. Place the straws and the container of liquid on the table.
2. Invite the child to take a straw and the container of liquid.
3. Tell her to put the straw into the container and to use the straw to drink the beverage.
4. Observe her as she sucks the liquid through the straw, watching for: (1) Drinking successfully using the straw, holding the straw gently with one hand; (2) Holding the container with one hand without spilling the liquid; (3) Blowing into the straw instead of sucking which causes sputters and bubbles; (4) Squeezing the top of the straw shut with her teeth or lips; (5) Stopping the liquid flow by pressing the straw in the middle with her fingers; (6) Playing with the straw; (7) Taking the straw out of the container and drinking the liquid.
5. Remember that children mature at different levels, and become independent at some skills at one time and other tasks at other times. Any assessment should consider the developmental level of the child, her experiences and attention span. This assessment is not meant to rank a child or to grade her in any way, but is meant to determine intervention strategies and for curriculum planning.

Credit: + Child sucks liquid through a straw while holding the container with one hand and the straw with the other hand.

Adaptations
Drinking through a straw seems unnatural to some children, because the inhale/exhale reaction is interrupted by swallowing. A child is use to inhaling or exhaling in an even airflow. Even if she is instructed to breathe in, hold her breath, and blow out, swallowing is not part of holding her breath. That is why her first attempts to drink through a straw usually result in either blowing into the straw or sucking the liquid into her mouth and then before swallowing it, it spurts out. Or she may close the top of the straw in an attempt to suck in, or she may use her hand to squeeze the straw closed so she can swallow what is in her mouth. To assist these children, model how to drink through a straw; for example: suck the liquid in, swallow, suck the liquid in again, and swallow. Be sure to hold the container with one hand and the straw gently with the other hand. After you model the

process several times, invite the child to use a straw and drink with you. Chant how to use a straw to give her additional help. Example:
"Suck the juice
Through the straw.
It taste so good,
Swallow it all."

6.154 Goes to toilet when necessary with infrequent accidents
Strand: 6-6   **Age:** 36-48m 3.0-4.0y

Definition
The child will indicate verbally, with a gesture, or by using a tangible object that he needs to be excused from the room to go to the bathroom.

Assessment Materials
An object that is used by the children to leave the room to go to the bathroom. These tangible objects may be: (1) A stuffed animal that in one position means that no one has left the room to go to the bathroom and that in another position means that someone has left; (2) A small flag that in an upright position means someone has left and that when in a down position means that no one has left to go to the bathroom; (3) A colored tag on a string: the string or tag has been placed on a hook to indicate someone went to the bathroom, and when that person returns he takes the string or tag down; (4) A small board that is colored red on one side and the other side is blue, the board is kept on a cup hook. When a child needs to leave the room he places the board so that the red side is showing, this indicates to other children that some one has left (particularly important if the classroom rule is that only one person may be excused at one time); (5) Ringing a bell and waiting for approval from the teacher; (6) Giving a hand signal and waiting for approval; (7) Raising their hand and asking permission to go to the bathroom; (8) Verbally requesting to go to the bathroom, etc.

Assessment Procedures
Grouping: Informally observe the child as he uses the bathroom watching for the procedures identified in the definition above. Informal observation is very effective as it is done in the environment in which the task is typically performed.
1. Observe the child as he uses the various options described above to leave the room to go to the bathroom.
2. Watch to determine if he uses the bathroom permission process correctly.
3. Watch to determine how many times he leaves the room.

Credit: + Child goes to the toilet when necessary, with infrequent accidents, after requesting to be excused to go to the bathroom.

Adaptations
Some children find asking permission to go to the bathroom or using a device to ask permission to go, is overwhelming, especially when they are in a hurry. Some children may forget the permission process if it is too involved or if recall is a concern. It is important to make sure that the child understands the classroom process to leave the room; "walk-him" through the steps several times, asking him to independently demonstrate the procedure. Also remember that emergencies do occur and understanding these situations is important.

6.155 Washes and rinses body areas
Strand: 6-5   **Age:** 48-56m 4.0-4.8y

Definition
The program-based components for this skill are not covered because washing/bathing involve skills usually dealt with at home - rather than in an educational setting. If washing/bathing is dealt with in the educational program, it is important to check with local agencies to determine appropriate policies. See the Appendix for information specific for children with special needs.

6.156 Runs comb/brush through hair
Strand: 6-5   **Age:** 56-72m 4.8-6.0y

Definition
The child places a comb or a brush in his hair. The child will hold the comb in an up-right position so that the teeth will go between hair strands. The child will put enough pressure on the brush so that the bristles will go between the hair strands.

Assessment Materials
A child's comb or brush and a mirror.

Assessment Procedures
Grouping: This skill should be assessed one-on-one with the child.
1. Observe the child as he uses his comb or brush to comb his hair.
2. Watch for placement, combing/brushing motion, position of the brush, etc.

3. If the child is having difficulty, assist him by using a hand-over-hand approach (your hand over the child's hand) to gently guide and direct his technique.
4. Often a mirror is helpful for observing position and placement.

Credit: + Child places a comb or brush in his hair and uses enough pressure on the brush so the bristles go between the strands of hair.

Adaptations

Some children find "sinking" a comb/brush in the hair difficult; the comb/brush often just "lays" on top of the hair rather than "sinks" into the hair to the scalp. To assist these children, place your hand over his and gently guide his motions. Combing/brushing a doll's hair or a wig are effective procedures for hair combing/brushing practice.

6.157 Adjusts water temperature to warm when shown by an adult

Strand: 6-5 **Age:** 36-48m 3.0-4.0y

Definition

The child will understand how to adjust cold water and hot water in a sink. The child will be able to turn the cold and hot faucets to the correct positions so the water will be the desired temperature, when shown by an adult.

Assessment Materials

/*\Safety Note: Be very careful and closely supervise the child with use of the hot water. A sink in the educational setting, which has hot and cold water available, and towels.

Assessment Procedures

Grouping: Informal observation is very effective as it is done in the environment in which the task is performed.
1. Observe the child as she washes her hands, looking for how she adjusts the faucets to secure warm water.
2. If the child has a concern, make sure that she is aware of which is the hot water and which is the cold water faucets, plus make sure she knows how to manipulate the faucets.

Credit: + Child adjusts water temperature to warm when shown by an adult.

Adaptations

Note: Any time the child deals with hot water, supervision is a must.

It is very important that children are aware of how to determine hot water faucets. Make sure that the child is aware of the hot water faucets in the classroom. This knowledge should occur prior to the child getting any water. It is also important that the child is made aware of how to determine hot water adjustments in other sinks; such as RED indicates hot and BLUE indicates cold, the words HOT and COLD written on the faucet handles, or the letters H and C written on the faucet. Have an adult model how to adjust the temperature of the hot and cold faucets to yield warm water first before letting the child attempt the skill. Allow the child to turn on the cold water and turn it off; allow the child to turn on the hot water (caution should be taken so that the child does not touch the hot water). To get warm water, explain to the child that she is to turn on the cold water first, place her finger under the water and GRADUALLY turn on the hot water, until her finger feels warm.

6.158 Undresses daily at designated times without being reminded

Strand: 6-2B **Age:** 48-56m 4.0-4.8y

Definition

Note: *Training in dressing or undressing is a real-life skill experience that occurs in a non-educational setting. However, certain aspects could and should be reinforced in the child's educational setting. It is important that local policies be adhered to when teaching dressing/undressing skills in the educational setting.*

6.159 Blows into tissue independently on request

Strand: 6-9 **Age:** 48-56m 4.0-4.8y

Definition

The child will blow into a tissue when she needs to or on request. The child will hold the tissue over her nose, blow, pinch the tissue off the end of her nose, and wipe around the nose area.

Assessment Materials

A box of tissues, a wastebasket.

Assessment Procedures

Grouping: Informally observe the child as she blows her nose watching for the procedures identified in the definition above. Informal observation is very effective as it is done in the environment in which the task is typically performed.

1. Observe the child when she needs to blow her nose.
2. Watch for the following: (1) The child uses a tissue, blows her nose, and wipes it clean of all residue; (2) The child does not blow her nose, she sniffs; (3) The child wipes her nose without blowing it; (4) The child needs to be reminded to blow her nose; (5) The child blows her nose once, needs to blow it again and neglects to blow a second time; (6) The child ignores the need.
3. Make sure that the child is aware of where the tissues are located and understands she is welcome to use them when needed.
4. Talk about what to do with the soiled tissues.

Credit: + Child blows into a tissue when she needs to, or on request. She holds the tissue over her nose, blows, pinches the tissue off at the end of her nose, and wipes around the nose areas.

Adaptations

Modeling how to blow one's nose is important. It may be helpful to verbally describe the nose blowing steps to the child. Remind her when she needs to get a tissue and blow her nose.

6.160   Wipes self after toileting
Strand: 6-6   **Age:** 48-66m   4.0-5.6y

Definition
The program-based components for this skill are not covered because toileting is a skill usually dealt with at home – rather than in an educational setting. If toileting is dealt with in the educational program, it is important to check with local agencies to determine appropriate policies.

6.161   Dresses independently when asked
Strand: 6-2A   **Age:** 48-66m   4.0-5.6y

Definition
Note: *Training in dressing or undressing is a real-life skill experience that occurs in a non-educational setting. However, certain aspects could and should be reinforced in the child's educational setting. It is important that local policies be adhered to when teaching dressing/undressing skills in the educational setting.*

6.162   Uses towel to dry body after washing
Strand: 6-5   **Age:** 48-60m   4.0-5.0y

Definition
The program-based components for this skill are not covered because washing/bathing involve skills usually dealt with at home - rather than in an educational setting. If washing/bathing is dealt with in the educational program, it is important to check with local agencies to determine appropriate policies. See the Appendix for information specific for children with special needs.

6.163   Disposes of tissue
Strand: 6-9   **Age:** 50-56m   4.2-4.8y

Definition
The child will throw a soiled tissue away in the appropriate container.

Assessment Materials
A box of tissues. Wastebasket.

Assessment Procedures
Grouping: Informal observation is very effective in assessing this skill.
1. Observe the child to determine if after he has blown his nose he throws the tissue away.

Credit: + Child throws his soiled tissue away in the appropriate container.

Adaptations
Some children neglect to throw away a tissue. Making sure that the child is aware of where he should throw the tissue is important. Assuring the child that there are more tissues should be emphasized. If the child feels unsure about where to throw the tissue, an individual sack/container attached to his work area may be considered, particularly when the child has a cold.

6.164   Drinks from water fountain without aid of adult
Strand: 6-3B   **Age:** 50-60m   4.2-5.0y

Definition
The child will drink from a water fountain without any assistance from another person. The fountain may be a faucet type, a button type, or an automatic release. While she learns how to turn the fountain on, she does not have to drink from it. She must be able to

reach the fountain independently, steps may be provided.

Assessment Materials
Available drinking fountain.

Assessment Procedures
Grouping: This skill can be assessed in a small group setting.
1. At break time, ask the children to line up for a drink at the water fountain.
2. Demonstrate how to turn the water on; ask several children to take turns turning the fountain on. Drinking from it is not necessary.
3. Observe each child as she takes a turn getting a drink from the fountain, watching for such drinking behaviors as: (1) Drinking the water successfully; (2) Has difficulty drinking and turning the water on at the same time; (3) Taking the water into the mouth but not swallowing; (4) Not opening her mouth, so the water sprays; (5) Demonstrates a concern in using the control mechanism to adjust the pressure of the water; (6) Places her whole mouth on the fountain; (7) Plays in the water with her hands; (8) Does not drink the water; (9) Spits the water out.
4. Note the type of drinking behavior the child exhibits.
5. This observational process is intended to provide information for modification of an inappropriate behavior or for program planning. This observational procedure considers only the ability of the child to drink from a fountain, and at the same time, to turn the water on. Other skills such as behaviors, conceptual understanding, and motor responses should also be considered.

Credit: + Child gets a drink of water from a water fountain without the assistance of an adult.

Adaptations
See #6.117.

6.165 (Removed, see page xviii)

6.166 Zips up front-opening clothing
Strand: 6-2A **Age:** 60-72m 5.0-6.0y

Definition
The child will zip up her clothing. The clothing should be front opening. The child will zip up her clothing by hooking the zipper base, holding the zipper tab and pulling up.

Assessment Materials
Clothes that zip up on the front.

Assessment Procedures
Grouping: Informally observe the child as she zips up her clothing watching for the procedures identified in the definition above. Informal observation is very effective as it is done in the environment in which the skill is typically performed.
1. Provide the child with front opening clothing that zips.
2. Ask the child to zip the jacket/coat.
3. Observe the child as she performs the task, watching for the way the child: (1) Holds the zipper base; (2) Holds the zipper tab with the other hand; (3) Pulls the zipper tab upward.

Credit: + Child zips up her front opening clothing by hooking the zipper base, holding the zipper tab and pulling up, independently.

Adaptations
Note: Usually children can unzip before they zip, so special attention should be given to connecting the two parts of the zipper at the base and then holding the bottom of the zipper as the other hand pulls the tab upward.

Some children have difficulty in zipping and unzipping. This difficulty may be related to: (1) Developmental delay in eye-hand coordination; (2) The necessary strength to pull up the zipper; (3) The patience to persist/continue until the task is complete; (4) The understanding of the need for zipping up and down (for warmth, cover-up, etc.) To assist these children: (1) Model the zipping and unzipping procedures; (2) Use physical assistance (hand-over-hand support) to perform the task; (3) Make sure that the learning experience is as directly related to where the zipping will occur as possible; (4) Allow for ample practice with support as needed, however the support should be gradually phased out. If the child finds zipping a problem, other closures should be considered or use a zipper pull to make pulling the zipper up easier. Fine motor and eye-hand coordination may be delayed, therefore, zipping may need to be introduced at a later time.

6.167 Uses toilet properly by self with no accidents
Strand: 6-6 **Age:** 52-60m 4.4-5.0y

Definition
The program-based components for this skill are not covered because toileting is a skill usually dealt with at home - rather than in an educational setting. If toileting is dealt with in the educational program, it is important to check with local agencies to determine appropriate policies.

6.168 Washes face and ears while in bath/shower
Strand: 6-5 **Age:** 52-62m 4.4-5.2y

Definition
The program-based components for this skill are not covered because washing/bathing involve skills usually dealt with at home - rather than in an educational setting. If washing/bathing is dealt with in the educational program, it is important to check with local agencies to determine appropriate policies.

6.169 Opens container and removes foods
Strand: 6-3A **Age:** 40-54m 3.4-4.6y

Definition
The child will open at least five different kinds of containers without any assistance. Examples of different kinds of containers are lunch boxes, milk cartons, juice box with straw, plastic containers, plastic bag, pre-packaged food items, threaded jar or bottle tops that have already had the seal broken.

Assessment Materials
Several different types of containers. These containers should represent at least seven different types of openings. Examples: (1) Lunch box, (2) Small cereal box, (3) Small milk carton, (4) Small juice box with straw, (5) Plastic bags, (6) Plastic containers, (7) Jar or bottle with a screw-on lid (seal already broken), (8) Pre-packaged food items.

Assessment Procedures
Note: Utensils may be needed by the child to empty the contents of the containers.
Grouping: Informally observe the child as she opens items during snack or lunch, watching for the procedures identified in the definition above. Informal observation is very effective as it is done in the environment in which the task is typically performed.

Level One:
1. Set the selected containers on a table.
2. Ask the child to come to the table.
3. Ask her to select one of the containers, open it, and empty its contents.
4. Observe her as she opens a container and removes the food, watching for: (1) Use of fine motor skills; (2) Understanding of the process needed to open and empty the container; (3) Strength and agility to open; (4) If she demonstrates patience; (5) If she cleans up any spills.
5. Ask her to select a different container and remove the contents. Observe her actions.
6. Continue with another container.
7. If she has not had experience opening and emptying any of the containers, she may have difficulty with this assessment.
8. Ask her to watch you as you open the container and empty its contents. As you model the procedure, verbally tell her what you are doing.
9. After the demonstration, ask her to select the same container and empty its contents.
10. Observe her actions.
11. The intent of this assessment is to determine a need for instructional strategies and to plan curriculum direction.

Level Two:
12. Observe the child as she opens a container (lunch box, thermos, jars, plastic bags, etc.) to determining the success, method, use of fine motor skills, and procedure she demonstrates.

Credit: + Child opens at least five different types of containers without assistance.

Adaptations
A child may have limited eye-hand control. If so, she may exhibit considerable difficulty controlling movements and may rely mostly on her vision for fine motor manipulation. Opening a milk carton, and taking the lid off a jar become arduous tasks when she is depending only on her visual abilities, and erratic movements result. If her motor skills or motor planning are the predominant aspect of the task, she may have a real problem. When she performs a task in which the motor skill is the principal skill, such as opening a milk carton, she needs to use more than her visual modality to do the task. When she opens the milk carton, she needs to hold the carton with one hand and to release the spout with the other. A firm hold is expected by one hand, and a squeezing motion is needed by

the other. Both hands are depending on motor reactions for completing the task, while the visual input is limited. When a child who uses visual control over motor movement finds it necessary to use motor control, training in eye-hand operation is recommended. Examples of the training steps include: (1) Give her a ball of clay, ask her to hold the clay in her hand, and squeeze it. As she squeezes it, tell her to use her other hand to pinch pieces of clay off; (2) Provide her with some lidded boxes and lidded jars, and ask her to take the lids off the boxes and to unscrew the lids off the jars. This activity requires her to hold the object firmly with one hand and remove the top with the other. Provide her with adequate practice, and soon the visual and motor skills will work to react as an equal team. When visual perception is required, the motor skills will respond, and when the motor movement becomes the predominant action, the visual will support it.

6.170 Washes face with soap when requested/on own
Strand: 6-5 **Age:** 54-62m 4.6-5.2y

Definition
The child will wash her face independently or when requested. She will use her hands or a cloth to wet her face, she will put soap on her hands or a cloth to put on her face, she will gently rub her soapy face, and she will rinse off her face with warm water and dry on towel.

Assessment Materials
A sink, soap, washcloth and a towel.

Assessment Procedures
Grouping: Informal observation is very effective as it is done in the environment in which the task typically takes place.
1. Observe the child as she washes her face.
2. Observe the child as she washes her face. Watch for the following: (1) Wets face with cloth or hands; (2) Applies soap; (3) Gently rubs face to get clean; (4) Rinses face; (5) Turns off water; (6) Dries face on a towel; (7) Puts the towel back or dispose of paper towels, etc.

Credit: + Child washes her face with soap and water on her own and when requested, without assistance.

Adaptations
Some children become confused as to the sequence of washing their face. They may place their hands under the water and splash the water, then dry their face, neglecting the soaping step. Or they will remember the soap step, but will put the soap on and forget to rinse it off before drying. To assist these children it is best to provide physical (hand-over-hand support) and/or verbal cues as you demonstrate the sequential steps. These steps are: (1) Turn on the water; adjust to warm; (2) Use a cloth or her hands to put water on her face; (3) Puts soap on a cloth or her hands and massages it into her face; (4) Rinses face with water; (5) Turns the water off; (6) Secures a towel; (7) Dries face on the towel; (8) Replaces the towel or if using a disposable towel throws it away.

6.171 Assists while another washes hair
Strand: 6-5 **Age:** 54-62m 4.6-5.2y

Definition
The program-based components for this skill are not covered because hair washing is a skill usually dealt with at home — rather than in an educational setting. If hair washing is dealt with in the educational program, it is important to check with local agencies to determine appropriate policies.

6.172 Opens all fasteners
Strand: 6-2B **Age:** 54-62m 4.6-5.2y

Definition
The child will open the fasteners on any article of clothing.

Assessment Materials
Clothing that has buttons, zippers, and snaps. Button board, zipper board, and snap board. Dolls with clothing that buttons, zips, and snaps.

Assessment Procedures
Grouping: Informal observation is very effective as it is done in the environment in which the task typically takes place.
1. Present the child with clothing that has various fasteners.
2. Ask her to put the clothing on herself or the doll.
3. Let her play in the dress-ups or with the doll for a few minutes.

4. Ask the child to remove her dress-up clothing or the clothing from the doll.
5. Observe the child as she removes the clothing and undoes the fasteners watching for: (1) Eye-hand coordination; (2) Appropriate pressure and strength needed to unsnap, unbutton, and unzip the clothing; (3) Using a trial and error approach; (4) Preservers and stays with the task until completed; (5) Gives up without asking for help.

Credit: + Child opens all fasteners on any article of clothing, independently.

Adaptations
See #6.96 and #6.133.

Some children have difficulty in unsnapping snap-type closures. This concern may be related to: (1) Developmental delays in eye-hand coordination; (2) The necessary strength to pull the snaps; (3) The patience to continue until the task is complete; (4) An understanding of the need to open the snaps; (5) The ability to open the snaps when the article of clothing is on the child. Opening snaps requires the child to "crinkle" the material around each snap, hold the bottom snap and pull. To assist children who have difficulty with this task, the following is recommended: (1) Model the unsnapping procedures; (2) Use physical assistance (hand-over-hand support) to perform the task; (3) Making sure that the learning experience is as directly related to where the unsnapping will occur as possible; (4) Allow for ample practice with support as needed, however gradually phased out support.

If the child finds unsnapping a huge problem, other closures should be considered. Development of fine motor skills and eye-hand coordination, may be delayed, and therefore, snapping needs to be introduced at a later time.

6.173 (Removed, see page xviii)

6.174 Spreads with a knife
Strand: 6-3A **Age:** 48-60m 4.0-5.0y

Definition
The child will use a knife (plastic) to spread a soft substance (e.g., butter, jam, cream cheese, apple butter) on a piece of bread, a cracker or a slice of toast.

Assessment Materials
/***Safety Note:** Be aware of special diets and allergies before doing this assessment. Carefully supervise use of knife.
A paper plate, napkins, knife (plastic), at least two pieces of bread for each child or crackers. A soft spreading substance (e.g., butter, jam, cream cheese, apple butter).

Assessment Procedures
Grouping: When you assess a child's ability to spread a soft substance on a piece of bread, the most effective procedure is observation. An observational assessment can be either spontaneous or occur in a semi-structured situation.
1. If the observational assessment is semi-structured, the following is a suggested procedure. At snack time, place a container of softened cream cheese, softened apple butter, jelly, or jam on the table.
2. Place the bread or crackers on the table along with the paper plates, a knife, and napkins.
3. At snack time, explain to the child that you have a special treat for her but that she must help with preparing it. For example, have her help by taking a cracker and spreading it with the jam (or another topping of her liking).
4. Observe her as she spreads jam on her cracker, watching for behaviors such as: (1) Successfully uses the spread; (2) Presses too hard when spreading; (3) Handles the knife inappropriately; (4) Uses too much spread or not enough; (5) Plays with the knife or the food; (6) Tries to convince another child to do the task for her; (7) Eats the spread directly from the utensil.
5. If she is unsuccessful at the task, model how to spread the cracker, and after the demonstration, ask the child to spread her own treat.
6 After your modeling, observe her as she spreads her cracker.
7. This assessment is meant to observe the fine motor skills and the eye-hand coordination needed to perform this self-help task. Any assessment should consider the developmental level of the child, her experiences, and attention span. Whenever the skill assessed relates to real-life function, it is best to interact with the child's home setting. This communication should include the way she performs the activity at home, ways her parents may assist her to perform

the skill, and strategies to determine her level of independence.

Credit: + Child uses a knife to spread a soft substance on a piece of bread or a cracker.

Adaptations

Some children have limited eye-hand coordination. These children may exhibit considerable difficulty controlling movements and may rely mostly on their vision for fine motor manipulation. When doing a task such as spreading jam on a cracker, the motor skill becomes the principal skill, so the child will have to use more than her visual modality to do the task. When she attempts to spread the cracker with a soft substance, she needs to hold the cracker with one hand and to move the knife across the cracker with the other hand, all the while knowing how much pressure to apply, how far to go, and when more spread needs to be added. A firm hold is expected by one hand and spreading motion is needed by the other. Both hands involved depend on motor reactions for completing the task, and the visual input is limited. For a child who uses visual control over movement and finds it necessary to use motor control, training in eye-hand operation through the following activities should be helpful: (1) Give her a brush (½ inch to 1 inch wide), colored water, and a sheet of paper. Tell her she is to "paint" the paper in a back and forth motion, as if she is spreading the paint. Tell her she is not to go off the paper and that when she runs out of "paint," she should dip her brush in the colored water. Make sure she understands that she needs to hold the paper with one hand and spread with the other; (2) Provide her with several wallpaper samples, glue, a plastic knife, scissors, and a large sheet of paper. Ask her to select one of the wallpaper samples and to spread the back with glue, using the knife, and then to attach it to the large sheet of paper. Make sure she uses the glue and knife in a spreading motion. This activity requires her to hold the paper firmly with one hand and to spread the glue with the other. Provide her with adequate practice, and soon the visual and motor skills will begin to react as an equal team. When visual perception is required, the motor skill will respond, and when the motor movement becomes the predominant action, the visual will support it.

6.175 Covers mouth with tissue, hand or the bend of the elbow when sneezing or coughing

Strand: 6-9 **Age:** 54-66m 4.6-5.6y

Definition
The child will use a tissue to cover his mouth when he sneezes or coughs. The child will use the tissue to wipe any residue from his nose and then will throw the tissue away. If a tissue is not available, the child will cover his mouth with his hand or aim the cough into the bend of his elbow. The child should wash his hands after sneezing, coughing, or blowing his nose to prevent the spread of germs.

Assessment Materials
Tissue. Wastebasket.

Assessment Procedures
Note: If the child has a cold, tissues should be easily obtainable by the child.

Grouping: Informally observe the child as he sneezes, coughs, or blows his nose, watching for the procedures indentified in the definition above. Informal observation is very effective as it is done in the environment in which the task is typically performed.

1. Observe the child when he sneezes or coughs to determine if he uses a tissue to cover his nose/mouth.
2. Make sure that the child is aware of where the tissues are located and that he knows he is free to use the tissues whenever needed.
3. If the child coughs or sneezes without covering his mouth/nose, remind him that he should use a tissue, his hand or his sleeve.
4. Remind the child that he should wash his hands after sneezing, coughing, or blowing his nose to prevent the spread of germs.

Credit: + Child covers his mouth with a tissue his hand, or the bend of the elbow when sneezing or coughing.

Adaptations
See #6.159.

6.176 Remembers to wash and dry hands after using the toilet

Strand: 6-6 **Age:** 54-72m 4.6-6.0y

Definition
The child will understand the importance of washing and drying hands before and/or after certain activities. These activities should include before

eating, before handling food, after toileting, after playing with dirty material, after working with materials such as clay, etc.

Assessment Materials
Faucet, soap, and disposable towels.

Assessment Procedures
Grouping: Informally observe the child as she washes her hands, watching for the procedures identified in the definition above. Informal observation is very effective as it is done in the environment in which the task is typically performed.
1. Observe the child as she washes and dries her hands.
2. During the observation, determine if the child automatically turns the water on, wets her hands, applies soap, rubs her hands together well, and then rinses, turns the water off and dries her hands.
3. Encourage the child to describe to you her hand-washing habits and why she feels she should or should not wash her hands before and/or after certain activities.

Credit: + Child remembers to wash and dry her hands after going to the bathroom, before eating, after playing with materials that can dirty her hands, etc.

Adaptations
Some children either overreact by washing their hands too many times, or they never bother to wash their hands on their own. A positive attitude about being clean is generally created by making "keeping clean" a pleasant activity. The children who would rather not wash, believe they have more important things to do. It is important to gently, and consistently, remind children of the benefits of washing and drying their hands to prevent the spread of germs.

6.177 Blows nose independently
Strand: 6-9 **Age:** 48-64m 4.0-5.4y

Definition
The child will blow his nose into a tissue without being reminded. The child will hold the tissue over his nose, blow, pinch the tissue off the end of his nose and wipe around the nose area.

Assessment Procedures
See #6.159 for assessment materials and procedures, as well as suggested adaptations.

6.178 Adjusts clothing before leaving bathroom
Strand: 6-6 **Age:** 48-66m 4.0-5.6y

Definition
The child will not leave the bathroom until she has her clothing adjusted. This includes all zippers up, skirts down, belts/sashes buckled/tied, shirts/blouses tucked in if appropriate, etc.

Assessment Procedures
Grouping: Informally observe the child as she leaves the bathroom, watching for the procedures identified in the definition above. Informal observation is very effective as it is done in the environment in which the task is typically performed.
1. Observe the child as she leaves the bathroom to determine if she has adjusted her clothing after using the facilities.
2. This should include such items as zippers up, skirts down, shirts in if worn that way, belts and buckles in place, etc.
3. If the child has not adjusted her clothing appropriately, recommend that she return to the bathroom and complete the dressing task.

Credit: + Child adjusts clothing before she leaves the bathroom.

Adaptations
Some children are often in too big a hurry to "re-dress" after using the bathroom. Zippers are forgotten, skirts are caught in pants, blouses/shirts are "turned lose," belts may be forgotten or not buckled, etc. It is important to let the child know that she needs to complete the step of adjusting her clothing. The most effective way of helping a child learn to adjust her clothing is to have her look in a mirror and ask her to evaluate her own appearance. Encourage the child to put herself back together.

6.179 (Removed, see page xviii)

6.180 Carries liquid in open container, without spilling
Strand: 6-3B **Age:** 58-70m 4.10-5.10y

Definition
The child will carry a container at least three-fourths full of liquid, without spilling. He may use both hands to carry the container.

Assessment Materials
A container, such as a pitcher used when watering potted plants.

Assessment Procedures
Grouping: When you assess a child's skill area, the most effective procedure is observation. An observational assessment can be either spontaneous or semi-structured.

1. If the choice is semi-structured, consider the following procedure: (1) Explain to the child that the plants need watering; (2) Give him a container to use to water the plants; (3) Put water in the container (at least 3/4 full); (4) Give him the container, and ask him to water the plants.
2. Observe him as he carries the container from the sink to the plants, watching for: (1) No spilling; (2) Moving very, very slowly, hands shaking, taking tiny steps; (3) Stops and puts the container down between the sink and the plants; (4) Spilling water; (5) Returns to the sink and pours some of the water out; (6) Chooses not to carry the water; (7) Tries to carry the container with one hand as the other hand covers the top of it.
3. Remember not to expect more of the child than he can do; conversely, let him do what he can do.
4. Make sure that modeling, verbal instruction, and physical assistance is available for him, if needed.

Credit: + Child carries liquid in a container, at least three-fourths full of liquid, without spilling.

Adaptations
If the child is having difficulty carrying liquid in an open container, it may be due to the following reasons: (1) Not having the strength to carry the container; (2) Moving too quickly; (3) Not paying attention to what he is doing. To assist the child: (1) Model how to hold the container and carry it from one location to another; (2) Use physical assistance (hand-over-hand support) to perform the task; (3) Put less liquid in the container to make the task easier to perform.

6.181 Ties shoes, following step-by-step demonstration/support
Strand: 6-2A **Age:** 60-68m 5.0-5.8y

Definition
The child will tie his shoelaces by pulling the laces, making and tightening a bow following step-by-step demonstration/support. The child will tie his shoes using the following steps: (1) Place one end of the laces in each of the child's hands, a pincer grasp is necessary; (2) Cross one lace over and then under the other lace; (3) Pull laces tight; (4) Physically assist the child, using hand-over-hand support, to make a loop with one lace; (5) Physically assist the child to make a loop with the other lace; (6) Help the child cross the loops; (7) Fold one loop over and then wrap it under and through the opening that is made at the bottom of the two loops; (8) Holding one loop in each hand with a pincer grasp, pull the loops simultaneously, forming a bow; (9) Tighten as necessary.

Assessment Materials
A shoe with laces, a lacing frame.

Assessment Procedures
Grouping: This skill should be assessed one-on-one with the child.

1. Provide the child with the shoe or the lacing board.
2. Ask the child to tie the shoe laces on either model.
3. Observe the child as he ties the laces, in particular the final tightening step. Watch for tightening the laces simultaneously, making sure that the bows are of equal size prior to tightening, making sure that the bow ends are nearly equal in length, and if the entire shoe tying process observed is done with a certain amount of natural movement, etc.

Credit: + Child ties his shoes, following step-by-step demonstration.

Adaptations
See #6.143.

6.182 Places a front opening garment on a hanger and hangs it up
Strand: 6-2B **Age:** 60-68m 5.0-5.8y

Definition
The child will place a front opening garment (sweater/blouse/shirt/etc.) on a hanger. The child will fasten (buttons/zips/snaps/etc.) the front opening garment after it is on the hanger.

Assessment Materials
A collection of "dress-up" clothes, which includes front opening items (sweater/blouse/shirt/ etc.) and coat hangers.

Assessment Procedures
Grouping: This skill should be assessed one-on-one with the child.
1. Ask the children to hang up the "dress-up" clothes on hangers and then hang the hanger on a rack, clothes line, rod, etc
2. Observe the child as she places the clothing on the hanger, closes any fasteners and places the hanger in the designated place
3. Watch for: (1) Placing a front opening garment on the hanger by first placing a single shoulder on the end of the hanger, next placing the other shoulder on the other end of the hanger, straightening the item and fastening the fasteners (button, zip, snap, etc.); (2) Hanging the hanger on the rack/clothesline/rod/etc.

Credit: Child places a front opening garment on a hanger and fastens the garment once it is on the hanger.

Adaptations
Some children find using a hanger a problem, particularly if the child is used to using hooks or drawers to store clothing. Placing a garment on a hanger requires: (1) Specific eye-hand coordination skills; (2) Using one hand to adjust the piece of clothing while the other hand is holding the hanger; (3) Understanding of the steps involved in placing a sweater/blouse/shirt/etc. on a hanger; (4) The importance of straightening the item after it has been hung; (5) Closing the front open garment fastening straight on the hanger, rather than closing a sweater/blouse/shirt when it is on their body. To assist these child, model the steps involved in hanging up a piece of clothing, allowing them to follow along with their own hanger and sweater/blouse/shirt/etc. Using clip clothespins to hold the first shoulder on the hanger is helpful to stabilize the item while the other shoulder is adjusted on the hanger. Allow the child to fasten the garment by placing the child behind the hanger and demonstrating how she can put her arms around the item as if it was on her body. If hanging up clothes on hangers is frustrating or too difficult for the child, allow her to fold the piece of clothing and put it in a box or hang it on a hook.

6.183 Selects and uses appropriate protective clothing per weather/settings
Strand: 6-2A **Age:** 60-70m 5.0-5.10y

Definition
The child will select the appropriate clothing for different weather conditions (rainy days, chilly times, hot weather, etc.) The child will select the appropriate clothing to wear based on the activity and setting (apron when using clay/water/cooking/etc.)

Assessment Materials
Paper dolls and paper-doll clothing, which can be purchased at teacher stores, department stores, etc. If unavailable, paper dolls and clothing are easy to make. Example: Catalogs, newspaper ads, coloring books are excellent sources to locate boys and girls as paper doll models. These models should be traced on thin paper and then glue the tracing on heavy paper before coloring them and cutting them out. To make the clothes for the dolls, draw around the dolls to get the correct size, put tabs on the clothes to hold them on the dolls, decorate and cut out. It is important that each doll have clothing for rainy days, cold days, hot days, clothes that are designed to protect other clothing, etc. It is easiest to make clothes for paper dolls when they have their arms and legs away from their bodies (sticking straight out). Each child should have a girl or a boy paper doll and a collection of clothing.

Assessment Procedures
Grouping: This skill can be assessed in a small group setting.
1. Give each child a paper doll and a collection of clothing.
2. Discuss the various pieces of clothing, what it is, under what conditions would you wear it, why would it keep you dry/warm/cool/etc.
3. Explain to the child that you are going to state a weather condition and they are to dress their doll in the appropriate clothing.
4. Example: (1) It is raining very hard and your doll needs to walk home. What would your doll wear to keep him/her dry? (2) It is very cold outside. What would your doll wear to help keep him/her warm? Continue with other scenarios.
5. Observe the child as he selects the appropriate clothing based on the situation presented.
6. Encourage the children to explain why they selected the article of clothing they did.

Credit: + Child selects and uses appropriate protective clothing based on the weather conditions or activity they will be involved in.

Adaptations

Some children have never been exposed to widely ranging weather conditions. To assist these children, show them pictures of different weather conditions and talk about the different pictures to provide an experience of how weather conditions can be in other places. Example: It is hard for a child in the southwest to understand a blizzard and freezing weather.

6.184 Uses paper towel from dispenser or cloth towel to dry hands in new situation

Strand: 6-5   **Age:** 40-52m 3.4-4.4y

Definition

When in a new situation, the child will either hang a hand towel or dispose of a paper towel after using it. The child will hang the towel on the appropriate hook or bar. The child will throw the disposable towel in the appropriate waste container.

Assessment Materials

A hand towel or disposable towels.

Assessment Procedures

Grouping: Informal observation is very effective as it is done in the environment in which the task is typically performed.
1. Observe the child in a new situation (field trip, sink at a another location in the building, etc.)
2. After the child washes his hands, observe what he does with the towel after he has dried his hands.
3. Watch for such issues as: (1) Hangs the towel up; (2) Throws away a disposal towel in the waste container; (3) Throws the towel on the floor; (4) Leaves the towel in the sink or around the area; (5) Does not use a towel; (6) Uses the towel as a toy; (7) Uses too many disposable towels.
4. It is important for the child to understand where to put the towel after using it. This needs to be modeled for him as well as allowing him to demonstrate his knowledge of the activity.

Credit: + Child uses a paper towel from a dispenser or a cloth towel to dry his hands when in a new situation. He will properly dispose of the paper towel or will hang up hand towel when he is done using it.

Adaptations

Some children often have a difficult time transferring a skill from one setting to another. These children learn a skill in a given situation and often do not realize that the same learned skill can be used in another similar setting with some modification. To assist these children as much as possible, change the components of the skill being learned without modifying the basic steps. Example: Place paper towels in a stack near the sink rather than from the dispenser. Place a folded cloth towel on a rod near the sink rather than on a hook.

6.185 Put laces in shoes and laces correctly

Strand: 6-2A   **Age:** 66-78m 5.6-6.6y

Definition

The child will put the laces in her shoes and correctly cross-lace (one end of the laces at a time) using alternate eyelets.

Assessment Materials

A shoe that does not have laces in it or a lacing board that has the laces removed.

Assessment Procedures

Grouping: This skill should be assessed one-on-one with the child.
1. Ask the child to put the laces in the shoes/board.
2. Observe the child as she proceeds, watching for: (1) Understanding that each end of the lace needs to be placed in one eyelet at a time; (2) Stays on task; (3) Uses trial and error methods if necessary; (4) Demonstrates the ability to pull the lace through the eyelet(s).

Credit: + Child puts laces in shoes and laces the shoe correctly.

Adaptations

Some children find lacing a tedious task and try to hurry through the process by pulling an end too far through, thereby making a short end. These children do not understand that cross-lacing through every other eyelet means that the laces need to be pulled through far enough to create equal lengths left. Use a hand-over-hand approach to assist these children and model the effective way to lace. Gradually phase out the physical support and replace it with pointing and verbally describing the process. It is also important to show patience as the child uses the trial and error approach.

6.186 Cuts with a knife

Strand: 6-3A **Age:** 60-72m 5.0-6.0y

Definition

The child will use a knife (plastic or table) to cut soft foods (e.g., banana, cake, Jello). He will begin cutting with a knife by using a down and pull motion. As he becomes skilled in cutting soft foods with a down and pull motion, he should be encouraged to cut harder foods, using a down, pull, and saw motion.

Assessment Materials

/*\Safety Note: Be aware of special diets and allergies before doing this assessment. Carefully supervise use of knife.

A paper plate, plastic silverware, napkins, a plastic or table knife, a soft food (e.g., a banana firm enough to be cut clean), solid *Jello*.

Assessment Procedures

Grouping: When you assess a child's ability to cut a soft food, the most effective procedure is observation. An observational assessment can be either spontaneous or occur in a semi-structured situation.

1. If the observational assessment is semi-structured, the following is a suggested procedure: At snack time, place a container of solid *Jello* (slightly score the *Jello* into sections to serve the number of children), a knife, paper plates, plastic silverware, and napkins on the table.
2. Explain to the child that you have a special treat, but that he must cut the treat so everyone may have a taste.
3. Show the child the *Jello*, and explain the scored lines to him.
4. Give him a knife, and ask him to follow the lines to cut the *Jello* into squares.
5. After he cuts the *Jello*, use a spatula to remove it from the pan, and put it on the paper plates for serving.
6. Observe him as he cuts the *Jello*, watching for behaviors such as: (1) Successfully cuts the food; (2) Does not apply enough pressure to cut completely through the food; (3) Demonstrates a problem following the guidelines; (4) Applies too much pressure when cutting; (5) Plays with the knife or the food; (6) Tries to convince another child to do the task for him; (6) Refuses to try.
7. If the child is unsuccessful at the task, model how to cut the *Jello*, and after the demonstration, ask him to cut it.
8. This assessment is meant to observe the fine motor skills and the eye-hand coordination needed to perform this cutting task. Children certainly mature at various levels, becoming independent at some skills at one time and other activities at other times. Any assessment should consider the developmental level of the child, his experiences, attention span, and objectiveness.
9. Whenever the skill assessed relates to a real-life function, it is best to interact with the child's home setting. These communications should include the way he performs the activity at home, ways the parent may assist him to perform the skill, and strategies to determine his level of independence.

Credit: + Child uses a knife to cut soft foods, using a down-and-pull motion.

Adaptations

See #6.174.

6.187 (Removed, see page xviii)

6.188 Identifies the correct restroom to use by recognizing the sex sign in a new setting

Strand: 6-6 **Age:** 65-78m 5.5-6.6y

Definition

The child will identify the correct restroom sign when shown several different signs (boys, girls, men, women, international signs, laddies and lassies, cowboys and cowgirls). The child should also be aware that some bathrooms are unisex, hence the sign may just read "bathroom" or "restroom."

Assessment Materials

Collect different restroom signs or make the common signs on 5 x 8-inch cards. The cards should include: (1) Boys, Girls; (2) Men, Women; (3) International signs; (4) Handicapped, etc.

Assessment Procedures

Grouping: This skill should be assessed one-on-one with the child.

1. Invite the child to a table. Begin a discussion about identifying the bathroom they would use.
2. Make sure the child understands that girls should go to a girl's bathroom and boys should go to a boys bathroom.
3. It is important that the child understands that these bathrooms are different than their bathroom at home.
4. Use the school bathrooms as examples.

© 2010 VORT Corporation. All rights reserved. Do Not copy.

5. Explain to the child that you are going to show her some signs and they represent signs that are on bathroom doors.
6. Request that when she sees a sign, she is to tell you if a girl or boy would use the bathroom that displays the sign on its door.
7. Show the child the sign and say, "Who would use this bathroom?"
8. Pause to allow the child time to respond.
9. If the child is unable to read the words, it may be necessary to point to and read the word.
10. Continue with the rest of the signs.

Credit: + Child identifies the correct restroom to use by recognizing the sign on the door, even in a new setting.

Adaptations

Some children do not have the background to respond to various restroom signs. They have probably been taken to the correct bathroom by someone else or when in a group, they have followed the rest of the children to the correct bathroom. To assist these children, provide them with varied experiences at different setting, as well as making them aware of signs that designate bathrooms.

6.189 Flosses teeth

Strand: 6-8 **Age:** 65-72m 5.5-6.0y

Definition

The program-based components for this skill are not covered because oral hygiene is a skill usually dealt with at home - rather than in an educational setting. If oral hygiene is dealt with in the educational program, it is important to check with local agencies to determine appropriate policies.

Most communities have people who work in the dental care field who are available to visit educational settings.

These resource people bring materials for demonstration on correct ways to brush teeth, and kits that include toothbrushes, toothpaste, dental floss and parent information packets.

These dental visitors are also prepared to talk about proper care of teeth, preventive dental care, the importance of a good diet, and visiting a dentist. Often they will bring models of teeth for the children to practice on, and they will leave a dental educational unit for further exploration and practice.

6.190 Uses proper brushing strokes to clean teeth

Strand: 6-8 **Age:** 65-78m 5.5-6.6y

Definition

The program-based components for this skill are not covered because oral hygiene is a skill usually dealt with at home - rather than in an educational setting. If oral hygiene is dealt with in the educational program, it is important to check with local agencies to determine appropriate policies.

Most communities have people who work in the dental care field who are available to visit educational settings.

These resource people bring materials for demonstration on correct ways to brush teeth, and kits that include toothbrushes, toothpaste, dental floss and parent information packets.

These dental visitors are also prepared to talk about proper care of teeth, preventive dental care, the importance of a good diet, and visiting a dentist. Often they will bring models of teeth for the children to practice on, and they will leave a dental educational unit for further exploration and practice.

6.191 Selects clean clothing, changes underclothes regularly

Strand: 6-2A **Age:** 66-72m 5.6-6.0y

Definition

The program-based components for this skill are not covered because dressing/undressing is a skill usually dealt with at home - rather than in an educational setting. If dressing/undressing is dealt with in the educational program, it is important to check with local agencies to determine appropriate policies.

6.192 Cuts with knife and fork

Strand: 6-3A **Age:** 66-78m 5.6-6.6y

Definition

The child will hold a knife and fork appropriately to cut food. She will hold a fork upside down (standard position with forefinger on top) in her non-dominant hand and a knife in her dominant hand (standard position with forefinger on top) to cut solid food. After she cuts the food, she will set the knife down and move the fork and food to her dominant hand for eating.

Assessment Procedures

/*\Safety Note: Be aware of special diets and allergies before doing this assessment. Carefully supervise use of knife.

See #6.174 and #6.186 for assessment materials and procedures.

Adaptations

A child may have a problem when cutting food with a knife and fork becomes part of the eating process. Developing the ability to grasp one utensil and cut with another may seem like an overwhelming challenge, making her feel clumsy and very unsuccessful. Any problems with motor skills and visual-motor integration certainly will affect her success level of this basic eating process.

The skill of cutting with a knife and fork entails doing a task analysis of the activity. For example, the prerequisite skills needed to use a knife to cut and a fork to hold the food being cut involve: (1) Ability to grasp the handle of the utensils. The child will hold a fork upside down (standard position with forefinger on top) in her non-predominant hand, and the knife in her predominant hand (standard position with forefinger on top) to cut solid food; (2) Ability to determine the amount of food to be cut and the efficient position of the fork; (3) Ability to maintain a steady hold with the fork and a moving motion with the knife; (4) Ability to release the knife, move the fork to the predominant hand, and move the food to the mouth; (5) Ability to follow directions.

6.193 Ties shoelaces independently

Strand: 6-2A **Age:** 66-78m 5.6-6.6y

Definition

The child will tie his shoelaces independently by pulling the laces, making and tightening a bow. The child will tie his shoes using the following steps: (1) Places one end of the laces in each of the his fingers, a pincer grasp is necessary; (2) Crosses one lace over and then under the other lace; (3) Pulls the laces tight; (4) Makes a loop with one lace; (5) Makes a loop with the other lace; (6) Crosses the loops; (7) Folds one loop over and then wraps it under and through the opening that is at the bottom of the two loops; (8) Holds one loop in each hand with a pincer grasp, pulls the loops simultaneously, forming a bow; (9) Tighten as necessary.

Assessment Materials

Shoe with laces, a lacing frame.

Assessment Procedures

Grouping: This skill should be assessed one-on-one with the child.

1. Provide the child with the shoe or the lacing board.
2. Ask the child to tie the shoelaces on either model.
3. If the child decides to use the lacing board, instruct him to take both ends of the lace on the board and put them through the eyelets alternately, forming an X-pattern. When the child comes to the end of the board, ask him to tie a bow.
4. Observe the child as he ties the laces, in particular the final tightening step. Watch for tightening the laces simultaneously, making sure that the bows are of equal size prior to tightening, making sure that the bow ends are nearly equal in length.
5. During the entire shoe tying process observe if it is done with a certain amount of natural movements.

Credit: + Child ties laces independently.

Adaptations

Note: When the child displays evidence of physical agility it is best to begin the training with a tie shoe on the child's foot.

Learning to tie ones shoes is a very difficult task for some children. Tying shoelaces requires well develop fine motor skills, the ability to use a pincer grasp, the need to hold the loops while moving them through the intersections, effective eye-hand coordination and on task patience. If the child is ready to lace his shoes the following steps are recommended: (1) Place the end of the laces in the child's fingers, a pincer grasp is necessary; (2) Physically assist the child, using a hand-over support by making a loop with one lace; (3) Physically assist the child to make a loop with the other lace; (4) Help the child cross the loops and holding in only one hand; (5) Using the other hand, place one loop through the opening that is made at the bottom of the two loops; (6) Holding one loop in each hand with a pincer grasp, pull the loops simultaneously, forming a bow; (7) Tighten as necessary. If the child is experiencing any developmental lag in fine motor skill, visual coordination, strength, sequencing concerns, task attending, it is best to delay the shoe tying activity.

6.194 Turns clothing right side out
Strand: 6-2B **Age:** 66-78m 5.6-6.6y

Definition
The child will turn an article of clothing right side out. The child will right side a closed front garment by taking the bottom of the item and pulling it through the neck area. The child will right an open-front garment by turning the shoulders inside out and then straightening the item.

Assessment Materials
Supply of clothes in the dress-up area.

Assessment Procedures
Grouping: Informally observe the child as she turns clothing right side out, watching for the procedures identified in the definition above. Informal observation is very effective as it is done in the environment in which the task is typically performed.
1. Invite the child to straighten up the clothing in the dress-up area.
2. Observe the child as she folds or hangs-up the clothing, making sure that the child turns those items that are wrong side out, right side out.
3. If the child needs assistance in adjusting these clothes, model how to reverse a garment and hang it up.
4. The intent of the clothing is to be used by the children to expand their creativity (creative dramatics, playtime, pretend time, etc.) not a "house-keeping" task.

Credit: + Child turns a piece of clothing right side out, on her own, and then straightens the item.

Adaptations
Some children find it difficult to turn clothing right side out. Often these children lack the motor skills to complete the task, do not see a need for righting clothing, becomes frustrated when the clothes become twisted, lack the eye-hand coordination to complete the activity, lack the experience of having to pick-up and put away clothing, etc. To assist these children it is important that the children are shown how to turn various style clothing right side out and to allow the child time to practice putting clothes away.

6.195 Brushes after meals or at designated times
Strand: 6-8 **Age:** 70-78m 5.10-6.6y

Definition
The program-based components for this skill are not covered because oral hygiene is a skill usually dealt with at home - rather than in an educational setting. If oral hygiene is dealt with in the educational program, it is important to check with local agencies to determine appropriate policies.

Most communities have people who work in the dental care field who are available to visit educational settings.

These resource people bring materials for demonstration on correct ways to brush teeth, and kits that include toothbrushes, toothpaste, dental floss and parent information packets.

These dental visitors are also prepared to talk about proper care of teeth, preventive dental care, the importance of a good diet, and visiting a dentist. Often they will bring models of teeth for the children to practice on, and they will leave a dental educational unit for further exploration and practice.